A HISTORY OF MAINE

●

A Collection of Readings
on the
History of Maine
1600-1970

by

Ronald F. Banks

University of Maine

KENDALL/HUNT PUBLISHING COMPANY
DUBUQUE, IOWA

Copyright © 1969 by
Ronald F. Banks

SBN 8403-0020-4

All rights reserved. No part of this book
may be reproduced in any form or by any
process without permission in writing from
the copyright owner.

Printed in the United States of America

Preface

The need for such a volume as this became apparent when the author was teaching a course in the history of Maine at the University of Maine. No work was or is available which could serve as a text for the course. The extent of the problem can be appreciated when one realizes that the last serious attempt at writing a history of Maine was that of Louis Hatch, published in 1919.

To write a history of a state one must rely on the efforts of others. If there exists a considerable body of scholarly monographic literature then one may produce a work of synthesis. The result will likely conform to a standard historical treatment of a state. Without such monographic literature it would be an act of folly to pretend to write an authoritative history.

It is precisely the absence of a large body of monographic literature which frustrates those who desire that a serious, scholarly history of Maine be written. Too little analytical scholarship in Maine's economic, political, and social history has been done to permit generalization in these crucial areas.

Faced with this reality, the editor of this volume has resorted to what can be described as a very poor substitute—a collection of readings. What follows is a series of selections from primary and secondary literature concerning different facets of Maine's past and present. No effort has been made to achieve total coverage. The traditional historical categories of analysis—economic, political, and social—are represented but not in a systematic narrative-descriptive manner.

Though much of the basic research is lacking to write a definitive history, it is nevertheless true that there has appeared some rather good work on certain phases of Maine's past and present. Much of this work is reprinted here and may serve to stimulate further research into significant problem areas.

In organizing the selections, I have followed a chronological plan. The book contains three divisions. The first deals with the "colonial" period down to 1820. The second is devoted to the nineteenth century and the third to the twentieth. The paucity of historical writing on developments in the twentieth century makes the third section the least historical and most impressionistic of all.

Ronald F. Banks
Assistant to the President and
Assistant Professor of History
University of Maine

Contents

Chapter   Page

Part I
INTRODUCTION: THE COLONIAL PERIOD, 1600-1820

1. A True Relation of Captain George Weymouth, His Voyage Made this Present Yeere 1605; in the Discouerie of the North Part of Virginia
   by James Rosier 7
2. The Popham Colony
   by Henry Burrage 23
3. A French Jesuit Mission Arrives at Mt. Desert
   by Father Pierre Biard, S.J. 38
4. The Plymouth Colonists in Maine
   by Henry S. Burrage 41
5. The Province of Maine
   by Richard A. Preston 51
6. The Jurisdiction of Massachusetts Accepted
   by Henry S. Burrage 64
7. The Germans Reach Broad Bay
   by Jasper J. Stahl 70
8. Organizing the Expedition
   by George Rawlyk 83
9. Domestic Life in Provincial Times
   by Charles E. Banks 92
10. Court House, Gaol, and Punishments
    by Charles E. Banks 100
11. The Capture of the Margaretta
    by George F. Talbot 109
12. The Burning of Falmouth, 1775
    by John C. Warren 115
13. The Proposed Province of New Ireland
    by Joseph Williamson 119
14. The Maine Frontier
    by Frederick Allis, Jr. 123
15. Maine's First Newspaper
    by Frederick G. Fassett, Jr. 136

Chapter		Page
16.	The War of 1812: A Turning Point in the Movement to Separate Maine from Massachusetts *by Ronald F. Banks*	143
17.	The September Election and the Brunswick Convention of 1816 *by Ronald F. Banks*	148
18.	The Maine Constitutional Convention of 1819 *by Ronald F. Banks*	161
19.	The Missouri Compromise: "The Mother Has Twins" *by Ronald F. Banks*	177

Part II
INTRODUCTION: MAINE IN THE NINETEENTH CENTURY, 1820-1900

20.	Maine and Its Public Domain—Land Disposal on the Northeastern Frontier *by David C. Smith*	191
21.	The Aroostook War *by Henry Burrage*	199
22.	Annual Reports of the Bath Temperance Society *by Anonymous*	207
23.	The Napoleon of Temperance *by Frank L. Byrne*	211
24.	Antislavery: Maine and the Nation *by Edward O. Schriver*	218
25.	The Flowering of a Lumber Town *by Stewart H. Holbrook*	228
26.	Frozen Gold: The Ice Industry on the Kennebec *by Ernest Marriner*	234
27.	The State of Maine Clippers *by William H. Rowe*	238
28.	Portland: Rival or Satellite *by Edward Kirkland*	248
29.	From Kittery to 'Quoddy *by Alvin F. Harlow*	260
30.	Wood Pulp Paper Comes to the Northeast, 1865-1900 *by David C. Smith*	270
31.	The Humble Potato *by Clarence A. Day*	280
32.	Manufacture of Beet Sugar—1838 *by Anonymous*	293
33.	The Beet Sugar Industry in Maine, 1875-1880 *by Ernest Thomas Gennert*	295
34.	Aroostook's "Sweet Potato" *by Editors of New England Business Review*	299
35.	Rise of the Knights of Labor and the A.F. of L. in Maine *by Charles A. Scontras*	303

Chapter		Page
36.	Bar Harbor: The Summer Colony *by Richard W. Hale, Jr.*	315
37.	How D'Ye Do, Colonel *by John J. Pullen*	324
38.	Maine and American Artists, 1710-1963 *by Jacqueline Davidson*	333

Part III
INTRODUCTION: MAINE IN THE TWENTIETH CENTURY

39.	The Trouble with Maine *by William S. Ellis*	339
40.	Issues and Decisions: Maine's Future *by George H. Ellis*	343
41.	Conservation and Economic Development *by Governor Kenneth M. Curtis*	347
42.	Poverty in Affluence *by The Staff of the Maine Business Indicators*	353
43.	Maine's "Income Gap" *by Edgar Miller*	357
44.	Maine's Sinclair Act *by Bailey, Frost, Marsh and Wood*	364
45.	"The Big Question?" Dickey-Lincoln Is Justified *by Senator Edmund S. Muskie*	370
46.	Dickey-Lincoln—It's Obsolete before It's Built *by Albert A. Cree*	373

PART I

THE COLONIAL PERIOD

The year was 1496. John Cabot, a Genoan born master mariner, had received the blessing of King Henry VII of England to go forth upon his "own proper costs and charges, to seek out, to discover and find whatsoever islands, countries, regions, or provinces of the heathens or infidels, in whatever part of the world they be, which before this time have been unknown to all christians."

Cabot, like Columbus before him, chose to sail west from Europe to find the land of the Great Khan. Instead, he became the first mariner sailing under the English flag to navigate the North American coast. He sailed along the coast working northward until he made a landfall in what is now Labrador. In the process, he became the first European, with the possible exception of the Norsemen, to lay eyes upon the Maine coast.

The Cabot voyage was only one of hundreds made to the new world by Europeans between 1492 and 1600. This was the Age of Discovery which had its genesis in the fertile imagination of the Portuguese Prince known as Henry the Navigator. During the 1500's, it was Spain who led in the exploration and colonization of the new world. In so doing, she became the first of the modern world powers.

The English were slow to adjust to the possibilities inherent in the opening of the new world. Not until Queen Elizabeth was crowned in 1558 did the future colonizers of the United States begin to experience the urge to enter the race for riches and power. Elizabeth was determined to wrest control of the Seven Seas from Spain and to place England in undisputed control of her own destiny as the world's leading power. She succeeded brilliantly.

The Elizabethan Seadogs, a coterie of clever mariners which included Walter Raleigh, Francis Drake and Humphrey Gilbert among others, harassed Spanish commerce and attacked Spanish possessions. In 1588, the moment of truth came with the defeat of the Spanish Armada. The balance of European power had been tipped in favor of the English.

With the victory, the way was now open for the English to intrude into eastern North America. At first, however, the colonization of North America would share the attention of Englishmen with the desire to find an all water route to India through the North American continent—the mythical Northwest Passage.

It was the search for both objectives which brought Bartholomew Gosnold to the New England coast in 1602. He was successful in neither. Blown off course, his voyagers became the first Englishmen to set foot on Maine soil, probably on the stretch of sandy beach which extends from Old Orchard to Kittery.

The following year, 1603, saw another English visitor come to the Maine coast. Martin Pring was sent by Bristol merchants to investigate the prospects for a lucrative trade in furs and fish. His glowing report, when added to the one Gosnold submitted, convinced influential people that New England and Maine were exploitable. The support of a number of wealthy men including Thomas Arundell, Ferdinando Gorges, and Sir John Popham was obtained and in 1605 these men underwrote the cost of the voyage of George Weymouth to the Maine coast. James Rosier accompanied Weymouth on this most important voyage and later wrote an account of it, (1).

After Weymouth's return to England, his chief sponsors, Arundell, Gorges, and Popham, decided to establish a colony. Joining with a number of other merchants from the towns of London and Plymouth, they asked the successor of Elizabeth I,

King James I, for a charter to establish a joint stock company as the instrument for colonizing. James obliged but for political reasons he created two companies. To the London Company he granted the right to plant a colony between the 34° and 41°. To the Plymouth Company (which included as proprietors Gorges, Arundell, and Popham) he granted the right to establish a colony between the 38° and 45°. In April 1607, an expedition sent by the London Company established the first permanent English colony in the new world at Jamestown. Three months later two ships under the command of George Popham and Raleigh Gilbert arrived on the Maine coast. Following the same course as Weymouth, they landed first by the St. George River but eventually settled at the mouth of the Kennebec River. For a year, the Popham colonists tried to make their venture a success. Finally, however, they were forced to return to England. Thus, the first English effort to establish permanency in New England (thirteen years before the Pilgrims settled Plymouth) ended in failure, (2).

Meanwhile, the French had evinced interest in the new world, an interest which eventually would place them on a collision course with the English. Throughout the 16th century, the French sent explorers to the new world. In 1598, they established a settlement on Sable Island off the coast of Nova Scotia. This effort failed but in 1603 one Sieur de Monts was granted trading and seignorial rights in what is now an area extending from Newfoundland to New York City.

In 1604, De Monts, his friend Samuel de Champlain, and a motley crew of settlers landed at St. Croix Island in the St. Croix River. This was nearly two years before the Popham colony was established. Thus the St. Croix colony, although lasting but a year, has the distinction of being the first attempt ever made by Europeans to establish a colony in Maine.

After the failure of the St. Croix colony in 1605, it was not until 1613 that a French settlement was again attempted in Maine. In that year a group of Frenchmen, among whom was a Jesuit priest, Father Pierre Biard, arrived at Port Royal in Nova Scotia. Biard had hoped to engage in missionary work among the Indians but found the population around Port Royal too sparse. Seeking a more populous area, he and his associates sailed from Nova Scotia to the Maine coast and up the Penobscot River to present-day Bangor (then known as Kadequit) at which was located an Indian village. The party returned to Port Royal to make preparations to settle at Bangor. Upon the return voyage they encountered a heavy fog and in desperation made their way up Somes Sound on Mt. Desert Island. It was here that they established a mission at a place the Indians called Pemetig, (3).

Later in the year, however, one Samuel Argall sailed from Jamestown to drive the French from what the English considered their soil. Argall entered the Sound with "the banner of England flying and three trumpets and two drums making a horrible din" opening fire on everything in sight. Biard and his party were taken prisoner bringing to an abrupt end the French colony or mission on Mt. Desert.

* * *

In 1608, when the Popham Colony dissolved, until 1620 when the Pilgrims came to Plymouth, the English made no effort to colonize further in New England. Even so, there was a good deal of activity along the New England coast. John Smith, of Jamestown renown, sailed along the coast between 1614 and 1616. A remarkably observant man, Smith drew what was probably the first map of the New England coast. Later, he penned his *A General History of New England* in which the term New England was employed for the first time.

During these years another activity in connection with the New England (especially Maine) coast engaged some Englishmen. In the spring scores of vessels would come to Maine to fish during the warm months. They dried their catch on the islands of the Maine coast where were pastured cows, hogs, goats, and other animals used by them as sources of foods. In the fall, they gathered up the thousands of pounds of dried fish and returned to England only to repeat the cycle the next spring.

In 1620 the original Plymouth *Company* was dissolved. In its place James I chartered the Council for New England, an organization designed to oversee the orderly settlement of the area north of present-day New York. The affairs of the Council were entrusted to forty-eight men among whom were John Mason and Ferdinando Gorges, the leading figures in early Maine history. In 1623, the Council appointed Mason and Gorges proprietors of the land lying between the Merrimac and Kennebec Rivers. In 1629, the two men agreed to divide their land at the Piscataqua River, the present-day boundary between Maine and New Hampshire. Gorges' share was the land between the Kennebec and the Piscataqua.

In 1621, the Council granted to the Pilgrims the land on which they settled around Plymouth. The first few years of the life of the colony were difficult. At one point, the settlers were saved from starvation only by the generous assistance of the above mentioned fishermen who willingly provided the Plymouth settlers with supplies. Yet, in the end the colony prospered. One reason for its success was again due to Maine. In 1629, the Council granted them a large chunk of land along the Kennebec River in the shape of a rectangle encompassing both shores. In the center of this land, the Pilgrims established a post which they called Cushenoc (Augusta). They had posts as well at present-day Castine and at the mouth of the Kennebec. Trading with the Indians, they soon amassed such amounts of capital they were able to pay off all of their debts. This happy situation continued until they sold their Maine grant in 1661, (4).

In the early 1630's there were numerous grants of land in Maine made by the Council and Gorges. One grant was made to Richard Vines who had first settled on it in 1623. The site of his settlement was at Saco and was very probably the first permanent settlement to be established in Maine. Charles II, a close friend of Gorges, moved to solidify his friendship which he needed in his struggle against the Parliamentary forces at home. It appears that Charles intended to reorganize New England which by now was a patchwork of competing colonies some quite unfriendly to the Crown. His plan was to appoint Gorges Governor of New England and to locate the capitol of the new domain at Agamenticus (York), a half-way point between the extremities of the region.

As the first step in implementing the plan, Gorges' grant to the territory between the Piscataqua and the Kennebec was confirmed by Charles I in 1639. In 1641, Gorges was declared Governor of the Province of Maine. Preliminary to the next step of becoming Governor of New England, Gorges established Agamenticus which he modestly named Gorgeana and made the first city in the new world. Gorges, who never set foot on Maine soil despite his forty year long infatuation with the area, sent his nephew Thomas Gorges to govern the jurisdiction in 1640. In that year, the first representative assembly or General Court was held in Saco. But the next step never came. The King became embroiled in Civil War. Gorges in siding with the King backed a loser, (5).

Because the "slight civil disturbance" in England did deflect Gorges from his interests in Maine, after 1643 the area was left to fend for itself. In 1647, Gorges died. His Maine lands passed to his heirs, or at least they were supposed to. However, with the Puritans coming to power in England, all properties of those who sided with the Crown were placed in jeopardy. The Puritans of Massachusetts encouraged by their counterparts in England abhorred the power vacuum left in Maine. Like iron attracted to a magnet, they moved into Maine and by 1658 declared themselves rulers over all the territory which had belonged to Gorges. Maine settlers were powerless to resist the intrusion and were left unimpressed by the Saints' claim that Maine had always belonged to Massachusetts by the terms of the Charter of 1629, (6).

After the restoration in 1660, Charles II pressured Massachusetts Bay to acknowledge the legitimacy of the claim to Maine which Gorges' heirs were pressing. Finally, in 1677, Massachusetts paid the sum of $6,000 to the heirs, thus bringing to an end the interest of the Gorges family in this area.

From 1677 to 1691, Maine was treated as a colony of Massachusetts Bay. A President, Thomas Danforth, oversaw the territory. From 1691 down to 1820, Maine was totally integrated with Massachusetts. Thus, from 1691 to 1820 there was no political or legal entity of Maine although the geographic fact of separateness served to remind those in both areas of the unnaturalness of the union.

* * *

Down to 1675, Maine people had enjoyed relative peace with the Indians of the area although the relationship between the two cultures was never cordial. In 1675, King Philip's War broke out in Massachusetts and soon spread to Maine. From that time until 1763, Maine was the scene of some of the bloodiest battles of the colonial period of American history.

Aggravating the situation between the two peoples was the fact that in 1689 the great contest for supremacy in North America known as the Second One Hundred Years War broke out. France, under Louis XIV, was determined to dethrone England as the leading western power as England had dethroned Spain earlier. Maine was strategically located between French Canada and English America, a most unenviable position. As happened elsewhere in the colonies, the French were able to ally themselves with the Maine Indians. As a result, the English settlements along the Maine coast experienced a double barreled threat. A number of villages were destroyed in the wars and at times the English settlers found themselves huddled in garrisons fearing to travel at all. These vicious wars also served as deterrents to further growth in population. For the one hundred years before the American Revolution, Maine for the most part stagnated.

One of the most interesting men to appear in Maine before the Revolution was a scion of a wealthy merchant family of Boston, Samuel Waldo. Actually, Waldo's interest in Maine was largely fortuitous. Back in 1631 the Council for New England granted to John Beauchamp and Thomas Leverett a large chunk of land along the coast from the Penobscot westward to almost the Kennebec, known as the Muscongus grant. In 1729, the heirs of Leverett, lacking funds to develop the grant, invited twenty persons into an association dedicated to that development. One of the "20 Associates," as they were called, was Jonathan Waldo, Sam's father. In 1732, when the father died, Sam inherited his father's interest in the grant.

Sam was an entrepreneurial type. He founded the first paper mill in Maine in 1731 in association with Thomas Westbrook. He was also one of the King's mast agents in Maine. Becoming impatient with the deliberateness of the "20 Associates," he got them to agree to grant him a portion of the grant as his own to develop. The area given him was that encompassing the territory between present-day Waldoboro and Thomaston.

Waldo was primarily interested in speculation in land. He knew that his land would not increase in value until settlers were brought to it to "mix their labor with the soil." But compared to other colonies, Maine was not an attractive area to prospective English or Scottish immigrants. He recognized this and consequently sought out peoples who were not as particular as most, namely a group of Palatinate Germans. What ensued was one of the most interesting if not edifying episodes in all of Maine's history, (7).

One of the historic events of this period in American and Maine History was the capture of the super fortress Louisbourg from the French in 1745. Maine men played an important role in the capture but none more than William Pepperrell, Jr., of Kittery who was chosen to lead the expedition, (8).

Everyday life in colonial America is always interesting to read about. Life in York during this period was no exception as the article dealing with this subject reveals, (9).

Americans have always been intrigued with battles waged by the "good guys" against the "bad guys." Colonial Maine had its share of bad guys at least judged by the standards of the day. Especially interesting to read about are the punishments meted out by the virtuous, (10).

* * *

From a military standpoint, Maine's role in the War for Independence was insignificant compared to developments in other parts of the colonies. Nevertheless, several incidents involving the British did occur in Maine. The most famous episode was the ill-fated Penobscot Expedition which took place in 1779. Unfortunately, no satisfactory account of this effort by Massachusetts authorities to expel the British from eastern Maine has ever been written. Another affair of as great renown was the expedition led by Benedict Arnold against Quebec in 1775. This colonial army, which included in its ranks such names as Aaron Burr, Daniel Morgan, and Henry Dearborn, as well as Arnold, went up the Kennebec River and crossed overland into Canada only to be ignominiously repelled at Quebec.

Less well known were two encounters between the English and Americans which occurred in 1775. Shortly after Lexington and Concord there took place at Machias what local tradition has claimed was the first naval battle of the Revolution. Although there is reason to doubt the veracity of the claim, the encounter did demonstrate to what extent relations with the mother country were ruptured a full year before the Declaration of Independence was promulgated,(11).

The second encounter began with the kidnapping of a British naval captain by overzealous patriots in May 1775, and ended with the same captain (Mowatt) returning to Falmouth (Portland) in October to bombard the town until three-quarters of it was totally destroyed, (12).

Not every colonist became a rebel. A sizeable minority chose to remain loyal to the Crown. These Tories, as they were called, found their lot a difficult one in many of the colonies. A large number of them were forcibly expelled and their property confiscated. Many fled to England but others, particularly New England Tories, went to Canada. The British authorities felt a special concern for their "patriots" and considered various schemes to provide for their welfare. One such scheme was hatched about 1779. The authorities hoped to detach from the American colonies all of the area in Maine between the Saco and St. Croix Rivers. This area would be named New Ireland and would become the north American sanctuary of the loyalists. Although the plan was never implemented, its consideration suggests that the English did not believe the jurisdiction which Massachusetts exercised over Maine (since 1658) was at all soundly based, (13).

Down to about 1785, Maine languished, her growth and development having been checked mainly by the numerous wars into which the area was drawn. By 1750, the population was estimated at only 10,000 people. After the Revolution, however, Maine embarked upon her first real period of sustained growth. Between 1785 and 1820, the population increased from 50,000 to 300,000. For the first time ever, capital began to be generated in substantial amounts. Shipping and lumbering flourished spurred on by great demand from Europe. In 1794, Bowdoin College was founded. In 1799, the first bank was established in the District of Maine at Portland. Of course, even these innovations looked pitifully inadequate compared to what needed to be done. The article entitled "The Maine Frontier", describes some of the problems and some of the opportunities facing the area in the 1780's and 1790's as it struggled to develop, (14).

One of the trappings of modern civilization is the newspaper. Among the innovations which occurred between 1785 and 1820 was the establishment of Maine's first newspaper. The first issue of the *Falmouth Gazette* appeared in January 1785, and contained the kind of news typical of newspapers of that period, (15).

The *Falmouth Gazette* and its various successors were organs of the Federalist political party which dominated the Maine scene down to 1804. With the election of the first Democratic-Republican President, Thomas Jefferson, in 1800, the Maine Democratic-Republican Party began to develop. By 1803 it was clear that the Federalist party had no future in Maine. From 1804 to 1820, Maine voted heavily Democratic. Indeed, down to the Civil War, Maine was a thoroughly Democratic state.

The movement to obtain a separation of Maine and Massachusetts began in 1785. At first, the movement was led by Federalist politicians but after 1807 the Democrats under the leadership of William King of Bath, Maine, took it over. Between 1785 and 1812, little enthusiasm for independence was evident in Maine. The War of 1812, however, became a turning point in the history of the movement, as the authorities in Massachusetts, especially Governor Strong, alienated many Maine people by their war policies. Particularly irksome was the refusal of the governor to lift a finger to expel the British from eastern Maine. In addition, the fact that the same authorities were more friendly to the British than their own government in Washington provided another source of irritation, (16).

In 1815, a group of Democratic politicians seized the opportunity given them by the war to push for immediate separation. The efforts of William King, John Holmes of Alfred, Albion K. Parris of Paris, and William Pitt Preble of Portland culminated in the famous Brunswick Convention of 1816. So eager were these men to achieve victory that when they discovered that they had fallen a few votes short, they resorted to bald faced diabolical tactics. Unfortunately for them, they were not masters of the art or science of chicanery and their efforts fell ignominiously to the ground, (17).

The leaders of 1816 learned much from their defeat of 1816, namely, that before they tried to achieve independence again they should carefully lay the groundwork. This was done by William King who travelled to Washington in the fall of 1818 to obtain the support of several key national politicians for the cause. In June 1819, the General

Court of Massachusetts consented to independence in an "Act of Separation." In October 1819, delegates from all over Maine met in Portland to draw up a constitution for the new state, (18).

In December 1819, the Congress was petitioned to admit Maine into the Union. At this point, Maine's forward motion was abruptly halted by a collision with the aspirations of the citizens of Missouri. For three months, the Missouri controversy raged until finally the forces of compromise led by one of Maine's congressmen, John Holmes, prevailed. On the 15th of March, 1820, Maine, which had existed in a kind of colonial status longer than any other territory in America, came into the Union as the twenty-third state, (19).

CHAPTER 1.

James Rosier accompanied George Weymouth to the coast of Maine in 1605. On returning to England, he wrote the following promotional account of his observations on the voyage.

A TRUE RELATION OF CAPTAIN GEORGE WEYMOUTH HIS VOYAGE, MADE THIS PRESENT YEERE 1605; IN THE DISCOUERIE OF THE NORTH PART OF VIRGINIA.*

by
James Rosier

1605 March

Vpon Tuesday the 5 day of March, about ten a clocke afore noone, we set saile from Ratcliffe, and came to an anker that tide about two a clocke before Grauesend.

From thence the 10 of March being Sunday at night we ankered in the Downes: and there rode til the next day about three a clocke after noone, when with a scant winde we set saile; and by reason the winde continued Southwardly, we were beaten vp and doune: but on Saturday the 16 day about foure a clocke after noon we put into Dartmouth Hauen, where the continuance of the winde at South & Southwest constrained vs to ride till the last of this moneth. There we shipped some of our men and supplied necessaries for our Ship and Voyage.

Upon Easter day, being the last of March, the winde comming at North-North-East, about fiue a clocke after noone we wayed anker, and put to sea. In the name of God, being well victualled and furnished with munition and all necessaries: Our whole Company being but 29 persons; of whom I may boldly say, few voyages have beene manned forth with better Sea-men generally in respect of our small number.

April

Munday the next day, being the first of Aprill, by sixe a clocke in the morning we were sixe leagues South-South-East from the Lizarde.

At two a clocke in the afternoone this day, the weather being very faire, our Captaine for his owne experience and others with him sounded, and had sixe and fiftie fathoms and a halfe. The sounding was some small blacke perrie sand, some reddish sand, a match or two, with small shels called Saint James his Shels.

The foureteenth of Aprill being Sunday, betweene nine and ten of the clocke in the morning our Captaine descried the Iland Cueruo: which bare South-West and by West, about seuen leagues from vs: by eleuen of the clocke we descried Flores to the Southward of Cueruo, as it lieth: by foure a clocke in the afternoone we brought Cueruo due South from vs within two leagues of the shore, but we touched not, because the winde was faire, and we thought our selues sufficiently watered and wooded.

Heere our Captaine obserued the Sunne, and found himselfe in the latitude of 40 degrees and 7 minutes: so he judged the North part of Cueruo to be in 40 degrees. After we had kept our course about a hundred leagues from the Ilands, by continuall Southerly windes we were forced and driuen from the Southward, whither we first intended. And when our Captaine by long beating saw it was but in vaine to striue with windes, not knowing Gods purposes heerein to our further blessing, (which after by his especiall direction wee found) he thought best to stand as nigh as he could by the winde to recouer what land we might first discouer.

---

*George Parker Winship, *Sailors Narratives of Voyages Along the New England Coast*, 1524-1624. (Boston: Houghton-Mifflin & Co., 1905), pp. 101-151.

May

Munday, the 6 of May, being in the latitude of 39 and a halfe about ten a clocke afore noone, we came to a riplin, which we discerned a head our ship, which is a breach of water caused either by a fall, or by some meeting of currents, which we judged this to be; for the weather being very faire, and a small gale of winde, we sounded and found no ground in a hundred fathoms.

Munday, the 13 of May, about eleuen a clocke afore noone, our Captaine, judging we were not farre from land, sounded, and had a soft oaze in a hundred and sixty fathomes. At fowre a clocke after noone we sounded againe, and had the same oaze in a hundred fathoms.

From ten a clocke that night till three a clocke in the morning, our Captaine tooke in all sailes and lay at hull, being desirous to fall with the land in the day time, because it was an vnknowen coast, which it pleased God in his mercy to grant vs, otherwise we had run our ship vpon the hidden rockes and perished all. For when we set saile we sounded in 100 fathoms: and by eight a clock, hauing not made aboue fiue or six leagues, our Captaine vpon a sudden change of water (supposing verily he saw the sand) presently sounded, and had but fiue fathoms.

Sankaty Head

Much maruelling because we saw no land, he sent one to the top, who thence descried a whitish sandy cliffe, which bare West-North-West about six leagues off from vs al along the shore, into which before we should enter, our Captaine thought best to hoise out his ship boate and sound it. Which if he had not done, we had beene in great danger: for he bare vp the ship, as neere as he durst after the boate: vntill Thomas Cam, his mate, being in the boate, called to him to tacke about & stand off, for in this breach he had very showld water, two fathoms and lesse vpon rockes, and sometime they supposed they saw the rocke within three or fowre foote, whereon the sea made a very strong breach: which we might discerne (from the top) to run along as we sailed by it 6 or 7 leagues to the Southward. This was in the latitude of 41 degrees, 20 minuts: wherefore we were constrained to put backe againe from the land: and sounding, (the weather being very faire and a small winde) we found our selues embaied with continuall showldes and rockes in a most vncertaine ground, from fiue or six fathoms, at the next cast of the lead we should haue 15 & 18 fathoms. Ouer many which we passed, and God so blessed vs, that we had wind and weather as faire as poore men in this distresse could wish: whereby we both perfectly discerned euery breach, and with the winde were able to turne, where we saw most hope of safest passage. Thus we parted from the land, which we had not so much before desired, and at the first sight rejoiced, as now we all joifully praised God, that it had pleased him to deliuer vs from so imminent danger.

Heere we found great store of excellent Cod fish, and saw many Whales, as we had done two or three daies before.

We stood off all that night, and the next day being Wednesday; but the wind still continuing between the points of South-South-West, and West-South-West: so as we could not make any way to the Southward, in regard of our great want of water and wood (which was now spent) we much desired land and therefore sought for it, where the wind would best suffer vs to refresh our selues.

Thursday, the 16 of May, we stood in directly with the land, and much maruelled we descried it nog, wherein we found our sea charts very false, putting land where none is.

Friday, the 17 of May, about sixe a clocke at night we descried the land, which bare from vs North-North-East; but because it blew a great gale of winde, the sea very high and neere night, not fit to come vpon an vnknowen coast, we stood off till two a clocke in the morning, being Saturday: then standing in with it againe, we descried it by eight a clocke in the morning, bearing North-East from vs.

Monhegan

It appeared a meane high land, as we after found it, being but an Iland of some six miles in compasse, but I hope the most fortunate euer yet discouered. About twelue a clocke that day, we came to an anker on the North side of this Iland, about a league from the shore. About two a clocke our Captaine with twelue men rowed in his ship boat to the shore, where we made no long stay, but laded our boat with dry wood of olde trees vpon the shore side, and returned to our ship, where we rode that night.

This Iland is woody, growen with Firre, Birch, Oke and Beech, as farre as we say along the shore; and so likely to be within. On the verge grow Gooseberries, Strawberries, Wild pease, and Wilde rose bushes. The water issued foorth downe the Rocky cliffes in many places: and much fowle of diuers kinds breed vpon the shore and rocks.

While we were at shore, our men aboord with a few hooks got aboue thirty great Cods and Hadocks, which gaue vs a taste of the great plenty of fish which we found afterward wheresoeuer we went vpon the coast.

Camden Hills

From hence we might discerne the maine land from the West-South-West to the East-North-East, and a great way (as it then seemed, and as we after found it) vp into the maine we might discerne very high mountaines, though the maine seemed but low land; which gaue vs a hope it would please God to direct vs to the discouerie of some good; although wee were driuen by winds farre from that place, whither (both by our direction and desire) we euer intended to shape the course of our voyage.

The next day being Whit-Sunday; because we rode too much open to the sea and windes, we weyed anker about twelue a clocke, and came along to the other Ilands more adjoyning to the maine, and in the rode directly with the mountaines, about three leagues from the first Iland where we had ankered.

St. George's Islands

When we came neere vnto them (sounding all along in a good depth) our Captaine manned his ship-boat and sent her before with Thomas Cam one of his Mates, whom he knew to be of good experience, to sound & search betweene the Ilands for a place safe for our shippe to ride in; in the meane while we kept aloofe at sea, hauing giuen them in the boat a token to weffe in the ship, if he found a conuenient Harbour; which it pleased God to send vs, farre beyond our expectation, in a most safe birth defended from all windes, in an excellent depth of water for ships of any burthen, in six, seuen, eight, nine and ten fathoms vpon a clay oaze very tough.

We all with great joy praised God for his vnspeakable goodnesse, who had from so apparent danger deliuered vs, & directed vs vpon this day into so secure an Harbour: in remembrance whereof we named it Pentecost harbor, we arriuing there that day out of our last Harbor in England, from whence we set saile vpon Easterday.

About foure a clocke, after we were ankered and well mored, our Captaine with halfe a dozen of our Company went on shore to seeke fresh watering, and a conuenient place to set together a pinnesse, which we brought in pieces out of England; both which we found very fitting.

Vpon this Iland, as also vpon the former, we found (at our first comming to shore) where fire had beene made: and about the place were very great egge shells bigger than goose egges, fish bones, and as we judged, the bones of some beast.

Here we espied Cranes stalking on the shore of a little Iland adjoyning; where we after saw they vsed to breed.

Whitsun-munday, the 20 day of May, very early in the morning, our Captaine caused the pieces of the pinnesse to be carried a shore, where while some were busied about her, others digged welles to receiue the fresh water, which we found issuing downe out of the land in many places. Heere I cannot omit (for foolish feare of imputation of flattery) the painfull industry of our Captaine, who as at sea he is always most carefull and vigilant, so at land he refuseth no paines; but his labour was euer as much or rather more than any mans: which not only encourageth others with better content, but also effecteth much with great expedition.

In digging we found excellent clay for bricke or tile.

The next day we finished a well of good and holesome cleere water in a great empty caske, which we left there. We cut yards, waste trees, and many necessaries for our ship, while our Carpenter and Cooper laboured to fit and furnish forth the shallop.

This day our boat went out about a mile from our ship, and in small time with two or three hooks was fished sufficiently for our whole Company three dayes, with great Cod, Haddocke, and Thornebacke.

And towards night we drew with a small net of twenty fathoms very nigh the shore: we got about thirty very good and great Lobsters, many Rockfish, some Plaise, and other small fishes, and fishes called Lumpes, verie pleasant to the taste: and we generally obserued, that all the fish, of what kinde soeuer we tooke, were well fed, fat, and sweet in taste.

Wednesday, the 22 of May, we felled and cut wood for our ships vse, cleansed and scoured our wels, and digged a plot of ground, wherein, amongst some garden seeds, we sowed peaze and barley, which in sixteen dayes grew eight inches aboue ground; and so continued growing euery day halfe an inch, although this was but the crust of the ground, and much inferior to the mould we after found in the maine.

Friday, the 24 of May, after we had made an end of cutting wood, and carying water aboord our shippe, with fourteene Shot and Pikes we marched about and thorow part of two of the Ilands; the bigger of which we judged to be foure or fiue miles in compasse, and a mile broad.

The profits and fruits which are naturally on these Ilands are these:

All along the shore and some space within, where the wood hindereth not, grow plentifully:
- Rasberries
- Gooseberries
- Strawberries
- Roses
- Currants
- Wild-Vines
- Angelica.

Within the Ilands growe wood of sundry sorts, some very great, and all tall:
- Birch
- Beech
- Ash
- Maple
- Spruce
- Cherry-tree
- Yew
- Oke very great and good
- Firre-tree, out of which issueth

Turpentine in so maruellous plenty, and so sweet, as our Chirurgeon and others affirmed they neuer saw so good in England. We pulled off much Gumme congealed on the outside of the barke, which smelled like Frankincense. This would be a great benefit for making Tarre and Pitch.

We stayed the longer in this place, not only because of our good Harbour (which is an excellent comfort) but because euery day we did more and more discouer the pleasant fruitfulnesse; insomuch as many of our Companie wished themselues setled heere, not expecting any further hopes, or better discouery to be made.

Heere our men found abundance of great muscels among the rocks; and in some of them many small Pearls: and in one muscell (which we drew vp in our net) was found foureteene Pearles, whereof one of prety bignesse and orient; in another aboue fiftie small Pearles; and if we had had a Drag, no doubt we had found some of great valew, seeing these did certainly shew, that heere they were bred: the shels all glistering with mother of Pearle.

Wednesday, the 29 day, our shallop being now finished, and our Captaine and men furnished to depart with hir from the ship: we set vp a crosse on the shore side vpon the rockes.

Thursday, the 30 of May, about ten a clock afore noon, our Captaine with 13 men more, in the name of God, and with all our praiers for their prosperous discouerie, and safe returne, departed in the shallop: leauing the ship in a good harbour, which before I mentioned, well mored, and manned with 14 men.

This day, about fiue a clocke in the afternoone, we in the shippe espied three Canoas comming towards vs, which went to the iland adjoining, where they went a shore, and very quickly had made a fire, about which they stood beholding our ship: to whom we made signes with our hands and hats, weffing vnto them to come vnto vs, because we had not seene any of the people yet. They sent one Canoa with three men, one of which, when they came neere vnto vs, spake in his language very lowd and very boldly: seeming as though he would know why we were there, and by pointing with his oare towards the sea, we conjectured he ment we should be gone. But when we shewed them kniues and their vse, by cutting of stickes and other trifles, as combs and glasses, they came close aboard our ship, as desirous to entertaine our friendship. To these we gaue such things as we perceiued they liked, when wee shewed them the vse: bracelets, rings, peacocke feathers, which they stucke in their haire, and Tabacco pipes. After their departure to their company on the shore, presently came foure other in another Canoa: to whom we gaue as to the former, vsing them with as much kindnes as we could.

The shape of their body is very proportionable, they are wel countenanced, not very tal nor big, but in stature like to vs: they paint their bodies with blacke, their faces, some with red, some with blacke, and some with blew.

Their clothing is Beauers skins, or Deares skins, cast ouer them like a mantle, and hanging downe to their knees, made fast together vpon the shoulder with leather; some of them had sleeues, most had none; some had buskins of such leather tewed: they haue besides a peece of Beauers skin betweene their legs, made fast about their waste, to couer their priuities.

They suffer no haire to grow on their faces, but on their head very long and very blacke, which those that haue wiues, binde vp behinde with a leather string, in a long round knot.

They seemed all very ciuill and merrie: shewing tokens of much thankefulnesse, for those things we gaue them. We found them then (as after) a people of exceeding good inuention, quicke vnderstanding and readie capacitie.

Their Canoas are made without any iron, of the bark of a birch tree, strengthened within with ribs and hoops of wood, in so good fashion, with such excellent ingenious art, as they are able to beare seuen or eight persons, far exceeding any in the Indies.

One of their Canoas came not to vs, wherein we imagined their women were: of whom they are (as all Saluages) very jealous.

When I signed vnto them they should goe sleepe, because it was night, they vnderstood presently, and pointed that at the shore, right against our ship, they would stay all night: as they did.

The next morning very early, came one Canoa abord vs againe with three Saluages, whom we easily then enticed into our ship, and vnder the decke: where we gaue them porke, fish, bred and pease, all which they did eat; and this I noted, they would eat nothing raw, either fish or flesh. They maruelled much and much looked vpon the making of our canne and kettle, so they did at a head-peece and at our guns, of which they are most fearefull, and would fall flat downe at the report of them. At their departure I signed vnto them, that if they would bring me such skins as they ware I would giue them kniues, and such things as I saw they most liked, which the chiefe of them promised to do by that time the Sunne should be beyond the middest of the firmament; this I did to bring them to an vnderstanding of exchange, and that they might conceiue the intent of our comming to them to be for no other end.

About 10 a clocke this day we descried our Shallop returning toward vs, which so soone as we espied, we certainly conjectured our Captaine had found some vnexpected harbour, further vp towards the maine to bring the ship into, or some riuer; knowing his determination and resolution, not so suddenly else to make return: which when they came neerer they expressed by shooting volleies of shot; and when they were come within Musket shot, they gaue vs a volley and haled vs, then we in the shippe gaue them a great peece and haled them.

Thus we welcomed them; who gladded vs exceedingly with their joifull relation of their happie discouerie, which shall appeare in the sequele. And we likewise gaue them cause of mutuall joy with vs, in discoursing of the kinde ciuility we found in a people, where we little expected any sparke of humanity.

St. George's River

Our Captaine had in this small time discouered vp a great riuer, trending alongst into the maine about forty miles. The pleasantnesse whereof, with the safety of harbour for shipping, together with the fertility of ground and other fruits, which were generally by his whole company related, I omit, till I report of the whole discouery therein after performed. For by the bredth, depth and strong flood, imagining it to run far vp into the land, he with speed returned, intending to flanke his light horsman for arrowes, least it might happen that the further part of the riuer should be narrow, and by that meanes subject to the volley of Saluages on either side out of the woods.

Vntill his returne, our Captaine left on shore where he landed in a path (which seemed to be frequented) a pipe, a brooch and a knife, thereby to know if the Saluages had recourse that way, because they could at that time see none of them, but they were taken away before our returne thither.

I returne now to our Saluages, who according to their appointment about one a clocke, came with 4 Canoas to the shoare of the iland right ouer against vs, where they had lodged the last night, and sent one Canoa to vs with two of those Saluages, who had beene a bord, and another, who then seemed to haue command of them; for though we perceiued their willingnesse, yet he would not permit them to come abord; but he hauing viewed vs and our ship, signed that he would go to the rest of the company and returne againe. Presently after their departure it began to raine, and continued all that afternoone, so as they could not come to vs with their skins and furs, nor we go to them. But after an howre or there about, the three which had beene with vs before came againe, whom we had to our fire and couered them with our gownes. Our Captaine bestowed a shirt vpon him, whom we thought to be their chiefe, who seemed neuer to haue seene any before we gaue him a brooch to hang about his necke, a great knife, and lesser kniues to the two other, and to euery one of them a combe and glasse, the vse whereof we shewed them: whereat they laughed and tooke gladly; we victualled them, and gaue them aqua vitae, which they tasted, but would by no meanes drinke; our beueridge they liked well, we gaue them Sugar Candy, which after they had tasted they liked and desired more, and raisons which were giuen them; and some of euery thing they would reserue to carry to their company. Wherefore we pittying their being in the raine, and therefore not able to get themselues victuall (as we thought) we gaue them bread and fish.

Thus because we found the land a place answereable to the intent of our discouery, viz.fit for any nation to inhabit, we vsed the people with as great kindnes as we could deuise, or found them capable of.

The next day, being Saturday and the first of June, I traded with the Saluages all the fore noone vpon the shore, where were eight and twenty of them: and because our ship rode nigh, we were but fiue or sixe: where for kniues, glasses, combes and other trifles to the valew of foure or fiue shillings, we had 40 good Beauers skins, Otters skins, Sables, and other small skins, which we knewe not how to call. Our trade being ended, many of them came abord vs, and did eat by our fire, and would be verie merrie and bold, in regard of our kinde vsage of them. Towards night our Captaine went on shore, to haue a draught with the Sein or Net. And we carried two of them with vs, who maruelled to see vs catch fish with a net. Most of that we caught we gaue them and their company. Then on the shore I learned the names of diuers things of them: and when they perceiued me to note them downe, they would of themselues, fetch fishes, and fruit bushes, and stand by me to see me write their names.

Our Captaine shewed them a strange thing which they soondred at. His sword and mine hauing beene touched with the Loadstone, tooke vp a knife, and held it fast when they plucked it away, made the knife turne, being laid on a blocke, and touching it with his sword, made that take vp a needle, whereat they much maruelled. This we did to cause them to imagine some great power in vs: and for that to loue and feare vs.

When we went on shore to trade with them, in one of their Canoas I saw their bowes and arrowes, which I tooke vp and drew an arrow in one of them, which I found to be of strength able to carry an arrow fiue or sixe score stronglie; and one of them tooke it and drew as we draw our bowes, not like the Indians. Their bow is made of Wich Hazell, and some of Beech in fashion much like our bowes, but they want nocks, onely a string of leather put through a hole at one end, and made fast with a knot at the other. Their arrowes are made of the same wood, some of Ash, big and long, with three feathers tied on, and nocked very artificiallie: headed with the long shanke bone of a Deere, made very sharpe with two fangs in manner of a harping iron. They haue likewise Darts, headed with like bone, one of which I darted among the rockes, and it brake not. These they vse very cunningly, to kill fish, fowle and beasts.

Our Captaine had two of them at supper with vs in his cabbin to see their demeanure, and had them in presence at seruice: who behaued themselues very ciuilly, neither laughing nor talking all the time, and at supper fed not like men of rude education, neither would they eat or drinke more than seemed to content nature; they desired pease to carry a shore to their women, which we gaue them, with fish and bread, and lent them pewter dishes, which they carefully brought againe.

In the evening another boat came to them on the shore, and because they had some Tabacco, which they brought for their owne vse, the other came for vs, making signe what they had, and offered to carry some of vs in their boat, but foure or fiue of vs went with them in our owne boat: when we came on shore they gaue vs the best welcome they could, spreading fallow Deeres skins for vs to sit on the ground by their fire, and gaue vs of their Tabacco in our pipes, which was excellent, and so generally commended of vs all to be as good as any we euer tooke, being the simple leafe without any composition, strong, and of sweet taste; the simple leafe without any composition, strong, and of sweet taste; they gaue us some to carry to our Captaine, whom they called our Bashabes; neither did they require any thing for it, but we would not receiue any thing from them without remuneration.

Heere we saw foure of their women, who stood behind them, as desirous to see vs, but not willing to be seene; for before, whensoeuer we came on shore, they retired into the woods, whether it were in regard of their owne naturall modestie, being couered only as the men with the foresaid Beauers skins, or by the commanding jealousy of their husbands, which we rather suspected, because it is an inclination much noted to be in Saluages; wherefore we would by no meanes seeme to take any speciall notice of them. They were very well fauoured in proportion of countenance, though coloured blacke, low of stature, and fat, bare headed as the men, wearing their haire long: they had two little male children of a yeere and half old, as we judged, very fat and of good countenances, which they loue tenderly, all naked, except their legs, which were couered with thin leather buskins tewed, fastened with strops to a girdle about their waste, which they girde very streight, and is decked round about with little round peeces of red Copper; to these I gaue chaines and bracelets, glasses, and other trifles, which the Saluages seemed to accept in great kindnesse.

At our comming away, we would haue had those two that supped with vs, to go abord and sleepe, as they had promised; but it appeared their company would not suffer them. Whereat we might easily perceiue they were much greeued; but not long after our departure, they came with three more to our ship, signing to vs, that if one of our company would go lie on shore with them, they would stay with vs. Then Owen Griffin (one of the two we were to leaue in the Country, if we had thought it needfull or conuenient) went with them in their Canoa, and 3 of them staied aborde vs, whom our whole company very kindly vsed. Our Captaine saw their lodging prouided, and them lodged in an old saile vpon the Orlop; and because they much feared our dogs, they were tied vp whensoeuer any of them came abord vs.

Powwow

Owen Griffin, which lay on the shore, reported vnto me their maner, and (as I may terme them) the ceremonies of their idolatry; which they performe thus. One among them (the eldest of the Company, as he judged) riseth right vp, the other sitting still, and looking about, suddenly cried with a loud voice, Baugh, Waugh: then the women fall downe, and lie vpon the ground, and the men all together answering the same, fall a stamping round about the fire with both feet, as hard as they can, making the ground shake, with sundry out-cries, and change of voice and sound. Many take the fire-sticks and thrust them into the earth, and then rest awhile: of a sudden beginning as before, they continue so stamping, till the yonger sort fetched from the shore many stones, of which euery man tooke one, and first beat vpon them with their fire-sticks, then with the stones beat the earth with all their strength. And in this maner (as he reported) they continued aboue two houres.

After this ended, they which haue wiues take them apart, and withdraw themselues seuerally into the wood all night.

The next morning, assoone as they saw the Sunne rise, they pointed to him to come with them to our shippe: and hauing receiued their men from vs, they came with fiue or six of their Canoas and Company houering about our ship; to whom (because it was the Sabbath day) I signed they should depart, and at the next Sun rising we would goe along with them to their houses; which they vnderstood (as we thought) and departed, some of their Canoas coursing about the Iland, and the other directly towards the maine.

This day, about fiue a clocke after noone, came three other Canoas from the maine, of which some had beene with vs before; and they came aboord vs, and brought vs Tabacco, which we tooke with them in their pipes, which were made of earth, very strong, blacke, and short containing a great quantity: some Tabacco they gaue vnto our Captaine, and some to me, in very ciuill kind maner. We requited them with bread and peaze, which they caried to their Company on shore, seeming very thankefull. After supper they returned with their Canoa to fetch vs a shore to take Tabacco with them there: with whom six or seuen of vs went, and caried some trifles, if peradventure they had any trucke, among which I caried some few biskets, to try if they would exchange for them, seeing they so well liked to eat them. When we came at shore, they most kindly entertained vs, taking vs by the hands, as they had obserued we did to them aboord, in token of welcome, and brought vs to sit downe by their fire, where sat together thirteene of them. They filled their Tabacco pipe, which was then the short claw of a Lobster, which will hold ten of our pipes full, and we dranke of their excellent Tabacco as much as we would with them; but we saw not any great quantity to trucke for; and it seemed they had not much left of old, for they spend a great quantity yeerely by their continuall drinking: and they would signe vnto vs, that it was growen yet but a foot aboue ground, and would be aboue a yard high, with a leafe as broad as both their hands. They often would (by pointing to one part of the maine Eastward) signe vnto vs, that their Bashabes (that is, their King) had great plenty of Furres, and much Tabacco. When we had sufficiently taken Tabacco with them, I shewed some of our trifles for trade; but they made signe that they had there nothing to exchange; for (as I after conceiued) they had beene fishing and fowling, and so came thither to lodge that night by vs: for when we were ready to come away, they shewed vs great cups made very wittily of barke, in forme almost square, full of a red berry about the bignesse of a bullis, which they did eat, and gaue vs by handfuls; of which (though I liked not the taste) yet I kept some, because I would by no meanes but accept their kindnesse.

Shad

They shewed me likewise a great piece of fish, whereof I tasted, and it was fat like Porpoise; and another kinde of great scaly fish, broiled on the coales, much like white Salmon, which the French-men call Aloza, for these they would haue had bread; which I refused, because in maner of exchange, I would alwayes make the greatest esteeme I could of our commodities whatsoeuer; although they saw aboord our Captaine was liberall to giue them, to the end we might allure them still to frequent vs. Then they shewed me foure yoong Goslings, for which they required foure biskets, but I offered them two; which they tooke and were well content.

At our departure they made signe, that if any of vs would stay there on shore, some of them would go lie aboord vs: at which motion two of our Company stayed with them, and three of the Saluages lodged with vs in maner as the night before.

Early the next morning, being Munday the third of June, when they had brought our men aboord, they came about our ship, earnestly by signes desiring that we would go with them along to the maine, for that there they had Furres and Tabacco to traffique with vs. Wherefore our Captaine manned the lighthorseman with as many men as he could well, which were about fifteene with rowers and all; and we went along with them. Two of their Canoas they sent away before, and they which lay aboord vs all night, kept company with vs to direct vs.

This we noted as we went along, they in their Canoa with three oares, would at their will go ahead of vs and about vs, when we rowed with eight oares strong; such was their swiftnesse, by reason of the lightnesse and artificiall composition of their Canoa and oares.

Pemaquid

When we came neere the point where we saw their fires, where they intended to land, and where they imagined some few of vs would come on shore with our merchandize, as we had accustomed before; when they had often numbred our men very diligently, they scoured away to their Company, not doubting we would haue followed them. But when we perceiued this, and knew not either their intents, or number of Saluages on the shore, our Captaine, after consultation, stood off, and wefted them to vs, determining that I should go on shore first to take a view of them, and what they had to traffique: if he, whom at our first sight of them seemed to be of most respect among them, and being then in the Canoa, would stay as a pawne for me. When they came to vs (notwithstanding all our former courtesies) he vtterly refused; but would leaue a yoong Saluage: and for him our Captaine sent Griffin in their Canoa, while we lay hulling a little off. Griffin at his returne reported, thay had there assembled together, as he numbred them, two hundred eighty three Saluages, euery one his bowe and arrowes, with their dogges, and wolues which they keepe tame at command, and not anything to exchange at all; but would haue drawen vs further vp into a little narrow nooke of a riuer, for their Furres, as they pretended.

These things considered, we began to joyne them in the ranke of other Saluages, who haue beene by trauellers in most discoueries found very trecherous; neuer attempting mischiefe, vntill by some remisnesse, fit opportunity affoordeth them certaine ability to execute the same. Wherefore after good advice taken, we determined so soone as we could to take some of them, least (being suspitious we had discouered their plots) they should absent themselues from vs.

Tuesday, the fourth of June, our men tooke Cod and Hadocke with hooks by our ship side, and Lobsters very great; which before we had not tried.

About eight a clocke this day we went on shore with our boats, to fetch aboord water and wood, our Captaine leauing word with the Gunner in the shippe, by discharging a musket, to giue notice if they espied any Canoa comming; which they did about ten a clocke. He therefore being carefull they should be kindly entreated, requested me to go aboord, intending with dispatch to make what haste after he possibly could. When I came to the ship, there were two Canoas, and in either of them three Saluages; of whom two were below at the fire, the other staied in their Canoas about the ship; and because we could not entice them abord, we gaue them a Canne of pease and bread, which they carried to the shore to eat. But one of them brought backe our Canne presently and staid abord with the other two; for he being yoong, of a ready capacity, and one we most desired to bring with vs into England, had receiued exceeding kinde vsage at our hands, and was therefore much delighted in our company. When our Captaine was come, we consulted how to catch the other three at shore which we performed thus.

We manned the light horseman with 7 or 8 men, one standing before carried our box of Marchandise, as we were woont when I went to traffique with them, and a platter of pease, which meat they loued: but before we were landed, one of them (being too suspitiously feareful of his owne good)

withdrew himselfe into the wood. The other two met vs on the shore side, to receiue the pease, with whom we went vp the Cliffe to their fire and sate downe with them, and whiles we were discussing how to catch the third man who was gone, I opened the box, and shewed them trifles to exchange, thinking thereby to haue banisht feare from the other, and drawen him to returne: but when we could not, we vsed little delay, but suddenly laid hands vpon them. And it was as much as fiue or sixe of vs could doe to get them into the light horseman. For they were strong and so naked as our best hold was by their long haire on their heads; and we would haue beene very loath to haue done them any hurt, which of necessity we had beene constrained to haue done if we had attempted them in a multitude, which we must and would, rather than haue wanted them, being a matter of great importance for the full accomplement of our voyage.

Thus we shipped fiue Saluages, two Canoas, with all their bowes and arrowes.

The next day we made an end of getting our wood aboord, and filled our empty caske with water.

Tuesday, the 6 of June, we spent in bestowing the Canoas vpon the orlop safe from hurt, because they were subject to breaking, which our Captaine was carefull to preuent.

Saturday the eight of June (our Captaine being desirous to finish all businesse about this harbour) very early in the morning, with the light horseman, coasted fiue or sixe leagues about the Ilands adjoining, and sounded all along wheresoeuer we went. He likewise diligently searched the mouth of the Harbour, and about the rocks which shew themselues at all times, and are an excellent breach of the water, so as no Sea can come in to offend the Harbour. This he did to instruct himselfe, and thereby able to direct others that shall happen to come to this place. For euery where both neere the rocks, & in all soundings about the Ilands, we neuer found lesse water than foure and fiue fathoms, which was seldome; but seuen, eight, nine and ten fathoms is the continuall sounding by the shore. In some places much deeper vpon clay oaze or soft sand: so that if any bound for this place, should be either driuen or scanted with winds, he shall be able (with his directions) to recouer safely his harbour most securely in water enough by foure seuerall passages, more than which I thinke no man of judgement will desire as necessarie.

Vpon one of the Ilands (because it had a pleasant sandy Coue for small barks to ride in) we landed, and found hard by the shore a pond of fresh water, which flowed ouer the banks, somewhat ouer growen with little shrub trees, and searching vp in the Iland, we saw it fed with a strong run, which with small labour, and little time, might be made to driue a mill. In this Iland, as in the other, were spruce trees of excellent timber and height, able to mast ships of great burthen.

While we thus sounded from one place to another in so good deepes, our Captaine to make some triall of the fishing himselfe, caused a hooke or two to be cast out at the mouth of the harbour, not aboue halfe a league from our ship, where in small time only, with the baits which they cut from the fish and three hooks, we got fish enough for our whole Company (though now augmented) for three daies. Which I omit not to report, because it sheweth how great a profit the fishing would be, they being so plentifull, so great, and so good, with such conuenient drying as can be wished, neere at hand vpon the Rocks.

This day, about one a clocke after noone, came from the Eastward two Canoas abord vs, wherein was he that refused to stay with vs for a pawne, and with him six other Saluages which we had not seene before who had beautified themselues after their manner very gallantly, though their clothing was not differing from the former, yet they had newly painted their faces very deep, some all blacke, some red, with stripes of excellent blew ouer their vpper lips, nose and chin. One of them ware a kinde of Coronet about his head, made very cunningly, of a substance like stiffe haire coloured red, broad, and more than a handfull in depth, which we imagined to be some ensigne of his superioritie; for he so much esteemed it as he would not for any thing exchange the same. Other ware the white feathered skins of some fowle, round about their head, jewels in their ears, and bracelets of little white round bone, fastned together vpon a leather string. These made not any shew that they had notice of the other before taken, but we vnderstood them by their speech and signes, that they came sent from the Bashabes, and that his desire was that we would bring vp our ship (which they call as their owne boats, a Quiden) to his house, being, as they pointed, vpon the main towards the East, from whence they came, and that he would exchange with vs for Furres and Tabacco. But because our Company was but small, and now our desire was with speed to discouer vp the river, we let them vnderstand, that if their Bashabes would come to vs, he should be welcome, but we would not remoue to him. Which when they vnderstood (receiuing of vs bread and fish, and euery of them a knife) they departed; for we had then no will to stay them long abord, least they should discouer the other Saluages which we had stowed below.

Tuesday, the 11 of June, we passed vp into the riuer with our ship, about six and twenty miles. Of which I had rather not write, then by my relation to detract from the worthinesse thereof. For the Riuer, besides that it is subject by shipping to bring in all traffiques of Marchandise, a benefit alwaies accounted the richest treasury to any land: for which cause our Thames hath that due denomination, and France by her nauigable Riuers receiueth hir greatest wealth; yet this place of it selfe from God and nature affoordeth as much diuersitie of good commodities, as any reasonable man can wish, for present habitation and planting.

The first and chiefest thing required, is a bold coast and faire land to fall with; the next, a safe harbour for ships to ride in.

Monhegan

The first is a speciall attribute to this shore, being most free from sands or dangerous rocks in a continuall good depth, with a most excellent land-fall, which is the first Iland we fell with, named by vs, Saint Georges Iland. For the second, by judgement of our Captaine, who knoweth most of the coast of England, and most of other Countries, (hauing beene experienced by imployments in discoueries and trauels from his childhood) and by opinion of others of good judgement in our shippe, heere are more good harbours for ships of all burthens, than England can afford, and far more secure from all winds and weathers, than any in England, Scotland, France or Spaine. For besides without the Riuer in the channell, and sounds about the ilands adjoining to the mouth thereof, no better riding can be desired for an infinite number of ships. The Riuer it selfe as it runneth vp into the main very nigh forty miles toward the great mountaines, beareth in bredth a mile, sometime three quarters, and halfe a mile is the narrowest, where you shall neuer haue vnder 4 and 5 fathoms water hard by the shore, but 6, 7, 8, 9, and 10 fathoms all along, and on both sides euery halfe mile very gallant Coues, some able to conteine almost a hundred saile, where the ground is excellent soft oaze with a tough clay vnder for anker hold, and where ships may ly without either Cable or Anker, only mored to the shore with a Hauser.

It floweth by their judgement eighteen or twenty foot at high water.

Heere are made by nature most excellent places, as Docks to graue or Carine ships of all burthens; secured from all windes, which is such a necessary imcomparable benefit, that in few places in England, or in any parts of Christendome, art, with great charges, can make the like.

Besides, the bordering land is a most rich neighbour trending all along on both sides, in an equall plaine, neither mountainous nor rocky, but verged with a greene bordure of grasse, doth make tender vnto the beholder of hir pleasant fertility, if by clensing away the woods she were conuerted into meddow.

The wood she beareth is not shrubbish fit only for fewell, but goodly tall Firre, Spruce, Birch, Beech, Oke, which in many places is not so thicke, but may with small labour be made feeding ground, being plentifull like the outward Ilands with fresh water, which streameth downe in many places.

As we passed with a gentle winde vp with our ship in this Riuer, any man may conceiue with what admiration we all consented in joy. Many of our Company who had beene trauellers in sundry countries, and in the most famous Riuers, yet affirmed them not comparable to this they now beheld. Some that were with Sir Walter Ralegh in his voyage to Guiana, in the discouery of the Riuer Orenoque, which echoed fame to the worlds eares, gaue reasons why it was not to be compared with this, which wanteth the dangers of many Shoules, and broken ground, wherewith that was incombred. Others before that notable Riuer in the West Indies called Rio Grande; some before the Riuer of Loyer, the Riuer Seine, and of Burdeaux in France, which although they be great and goodly Riuers, yet it is no detraction from them to be accounted inferiour to this, which not only yeeldeth all the foresaid pleasant profits, but also appeared infallibly to vs free from all inconueniences.

I will not prefer it before our riuer of Thames, because it is Englands richest treasure; but we all did wish those excellent Harbours, good deeps in a continuall conuenient bredth, and small tide-gates, to be as well therein for our countries good, as we found the here (beyond our hopes) in certaine, for those to whom it shall please God to grant this land for habitation; which if it had, with the other inseparable adherent commodities here to be found; then I would boldly affirme it to be the most rich, beautiful, large & secure harbouring riuer that the world affoordeth.

A bend or narrow portion

Wednesday, the twelfth of June, our Captaine manned his light-horseman with 17 men, and ranne vp from the ship riding in the riuer vp to the codde thereof, where we landed, leauing six to keepe the light-horseman till our returne. Ten of vs with our shot, and some armed, with a boy to carry powder and match, marched vp into the countrey towards the mountaines, which we descried at our first falling with the land.

Camden Hills

Vnto some of them the riuer brought vs so neere, as we judged our selues when we landed to haue beene within a league of them; but we marched vp about foure miles in the maine, and passed ouer three hilles: and because the weather was parching hot, and our men in their armour not able to trauel farre and returne that night to our ship, we resolued not to passe any further, being all very weary of so tedious and laboursom a trauell.

In this march we passed ouer very good ground, pleasant and fertile, fit for pasture, for the space of some three miles, hauing but little wood, and that Oke like stands left in our pastures in England, good and great, fit timber for any vse. Some small Birch, Hazle and Brake, which might in small time with few men be cleansed and made good arable land: but as it now is will feed cattell of all kindes with fodder enough for Summer and Winter. The soile is blacke, bearing sundry hearbs, grasse, and strawberries bigger than ours in England. In many places are lowe Thicks like our Copisses of small yoong wood. And surely it did all resemble a stately Parke, wherein appeare some old trees with high withered tops, and other flourishing with liuing greene boughs. Vpon the hilles grow notable high timber trees, masts for ships of 400 tun: and at the bottome of euery hill, a little run of fresh water; but the furthest and last we passed, ranne with a great streame able to driue a mill.

We might see in some places where fallow Deere and Hares had beene, and by the rooging of ground we supposed wilde Hogs had ranged there, but we could descrie no beast, because our noise still chased them from vs.

We were no sooner come aboord our light-horseman, returning towards our ship, but we espied a Canoa comming from the further part of the Cod of the riuer Eastward, which hasted to vs; wherein, with two others, was he who refused to stay for a pawne: and his comming was very earnestly importing to haue one of our men to go lie on shore with their Bashabes (who was there on shore, as they signed) and then the next morning he would come to our ship with many Furres and Tabacco. This we perceiued to be only a meere deuice to get possession of any of our men, to ransome all those which we had taken, which their naturall policy could not so shadow, but we did easily discouer and preuent. These meanes were by this Saluage practised, because we had one of his kinsemen prisoner, as we judged by his most kinde vsage of him being aboord vs together.

Thomaston

Thursday, the 13 of June, by two a clocke in the morning (because our Captaine would take the helpe and aduantage of the tide) in the light-horseman with our Company well prouided and furnished with armour and shot both to defend and offend; we went from our ship vp to that part of the riuer which trended Westward into the maine, to search that: and we carried with vs a Crosse, to erect at that point, which (because it was not daylight) we left on the shore vntill our returne backe; when we set it vp in maner as the former. For this (by the way) we diligently obserued, that in no place, either about the Ilands, or vp in the maine, or alongst the riuer, we could discerne any token or signe, that euer any Christian had beene before; of which either by cutting wood, digging for water, or setting vp Crosses (a thing neuer omitted by any Christian trauellers) we should haue perceiued some mention left.

But to returne to our riuer, further vp into which we then rowed by estimation twenty miles, the beauty and goodnesse whereof I can not by relation sufficiently demonstrate. That which I can say in generall is this: What profit or pleasure soeuer is described and truly verified in the former part of the riuer, is wholly doubled in this; for the bredth and depth is such, that any ship drawing 17 or 18 foot water, might haue passed as farre as we went with our light-horsman, and by all our mens judgement much further, because we left it in so good depth and bredth; which is so much the more to be esteemed of greater woorth, by how much it trendeth further vp into the maine: for from the place of our ships riding in the Harbour at the entrance into the Sound, to the furthest part we were in this riuer, by our estimation was not much lesse than threescore miles.

From ech banke of this riuer are diuers branching streames into the maine, wherby is affoorded an vnspeakable profit by the conueniency of transportation from place to place, which in some countries is both chargeable; and not so fit, by cariages on waine, or horse backe.

Heere we saw great store of fish, some great, leaping aboue water, which we judged to be Salmons. All along is an excellent mould of ground. The wood in most places, especially on the East side, very thinne, chiefly oke and some small young birch, bordering low vpon the riuer; all fit for medow and pasture ground: and in that space we went, we had on both sides the riuer many plaine plots of medow, some of three or foure acres, some of eight or nine: so as we judged in the whole to be betweene thirty and forty acres of good grasse, and where the armes run out into the Maine, there likewise went a space on both sides of cleere grasse, how far we know not, in many places we might see paths made to come downe to the watering.

The excellencie of this part of the Riuer, for his good breadth, depth, and fertile bordering ground, did so ravish vs all with variety of pleasantnesse, as we could not tell what to commend, but only admired; some compared it to the Riuer Seuerne, (but in a higher degree) and we all concluded as I verily thinke we might rightly) that we should neuer see the like Riuer in every degree equall, vntill it pleased God we beheld the same againe. For the farther we went, the more pleasing it was to euery man, alluring vs still with expectation of better, so as our men, although they had with great labour rowed long and eat nothing (for we carried with vs no victuall, but a little cheese and bread) yet they were so refreshed with the pleasant beholding thereof, and so loath to forsake it, as some of them affirmed, they would haue continued willingly with that onely fare and labour 2 daies; but the tide not suffering vs to make any longer stay (because we were to come backe with the tide) and our Captaine better knowing what was fit then we, and better what they in labour were able to endure, being verie loath to make any desperate hazard, where so little necessitie required, thought it best to make returne, because whither we had discouered was sufficient to conceiue that the Riuer ran very far into the land. For we passed six or seuen miles, altogether fresh water (whereof we all dranke) forced vp by the flowing of the Salt: which after a great while eb, where we left it, by breadth of channell and depth of water was likely to run by estimation of our whole company an unknowen way farther: the search whereof our Captaine hath left till his returne, if it shall so please God to dispose of him and vs.

For we hauing now by the direction of the omnipotent disposer of all good intents (far beyond the period of our hopes) fallen with so bold a coast, found so excellent and secure harbour, for as many ships as any nation professing Christ is able to set forth to Sea, discouered a Riuer, which the All-creating God, with his most liberall hand, hath made aboue report notable with his foresaid blessings, bordered with a land, whose pleasant fertility bewraieth it selfe to be the garden of nature, wherin she only intended to delight hir selfe, hauing hitherto obscured it to any, except to a purblind generation, whose vnderstanding it hath pleased God so to darken, as they can neither discerne, vse, or rightly esteeme the vnualuable riches in middest whereof they live sensually content with the barke and outward rinds, as neither knowing the sweetnes of the inward marrow, nor acknowledging the Deity of the Almighty giuer: hauing I say thus far proceeded, and hauing some of the inhabitant nation (of best vnderstanding we saw among them) who (learning our language) may be able to giue vs further instruction, concerning all the premised particulars, as also of their gouernours, and gouernment, situation of townes, and what else shall be conuenient, which by no meanes otherwise we could by any obseruation of our selues learne in a long time: our Captaine now wholy intended his prouision for speedy returne. For although the time of yeere and our victuall were not so spent, but we could haue made a longer voyage, in searching farther and trading for very good commodities, yet as they might haue beene much profitable, so (our company being small) much more preiudiciall to the whole state of our voyage, which we were most regardfull now not to hazard. For we supposing not a little present priuate profit, but a publique good, and true zeale of promulgating Gods holy Church, by planting Christianity, to be the sole intent of the Honourable setters foorth of this discouery; thought it generally most expedient, by our speedy returne, to giue the longer space of time to make prouision for so weighty an enterprise.

Friday, the 14 day of June, early by foure a clocke in the morning, with the tide, our two boats, and a little helpe of the winde, we rowed downe to the riuers mouth and there came to an anker about eleuen a clocke. Afterward our Captaine in the light horseman searched the sounding all about the mouth and comming to the Riuer, for his certaine instruction of a perfect description.

The next day, being Saturday, we wayed anker, and with a briese from the land, we sailed vp to our watering place, and there stopped, went on shore and filled all our empty caske with fresh water.

Our Captaine vpon the Rocke in the middest of the harbour obserued the height, latitude, and variation exactly vpon his instruments.

1. Astrolabe.
2. Semisphere.
3. Ringe instrument.
4. Crosse staffe.
5. And an excellent compasse made for the variation.

The certainty whereof, together with the particularities of euery depth and sounding, as well at our falling with the land, as in the discouery, and at our departure from the coast; I refer to his owne relation in the Map of his Geographicall description, which for the benefit of others he intendeth most exactly to publish.

The temperature of the Climate (albeit a very important matter) I had almost passed without mentioning, because it affoorded to vs no great alteration from our disposition in England; somewhat hotter vp into the Maine, because it lieth open to the South; the aire so wholesome, as I suppose not any of vs found our selues at any time more healthfull, more able to labour, nor with better stomacks to such good fare, as we partly found.

Sunday, the 16 of June, the winde being faire, and because we had set out of England vpon a Sunday, made the Ilands vpon a Sunday, and as we doubt not (by Gods appointment) happily fell into our harbour vpon a Sunday; so now (beseeching him still with like prosperity to blesse our returne into England our country, and from thence with his good will and pleasure to hasten our next arriuall there) we waied Anker and quit the Land vpon a Sunday.

The Fishing Banks

Tuesday, the 18 day, being not run aboue 30 leagues from land, and our Captaine for his certaine knowledge how to fall with the coast, hauing sounded euery watch, and from 40 fathoms had come into good deeping, to 70, and so to an hundred: this day the weather being faire, after the foure a clocke watch, when we supposed not to haue found ground so farre from land, and before sounded in aboue 100 fathoms, we had ground in 24 fathomes. Wherefore our sailes being downe, Thomas King boatswaine, presently cast out a hooke, and before he judged it at ground, was fished and haled vp an exceeding great and well fed Cod: then there were cast out 3 or 4 more, and the fish was so plentifull and so great, as when our Captaine would haue set saile, we all desired him to suffer them to take fish a while, because we were so delighted to see them catch so great fish, so fast as the hooke came down: some with playing with the hooke they tooke by the backe, and one of the Mates with two hookes at a lead at fiue draughts together haled vp tenne fishes; all were generally very great, some they measured to be fiue foot long, and three foot about.

This caused our Captaine not to maruell at the shoulding, for he perceiued it was a fish banke, which (for our farewell from the land) it pleased God in continuance of his blessings to giue vs knowledge of: the abundant profit whereof should be alone sufficient cause to draw men againe, if there were no other good both in present certaine, and in hope probable to be discouered. To amplifie this with words, were to adde light to the Sunne: for euery one in the shippe could easily account this present commodity; much more those of judgement, which knew what belonged to fishing, would warrant (by the helpe of God) in a short voyage with few good fishers to make a more profitable returne from hence than from Newfoundland: the fish being so much greater, better fed, and abundant with traine; of which some they desired, and did bring into England to bestow among their friends, and to testifie the true report.

Cod-liver oil

After, we kept our course directly for England & with ordinary winds, and sometime calmes, vpon Sunday the 14 of July about sixe a clocke at night, we were come into sounding in our channell, but with darke weather and contrary winds, we were constrained to beat vp and downe till Tuesday the 16 of July, when by fiue a clocke in the morning we made Sylly; from whence, hindered with calmes and small winds, vpon Thursday the 18 of July about foure a clocke after noone, we came into Dartmouth: which Hauen happily (with Gods gracious assistance) we made our last and first Harbour in England.

Further, I haue thought fit here to adde some things worthy to be regarded, which we haue obserued from the Saluages since we tooke them.

First, although at the time when we surprised them, they made their best resistance, not knowing our purpose, nor what we were, nor how we meant to vse them; yet after perceiuing by their kinde vsage we intended them no harme, they haue neuer since seemed discontented with vs, but very tractable, louing, & willing by their best meanes to satisfie vs in any thing we demand of them, by words or signes for their vnderstanding: neither haue they at any time beene at the least discord among themselues; insomuch as we haue not seene them angry but merry; and so kinde, as if you giue any thing to one of them, he will distribute part to euery one of the rest.

We haue brought them to vnderstand some English, and we vnderstand much of their language; so as we are able to aske them many things. And this we haue obserued, that if we shew them any thing, and aske them if they haue it in their countrey, they will tell you if they haue it, and the vse of it, the difference from ours in bignesse, colour, or forme; but if they haue it not, be it a thing neuer so precious, they wil denie the knowledge of it.

They haue names for many starres, which they will shew in the firmament.

They shew great reuerence to their King, and are in great subiection to their Gouernours: and they will shew a great respect to any we tell them are our Commanders.

They shew the maner how they make bread of their Indian wheat, and how they make butter and cheese of the milke they haue of the Rain-Deere and Fallo-Deere, which they haue tame as we haue Cowes.

They haue excellent colours. And hauing seene our Indico, they make shew of it, or of some other like thing which maketh as good a blew.

One especiall thing is their maner of killing the Whale, which they call Powdawe; and will describe his forme; how he bloweth vp the water; and that he is 12 fathoms long; and that they go in company of their King with a multitude of their boats, and strike him with a bone made in fashion of a harping iron fastened to a rope, which they make great and strong of the barke of trees, which they veare out after him; then all their boats come about him, and as he riseth aboue water, with their arrowes they shoot him to death; when they haue killed him & dragged him to shore, they call all their chiefe lords together, & sing a song of joy: and those chiefe lords, whom they call Sagamos, divide the spoile, and giue to euery man a share, which pieces so distributed they hang vp about their houses for prouision: and when they boile them, they blow off the fat, and put to their peaze, maiz, and other pulse, which they eat.

* * *

A briefe Note of what profits we saw the Countrey yeeld in the small time of our stay there.

Trees

Oke of an excellent graine, strait, and great timber.
Elme.
Alder.
Cherry-tree.
Ash.
Beech.
Birch, very tall & great; of whose barke they make their Canoas.
Wich-Hazell.
Hazell.
Maple.
Yew.
Spruce.
Aspe.
Firre.
Many fruit trees, which we knew not.

Fowles

Eagles.
Hernshawes.
Cranes.
Ducks great.
Geese.
Swannes.
Penguins.
Crowes.
Sharks.
Rauens.
Mewes.
Turtle-doues.
Many birds of sundrie colours.
Many other fowls in flocks, vnknown.

Fishes

Whales.
Seales.
Cod very great.
Haddocke great.
Herring great.
Plaise.
Thornebacke.

Rockefish.
Lobstar great.
Crabs.
Muscels great, with pearles in them.
Cockles.
Wilks.
Cunner fish.
Lumps.
Whiting.
Soales.
Tortoises.
Oisters.

Beasts

Raine-Deere.
Stagges.
Fallow-Deere.
Beares.
Wolues.
Beauer.
Otter.
Hare.
Cony.
Hedge-Hoggs.
Polcats.
Wilde great Cats.
Dogges: some like Wolues, some like Spaniels.

Fruits, Plants, and Herbs

Tabacco, excellent sweet and strong.
Wild-Vines.
Strawberries.
Raspberries.
Gooseberries.   } abundance.
Hurtleberries.
Currant trees.
Rose-bushes.
Peaze.
Ground-nuts.

Angelica, a most soueraigne herbe.

An hearbe that spreadeth the ground, & smelleth like Sweet Marioram, great plenty.

Very good Dies, which appear by their painting; which they carrie with them in bladders.

The names of the fiue Saluages which we brought home into England, which are all yet aliue, are these.

1. Tahanedo, a Sagamo or Commander.
2. Amoret.   or Nahanada
3. Skicowaros, Gentlemen.
4. Maneddo
5. Saffacomoit, a seruant.   or Skidwares

CHAPTER 2.

As a consequence of the Weymouth voyage, several Englishmen combined their resources in 1606 to form the Virginia Company in order to establish a colony in America. In 1607, the company sent colonists to the coast of Maine where, at the mouth of the Kennebec River, the Popham Colony was established.

THE POPHAM COLONY*
by
Henry Burrage

The Southern Virginia Company had already despatched colonists to the new world. There also was a movement for a like undertaking on the part of the Northern or Plymouth company. Conferences were held by the members of the company with others interested in the expansion of England's territory and trade. With enthusiasm the work of organizing the proposed colony was commenced. As this work, at least for the most part, was carried forward at Plymouth, Gorges, who was in command of the fort at that place, may be regarded as most conspicuous in this service, as well as in making preparations for the voyage. Difficulties were encountered as the work proceeded. A glimpse of these is afforded in a letter which the mayor of Plymouth addressed May 10, 1606, to Lord Salisbury, King James' Secretary of State, suggesting some modifications of the charter. Sir John Popham, he wrote, had invited the co-operation of some of the prominent citizens of Plymouth; but some of the provisions of the charter were objectionable, especially the provision that placed the direction of the affairs of the colony in the control of a council, the majority of whose members were "strangers to us and our proceedings". They accordingly asked the prime minister's protection and help. This complaint was not sent to Lord Salisbury without the knowledge of Sir Ferdinando Gorges; for on the same day Gorges addressed a letter to the prime minister, explaining further the position taken by the men of Plymouth, who, he wrote, were at first well disposed and ready "to be large adventurers", but had now withdrawn their aid and refused to have anything to do with the work to be undertaken. Evidently, Gorges considered this a very undesirable situation, and he urged a change in the provisions of the charter to which objection had been made, believing that in this way the interest of "many worthy and brave spirits" could be secured. The complaint of the mayor of Plymouth and his associates was laid before Lord Salisbury by Captain Love, the bearer of the letter. No word concerning the result has been preserved, so far as is known. Such, however, was the success of the efforts of the chief justice in connection with the fitting out of the Popham colony, that harmony of action among those interested in the enterprise seems at length to have been reached.

Two vessels, the Gift of God and the Mary and John—the tonnage of both unknown—were secured for transporting the colonists and their stores to the selected location of the colony. Concerning the number of the colonists, and the manner in which they were obtained, there is little information. Gorges makes mention of "one hundred landsmen". Probably he does not include in this designation "divers gentlemen of note", who are said to have accompanied the expedition. Strachey says the Gift of God and the Mary and John carried "one hundred and twenty four planters". To this number, of course, must be added the number of the crews of the two vessels in order to make up

---

*Henry S. Burrage, *Beginnings of Colonial Maine* (Portland: Marks Printing House, 1914), pp. 63-99.

the full number of persons connected with the enterprise.

In providing the funds that were necessary for the purpose of fitting out and establishing the colony, Sir John Popham doubtless had a prominent place. He not only made large contributions when calls for money came, but he interested many of his friends and acquaintances in the work to which, with so much enthusiasm, he had put his hands. In one way or another the funds were raised and the expedition was made ready. May 31, 1607, was the sailing day. The Gift of God and the Mary and John—the former commanded by George Popham and the latter by Raleigh Gilbert—lay in the old harbor of Plymouth, now known as Sutton's Pool, the same harbor from which the Mayflower sailed thirteen years later. Gorges, doubtless, was present at the departure of the colonists. Doubtless, too, Sir John Popham was there, having laid aside his official robes and left London in order by his presence to give forceful expression to the hopes he entertained, both for himself and the nation, in establishing an English colony in northern Virginia. All Plymouth, too, was there, prominent merchants, military and other professional men, fishermen and seamen, all much interested in an enterprise that was designed to bring the old and new worlds into close and prospering relations. As the Gift of God and the Mary and John sailed out of the harbor, the vessels were saluted by the guns of the fort, while from the Hoe the heartfelt benedictions and best wishes of a great company followed the colonists until the vessels had disappeared upon the horizon.

A brief account of the fortunes of the Popham colony appeared in 1614 in Purchas's *Pilgrimes*. This was followed in 1622 by a short statement in *A Briefe Relation of the Discovery and Plantation of New England* by the president and council. In 1624, Captain John Smith included in his *General History of New England* a brief record of the Popham enterprise. These were the principal sources of information concerning the colony until 1849, when the Hakluyt Society published William Strachey's *Historie of Travaile into Virginia Brittania*, written about 1616. Evidently the narrative was based upon sources not in the possession of the earlier writers, and Strachey's account of the experiences of the Popham colonists was the best available until 1875, when a manuscript, once in the possession of Sir Ferdinando Gorges, and containing a journal, written by one connected with the colony, was discovered in the library of Lambeth Palace, London. It covers a period of about four months, that is, from the departure of the expedition from the Lizard, June 1, 1607, to September 26, 1607. With this last date the manuscript abruptly closes; but as Strachey, by many evidences which his narrative furnishes, is believed to have used this manuscript in preparing his account of the Popham colony, his continuation of the story from September 26 is believed, for the same reason, to have been based upon that part of the Lambeth Palace manuscript, which in some way was afterward lost and is still lacking. Although in the title of the manuscript the name of the author is not mentioned, indications in the narrative point almost unmistakably to the conclusion that the writer was James Davies, one of Gilbert's officers on the Mary and John, and otherwise prominently connected with the colony.

The narrative of the voyage begins at "the Lizard" on the first of June, the day after the vessels sailed out of the harbor of Plymouth, fifty miles away. Thence both vessels, instead of taking the direct westerly course to the American coast, as did Gosnold and Pring, followed Weymouth's course in the Archangel, and sailed southerly to the Azores islands, which were reached in twenty-four days. June 27, at the island of Flores, a landing was made for wood and water. Continuing the voyage, Popham and Gilbert fell in with two Flemish vessels June 29, and Captain Gilbert, as a token of friendly feeling, invited the captain of one of the vessels to come aboard the Mary and John. The invitation was accepted, and the Flemish captain was kindly received and hospitably entertained. On his departure, the guest cordially invited Gilbert and a few others on the Mary and John to accompany him to his ship, apparently moved thereto by the kindly reception he himself had received. To this "earnest entreaty," Gilbert and those with him, yielded; but, to their surprise, on reaching the Flemish vessel, they were treated as prisoners, some of the party being placed in the "bibows" (bilboes), and others being subjected to "wild and shameful abuses." It happened, however, that in the crew of the Flemish vessel were English sailors, who, noticing this affront to their countrymen, found opportunity to make known to Gilbert their determination to stand by him and his companions. When the Flemish captain discovered this evidence of a threatened uprising on the part of his own men, the situation was not pleasing to him. He accordingly hastened to release the prisoners, and returned them to their own ship to their "no small joy".

Meanwhile, Popham, in the Gift of God, either had not seen or failed to answer the signals of distress made by the Mary and John. His action is not explained in the narrative, which seems to imply unworthy conduct on his part in sailing away without an attempt at assistance. The two vessels thus fell apart, and did not again come together until their arrival on the American coast.

When this affair with the Flemish ship occurred, the Mary and John was ten leagues southwest of Flores. Continuing the voyage to the American coast, the vessel reached soundings July 27, in latitude 43°, 40', and July 30, land was descried, evidently the Nova Scotia coast. Gilbert anchored and landed, but his stay was brief, and he proceeded down the coast on his way to the appointed rendezvous. August 5, land again was sighted. In the narrative there is an outline sketch of the view that was obtained by the voyagers in thus approaching the coast—a view of the high mountains "in upon the main land near unto the river of Penobscot". Such they knew them to be from the maps of Weymouth and Pring in their possession. Both the sketch and the narrative make it evident that the Mary and John, in now approaching the coast, must have been some distance southeast of the Matinicus islands. The mountains were the Camden mountains, noteworthy features of the coast to any mariner approaching the land at this point. Gilbert and his men now knew that the designated meeting-place of the vessels, in case of separation, was not far away.

Proceeding in toward the coast, the Mary and John, her entire ship's company alert with interest, came at length to the Matinicus islands easily recognizable from the narrative. A second outline sketch of the mountains toward which the Mary and John was moving is here inserted in the Lambeth manuscript, showing the changed appearance of the mountains, as seen from this nearer point of approach. At these islands the vessel's course was made "west and west by north" towards three other islands, eight leagues from the islands before mentioned. Differences of opinion have found expression as to the three islands to which reference is thus made. The record is brief, and it is difficult to obtain from it that accurate information which a fuller statement would have supplied. But the general direction seems unmistakable. Following down the coast from the Matinicus islands, the course of the Mary and John must have been in the direction of the St. George's islands. A careful examination of the narrative in the light of such facts as are now attainable warrants this statement. It was ten o'clock at night when an approach to these islands was made. "We bore in with one of them", is the record, and the reference is that other islands were near. In fact, in the clear light of the morning that followed, the voyagers on the Mary and John found themselves "environed" with islands, and the narrative adds "near thirty", evidently an estimate. The anchorage, therefore, was not at Monhegan, as some have maintained. The *Relation* excludes any such view. No mariner, anchored at Monhegan, would refer to his vessel as "environed" with "near thirty islands". On the other hand, if the Mary and John, guided by directions derived from the narratives of the voyages of Weymouth and Pring, anchored in what is now known as St. George's harbor, the mention of environing islands—"near thirty"—is in harmony with easily recognized facts as to distance and direction.

It should be added, furthermore, that the *Relation* makes the anchorage of the Mary and John not far from the island on which Weymouth erected a cross as a token of English possession. The statement is, "We here found a cross set up, that which we suppose was set up by George Wayman". Rosier's narrative of Weymouth's voyage affords no foundation whatever for the supposition that the cross, which Weymouth erected upon an island on the coast of Maine, was erected on Monhegan. His brief visit to that island was from his anchorage north of it on his first approach to the coast, and was for the purpose of obtaining wood and water. On the following day, from that anchorage, he brought the Archangel "along to the other islands more adjoining to the main, and in the road directly with the mountains" he had seen on approaching the coast. The St. George's islands, extending in a line nearly north northeast and south southwest for about five miles, answer fully to this description, as has already been stated. Gilbert and his men were not long in finding the cross Weymouth erected on one of these islands, confirming the other facts in their possession, that the designated place of rendezvous had been reached.

Gilbert's first anchorage, which was made somewhat hastily under the circumstances, was not found to be satisfactory, and a better one was secured on the following day. While the necessary examination was in progress, and the Mary and John was "standing off a little", a sail was descried at sea, but "standing in towards this island", namely the island near which the Mary and John had been anchored. Gilbert at once sailed out to meet the stranger, and it was soon discovered that the new arrival, as hoped for, was Gilbert's consort, the Gift of God. Evidently, differences as to the cause of the separation were at once forgotten; and in the joy of their "happy meeting" the two vessels sailed into the appointed haven, and "there anchored both together".

The language of the *Relation* is plain, and there is no warrant whatever for the view, maintained by some writers before the discovery of the Lambeth Palace manuscript, that this anchorage was at Monhegan. The island near which both vessels anchored was no other than the island in the vicinity of which the Mary and John anchored on her arrival on the coast; and this, as has already been shown, was not the island of Monhegan, but one of the St. George's islands and probably the one on which Weymouth set up a cross. If Monhegan had been the place of rendezvous, Popham would have sought an anchorage there. On the contrary, he was heading for islands farther in toward the main when the Gift of God was sighted from the deck of the Mary and John, and thence was led by her into the island harbor, which, evidently on the part of both captains, was the predetermined location for anchorage on reaching the American coast.

One of the five Indians captured by Weymouth was included in the company on board the Mary and John. In the Lambeth Palace manuscript he is mentioned as "Skidwarres". Rosier, in his *Relation*, calls him "Skicowaros". Probably he was one of the Indians assigned by Weymouth to Sir John Popham, and doubtless very much was expected from him in matters connected with the settlement of the colony, especially in the relation of the colonists to the Indians. Very naturally Skidwarres, on reaching these familiar scenes, was anxious to be set on shore at once, in order to join his people from whom he had so long been separated. Just as anxious, apparently, was Gilbert to further the wishes of Skidwarres, and so, with the first opportunity, to place himself in friendly relations with the natives of the country. Accordingly at midnight, following the arrival of the Gift of God, Gilbert and some of his men, in one of the ships' boats, rowed westward past "many gallant islands," and landed Skidwarres, by his direction, in a little cove on the mainland, on the east side of the Pemaquid peninsula, and evidently at what is now known as New Harbor. Then, still guided by Skidwarres, they marched across the peninsula, a distance of "near three miles" to the Indian encampment. The chief of the Indians was none other than Nahanada, also one of Weymouth's captives, who had been returned by Hanham and Pring the year before; but though the Indians very naturally were inclined at first to hold themselves somewhat aloof, the assuring words addressed to them by Skidwarres and Nahanada caused them to lay aside their fears, and assurances of mutual friendship followed. Gilbert and his men remained at the Indian village two hours, and then, accompanied by Skidwarres, they returned to the ships in Pentecost harbor.

The next day was Sunday. Concerning its religious observances by the colonists, the *Relation* contains this record: "Sunday, being the 9th of August, in the morning the most part of our whole company of both our ships landed on this island, that which we call St. George's island, where the cross standeth, and there we heard a sermon delivered unto us by our preacher, giving God thanks for our happy meeting and safe arrival into the country, and so returned aboard again." The place of this first recorded observance of Christian worship in New England is here clearly indicated. It was on the island near which Weymouth anchored the Archangel after leaving his anchorage north of Monhegan, and on which Weymouth's cross stood. No appeal can be made to the fact that this island is called in the narrative "St. George's island"—the name given by Weymouth to Monhegan. Its mention here—the writer being familiar with Rosier's *Relation*—is evidence only to the well-known fact that thus early the name St. George had been transferred from Monhegan to the island on which Weymouth's cross was erected, and later was made to include the whole group of islands since known as the St. George's islands.

The character of the service is also clearly indicated in the *Relation*. Though the words "sermon" and "preacher" are very suggestive of religious conditions in England at that time, and may have been due to the writer's habit of expression, it is probable that the preacher, Rev. Richard Scymour, was a clergyman of the Church of England. With such promoters as those most interested in the colony—Popham, chief justice of England, and Sir Ferdinando Gorges, an ardent royalist and churchman—it is not likely that English dissent would furnish religious leadership in the undertaking. If there were differences of religious belief among the colonists, these were laid aside; and devout hearts found abundant occasion in the experiences of the voyage for glad expression of thanksgiving and praise. It was certainly a most fitting service in connection with an enterprise that meant so much both for the old world and the new.

On the following day, August 10, both captains—Popham in his shallop with thirty men and Gilbert in his ship's boat with twenty men—taking with them Skidwarres, passed around Pemaquid point, evidently to avoid the march across the peninsula, and visited the Indians at the place where Gilbert had met them two days before. As at the previous interview, the establishment of kindly relations with the Indians was the purpose of the visit; but apparently the memory of the natives, who were captured by Weymouth with Skidwarres and Nahanada and had not been returned, lingered in the hearts of the members of the tribe, and there was an evident lack of cordial feeling. The visitors spent the night by themselves on the other side of the Pemaquid river. Better relations were not secured on the following day; and the visitors, leaving Skidwarres, who now expressed a determination to remain with his people, returned to their ships.

That night the vessels remained at the place of rendezvous. But the summer was rapidly passing, and the planting of the colony was now a matter of pressing interest and importance. Accordingly, on the following morning, Wednesday, August 12, anchors were weighed, and both vessels, moving out from their island harbor into the open sea, were headed westward down the coast. Pring's explorations of the preceding year had called attention to the river Sagadahoc as a larger and more important river than that which Waymouth discovered in 1605, and therefore one upon which a more suitable location for the settlement of a colony could be found. It is a clear inference from the *Relation* that before the Gift of God and the Mary and John left England it had been decided that the colonists should proceed to the Sagadahoc, and establish themselves there. In accordance with this decision, Popham and Gilbert now sailed westward, instead of moving in toward the main land and the river of Weymouth's exploration.

In reaching the sea, the Kennebec river, the ancient Sagadahoc, does not present an opening that is discoverable from vessels passing along the coast. Popham and Gilbert had been made acquainted with this fact, and careful directions for gaining an entrance to the river had been placed in their hands. Accordingly, when night drew on, in order not to pass too far to the westward and so "over shoot" the mouth of the river, both vessels struck their sails and thus remained from midnight until morning. With the break of day, they were about half a league south of the "island of Sutquin." The writer of the *Relation* adds here two rude but good drawings of Sequin as seen from different points; and in referring to the island he mentions the fact that the island is situated "right before the mouth of the river of Sagadahock." Popham and Gilbert, therefore, had an excellent guide to the mouth of the river. But Gilbert, in the Mary and John, not convinced that the island was "Sutquin," continued to stand to the westward in search of it. On the other hand, Popham, in the Gift of God, sending his shallop landward from the island which he held to be the "Sutquin" of his directions, found the mouth of the Sagadahoc, and at the close of the day brought his vessel safely into the river and anchored.

That night a heavy storm from the south broke upon the Mary and John, and with difficulty the vessel was rescued from many perils upon a lee shore; but at length a refuge was found under the shelter of two islands. Here Gilbert remained until

Saturday, August 15, when the storm having spent itself, he headed his vessel again for "Sutquin." On his return, however, by reason of an offshore wind, he was unable to bring the vessel into the river. On the following day, Popham in his shallop came to the assistance of his consort, and before noon the Mary and John found anchorage in the Sagadahoc alongside of the Gift of God.

The location of the colony was now the matter of first importance with the colonists, and on the following day, August 27, Popham in his shallop with thirty others and Gilbert in his ship's boat and eighteen others—fifty in all—proceeded up the river in search of the most suitable place for the plantation. "We find this river," says the *Relation*, "to be very pleasant with many goodly islands in it and to be both large and deep water having many branches in it; that which we took bendeth itself towards the northeast." From these words it may be inferred that, after reaching Merrymeeting bay, the explorers passed into the Kennebec; but concerning the distance made in that part of the river there is no statement, or any words even from which an inference can be drawn. It is evident, however, that in their search the explorers found no place for a plantation preferable to that which was observable from the vessels in the river. Accordingly, after their return they "all went to the shore and there made choice of a place for our plantation, which is at the very mouth or entry of the river of Sagadahock on the west side of the river, being almost an island of a good bigness." The record affords no opportunity for doubt with reference to the place selected. It was at the mouth of the Sagadahoc, and on the west side of the river. The added statement, that the land selected for the plantation formed "almost an island of a good bigness," describes in general terms the peninsula of Sabino, "a huge misshapen triangle" between Atkins bay and the sea. Examination of this tract of land establishes its fitness for plantation purposes. Just as clearly as the *Relation* establishes the general location of the Popham colony on the west side of the river, so another discovery, since that of the Lambeth Palace manuscript, enables us to fix the precise location of the fortified settlement, which Popham and his associates made at the mouth of the Sagadahoc.

The choice of this precise location of the settlement was made August 19. "All went to the shore" for this purpose, and after the selection there was a religious service. To the colonists this meant much more than that held a few days before on one of the islands of St. George's harbor. Then, the service was one of thanksgiving for their safe arrival in the new world. Now, they were about to lay the foundations of civil government; and as their own hopes, and the hopes of those most deeply interested in the welfare of the colony, extended into an unknown future, their preacher, in the presence of all the colonists, implored the blessing of God on the great undertaking upon which they now formally entered. "After the sermon," adds the *Relation*, "our patent was read with the orders and laws therein prescribed." The patent—if patent there was—must have been a copy of that granted by James I on April 10, 1606, providing for two colonies in America, designated as the first and second, the former known as the southern colony and the latter as the northern colony. The document is a lengthy one and its reading could have added little interest to the occasion, as its provisions were already known. But as the words in the *Relation* "therein prescribed" make the patent the source of the "orders and laws" now read to the colonists, the writer doubtless had reference to the instructions of the King promulgated November 20, 1606 for the government of the colonies. These were prepared "for the good Order and Government of the two several Colonies and Plantations to be made by our loving subjects in the Country commonly called Virginia and America." A copy of these instructions was furnished to the heads of both colonies, southern and northern. The copy received by the Popham colonists has not been preserved. Happily, however, the copy carried to Virginia by the Jamestown colonists has come down to us in full, with its provisions for orderly government, appointment of officers, administration of justice, trial by jury, punishment of offenders, etc., the foundation principles of the civil government which the colonists were to organize.

First of all, these instructions established in England a "King's council of Virginia," having full power to give directions for governing the colonists "as near to the common laws of England and the equity thereof as may be." This King's council was authorized to appoint for each colony a council, and the council was made the governing body of the colony. The president of the colony, serving one year, was appointed by the colonial council from its own membership. His successor, in case of death, or absence, received appointment from the council, and for any just cause the council could remove the president from office. In cases of criminal offense, the president and council pronounced judgment. Provision was made for reprieve by the president and council, and for pardon by the King. The president and council also had power to hear and determine all civil causes. They could also from time to time "make and ordain such constitutions, ordinances and officers for the better order, government and peace of the people," these always, however, to be "in substance consonant unto the laws of England, or the equity thereof." Then follow these words:

"Furthermore, our will and pleasure is, and we do hereby determine and ordain, that every person and persons being our subjects of every the said colonies and plantations shall from time to time well entreat those savages in those parts, and use all good means to draw the savages and heathen people of the said several places, and of the territories and countries adjoining to the true service and knowledge of God, and that all just, kind and charitable courses shall be holden with such of them as shall conform themselves to any good and sociable traffic and dealing with the subjects of us, our heirs and successors, which shall be planted there, whereby they may be the sooner drawn to the true knowledge of God and the obedience of us, our heirs and successors, under such severe pains and punishments as shall be inflicted by the same several presidents and councils of the said several colonies, or the most part of them within their several limits and precincts, on such as shall offend therein, or do the contrary."

In other words, both the colonists and the natives of the country, in their mutual relations, were to be under a reign of law that would aim to secure the rights and happiness of all. In the King's instructions with reference to the government of the two colonies, the rights of the colonists, so far as personal liberty is concerned, received no recognition. The officers were to be elected by the King's council, and not by popular vote. Strachey, indeed, says that after the reading of the laws under which the Popham colonists were now placed, "George Popham, gent, was nominated president; Captain Raleigh Gilbert, James Davies, Richard Seymour, preacher, Capt. Richard Davies, Capt. Harlow . . . . . . were all sworn assistants." Captain John Smith, however, puts the case very differently, when in referring to the Popham colony in his *General History of New England,* he says: "That honorable patron of virtue, Sir John Popham, Lord Chief Justice of England, in the year 1606, procured means and men to possess it (i.e. that part of America formerly called Norumbega, & c.,) and sent Captain George Popham for president; Captain Raleigh Gilbert for admiral; Edward Harlow, master of the ordinance; Captain Robert Davis, sergeant major; Captain Ellis Best, marshal; Master Leaman, secretary; Captain James Davis to be captain of the fort; Master Gome Carew, chief searcher."

The natural inference from these words is that the officers of the colony were appointed in England by Sir John Popham. But the name of the chief justice is not included in the list of members of the "King's council of Virginia" which appears in the instructions for the government of the colonies. In that council, however, the Popham family was represented by Popham's son and heir, Sir Francis Popham. Captain Smith, making the above record in 1624, probably was in error in implying that the officers of the colony were appointed by Sir John Popham. The latter's enthusiastic exertions in financing the undertaking entitled him to honorable mention in any reference to the northern colony; but unquestionably there is no ground for the inference that the King's instructions were not strictly followed in the appointment of all the officers of the Popham colony.

On the following day, Thursday, August 20, the whole company again landed, and work at once was commenced on the fort that was to inclose the colonist's settlement. It was a large earthwork, occupying the level plot of ground at the northern extremity of Sabino head. President Popham "set the first spit of ground." The rest followed, and "labored hard in the trenches about it." As within the inclosure necessary buildings were to be erected later for the use of the colonists, there was need of busy endeavor in order to complete the required work before the winter opened.

On the next day, the colonists continued their work, some in the trenches and others in the woods preparing fagots for use in the construction of the fort. Thus early, also, under the direction of the head carpenter, those who were familiar with shipbuilding repaired to the woods and commenced to cut timber for the construction of a small vessel, which would be needed by the colonists on the return of the Mary and John and the Gift of God to England before the close of the year.

On Saturday, August 22, President Popham proceeded in his shallop up the river as far as Merrymeeting bay. From that large body of water, in his former exploration, he had entered the Kennebec, and noted its characteristics and opportunities for trade with the Indians. This time he turned westward from this point, and entered the ancient Pejepscot, now the Androscoggin. Probably he proceeded as far as the falls at Brunswick. There, or at some other part of the river, he held a parley with a body of Indians, who informed him that they had been at war with Sasanoa, the chief of the Kennebec Indians, and had slain his son. He also learned that Skidwarres and Nahanada were in this fight. Having completed his exploration, President Popham returned with his party to the mouth of the river on the following day.

With the new week that had opened, the colonists continued the work upon which they had entered with so much energy and enthusiasm. Meanwhile Captain Gilbert had in contemplation exploration to the westward after the return of President Popham. By unfavorable weather, however, he was delayed until Friday, August 28, when, in his ship's boat with fifteen others, he sailed out of the river and proceeded westward along the coast. Mention of "many gallant islands," evidently the islands of Casco bay, is made in the *Relation*. It was a picturesque scene which Gilbert and his companions had before them, as in the afternoon, with a favoring breeze, they sailed past these many wooded islands. That night, the wind having now shifted and being strong against them, they anchored under a sheltering headland called Semeamis. Because of meager details in the *Relation,* the exact location of this headland cannot now be determined with certainty. Thayer, who has carefully sought for a location in the light of these scanty materials, expresses the opinion that it is to be found on some part of Cape Elizabeth, not far from Portland head light, in what is known as Ship cove.

The next morning, Captain Gilbert, against a strong head-wind, continued his course along the coast. There was hard rowing in a rough sea, and progress was slow. At length as the day drew to a close, escaping the baffling billows that had assailed them so many hours, they came to anchor under an island "two leagues from the place" where they anchored the night before. The indications are clear that this island was no other than Richmond's island. Here Gilbert remained until midnight, and then, the wind having subsided, he and his companions left the island "in hope to have gotten the place we desired." But soon after the wind again swept down upon them—a strong wind from the southwest—and they were compelled to return to the anchorage they had just left. Concerning the desired place which Gilbert hoped to reach, there is no information. Something, evidently, he had learned from Pring, or earlier explorers, led him onward and the head-winds that beset him, and drove him back, brought disappointment.

The next day was Sunday, and the southwest wind being favorable for the return to the Sagadahoc, the baffled voyagers directed their boat thitherward. Again they entered Casco bay, and again the writer of the *Relation* extolled its "goodly islands . . . . . . so thick & near together that you cannot well discern to number them, yet may you go in betwixt them in a good ship, for you shall have never less water than eight fathoms. These islands are all overgrown with woods very thick as oaks, walnut, pine trees & many other things growing as sarsaparilla, hazle nuts & whorts in abundance." The return journey was successfully made, and the mouth of the Sagadahoc was reached at the close of the day. It was a very favorable run from Richmond's island.

Attention was now given not only to work on the fort, but also to the erection of a storehouse within the inclosure. Any relation with their Indian neighbors was a matter of very great interest. On the first day of September a canoe was discovered approaching the fort, but its occupants, when at the shore, acted warily, not allowing more than a single colonist to come near at a time. The writer of the *Relation* makes mention of two "great kettles of brass" that he saw in the canoe, an evidence apparently of earlier trading relations with European fishing and trading vessels on the coast.

A few days later, September 5, nine Indian canoes entered the river from the eastward. They contained about forty men, women and children, and among them were Nahanada and Skidwarres. All were kindly welcomed and entertained. The larger part of the visitors, after a while, withdrew to the opposite side of the river and made their camp there; but Skidwarres and another Indian remained with the colonists until night. Then, as both wished to rejoin their own people, Captain Gilbert and two other officers conveyed them across the river, and stayed that night with the Indians who were to depart in the morning. When, at that time, the Indians set out on their return to Pemaquid, Gilbert obtained from them a promise that on a certain day, agreed upon by both parties, they would accompany him to the place on the Penobscot river where the "bashabe," or principal chief of that region, resided.

This promise evidently gave great satisfaction to the colonists, and strengthened the hope that thus early strong friendly relations would be opened with one of the most powerful of the neighboring Indian tribes. Accordingly, three days later, Tuesday, September 8, Gilbert, accompanied by twenty-two others, started eastward, taking with them various kinds of merchandise for traffic with the Indians. But again the wind was contrary, and in waiting for more favorable weather conditions, they delayed so long that they were not able to reach Pemaquid at the appointed time. When they finally came to the place, the Indians, whom they were to meet, and who were to conduct them to the "bashabe", had left. They "found no living creature. They all were gone from thence". This is a noteworthy record in the *Relation,* inasmuch as it furnishes information with reference to conditions existing at Pemaquid at that time. Indians were its only inhabitants, and they had now left. If Gilbert and his men, in their search for the Indians, found at Pemaquid any traces of other inhabitants or of an earlier European civilization, they failed to record the fact. Early references to Pemaquid make mention only of Indian occupation, or traces of such occupation.

But Gilbert and his companions, disappointed in not finding the Indians, and especially Nahanada and Skidwarres, did not abandon the expedition, but sailing around Pemaquid point, Gilbert directed his boat to the eastward in the hope of reaching by water the seat of the "bashabe" upon the Penobscot river. Three days were spent in this endeavor, but the river did not open to them in that time, and their food supply not warranting a farther search, the explorers were at length compelled to turn about and make their way back to their companions at the mouth of the Sagadahoc.

Meanwhile the storehouse within the fort had been so far completed, that September 7, the removal of supplies from the Mary and John began. But work on the fort was not discontinued. The season, however, was advancing so rapidly that it seemed desirable to make a more extended exploration of the river before it should be closed by ice. Accordingly, September 23, Gilbert and nineteen others started "for the head of the river of Sagadahock". For two days and a part of a third day, the course of the Kennebec was followed as far as the falls at Augusta. With some difficulty these were successfully passed, and Gilbert and his companions ascended the river about a league farther. But night coming on they landed and went into camp. The evening had not far advanced when their rest was disturbed by a call in broken English from some Indians on the opposite side of the river. A response was made, but the strangers soon withdrew and the night passed without added interruption. The use of broken English by these savages indicated an earlier contact with Englishmen in American waters. Possibly this was in the preceding year when Hanham and Pring were on the coast. It is perhaps more probable that the "broken English" of these Indians was the result of trading relations with English fishermen, whose vessels had visited American waters from the opening of the century, or at least shortly after its opening.

On the following morning, Saturday, September 26, four Indians appeared and made themselves known as the Indians who had called to them from the opposite side of the river the evening before. Evidently they had received information of the progress of Gilbert and his men up the river, and wished to learn the significance of the presence of the visitors. One of the four announced himself as "Sebanoa . . . . . . Lord of the river of Sagadahock."

With this announcement, the manuscript *Relation,* followed in this narrative thus far, abruptly closes at the bottom of a page. There can be little, if any doubt whatever, that originally there were added pages which in some way became detached, and so were finally lost in the vicissitudes through which the manuscript passed before it found a safe resting place in the library of Lambeth Palace. The story of the Popham colony that is found in William Strachey's *Historie of Travaile into Virginia,* follows so closely the *Relation* to this point as to leave little doubt from the character of the rest of the story, that Strachey had all the missing pages of the manuscript before him while writing his narrative. As there is reason to believe that the manuscript—doubtless prepared for the information of the patrons of the enterprise—was continued only to October 6, 1607, the probable date of the sailing of the Mary and John for England, the loss is not a great one, and happily is in part at least supplied by Strachey's narrative, supplemented from other sources than those available now.

Strachey's narrative continues the story of Gilbert's interview with Sebanoa, recording acts of duplicity and treachery on the part of the Kennebec Indians as well as other acts of kindness and good-will. Gilbert seems to have conducted himself with tact and discretion under circumstances that were full of peril to himself and his party. It was his declared purpose in the exploration to go "to the head of the river", but the rapids he had now reached made progress difficult. His experiences with the Indians, also, had been by no means what he desired. At all events he now abandoned farther advance up the river, and having erected a cross at the highest point he had reached, he set out on his return to the settlement. On the way down the river, search was made for the "by river of some note called Sasanoa", by which plainly was meant the tidal river that connects the Kennebec opposite Bath with the waters of Sheepscot bay. Concerning this inland passage into the Sagadahoc, information doubtless had been received from Indians they had met in interviews already mentioned; but though Gilbert and his party looked for it carefully, a fog at length settled down upon them and they were obliged to make their way homeward as best they could.

They reached the fort on September 29. September 30 and October 1 and 2, all were busy about the fort. On the Mary and John, too, now nearly ready to sail on her return voyage to England, there were doubtless many evidences of preparations for the voyage. September 3, Skidwarres, crossing the river in a canoe, brought a message to President Popham, saying that Nahanada, also the bashabe's brother and other Indians, were on the opposite side of the river, and would visit the colonists on the following day. This they did, two canoes conveying the party, which included Nahanada and his wife, Skidwarres, the bashabe's brother and a chief called Amenquin. Popham entertained his guests with kindness and generosity during two days, the last day being Sunday, on which "with great reverence and silence" the Indians attended the religious services of the colonists both morning and evening. With the exception of Amenquin, all the Indians departed on Monday, October 6, and on this date the daily journal in Strachey's narrative ends. This abrupt suspension of the daily record of the Popham colony gives probability to the inference that it was brought to a close because of the sailing of the Mary and John about this date; the journal having been kept apparently for the purpose of affording the patrons of the colony in England eagerly awaited information at the earliest possible opportunity. As the plan of Fort St. George, already mentioned, bears the inscription "taken out on the 8th of October, 1607," it is possible that in these few words is recorded the exact date on which the Mary and John sailed out of the river homeward bound.

The vessel arrived in the harbor of Plymouth, England, on the first day of December. No one with a deeper personal interest welcomed the tidings the Mary and John brought from the colonists than Sir Ferdinando Gorges. The journal was placed in his hand, and added information with reference to the colony was communicated by the officers of the vessel. It was "great news", and the commander of the fort at Plymouth late that very night—evidently having spent the preceding hours in personal interviews with the returning voyagers—hastened to make known to Secretary Cecil at Hatfield house the information he had received. The colonists he wrote, had successfully established themselves in a fertile country, with gallant rivers, stately harbors and a people tractable, if only they were discreetly dealt with. To be sure, the Mary and John had brought no such cargo as would satisfy the expectation of those who had furnished the funds for financing the undertaking, and this fact, he said, might be used to the disadvantage of the enterprise; but it should be remembered, he added, that the colonists during the two months following their arrival at the mouth of the Sagadahoc had been busily engaged in establishing themselves in a secure position there. But this was not the whole story, and Gorges was compelled to add that already among the colonists there were discordant elements, occasioned by the "defect and want of understanding of some of those employed, to perform what they were directed unto from whence there did not only proceed confusion, but, through pride and arrogancy, faction and private resolution," concerning which he would inform his lordship more fully at another time.

But though Gorges evidently was considerably discouraged on account of the reported condition of things among the colonists, he had no difficulty in finding excellent reasons why his associates in the enterprise should not steadfastly resolve to follow it up with energy and hopefulness. Such reasons he found in "the boldness of the coast, the easiness of the navigation, the fertility of the soil, and the several sorts of commodities that they are assured the country do yield, as namely fish in the season in great plenty, all along the coast mastidge for ships, goodly oaks, and cedars with infinite other sorts of trees, rosin, hemp, grapes very fair and excellent good, whereof they have already made wine, much like to the claret wine that comes out of France; rich furs if they can keep the Frenchmen from the trade; as for metals, they can say nothing, but they are confident there is in the country, if they had means to seek for it, neither could they go so high as the alum mines are which the savages doth assure them there is great plenty of." The manufacture of alum from pyritic shale was at that time exciting public interest not only in England but upon the continent; and the fact that thus early the colonists had satisfied themselves of the existence of deposits of pyritic shale in the Sagadahoc country was one especially welcome to Gorges.

In a second letter to Cecil, dated December 3, 1607, Gorges gives fuller expression to the reports he had received with reference to the general confusion already existing among the colonists. President Popham, he described as "an honest man, but old and of an unwieldly body, and timorously fearful to offend or contest with others that will or do oppose him; but otherwise a discreet, careful man." Concerning Gilbert, the second in command, Gorges says he is described by those who returned in the Mary and John as "desirous of supremacy and rule, a loose life, prompt to sensuality, little zeal in religion, humorous, headstrong and of small judgment and experience, other ways valiant enough." Of the other officials, the preacher, Rev. Robert Seymour, was especially commended "for his pains in his place and his honest endeavors." Honorable mention was also made of Captain Robert Davies and Mr. Turner, the company's physician. But of the colonists in general, little was said. Evidently they were regarded by Gorges as unfit for employment in such an undertaking. "Childish factions" had already developed among them.

Naturally, Gorges was disturbed on account of this condition of things in the new colony; and he expresses to Cecil the wish that the king, "unto whom by right the conquest of kingdoms doth appertain," would take the matter into his own hands, and so not allow the project to fail. Delicacy did not allow Gorges to withhold the suggestion that in case this were done he would be "most happy to receive such employment" from the king as his highness shall deem him fitted, and he had no doubt that, with "very little charges", he would be able "to bring to pass infinite things."

In all probability Cecil laid before the king this discouraging report. We have no reason to believe, however, that it gave the easy-going monarch any part of that deep anxiety that disquieted his devoted servant in command of the fort at Plymouth; and Gorges' suggestion concerning the man for the hour evidently received no consideration whatever. But there was occasion for anxiety, as Gorges well knew. If, as he desired, government assistance in supporting the colony could not be obtained, there was no lack of whole-heartedness in his continued endeavors to render all possible aid with reference to English colonization in the new world.

Information concerning affairs at the mouth of the Sagadahoc after the departure of the Mary and John is derived for the most part from Strachey's narrative; but such information is exceedingly meagre. The colonists, he says finished the fort and fortified it with twelve pieces of ordnance. They also built fifty houses within the inclosure, besides a church and a storehouse. In this mention of the number of houses erected by the colonists there is evidently an error. No such number was required for present occupancy. Moreover, the plan of the fort found in the library at Simancas, which apparently was drawn with reference to completeness of design, shows not a third of the number of buildings mentioned by Strachey. To have completed, before winter set in, even the number indicated on the plan, would have required a force of workmen far beyond that which was at Popham's command. The most that was attempted, doubtless, was to provide for the colonists as comfortable quarters as the means at their disposal admitted.

Added information with reference to the colonists is furnished in a letter written by Gorges February 7, 1608, to Secretary Cecil, informing him of the arrival of the Gift of God in the harbor of Plymouth. Probably the date of the letter is the date of the arrival of the Gift, as Gorges was not likely to lose any time in conveying to the government this latest intelligence from the mouth of the Sagadahoc. First of all, he refers to the severity of the cold at Sagadahoc, by which the colonists had been sorely pinched, although it was probably not later than the middle of December when the Gift's return-voyage was commenced and the winter then was only in its early stages. The health of the colonists, however, was good. But the troubles among them which had appeared even before the departure of the Mary and John were still operative, and Gorges was compelled to report "idle proceedings" and the existence of "divisions," "factions," each "disgracing the other, even to the savages". The picture was a dark one and might have been made even darker. Certainly Gorges could have found in the report little encouragement, either for himself or Cecil, with reference to the success of an undertaking to which he had given his best endeavors. In fact, his only hopes in connection with English colonization upon American soil seemed now to hang upon the king, "the chief spring of our happiness . . . . . . who at the last must reap the benefit of all our travail, as of right it belongs unto him"; and so he urges upon the secretary careful consideration of the whole matter, adding his own public and private reasons in seeking to extend the glory of England beyond the sea—namely "the certainty of the commodities that may be had from so fertile a soil as that is, when it shall be peopled, as well for building of shipping, having all things rising in the place wherewith to do it." This, also, would be for "the increase of the king's navy, the breeding of mariners, the employment of his people, filling the world with expectation and satisfying his subjects with hopes, who now are sick in despair and in time will grow desperate through necessity." Moreover, to abandon American colonization would afford an opportunity for others to seize the prize, which England might have. "At this instant", adds Gorges, "the French are in hand with the natives to practice upon us, promising them, if they will put us out of the country, and not trade with none of ours, they will come unto them," etc. "The truth is," he adds, "this place is so stored with excellent harbors and so bold a coast, as it is able to invite any actively minded to endeavor the possessing thereof, if it were only to keep it out of the hands of others." These words of Gorges indicate a strong and even statesmanlike grasp upon problems that had much to do with the future of the island kingdom; and they admirably illustrate the prevalent thought and purpose of those best informed in England, not only then but in the generations that followed, until the inspiring dream of England's hold upon American soil had finally been realized.

Of course, in the present state of affairs at the mouth of the Sagadahoc, if anything was to be done by the government, it must be done quickly; and Gorges suggests to Cecil that the king furnish for the undertaking "one of his middle sort of ships, with a small pinnace, and withal to give his letters, and commission, to countenance and authorize the worthy enterpriser." This would put new life into the colony, and Gorges, ready to serve his sovereign and the country, declared his willingness to take command for the discovery of the whole American coast "from the first to the second colony".

In this letter to Cecil, Gorges makes no mention of the fact that a part of the colonists returned to England on the Gift of God. Purchas, however, in his *Pilgrimes,* published in 1614, says in his reference to the Popham colony that "forty-five remained there, after the departure of the Gift," and refers to a letter written by President Popham as his authority for the statement. Captain John Smith, in his *General History of New England,* published ten years later, says, "They were glad to send all but forty-five of their company back again." As none of the colonists returned in the Mary and John, so far as is known, the reference must be to the colonists who returned in the Gift of God. Such a lessening of the number of the colonists before even a single winter had passed was the most discouraging fact which the arrival of the Gift revealed to Gorges, and he had no heart to make it known to Cecil in this first report of the arrival of the second vessel.

One added report from the colony is found in a letter to King James written by President Popham, December 13, 1607. Gorges makes no reference to it, and of its existence there was no knowledge until it was discovered a little more than half a century ago by George Bancroft, the historian, while making some researches in the Records Office in London. The letter was written in Latin that cannot be called classic, and abounds in those flattering, adulatory words and phrases that were so pleasing to the heart of the king. Popham makes no mention of discouraging circumstances. He had no reference even to the winter cold that had chilled so thoroughly the interest of so many of the colonists. It is his "well-considered" opinion "that in these regions the glory of God may easily be evidenced," the empire enlarged, and its welfare speedily augmented. His report concerning the products of the country, however, is not so well considered; for he informs the king that "there are in these parts shagbarks, nutmegs and cinnamon, besides pine wood and Brazilian cochineal and ambergris, with many other products, and these in the greatest abundance." Allowance must be made for the exaggeration of enthusiasm, but evidently the president's nutmegs, cinnamon and Brazilian cochineal were the products of excited imaginations.

February 5, 1608, two days before Gorges wrote to Cecil concerning the arrival of the Gift of God, President Popham died. Gilbert and the remaining colonists doubtless gave him fitting burial within the enclosure of Fort St. George. Gorges says, "he had long been an infirm man." High aims and purposes, however, still animated him. He was not one who would turn back in any worthy enterprise. The opportunity for securing for his king and country a stronghold upon the American continent, he clearly saw, and he embraced it with whatever of toil and hardship it might bring to him personally. We have no information concerning his last days. No other member of the colony died from sickness that winter. In fact, the health of the colonists throughout the winter season was exceedingly good. In all probability on account of extreme age, the leader of the enterprise was ill-prepared to endure the exposures to which an unusually severe winter subjected him and his followers. Whether, however, the end came suddenly, or after prolonged illness, Popham manfully fulfilled all the duties devolving upon him as the head of the colony, and worthily finished his course. Gorges, writing many years afterwards, paid beautiful tribute to Popham's steadfast loyalty to God and native land, in the words: "However heartened by hopes, willing he was to die in acting something that might be serviceable to God and honorable to his country."

Meanwhile Gorges, Sir Francis Popham and others, were busily employed in securing supplies and forwarding them to the colonists at the mouth of the Sagadahoc. Writing to Cecil March 20, 1608, Gorges said: "As concerning our plantation, we have found the means to encourage ourselves anew, and have sent two ships from Topsham for the supplies of those that be there, with victuals and other necessaries, having set down the means how we shall be able by May next to send one more of two hundred tons." The two vessels thus despatched brought to the colonists the intelligence of the death of Sir John Popham in the preceding June. This was a loss as unexpected as it was severe. But the welcome arrival of these two ships with abundant supplies was ample testimony to the fact that the colonists still had in England ardent friends of the enterprise. In the reports that have come down to us concerning the arrival of these two vessels, there is no mention of any increase in the membership of the colony by recruits from England. Gorges refers to supplies only. Of course there was need of these; but it was not by any means the only need of the men, who, notwithstanding past discouragements, were loyally sustaining Sagadahoc interests; and it is impossible to think of any such gathering of supplies by Gorges and his associates that was not at the same time accompanied by the most earnest efforts to reinforce the little company of forty-five left with Popham and Gilbert on the departure of the Gift of God in the middle of December. Such efforts, however, seem to have been unsuccessful.

But the affairs of the colonists brightened with the arrival of the two vessels from England. The winter with its cold and storms was behind them. Gilbert had succeeded George Popham as president of the colony. The Virginia had been launched and was ready for service. With the promise of a third vessel and added supplies soon to be on their way, the outlook for the future of the colony was certainly a more favorable one. Evidently neither on the part of the supporters in England, nor on the part of the leaders of the enterprise at Fort St. George, was the possible abandonment of the undertaking in any way under consideration.

Concerning the condition of affairs under the direction of Gilbert we have no information whatever. All we know is that his presidency was brought to an unexpected end by the tidings brought to the Sagadahoc by the third vessel despatched thither. When Gorges, March 20, wrote to Secretary Cecil concerning this third vessel, he thought it might be ready to sail in May, but for some reason unknown there was delay in the preparation for the voyage, and in all probability the vessel did not leave England until July. This is a well-founded inference from the fact that Sir John Gilbert, the elder brother of President Raleigh Gilbert, died July 5, 1608. The third vessel, bringing this intelligence to President Gilbert, could not have left England before that date. Probably there was not much added delay in despatching the vessel and if this was the fact the arrival of the vessel must be placed about the first of September, or a little later. President Gilbert was his brother's heir, and on account of the large personal interests involved in this fact, it became necessary for him to make preparations for an early return to England. The situation was a peculiar one. Among the little company remaining there was no one who possessed the requisite qualifications for the successful administration of the affairs of the colony. To continue the enterprise, therefore, seemed out of the question. Accordingly, the complete abandonment of Fort St. George and all for which it stood followed, and preparations at once were made for dismantling the fort and removing the ordnance and stores to the vessels anchored near by. How much time was required in accomplishing this transfer is not known. In all probability the embarkation of the colonists occurred as early as the close of September. In the records that have come down to us concerning the return of the colonists there is not a hint that the departure brought any sorrow or even disappointment to those who constituted the great body of Gilbert's company. Their interest in the undertaking was of the slightest kind. In all probability the experiences of a single winter at the mouth of the Sagadahoc made welcome to them an opportunity to return thus early to more desirable conditions of life in their native land. Far otherwise was it with Gorges and other steadfast friends of English colonization in America, when about the close of November, or early in December, the three vessels and the pinnace Virginia, built by the colonists, arrived in Plymouth harbor and announced the abandonment of the colony. This was chilling information, and years afterward, Gorges, in referring to its effect upon himself and other patrons of the undertaking, could only say: "all our former hopes were frozen to death". The collapse of the colony was complete. Strachey says: "all embarked . . . . . . and set sail for England."

Why was not the Popham colony assigned to a more southerly location on the American coast, one in which the colonists would have avoided that severity of the winter season to which they were unaccustomed in their English homes? Certainly it was not from any lack of knowledge concerning the unfavorable conditions in which they found themselves after the location of the colony. Nor was it because of insufficient information with reference to the character of the country farther down the coast. There had been careful exploration of the territory to the southward as far nearly as Narraganset bay. Pring, whose explorations largely determined the location of the Popham colony, was familiar with the coast as far as Massachusetts bay. What advantage, then, had the location at the mouth of the Sagadahoc over places in a more congenial climate?

Evidently one of the determining factors in its selection was the great value of the fisheries in the immediate vicinity of Fort St. George. The early explorers on the coast, in their printed reports, and much more by word of mouth, had called attention to the rich returns that these fisheries promised. English fishermen also were already acquainted to some extent with the fishing privileges in these waters. Those who were especially interested in the establishment of the colony were merchants of Plymouth and Bristol, long connected with fishing interests, and attracted hither by the reports of the greater abundance of fish on the American coast. Certainly, these fishing grounds had a value that could not be overestimated. France was endeavoring to seize and hold these grounds, but England claimed them and their possession was deemed worthy of a supreme effort on the part of the English nation.

Another determining factor in the location of the Popham colony is to be found in the opportunity that the river Sagadahoc offered for profitable trade with the Indians, especially in valuable furs. There was no such opportunity farther down the coast.

From a commercial point of view, therefore, the location of the Popham colony seems to have been amply justified.

Why, then, did the colony fail? Primarily, the death of the Pophams, Sir John in England and Captain George, the president of the colony, in Fort St. George, was a heavy blow at the enterprise. Then, too, Gilbert's recall to England on account of the death of his brother was doubtless a heavy stroke, inasmuch as among the other colonists no one could be found who was capable of taking Gilbert's place. This statement, however, reveals only partially the difficulties of the situation. Not only were the Popham colonists generally lacking in those sturdy qualities that such an enterprise demands, but if we may accept the testimony that is furnished by contemporary writers, the company comprised the vagrant and the dissolute to such an extent that Gorges is believed to have stated the fact mildly when he wrote, that they were "not such as they ought". Indeed, as later he reflected upon the disastrous ending of the undertaking, he felt, and had reason for feeling, that if he and others interested in American colonization would achieve success in connection with their desires and endeavors, "there must go other manner of spirits" than were found so largely in the Sagadahoc colony.

CHAPTER 3.

After the failure of the Popham Colony in 1608, no further effort was made to establish a colony in Maine until 1613 when Father Biard, a Jesuit priest, led a group of Frenchmen to Mt. Desert Island where at the mouth of Somes Sound they established themselves.

A FRENCH JESUIT MISSION ARRIVES AT MT. DESERT*
by
FATHER PIERRE BIARD, S.J.

They fitted up a ship in France to take the Jesuits away from Port Royal, and to found a new French settlement in a more suitable place.

The chief of this expedition was Captain la Saussaye, who was to winter in the country with thirty persons, counting in the two Jesuits and their servant, whom he was to take up at Port Royal. He had with him, besides, two other Jesuits, Father Quantin and Gilbert du Thet, whom he was to take there, but they were to return to France in case two at Port Royal were not dead, of which there was some doubt. The entire company, counting the Sailors, numbered 48 persons. The master of the ship was Charles Flory of Habbeville, a discreet, hardy and peaceable man. The Queen in her goodness had contributed four of the King's tents or pavilions, and some munitions of war. Sieur Simon le Maistre had devoted himself earnestly to the freighting and provisioning, and Gilbert du Thet, the Jesuit lay brother, a very industrious man, had not spared himself; so they were amply provided with everything for more than a year, besides the horses and goats which were being taken over for domestic purposes. The ship was of a hundred tons burthen.

This expedition, thus fitted out, departed from Honfleur on the 12th of March, 1613, and landed first at Cap de la Hève on the coast of Acadie, on the 16th of May, having consumed two entire months in the passage. At Cap de la Hève Mass was said and a Cross erected, upon which was placed the coat of arms of Madame la Marquise de Guercheville, as a sign of having taken possession of it in her name. Thence putting to sea again, they came to Port Royal.

At Port Royal they only found five persons; namely, the two Jesuits, their servants, the Apothecary Hebert, and another. Sieur de Biencourt and the rest of his people were all quite far away, some here, some there. Now because Hebert was taking the place of the sieur, they presented to him the Queen's letters, which contained the royal command to release the Jesuits and to let them go wherever they pleased so the Jesuits took away their property in great peace. And on that day as well as on the following, they made it as pleasant for Hebert and his company as they could so that this arrival would not be a cause of sadness to them. At their departure, (although they were not in need of anything) they left them a barrel of bread and some bottles of wine, that the Farewell might be received with equally good grace.

Unfavorable winds kept us about five days at Port Royal, and then a propitious Northeaster arising, we departed, intending to go to the river Pentegoet, to the place called Kadesquit, the site destined for the new colony, and having many great advantages for such a purpose. But God ordained otherwise. For when we were to the Southeast of the Island of Menano, the weather changed, and there came upon the sea such a dense fog that we could see no more by day than by

---

*The Jesuit Relations: the extract given as translated in Forerunners and Competitors of the Pilgrims and Puritans, edited by Charles Herbert Levermore (Brooklyn, N.Y.: The New England Society of Brooklyn, 1912).

night. We had serious misgivings in this time of danger, because in this place there are breakers and rocks, against which we were afraid of striking in the darkness; the wind not permitting us to draw away and stand out to sea. We continued thus two days and two nights, veering now to one side, now to the other, as God inspired us. We were moved by our affliction to offer prayers and vows to God, that he might be pleased to deliver us from the danger, and direct us to some place for his glory. In his goodness he hearkened to us, for when evening came on we began to see the stars, and by morning the fogs had all disappeared. We recognized that we were opposite Mount Desert, an Island, which the Savages called Pemetig. The pilot turned to the Eastern shore of the Island, and there located us in a large and beautiful port, where we made our thanksgiving to God, raising a Cross and singing to God his praises with the sacrifice of the holy Mass. We called this place a, port Saint Sauveur.

Now here in this Port of St. Sauveur a great contention arose between the Sailors and our company, or us other passengers, because the charter party and contract, drawn up in France, stipulated that the Sailors should be held at anchor in a Port of Acadie, which we should name to them, and should remain there for the space of three months; the sailors maintained that they had arrived at a Port of Acadie, and that therefore the said term of three months should begin to run from the time of this arrival. It was explained to them that the Port was not the one that had been designated to them by the name of Kadesquit, and therefore the time would not begin to be counted until they were there. The pilot obstinately opposed this, maintaining that a ship had never gone as far as Kadesquit, and that he had no intention of becoming a discoverer of new routes; there was also some mistake about the name Acadie meaning Norambegue, which strengthened the dispute; reasons here, reasons there; nothing but argument, a bad augury for the future.

During these quarrels, the Savages signaled to us with smoke. This means that we can go and find them if we need them, which we did. The Pilot incidentally remarked to these Savages that the Port Royal Fathers were in his ship. They answered that they would like very much to see the one with whom they had become acquainted two years before at Pentegoet. This was Father Biard, who went immediately to see them, and in asking about the route to Kadesquit, said he wished to go there to live. "But," said they, "if thou wishest to stay in these regions, why dost thou not rather remain here with us, who have truly as good and beautiful a place as Kadesquit?" And they began to sing the praises of their home, assuring him that it was so healthy, and so agreeable, that when the Savages are sick in other parts, they have themselves brought to this place and here recover. These blessings did not affect Father Biard much, for he knew that the Savages did not lack that with which almost everyone is abundantly provided, namely, the ability to praise their own wares. But they knew well how to use their machinations against him to carry him off. "For," said they, "it is necessary that thou comest since Asticou, our Sagamore, is sick unto death; and if thou dost not come he will die without baptism, and will not go to heaven. Thou wilt be the cause of it, for he himself wishes very much to be baptized." This argument, so naively deduced, astonished Father Biard, and fully persuaded him to go there, especially as it was only three leagues away, and in all there would result no greater loss of time than one afternoon; so he got into one of their canoes with sieur de la Motte, Lieutenant, and Simon the interpreter, and went off.

When we arrived at Asticou's cabins, we found him truly sick, but not unto death, for it was only a cold that troubled him; so having assured ourselves of his good condition, we had plenty of leisure to go and visit this place, so greatly boasted about and so much better for a French settlement than Kadesquit. And in truth we found that the Savages were not wrong in praising it so highly, for we ourselves were wonderfully astonished; and having carried the news to the chiefs of our company, and they having come to view the place, all unanimously agreed that we ought to stay there and not look for anything better, especially as it seemed as if God told us to do so through the fortunate events which had happened to us, and through an evident miracle, which he performed in the restoration of a child of which we shall speak elsewhere.

This place is a beautiful hill, rising gently from the sea, its sides bathed by two springs; the land is cleared for twenty or twenty-five acres, and in some places is covered with grass almost as high as a man. It faces the South and East, and is near the mouth of the Pentegoet, where several broad and pleasant rivers, which abound in fish, discharge their waters; its soil is dark, rich and fertile; the Port and Harbor are as fine as can be seen, and are in a position favorable to command the entire coast; the Harbor especially is as safe as a pond. For, besides being strengthened by the great Island of Mount Desert, it is still more protected by certain small Islands which break the currents and the winds, and fortify the entrance. There is not a fleet which it is not capable of sheltering, nor a ship so deep that could not approach within a cable's length of the shore to unload. It is situated in latitude forty-four and one-third degrees, a position still less northerly than that of Bourdeaux.

Now having landed at this place and planted here the Cross we began to work; and with the beginning of work also began the quarrels, a second sign and augury of our ill luck. The cause of these dissensions was principally that la Saussaye, our Captain, amused himself too much in cultivating the land, while all the chiefs of the enterprise were urging him not to employ the laborers for that purpose, but to get to work without delay upon the houses and fortifications, which he did not wish to do. From these disputes sprang others, until the English brought us all to an understanding with each other, as you will hear immediately.

CHAPTER 4.

The Pilgrims of Plymouth came to Maine in 1629 after receiving a grant along the Kennebec from the Council of New England. As a result of their lucrative trade with the Indians they were able to pay off their debt owed in England.

THE PLYMOUTH COLONISTS IN MAINE*
by
HENRY S. BURRAGE

A new interest has been awakened in the Pilgrim Plantation at Plymouth by the recent publication of Bradford's History, from the original manuscript, now in the possession of the Commonwealth of Massachusetts. In its main features this story of heroic endurance and sublime faith is well known to all who have given any attention whatever to our early New England history; yet he has missed much who has not traced the fortunes of the Pilgrim Fathers in the quaint narrative of their first governor. To us, living in Maine, however, the story as told by Bradford has a peculiar interest from his frequent allusions to places and events within our own borders; and in reading the narrative one is soon impressed by the fact that a closer relation existed between the Plymouth Colony and what is now the state of Maine than has hitherto been indicated.

When the Pilgrims, during their residence in Holland, were considering the question of a removal to some part of the new world, there were those in their number who expressed a very decided preference for Guiana, in South America, concerning which such glowing accounts had been written by Sir Walter Raleigh. Others favored a settlement within the limits of the Virginia Company, but not in connection with the colony already established on the banks of the James River, where again they might be brought into conflict with the English church. New England had no attractions for them on account of the severity of its climate, reports concerning which had been preserved in the records of the Popham Colony and in the relations of various voyagers. All things considered the country about the Delaware River seemed to offer the most favorable opportunity for the successful establishment of a permanent colony. The Virginia Company, whose territory extended from Cape Fear to Long Island Sound, was willing to co-operate with the Pilgrims, and offered to grant them a tract of land with all the rights of self government which the Company itself possessed. Such a grant accordingly was secured, not in the name of the Pilgrims, however, but of Mr. John Wincob, an English gentleman who was interested in the movement and proposed to throw in his fortunes with theirs. "But God so disposed," says Bradford, "as he never went nor they ever made use of this patente." Some Dutchmen at Manhattan, also, made "faire offers," proposing to transport the entire company to that trading post at the mouth of the Hudson River and conceding to them the right of self government in their internal affairs. In response to this offer, early in 1620, a statement was made to the stadtholder giving the conditions on which the Pilgrims would consent to establish their colony at Manhattan. These conditions were at length rejected, but before the reply was received negotiations with the Dutch on the part of the Pilgrims had been broken off by the advice of Mr. Thomas Weston, a London merchant, who visited Leydon and persuaded the Pilgrims "not to medle with ye Dutch, or too much to depend on ye Virginia Company; for if that

---
*Henry S. Burrage, *"The Plymouth Colonists in Maine"* Collections of the Maine Historical Society, (Portland, Published by the Society, 1904), 3rd Series, I, pp.116-145.

failed, if they came to resolution, he and such marchants as were his freinds (togeather with their owne means) would sett them forth;... Aboute this time also," adds Bradford, "they had heard, both by Mr. Weston and others, y^t sundrie Hon^{bl}: Lords had obtained a large grante from ye king, for ye more northerly parts of that countrie, derived out of ye Virginia patente, and wholy secluded from their Govermente, and to be called by another name, viz. New England." The reference is to what is now known as the New England charter.

It was not the purpose of the Pilgrims in following the advice of Weston and others to settle in that part of New England to which they came in December, 1620. This is made clear by Bradford. Referring to the Voyage of the Mayflower, he says: "After large beating at sea they fell with that land which is called Cape Cod; the which being made & certainly knowne to be it, they were not a little joyfull. After some deliberation had amongst themselves & with ye m^r of ye ship, they tacked aboute and resolved to stande for ye southward (ye wind and weather being faire) to finde some place aboute Hudsons river for their habitation." But the Pilgrims soon found themselves among the "deangerous shoulds and roring breakers" off the southerly part of the Cape and perceiving their peril they bore "up againe" for the Cape and the next day anchored in "ye Cape-harbor." The settlement at Plymouth followed. The Mayflower voyagers had long enough braved the wintry Atlantic, and were glad to find a resting place even if it were on the bleak, inhospitable shores of New England.

About two months after the Pilgrims landed at Plymouth, an Indian walked down the street on which they had built the log-huts of their little settlement. To the surprise of the colonists who met him he addressed them in broken English. His name was Samoset, and he told them that he had obtained his use of their language from the captains and sailors of English fishing vessels that came each year to "ye easterne parts" to fish. From him the Pilgrims derived much valuable information. He told them about the Indians in their vicinity, their names and number. Later he made them acquainted with Squanto, or Tisquantum, to whom they were so much indebted subsequently; also with the great chief, Massasoit. Samoset also told them "many things concerning ye state of ye country in ye east-parts wher he lived, which was afterwards profitable unto them"—how profitable Bradford makes known in the further unfolding of his narrative. Doubtless the Indian's story was not fully intelligible, but from his imperfect use of the English language the Pilgrims learned enough to give them some acquaintance with a region not very remote to which their own countrymen had made more or less profitable voyages for fishing or trading purposes since the days of the Popham Colony; and what they thus learned, as Bradford intimates, was not forgotten.

The merchant adventurers in London, who furnished the capital for the Pilgrim enterprise, expected large returns for their venture. Very naturally the colonists desired to meet their just expectations. But the early years of Bradford and his associates at Plymouth were spent almost wholly in the eager struggle for existence. Squanto taught them how to raise Indian corn, but from their scanty harvests it was difficult at first to procure subsistence sufficient for their own necessities. The Mayflower returned to England without lading. But the Fortune, in 1621, on her return voyage carried "good clapbord as full as she could stowe," manufactured by the hard labor of the Pilgrims during the preceding winter doubtless. She also carried two hogsheads of beaver and other skins, which for a few trifling articles they had purchased of the Indians. The Fortune unfortunately was captured on the voyage by Frenchmen and taken to a French port, where before the release of the vessel everything of value on board was confiscated. The loss of the cargo was a grievous disappointment to the Pilgrims as well as to the merchant adventurers impatiently awaiting the arrival of such products of the new world as the colonists could send to repay the money and goods they had advanced.

About the end of May, 1622, when the provisions of the Pilgrims were nearly exhausted, they discovered a boat at sea which at first they thought to contain Frenchmen, but which proved to be a shallop from a fishing vessel at Damariscove. The shallop had seven passengers who had crossed the Atlantic in this vessel. With this addition to the colony, however, there came no supplies to the hungry colonists. Among other letters which the shallop brought, however, was one from the master of a fishing vessel at Damariscove, one John

Huddlestone. Huddlestone was a stranger to the Pilgrims, but from some one of the vessels that had come from Virginia he had heard of the massacre of the colonists there by the Indians, and his letter was intended to put the Pilgrims on their guard lest a like fate should befall them. Bradford wrote a letter of grateful acknowledgement in response, and Mr. Winslow, in a boat belonging to the colony, accompanied the shallop to Damariscove on its return, with instructions to procure for the colonists "what provisions he could of ye ships." Huddlestone not only furnished Mr. Winslow with such supplies as he could spare from his own stores, but he gave him letters to the captains of other fishing vessels in the vicinity, who treated him in a like generous way, by which, says Bradford, "ye plantation had a double benefite, first, a present refreshing by ye food brought, and secondly they knew ye way to those parts for their benefite hereafter."

By the supplies received from the fishing vessels at and near Damariscove the Pilgrims were enabled to subsist, though most frugally, until the welcome time of harvest arrived. But the corn they then obtained did not furnish the colonists with a full year's supply, and there would have been hunger in their log cabins, if they had not obtained subsistence from the neighboring Indians. No attempt to add to their stock from the "eastward," however, was made until early in March, 1624, when the pinnace was newly fitted out and despatched thitherward on a fishing cruise. She arrived safely at a place near Damariscove and, as Bradford says, "was there well harbored in a place wher ships used to ride, ther being also some ships allready arrived out of England. But shortly after ther arose such a violent & extraordinarie storme, as ye seas broak over such places in ye harbor as was never seene before, and drive her against great roks, which beat such a hole in her hulke, as a horse and carte might have gone in, and after drive her into deep water, wher she lay sunke." The master of the pinnace and one of the men were drowned, while the rest rescued themselves with the greatest difficulty, and at length made their way back to Plymouth and reported the disaster. Later in the season, some of the masters of the fishing vessels at Damariscove sent word to the Plymouth colonists that it was a pity so fine a vessel should be lost and they offered, provided the Pilgrims would defray the cost, to raise the wreck, and provide ship carpenters "to mend her." The Pilgrims thanked the captains for their kindly offer, and sent men to Damariscove and also beaver to provide for the expense. A large number of empty casks were fastened to the wreck at low water, and when the tide rose and the wreck was lifted, they drew it to the shore "in a conveniente place wher she might be wrought upon; and then hired sundrie carpenters to work upon her, and others to saw planks, and at last fitted her & got her home." But the venture as a whole proved a very unremunerative one.

Meanwhile Bradford and his associates at Plymouth were not only exerting themselves to the utmost to provide subsistence for the members of the colony, but at the same time they were earnestly endeavoring to pay their indebtedness to the merchant adventurers in London. In 1625, after harvest, which was the most abundant they had gathered since the establishment of the colony, they dispatched a boat's load of corn to "ye eastward, up a river called Kenibeck." This is Bradford's first mention of the Kennebec, but the name must have been a familiar one to him from the time of their acquaintance with Samoset. The boat in which the corn was carried for this venture was one of two which the carpenter of the Pilgrims had built during the preceding year. "They had a little deck over her midships to keepe ye corne drie," says Bradford, "but ye men were faine to stand it out all weathers without shelter; and y^t time of ye year begins to grow tempestuous." Mr. Edward Winslow was in charge of this Kennebec venture. Proceeding up the river, he found the Indians exceedingly well disposed, and had no difficulty in exchanging his store of corn for beaver, of which he obtained seven hundred pounds. When Winslow at length dropped down the river on his return homeward, he had laid the foundations of an exceedingly profitable trade, and he made his way back to Plymouth with high hopes that from this trade the colony would be able to discharge ere long its financial obligations in London. These hopes were not doomed to disappointment. The sight of the beaver, as Winslow and his boat's crew landed at Plymouth the proceeds of this Kennebec venture, was one with which the Pilgrims became more and more familiar as the years went by.

Little time was spent by the Plymouth men in fishing, but the colonists devoted themselves to "trading and planting," and this with "ye best industrie they could." They had now learned the value of corn for trading purposes, and the amount planted was considerably increased, the governor and those who were associated with him in managing the traffic for the benefit of the colony using all diligence in promoting the general welfare.

But in their traffic with the Indians other commodities than corn were desirable, and learning that the plantation at Monhegan belonging to certain merchants in Plymouth, England, was to be broken up and that "diverse usefull goods" brought there by these parties were to be sold, Governor Bradford and Mr. Winslow, with some other of the colonists, proceeded thither in a boat. Evidently they made their way along the coast, and when they reached Piscataqua, Mr. David Thompson, who resided there, "took opportunitie to goe with them," an unfortunate decision for the Plymouth men. For when they came into the harbor at Monhegan, the traders there had two bidders for their goods instead of one. They made a profitable use of their advantage, and the visitors at length, in order that they might not further work to each other's injury, bought the goods in common and then divided them equally. Various commodities obtained from the wreck of a French vessel had fallen into the hands of the traders at Monhegan and Damariscove. These, also, were bought in partnership, and the amount paid by the Pilgrim colonists was upward of 500 pounds. This payment was met by the beaver and other furs which they secured from the Indians of the Kennebec. The Plymouth men were now well supplied with articles for their traffic on that river. "With these goods," says Bradford, "and their corne after harvest, they gott good store of trade, so as they were enabled to pay their ingagements against ye time & to get some cloathing for ye people, and had some comodities beforehand."

Meanwhile the relations of the Pilgrims to the London merchant adventurers became more and more unsatisfactory. The adventurers had failed to secure the large returns they had expected from their venture, and in 1625 the majority of them deserted the colony. At the same time the Plymouth men, who better understood the difficulties encountered, were not pleased with the reproaches heaped upon them by their English promoters. In order to a better mutual understanding, the Pilgrims in 1625 sent Capt. Miles Standish to England. They desired also better terms in purchasing goods and lower rates of interest. "But he came in a very bade time," says Bradford, "for ye State was full of trouble, and ye plague very hote in London, so as no business could be done." Standish spoke with some of the Council, however, who promised helpfulness according to their ability, but little money was in circulation on account of the plague. With much "adooe" says Bradford, he borrowed "150 pounds at 50 per cent," which, after paying his expenses he laid out in goods and returned to New England in a fishing vessel. In the following year Mr. Allerton continued the negotiations with the creditors in London, and an agreement was at length reached by which the Plymouth colonists were to pay the London adventurers 1800 pounds, of which 200 pounds were to be paid annually until the whole debt was provided for, the first payment to be made in 1628. "This agreemente," says Bradford, "was very well liked of, & approved by all ye plantation, and consented unto: though they knew not well how to raise ye payment, and discharge their other ingagements, and supply the yearly wants of ye plantation, seeing they were forced for their necessities to take up money or goods at so high interests." But the trade with the Indians on the Kennebec inspired hopefulness in the colonists. They needed for this trade, however, a larger boat than they now possessed. They ran a great hazard in their trips along the coast in a small craft, especially in the winter season. In their perplexity the house carpenter of the colony was consulted. He was an "ingenius man," according to Bradford, and had wrought with the ship carpenter, now dead, when he built the boats they had used hitherto. So he was asked to make trial of his skill in the same art. This he did. Selecting one of the largest of the boats he sawed it "in ye midle and so lenthened her some 5 or 6 foote, and strengthened her with timbers, and so built her up and laid a deck on her." The result was a convenient and serviceable vessel, which the colony used for trading purposes on the Maine coast seven years.

But the Pilgrims needed not only a larger vessel for their increased Indian traffic on the Kennebec, but such a foothold there as vested rights alone would secure. This very soon became evident. There were those who let it be known that they desired to obtain at least a share of this profitable traffic. Among others, the traders at Piscataqua had their eyes directed thitherward, and there were parties also farther to the eastward who were eager to extend their trade in that direction. Then, too, there were the masters of fishing vessels on the coast, who very naturally wished to add to their profits by traffic with the Indians. Indeed the threat was made of procuring in England a land grant of the region and of excluding the Plymouth men from the Kennebec by means of such a grant. The Pilgrims, therefore, as Bradford says, "thought it needfull to prevent such a thing." Only a hint with reference to this proposed action was necessary to move them promptly in the same direction. Mr. Allerton was about to go to England for the purpose of adjusting financial matters with the merchant adventurers. They now directed him to secure for the Plymouth colonists a patent for such a tract of land on the Kennebec as would enable them to control the Indian traffic of the river. Mr. Allerton was successful in his undertaking so far as the financial affairs of the colony were concerned. He also secured "a patente for Kenebeck," but its terms were unsatisfactory to the Pilgrims. "It was so straite & ill bounded," says Bradford, "as they were faine to renew & inlarge it the next year."

This was done and the patent was issued January 13, 1629, "for and in consideracon, that William Bradford and his Associates, have for these nine years lived in New Englande aforesaid, and have there inhabited and planted a Towne, called by the name of New Plymouth, att their owne proper Costs and Charges; and now seeinge that by the spetiall Providence of God, and their extraordinary Care and Industry, they have encreased their Plantacon to neere three hundred People, and are vppon all Occasions able to releive any new Planters, or other his Majestie's Subjects, whoe may fall vppon that coaste." The first part of the patent confirmed to the colonists at New Plymouth the tract of land on Massachusetts Bay on which their colony was planted. But to this grant was added another in these words: "And forasmuch as they have noe convenient Place, either of Tradinge or Fishinge within their own precincts, whereby (after soe longe Travell and great Paines) soe hopefull a Plantacon may subsiste, as alsoe that they may bee incouraged the better to proceed in soe pious a Worke, which may especially tend to the Propagation of Religion, and the great Increase of Trade to his Majestie's Realmes and Advancements of the publique Plantacon," the Council also granted to William Bradford for the Plymouth Colonists, "all that Tracte of Lande or Parte of New Englande in America aforesaid, which lyeth within or betweene, and extendeth itself from the vtmost Limitts of Cobbiseconte alias Comuseeconte, which adioneth to the River of Kenebeke, alias Kenebekike, towards the western Ocean, and a Place called the Falls att Nequamkike, in America aforesaid, and the space of fifteen Englishe miles on each side of the said River commonly called Kenebek River, and all the said River called Kenebek, that lies within the said Limitts adand bounds eastward, westward, northward, or southward laste aboue menconed.... together with free Ingresse, Egresse and Regresse with Shipps, Boats, Shallops and other vessels from the Sea commonly called the Westerne Ocean, to the said River called Kennebek, and from the said River to the said Westerne Ocean."

It should be noticed that the patent makes prominent the fact that the Kennebec afforded facilities for trading with the Indians which Plymouth and the neighboring localities did not furnish. It should also be noticed that while this grant to the Pilgrims did not extend to the mouth of the Kennebec river, it secured to them the right to pass in and out, and they could easily hold the trade of the river, having the first chance of meeting the Indians as they descended the stream in their fur-laden canoes. Not any too soon, however, had the Plymouth colonists obtained this advantage. Without it, as subsequent events showed, they would have found it much more difficult to keep back their eager and troublesome rivals.

On the banks of the Kennebec, upon this tract of land thus secured, the Pilgrims erected a fort and trading house. Concerning the location upon which these stood there have been various opinions. Sullivan in his *History of the District of Maine,* says with some hesitancy that "it was on what is now called Small Point; on the west side of the river, and near the sea. Tradition," he adds, "assures us that Popham's party made their landing on the island now called Stage Island; and as there are the remains of an ancient fort on Small Point, and wells of water of long standing, with remains of ancient dwelling houses there ... it may be concluded that the Plymouth Fort was at that place." By Small Point Sullivan plainly has in mind the whole tract of land between the Kennebec and Casco Bay, and the Pilgrim's fort and trading house in his view therefore was located on the eastern part of this tract bordering on the river and not far from its mouth. Williamson, in his *History of Maine,* however, says that the Pilgrims in prosecuting the trade of the river had three stations for local traffic, one at Popham's fort, one at Richmond's landing and one at Cushnoc. In another place he says that the Pilgrims had two trading stations on the river, "one at Fort Popham and one at Cushnoc." There is no evidence, however, that the Pilgrims established a trading post at the mouth of the river. This was not within the limits of their patent. Moreover the early Pilgrim writers make mention of only a single trading house on the river. Bradford, writing of events that occured in 1631, mentions "ye house ther." Again, writing of events that occurred in 1634, he refers to some who "would needs goe up ye river aboue their house (towards ye fall of the river) and intercept the trade that should come to them," i.e. the Pilgrims. If the Plymouth Colony had more than one trading house on the Kennebec, Bradford could hardly have failed to mention the fact. It is accordingly the accepted view at the present time that the Pilgrims had a single trading post only on the Kennebec, and that this was at Cushnoc, the present Augusta.

After they had thus firmly established themselves on the Kennebec, Bradford and his associates came into possession of a trading house on the Penobscot. In 1629, some of the English merchant adventurers, who were interested in the Pilgrim enterprise, entered into business relations with one Edward Ashley and furnished him with goods for trading purposes. Bradford describes Ashley as "a very profane younge man," who had "for some time lived amonge ye Indians as a savage." Though he had "wite and abillitie enough to menage ye business," Bradford "feared he might still rune into evill courses (though he promised better)," and that "God would not prosper his ways." Ashley opened a trading post "at Penobscot." While the Pilgrims had no confidence in the man, they foresaw that a trading post on the Penobscot in unfriendly hands would be prejudicial to their Kennebec interests. So "to prevente a worse mischeefe," as Bradford puts it, they "resolved to joyne in ye bussines" and furnished Ashley with supplies. But Ashley soon exhibited his true character and having been detected in selling powder and shot to the Indians (which he was under bonds not to do) he was arrested by parties not mentioned and taken to England where he was imprisoned in the Fleet. Ashley, however, had influential friends, who at length secured his release, and he was planning to return to New England when he received an offer from certain London merchants to go to Russia in their interest. This offer he accepted, but on his return he "was cast away at sea; this," adds Bradford, "was his end." The trading post at Penobscot meanwhile had been maintained by the Pilgrims and it passed in this way into their hands, so that although Mr. William Pierce "had a parte ther" it was "wholy now at their disposing."

This trading post at the Penobscot was not altogether a source of profit to the Pilgrims. In 1631, the house was robbed by some Frenchmen, who secured beaver and goods to the value of from four hundred to five hundred pounds. Bradford's account of the affair is as follows: "The M^r of ye house, and parte of ye company with him, were come with their vessell to ye westward to fecth a supply of goods which was brought over for them. In ye mean time comes a smale French ship into ye harbore (and amongst ye company was a false Scott); they pretended they were newly come from ye sea, and knew not wher they were, and that their vesell was very leake, and desired they might hale her a shore and stop their leaks. And many French complements they used, and congees they made; and in ye ende, seeing but 3 or 4 simple men, y^t were servants, and by this Scoth-man understanding that ye maister & ye rest of ye company were gone from home, they fell of comending their gunes and muskets, that lay upon racks by ye wall side, and tooke them downe to looke on them, asking if they were charged. And when they were possesst of them, one presents a peece ready charged against ye servants, and another a pistoll; and bid them not sturr, but quietly deliver them their goods, and carries some of ye men aborde, & made ye other help to carry away ye goods. And when they had tooke what they pleased they sett them at liberty, and went their way, with this mocke, biding them tell their M^r when he came, that some of ye Ile of Rey gentlemen had been ther."

Of course the Plymouth colonists could not expect reparation for their loss, and Bradford closes his account of the affair without comment, but evidently not without a groan.

The trading house on the Kennebec was a larger source of revenue to the Pilgrims than the trading house at Penobscot, but it was not an unmixed blessing. From the first other parties desired to secure at least a part of the traffic with the Indians whose villages were on the Kennebec or who made the river a thoroughfare. In 1634, one John Hocking, who lived at Piscataqua, agent for Lords Say and Brooke and other Englishmen interested in the settlement there, made his way to the Kennebec, purposing to proceed in his vessel up the river beyond the Pilgrim trading house, and so to secure trade with the Indians that otherwise would fall into the hands of the Plymouth colonists. John Howland, who was in command of the Pilgrim trading post, protested against this effort on the part of Hocking, insisting that it was an infringement of rights secured to the Pilgrims by their patent. The appeal was to that clause in the grant which authorized Bradford and his associates "to take, apprehend, seize and make prize of all such persons, there Shipps and Goods, as shall attempt to inhabit or trade with the savage People of that Country within the several Precincts and Limitts of his and their several Plantacon." But Hocking refused to heed the protest made by Howland. He said, as Bradford puts it, that he "would goe up and trade ther in despite of them and lye ther as long as he pleased," and in the effort to make good his words he sailed past the Pilgrim fort and anchored. Howland then went to Hocking, and having again called his attention to his unjustifiable action he urged him to take his vessel down the river; but Hocking still refused. He was in a position to have the first chance for trade with the Indians as they descended the river in their canoes, and he intended to make the most of it. Howland accordingly proceeded to action. Instructing his men not to fire their guns upon any provocation, he sent two of them to cut the cable of Hocking's vessel. This they succeeded in doing, and as the vessel started down the stream, Hocking seized a musket and killed one of the Plymouth men, Moses Talbot. His companion in the canoe, who "loved him well," as Bradford says, could not restrain himself, and levelling his musket at Hocking he shot him in retaliation. The vessel continued on its course down the river, and Hocking's men, on their return to the Piscataqua, carried the tidings of the affair thither.

This report in due time reached Lords Say and Brooke in England. In it the fact was withheld that Hocking, who was infringing on the rights of the Pilgrims, had killed one of the Plymouth men; and Lords Say and Brooke were indignant at the treatment Hocking had received on the Kennebec. The same version of the affair, either from the Piscataqua or from England, was carried to the colonists of Massachusetts Bay. When, not long after, the Plymouth colonists sent their vessel to Boston, the authorities there arrested John Alden, who was at the Kennebec trading post when Hocking was killed, though not a participant in the affair. The Plymouth colonists regarded Alden's arrest as an unfriendly proceeding on the part of the Massachusetts officials, and sent Capt. Miles Standish to Boston with letters from Bradford and others to secure Mr. Alden's release. This was effected, but at the same time Capt. Standish was put under bonds to appear at the next court, June 3, 1634, with a certified copy of the patent showing the rights of the Plymouth colonists on the Kennebec. At this meeting of the court the Massachusetts Bay authorities made it evident that they did not wish to give offence to the Plymouth colonists, but it was equally evident that they desired to make in England a favorable impression in their own behalf, as if they were the special guardians of law and order in New England. Governor Dudley in a private letter counselled patience on the part of the authorities at Plymouth. After a while Mr. Winthrop suggested a conference in which the Plymouth colonists, the colonists at the Piscataqua, and those of Massachusetts Bay should be requested "to consult and determine in this matter, so as ye parties meeting might have full power to order and bind," "and that nothing should be done to ye infringing or prejudice of ye liberties of any place." Such a conference was held in Boston, but only the Plymouth and Massachusetts Bay colonists were represented. The matter, however, was fully discussed, and an opinion of each representative, both magistrates and ministers, was requested. The result was that while "they all wished these things had never been, yet they could not but lay ye blame & guilt on Hockins owne head." At the same time "grave and godly exhortations" were made to the Plymouth men, which they "imbraced with love & thankfullnes, promising to indeavor to follow ye same," and there was no further agitation of the matter. Mr. Winslow was sent to England not long after in order to see that no harm should come to the colony in consequence of this affair, but he found that the agitation had ceased there also.

The extent of the Pilgrim trade on the Kennebec at this time may be inferred from the fact that Mr. Winslow took with him to England 3,738 pounds of beaver, "a great part of it being coat-beaver sould at 20^s p^r pound" the proceeds of the sale of which went into the hands of the London merchants to whom the colonists were indebted. According to Bradford, between November, 1631, and June 24, 1636, the Pilgrims sent to England 12,530 pounds of beaver, the most of which was obtained from the Indians on the Kennebec. It was from the sale of this beaver in a great measure that they were able at length to extricate themselves from the financial difficulties in which they had become involved through their London agents.

But their troubles at Penobscot were not ended. At the trading house there they suffered a still greater loss from the French in 1635. Chevalier Charles de Menou, or as he is usually styled D'Aulnay Charnisay, appeared one day in the harbor, sent thither by Sir Isaac de Razilli, who had command of the French forces in Canada. His orders were to expel the English as far as Pemaquid. D'Aulnay at first was lavish in compliments, but he soon revealed his true character and purpose by taking possession of the trading house. Declining to make payment for the goods with which the house was stored, although he said he would settle with the Pilgrims when convenient, D'Aulnay bestowed upon the Pilgrim party at the post some provisions and sent them back to Plymouth in their shallop. On their arrival at Plymouth they rehearsed these facts. The Pilgrim spirit was stirred, and at once the Plymouth men proceeded to consult their brethren of Massachusetts Bay. The affair was one in which they were interested as well as the Plymouth colonists, as it was not desirable for English interests that the French should obtain a permanent foothold at Penobscot. When, therefore, the Pilgrims proposed to hire a vessel for the purpose of retaking the trading post at Penobscot, the Bay colonists gave their approval to the project. The vessel secured for this purpose was commanded by one Girling, who agreed to drive off the French and deliver the trading post again into the hands of the Plymouth men for seven hundred pounds of beaver, which was to be delivered to him there when he had accomplished the undertaking. If he failed Girling was "to lose his labor and have nothing."

Capt. Miles Standish with twenty men accompanied Girling in a Pilgrim vessel on which was the promised beaver. Standish piloted Girling to the harbor on the shore of which the Pilgrim trading house was located. Before the trading house was within reach of his guns, however, Girling began to blaze away. Miles Standish was indignant and remonstrated with Girling at this display of folly. But Girling had already exhausted his supply of powder, and could do nothing else but retire. When he made known this state of things to Capt. Standish, the latter, in order that the expedition might not prove a failure, offered to get a supply of powder at the nearest plantation. The offer was accepted and Standish bore away; but subsequently, learning that Girling intended to seize the beaver, Standish sent to Girling the promised powder supply, but took the beaver home. Girling made no further attempt to recover the trading house at Penobscot and went his way.

The Plymouth men now laid the matter again before the authorities of the Massachusetts Bay colony, believing that the French would at once endeavor to strengthen their position at Penobscot. At first the Massachusetts men were inclined to furnish the needed assistance in driving away the French. Soon, however, they not only declared their inability to do anything, but began to trade with the French at that point, furnishing them with provisions and ammunition; and so, as Bradford asserts, became "the cheefest supporters of these French." The colonists at Pemaquid also furnished the French both supplies and information, adding guns and ammunition for the Indians, to the great amazement of Bradford and his associates, who made no further attempt to regain possession of their trading house at Penobscot.

After the Pilgrims had settled their accounts in London so that they were no longer indebted to the merchants there for both outfit and subsequent advances of money and goods, but had become independent, each member of the colony working for his own interest, the trade with the Indians on the Kennebec was leased to parties interested in its maintenance. In 1640, Bradford surrendered the patent of the lands occupied by the colony to the free men of the colony, the patent, including the Kennebec grant having been issued to him, his heirs and associates and assigns. At a General Court held at Plymouth June 8, 1649, a committee was appointed to treat of and let the trade at the Kennebec, which accordingly on the 4th of July following they did for the term of three years, the colony retaining only civil jurisdiction there. June 29, 1652, it was agreed to sell the trade at Kennebec to those who formerly had it, on the same terms as before and for the same number of years. But to the Pilgrims it seemed more and more desirable as the colonists upon the New England coast multiplied to secure an extension of their grant on the Kennebec so that it should include lands on both sides of the river to the mouth of the river. In the Calendar of State Papers occurs the following record: "March 8, 1652, an order of the Council of State was passed for a report to be presented to Parliament upon petition of Edward Winslow, on behalf of William Bradford, Governor of New Plymouth in New England, and his associates, wherein he sets forth that for many years the plantation has had a grant for a trading place in the river Kennebec, but not having the whole of the river under their grant and government, many excesses and wickednesses have been committed, and the benefit of the trade for furs, one of the greatest supports of their plantation, has been taken from the inhabitants of New Plymouth, and prays for a grant of the whole river of Kennebec: recommending the desire of the petitioners be granted, with a saving in the grant of the rights of any of the people of the Commonwealth, the grant to pass under the Great Seal, if Parliament think fit."

An added record, under date of April 29, 1652, shows that the petition of Mr. Winslow was referred to the Committee for Foreign Affairs to report upon what had been done in cases of like nature. March 16, 1653, the committee made a report recommending to the Council of State "that the government of the whole river of Kennebec in America be granted to the town of New Plymouth, in New England, for seven years, by way of probation." The committee's report was evidently adopted. In other words the grant of land was not extended, but the jurisdiction of the Pilgrim authorities was extended over the territory to the mouth of the Kennebec for a limited period.

In accordance with this order, at a General Court held at Plymouth March 7, 1653, Mr. Thomas Prence, one of the magistrates of Plymouth, was authorized to summon all the inhabitants dwelling on the Kennebec to some convenient place "to receive from him such instructions and orders" as he had received from the General Court. The records of the Plymouth colonists make it abundantly evident that it was only "the government of the aforsd inhabitants," living on either side of the Kennebec from its mouth to the southern limit of the Pilgrim patent, that was conferred upon the Plymouth men by the mother country. This governmental authority was exercised by the Pilgrims and in 1648 and again in 1653 they protected and extended their land interests to the northward by deeds of land from the Indians.

But things grew worse instead of better on the Kennebec. At a General Court held at Plymouth June 7, 1659, the following action was taken: "Forasmuch as we have good information that Things are in such a Posture at Kennebec, in Reference to some Troubles among the Indians, some of whom being slain, some carried away and thereby also discouraged, that there is a present desisting from their Hunting, and so a cessation of the Trade, whereby such as have rented the Trade of the Country, are so far discouraged, that they see, and it probably appeareth, that they will not only be disabled for paying the expected Rent, but will be likely to suffer great Losses; and do also fear they may be forced wholly to desist and to call Home their Estate there; whereby the Trade may be indangered to be lost for the future, if some Course be not taken about it. The Court do therefore recommend to the several Townships Consideration, and desire they would depute some men whom they can betrust, to signify their minds at the Sitting of the General Court in October next; and to impower them to act in the Premises."

At this meeting of the Court the rent of the Kennebec trade for the year 1659 was remitted, and it was agreed that the "Farmers of the Trade" should pay ten pounds to the colony for the year next ensuing; and at the end of said term, viz. November 1, 1660, the said Farmers should leave the Kennebec trade to the disposal of the colony, the Farmers agreeing also not to have any trade with the Indians on the Kennebec later than November 1, 1660.

When the General Court met at Plymouth June 6, 1660, it was voted that if 500 pounds could be obtained for the colony's interest on the Kennebec, it should be sold. In accordance with this vote, the Pilgrims in 1661 sold all their lands on either side of the Kennebec, secured by their patent, also by deeds from the Indians, to Antipas Boies, Edward Tyng, Thomas Brattle and John Winslow. These persons and their heirs held their Kennebec lands nearly a century, making no endeavor to colonize them, but holding them for trading purposes only. In September, 1749, a meeting of the proprietors was held with a view to the introduction of settlers. Other proprietors were admitted, and in June, 1753, in accordance with an act passed by the General Court of Massachusetts permitting persons holding lands in common and undivided to act as a corporation, a corporation was formed under the title of "The Proprietors of the Kennebec Purchase from the late colony of New Plymouth," although the usual designation was the Plymouth Company. The land claim under this purchase greatly exceeded the claim of the Pilgrims and extended from Casco Bay to Pemaquid, and from the ocean to Carratunk Falls. But there were rival claims for a part of this territory. In 1758, it was decided that Clarke and Lake's north line on the east side of the Kennebec as claimed by Indian deeds should be that of the north line of the present town of Woolwich. The claim of the Wiscasset Company, also based on Indian deeds, was settled in 1762, and the dividing line between the two was fixed at half way between the Sheepscot and Kennebec rivers. In 1758, but finally consummated in 1766, the Pejepscot proprietors released to the Plymouth Company the lands between the Kennebec and New Meadows, including Bath and Phippsburg, the west line to be fifteen miles from the Kennebec. The fourth settlement was with the Pemaquid proprietors in 1763. The Kennebec territory, as thus determined, extended from the ocean on the west bank of the river to Norridgewock, and was about thirty-one miles in width, with the river in the center.

CHAPTER 5.

The leading figure in colonial Maine history was Ferdinando Gorges of Plymouth Fort, England. In 1639 he was given by King Charles I all of Maine west of the Kennebec. Named the Province of Maine, this area loomed large in the planning of both the King and its proprietor, Gorges.

THE PROVINCE OF MAINE*
by
Richard A. Preston

"If in the conclusion of my undertaking and expense of my fortunes, to advance the honour and happiness of my nation, I have settled a portion thereof to those that in nature must succeed me, you may be pleased to remember that the labourer is worthy of his hire."

Sir Ferdinando Gorges

Gorges' charter for Maine was affixed with the Great Seal on April 3, 1639, two years after he was commissioned as royal governor. Not long afterwards he busied himself with writing *A Briefe Narration of the Originall Undertakings of the Advancement of Plantations into the Parts of America, Especially, Shewing the Beginning, Progress, and Continuance of that of New-England.* The *Brief Narration* stands in relation to the Maine charter much as the *Brief Relation* stood in the charter of the Council for New England. Both contained historical accounts of the exploration and organizing activity which had preceded the issue of a charter, both described the benefits of American planation, and both outlined Gorges' intentions and plans. They were obviously produced as publicity to attract support, but if that fact is fully recognized they are both valuable as sources of information about Gorges and his work and his hopes.

Taken along with the Maine charter, the *Brief Narration* reveals the way in which Gorges hoped to build his colony in America. He had obtained a royal grant giving him, along with a land title without other overlord than the King, the right to create a colonial government without the necessity of relying on associates. However, in view of his many failures to harness the state and various supporters to the task of colonization, the proposals outlined in the *Brief Narration* and in his 1639 charter must be regarded as the end to which he had been forced rather than as the ideal for which he had long striven.

The extent of the grant was princely. It did not stretch from sea to sea like the territory of the Council for New England; but it did extend much further along the coast than the fortieth share of the New England patent which Gorges had received in the division of 1623. The new charter conveyed to him that eighth portion of the New England territory which had fallen to him in the division of the Grand Patent in 1635 and which he had already named New Somersetshire. As precisely delimited in the charter its bounds ran from the mouth of the Piscataqua to the Kennebec and up into the mainland for a hundred and twenty miles. It included also the northern part of the Isles of Shoals and other islands. This territory was to be called the Province or County of Maine. In addition, as a kind of relic of the interest he had shown in more southerly territory earlier in his career, and also as a remnant of that minor share in the "public plantation" or an equivalent thereof which had been a feature of all his earlier plans, Gorges received the two islands south of Cape Cod, "Capawock" and "Nautican", that is to say Martha's Vineyard and Nantucket. With the land

---

*Richard A. Preston, *Gorges of Plymouth Fort* (Toronto: University of Toronto Press, 1953), pp. 321-345. Reprinted by permission of the publisher.

went the woods and rivers, fauna and flora, the fisheries (including pearls, whales, and sturgeon), the mines of gold, silver, and other metals, and the patronage of the livings of all the churches to be established in the province.

Along with these extensive property rights the King granted to Gorges all such "rights, jurisdictions, privileges, prerogatives, royalties, liberties, franchises, pre-eminences, and hereditaments" in the Province as the Bishop of Durham had or ought to have in the Bishopric or County Palatine of Durham. This important "Bishop of Durham clause", first used in the grant of Avalon (Newfoundland) to Calvert in 1623, was at this time becoming the significant feature of those colonial grants which were later to be known as the "proprietary provinces" of the first British Empire. They were created in conscious imitation of the great feudal provinces which had grown up during the Middle Ages and which had come to be accorded special treatment because they formed a protective barrier on the frontier. The holders of mediaeval "palatinates" like Durham in the North of England had been allowed a relatively large authority in civil government and had come to possess many rights and privileges which elsewhere in the Kingdom were regarded as "regality" and reserved for the Crown. In the early seventeenth century similar privileges were granted to the proprietors of American provinces because their provinces were, like those of the marcher lords of the Middle Ages, remote from royal authority and so were presumed to need special treatment.

The Maryland charter, granted to Calvert in 1632, had conferred on the proprietor all the powers that any Bishop of Durham had ever had; but this had apparently come to be regarded as too sweeping and so the "Bishop of Durham clause" in the charter of 1639 granted to Gorges only those powers which legally belonged to the contemporary Bishop of Durham. However, the "Bishop of Durham clause" was followed by a detailed statement of the privileges that Gorges was to enjoy in Maine and these actually included many judicial rights which had been lost by the Bishop as a result of the Act of Resumption of 1536. Clearly the "Bishop of Durham clause" was not intended as a precise statement of the rights which Gorges was to exercise but was placed in the charter to indicate the general nature of the proprietary government which was to be established in Maine.

Thus, whereas in the early seventeenth century the King's writ ran in Durham, judicial appointments there were made by the Crown, appeals could be made to the King's courts, and pardons were granted by the King and not by the Bishop, in Maine all these "royal" functions were to be exercised by Gorges as Lord Proprietor. And whereas in Durham the laws of England had legal force unless the Palatinate was specifically exempted, in Maine the source of law was to be the Proprietor with the assent of an assembly of freeholders. Furthermore, in emergency the Proprietor could rule Maine by ordinance provided the ordinances were reasonable and not repugnant to the law of England. Gorges was also granted other jealously guarded royal rights like the claim to royal fish (sturgeons and whales), treasure-trove, wreckage, mines of precious metals, base metals, and other minerals, and also escheats taken from felons; and he was given power to muster an army of residents for defence, to build fortifications, to transport ordnance to the colony, to exercise admiralty jurisdiction (with reservation of the rights of the Lord High Admiral in England), to incorporate boroughs by charter, and to set up markets, tolls, and customs duties. All these rights and privileges were normally retained jealously by the Crown and some of them had long been taken away from the Palatine Bishop of Durham. They were granted to the Lord Proprietor by the Charter of Maine in 1639 on the theory that a distant American provincial lord needed some extraordinary powers and privileges.

But the Maine charter included at the same time certain clauses which deliberately curbed the independence of the Proprietor. The charter stated categorically that the Province of Maine was "immediately subject to our Crown of England and dependent upon the same for ever"; and the residents in the colony were "reputed to be of the allegiance of Us, Our Heirs and Successors and . . . esteemed to be the natural born subjects of Us, etc." More important still, it also specifically declared that, although all that concerned the "propriety" (the territorial rights) of the Province, and the appointment of provincial officials, was to be left to Gorges (much as was still the case in

Durham), his power in civil and ecclesiastical matters was to be "subordinate and subject" to the Lords Commissioners for Foreign Plantations. This was in conformity with the situation in Durham in the seventeenth century where an important supervision was exercised by the prerogative Council of the North from its seat in York. Thus, while Laud had finally agreed to the granting of the Charter of Maine and to the establishment of the proprietary colony for which Gorges had been asking for four years, he had succeeded in including conditions which ensured that, if the system of governing the colonies by his royal "commission" which he had started in 1634 continued to operate, the government of Maine would remain to some extent under royal control. Royal support and supervision was what Gorges himself had always recommended.

Another, and equally important curb upon the power of the Proprietor of Maine, was written into the charter and was also endorsed by Gorges in the *Brief Narration*. Despite the fact that this was the time of the Stuart "despotism" in England the charter provided that legislation was to be made by the Proprietor "with the assent of the greater part of the freeholders" of the Province provided it was not repugnant to the laws of England. Very different was the position in Durham where law made in the English Parliament operated automatically unless the Palatinate was specifically exempted and where the local "assembly" had failed to develop as a law-making body. In the *Brief Narration* Gorges gave fuller details about the representative rights to be enjoyed by the settlers. He said that he had created a Council of officials to be known as the "standing Counsellors ... to whom is added eight deputies, to be elected by the freeholders of the several counties, as counsellors for the state of the country, who are authorized by virtue of their places to sit in any of the ... courts and to be assistants to the Presidents thereof, and to give opinions according to justice, etc."

He went on,

> There is no matter of moment can be determined of, neither by myself, nor by my Lieutenant in my absence, but by the advice and assent of the whole body of the Council or the greater part of them, sufficiently called and summoned to the Assembly, That no judge or other minister of state to be allowed of, but by the assent of the said Council, or the greater part of them, as before. That no alienation or sale of land be made to any, but by their counsel and assent, be it by way of gift for reward, or service, or otherwise whatsoever. That no man to whom there hath been any grant passed of any freehold, shall alienate the same without the assent and licence of the said Council, first had and obtained. That in case any law be to be enacted, or repealed, money to be levied, or forces raised for public defence the summons thereof to the several bailiwicks, counties, is to be issued out in my name, but with the consent of the said Council; by virtue whereof, power is to be given to the freeholders of the said counties respectively, to elect and choose two of the most worthy within the said county as deputies for the whole, to join with the Council for performance of the service for which they were called to that assembly, (and to hear) all appeals made for any wrong or injustice committed by any the several officers of any of the standing courts of justice, or authority of any other person or persons.

The delimitation of the different functions of the Standing Council and of the elected "Assembly" of freeholders is not made clear in this passage; but even so it is abundantly made evident that Gorges was not planning to create a little despotism in America. The seeds of "government by consent" were deliberately planted in the charter; and the legislative and administrative machinery which he planned for the Province bears strong resemblance to the system of colonial government by a mixed council of official and elected members which was later to become a regular feature of British colonial government in later centuries.

Thus the political powers of the Lord Proprietor, although more extensive than those of the contemporary Bishop of Durham in the Palatinate, were definitely curtailed by the charter. But his property rights, like those of the Bishop, were not subject to similar limitation. Gorges was to be the supreme feudal landholder of Maine and, despite the mediaeval statute of *Quia Emptores* which forbade subinfeudation, he was authorized to distribute the land of the Province to be held of himself. He could set up manors and he could grant to the manorial lords the right to hold courts baron and courts leet, that is to say feudal courts for the settlement of civil disputes and for dealing with crime. Landholders already in the area were to lay down their *jura regalia* and were henceforward to hold their land of Gorges. The Proprietor was also empowered to monopolize the trade "unto in or from" the Province and to control immigration into it. It is noticeable, however, that as a result of the opposition which Gorges had had to face in the Parliaments of the 1620's, liberty of fishing was allowed to all English subjects who were also specifically permitted to dry fish and nets on shore provided no "notable damage or injury" was done to the harbours, the creeks, or the woods belonging to Gorges or to the inhabitants of the Province.

The charter and the *Brief Narration,* which contain Gorges' ideas at this time, were produced for different purposes and this explains one very noticeable difference in their contents. While the charter contains those quasi-feudal, or proprietary clauses which show the nature of the government intended, the *Brief Narration* gives no details of feudal institutions to be introduced into the colony. It may be said that this merely means that Gorges was getting wiser with age. The non-feudal charter of the Council for New England of 1620 had been accompanied by strikingly feudalistic proposals in the *Brief Relation* in 1622; and the Council had failed. So it may be that in 1639, remembering his earlier failure, Gorges wrote his feudal proposals into the charter but carefully omitted them from the accompanying publicity.

Similarly it is noticeable that the *Brief Narration,* in the part devoted to the frame of government to be established in the Province, speaks only, and at length, of Sir Ferdinando's intention to introduce representative government and obviously this was done with the aim of attracting settlers. But this reference to representative government must not *ipso facto* be regarded as insincere. As has been shown, the charter, which was legally binding on the recipient, included a similar, though briefer, reference to representative government. The explanation is simple. Just as the *Brief Narration* was written to please potential settlers who might read it, the charter was likewise drafted to please those for whose eyes it was intended, namely the Crown lawyers whose jargon was still the feudal land law of England, and the ministers of the Crown, especially Laud, who would see in its conservative feudal clauses a stabilizing influence for a wayward land.

For this princely American estate, and for these great powers, Gorges was to make the easiest possible returns to the King. He held his Province "as of the manor of East Greenwich in the County of Kent by fealty only in free and common socage and not *in capite* nor by knight's service," a hybrid arrangement which would have been regarded with horror in the Middle Ages. Socage tenure, holding by the plough, was the tenure of the men who worked the soil. A mediaeval prince who could create manors would have scorned to hold by so lowly and base a tenure. But by the sixteenth century the quit-rents owned by socage tenants in lieu of labour service had, in general, become so small in real value as to be not worth collecting. As other obligations were still attached to the higher and more honourable tenures, socage had thus become the easiest and the most desirable tenure by which to hold land. Furthermore new tenants were inclined to refuse to accept land which had to be held directly of the King, as a tenant-in-chief or *in capite,* because that kind of vassalage entailed certain obligations which could be avoided if the same land were held *ut de manore,* that is to say as if it were part of one of the royal manors. Thus the Maine charter granted Gorges the Province in the simplest way then consonant with English law: socage tenure as of the manor of East Greenwich.

The charter prescribed payments to the King consisting only of one quarter of wheat annually, one-fifth of the profit of gold and silver mines, one-fifth of all free gold found upon the sea shore or in rivers or elsewhere within the bounds of the Province, and one-fifth of the profits of pearl fishing. Clearly such payments might be negligible by comparison with the potential profits from the Province. This great disparity between what Gorges had to pay and his chance of earning an immense income can only be understood if it is realized that American colonization was still a very risky procedure, that it was fully realized that the first few years were bound to bring loss, and that the scheme might soon collapse, as indeed it did.

The Crown had given away something which it did not yet really possess and which had cost nothing but which, if the project proved successful, would lead to enormous and incalculable gain to England. Moreover, there was no alternative means by which the same end, the colonization of New England by an agency which would recognize the authority of the Crown, could be attained. In 1639 royal support for plans of colonization was less likely than ever before. Early in that year the Scottish rebellion had dashed the high hopes of the centralizers and the authoritarians. As has been seen, even Laud, who disliked the idea of proprietary government, had been brought to accept it as the only way in which the plantation of loyal colonies could be established and by which the dangerous centrifugal forces generated by Puritanism in New England could be held in check. Furthermore, if a proprietary colony could be set up in New England the ever-present fear that foreign rivals might shoulder England out would be finally allayed. So the King had everything to gain and nothing to lose by the grant of Maine to Gorges.

Gorges was the recipient of what was virtually a gift largely because there were few other interested individuals who would be willing to undertake the development of the Province and who could be trusted to keep it loyal to King and Church. For instance, the courtiers and favourites among the eight men who had agreed in 1635 to divide New England between them had not maintained their interest; and only Gorges had followed the business with sufficient persistence to gain the necessary royal charter. In the early seventeenth century few Englishmen were filled with that fanatical zest for imperialist expansion which coloured the whole of Sir Ferdinando's outlook and career. It is true that religious dissentients were prepared to risk their lives in colonizing distant and dangerous places for the sake of gaining the right to worship in the way they pleased; merchants would finance ventures which would bring immediate returns within the year; and a few of the nobility and gentry had shown interest in overseas plantations. But the promise of great estates in New England had proved inadequate to keep alive the ardour of the gentry. Samuel Argall and Barnabe Gooch had worked hard with Gorges in the early days. Both were now dead. John Mason had supported him later and had drafted a charter for his own province of New Hampshire in 1635; but he too, had died. Lord Gorges has been a loyal supporter of his cousin's schemes; but he had become financially embarrassed himself. Sir Ferdinando alone had struggled on to the very end. The charter of Maine was thus a reward for Gorges' extraordinary persistence as well as a recognition of the fact that if anyone could and would plant a great royal settlement in New England he was the man.

Gorges' adoption of, or adherence to, what are sometimes described as antique and outmoded feudal institutions may need further explanation. It must be remembered that the origin of the English land law was feudal and that its language still used (and still, to a lesser degree, uses) feudal terms. In the seventeenth century this usage was more than mere "legal jargon". Modern "fee simple" or "freehold", that is to say tenure without a lord, was still unknown. New land must therefore automatically be "held of a lord". In Massachusetts a practice was rapidly developing at this very time of granting land in "fee simple" which was in fact more like the "allodial tenure" of mediaeval Europe, that is to say tenure without a lord. This was a revolutionary development. It occurred because the leaders went themselves to the colony and so came to understand American conditions. Men like Gorges, who remained in England, could hardly be expected to introduce so radical an innovation in the technicality of the land law. Instead, they tried to recreate a land system in New England similar to that which they knew and understood in England. They used the language of feudalism because that was the language they used at home. They granted land in America in the way in which they believed their ancestors had received their lands in the remote past when the Normans conquered England and introduced the land law. Gorges, then, was not trying to revive and reintroduce the dead past but was merely prescribing for America the living society which he knew in contemporary England.

Yet, at the same time, it is obvious that the combination of political and territorial rights inherent in the feudal type of tenure seemed to many men of that time, and especially to men of Gorges' class, to suit the conditions of colonization in a distant and dangerous land. It was logical in their eyes that political and military leadership should be given to the natural leaders, the landowners. It must not be forgotten that in contemporary England even though political feudalism was dead, the landlords still controlled local government and were the military leaders of their tenants and neighbours. Their leadership was not "feudal" and was now exercised by virtue of unpaid office under the Crown as magistrates or officers of the militia; but it differed little from that of their ancestors. It was natural in seventeenth century England for the landed classes to rule and lead. That leadership, strengthened by being related to the holding of particular land grants, seemed reasonable for American conditions.

Yet Gorges was not entirely without some understanding of the real conditions of the new world. Indeed he tried to bring an accommodation between both the worlds with which he had to deal. In addition to creating a society bound by strong feudal ties he promised liberal terms of representative government; and he also accepted conditions by which the colony would come under the control of the Royal Commission for Foreign Plantations. These were of course gestures to please potential settlers on the one hand and Laud on the other. But they were also in conformity with his earlier colonial plans. It must be remembered that he was still the royal governor-designate of all New England. Also, a little earlier, he had proposed to the Crown that he should be given a proprietary province to finance his government and that he should be allowed to grant liberal terms to the settlers already settled in Massachusetts. Gorges' plan for New England, a feudal proprietary with liberal terms of self-government and with a great degree of royal control, was what he had come to regard as the only way in which, especially in the plight of royal government in England in 1639, the intransigeance of Massachusetts might be overcome and the security of the English position in New England maintained.

His formula for American colonization had changed little with the years, but he himself was changing. On April 3, 1639, when Gorges came into legal possession of the American lands for which, as he said with pardonable exaggeration, he had "travailled ... above forty years", he was nearly seventy-one years of age. The best part of his life, "laden with troubles and vexations from all parts", was behind him. There were signs that his strength was failing and that he had come into possession at a time when his own personal powers were unequal to the difficult task. Within the last few years illnesses had made him painfully aware that he was growing old. In 1637, for instance, he had written to his step-son to say that he had been "seized with an extraordinary weakness for want of a stomach to eat"; and he had had to borrow a bed-coach in order to creep by easy stages back from London to Ashton to seek, as he said, "the comfort ... of that air which, if that help not, I shall commit myself to Him who best knows how to dispose of me".

In the same year, when recommending for military employment his nephew William who had served as his deputy in the Plymouth fort and in the New Somersetshire colony, Sir Ferdinando had slipped in a hint that he would like military employment for himself; but he had confessed that physically he was not ready fit for command. He had broached the subject in that indirect way which is a feature of some of his letters to the King's ministers. He wrote to Coke, "Besides I am grown a little doubtful of the state of my own body, not able to endure the sea any long time, and, therefore, if my service may be accepted of, I must humbly pray to be left at liberty to retire myself when ever I have settled the business in such a way as may give His Majesty and their Lordships satisfaction in what I have propounded." A little later he apologized for sending a nephew to attend the Privy Council about his colonial affairs because, as he said, old age was "overtaking" him and he was not well enough to make a personal appearance.

But he was loth to admit that he was past his prime. Despite the growing weaknesses of age his physicians had pronounced his constitution sound; and he had continued to play a vigorous part in local affairs. Strong enough at sixty-four to ride in a horse race, at sixty-seven he was appointed Marshall of the Field at the muster of the train-bands of Dorset; and at sixty-nine, in the year of the illness to which reference was made above, he was a Justice of the Peace and concerned with the vexatious business of apportioning the levies of ship-money on the parishes of Somersetshire. Moreover, he was confident that age and experience were valuable assets. For instance, he believed that if he were allowed to advise the King on Turkish piracy in the Mediterranean and on the military situation in Germany, all would go well. He was also convinced that his long experience of American affairs fitted him to deal with all the problems of New England. He was certain that, if given the opportunity, he could solve the foreign and colonial difficulties of the Crown.

Apparently he still maintained the hope that he could go to New England as royal governor. He had been thwarted for four years by the difficulties he experienced in obtaining from the Crown, first his royal commission as "General Governor" and then his patent for the Province of Maine to support his government. After he had obtained the commission in 1637 and the charter in 1639, there appeared to be no further reason for him to linger in England.

Furthermore, conditions in New England made it urgent that he should hasten to take up his public appointment and to look after his private affairs. New England outside that area controlled by the Massachusetts Puritans had rapidly fallen into disorder after William Gorges had abruptly returned to England in 1637. There are no "Court Records" for the Maine settlements for the ensuing two or three years and it is reasonably certain that no government existed. Laud's confidant, the Reverend George Burdett, who had settled in Maine after being driven from Massachusetts and who had grown to be a power in the land, was an evil influence. The Trelawny Papers describe the anarchy which prevailed. Winter, an agent of a Plymouth merchant, Robert Trelawny, who had set up a colony and fishing station in the Maine area on the basis of a grant from the Council for New England, complained in a letter to his master, "To certify you of the estate of this Country, I know no alteration but as it hath formerly been: here lacks good government in the land, for a great many men deal very ill here for want of government." At another time he wrote "for here is neither law nor government with us about these parts to right such wrongs, & I am but one man"; and again, "For I have a bad company to deal withall, being in a lawless country."

Gorges had long been aware of this need for the establishment of law and order. In a petition to the Privy Council asking for a dispensation for those going to Maine from restrictions on emigration which had been reimposed in 1637, he had spoken of the necessity for the "reformation of disorders" by the despatch of those who would conform to the Church of England. This was a reference not merely to the disorder of religious dissent but also to the lack of civil authority. Later, in 1640, in a letter to Windebank he hinted again at disorder in New England, saying that he had learned by letters that, had he not received the royal grant, he would own no more land there than that on which his house stood and where his trusted servants were settled. He said that his title to the rest of the Province had been disputed by one and another and that some of the claimants had appealed to Massachusetts for support. During the hiatus in a legal civil authority, from the time of the dissolution of the Council of New England in 1635 to the creation of the Province of Maine in 1639, squatting had spread in the northern territory and was accompanied by civil disorder and by the spread of nonconformity. William Gorges' brief stay in Maine had failed to check disorder and his abrupt departure had probably increased the open defiance of Gorges' authority which was based only on the arrangements made in 1635 for the division of the authority of the Council for New England.

The appeals by squatters to Massachusetts were ominous. Obviously the Puritans were the ones who stood to gain unless Gorges' authority could be established. Anarchy in Maine would lead to the strengthening of religious nonconformity to the loss of Gorges' property rights, and, most important of all, to the complete collapse of his plan to assert royal control over New England. Thus the security of the English hold on North America would be weakened; for it was inconceivable to men of Gorges' beliefs that the Puritans could defend themselves or that New England could remain a part of England's possessions if they resisted royal control. Gorges' attitude to the Massachusetts problem was based not so much on a dislike of Puritanism as on a desire to see a strong British Empire overseas.

Although the Maine charter passed the Great Seal in April 1639 it is likely that it was not delivered to Sir Ferdinando until several months later. Therefore, his first commission of government, to establish a provisional government over the existing scattered settlements in Maine, which he sealed on September 2, 1639, was probably issued as soon as he had actually gotten his charter in his hands. This first commission was a necessary temporary expedient until Sir Ferdinando could go to his province. By it Gorges invested authority in a number of magistrates led by Sir Thomas Jocelyn, an old man of seventy-eight years, who was at that time paying a visit to his son in New England. But for some reason this first commission seems not to have been sent over at the time of its issue.

A few months later, in January 1640, Gorges wrote to tell Secretary Windebank that he would not "take shipping" to go to America himself until he had attended upon the King and the Privy Council in order to receive instructions. No reason for his delay was given but it is probable that he could not finance an expedition on a scale fitting the Lord of the Province of Maine and the potential General Governor of New England. As he would not want to sneak into his domain by the route which most travellers to Maine followed at that time, namely as a passenger on a ship bound to Boston, he was anxious to obtain royal support. A few months later he drafted a second commission which also nominated Jocelyn as his leading deputy. But before this new document could be forwarded to New England Sir Ferdinando learned that Jocelyn had arrived back home. Accordingly, he at once issued a third commission which was despatched along with the first one issued the previous September, perhaps to prove that there had been no failure to create a government since the time of the grant of the charter. The documents were probably sent in the care of Thomas Gorges who in the latest commission was named Secretary and, in effect, the leading member of the new government of Maine. The choice of this young relative seems to have been an acknowledgement by Sir Ferdinando that he could not himself go to his Province.

Thomas was only a distant cousin of Sir Ferdinando's but he belonged to a branch of the family which had maintained very close relations with Sir Edward Gorges, Sir Ferdinando's elder brother, whose seat at Wraxall was near to their house at Batcombe. Thomas was also related to the Hydes, of whom Lawrence was Attorney-General at this very time and Edward was to become Lord Chancellor in a future reign. Mr. Raymond Gorges suggests that it was perhaps as a result of the Hyde connection that all brothers in the Batcombe branch of the Gorges family had been sent to the Inns of Court to be trained in law. Thomas had just completed his course when Sir Ferdinando selected him to go to Maine as his deputy.

A few days after appointing Thomas, Sir Ferdinando wrote to Governor Winthrop in a final attempt to conciliate the men of Massachusetts by a direct approach. He said that the new deputy he was sending out had been given particular instructions to maintain good relations with the Bay colony and he added that when he himself came to rule the province he would work for a "union or conformity of all parties or at least a patient and charitable bearing with each other's errors or self-affections that so our Lord the King may be assured of our subjections, the public be not disturbed, the common cause of justice made free, and the country's defences provided for." Political unity was paramount in his mind. Religion, although a matter of personal concern, was secondary. Just as he had been unable in the 1620's to comprehend the nature of the constitutional struggle which raged around him, so in the 1630's he was unable to understand the determination of the Puritans to defend their concept of the church. For Sir Ferdinando was just as fanatical about colonial expansion as the Puritans were about their religion and the Parliamentarians were about their constitutional doctrines. Hence he was blind to all obstacles and he sincerely believed that Massachusetts could, by a wise and diplomatic handling, be brought into a strong colonial empire.

Gorges was prepared to appease the men of Massachusetts. The Ordinances in which he set out his instructions to the new deputy, Thomas Gorges, included express orders for the strict suppression of, among other crimes, fornication, incest, swearing, and drunkenness, crimes against which the Puritans themselves regularly inveighed. To enforce a policy which would stamp upon Maine a moral code not unlike that of the Bay colony itself, Gorges sent a governor who was either a Puritan or who was not far from Puritanism in his outlook. The branch of the Gorges family to which Thomas belonged was, if not already Puritan, very sympathetic to the religious ideas of the men who had settled in Massachusetts. Thomas' reception in Boston seems to prove his Puritanism. He had travelled to Maine by way of Boston and he had stayed there awhile to listen attentively to the advice of the Puritan magistrates. Winthrop thought him "sober and well-disposed" and found no fault with his administration of Maine even though he must have been aware that Thomas' appointment was a step towards the intended enforcement of royal authority over the whole of New England. Sir Ferdinando was not fanatically opposed to the Puritans on religious grounds and he had selected his young relative with the deliberate intention of conciliating Massachusetts. It was a wise and moderate step towards the achievement of his ends, the secure colonization of New England under the close supervision of the Crown.

Gorges wrote to Winthrop on March 26, 1640 for the purpose of telling him why he was not coming at this time to his province. He explained, "The sudden approach of our long wished-for Parliament (the Short Parliament) invites me to attend (await) the happy issue thereof." This was probably not the whole truth. Age and poverty were the chief stumbling blocks; but Gorges would hardly admit them to the Puritan leader. Yet his explanation was not hypocrisy. His natural loyalty was to the King, but it will be remembered that during the ascendancy of Buckingham he had been friendly with Eliot and Warwick and had hoped that England's patent weakness could be solved by the restoration of the Tudor balance between King and Parliament. That was still his sincere desire.

Such an accommodation would solve his own personal problems and further his colonial plans. If Charles and Parliament could come to an agreement, the financial difficulties of the Crown would be eased and royal support might then be made available for colonial projects. Gorges had never been wealthy enough to undertake large-scale plantation without help. His failure to enlist the support of the Crown and of private individuals had driven him to adopt a proprietary form for his colony. By 1639, when his charter authorized him to act on his own, he was less able than ever before to support colonization. The Laconia project had bankrupted him; the estate of his wife, his chief support, could not finance the plantation of Maine; and his former backer, Lord Edward Gorges, was no longer able to help. Only by royal aid could he hope to carry on with his plans. A moderate backing by the King might bring to life the grand plan for the plantation of Maine in accordance with the plans set out in the charter and the *Brief Narration*.

By 1640, however, the Scottish resistance to Laud's religious innovations had become dominant in the English political scene. In 1639 the Scots had appointed a Commander-in-Chief, Alexander Leslie, and Charles' attempt to use the train-bands of the northern counties to force them to submit had proved futile. As a result, on the advice of the Earl of Strafford and of Laud, the King had decided to end the attempt to rule without the aid of Parliament. But the Parliament which had met on April 13, 1640 had insisted that the nation's grievances should be redressed before it would vote supplies to the King to bring Scotland to heel. Hence, within three weeks, it had been dissolved, so soon that it became known as the "Short Parliament." The financial embarrassment of the Crown remained; and there was no prospect that Gorges could gain royal support for his colonial plans. As a consequence, Sir Ferdinando had to stay in England. Maine continued to be ruled by his deputy.

At first, things went very well under Thomas. There was no great new movement of peoples to fill up the new Province but the young man proved to be a most successful governor of those settlements which already existed. In the area covered by the charter there were little plantations in the Piscataqua area, on the Saco, on Casco Bay, and up as far as the Kennebec and the area near Damariscove and Monhegan, the early fishing posts. Thomas set up an annual "General Court" for the whole province at Saco, the first one assembling on June 25, 1640. Its members were Richard Vines, Sir Ferdinando's Steward-General, Henry Jocelyn, and Edward Godfrey. Thomas Gorges was apparently not present himself in person. But he was undoubtedly responsible for establishing the provincial government which William Gorges had let fall.

When the General Court covened, the settlers on the Agamenticus formally acknowledged the jurisdiction of Sir Ferdinando as Lord of the Province of Maine but registered with the Court a reservation claiming certain rights of local government. Perhaps to meet this protest the General Court ruled that minor courts should meet thrice yearly at Agamenticus as well as Saco. The settlers from the Piscataqua area also complained that Saco was too distant for them to attend conveniently; so they were granted the right to attend at the minor courts either at Agamenticus or at Saco as they found convenient. The new regime thus provided for the administration of justice throughout the settled parts of Maine and made some provision for decentralization to suit actual conditions.

The records of the meeting of the first annual Court and of one minor court at Saco, which are all that are now extant, show that the arrival of Thomas brought order to a troubled land. Thomas' legal training is fully evident throughout and he tackled the most difficult problems with vigour and courage. His treatment of the Reverend George Burdett, the exile from Massachusetts who had come to be an evil influence in Maine in the last few years, amply demonstrates that the new regime was both impartial and strong. Burdett complained to the Court that he had been slandered by his neighbours. The slanderers were fined by the Court after having been found guilty by a jury on the legal ground of that time that truth was no defence against a charge of slander. But immediately afterwards, Burdett was charged with and convicted of immorality and adultery, the very crimes of which the slanderers had accused him. Thereupon, many of Burdett's parishioners refused to pay him his wages, feeling, no doubt, that a convicted lecherer was not worthy of hire as a minister of God. The Court promptly ordered that anyone who failed to pay what was due to Burdett would be called to account at the next session. Thus the administration of Thomas Gorges, with a nice regard for the law and justice, dealt effectively with a dangerous character and a very difficult problem.

Thomas was not afraid of greatness. Burdett's connections with Archbishop Laud had not saved him. Similarly in the tangle of legal disputes between George Cleeve and John Winter he acted with regard for law and justice rather than for favour and influence. John Winter, the agent of the Plymouth merchant Robert Trelawny, was in charge of the Trelawny interests in Maine based on a patent issued by the Council for New England in 1631. During the interregnum between William Gorges and Thomas Gorges, Winter had complained to his master of the lawlessness of New England. But actually he was himself a most aggressive character and was determined to expand the land grant which he administered. At the same time he ran a fur-trading post on the harshest terms. As soon as Thomas Gorges appeared in the country a Grand Jury of Winter's neighbours accused Winter of profiteering by charging high prices and by simultaneously under-valuing the furs which he accepted in trade. Not long afterwards George Cleeve, who had come to New England a little before the first settlers sent out by Trelawny, claimed before the Court that he had been evicted by Winter from land which he had developed in consequence of a promise by Sir Ferdinando that he could settle "in any place unpossessed." Winter replied to this latter charge by declaring that this particular dispute had already been submitted to Sir Ferdinando Gorges who had ruled in his favour and that Vines, on the Proprietor's instructions had confirmed Trelawny's possession. The Court, however, found for Cleeve. They knew that many grants in the early days had been given on the same basis without any details of bounds or even location. Vines, who was a member of the Court, abstained from participating in the judgment, presumably because he was involved in the dispute not merely as the agent who had enforced Sir Ferdinando's previous ruling but also as an opponent of Cleeve when the latter has persuaded the elder Gorges to nominate him as Deputy Governor a few years earlier. Trelawny, having appealed to Sir Ferdinando in England, wrote to tell Winter that the verdict was to be reversed. But the administration in Maine seems to have stuck to its guns. Thus the regime set up by Thomas acted with a remarkable degree of impartiality even in cases in which members of the Court were involved, and even when the Proprietor himself seemed likely to interfere. Thomas Gorges went a long way towards building up a sound government in Maine.

It is important to notice that his justice ran in the name of "our Sovereign Lord the King and the Lord of this Province"; the fines which he collected were collected for the King or for the costs of the court; and recognizances were owed to the King. Furthermore, there was no sign of the creation of a feudal administrative system. Although Thomas took over Sir Ferdinando's so-called "manor of Point Christian" there is no evidence that he established a manorial court. His government was tailored to fit the needs of the young Province rather than the pattern of the charter or any outdated feudalistic model. He successfully laid the foundations for the implementation of Sir Ferdinando's plan of extending royal control throughout New England by the device of establishing a vigorous proprietary colony; and that colony was administered much as any royal colony would have been and without any of the encumbrances of mediaeval feudalism upon which the charter seemed to lay so much stress.

Back in England Sir Ferdinando, prevented by the deteriorating political situation from going in person to New England, continued to interest himself from afar in the work of plantation. It was probably at this time that he wrote the *Brief Narration*. The development of his ideas of representative government in that book may thus derive from the fact that, six months after the dissolution of the Short Parliament had blighted Gorges' hopes of going to America, the Long Parliament had met on November 3, 1640.

In other ways, also, Sir Ferdinando showed a capacity for adjusting his plans to the temper of the times. Using the powers which were granted to him in the charter for the incorporation of boroughs, he went much further even than his Deputy, Thomas Gorges, to satisfy the demand of the scattered communities in Maine for autonomy. Sir Ferdinando incorporated Agamenticus as a borough on April 10, 1641, with Thomas Gorges its "first and next mayor." There were to be other officials similar to those of contemporary English boroughs. On March 1, 1642, the charter of Agamenticus was replaced by a second charter by which the borough was extended in area, raised to the dignity of a city (which in English usage meant that it would be the seat of a bishopric), renamed Gorgeana, and given a yet more elaborate system of government including mediaeval city officials called "sergeants of the white rod." But the significant feature of the new charter was neither the implication that episcopacy was to be introduced, nor Gorges' desire to glorify his name by giving it to the first city in New England, nor his creation of an over-elaborate governmental system with officials already becoming ornamental rather than functional in England. The really important thing about the Gorgeana charter was the introduction of local self-government. Agamenticus had been a closed corporation like contemporary English boroughs. Gorgeana, on the other hand, was to have a council chosen by the settlers and this council was to select the magistrates. It was thus to be more representative in its form of government than was customary in English local government at that time.

As it turned out, however, Gorges' charters built only castles in the air. Thomas had indeed established law and order in Maine and had asserted the authority of the King and the Proprietor; but he was building on sand. Neither he nor Sir Ferdinando could produce in Maine an accommodation of the royal and the representative systems of government at the very time when England was rushing headlong into war because of the conflict between those two forms of government.

The Long Parliament, its existence made secure by the presence of the Scots on English soil, had imprisoned Strafford and Laud and had proceeded to introduce measures to limit royal authority. Then it had turned to religion. Here, however, a party which favoured Episcopalianism had appeared in the Commons and had provided the King with the support which he had long lacked. As a result, he was enabled to resort to force. War broke out between King and Parliament.

In Maine, Thomas Gorges was torn in his allegiance. Towards the end of 1643 he abandoned his task in New England and returned to England to fight on the side of Parliament. Nevertheless, Vines succeeded him as Governor in Maine and the edifice which Thomas had founded, despite its newness, proved strong enough to endure for several years the neglect caused by the Civil War. Thomas had built well. But the ultimate fate of the Province obviously depended on the verdict of the fighting in England.

Meanwhile Sir Ferdinando had also been swallowed up in the maelstrom of war and was once again diverted from his lifetime interest in colonization. When active warfare broke out in 1642 he was seventy-four, a phenomenal age for those times when men aged more rapidly than they do today. He had never believed that the differences between King and Parliament were irreconcilable; and though he was a faithful servant of the Crown, during the ascendancy of Buckingham he had grown familiar with some of the Parliamentary leaders. In the period when Charles was attempting to rule without Parliament Gorges had been looking toward the recall of Parliament as the means by which an agreement between the two essential elements of the constitution might best be effected; but when the summoning of the Long Parliament had led only to war his natural loyalty to the King, whose predecessors he had served so faithfully for forty years, had determined his course of action. He was too old for continuous campaigning; but he sought an opportunity to strike a blow for his King.

In July 1642 Gorges, with Thomas Smyth, raised a troop of horse from the gentry of Somerset and Gloucester and in the name of the King summoned the City of Bristol to admit him. Bristol, the second port of the Kingdom, would have been a great prize. The Mayor, however, refused to allow Gorges within the city claiming that Charles had ordered the citizens to keep and defend the city for his own use but had not expressly commanded them to admit troops. As the city could not be forced by cavalry, Gorges had to withdraw. A few weeks later the Earl of Essex, with a Parliamentary force, gained entry and proceeded to organize Bristol as an outpost in the heart of the Royalist West Country.

Sir Ferdinando, despite his age, was still out in the field. With Thomas Smyth and Lord Poulett, Smyth's father-in-law, he joined the Marquis of Hertford at Wells. But the Royalists were driven back to Sherborne and then compelled to evacuate North Devon by sailing from Minehead to South Wales. At Cardiff Thomas Smyth died and Sir Ferdinando brought his body back to Ashton Court for burial. The old man himself probably retired from campaigning at this time. Sir Ferdinando's activities had, however, attracted the attention of Parliament. Thomas Smyth and Lord Poulett had been declared delinquents by both Houses of Parliament for enforcing the royal commission of array. As Sir Ferdinando was known to have taken part in a Royalist action at Shepton Mallet Parliamentary commanders in the west were instructed to watch him.

But Gorges, although not now on active service, was still able to aid the King's cause. When Prince Rupert advanced into the west in 1643, it was he who was probably instrumental in bringing Bristol into the King's hands. He wrote to tell the Prince that the city's defences had been weakened by the over-extension of its defences; and he provided detailed instructions and a map to show how the Prince could approach and seize the town by detaching 3,000 foot and 2,000 horse and distracting the enemy's attention with the main force. Bristol fell to Rupert shortly afterwards and was held by the King for two years.

During the closing years of the Civil War, amidst the general confusion of the time, Sir Ferdinando disappears from view. From about 1642 or 1643 the people of his Province of Maine lost touch with him and attempts were made by some of the disaffected elements to overthrow his proprietorship. George Cleeve went to England and persuaded a prominent Member of Parliament, Sir Arthur Rigby, to buy up the old "Plough Patent" of Lygonia from the Familists. The exact details of the transaction, and even the extent of the claim, are not known but it appears to have given Rigby and Cleeve title to the territory between Casco Bay and Cape Porpoise, a considerable part of the Province of Maine and including territory already settled by Gorges' followers. As English authority over New England had been suspended by the constitutional and military conflict, the rival claimants appealed to Massachusetts; but the wily Puritans abstained from favouring either side. They had designs on the territory themselves. For a time the dispute remained unsettled.

By October 1645, no word having been received from the Proprietor for a long time, the settlers in Maine found it necessary to confirm the government of Richard Vines as Deputy Governor by an Order of the General Court. His government was to continue for one year and it was decided that a Deputy Governor would be elected annually. At the same time the Court gave Vines the power of attorney over Sir Ferdinando's estates in Maine. But news of Cleeve's success in obtaining strong claims to the Lygonia area discouraged Vines. He had lived in Maine for thirty years and for much of that time had been Sir Ferdinando's chief agent. When Sir Ferdinando's support was gone, Vines felt that he could no longer carry on. Cleeve was his personal enemy; and the triumph of Parliament over the King in 1645 obviously meant that Sir Ferdinando's hold on Maine would be weakened. Hence, Vines abandoned the land which had long been his home and took his family off to Barbados.

Vines was succeeded as Deputy Governor by Henry Jocclyn who had been named by the Court in 1645 as next in succession. For two years Jocelyn continued to rule in the name of the Proprietor and to look after Sir Ferdinando's property rights. Early in 1647, Sir Ferdinando's Manor House at Point Christian was handed over to one Robert Nanney as security for a paltry debt of 11 pounds. No doubt, this was a convenient way of installing a bailiff until such time as Sir Ferdinando or his heirs made other arrangements. A little later the General Court took a bond from John Alcock of Agamenticus for a debt owed to the Proprietor; and the Court also dealt with such minor matters as the fencing of the boundary of his estate. The regime established in Maine by Thomas Gorges continued to operate with a considerable degree of success despite lack of direction from England and despite the departure of two of its most important leaders.

While it is not clear where Sir Ferdinando was during this vital period, it is possible that he was in the vicinity of Bristol; for when the city was recaptured by the Parliamentarians under Sir Thomas Fairfax in 1645, Gorges is said to have been treated courteously by the general whose grandfather had campaigned with him at Rouen over fifty years earlier. Furthermore, Sir John Poulett, son of his old friend Baron Poulett of Hinton St. George, who had made his peace with the Parliamentarians by payment of a delinquency fine, was able to tell Gorges that Baron Fairfax, father of Sir Thomas, had spoken of his old acquaintance with the old man and had expressed a willingness to comfort him in his "untimely sufferances."

Accordingly, on June 1, 1646, Sir Ferdinando wrote to the elder Fairfax to express his gratitude for the courtesy with which he had been treated by the son and to say that he had never "swayed . . . further than an obedient servant only careful of my Country's happiness" and that he had "been fearful to side with either party as not able to judge of so transcendent a difference but sorrowing in the highest degree to find such a separation threatening so much the ruin of all." He said that he hoped that the King's decision to accept the advice of Parliament would restore the "happiness we once enjoyed," in other words, the balanced constitution of the Tudors. And he expressed a desire to wait upon Fairfax to explain how he had passed his time "in these sad seasons." But his longing for a return of the balance between King and Parliament was entirely unrealistic in view of the complete military victory of Parliament and of the unwillingness of Charles to accept the verdict of the field.

Apparently the personal friendship of the Fairfaxes did Gorges little good. A report reached New England that he had been "plundered" and imprisoned. And a little later came the news that he was dead. At about the same time, Parliament sent instructions that Rigby's claim to Lygonia was valid. Jocelyn, whose interests lay within Rigby's area, immediately withdrew from the Deputy Governorship of Maine. The settlers in the remainder of the Province then joined together under the leadership of Edward Godfrey, one of Gorges' magistrates, and when they were unable to make contact with Sir Ferdinando's heirs they continued the practice started in 1645 of electing the Deputy Governor. In July, 1649, this practice was confirmed by a "compact" between them. Thus what was left of Gorges' Province remained a little republic until, at the end of 1652, Massachusetts began to swallow up the northern settlements piece-meal. The process of annexation was completed by 1658.

Sir Ferdinando had died at Ashton Phillips in Somerset where he had lived ever since his marriage to Elizabeth Smyth. His will, dated May 14, 1647 ten days before his death, bequeathed to Lady Elizabeth all his goods and chattels, except 20 pounds which was to be distributed to the poor. The will makes no mention of land or estates. Sir Ferdinando had long ago returned to his brother Edward the Manor of Birdcombe which he had received from his father. He had no other estates in England; and the land on which he lived at Ashton was the property of his wife. His American estates were not mentioned in the will. Sir Ferdinando's optimism about America and about his plans for New England and Maine had at last been quenched. He died knowing that he had failed.

The epilogue to Gorges' story is brief. His claims to Maine passed to his grandson Ferdinando, that young man to whom Agamenticus had been granted as long ago as 1631. After the Restoration, Ferdinando Gorges Junior and John Mason both tried to claim the estates originally owned by their grandfathers in New England but with no great success. In May, 1677, young Ferdinando accepted 1,250 pounds for the surrender of his claims in Maine. Although a paltry sum it was some degree of recognition by the Puritans that those claims had had some validity; but this sale finally extinguished the interests of the Gorges family in those American lands which Sir Ferdinando had laboured to develop as a proprietary province owing a close allegiance to the Crown. New England was thus left to follow a very different destiny from that which Sir Ferdinando, throughout his long life, had planned.

CHAPTER

6.

Massachusetts Bay extended its power over Maine in the 1650's. The submission of all coastal towns was complete by 1658 even though many inhabitants resisted to the last.

THE JURISDICTION OF MASSACHUSETTS ACCEPTED*

by

Henry S. Burrage

The members of the general court of Massachusetts, in their search for the northern boundary of the colony, perused the colonial charter on May 31, 1652. The attention of the general court had been called to the boundary matter in the preceding year. In fact, in October, 1651, they had reached the conclusion that from an extension of the northern boundary line of the colony, "it doth appear that the town of Kittery, and many miles to the northward, is comprehended within our grant." In reaching this conclusion, the members of the general court were doubtless influenced by an effort on the part of several persons in Kittery to induce the residents there ("who govern now by combination") to present a petition to Parliament for a grant of the place. This, it was said, a majority of the inhabitants refused to do, many of them expressing their willingness "to submit themselves to the government of the Massachusetts". Under these circumstances the members of the court, taking into consideration the "commodiousness" of the Piscataqua river, and the fact that it would be prejudicial to the Massachusetts government if Kittery and the Piscataqua river should be held by those who were unfriendly to the Bay colony, it was ordered, "that a loving and friendly letter" be sent to the inhabitants of Kittery informing them that Kittery was within the Massachusetts grant, and that a commission had been appointed consisting of Simon Bradstreet, Major Daniel Denison and Captain William Hawthorne to treat with them in accordance with their instructions, and to receive them under the Massachusetts government provided "terms of agreement can be concluded upon by mutual consent". If, however, the inhabitants of Kittery declined to enter into such an agreement, the commissioners, having "laid claim to the place", were to protest against any further proceedings "by virtue of their combination or other interest whatsoever".

Information concerning this action reached the Province of Maine soon after the action was taken, and Edward Godfrey, as governor of the province, summoned a provincial general court to meet December 1, 1651. On the third day of the session, the court directed Mr. Godfrey, Mr. Leader and Mr. Shapleigh to draw up a petition to Parliament for a confirmation of the existing provincial government. This petition, prepared by Godfrey, professing free and willing submission to the government of England as then established "without a King or House of Lords", called attention to the circumstances under which the colonists had been compelled to take upon themselves the government of the province, making mention especially of the death of Sir Ferdinando Gorges, and the failure of his son and heir to identify himself with the interests of the province. Having thus been forced "by way of combination to govern and rule according to the laws of England", in behalf of the general court the governor asked for a confirmation of the government thus established and requested that the inhabitants of the

---

*Henry S. Burrage, *Beginnings of Colonial Maine* (Portland: Marks Printing House, 1914), pp. 370-382.

province, as free-born Englishmen might be declared members of the Commonwealth of England.

But Godfrey did not cease his opposition to the proposed action of Massachusetts with the preparation of this petition. Toward the close of May, 1652, he addressed an earnest letter to Edward Rawson, secretary of the general court of Massachusetts, challenging the claim of the Bay colony to Maine territory as included within Massachusetts limits. In his reply, which was by order of the general court, Rawson defended the action against which Godfrey had remonstrated. To this communication Godfrey made a vigorous answer July 9, 1652. "For our perusal of your patent and your line", he wrote, "we apprehend the bounds thereof were set more than twenty years last past, at the sea-side and so up into the country from the sea three miles on this side Merrimac, as all other patents were which are no less than ten in number, that we perceive by the extension of your unknown line you now willingly labor to engraft". Against such pretended jurisdiction Godfrey earnestly protested. "We are loath to part with our precious liberties for unknown and uncertain favors", he wrote. "We resolve to exercise our just jurisdiction till it shall please the Parliament, the Commonweal(th) of England, otherwise to order under whose power and protection we are."

The general court of Massachusetts made no haste in the procedure. The action of the court in connection with the perusal of its charter did not take place until May 31, 1652. The commissioners did not receive their instructions to repair to Kittery until June 11, 1652. On account of a change in the membership of the commission as finally constituted, William Hawthorne, John Leverett and Henry Bartholomew represented the colony of Massachusetts bay in the Kittery conference, which seems to have been held July 9, 1652. Edward Godfrey, Richard Leader, Nicholas Shapleigh, Thomas Withers and Edward Rishworth, who declared themselves "to be persons in present power for the ordering and managing of whatsoever might be of concernment to the people", represented the Province of Maine. There is no record of the proceedings of the conference. Doubtless there was much discussion, but Godfrey and those associated with him declined to accept the overtures of the Massachusetts commissioners.

Because of this action it only remained for the commissioners to present the protest of Massachusetts as their instructions required. It did not appear to them, the commissioners said, that Godfrey and others, representing the Province of Maine, possessed any rightful authority, inasmuch as the provincial territory was included in the limits of the patent of the Bay colony, and so by grant and charter, under the great seal of England, was under the jurisdiction of Massachusetts. But they were authorized to say that those submitting themselves thereunto should "freely and quietly possess and enjoy all the lands, goods and chattels appertaining to and possessed by any or every of them" and that they should have "right and equally share" in all acts of favor and justice which by virtue of government the inhabitants of Massachusetts "do or may expect to enjoy". Then followed the protest of Massachusetts against any person or persons within the Province of Maine exercising jurisdiction over the inhabitants of the province, or any part thereof, after October 10, 1652, without order from the general court or council of the colony of Massachusetts bay.

The commissioners' announcement of this protest was dated July 9, 1652. This, also, was the date of Governor Godfrey's answer to Secretary Rawson's letter of June 12, 1652, to which reference has already been made. It was also the date of the answer made by Godfrey and his associates, "sworn magistrates" of the Province of Maine, to the Massachusetts protest. Evidently, July 9, 1652, was a busy day in Kittery. The answer made to the protest by the magistrates of the Province of Maine was plainly the work of Governor Godfrey. It assailed again the action of the Bay colony in attempting to extend its jurisdiction northward. "The truth doth and shall appear", it was said, "that where their bounds were set up more than twenty years passed, and both before and since many patents (have been) granted for the populating and propagating of the land". In this way, it was added, a large sum of money had been expended. Also lawful jurisdiction had been exercised by officers "acknowledged and owned by you of the Massachusetts", and "approved and justified in England". And now, for these gentlemen to come "in the name only and behalf of the jurisdiction of the Massachusetts", saying that the inhabitants who "shall submit unto them shall freely and quietly possess and enjoy all the lands, goods, chattels, and that we shall enjoy equal favors in acts of government,—these proposals are not in our judgment meet; the time, places and persons considered we patiently bear them, and submit to be judged by those whom we acknowledge to be our supreme judges. Against exercise of jurisdiction, we resolve and intend to go on till lawful power command us the contrary, as subordinate and depending upon the Commonwealth of England."

On receiving the report of the commissioners, the general court of Massachusetts evidently saw no reason for discouragement. Its conference had revealed the attitude of the provincial officers only. It was now resolved to appeal to the inhabitants as a whole. Accordingly, October 23, 1652, the court appointed six commissioners to settle the civil government amongst the inhabitants of Kittery, the Isles of Shoals, "and so to the most northerly extent" of the colony's patent. By their instructions, the commissioners were to proceed to the territory north of the Piscataqua, and summon the inhabitants to assemble in places deemed by the commissioners most convenient and require their submission, granting unto them at the same time equal protection and privileges with the inhabitants of the Bay colony. They were also to establish courts for hearing and determining all causes, civil and criminal, to appoint commissioners, constables and such other officers as they deemed needful for preserving peace and good order, "and otherwise to act in the premises" as the general court shall direct, doing whatever in their wisdom and discretion would be most conducive to the glory of God, the peace and welfare of the inhabitants and the maintenance of their own "just rights and interests."

Four of the six commissioners, namely, Simon Bradstreet and Samuel Simonds of Boston, Captain Thomas Wiggin of New Hampshire and Bryan Pendleton of the Province of Maine, proceeded to Kittery, where they opened a court November 15, 1652, and issued a summons to the inhabitants to assemble on the following day, between seven and eight o'clock in the morning at the house of William Everett. The inhabitants appeared as summoned, and the conference was opened by the Massachusetts commissioners, who presented evidence of their appointment and also the instructions they had received. For four days there was full and free discussion. In general, the temper of both parties was good, but evidences of strong feeling are reported and mention is made of the offensive bearing and words of one John Bursley, who, towards the commissioners and some of the residents of Kittery that apparently were ready to subscribe their submission, indulged in threats to such an extent that at once he was brought to trial and confession for his misbehavior. Finally, the inhabitants declared their willingness to give written consent to the jurisdiction of Massachusetts, provided certain conditions offered by them were accepted. This offer the commissioners declined on the ground that their instructions required the submission of the inhabitants first; then, a guaranty of rights and of ample privileges would follow. Evidently further opposition was thought to be useless, and November 20, 1652, forty-one of the inhabitants of Kittery subscribed to the following declaration: "We whose names are underwritten do acknowledge ourselves subject to the government of Massachusetts bay in New England."

In fourteen articles the commissioners then enumerated the rights and privileges the people of Kittery were to possess under the government of Massachusetts. The territory north of the Piscataqua was to comprise a county known as Yorkshire. The inhabitants were to have "protection and equal acts of favor and justice" with those dwelling on the south side of the Piscataqua. Kittery was to remain a township, and enjoy the privileges of other Massachusetts towns. Titles to property in houses and lands "whether by the grant of the town or of the Indians", or of those justly holding them. Kittery was promised a deputy to the general court, and two if "they think good". All the present inhabitants of the town were to be regarded as freemen of the country, and having taken the oath as freemen they were to have liberty to vote for "governor, assistants and other general officers of the country". Moreover, the county of York was to have county courts in the most commodious and fit places, "as authority shall see meet to appoint". Provision also was made for every township to have three men appointed by the county court for the trial of minor causes, in places where there was no resident magistrate or commissioner. The county, also, was to have three associates to assist such commissioners as the present commissioners, or such as might afterwards be sent. Furthermore the men of the whole county of York were not to be drawn upon for any ordinary general trainings out of their own territory without their consent.

How many of the inhabitants declined to acknowledge their submission to Massachusetts at that time is not known. It is said there were some; but the forty-one who yielded, and by subscription acknowledged themselves subjects to the government of Massachusetts, comprised a majority and probably a large majority of the freemen of the place.

Having completed their labors at Kittery, the commissioners on Monday, November 22, proceeded to Agamenticus, Gorges' Gorgeana, where, in response to the commissioners' summons, the inhabitants assembled at the house of Nicholas Davis. Prominent among them was Edward Godfrey, still representing the Gorges interests. Doubtless during the conference of the preceding week at Kittery he had been in close touch with friends there holding like views with reference to the claims of Massachusetts; and in the submission of Kittery's inhabitants he could hardly have failed to foresee the issue of the conference in his own town. None the less, however, in a day of "debatements", his voice rang out loud and clear in opposition to any encroachment upon territory that had long been known as the Province of Maine. But it was of no avail. At the close of the day, when the vote was taken, the inhabitants of Agamenticus took the same action as the inhabitants of Kittery on the preceding Saturday. As recorded by the commissioners the vote was as follows: "Mr. Godfrey did forbear until the vote was passed by the rest, and then immediately he did by word and vote express his consent". According to Godfrey's own statement, however, his submission was with a mental reservation. In a later appeal to Parliament, he wrote, "Whatever my body was inforced unto, heaven knows my soul did not consent unto". The statement seems to belong to a considerably later period in Godfrey's life, as in the endorsement at the close of the petition occur the words, "This was after Richard Cromwell was out", and therefore after April 22, 1659. In no sense could it be said that Godfrey was under any outward compulsion in yielding submission to the government of Massachusetts. His submission, it is true, was an unwilling one, but the act was his own. Of course, his conviction with reference to his rights remained unchanged. To the best of his ability he had opposed the onward advance of Massachusetts into territory north of the Piscataqua. But now, even his fellow townsmen were not in agreement with him; and when this fact was made clear by their votes at the close of the conference, he yielded and added his vote to the forty-nine votes already recorded.

This concession on the part of Godfrey has been called a mistake. Rather it seems to have been the only course open to him if he was to have any helpful influence at Agamenticus. The opportunity for such helpful influence appeared when he received an appointment as the first of four commissioners to whom, with one assistant of the Massachusetts government, was given authority to keep one county court at York each year, while any three of them were authorized to try cases without a jury. They were also empowered to conduct the affairs of the county in general. This position Godfrey held for three successive years. But the fires of resentment continued to burn in his breast; and at length, probably in 1655, he left Agamenticus and made his way to England in the hope of securing from the home government redress for the losses he had sustained. During Cromwell's Protectorate, however, and also during the Protectorate of his son Richard, conditions were unfavorable for a successful presentation of his case. In 1660, however, with the restoration of Charles II, the withered hopes of Godfrey and the heirs of Gorges and Mason suddenly brightened. Yet, under even these changed circumstances, disappointment upon disappointment followed; and when we obtain our last glimpses of Godfrey, he is an inmate of Ludgate jail, London, hopeless, friendless, bending under the weight of more than fourscore years; and there, on an unknown date, it is supposed that he died. His burial place, like that of Robert Trelawny, is unknown.

Thus, in 1652, by a direct appeal to the people, Massachusetts succeeded in extending her jurisdiction over the nearest of the Maine settlements. Her success foreshadowed such added action on the part of the Bay colony as would bring to an end any exercise of authority derived from the proprietary governments of Gorges and Rigby. Yet again there was no hasty action in further procedure. In May, 1653, the general court of Massachusetts admitted two representatives from Maine, one from Kittery and one from York. Shortly after, however, having approved the wise and successful work of the commissioners at Kittery and York, the court appointed commissioners to extend the jurisdiction of the colony still farther northward so as to include Wells, Saco and Cape Porpoise. Equal success attended the efforts of the commissioners in these settlements, and July 5, 1653, their inhabitants by their votes placed themselves under the jurisdiction of Massachusetts.

About this time the Plymouth colonists, somewhat tardily indeed, were directing attention to the lack of good government in its Maine territory on the Kennebec. Some one, evidently, had reminded the Pilgrims of their failure to comply with the requirement of their charter that the English settlers on the river within the colony's territorial limits "should be orderly governed and carried on in a way of peace for their common good in civil concernments". This requirement they had not fulfilled, and the general court of the Plymouth colony now authorized Thomas Prence, one of the colony's honored magistrates, to proceed to the Kennebec and call together the inhabitants along the river "for the settling of a government". Mr. Prence made his way thither, and May 23, 1654, the people assembled at the house of Thomas Ashley at Merrymeeting bay, where sixteen persons, including Thomas Purchase, took the oath of fidelity to the Commonwealth of England and Plymouth colony, and agreed upon a series of articles designed to secure a proper observance of law and order within the limits of the Pilgrim grant.

As yet, still farther to the eastward, there was little if any endeavor to make proper provision for securing the benefits of good government. The necessity was recognized, but the ways and means were not discoverable. And still Massachusetts, while watchful of the territory beyond Saco, delayed added action in extending her jurisdiction. There, men of considerable influence, like Henry Jocelyn, Robert Jordan and Arthur Mackworth, continued their opposition to the claims of Massachusetts as also did George Cleeve; the former on religious and political grounds, and the latter in an endeavor to retain his place in connection with the Rigby interests which otherwise would be blotted out. To Cleeve's protest against any further encroachment Massachusetts made reply: "We have not endeavored to infringe the liberties of the planters of those lands, but have offered them the same with ourselves; nor to nourish or ease ourselves by taxing of their estates, to ease ourselves. We expect no more than what they formerly did, namely, bear their own charges; nor do we seek to put upon them that which we ourselves would count unequal, namely, to subject (them) to such laws and constitutions made by others without their consent, it being the portion of most of our present inhabitants, as of the subjects of most countries, to be in no other capacity; the constitutions of government and new model of laws not being made in every age of men, or upon the arrival of new comers to a colony".

But all the while, Massachusetts held firmly to her purpose. At length, having received "divers complaints" for want of government at the westward, the Massachusetts authorities May 15, 1657, addressed a letter to Henry Jocelyn and Robert Jordan, requesting them to meet the commissioners of the colony at the next county court at York, to assist in settling "those parts beyond Saco", to the utmost bounds of the Massachusetts charter. As neither appeared in answer to this request, Massachusetts proceeded to summons the inhabitants in the territory mentioned to present themselves at the general court to be held in Boston, October 14, 1657. Again there was default. Cleeve, however, responded by a protest against the legality of the action of Massachusetts in extending her jurisdiction into Maine territory, adding an announcement that the inhabitants had resolved not to yield submission to the government of the Bay colony.

To this protest the general court of Massachusetts, October 23, 1657, replied by a "declaration and protestation", reaffirming its "right and claim to those parts", but asserting its purpose to "surcease any further prosecution", at the same time insisting that "if any mischief or inconvenience" should result "by means of their own differences, or for want of a settled government . . . . . . all the blame and danger must and ought to be imputed" to the inhabitants themselves. Here, also, it was made to appear that Jocelyn, Jordan and Cleeve, in their attitude toward Massachusetts, did not represent the people among whom they lived; and in response to added complaints of unsettled conditions, commissioners, appointed by the general court, were directed to repair to Black Point, Richmond's island and Casco to receive the submission of the inhabitants. In attending to this duty, the commissioners held a court, July 13, 1658, at the house of Robert Jordan, at Spurwink. Hither came a majority of the residents in the places mentioned. As at Kittery, York, Wells, Saco and Cape Porpoise, there was "serious debate", but final unanimity, "the inhabitants of Black Point, Blue Point, Spurwink and Casco bay, with all the islands thereunto belonging", acknowledging themselves to be subject to the government of Massachusetts bay. Twenty-nine persons signed the form of submission. Among them appear such familiar names as George Cleeve, Robert Jordan and Michael Mitton. In the articles of agreement it was announced that the places formerly known as Black Point, Blue Point and Stratton's islands would be called Scarborough henceforth. Those places, hitherto known as Spurwink and Casco bay from east side of Spurwink river to the Clapboard islands in Casco bay, and running back into the country eight miles, would be called henceforth Falmouth, Henry Jocelyn, Robert Jordan, George Cleeve, Henry Watts and Francis Neale were appointed commissioners for the year ensuing and were invested with full power, or any three of them, for the trial of all causes without jury, within the limits of Scarborough and Falmouth; while Henry Jocelyn, Robert Jordan, Micholas Shapleigh, Edward Rishworth and Abraham Preble were invested with magisterial power throughout the county of York.

The purpose of Massachusetts, at least the initial purpose, in her invasion of Maine territory, was now accomplished. It was not without watchfulness and skilful management, however, that under changed political conditions in England she succeeded in retaining her hold upon the territory thus secured. The stars in their courses seem to fight on her side, and she was able at length to extend her jurisdiction into the larger territory still farther to the eastward.

CHAPTER

7.

Samuel Waldo was among the first Americans to attempt to make his fortune in the wilderness that was colonial Maine. A dealer in lime, a founder of Maine's paper industry, and a mast agent of the King, Waldo also was responsible for bringing to the Maine coast a group of German Protestants. The following account of the German immigration was written by Jasper Stahl and represents one of the most impressive efforts of a local historian in historical scholarship.

THE GERMANS REACH BROAD BAY*
by
Jasper J. Stahl

In the researches of those who have interested themselves in the early history of Maine and of Lincoln County, the view persists that the colonization of the Waldoborough area by the Germans was started as early as 1739. The grounds for this belief are based on a number of sources, some of which have been long known to historians, while others confirming this conclusion have only recently been brought to light and are being presented in this chapter for the first time.

The older sources for a German settlement as early as 1739 seem to be twofold. The first was a letter written by the Lutheran pastor at Waldoborough, the Reverend John William Starman, to William Willis, the Portland historian. This was published in the *Collections of the Maine Historical Society*. In this letter the Reverend Starman states: "A few German immigrants began the original plantation of Waldoborough; it is supposed that they came over in the summer or autumn of 1739. It was first the abode of only two or three families to which accessions were made in 1740." This same view is represented by William D. Williamson, who adds that they came on a vessel "which brought to New England that year letters of marque and reprisal from the King of England against the subjects of Spain." The evidence offered by the Reverend Starman should unquestionably carry weight, for he resided in the community from 1812 to his death in 1854. The span of his ministry in the town was coextensive with the lives of a goodly number of the older German settlers.

Conrad Heyer, for example, was a member of the Lutheran parish during Starman's entire ministry; and the reverend gentleman unquestionably knew him intimately. Likewise, Jacob Ludwig who died in 1826 was an officer in the Lutheran congregation in the early years of Starman's ministry; and from him, too, the pastor must have become very familiar with the history of the earliest days. But neither Heyer nor Ludwig was among the very earliest German settlers, for Heyer was born at Broad Bay in 1749, and Ludwig came as a boy in his teens in 1753. There were, however, those of the earliest colonists who were still living when Mr. Starman came to Waldoborough, whose association with him as their pastor was unquestionably a particularly intimate one. In those days of no newspapers and a very limited communication with the outside world, the facts and doings of the past were in the minds of all a part of the living present, and Starman, as well as Heyer and Ludwig, must have been as familiar with the history of the earliest days as though they themselves had lived it. Hence despite the absence of documentary data, it is difficult, indeed, to disregard the testimony offered by the Reverend Starman. Furthermore, the conclusion offered by Judge Williamson receives collateral support from a communication of Governor Shirley to the General Court, reported in the *Boston Gazette* of September 24, 1739, to

---

*Jasper Jacob Stahl, *History of Old Broad Bay and Waldoboro* (Freeport: Bond-Wheelwright Co., 1956), I, pp. 92-116. Reprinted by permission of the publisher and the author.

the effect that a ship arrived in Boston from England in mid-September of that year bearing from the King "the Commissions of Marque and Reprisal" which bore the London date of July 20, 1739. That there were a few German families aboard this ship is strongly within the range of probability, for Samuel Waldo was in Europe at that time primarily in the interests of his projects in "Eastern parts." From the constant flow of German emigrants, all of whom stopped at English ports for clearance, he may well have induced a few families to effect contact with his agents in Boston relative to settling on his lands in the Province of Maine. That this matter was uppermost in his mind is clear from the following advertisement which he placed in the *Boston Gazette* of July 13, 1739. "Samuel Waldo of Boston, Merchant, intending to take his departure for Great Britain with Captain Hall, gives notice that all desiring to settle in the Eastern Parts of this Province, should apply in his Absence to his Agents at his House in Queen Street."

The second of the older sources for the belief in a settlement by the Germans at Broad Bay prior to 1742 was Cyrus Eaton of Warren. Eaton was born at Framingham, Massachusetts, in 1784 and came to Warren in 1804. He was self educated, but despite this fact was an extremely careful and reliable scholar. In his life span of ninety years he was an assiduous fact-gatherer from any and all sources. He early came to know some of the first Broad Bayers; and from a period in his life when he was a teacher in Waldoborough, he was able to widen the circle of his friends among the early Germans and to gather data firsthand. He seems to have drawn much of his material from Joseph Ludwig, who came to Broad Bay in 1753. With such sources at his disposal Eaton states: "The same year, 1740, forty German families from Brunswick and Saxony, tempted by the imposing offers which the indefatigable Waldo had made and caused to be circulated in their language, after first landing at Braintree, Massachusetts, arrived at Broad Bay and laid the foundation of the present town of Waldoborough." There is no necessary contradiction involved here with the Starman date of 1739, for it is a verifiable fact that some migrations split on reaching Boston, part remaining in the Boston district and others coming to Waldo's grant in eastern parts. It is known that the ship bearing the Commissions of Marque and Reprisal reached Boston in mid-September, 1739; and if it did bring a load of German immigrants, it is entirely probable that a few families came to Broad Bay in the autumn of that year, and that the others wintered in the German settlement at Germantown (Braintree), and then joined their fellow migrants at Broad Bay the following spring, when Waldo's agents could have made more detailed arrangements for their care and settlement. These would have been the "accessions" which the Reverend Starman reported "were made in 1740."

A substantial body of new material, presented here for the first time, supplements and strengthens the hypothesis that 1739-1740 was the period when Germans first settled in Waldoborough. Waldo, as has become abundantly clear, was a dogged and constant worker in the promotion of his projects. That the evidence for the 1739-1740 settlement is not more abundant may well have arisen from the fact that in these years he was disposed to screen his activities. It was while he was in England from 1738 to 1740, working and intriguing for the unseating of Governor Belcher, that Waldo renewed contact with a Swiss by the name of Sebastian Zuberbuhler with whom he had had dealings several years before.

Zuberbuhler was born at Linden in the Canton of Appenzell which is in the northeast corner of Switzerland, just south of Lake Constance. In 1734 he was sent by his own countrymen to South Carolina to investigate the possibilities of locating a colony of Swiss in that district. Already in 1732 John Peter Purry of Neufchatel, Switzerland, had founded Purrysburg on the Savannah River and had settled one hundred and seventy colonists there. Their report of conditions had been most favorable; and the next year, 1733, close to two hundred Swiss Germans and Germans were sent out to the Savannah.

It is possible that Zuberbuhler came in this transport in order to follow in Purry's footsteps as a land speculator. He had associated himself with a Herr Simon who had a ship and a ship's chandler business in Rotterdam, and with another Swiss, Tschiffeli by name, in order to settle a colony of Appenzeller Swiss on the Santee River close to the border of North Carolina. For this purpose they had acquired from the English proprietors a considerable area of land. In these ventures Sebastian's brother, the Reverend Bartholomew Zuberbuhler, was also associated. Just how successful this project was is not known, for at this point Zuberbuhler disappears from view for a number of years. For the greater part of this period Zuberbuhler and Samuel Waldo had had contact with one another, as is made clear by a letter of Governor William Shirley to the Duke of Newcastle, dated at Boston, August 30, 1742. In this communication Shirley made it clear to the Duke that affairs in the settling of eastern parts were at a standstill, "which has prevented Mr. Zuberbuhler from transporting 100 Protestant families *more* from the Swiss Cantons, as he had in 1735 contracted with Mr. Waldo to do."

The meeting in London between Waldo and Zuberbuhler was to draw thousands of men living in all parts of the United States into the causal sequence of Broad Bay and American history. To Waldo, Zuberbuhler must have seemed the perfect instrument for his purposes. The Swiss knew both America and Europe, he was German, English, and perhaps French speaking, and for several years had had experience in recruiting emigrants on the continent and transporting them to the New World. These facts fitted perfectly into Waldo's plans; and the two men struck a bargain whereunder Samuel Waldo promised and obligated himself to convey to Sebastian Zuberbuhler, "or his order at the charge of the said Waldo by good and sufficient Deeds in the Law, 12,000 acres of land—to be laid out between Muscongus and Penebscot rivers . . . *adjoining to the settlement of the Germans.*" The land here in question was a part of the Muscongus tract; and the instrument promising to make the conveyance of this acreage was drawn up in London and bears the significant date of February 19, 1740. It was not a formal conveyance of title, but merely an agreement under which Waldo obligated himself to convey title to 12,000 acres, probably at a time when both men would be in New England, where the surveying of bounds could be done which would be essential to making the conveyance a meaningful and binding legal agreement. It is extremely doubtful if the actual conveyance ever was made, since nowhere is it a matter of record. Zuberbuhler, however, was still sufficiently hopeful of his ultimate title in 1745 that on March 25 of that year, as he was leaving Broad Bay for the Louisburg campaign, he conveyed 6,000 acres of this land to George Tilley of Boston, as part collateral of a loan of 96 pounds made to him by Tilley. It is significant that the only claim Zuberbuhler could make at this time to the grant was based solely on the London agreement of 1740.

The main significance of the London agreement is not that it reveals the character of some of Mr. Waldo's deals, but rather that it casts light on the first German settlement at Broad Bay. The 12,000 acres involved in Waldo's promise were to be laid out "adjoining to the settlement of the Germans." If these words are to be taken in their literal sense, they can only mean that there was already a settlement of Germans on the Medomak by February 19, 1740, probably the few families who had come in 1739 on the ship bringing the letters of Marque and Reprisal from the King of England against the subjects of Spain. Hence it is likely that this "settlement of the Germans" should be construed as including the balance of this migration that passed the winter of 1739-1740 at Braintree, and was scheduled to join the settlement at Broad Bay the following spring, for this seems to have been a certainty that was entering into Waldo's calculations at this time. Further migrations to Broad Bay were unquestionably a part of the plans being formulated by Waldo and Zuberbuhler in London in the late winter of 1740, for Waldo was not a philanthropist haphazardly scattering his bounty on the waters. When Waldo made a promise, there was usually a *quid pro quo* involved, which in this situation meant that for 12,000 acres Zuberbuhler had to return plenty in value for value received. From this time forward for a number of years, Zuberbuhler was Waldo's agent in the program of colonizing the lands at Broad Bay with Germans. We know much of his activities in the year 1741, but where he was and what he was doing for the balance of the year 1740 after having completed his agreement with Waldo in February of that year is not known. We may be reasonably certain that as Waldo's agent he did not pass the spring, summer, and autumn of 1740 in idleness. We are venturing the conjecture that in the late winter of 1740 he returned to his home, Canton of Appenzell, where his repute was high, and early the following spring recruited a migration of thirty-odd Swiss families which during the summer he transported and settled on Mr. Waldo's grant at Broad Bay.

In Waldoborough history there has been from the early days a persistent, long-lingering tradition or fable of a lost colony—a tale of a traveller or hunter who in the 1740's wandered along the banks of the river and found cabin after cabin vacated and not much in them disturbed "as though the occupants had just stepped out for a short while." It is possible that that which has lingered so long as romance or tradition is also history, for it now seems very probable that there was such a colony. In all likelihood they found the winters too severe, or the soil too stony, or the hazards of Indian warfare more than they cared to endure. Whatever their reasons, they disappeared during the War of the Austrian Sucession while General Waldo was with his troops at Louisburg. It is apparent that they dispatched on one of the cordwood coasters one or more of their number to Boston, who chartered a ship which returned to the Medomak, where the unhappy Swiss colony embarked for parts unknown.

William Shirley, Governor of the Colony of Massachusetts Bay, writing in 1746 to the Duke of Newcastle, His Majesty's Minister for Foreign Affairs, and seeking either recognition or compensation for General Waldo, for the losses sustained by him in his personal affairs by reason of his long absence in the King's service at Louisburg, states:

> ... One instance of which (loss) is that after suffering otherwise in his eastern settlements, *no less than thirty-four Swiss families,* which he had transported on his lands at a great expense from the protestant Cantons, are now quitting them togeather, to the entire breaking up of one of his settlements occasioned chiefly by his attendance upon His Majesty's Service at Louisburg, which I engaged him to do upon my leaving it, for the sake of keeping the soldiers easy.

This is weighty evidence indeed, for up until the time when he was appointed governor in June, 1741, William Shirley had been Samuel Waldo's personal attorney, had represented Waldo's interests in America while the latter was in England, and on becoming governor had collaborated with Waldo in a common program of settling the eastern parts with Protestant Germans. Surely there was no one who knew Waldo's business better than Shirley, and no one more thoroughly familiar with conditions on the Maine frontier, the settlement of which was one of his pet policies. Even if Shirley and Waldo had not been close collaborators over the years, this evidence would still carry great weight; for in the summer of 1742 the Governor made a trip to the eastern parts as far as the settlement on the Georges River, and spent some time at Broad Bay. In other words, he was on the spot; he saw and he knew, and reported on conditions to the General Court on September 3, 1742.

Where the Swiss families went is a matter of conjecture, but it would seem reasonable to conclude that they joined their Swiss brethren in the Carolinas, where they had migrated before them under the guidance of this same Sebastian Zuberbuhler. It cannot be denied that these events, though real, impart to the history of these early days a certain colorful romance of "old, unhappy, far-off things," only dimly seen in retrospect, of which the sharper details will remain shrouded from human ken forever.

History, which Alexis Carrel calls "the conjectural science," offers no certain answer. There are historians who mention two southern areas as the scenes of Broad Bay migrations, Orangeburg and Londonderry, both in South Carolina. A study of the Orangeburg area, made, to be sure, at a considerable distance, reveals no trace of any such migration, whereas Londonderry does offer clues. Professor R.H. Taylor writes: "Regarding the group of German settlers who migrated from Waldoboro, Maine to Londonderry, Abbeville District, S.C., I have found a few references. In Wallace, *History of South Carolina,* Vol. II, pp. 44-46, this group is mentioned—In Wittke, *We Who Built America,* a new book, the Waldoboro group is mentioned, p. 67."

From this we may infer that there was a migration from Waldo's estates to the "Abbeville District." Whether it was made up of German Palatinates or German Swiss, we do not know. Perhaps some later historian will be able to make this a matter of on-the-spot investigation through contact with the descendants of these families still living in that area.

Waldo's colonizing projects at Broad Bay in these years were wholly in line with a larger policy of the Massachusetts government; and the aims of the Governor and of himself had much, indeed, in common. It was Waldo's plan to settle the western part of his Patent with Protestant Germans, and it was Shirley's policy to settle western Massachusetts and the more exposed portions of the Province of Maine west of the Penobscot likewise with Protestant colonists from Germany. The thought in Shirley's mind was that such settlements would serve as a buffer against the Indians, and that by increasing the number of inhabitants on the frontier, these outposts would be made more defensible and secure against the pressure of the French. It was Waldo, who, with his first colonies of Germans and Swiss-Germans, had taken the first step. Shirley was a close observer and an interested backer, since these first colonies could serve him as an experiment, and if they stuck, as a model for his own plan. So impressed was he by results that in 1742 he laid his own colonizing program before the General Court, which appointed a committee of its members to investigate, consider ways and means, and report. This was as far as the matter went at this time; for the War of the Austrian Succession (1743-1748) blocked further moves in this direction; but on the return of peace, Shirley again moved to set his program in immediate operation.

Before the advent of the war, Waldo had carried his plans, as is already apparent, considerably further than Shirley; and in 1742 they were in full swing. In the case of the migration reaching Broad Bay in this year, we find ourselves on sound historical ground, where the evidence is ample and sufficiently conclusive to offer a rather detailed story of the origin and of the coming of one of the larger of the German migrations. In the day of slow transportation in which Waldo lived, he had found that promoting his colonizing schemes both in Europe and New England at the same time was rather a large undertaking for one man. A journey to Europe could take six weeks. Then, too, moving from place to place on the continent by coach was likewise slow; and the journey back to America might require another six weeks, depending on wind and weather. In the mid-eighteenth century one man just could not devote himself to interests in both places. By engaging the services of Sebastian Zuberbuhler, Waldo hoped to avoid the necessity of further European trips on his own part.

Early in 1741 Zuberbuhler was back in Europe and had set up headquarters in Speyer at the Inn of the Golden Lion. Speyer was a strategic spot. It is situated on the south, or French side, of the Rhine below Mannheim and in the eighteenth century was in the Bishopric of Speyer between the Palatinate and Baden-Durlach, with Wurtemberg just east. This is the general area from which so many of the Broad Bay founders came. From this point he could operate in all three of these territories, and throughout this region he distributed the first known of "Waldo's circulars" which was printed in Speyer in 1741.

From other sources examined, the existence of such a document had become clear, and in October 1938 it was brought to the light of day. It is here presented for the first time, as a part of our history. It is an interesting and illuminating paper, since it lays down in detail the conditions under which some of the earliest Germans were led to embark on the great enterprise. Its formal and somewhat obsolete legal phraseology balks in spots at translation, and in such passages a freer rendering is necessary. Otherwise the document follows in a literal form:

> A short description of the Province of Massachusetts Bay in New England, especially of the tract of land on Broad Bay belonging to the Imperial British Colonel, Samuel Waldo, Hereditary Lord of Broad Bay, along with the principal conditions under which foreign protestants may settle there. Speyer, printed and available in the Gotselchen Printing House, 1741.
>
> The Province of Massachusetts Bay lies on the Atlantic Ocean and extends in general east, northeast and south southwest from the forty-first to the forty-third degree, north latitude, and is situated five hours west of the London meridian. The land consists of great strips or divisions, parts of which belong to the government, parts to the first colonists, and also to such hereditary lords as dwell in England to whom an hereditary title has been granted by the Crown, as is the case of Pennsylvania; hence the economy and the form of government rests on the same basis as in this latter colony; with this exception, that each of these provinces or districts may adopt its own regulations or laws, without having to depend on the General Assembly for them, an advantage which cannot be had elsewhere.
>
> Boston, the Capitol of this Province, has been built upwards of a hundred and fifty years and is owned and occupied by a great number of prosperous English residents. The city lies about half way between Philadelphia and Halifax in Nova Scotia.— From this latter province it is about five hundred English or approximately one hundred German miles distant and is separated from it by a large bay which is known as the Bay of Fundy. The climate here, as one can well imagine, is very healthful and the soil extremely fruitful and yields all kinds of produce as in Germany, especially, however, hemp and flax in great perfection. It is the same with the wood which grows here which is for the most part oak, beech, ash and maple. Game also is most plentiful in these forests and the streams abound with fish. Everyone is allowed to fish and to hunt. Since the previously mentioned Imperial British Colonel, Samuel Waldo, Hereditary Lord of Broad Bay, possesses there a large and fruitful grant of land yielding to none in its richness and quality, and is minded to set up there plantations and colonies, he invites all such Protestants of the Palatinate who are skillful and

industrious artisans or farmers and who so wish, to emigrate to America and to settle there on his estates, under the following terms or conditions. All those so inclined may present themselves to the accredited Agent or Commissioner of the previously mentioned Colonel and Hereditary Lord, Samuel Waldo, Mr. Sebastian Zuberbuhler, who is possessed of plenary power as well as the most gracious approval of his Serene Highness, the Elector. Mr. Zuberbuhler may be found at the Inn of the Golden Lion in Speyer and will be ready to impart all desired data or information.

There follows the advantages accorded to the colonists along with the terms and conditions:

1. Such Protestants of the Palatinate as may be inclined to emigrate to these estates of the Colonel Samuel Waldo, Hereditary Lord, etc., will present themselves to the previously mentioned Commissioner, Mr. Sebastian Zuberbuhler, where they will have to complete and sign the written articles and contracts. Then there is to be made a deposit of five imperial crowns for each adult, and the half for each person under fourteen years of age. This will serve as a guarantee that they are minded to fulfill loyally the stipulations of these articles and contracts.

2. On a day to be determined and set by the said Commissioner, Mr. Sebastian Zuberbuhler, those desirous of emigrating and the contracting parties, will report in Rotterdam, where the before mentioned Colonel Samuel Waldo, Hereditary Lord, etc., will have in readiness a ship or several ships for the transportation of such numbers of Palatinates as may present themselves. Should such a ship or ships be not there and in readiness for sailing within one week after arrival of the Palatinates in Rotterdam, then the said Colonel Samuel Waldo, Hereditary Lord, etc., is to pay them for each day after the expiration of the said seven days thirty pounds sterling as demurrage; and should the ship or ships be retarded or delayed by the Palatinates, then the Palatinates are to pay the said Waldo, Hereditary Lord, etc., fifteen pounds sterling as demurrage for each day of delay.

3. Samuel Waldo, Colonel and Hereditary Lord, etc., promises and obligates himself against the time of the arrival of the Palatine emigrants at Broad Bay in New England, to build and complete at his own expense, two houses for their domiciling—each house to be thirty-five feet square and two stories high and likewise a church; in the construction of these houses he promises to pay for each of the same one hundred pounds sterling, and for the church two hundred pounds sterling.

4. Samuel Waldo, Colonel and Hereditary Lord, etc., promises and obligates himself at his own expense to settle in the colony and to pay an engineer or a surveyor a yearly salary of one hundred pounds sterling for three years; a physician or surgeon a yearly salary of one hundred pounds sterling for five years; a preacher a yearly salary of seventy pounds sterling and a schoolmaster a yearly salary of thirty pounds sterling, each for a period of ten years.

5. Samuel Waldo, Colonel and Hereditary Lord, etc., promises and obligates himself to delimit and to lay out for the said Palatine emigrants or colonists a suitable area of land for a city, and therein to prepare and reserve for each family one quarter *morgen* or acre of ground for a house and lot. At the same time he will set aside sixty thousand *morgen* or acres of land adjoining the said city, and each settler shall receive for himself and his heirs in perpetuity a tract of fifty *morgen* or acres against the payment of a price of two shillings and a half pence for each *morgen* or acre—The said price to be paid within three years of the date of the arrival of the colonists in Broad Bay.

6. Samuel Waldo, Colonel and Hereditary Lord, etc., promises and obligates himself, for the housing maintenance of the said colonists, for a period of one year, to provide and deliver the following foodstuffs, namely; one hundred and twenty thousand pounds of beef, twenty thousand pounds of pork, sixty thousands pounds of wheat-flour, sixty thousand pounds of coarse or unbolted flour, four thousand bushels of Indian corn, four thousand bushels of salt, the one half of the above to be delivered on their arrival and the other half six months thereafter in the following manner: each person over ten years of age to receive one hundred and fifty pounds of beef, fifty pounds of pork, one hundred and fifty pounds of wheaten-flour, one hundred and fifty pounds of coarse or unbolted flour, ten bushels of Indian corn, and one bushel of salt: each person under ten years of age is to receive one half of the above.

7. Samuel Waldo, Colonel and Hereditary Lord, etc., promises and obligates himself further to furnish and to deliver to each family the following things, one cow and calf, a pregnant sow, three axes, four hoes, a spade and a handsaw. At the same time each colonist is to have the privilege and the right in the forests of the said Waldo, Colonel and Hereditary Lord, etc., to cut as much wood as he may find necessary for his own needs, *or for sale on the banks of the rivers and sea, where many vessels are ready to buy all such at four shillings a cord.*

8. These and other advantageous circumstances and conditions may, it is to be assumed, influence here and there certain Palatine and German folk to emigrate to such a fruitful country, so conveniently located on the sea and its rivers, so highly privileged, and so well governed, where the occupants enjoy so many good rights, which belongs to such a powerful and gracious Lord and which is ruled with such paternal favour. He (the gracious Lord) makes and extends this offer to all those who are in a position to defray the costs of emigrating thither, without his ever hoping or expecting to receive the slightest pay or profit for himself, and where they according to their protestant faith may worship their God undisturbed in their own right and according to their own conscience and where they may be in a position to maintain and amply support themselves and others.

Signed at Speyer on this fourteenth day of July, A.D. 1741
Samuel Waldo
Colonel and Hereditary Lord of Broad Bay in New England
Sebastian Zuberbuhler
Commissioner with plenary powers.

This is a document which glows with the promises as well as the egotism of the proprietor. Its details should be carefully noted, for many of the important episodes of the following decades is implied within them.

In the course of the winter of 1741-42, Zuberbuhler succeeded on the representations of this circular in securing a goodly number of colonists purposing to settle on Waldo's grant. In short, there were more than two hundred Palatinates and Wurtemburgers. They were Lutherans in considerable part and people in tolerable circumstances. They were in a measure moved to emigrate in consequence of the pressure exercised on them by a hostile Catholic-Reformed Church coalition. There were other factors behind their urge to leave the Old World, but it was this religious situation which tipped the scales and led them to break loose and seek a land where they could, according to Waldo's promise, practice their religion in peace. With them they had a learned, if not a pious, preacher. It was true of all the Germans that they were little prone to emigrate unless a minister accompanied them. Hence most of the agents sought a clergyman as the nucleus around which they could assemble their recruits. The spiritual leader of this colony was the Rev. Philipp Gottfried Kast, *Doktor der Theologie.* It may be inferred from later developments that Doctor Kast had collaborated with Zuberbuhler in recruiting the colony, and for his service had received a per capita commission, and that he had taken Zuberbuhler's note in payment, since at the time of their arrival at Broad Bay the latter owed him a considerable sum of money which was to become the subject of later litigation. There was also Doktor Jacob Friedrich Kurtz, *Doktor der Medezin,* as well as an engineer or surveyor whose name we do not know, and a schoolmaster, most probably John Ulmer, who was to become one of the outstanding figures in early Broad Bay history. Several of these colonists were well to do, but had sold their houses and lands to found this plantation in a new world, as it seemed to them, of freedom and unbounded promise.

It was stipulated that the migration should assemble at Mannheim, a city in the Rhenish Palatinate halfway between Worms and Speyer, on the east side of the Rhine and located on the Neckar River just above its confluence with the Rhine. Thither Zuberbuhler led those from the Palatinate. They proceeded in small river boats from Speyer down the Rhine in March, 1742. Shortly after their arrival at Mannheim, they were joined by the contingent from Wurtemburg which had proceeded in small boats down the Neckar from Heilbronn, possibly under the leadership of either Kast or Kurtz. Here the whole company transferred to larger boats for the trip down the Rhine to Rotterdam. The day of their departure from Mannheim is not known, but on the 22nd of April they reached Muhlheim just below Cologne. Here they were stopped by the intervention of the Dutch Government which demanded a guarantee that they would not be held up for any length of time in Holland without means of support. In other words, the Dutch were seeing to it that if there were delay in Rotterdam, they would not become charges of the city. This was a problem for Zuberbuhler as he did not know whether Waldo had a ship waiting to receive them or not. So he hastened on alone to Rotterdam, where he ascertained that Waldo's shipping agents had not as yet been able to make any arrangements for the reception and transportation of the emigrants. Thereupon Zuberbuhler set out for London to get information as to procedure from Waldo's agents in that city, Messrs. Sedgwick and Kilby. Because there were no ships available this firm refused to give him any idea of what he might expect. Hence the unfortunate colonists had to tarry for more than eight weeks at Muhlheim in the electorate of Cologne until relief came in the middle of June.

The time taken up by the trip from Mannheim to Cologne is uncertain. Usually at that time a journey from Speyer or Heilbronn to Holland lasted from four to six weeks by reason of the fact that Germany was split up into several hundred independent or semi-independent political units, each maintaining its own customs offices and tariffs. These were a source of indefinite delays in travelling. Some idea of this nuisance is given us by Dr. Friedrich Hermann, Professor in Lubeck. In 1804, Hermann made a tour of America and recorded his impressions in a book entitled *Die Deutschen in Amerika.* In this work he states that from Heilbronn to Rotterdam there were no less than thirty-six customs stations, at which the boats were visited by officials, concerning which he adds—"ein Gaschaft wobei die Zollbeamten mehr auf eigene Bequemlichkeit, als auf die Schnellige Abfertigung der Schiffe Rucksicht nahmen." The costs of so long a journey plus the two months sojourn in Cologne greatly depleted the slender resources of some of the emigrants. The difficulties in this respect were exacerbated by the outbreak of war between England and Spain. The activities of Spanish privateers and pirates added greatly to the hazards of trade and had markedly increased the costs of food stuffs, especially in the Netherlands. The outbreak of this war with its threat to shipping was probably also the reason why there were no ships immediately available.

We should note here an added touch of either thrift or cunning on the part of Waldo or his agent. For this we go back to the terms of the agreement, from which I quote: "Should such a ship or ships be not there and in readiness for sailing within one week after the arrival of the Palatinates in Rotterdam, then the said Colonel Samuel Waldo, Hereditary Lord, etc., is to pay them for each day after the expiration of the said seven days, thirty pounds sterling as demurrage." In other words, for

The Germans Reach Broad Bay

Zuberbuhler to have given the Dutch Government the needed assurance and taken the emigrants on to Rotterdam would have cost Waldo a tidy sum of money, whereas by holding them in Cologne they were obligated to defray their own living costs. So after many difficulties, sufferings, and delays, during which Zuberbuhler was compelled to make two trips to England, they finally reached Rotterdam on June 20, 1742. Even here their troubles were not at an end, for a ship was not at hand. The Spanish privateers made transportation precarious; and the Pennsylvania trade in emigrants, greatly on the increase and highly remunerative, made it difficult to procure a ship. Here in Rotterdam, however, after the expiration of the seven-day period, Waldo had to bear the living costs of his colonists—their first break on this unhappy journey.

In the meantime the best season of the year was passing. Spring was gone and summer was well on its way. Naturally impatience and discontent were rife. About thirty colonists, listening to the blandishments of competing shipping agents, abandoned the migration and proceeded to Pennsylvania. Others turned back home; some of the younger men enlisted as hirelings in the English army, so that the number of the colonists seems to have been reduced to a hundred and fifty or sixty. From the materials at hand, it can be inferred that Zuberbuhler was a man of considerable honesty and rectitude and a finer humanitarian than most of the professionals of this period who were engaged in this traffic. To give a completer picture of the difficulties which beset him, there is offered at this point one of his letters to Waldo written from London apparently on the occasion of his second trip to that city for the purpose of securing transportation for his group:

> Sir: It is impossible for you to conceive ye fatigues & troubles & extraordinary expenses I have gone to in this undertaking of wch I shall let you know further particulars when I see you—I have been obliged to come over to England from Germany twice to get yr Agents Messrs Sedgwick & Kilby to do their part and now that I have brought ye people down and things bean more than could be expected all Impediments considered as I shall give you a full Relation of with ye causes more at large—Thes (e) delays gave rise to suspicions among ye people being 120 full familys wch had agreed to go but have been prevented by many artifices also made use of from Merchts in Holland concerned (in) ye Pensilvania trade and who will be affected by ye success of this affair—& if these People now coming wch consists of above 200 ye greatest part young people fit for business are well received & used upon, their Report to their Friends in Germany who only send them for an essay of ye Country & usage: ye rest who are ye chief & Substantial persons all declare that they will follow next year on being satisfied of ye Solidity of ye undertaking. Thus ye whole burthen has been upon my shoulders, but as I consider that ye Intentions will be fully answered by this first small transport & that ye charges will be much lessened in ye article of provisions & they may be more easily accommodated in other respects & indeed it would have been ye more he(a)vy upon me had not Mr. Stanton encouraged & assisted me to ye thro: it being persuaded of ye good effects of it in ye end designed for yr advantage in making a flourishing settlement wch may be completed in a year more—The Minister & other officers who are men of great alliances Interests & Considerations are among these of ye first transport. Mr. Stanton & I will give you a full acct of ye money received wch is lessened by reason that ye 40 people who were to go passage free are come down among those few & their waiting for ships at charges ever since ye 20th of June wch you must imagine has greatly consumed ye Effects of ye poorer sort so that ye money paid will be but barely sufficient to Victual them—& there is but one ship ready to transport them wch is properly fitted up for ye purpose whose Owners demand 300 pounds for ye run & 40 more for ye beddings Coppers & other necessaries of wch we can get one no cheaper—Therefore am obliged to give Bills drawn on ye for ye paymt of that Sum 30 days after ye landing of ye people in New England wch I give you notice of that you may prepare for ye payment. I hope to find you in good Health & with all success to ye Undertaking wch God grant, I am Sr yr Very Hble Servt.
>
> S. Zouberbuhler.
>
> London ye 5th July 1742
>
> P.S. I set out for Holland in a few hours & expect we shall be ready to sail in 10 days or a fortnight after wch must regulat(e) yrself in sending out ye Pilot Ship to meet, as for ye Captain is a Stranger to those Ports & Coasts.

This letter provides a goodly number of historical facts and hints: the extreme difficulties under which Zuberbuhler worked; the additional expense incurred; the original number of the families; the reduction of their number through the seductions of the Rotterdam shipping merchants; the justifiable suspicion among the emigrants; the final number in the colony of two hundred souls—mostly young people; the number of the poorer folk who were to go passage free; and the cost of the voyage across.

Finally a ship was chartered, and amid great rejoicing on the part of these poor souls they sailed from Rotterdam in August. The vessel was the *Lydia* commanded by Captain James Abercrombie. On August 14th they reached Deal on the east coast of England, about twenty miles north of Dover. Here the ship remained lying for four days and from here Zuberbuhler wrote to Waldo as follows:

> Deal
> August 17th, 1742
>
> Sir:
> I arrived here three days ago with about 140 full passengers all in perfect health, ye ships name is *Lydia*, ye Capt. James Abercrombie—he never was in New England, but intends however to go directly for St. Georg River, or Cascobay. I hope all things are got ready for their reception—I expect Mr. Kilby

here to day. I wish you well ye Gentlm is just going so I can't write you more.

I am Sr your most humble servant
S. Zouberbuhler.

P.S. To morrow we shall set out & according ye wind is we shall go North about, ye people fight bravely, so there is no fear about ye Spaniards.

To Mr. Samuel Waldo Mercht. &c.
Pr. Mr. Austin Bolton.

In his letter under date of July 5th Zuberbuhler had indicated that the transport contained "above 200 passengers." From Deal on August 17th he wrote that there were on board the *Lydia* "about 140 full passengers." There had, then, been some shrinkage in the interim due to causes already noted. If, in Zuberbuhler's awkward and inexact English, this term meant full-paid "freights," as they were commonly called, the forty who were to go passage free would swell the number of the migration to an approximate figure between one hundred and seventy-five and two hundred. As these were for the most part "young people fit for business," it would follow that the number of children in the transport would be somewhat below the number usual in such migrations. Furthermore, Zuberbuhler's confusion in sometimes speaking of freights and at other times of families renders a numerical estimate difficult and uncertain.

In almost every transport to America there were a number of Germans too poor to pay the cost of passage. As previously indicated, such, on their arrival in the colonies, commonly bound themselves out to work for a number of years to whomsoever would defray the costs of their passage. In this transport there were forty such free freights and no one at the receiving end to pay their costs of passage. In this case they could only have arrived at Broad Bay as redemptioners under contract to work for Waldo for a stipulated period of years. Of such an arrangement nothing is known, although it remains a possibility that the Colonel had planned to use them in the construction of the houses and church which he had obligated himself to erect. It is also probable that they were used in 1743-1744 for work on his mills and the forts and stockades. There were also certain members of this migration who arrived in debt to Zuberbuhler. The considerable lapse of time between starting from their homes and embarking at Rotterdam had exhausted the reserve capital of some, and in order to live they had seemingly been compelled to borrow funds of Zuberbuhler. In return they had given notes to him, all payable on September 4, 1747. Among such was Joachim and Conrad Heiler who gave notes for 7 pounds 14s. 3½d., David and Phillip Rominger, with a note of 7 pounds 12s. 5d., and Hans Georg Vogler and Philip Christoph Vogler with a note for 6 pounds 10s. 9d.

On the 18th of August, then, in 1742, after four months of delay at Cologne and in Holland, and six months after they had left their homes, the *Lydia* headed out to sea. Little is known of the specific details of the trip across. War was on and in order to escape Spanish and possibly French cruisers, they sailed to the north of England and Scotland as we may infer from Zuberbuhler's letter to Colonel Waldo. The Atlantic passage took, in all probability, between six and seven weeks. At this season of the year bad weather was undoubtedly encountered which extended the normal summer duration of such a voyage. The ship, however, was clearly not overcrowded. Hence we may infer that by comparison with the Pennsylvania traffic health was good. If the ship was well provisioned, the trip must have been made in reasonable comfort. Disease, deaths, and births undoubtedly occurred, but of such History is silent.

Sometime in the early days of October, the *Lydia* reached Marblehead, which was not Captain Abercrombie's intended landfall. In the letter already quoted of Zuberbuhler to Colonel Waldo from Deal (August 17, 1742) the agent observes near the end of the epistle: "I expect Mr. Kilby here today." It is probable that Kilby brought last-minute instructions, which he had received at London from Waldo, to touch at Marblehead; for it was Waldo's plan, as will be seen, for the *Lydia* to take on additional settlers there for conveyance to his settlement on the Georges River. There were other plans, too. At Marblehead the Germans could be and were to be given something like a state reception. From this point their first letters would be sent back to relatives and friends in the Fatherland. If the reception was favorable and the reports were good, according to Zuberbuhler, those waiting on the other side for such a word could be easily induced to come the next season. So the ship made Marblehead and lay there at anchor for a few precious days. I say "precious days" because winter was steadily creeping forward. So here these unsuspecting victims of dire times ahead awaited their reception. In a few days it came—Governor Shirley and his staff, Colonel Waldo, a number of the honorable members of the General Court and the Governor's interpreter, one A. Keller by name. Colonel Waldo even brought his daughters with him. The souls of these humble Germans, unused to such honor from above, must have thrilled again and again at this show of favor from the *Obrigkeit*. Their illusionment, however, was destined to be brief. But for the moment every effort was made to give the new arrivals a favorable impression. They were dined, wined, and entertained. The letters were sent back to the old home. Then the *Lydia* headed for "eastern parts" with Zuberbuhler and Waldo himself on board, while Governor Shirley and the honorable members of the General Court returned to Boston.

In late October the colonists reached St. Georges Bay, where a number of Scotch settlers taken on at Marblehead were landed at the Georges River Settlement. Here Colonel Waldo transferred himself to another vessel, Boston bound. Anchors were then weighed and the *Lydia* entered the mouth of the Medomak and made her way up to Broad Bay, for a reception of a somewhat different order. Here there was no town, no church; no buildings stood ready for their accommodation. But there was wilderness on every hand, with the banks of the river possibly touched here and there with the tones of a late autumn glory. On the east side of the bay and river, cabins with little clearings by the shore, and on the west side and on the Neck a few more cabins and rough clearings met their gaze, relieving in a measure, perhaps, the feeling of awe and dread inspired by the lonely and interminable forests.

THE FIRST YEAR AT BROAD BAY

The *Lydia* in all probability made her way up into Broad Bay no farther than Schenck's or Trowbridge's Points, for here the channel makes in reasonably close to the shore, and here she could logically anchor and put her cargo of freight and humans ashore in small boats. Since the whole river was uncharted and perhaps unmarked, it seems hardly reasonable that the upper reaches of shallower water would have been essayed by a ship of her size. Furthermore it should be remembered that there was no concentration of population on the river at so early a date, and Trowbridge's Point was central to all the cabins scattered along the banks, and even at this time was used as a landing place for all sailing vessels coming to Broad Bay. Indeed, it became and remained the "town landing" until the development of the village at the head of tide in the early decades of the nineteenth century.

The scene that unrolled before the eyes of the Germans as the *Lydia* slowly sounded her way through the "Narrows" and up the bay, could hardly have been in line with their expectations. It was late October. Before them, along the bay and river, crude little log cabins hugged close to the banks; behind these were a few acres of cleared land, in some places still studded with stumps and formidable boulders. Beyond was an unending wilderness of evergreen broken by the fading colors of the deciduous trees. There was no sign of a "city" or village and no trace of the two large "long houses" for their winter shelter, or of the church as called for in the articles of agreement. In short, the prospect must have been not only disappointing but disquieting; and in the hearts of some there must have been a consciousness of cruel deception, as well as a vague sense of betrayal, as they gazed for the first time in their lives on the vast, untenanted wilderness.

This first impression of their new home raises the old, uncritically accepted view of General Waldo's perfidy—a view which an unbiased examination of the facts must to a very considerable degree reject; for in a large measure he, as well as his settlers, was the victim of circumstances which rather sadly messed up his plans for the successful planting of this colony. Unquestionably Waldo was somewhat unscrupulous in his business dealings, a hard bargainer, and self seeking, but so were most of the prominent business leaders of his period. It was in no sense his practice, however, to act counter to his own self-interest. At this time the major object of his life was to develop these lands in eastern parts, and it would hardly have been in keeping with his purpose to incur the very considerable expense of recruiting and transporting these settlers from Europe and then leave them to starve and die on the lands he so dearly wished to populate. Such a policy would not have been consonant with the quality of self-interest so clearly characteristic of him, and certainly Colonel Waldo was not a man given to committing absurdities.

The actual conditions faced by the Germans at Broad Bay in the winter of 1742-1743 were not as harsh as has long been depicted by popular tradition. To be sure, there was much discomfort, some suffering, and a few deaths—none of which can be categorically charged to Colonel Waldo's indifference or neglect. Rather should we give the Colonel his just, historical due by viewing conditions in the light of motives and circumstances operating at that time in this specific situation. Waldo had only recently ended a long sojourn in England, where he had successfully finished a fight to oust from the governorship of Massachusetts Bay his enemy, Jonathan Belcher. During this costly political battle and his long absence from business affairs, his fortune had been substantially reduced. In consequence he had been compelled to borrow money from his cousin, Cornelius, and to mortgage his Boston home. He was in reality close to bankruptcy, but was not a man to end his career in so abject a fashion. With his accustomed vigor he recouped his failing finances in a ruthless fashion characteristic of the business practices of the period, by bringing about in 1743 a foreclosure action against his former partner, Colonel Thomas Westbrook, and thereby acquiring all of Westbrook's properties. This was an event which led the chronicle-minded Parson Thomas Smith of Falmouth to make the following entry in his famous *Journal* under date of June 14, 1743: "Mr. Waldo came to town with an execution against Col. Westbrook for 10,500 pounds and charges."

A still more important congeries of facts throwing light on the colony at Broad Bay and its condition that first winter must be traced back to their inception in the European scene. The Germans had left their homes in the Palatinate and Wurtemberg in March 1742, consequently Waldo had good reason to believe that they would reach Broad Bay by early July at the latest, but here, as we have seen, fate again intervened, for war broke out in Europe. The Spanish privateers made English merchant shipping a precarious affair. Apart from the usual discrimination against shipping Germans to New England on the part of the Rotterdam shipping houses, the war made it more difficult to secure vessels. Despite this fact Waldo apparently continued to wait with the thought that if the colonists arrived by midsummer he could provide the lumber and have the houses and church built by the Germans themselves. This was shrewd and reasonable, since it would save him the cost of importing labor as well as that of wages and food. As the summer advanced he continued to delay and take chances, largely because of his lack of cash or credit. This proved to be a gross misjudgment, and for the colonists a tragic error—an error of judgment, however, rather than deliberate intent on the part of Mr. Waldo.

These facts and conditions make it reasonably clear why, when the Germans arrived at Broad Bay late in October 1742, so few arrangements had been made for their accommodation. The *Lydia* undoubtedly had taken aboard at Marblehead a substantial store of food, as well as the axes, hoes, spades, handsaws, and other tools specified in the original contract; for without these, of course, few settlers could have survived the winter. It has always been generally assumed that such tools and equipment were brought by the colonists from Germany, but such was not the case. The long journeys overland and by small river boats precluded this, and besides it was not allowed by the Rotterdam shipping firms which made their profits in this trade by packing in a maximum of human cargo and a minimum of personal belongings. Whether in the Pennsylvania or New England traffic, each adult was allowed a single wooden chest which contained his clothing, a little bedding, small personal articles, in some cases a few pieces of gold or silver, a copy of family marriages, births, and deaths copied from the Church Register in the Old Country, a Bible, a Prayer or Hymn Book, a copy of Arndt's *Das Wahre Christentum*, the Augsburger Confession of Faith, and Luther's Catechism if they were Lutherans, and the Heidelberger Catechism if they were of the Reformed Church. The chest of the immigrant, Feyler, who came in this colony is still in the possession of the Feyler family at Broad Bay, and it may be regarded as typical. It is four feet and nine inches in length; two feet in depth and twenty-three inches in width. It is made of semi-hard boards, mortised at the four corners—

boards seven-eighths to one inch in thickness. The cover is secured on the back by two handmade hinges which are each a part of a handmade iron strap running around the chest and ending on the front side, a couple of inches below the cover, in an eye. Directly above this in the cover is a rough eye bolt. The chest was made fast by a lashing passed between these two eyes and secured. This or chests similar in size and construction were standard equipment for all the German migrants to the New World.

Once ashore along the waterfront Mr. Zuberbuhler and the engineer assumed the roles of guidance and leadership. It was a chore of no small order to organize and direct the energy and activity of upwards of two hundred people toward the detailed and complicated task of establishing themselves in a wilderness with so little time separating them from cold weather. The first act of settlement must have been to set up shelters for their stores, and to erect crude, open-air fireplaces for the preparation of food. It is possible that during the night the newcomers were sheltered in the sheds, lean-tos and in some cases the cabins of those who were already mercifully settled in their own homes. Then there were doubtless those who spent the first nights around campfires in the open, until rough, temporary structures were built for sleeping and protection against the weather. What these were we can only conjecture—possibly shelters of interwoven brush, or conical huts of branches laid up with turf, such as the charcoal burners used in England, or holes dug in the river banks with timbered-over ceilings. All such structures had been used as their first homes by the earliest settlers in Massachusetts, and certainly it was an architectural pattern well known to the English-speaking settlers already located at Broad Bay. The weather during these fall days was mercifully mild. Parson Smith was a faithful weather recorder, and the entries in his useful *Journal* indicate an unusually late autumn. Under October 18, 1742, we learn of "some unusually hot days about this time," and another most revealing comment on December 23: "Wonderful weather for about ten days past; *there has been no cold weather yet*." These entries provide the assurance that after their landing the colonists had a full eight weeks of tolerable weather before winter set in in earnest around them. There is also good reason to believe that in this period Mr. Waldo was busy in their interests; for there is a letter written to him by a Joseph Plaisted, dated York, October 19, 1742, in which a report is given on certain problems connected with the raising of money, on the prices of certain food supplies, and on the strong possibility of Plaisted being able "to git five or six yoke of oxen." It is somewhat difficult to avoid the conclusion that coming just at this time, these activities were in the interests of the new Broad Bay settlers.

Amid the uncertainties faced, Providence was at least beneficent in vouchsafing to these strangers a chance to construct log cabins before the advent of harsh weather. Mr. Zuberbuhler, the engineer, and possibly Mr. Waldo took the lead in assigning lots to each family. These were in the main on the east bank of the river, in an area stretching roughly from the present farm of Foster Jameson up along the river to the district above the first falls. These lots were contiguous save here and there where a lot was pre-empted by an older settler. It is probable that the lots were already surveyed and staked out, but if such were not the case it is reasonably certain that at this time the engineer would have done little more than survey the shore frontage, mark the bounds with numbered stakes and then from these stakes run the lines back into the woods for a short distance, in order to give each settler in the briefest time an area on which he could cut his logs and build his cabin. Most of the lots were laid out with a frontage on the river of twenty-five rods from which the lines were run back into the country on a due east course for a sufficient distance to embrace one hundred acres. This method of apportioning land was the one almost universally employed in locating settlers on all Maine rivers; but it was not in line with the plan of the original contract, under which the settlers would have been concentrated on quarter-acre lots in a compact village settlement with their farm lands set aside in lots scattered through the surrounding country, as was and is the case today in the more thickly populated areas of Germany.

Taken as a whole, the evidence is reasonably conclusive that the abodes of the Broad Bay Germans this first winter were log cabins. Contrary to general belief log cabins were not an original American type of dwelling. They were introduced into the New World by the Swedes and Finns on the Delaware and did not appear on the New England frontier until the eighteenth century. They were, however, a well-established architectural type by the time the first Germans arrived at Broad Bay. The settlements on the Georges, along the sound, and the few scattered dwellings on the Medomak were of this type, so the Germans had models ready at hand. Their first cabins, however, were crude, constructed as they were in a race with winter. The material was ready at hand, and as they felled the trees for their dwellings they were preparing their land for crops the next spring. About a month is required for the construction of a log cabin, but the Germans, being new at such a task, required somewhat more time despite the goodly number of carpenters in this migration.

These cabins of the first winter were one- or two-room structures with a floor of clay or flat field stones, and with the chinks between the logs filled in with clay in which dried grass was used for a binder. There was no time to build chimneys, nor was the material available. In lieu of these a rough stone fireplace was erected near the end or corner of the room and the smoke escaped through a hole in the roof. There was no dearth of firewood, but the character of the log structures was not such that a maximum of warmth could be utilized. The long and providential Indian summer was a period of strenuous effort which enabled the colonists to make a fair provision against the advent of winter and Colonel Waldo to get supplies to the settlement before the river was closed by ice. We catch a glimpse of the awkward activity of these Germans, operating under conditions frighteningly strange to them, from a letter of complaint written by one of their English neighbors to Colonel Waldo, of which a relevant portion is here cited:

Broad Bay, December 9, 1742

...This is to lett know my Missfortunes since you wass with us last. Ye Ingeneares man Hass Kilt a Steere of mine and Settled with ye Ingenear about Itt. He fell a tree on him and Brooke his back. They Killed and Kept him for nine Days, and sent ye 4 Quarters and hide to my house with a Gard of men, thru them in and went thire way, nobody a tome but my wife. I would Doo nothing to him until I sent you—. If there is not Method taken with them they may kill All ye Creaters wee have.

(Signed) James Littell

From this letter a number of interesting inferences may be derived: the Germans were clearly organized and operating under the leadership of the engineer; a considerable friction and ill-will already existed between them and the older English, Scotch-Irish settlers of 1736; and Colonel Waldo was on the scene in person during these strenuous days of preparation, which was entirely to his credit and indicative of his concern and interest. Furthermore it is clear evidentially that he lived up to contract in the matter of food supplies before the ice closed the river for the winter. Mr. Zuberbuhler remained with the colony until well into December, and doubtless left on one of the last supply or cordwood coasters before the closing of the river.

Such preparations, under conditions faced, were good insurance against the advent of cold weather, but could not have been adequate against exposure sickness. A serious drawback was to be found in the fact that few of the Germans at this time possessed firearms, which made it impossible to draw fully on wild life for a supply of fresh meat, but there was fish and shellfish a plenty, which could be drawn upon richly to supplement the food. Despite all this there was suffering, disease, and death. Among the victims, probably of exposure, was the unnamed engineer or surveyor who left a widow and some small children. His death was unquestionably a grave loss to the little community, which in its extreme isolation could ill afford the loss of a trained leader, and especially so in the midst of winter when the problem of survival was most acute.

CHAPTER 8.

The following account describes the preparations made by the Massachusetts authorities to organize the great expedition against Louisbourg. Maine men, as will be apparent, played a significant role in this famous battle.

ORGANIZING THE EXPEDITION*
(February-March, 1745)
by
George Rawlyk

Preparations for the expedition against Louisbourg began on February 5, 1745. After reluctantly agreeing to send the expedition, the General Court of Massachusetts outlined the broad framework of policy within which it expected the governor to work. Shirley was instructed to raise a force of 3,000 volunteers and to appoint all necessary officers. Each noncommissioned volunteer was to be paid 25 shillings per month and was to be given one blanket. To facilitate recruiting, the governor was empowered to offer the volunteers one month's pay in advance, as well as to promise that they would be "entital'd to all the Plunder." In addition, unspecified arrangements were to be made "for the furnishing of necessary Warlike Stores for the Expedition" and for the securing of four months' provisions. A committee of the General Court was to be appointed to procure and to fit out vessels to transport troops and supplies to Louisbourg and it was hoped that these vessels would be ready to sail by March 12. Moreover, the governor was to write to the "Governments of New York, the Jerseys, Pennsylvania, New Hampshire, Connecticut & Rhode Island to furnish their respective Quotas of Men & Vessels to Accompany or follow the Forces" of Massachusetts. Finally, to prevent the enemy from learning of the expedition, Shirley was to place an embargo upon all Massachusetts shipping, presumably until the expedition finally sailed from Boston. Furthermore, all French nationals and other "suspected persons" were to be arrested and special "Watchmen" were to be stationed on various roads throughout the colony "to search suspected passengers." Once put into force the embargo not only proved successful in keeping the French ignorant of the projected expedition until after it sailed, but also made available numerous vessels to transport men and supplies to Louisbourg.

It was clear to Shirley and to many of the members of the General Court that few men would volunteer to serve in the expedition until an unusually popular commander-in-chief was appointed. One critical observer went so far as to maintain that:

> Fidelity, resolution and popularity must supply the place of military talents; . . . It was necessary that the men should know and love their General, or they would not enlist under him.

Even though Shirley possessed the power to appoint such an officer independently, he nevertheless preferred to consult the General Court before making his final decision. He realized that if the General Court was to maintain its enthusiasm for the Louisbourg venture its approval of the commander-in-chief was imperative.

Four men eagerly offered their services to Shirley—William Vaughan, Samuel Waldo, Lieutenant-Governor Benning Wentworth of New Hampshire and John Bradstreet. Vaughan's offer was never taken seriously by Shirley, who like many members of the General Court regarded Vaughan as a "whimsical wild projector" and as an ambitious "outsider." Shirley did not wish to see

---

*George Rawlyk, *Yankees at Louisbourg* (Orono: University of Maine Press, 1967), pp. 41-57. Permission to reprint granted by the publisher.

Vaughan receive all the credit and the reward for originating and carrying out the expedition. As far as Shirley was concerned, Vaughan had served his purpose and now could be discarded.

Samuel Waldo was an active member of the General Court and one of Shirley's closest friends. A land speculator on a grand scale, Waldo had purchased the questionable Alexander land rights to Nova Scotia in 1730. In 1745, confronted by serious financial difficulties, Waldo saw in the Louisbourg project an excellent opportunity to have his claim to much of Nova Scotia recognized by the British government. However, Waldo lacked the required popular appeal, and his close association with Shirley was resented by the General Court. Shirley probably resisted a temptation to accept Waldo's offer, realizing that such an appointment would result in violent criticism and lack of support in the General Court and throughout the colony. Waldo had to be satisfied with a brigadier-general's commission.

Wentworth, apparently temporarily dissatisfied with his position as Lieutenant-Governor of New Hampshire, considered himself to be admirably qualified to lead the expedition. When the gouty governor informed Shirley of his willingness to sail to Louisbourg, the startled Shirley immediately shattered Wentworth's dream:

> Upon communicating y^r offer of your taking the Command of the Expedition and proceeding in it, to two or three Gentlemen in whose prudence & judgm^t I most confide, I found 'em clearly of opinion y^t any alteration of the present command would be attended with great risque, both with respect to our assembly and soldiers being intirely disgusted.

John Bradstreet, who had had some limited military experience at Canso, regarded himself as a military strategist and leader of considerable note. Shirley was evidently impressed with Bradstreet's ability and, if Bradstreet's journal is to be taken seriously, offered him the command of the expedition. However, "finding it would be difficult to raise a Sufficient Number of Men Unless under the Command of one of their own Country Men," Shirley was forced to withdraw his offer. In all likelihood Shirley's offer was not made in good faith. He realized that Bradstreet did not have the necessary qualifications. But in order to cajole Bradstreet into joining the expedition, Shirley felt compelled to offer him the command with one hand and then immediately take it back with the other. Shirley was an astute judge of character; Bradstreet eventually joined the expedition as the commander-in-chief's special military adviser.

One man, William Pepperrell, towered above all possible candidates, but he showed little enthusiasm at first to lead the expedition. Shirley soon came to realize that Pepperrell, who had been a member of the General Court since 1727 and who in 1745 was president of the Council and colonel of the Maine militia, was the only man with the necessary qualifications to serve as commander-in-chief. Pepperrell was an unusually successful merchant "of unblemished reputation, of engaging manners, extensively known both in Massachusetts and New Hampshire, and very popular." His military experience, however, had been limited to the none too exacting inspection of frontier defences and to the general organization and training of the Maine militia. But there were very few Massachusetts residents who had more military experience than Pepperrell, and there was certainly no one who had any satisfactory training or experience in the technical side of warfare.

Almost immediately after the General Court accepted the resolution of the special committee under the chairmanship of Pepperrell to undertake the Louisbourg expedition, Pepperrell was approached by Shirley and leading members of the General Court "to head ye forces." Pepperrell politely yet firmly refused—"Mrs. Pepperrell being in an ill state of health & my business unsettled." Pepperrell's refusal spurred Shirley and the Court members into increasing their pressure upon the reluctant Piscataqua merchant. They emphasized that unless he acceded to their request, there would be no expedition. Instead the French from Louisbourg would probably invade "ye eastern part of New England, & Newfoundland would have stood but a poor chance, so that ye greatest part of ye codd fishery in a short time would have been in ye French hands, and great part of our trade to New England, Verginia, etc. intercept^d by y^m." Pepperrell found himself on the horns of a dilemma. He did not want "to undertake so dangerous and fatiguing an Enterprize," but he also did not want to jeopardize the sending of the expedition. Thoroughly confused and burdened by the fear that his refusal might in fact lead to the destruction of Massachusetts, Pepperrell sought the advice of a close friend, the evangelist George Whitefield who was in Boston conducting "a hopeful Revival of Religion." Whitefield assured Pepperrell that:

> ...if he did undertake it, he would beg of the Lord God of armies to give him a single eye; that the means proposed to take Louisbourg, in the eye of human reason, were no more adequate to the end, than the sounding of rams' horns to blow down Jericho; but that, if Providence really called him, he would return more than conqueror.

After much prayer and after receiving the "free consent" of his wife, Pepperrell on the following day, February 11, declared that he would accept Shirley's offer to lead the expedition and was commissioned Lieutenant-General and Commander-in-Chief of all land and sea forces.

Pepperrell's appointment "paid enormous political dividends to Shirley." By gaining the wholehearted support of the powerful Pepperrell faction in the General Court, Shirley had at last been able to unite formerly warring factions under his own firm leadership. In February 1745 Shirley's position in Massachusetts had never been stronger. To consolidate his position further, Shirley appointed his friends and allies—men such as Joseph Dwight, Robert Hale, John Choate, Shuball Gorham—to the vitally important and financially remunerative colonelcies in the expedition force.

With Pepperrell's acceptance the recruiting campaign began in earnest. The campaign was carefully planned by Shirley and his supporters. A concerted propaganda barrage was intended to prepare the way for the recruiting officers. Across the length and breadth of Massachusetts, supporters of the expedition led by the energetic Vaughan proclaimed that the capture of Louisbourg was simply a matter of sailing there. The French fortress was "slenderly Fortified" and its garrison was eager to surrender to an invading force. Moreover, it was stressed that the Louisbourg merchants and officers possessed vast sums of money and other valuables—readily obtainable plunder that would doubtless make each volunteer a rich man. Some ministers of the gospel, but not all, joined the propaganda chorus. By giving the expedition the motto *'Nil desperandum Christo duce'* Whitefield tried to transform it into a Protestant crusade. One poetic divine declared:

> For Zion's Sake hold not your Peace
> While She's in such Distress,
> Compressed by Vast Thousands of
> The Sons of Wickedness. . . .
>
> 'Tis nothing less than Christ himself,
> These Anti-Christians fight,
> And if it were but in their power
> They'd ruin his Kingdom quite. . . .
>
> Ev'n so, Lord Jesus, quickly come,
> In thine almighty Power,
> Destroy proud Antichrist, O Lord,
> And quite consume the Whore.

Another pious Calvinist exclaimed:

> . . . And how sweet and pleasant will it be . . . to be the person under God that shall reduce and pull down that stronghold of Satan and sett up the kingdome of our exalded Saviour. O, that I could be . . . in that single church [in Louisbourg] to destroy ye images their sett up, and ye true Gospel of our Lord and Savior Jesus Christ their preached.

To other ministers, the Louisbourg expedition was imperative to see clearly whether their God was pleased with the spiritual growth of the Massachusetts Church. The capture of Louisbourg would be convincing proof that their God was still their "great Preserver and Benefactor."

From the beginning of the campaign there was "a considerable readiness in many to enlist," especially in the Maine region. Many men sought commissions for other reasons than their anti-Roman Catholic feeling or their fear of a possible French invasion. They wanted commissions because of "a hope, well or ill grounded, that if the place be taken they may have their commissions confirmed at home, and so have either a full sterling pay, if they are employed, and if they are dismissed a half-pay." One frank father wrote Pepperrell:

> The Prospect of Profit either by Wages or Plunder had no Weight in ye Scale to induce my Son to engage in the expedition... what he principally aimed at is a Capt[s] Commission in the King's Pay. I have been told the Company of Volunteers who went to Annapolis last summer were (as soon as advice of it got home) put in the British Pay and if that be true, I suppose Cape Breton if it be reduced will be garrisoned in part by New England Volunteers upon the Same Establishment and the Officers have commissions from the Crown, as it should be so.

After receiving their commissions from Shirley authorizing them "to beat . . . Drums" within a certain militia regiment "for the enlisting of Volunteers," some officers went to great lengths to persuade volunteers to enlist:

> [Captain Sewell] called his men to his own house & generously entertained them all with a dinner & much encouraged them to engage in the present expedition, promising to as many . . . as would go that he w[d] give them out off his own pocket so much as with the Province pay they sh[d] have 8£ p[r] month. And that if any of their familys were in want he would supply them so that they sh[d] not suffer.

James Gibson, a Boston merchant and former officer in the Royal Regiment of Foot Guards in Barbados, raised "some hundreds" of volunteers at his own expense. Vaughan was so successful in raising men that the jealous Shirley eventually ordered him "to stop enlisting." A few audacious individuals recruited volunteers without first receiving commissions from Shirley. After they had collected together a regiment of volunteers, they demanded commissions. Usually Shirley gladly met their demands.

The rank and file had various reasons for enlisting. The desire for plunder was probably the most important single reason. Only a few years earlier, hundreds in Massachusetts had rushed to volunteer to participate in the Carthagena expedition to the Caribbean. So many volunteered in Massachusetts, in fact, that a large number had to be turned away. These men were not primarily interested in driving the Spanish from the West Indies; they were concerned with filling their empty pockets with Spanish gold. The Louisbourg expedition was regarded in a similar light, though some men were motivated by "The Expectation of Seeing Great things, etc." and others were convinced that unless the French were driven from Louisbourg the French fortress "was Like to prove Detremental if not Destroying to our Country." It seems that only a relatively small number of men volunteered solely because of their strong anti-Roman Catholic feeling.

To stimulate further the recruiting campaign the General Court on February 18 adopted a wage list for volunteers serving in the land force and also clarified certain details regarding bounty payments and subsistence and other allowances. Colonels were to receive £15 new tenor monthly, Captains £4, 10 shillings, Lieutenants £3, Chaplains £4, 10 shillings, Corporals £1, 8 shillings. Ordinary soldiers were to be allowed, in addition to their monthly pay of 25 shillings, £1 bounty money on enlisting and a weekly subsistence allowance of 5 shillings. Also they were to be given "a Gill and half of Rum pr Day for the first Month and one Gill pr Day afterwards." There is evidence to suggest that the General Court went even further "to Incourage men to Inlist" by proposing:

> ... that the Widows or nearest relatives of any officer or soldier that is slain or shall otherwise loose his life in the service, shall be entitled to four months pay.
> And that the wives of any officer or soldier in the Expedition or any other person that appears with a power of Attorney duly authenticated, shall at the end of every month receive out of the Treasury half or all the wages of such officer or soldier.

There may have been good financial reasons therefore for the women of Massachusetts supporting the Louisbourg expedition with such unusual vigour! Two days later the Court resolved to give each captain "two Shillings and six Pence for the Charge of inlisting each effective Man." Two weeks earlier the Court had agreed "That half a Pound of Ginger, and one Pound and an half of Sugar, be allowed each Soldier that proceeds in the intended Expedition against Louisbourg."

The recruiting campaign met with vigorous opposition in certain quarters, and this opposition was partly responsible for preventing the expedition from sailing on the intended date, March 12. There were three main centres of opposition in Massachusetts. First, an undetermined number of fishing entrepreneurs discouraged their workmen from volunteering, in the hope that when the embargo on shipping was lifted they would be able to fish on the Sable Island Bank and elsewhere without any immediate fear of French attacks. Would not the French in Louisbourg be far more concerned with the New England invading force than with a few harmless fishing vessels? Second, a small number of clergymen vociferously argued that those who volunteered "would dye there [at Louisbourg] and be dammn'd to[o]." The souls of too many of the potential volunteers were still unregenerate and thus death would open wide the gates to everlasting torment. Third, frontier inhabitants, fearing possible Indian attacks, did all in their power "to keep the people at home." In spite of the concerted opposition to the expedition, by April 4 over 3,000 Massachusetts residents had volunteered to serve in the land force and some 1,000 to man the expedition's ships.

The unexpected delay in the sailing of the expedition—the first Massachusetts contingent did not sail until April 4 and the second until two days later—was only partly the result of the persistent opposition to the scheme. The delay was also caused by the unexpected difficulty in obtaining supply and transport ships and sailors to man them, by the belated and often negative response of the other colonial governments to Shirley's urgent appeal for aid, and by Shirley's decision to wait until the last possible moment to see whether British warships from the Caribbean would join the expedition.

Apparently the General Court accepted without question Vaughan's wild claim that the Marblehead merchants themselves would supply a sufficient number of ships to transport 3,500 troops and the necessary provisions to Louisbourg by the middle of February. As a result, the Court concentrated upon the raising of a land force and did very little to encourage owners to offer their vessels and sailors to volunteer to man them. By early March, however, the complacency of the Court about the naval aspects of the expedition was shattered by the realization that unless transports were immediately found, the expedition could not sail in time to take advantage of Louisbourg's weaknesses. On March 10 the Court resolved to pay each captain of a transport vessel sailing in the expedition £3 monthly, each mate £2, 10 shillings, and each ordinary seaman £2. It is interesting to note that the ordinary seaman received a higher monthly wage than the ordinary volunteer in the land force. If such an arrangement had been made at the start of the recruiting campaign, it is highly doubtful that very many men from the coastal areas of Massachusetts would have volunteered to serve in the land force. By March 10, however, the recruiting of land forces had advanced so favourably that the Court could offer sailors more pay, especially since there was a greater need for seamen. In order to obtain ships, the Court decided on March 12:

> ... That the several Vessels that are or shall be taken up in the Service of the Province in the intended Expedition, be and they hereby are insured by the Government, according to the several Apprizements taken by Persons under Oath."

Eventually the money the shipowners were undoubtedly promised for the use of their vessels and the inability of the owners to make profitable use of their vessels in any other way because of the embargo, induced a sufficient number of them to come to the aid of the Court, but not until after the original departure date.

In his circular letter of February 9, sent to all the colonial governors north of and including Pennsylvania, Shirley requested "Land & Sea" assistance for the Louisbourg expedition. He argued that such an expedition would provide for "the safety of the trade and navigation" of all the colonies north of Pennsylvania. Shirley further promised that the British government would dispatch a sizeable fleet of warships to "Support us in our Design." Shirley's letter was carried to the various governors by members of the Massachusetts General Court chosen because of their persuasive powers.

The New Jersey government brusquely rejected Shirley's request. Seeking a scapegoat, Governor Lewis Morris declared that the powerful Quakers were responsible for his government's refusal to support the expedition. He would have been closer to the mark if he had maintained that there was really no concern in New Jersey about the Louisbourg threat and consequently little interest in the proposed expedition.

Governor George Thomas of Pennsylvania laid Shirley's request before the Assembly during a special session, which was not called, however, until March 8. Thomas urged the Assembly to send Shirley a "Provision of Money." He pointed out that:

> The Conquest of Louisbourg, which is the only French Port of Consequence in this Part of the World, either for Strength or the Accommodation of large Ships, will banish all apprehensions for the future of Maritime Attempts upon the Colonies, or their Trade upon this Coast, ... Dispatch, you will see, is the life of the undertaking.

But the Quaker-controlled Assembly refused to accept Thomas' recommendation. One member declared:

> We have often been importun'd to do something in our own Defence, and have always refus'd: Therefore it will not become us to raise Men and Money to go and disturb those that neither meddle nor make with us; People with whom we have nothing to do.

Some members who did not share *"the religious Principles* of the Majority agreed with Benjamin Franklin when he wrote to his brother in Massachusetts:

> Fortified towns are hard nuts to crack; and your teeth have not been accustomed to it. Taking strong places is a particular trade which you have taken up without serving an apprenticeship to it. Armies and veterans need skilful engineers to direct them in their attack. Have you any? But some seem to think forts are as easy taken as snuff.

The consensus of the Assembly members was that since they had not been consulted beforehand regarding the expedition, and since there were no instructions from Whitehall, it would be extremely imprudent "to unite in an Enterprize where the Expence must be great, perhaps much bloodshed, and the Event very Pennsylvania's money could be spent on much more worthwhile projects.

In spite of a ringing appeal to the New York Assembly to provide men and ships for the expedition, Governor George Clinton had to be satisfied with lending Shirley ten 18-pound cannon with their carriages and other equipment. The Assembly refused to support the expedition in any other manner because its members wished to concentrate New York's military effort on its exposed northern frontier. Moreover, the Assembly was locked in bitter dispute with the governor and stubbornly refused to adopt his Louisbourg policy largely because he had advocated it. Shirley was overjoyed on hearing on March 13 of Clinton's offer to lend the ten cannon. Up to that date Shirley had serious reservations regarding whether the expedition should sail with what he considered to be totally inadequate artillery. Clinton's offer drove all doubts from Shirley's mind and the Massachusetts governor quickly abandoned his

On February 16 the Rhode Island Assembly considered Shirley's request for assistance. "After a long and Tedious Debate" the Assembly decided to raise 130 seamen to man the Colony sloop *Tartar*. The *Tartar*, after being "equipped with all necessary warlike stores," was to join the Massachusetts expedition "at the place of rendezvous." The Assembly, however, refused to raise a land force since there was no guarantee that the expedition would be supported by the British government or even by the Massachusetts people. Had not the resolution favouring the expedition been "carry'd but by one single Vote?" Furthermore, most of the members of the Assembly resented the fact that the Massachusetts government had undertaken "the Conquest of Cape Breton, without previously consulting their Neighbours."

Shirley was totally dissatisfied with what he considered to be Rhode Island's miserable response to his reasonable request. He was grateful for the promise of the *Tartar* and also pleased that two Newport merchants had consented to have two of their privateers, the *Fame* and *Caesar*, chartered by the Massachusetts government. But the governor wanted some Rhode Islanders to join the land force. He therefore wrote to Governor William Greene of Rhode Island on March 15 and insisted that Rhode Island supply at least a token land force for the Louisbourg expedition.

On receiving Shirley's letter, which promised among other things that the expedition would definitely be supported by "some of his Majesty's Ships of War from the West Indies and Great Britain," the Rhode Island Assembly completely reversed its former Louisbourg policy. One hundred and fifty men were to be "enlisted as soldiers" and nine men as commissioned officers. Apart from the bounty of 30 shillings new tenor, 10 shillings more than the Massachusetts bounty, the wages to be paid the volunteers and other arrangements were exactly patterned after those of Massachusetts. Furthermore, the Assembly empowered Shirley to enlist up to 350 Rhode Islanders to serve in the Massachusetts contingent, offering 10 shillings bounty, in addition of course to the Massachusetts bounty, to those who volunteered.

There were probably two main reasons for the Assembly's reversal of policy. First, the bitter boundary controversy between Rhode Island and Massachusetts had not as yet been settled by the British authorities. The Rhode Island Assembly members feared that if the Louisbourg expedition succeeded and there were no Rhode Islanders in the land force, inevitably the British government would support the Massachusetts claims in the boundary question. Second, on hearing that Connecticut and New Hampshire had decided to send sizeable land forces to Louisbourg, pride compelled Rhode Island to do likewise.

To enunciate a policy was one thing; to implement it successfully was another. Rhode Islanders refused to volunteer, many hurried off instead to man the large number of privateers. Only some ninety men served on the *Tartar*, which was destined to play an important role in the expedition. Eventually the government was forced "to impress Men to compleat the Companies," but before the Rhode Island force could sail Louisbourg had already fallen.

Unlike its sister "Old Charter" government, the Connecticut Assembly, on first being informed of Shirley's Louisbourg scheme resolved "(relying on the blessings of Almighty God) to joyn . . . in the intended expedition." It was agreed that a land force of 500 men was to be raised under the command of the deputy-governor of the colony, Roger Wolcott. Wolcott more than any other man was responsible for this decision. He wanted to see the French driven from Louisbourg and he vigourously asserted the importance of sacrificing "domestic ease and. . .private interests, to the more important concerns of the public." The

Connecticut volunteers were to receive higher bounties and wages than those in Massachusetts. In addition, the colony's guard sloop, the *Defence,* was to be "equipped and manned with her full complement of officers and men" to convoy the Connecticut transports from New London to Canso.

Armed with the Assembly's Louisbourg resolutions, two of its most prominent members, "Jonathan Trumble and Elisha Williams," made their way to Boston fully prepared for some hard bargaining with Shirley. They demanded that Wolcott be appointed second-in-command to Pepperrell. Only if this were done, would they guarantee that 500 volunteers would be raised in Connecticut. After consulting Pepperrell, who regarded Wolcott as "a Gentleman of ... Wisdom & Experience," Shirley gave Wolcott "the Second Command over the Forces raised for the Expedition against Cape Breton." When news of Shirley's decision reached Connecticut, probably on March 20 or 21, the recruiting campaign began in earnest. Eventually 516 men, including commissioned officers, were enlisted largely because of Wolcott's unusual popularity. But the scarcity of guns, ammunition, supplies, and transport vessels and generally bad organization prevented the Connecticut fleet from sailing from New London until April 25, some three weeks after the Massachusetts fleet left Boston. The Connecticut fleet consisted of seven transports and two armed vessels, the *Defence* and the *Tartar.*

Shirley had confidently expected that Benning Wentworth, could persuade the members of the New Hampshire House of Representatives to provide men and supplies for the expedition. By so doing, the New Hampshire government would serve as an excellent example for the other colonies. Shirley, however, had underestimated the growing independence of the New Hampshire House and over-estimated the political power of Wentworth.

After carefully examining Shirley's request for aid, the members of the House of Representatives, on February 13, declared that they were in favour of raising at least 250 volunteers but only "if proper methods may be concluded on for defraying the charge." By "proper methods" they meant the printing of £4,000 of new money. Three days later the House further clarified its policy. They asked Wentworth to have £10,000 printed "towards the Defraying the charge of the said Expedition for the Reduction of Louisbourg & the further carrying on the warr against his Majesty's Enemies & for the necessary support of this his Majesty's Government." Special taxes to be levied during the period 1755 to 1765 were to provide funds "for Drawing in & Sinking the said Bills." In advocating such an inflationist policy, the New Hampshire House was following the example of the Massachusetts House of Representatives which had had £50,000 printed, "for putting the Province in a better Posture of Defence." The New Hampshire House of Representatives was controlled by paper-money advocates who saw in the Louisbourg affair an extraordinary opportunity to force their inflationary views upon a hitherto hostile Council and lieutenant-governor. The House stressed that unless Wentworth acceded to their request regarding the issue of paper money, they would refuse to pass the necessary legislation for the recruiting of Louisbourg volunteers. By February 16 the battle lines were clearly drawn and neither side contemplated surrender or even compromise. The stubborn Wentworth maintained that he had received definite instructions from Whitehall not to print "any more money than what is now Extant." On the other hand, the members of the House vehemently argued that unless money was printed there would be no New Hampshire contingent in the Louisbourg expedition and in all probability the "naked and defenceless" frontiers of the colony would be overrun by Indian allies of the French. To the House the capture of Louisbourg was of great significance, but the successful defence of the immediate frontiers of the colony was considered to be of far greater consequence.

Confronted by the unexpected New Hampshire impasse, the disconcerted Shirley proposed to Wentworth that five or six companies of volunteers be raised in New Hampshire to serve in the Massachusetts force and to be paid by the Massachusetts government. Shirley also tried to persuade Wentworth to "consent to the Emission of a further sum in bills" because of the "extraordinary Emergency." Shirley was not the only one who was disappointed with New Hampshire's refusal to support the Louisbourg expedition. Many New Hampshire residents, stirred by Vaughan's vision and encouraged by Pepperrell, began to exert considerable pressure upon Wentworth. Finally on

February 23 and 24, after the House of Representatives had resolved to raise 350 volunteers and pay them according to the Massachusetts scale, Wentworth agreed to the emission of £13,000. It should be noted, however, that the House intended to spend less than one half of the £13,000 on the Louisbourg expedition. The New Hampshire House of Representatives had indeed won a notable victory.

On hearing of the resolution passed by the New Hampshire House and agreed to by Wentworth, Shirley decided that only 150 men should be raised in New Hampshire and paid by the Massachusetts government. Furthermore, he ordered these men to serve under the officer in charge of the New Hampshire-paid volunteers, Colonel Samuel Moore. When the New Hampshire fleet of transports sailed for Canso on April 3, only 456 volunteers were on board, including the thirty-odd men who manned the colony guard vessel. The number of New Hampshire volunteers had fallen some fifty short of the desired goal.

Since he had serious reservations regarding the strong emphasis placed upon the element of surprise in the plan to capture Louisbourg accepted by the Massachusetts General Court, Shirley on February 9 wrote to Sir Chaloner Ogle, commander of the British squadron stationed at Jamaica, and to Commodore Peter Warren, commander of the Leeward Islands squadron, asking for naval assistance. In his letter to Ogle, Shirley stressed that the success of the expedition depended to a considerable degree upon the arrival in Louisbourg waters by at least May of some British warships. By blockading the French fortress with British warships, Shirley hoped to prevent the landing of the expected French reinforcements and supplies and thus provide "the finishing hand to this important Enterprise." He was confident of naval aid:

> [since] the success of this affair will be attended with such Advantages to the Crown and the Trade, not only of all the Northern Plantations in America, but even of Great Britain itself, by securing to his Majesty the Fortress of Annapolis Royal, and the whole province of Nova Scotia, and by preserving that valuable Branch of our Trade which depends on our Fishery . . . I doubt not but you will contribute everything in Your power to Our Assistance.

Ogle did not receive Shirley's letter until March 25 when his command was at an end. He forwarded it to his successor Admiral Davers with a trenchant remark—"I am of opinion that it is not in Your power to comply with Mr. Shirley's request." Ogle's advice to Davers was undoubtedly correct, since Davers in the early months of 1745, with few ships at his disposal, was in no position to send naval aid to anyone. However, there was no good reason for Ogle's own refusal to come to Shirley's aid. Ogle was about to sail to England with one small and four large warships, all of which had been recently refitted. He could easily have sailed to Cape Breton but he lacked the necessary initiative.

Warren, on the other hand, regarded Shirley's request in an entirely different light. He was unable to treat it with the superciliousness of Ogle. For in September, 1744, Warren had proposed to the Lords of the Admiralty that it was of vital importance for the British cause in North America to drive the French from Louisbourg. Shirley's scheme, therefore, struck a responsive chord in Warren.

In 1745 Warren was only 42 years old, but he had received his captain's commission eighteen years earlier. Having spent some years stationed in North American waters and having married a resident of New York, Warren tended to look at strategic problems in the same way as Shirley did. In addition, Warren was an unusually ambitious man who in 1744 and 1745 desperately wanted to be appointed governor of one of the northern colonies, preferably New York. He believed that if he could carry out successfully some brilliant military stroke against the French, he would receive this desired reward.

Shirley's letter reached Warren at Antigua on March 5. The Massachusetts governor used all of the persuasiveness at his command in urging Warren to send warships to support the proposed expedition. Shirley even offered Warren "the command of the expedition . . . a most happy event for his majesty's service and your own honour." Warren immediately called the captains of his squadron together to discuss Shirley's letter. After a prolonged discussion, it was decided that it would be extremely unwise to send ships to Cape Breton without first receiving instructions from the Admiralty. Nevertheless, it was decided to send two ships, the *Launceston* and the *Mermaid*, to Boston and New York respectively where they were to await further "directions from the Lords of Admiralty."

But the *Launceston* and *Mermaid* were never sent to Boston and New York. For on March 19 Warren received instructions from the Admiralty to proceed immediately "either to the Relief & Succour of Annapolis Royal . . . or for making any Attempts on the enemy." The only brake on Warren's desire to support Shirley had been removed. Warren called together his captains once again and informed them of the instructions he had just received from the Admiralty. The captains, together with the Governor and Assembly of Antigua, pleaded with Warren not to sail to Cape Breton. They had heard rumours about a large French squadron making its way towards the Caribbean. Warren refused to be intimidated and he refused to be tied to the decision made by the council of war:

> Warren was prepared to take the risk that the French were not coming, or that if they were a British force equal to them would follow. Realizing that in war risks must be taken, he was sure that this was one that was justifiable.

On March 24 Warren sailed from Antigua with the *Superbe,* 60 guns, the *Launceston,* 40 guns, and the *Mermaid,* 40 guns. He also sent orders to the *Eltham* at Piscataqua and the *Bien Aimé,* a prize at Boston, to join him off Cape Breton.

Shirley knew nothing about Warren's departure until after the Massachusetts troops had left Boston for Canso. On April 4, having in his possession Warren's negative response to the request for naval assistance, Shirley had no good reason to delay the sailing of the expedition any longer. However, he kept the volunteers ignorant of the potentially explosive intelligence, and consequently when they sailed from Boston they were convinced that "Commodore Warren is coming to our assistance, which with the blessing of God will be of great advantage."

Without question the departure date of the expedition was delayed more by Shirley's decision to wait for Warren's answer to his request than by any other single factor. Nevertheless, the procrastination of the other colonies and the difficulty in obtaining transports also caused delay.

Before the expedition sailed, Shirley sent six armed colonial vessels "to cruise before the harbour of Louisbourg in order to intercept any intelligence, Recruits or Supplys, which might be sent to the Enemy before the arrival" of the invading army. *The Prince of Orange,* 14 guns, the *Boston Packet,* 12 guns, and the *Fame,* 24 guns, sailed for Cape Breton waters sometime before March 24. The *Molineux,* 24 guns, the *Caesar,* 14 guns, and the *Massachusetts,* 22 guns, followed on March 27. The *Prince of Orange, Boston Packet* and the *Massachusetts* were owned by the Massachusetts government, while the other vessels were hired by it. On March 28, to prepare the way for the expedition, the *Resolute,* 10 guns, and *Bonetta,* 6 guns, were sent to Canso.

At four o'clock in the afternoon on Sunday, April 4, the first Massachusetts contingent of some 2,800 men, in fifty-one transport vessels under the convoy of the *Shirley,* 24 guns, sailed from Boston. Two days later, the second contingent of 200 sailed.

The selection of Sunday for the sailing date for the main body of the expedition was significant. It was a public declaration by the Massachusetts residents of their belief that without the direction and blessing of the Almighty the expedition would be a failure. As the ships slowly vanished out of sight, an unprecedented campaign of prayer began in Massachusetts to ensure the success of the Louisbourg expedition. This prayer campaign was caustically criticized by Benjamin Franklin in a letter to his brother in Massachusetts:

> You have a fast and prayer day for that purpose [fall of Louisbourg]; in which I compute five hundred thousand petitions were offered up to the same effect in New England, which added to the petitions of every family morning and evening, multiplied by the number of days since January 25th (O.S.) make forty-five millions of prayers; which, set against the prayers of a few priests in the Garrison, to the Virgin Mary, give a vast balance in your favor. . . . in attacking strong towns I should have more dependence on *works,* than on *faith;* for, like the kingdom of heaven, they are to be taken by force and violence; and in a French garrison I suppose there are devils of that kind, that they are not to be cast out by prayers and fasting, unless it be by their own fasting for want of provisions.

CHAPTER

9.

Little has been written about every day life in colonial Maine. The following account offers some insights into what life may have been like.

DOMESTIC LIFE IN PROVINCIAL TIMES*
by
Charles E. Banks

The eighteenth century opened with York slowly rising from the ashes and sorrows of the past. Mourning in almost every family gave life a solemnity which time only could assuage. For many years the sight of garrison houses revived the dread of savages lurking in the forests, coiled and ready to strike unawares like the deadly rattler. Six formal wars, aimed against these savages and their French coadjutors, rendered life in the first half of this century a recurring panorama of military alarums with short periods of disturbed peace intervening. Each decade found the town growing, and it became less of a frontier settlement as the years went by. Berwick on the north and Wells on its eastern boundary became the buffers that gave an increasing sense of security. Yet with demands on the people in the first half of the century to offer themselves and their sons as cannon fodder in the local repercussion of European wars devised for the "glory" of the Hanoverian and French royal families, the social development of this century was retarded much more than in the previous one. The original settlers had practically fifty years of peace to lay the foundations of a settled community. It was not till 1763 that the last quota of men from this town were called upon to do military duty beyond its borders for the security of the Province and the country at large.

Under these circumstances the thoughts and activities of the townspeople were engaged in the pressing work of conserving life and maintaining the civilization and culture of English institutions which their grandsires had planted. They had slowly overcome the aboriginal menace and at the last were in conflict with their ancient French rival for supremacy. If it was not conducive to the development of the higher values of art, science and literature, it was contributory to the future of the continent. To this important result York contributed her blood and treasure.

With these inevitable events which turned the thoughts of a small community into the atmosphere of military quarters and barracks, the stimulus of conflict kept it alive to its possibilities and prevented that stagnation which is the handmaid of profitless inactivity. York did not give up to a vegetable existence and watch itself grow. As soon as it emerged from this half century of conflict it began to take on rapidly the habiliments of a fully developed Colonial community. Victorious in war, it became expansive in peace. Although still on the extreme northern edge of English settlements, the developments in the comforts and amenities of life in the colonies south of us (where the conflicts rarely disturbed material progress) rapidly found an appreciative acceptance here. It will be asked what problems engaged their daily existence and in what way did they meet the new day that had dawned? To the present generation with all the devices and diversions which embellish modern living it is an unanswered wonder how our ancestors in that era kept themselves from yawning for lack of excitement. The answer is that they were a

---

*Charles E. Banks, *History of York, Maine,* (Boston: Murray Printing Company, 1935), II, pp. 328-345.

self-contained people and never knew the need of external means to keep them refreshed.

In 1765 York was a community just as large as it is today, numerically, and it is easy to see that enough was going on in their ordinary routine of life. The "country road" of 1699 was lined with houses as it is today from Stage Neck to Brixham. The village had as many people busily in and out of its houses and shops as can be seen at present, while the water front and the harbor could show more vessels entering and leaving and more activity than exists now. Visualize the roads, without their present finished surfaces, and with ponderous wains being slowly dragged by deliberate oxen, and an occasional horse-drawn wagon toiling along through the sandy ruts, and the external picture of the town is before us. There was nothing much to distract the attention of the people, or to help them "kill time" beyond the ordinary happenings of the human race in its seven stages of existence. They were dependent on themselves for topics of conversation and mental development. "Learning" as such was not a common privilege, although in the chapter on schools evidence from the records will show that the standards set by the Province at large were available here. It is not known that any lay resident of the town had acquired a college education, though the ministers provided examples of liberally trained minds who could give tone to ordinary social intercourse. Wigglesworth Toppan, who had come to York from Newbury about 1730 and became a Deacon of the church, was a descendant of the famous author of "The Day of Doom," that much printed piece of lugubrious poetry which scared the children of his generation out of a year's growth. Doubtless he inherited the literary tendencies of his distinguished clerical ancestor, and Judge Sayward in recording his death in 1781, stated that he was "a man of Great Reading & Tenatious Memory. I suppose he had the Biggest Library in the County." During the half century he lived here, his home must have been the center of literary culture in this vicinity.

It was a community of hardy and enterprising men when finally released from the demands of military service. They did not lapse into a life of ease, but promptly seized upon the raw materials provided by nature to bring forth and turn into wealth and make themselves independent. There were few idlers. He that did not work could not eat. Sea-borne traffic with the larger communities south of us, with agrarian pursuits as a sure foundation for a stable existence, occupied their energies, and the town was rarely destitute of the common necessaries of life as often happened in towns like Falmouth where the farming interests were neglected for industrial pursuits. When three-quarters of the century had been reached there was a distinct class of wealthy citizens who had accummulated a competency as a result of their energy and thrift.

The outward condition of the people in their style of habitations bore no comparison to the grandeur of the present day. The buildings, with one known exception, were all of wood, generally unpainted and most of them but one story high. Only a few of them survive today, either from decay of material or from abandonment and replacement by larger and more convenient structures. The mansion of Jonathan Sayward survives as a relic of the earlier part of the century; the Emerson residence, of somewhat later construction, yet houses a remarkable collection of contemporary antiques owned by his descendants, while the frame of the "grand new house" of Judge Sewall, as described by Judge Sayward, was not "raised" till 1794 and now exists as "Coventry Hall." It stands almost as staunch as when it was built, a beautiful monument of Colonial architecture; "one of the grandest bilt in the county," added the Judge in his diary. These represented the accumulated wealth of the slowly growing aristocracy of the town.

To adequately express their significance required the intimate touch of the women of York. As always, the female element of society is the first to put on the external adornments which accompany a more leisurely existence. By 1765 the wives and daughters of the well-to-do were wearing high headdresses, attractive stomachers, gowns of ample folds, ruffles at neck and elbows, high heeled shoes and cloaks in colors for occasions of a social character. Nor were the men who had money to loan on mortgages or fumbled with warrants for soldiers' wages far behind their women folk in personal dress. The office, shop or warehouse being closed, they emerged in the evening in habits so different from their working clothes that they presented an entirely new appearance. Like characters on the stage they paraded in cocked hats, full bottomed wigs, ruffles at the wrists, embroidered vests, small clothes with dazzling buckles at the knees and on their shoes, silken hose and silver-headed canes. Scarlet was the favorite color for cloaks *en fete*; in this brave apparel the gayeties of birthdays and weddings were enjoyed.

Evidence of the growth of the town in its observance of the official and social amenities of life is strikingly portrayed in a contemporary account of an escort prepared for the arrival of the Judges of the Supreme Court of the Province in the year preceding the outbreak of the Revolution. It is told by John Adams in a letter to his wife, June 29, 1774, and reads as follows:

> When I got to the tavern on the eastern side of Piscataqua river, I found the Sheriff of York (Jotham Moulton), and six of his deputies, all with gold laced hats, ruffles, swords, and very gay clothes, all likely young men, who had come to that place ten miles, to escort the Court into town. This unusual parade excited my curiosity and I soon suspected that it was to show respect and be a guard of honor to the Chief Justice, if he had been coming to Court.

This brave array of mounted civil officials in cocked hats, scarlet coats, short clothes, knee and shoe buckles, armed with swords, shows how far York had traveled since the lean and drab days of the early part of the century.

The references made elsewhere in this history to the social proclivities of Judge Sayward might convey the impression that his mansion was the only center of hospitality and conviviality in the town. This was far from the case, as other families like the Emersons, Lymans and Sewalls shared with him the leadership in social functions. On April 12, 1771, Dr. Job Lyman gave an entertainment and reception to the Court and "society" in the town to celebrate his appointment as a Justice of the County of York. At his house on the main street the elite gathered to congratulate him and partake of his decorated pasties and authoritative punch. These affairs lacked none of the gorgeousness of Provincial dress and gayety. Myriad candles whose rays were multiplied in the pendant glass prisms of the chandeliers gave brilliancy to the scene while the music of viols and harpsichords helped to lure the young to show their gracefulness in the minuet. When the affair was over Mr. Justice Lyman knew that he had been properly installed in his new office with popular approval.

On the occasion of reaching his majority young Edward Emerson gave an entertainment January 19, 1786, to the young gentlemen and ladies of York at the fort. For an adventure of this kind in midwinter, only youth could enjoy. According to one who chronicled the event "it was exceeding bad traveling, notwithstanding the young ladies were so much ingaged in the Frolic that they went knee-deep in snow to honor Mr. Emerson and see and get sweethearts." It can be safely said that life in York in the Provincial period was not lacking in opportunities for social enjoyment, and for picturesqueness it has no equal at the present day.

The institution of marriage as a part of the social system was originally separated, as far as possible, from any connection with the church, but in the Provincial era the clergy had recovered, to a great extent, their lost jurisdiction over the marriage ceremony. It was from the first regarded as a civil function in which the minister derived his authority from the State and acted as its agent in performing the legal act of marrying. The basis of our social fabric has been as much under the control of Justices of the Peace as of the clergy.

Following the English and Continental customs, without their formalities of betrothal, it was a part of the program for the bride's father to give her a marriage "portion," or dower, and this was usually in the form of a lot for a homestead or gifts in money or in kind, depending on the material wealth of the parent. The calling of the banns in public meeting was also enjoined, as was the law in England, and in addition a license to marry was required by the town officials. If one of the parties resided in another town a license was required in both places. Instances of objection to the granting of licenses are recorded here, sometimes by the parents of the proposed bride and often by some disappointed suitor who forbade the ceremony on the plea that a prior "engagement" already existed in his or her favor.

Like all other occasions when rejoicing was an acceptable part of a social event, weddings were the opportunities of relaxation and mirth for the somber atmosphere of a Provincial town, and the usual festivities attendant upon the ceremony, which usually took place in the evening, were indulged by the family, neighbors and friends of the happy couple in proportion to their ability to provide the settings of a feast. But this age-old custom was not always to be enjoyed, as there grew up in New England, borrowed from the old country, an example of thrift on the part of the bridegroom which, fortunately, did not obtain much transplanted popularity. When marrying a widow, the prospective husband, wishing to give public notice that he took his new wife dowerless and without obligations to pay any debts of the previous husband, required that the bride should be married naked or lightly clad in a chemise or smock as evidence that she brought nothing of her former marriage to their new relationship. It was the custom for the woman to cross the King's Highway thus clad at night as an ocular demonstration of this legal relief, and sometimes she was married standing in a closet in this semi-nude state, reaching out her hand and arm to enact her part of this strange cermony. The bridegroom provided a complete wardrobe for his bride who was then dressed by her friends. These deliberate legal quibbles to save the bridegroom harmless were known as "shift" or "smock" marriages and were rather common in New England until the beginning of the nineteenth century. In fact, one occurred in England as late as 1900.

This town had an example about 1730, when William Bracey, a resident of York, went through this solemn farce, when taking for his third wife, the Widow Rylance, as testified by the witnesses. Two of her women friends made oath:

> ... that before William Brasey married the widow Rylance, he brought her cloath to us the Deponents both Linning and Woolling and all things that was needful for the Dressing of a woman and delivered us to dress the aforesaid woman to be married in and we were present and saw the said Brassey married to the sd Rylance in those cloathes before mentioned.

In the material improvements of life the increasing facilities of travel and communication brought to the town some of the privileges enjoyed by the big towns of New England. While Boston, Newburyport and Portsmouth had the advantages of a regular "post," it was not till 1760 that a weekly mail service was established to the eastward. Elsewhere is related the development of this novelty which was an external aid in bringing York in touch with the outside world. Until then the only "news" brought to town came from the casual coasters who entertained the townsfolk with relations of their visits to Boston, New York and Charleston, or the more frequent travelers to Portsmouth who brought back the intimate gossip of that town for home consumption.

With the regular mails brought by the post-rider came copies of the *Boston News Letter* or the *New Hampshire Gazette.* It is not known to whom the honor of early patronage of this adjunct of modern life belongs, but as far as recorded evidence permits a decision, it belongs to Capt. John Bradbury, as established by the following entry in his Diary:

> York July the 29 1763. This day entered my name to take the hamshire papers for one year Capt James Carlisle paying one half to Daniel Fowle.

In 1771 Jonathan Sayward notes his subscription "for one year newspapers to Thomas Fleet" of Boston, publisher of the *News Letter,* although he had probably been a reader of this much earlier. In 1759, James Sayward was the local agent of the Portsmouth paper as appears by the notice he inserted in an issue of December of that year:

> This is to desire those Persons in the County of YORK who entered their Names or engage to take the NEW HAMPSHIRE GAZETTE of me the Subscriber, to pay what is due for the same.
>
> JAMES SAYWARD

As early as 1761, Edward Emerson and Jonathan Sayward had inserted advertisements in the Portsmouth paper and presumably both were subscribers. A careful inspection of the files of the *Boston News Letter* shows that items of "news," as then interpreted, were being sent to it from here as early as 1707 and intermittently thereafter. At first they were tales of Indian depredations, but in 1728 an obituary notice of ten lines reporting the death of "the vertuous and Pious Wife" of Parson Moody appeared in the *News Letter,* concluding with the "full assurance that she had entered on her Eternal jubilee." In 1752, the birth of triplets to the wife of David Preble enlivened the issue of January 30. As these were their first-born, it may be said that it was an excellent start in raising a family. There can be no doubt that this event was a sensation in the town, but not an example to be generally adopted.

The execution of Tony, a Negro slave, who had killed his master's daughter and behaved "very penitently" on the gallows, appeared in July 1759 as an item of local concern. Arrivals and departures of vessels, shipwrecks, eclipses in 1758 and 1765, and accounts of the earthquakes which stirred the superstitious here, as frowns of a vengeful God, made up the bulk of the news. One item, however, printed in 1761, tells of the performance of a surgical operation on a York lady of the age of threescore and ten years by Dr. Jackson of Portsmouth. She "having labour'd under a Dropsy of the Belly for a long Time was tap'd and near five gallons of water came away," and it was reported as successful a month later. In 1760, James Sayward, "who is now gone on the present Expedition," local agent for the *Gazette,* requested delinquents to pay their dues for the paper to David Sewall or Thomas Moulton.

Of course, no account of the life of the people in the eighteenth century could be complete without a reference to the universal acceptance of and indulgence in the social glass, sanctioned by the clergy and approved by centuries of racial tradition. Liquor appeared everywhere on all sorts of occasions from the ordination of ministers, funerals and weddings, to raising the frame of a barn. Probably every family was supplied with "spirits," as West India rum was designated, and the various hot concoctions prepared from it on cold winter days and nights were part of the routine of their lives. For the casual visitors and transient residents the taverns provided ample opportunity for indulgence and in them congregated the gregarious townsmen who had a tenacious respect for royal birthdays and national holidays. Toasts to the king were easily offered on all occasions, but someone was always present with a prodigious knowledge of the natal days of princes and statesmen who could induce all present to fill their glasses in honor of the alleged event. Appointments to office, commissions in the military establishment and training days sufficed to fill in any lack of birthdays as an excuse for drinking healths. Of course this custom resulted in some abuses, but when it is considered that they had little of outside entertainment to lighten the dullness of their restricted environment we can at least look on their social indulgences with tempered approval. Even such excitement as the earthquake on Sunday, June 3, 1744, when the congregation thought it was an Indian attack and the men seized their guns for action, could not furnish indefinitely a reason for social interchange. To this pleasant aid in passing the long hours of leisure there may be added the general use of the comforting pipe of tobacco. Evidences of it here in 1762 and 1771 are available, but it is a certainty that it was a part of the equipment of both men and women much earlier.

There are no indications that evening entertainments, as we understand them, came to town with that century. It is certain that a community must creep before it walks in the development of its community life, and enough has been shown to establish the gradual growth to a civilized stature in the last half of the eighteenth century. It is true that all of it was not uplifting, as our modern reformers would say, but it paralleled the customs of other communities of its size in taking on new offerings of interest. The gambling instinct of the English people found opportunity here in the local lotteries. There is an Arabian proverb which says: "If God purposes the destruction of an ant He allows wings to grow on her," and while this method of finance was not sound yet the spirit of adventure in taking a "flyer" was strong. Early in 1758 the York County Lottery was advertised to be drawn at our Town House, and tickets were sold to secure funds to build bridges across the Saco and Presumpscot Rivers, and Daniel Moulton, who seemed to be the local manager, announced that he would take "Province Notes for the Tickets." It is to be remembered that lotteries were a common device to raise money for strictly moral purposes and even Harvard College and the immortal George Washington gave their approval to the practice, the former to build a new hall and the other to aid the construction of a canal.

Perhaps the most interesting event happening in this period was the visit of the Rev. George Whitefield, the famous English evangelist, to York in 1744, and his occupancy of the pulpit of the First Church on Sunday, November 4, that year. He had come directly from London and had put in here on account of weather conditions at sea, but it was not his first visit to America. Probably no minister of the gospel encountered so much hostility in New England even in the halcyon days of Puritan persecution as this stormy petrel of the new religion. It was his methods and manners in the pulpit rather than his character as a clergyman that aroused the bitterest hostility as well as the most ardent champions of his cause. He disdained droning out long sermons divided into firstlies and fifthlies and spoke without notes. He was the advance prophet of the itinerant preachers of a half century later and as such had a common bond of sympathy with Parson Moody, as their methods were much alike. His invasion of Maine caused the greatest upheaval in the life of the local churches. One diarist wrote: "the Parish are like to be in a flame on account of Mr. Whitefield's coming, the leading men violently oppose him." His meetings became scenes of emotional extravagance, confusion and disorder owing to his dramatic appeals to "sinners" to come to repentance, and the staid, conservative element was shocked at his influence over the people. The old guard of the Puritan theocracy resented any innovations which disturbed the comfortable doldrums characteristic of the Dark Ages in religious New England. In the course of years Whitefield finally overcame these prejudices and a quarter of a century later he occupied this same pulpit Thursday, September 27, 1770, by favor of Rev. Isaac Lyman, preaching from John XIV:6, "I am the way." He was accompanied on this visit "by a number of Ladies and Gentlemen of Portsmouth." This proved to be his last sermon and public appearance as he died suddenly on Sunday morning three days later at Newburyport.

On July 17, 1785, the town was treated to the unusual spectacle of a visiting Italian nobleman. This was Count Luigi Castiglioni, Cavaliere dell Ordine di S. Stefano, a citizen of Milano. He was a young man about twenty-three years of age who evidently came to York with a letter of introduction to Judge Sewall and by him was presented to Judge Sayward. "He speaks so much inglish,"wrote the latter, "as to be well understood. He is making the tower of the States (and) hath been as far as Baggaduce." The Count was traveling with a suite, as Judge Sayward noticed that "his waitting men appear Dressed better than himself which I am assured is the Common Practice." Whatever the source of this assurance it is evident that the Count was dressing as a Democrat in a Democratic country.

The observations of Count Castiglioni relative to the people of this town and their economic situation is worth repeating:

> The land of old York is dotted with poor cabins where dwell the cultivators who came only a few years ago and whose food consists of rye bread, and maize with pork and salt beef, and whose drink is Grog and spruce beer. This is obtained by boiling the young shoots of pitch pine to extract the flavor from the bark and then mixing that decoction with a sufficient quantity of molasses. Cider is not so abundant as in the more Southern parts of Massachusetts, because the orchards are not yet numerous enough and the Grog which is made from Rum mixed with water is the most common liquor. The progress of agriculture is quite considerable in proportion to the brief time since the beginning of cultivation in this country. The homes of the inhabitants are quite distant from each other.

The visit of Governor Shirley has already been described (Volume I, p.370) and on June 24, 1791, the famous first signer of the Declaration of Independence, Gov. John Hancock and his equally famous wife, "Dorothy Q." with the Governor's official suite visited York as guests of Judge Sayward. The Governor and the Judge were old friends in pre-Revolutionary times and a bond of local interest existed as a topic of conversation between them, for the Governor's grandfather preached at York for a season prior to the settlement of Parson Moody. In 1767, Jonathan Sayward had built a brig for Hancock, but in the years following, their political paths on which they had recently started had widely diverged. Now Hancock was in the height of his public career as a result of his political acumen while the reputation of Sayward had long been in eclipse. It was a gracious gesture for this Republican statesman to show to this upholder of the Royal prerogative after the clash of arms had brought the latter to defeat. The Judge records the circumstance in his Diary:

> Governor Hancock & Lady & his Sute paid me an agreeable visit and dined with a large company with which he honoured me and in confidence regained my judgment of men for the good of the country in which I hope I have done some service.

Under the mellowing influences of old wines to aid the digestion of a well-stocked table, these political antagonists could forget the asperities of the past and the mansion once more was the scene of a brilliant entertainment in which the Judge regained his good opinion of the men he had so long but unhappily opposed.

In keeping with the general dislocation of the times—social, political and religious—an eminent Quaker, Mr. David Sands, came to town as an exponent of the religion made famous by William Penn. While the privileges of the church building were not extended to him although it was not occupied on Thursday, April 8, the date of his visit, nevertheless he was accommodated at "the Brick house in this town," (Ingraham's Tavern, near the site of "Coventry Hall"). He preached there "to a large congregation to acceptance," and thus added his mite to the liberalizing tendencies of the era in Maine. There were two Quakers who had been living here for several years before his appearance. But this sect, advocating resistance to war as one of their doctrines, found its greatest support in the midst of a distressing conflict and during the period of prostration which followed, and when these conditions ceased the sympathetic interest in their peaceful system lost its appeal and never was revived. It was against the spirit of a dominant pioneering race.

NEGRO SLAVES

In view of the attitude, in the last century, of this section of New England, on the moral question of human slavery, as expressed in opinions and emphasized in actions in the Civil War, it seems strange that the records of this town give ample evidence that Negro slavery was an accepted and acceptable part of the social life in York in Colonial times and down to the early part of the last century. It had the unhesitating approval of Parson Moody and the people. In fact the parish actually bought a slave for the Parson. At a meeting held January 9, 1732-1733, it was

> VOTED that there be a Slave Bought by the Parish to be Imployed for the use of said Parish in Labouring for the Rev. Mr. Samuel Moody/
> VOTED that Samuel Came Esqr, Elder Richard Milberry and Mr. Joseph Holt be Imployed as agents for the Parish to purchase a Slave for said Parish/

The committee bought a Negro but on December 26, 1735, it was voted that if the "Negro Man cant do for Mr Moody that the Assessors Hire a Man for Mr Moody." In 1736, he had a girl slave called "Phyllis."

An earlier slaveholder, however, was none other than an Elder in the church, Joseph Sayward, who had an Indian bond servant in 1730, named "Boneto," (purchased of Thomas Pickering), to whom he agreed to give freedom, if at the end of nine and a half years he should "behave himself faithfully, soberly & temperately as a Servant ought to do." This is the only instance of Indian slavery that appears in the records.

It is not easy to state accurately how early Negro slavery was introduced into York, but probably not before 1700, but it soon became a common practice among those able to buy and keep slaves. In 1736, Jedediah Preble had a slave named "Andrew," and in 1737, Joseph Swett, two, "Pompey" and "Betty," who were married that year. Peter Nowell seems to have been the largest slaveholder in his day. In 1737, he gave by deed to his son Abraham a "Negro Girl named Diner," and in his will in 1738, he bequeathed to his wife the choice of three slaves, named Flora, Phillis and Peg.

In 1754, there were twenty-four slaves in the town and in the census of 1765, twenty female and thirty-six male Negroes were listed in the town, fifty-six in all. Probably all of them were in slavery. In 1769, Edward Grow advertised in the New Hampshire Gazette a reward of four dollars for the return of a runaway slave named, "Tony." Two slaves were married in 1770: "Caesar, a slave belonging to Richard Talpey, and "Rose," belonging to Joseph Weare. It is known that the Moultons of Cider Hill owned slaves, and the Came family, also of the same neighborhood, had a Negro named "Sharper" who was a crony of "Caesar" belonging to the Plaisteds. It is related that on one dark evening "Sharper" visited "Caesar" and when it came time to go home the darkness had not decreased, and he asked "Caesar" to accompany him to his home, which "Caesar" obligingly did. But when they arrived at Came's house, it was just as dark, so he went back with "Caesar" by request of the latter, and so they went back and forth all night until daybreak. This may not be history, but it is African psychology.

On April 21, 1775, a Negro also named "Caesar," which was a popular name for gentlemen of color, accompanied Captain Moulton's company to Concord when the news of that battle reached here, a fact which warrants a separate paragraph to record his patriotic act. He was living in 1800, a free Negro, with a family of three.

FREE NEGROES

The Census of 1790 shows twenty-six Negroes credited to the following families: three to the Weares at Cape Neddick, and one each to Samuel Trevett, Nicholas Sewall, Jonathan Sayward, Mrs. Sarah Swett, Joseph Thompson, Ebenezer Thompson and Jedediah Blaisdell, and two to John Main. Giles Scott was a free Negro living here at that time, who had come originally from Jamaica to be educated.

In 1800, there were twenty-one Negro slaves of whom one was "yellow," and in 1810, nineteen Negroes including Caesar Talpey with a family. Most of them were dependents living in a state of modified bondage. After that they disappear from the enumerations. The Misses Raynes kept two of the last generation of these unfortunate beings, called "Phyllis" and "Dinah Prince." The latter had lived in her younger days near the Mill Dam between Meeting House Creek and the River, and was popularly supposed to have occult powers.

"Black Isaac," the fiddler, was a Virginia slave according to his own story and escaped from his master. He wandered into Maine from Long Island, stopped here to woo and win a dusky mate, Chloe, daughter of Caesar Talpey, and married her. They were blessed with fourteen ebony pickaninnies. He was a regular feature at the annual training days in York, and with his fiddle accumulated stray pennies fiddling for dances at three pennies a dance. His repertoire was limited to a few tunes, but he was in demand all day at these functions. He added his voice to his instrument in scraping out his favorite ballad, "When I am dead and gone to roost," which he sang and played with all the vim of a modern jazz artist, according to tradition. His adopted name was Davis and he was probably a free Negro when he came here. In 1850, there were but six Negroes in York, and these were the ravel ends of a race that at one time had lived in comfort and even luxury in the homes of the "quality" of York before the Revolution.

In 1789, slavery was abolished in Massachusetts, shortly after the adoption of the Constitution. Judge Sayward rather sadly notes the death of his old servant "Prince," of whom he says: "the New Constitution made him free. He was Babtized on his death bed. I perposed to bury him at my Cost, as I have supported him in his Last sickness."

In this recital of the peaceful, bucolic life of the people of York in that century we are prepared to learn that longevity was a natural accompaniment of such an existence. In 1780, there were eighty-seven persons then living in the town upwards of seventy years; twenty-two upwards of eighty, and four nonagenarians, or nearly a hundred persons who had passed threescore and ten out of a population of twenty-six hundred. Centenarians of the native stock have lived here in the last three centuries, a silent tribute to the soundness of the race.

The closing years of the century found the people here following the general trend of sentiment of the nation in adopting the manners, dress and customs of our late allies, the French. The War for Independence had created a distaste for anything English and these antagonisms were not easily overcome. Nor was this hostility much lessened for many years. The French Revolution of 1789, so closely following our own, had leveled all ranks and made for a spiritual brotherhood which has not ceased to function. With the creation of "Liberty, Equality and Fraternity" in France went out the short clothes of the *ancien regime,* and the simpler habiliments marking the citizen class were adopted here with enthusiasm.

The end of his days for a citizen of York in this century was marked by every-increasing formality as he was carried to his last resting place. Women wore special hoods and mourning scarves at first, but these were discarded before the Revolution, and mourning rings became a part of the last rites of the well-to-do. Burial services attracted large neighborhood attendance, according to the standing of the deceased. In 1746, the death of a child of Rev. Samuel Chandler in "Scotland," only a few days old, drew from him this entry in his Diary: "funeral of our child pretty large for an Infant." In 1793, the town appointed a committee of seven "marshalls" to regulate the order of processions at funerals, a practice that was continued for several years. It would seem that these ceremonies had become popular demonstrations and required "Marshals" to keep the marchers in orderly procession to the grave. Hearses came into use as the new century was opening. York had now discarded its youthful clothes and merged into the long pants of a vigorous manhood.

CHAPTER

10.

A further view of life in colonial Maine is observable through the working of the legal system. The harshness of that system, while revolting to modern minds, was not unusual, for in England and in other colonies the law was equally severe.

COURT HOUSE, GAOL, AND PUNISHMENTS*
by
Charles E. Banks

THE SHIRE TOWN

With the judicial system of the Province this history has no concern, except as it relates to the seat of government and sittings of the Courts. Almost from the first this town held that relation to the Province. It was more frequently used as the place where Provincial and County Courts were held than any other. In 1640, it was ordered that three sessions of the Quarterly Courts should sit at Agamenticus and one at Saco. After Massachusetts took over the government the sessions were held alternately at Kittery and York, but the presence of the County records, then kept by Rishworth, who resided here, automatically made York the shire town in practice. In 1668, the famous "military" court assembled here when Massachusetts used armed force to reassert her authority, and in 1670, John Josselyn, the traveller, called York "the Metropolitan of the Province," meaning its seat of government. The extent of the Province, however, with settlements miles apart, made it necessary to hold court sessions elsewhere, occasionally, to accommodate inhabitants living between Kittery and the Sagadahoc. In 1680, when the Charter government was organized it met in this town, and the courts also were held here for the following five years. The Andros regime caused a general dislocation of all governmental customs, but after his overthrow the courts resumed sittings at York. When the charter of William and Mary, dated October 7, 1691, came into operation all the former methods had to be revised to meet its provisions. Under the rearrangement of officials and offices, it was provided that the four sessions of the courts should be held in York and Wells alternately. The Indian wars, which followed almost immediately, with the destruction of York and Wells, turned York into a garrison outpost and interfered with orderly government for a decade. With the beginning of the resettlement of abandoned towns in Maine the old arrangement was resumed, but with the gradual growth of places further east there came agitations for court sessions in that section, with the possibility of changing the location of the shire town. To forestall this the residents of York and Wells, through Lewis Bane and William Sawyer, in June 1717, petitioned "that the Town of York be now restored to their Right and Priviledge as the Shire Town of that County." In November Abraham Preble, Richard Milberry and Samuel Came petitioned the General Court that the Registry of Deeds may not be kept at Kittery, as it now is, but be removed and kept at York the Shire Town. The Town voted on February 11, 1717-8 that Abraham Preble be chosen "to assist in the Towns behalfe to Git the Generall Corts Confirmation that this Town of York is the Sheir Town of this County of York, that so the Ridgistry of Deeds &c may be kept according to Law." In June, 1718, the General Court acted on this matter favorably, and ordered "that the Registry of Deeds be kept and the Superior Court of Judicaturs &c be held henceforth in the said Town of York." Thus York was confirmed in her

---

*Charles E. Banks, *History of York, Maine*, (Boston: Murray Printing Company, 1935), II, pp. 228-244.

ancient rights as the "Metropolitan of the Province." This situation continued until 1735, when the growth of the Eastern towns made it necessary to recognize their convenience, and in that year Falmouth (now Portland) was authorized to share this honor. At the division of the county, in 1760, when Cumberland and Lincoln counties were set off from York County, which had hitherto embraced the whole Province, this town remained the shire town of the old County of York. In 1802, the town of Alfred was chosen to share the privilege with York as Falmouth had done previously. The courts were retained here until 1832, when, on account of the requirements of centralization from a geographical standpoint, Alfred was finally adopted as the shire town. The office of County Treasurer had been removed there in 1813, the Registry of Deeds in 1816, and the Probate Office in 1820, together with the office of the Clerk of Courts.

COURT HOUSE

That Sir Ferdinando Gorges planned to build a Court House is certain from his letter of "Instructions" (the second set), dated March 10, 1639, in which he directed "that there may be a place appointed for the hearing & determining of causes, I have thought to assigne the same to be as nere as may be in the midst of that parte of the Province which is most inhabited, and that there be a house builte for that purpose at my one chardge if it cannot otherwise be setled." As this town was in the centre of the "most inhabited" part of the Province, at that time, such a building may have been erected, but there is no record of it here or elsewhere.

It has already been explained that the ancient courts were held in the meetinghouses and as population increased the use of these edifices not built for the purpose became unsatisfactory and public opinion demanded that a suitable building be provided for this civil function. At a town meeting held December 5, 1733, the sum of 100 pounds was voted towards building a courthouse and on the 20th of the same month it was

> "Voted that Decon Abiel Goodwin, Capt. Peter Nowell and Mr. Joseph Holt be a Committee to Joyn with the Courts Committee in carrying on this Towns Part in building a Court House in this Town."

The joint committee were authorized "to appoint a Place to set sd House upon." On January 28, 1733-34, the town took additional action as expressed in the following vote:

> "That this Town will Joyn with the County in building of a Court House in this Town which House shall be for the use of sd County to hold Courts in & for a Town House for the use of this Town to meet in on all Publick Times if they see cause: The Dementions of sd House to be as followeth viz: Thirty Five Foot Long & Twenty Eight Foot Wide: Twenty Foot Stud: the lower Story Eight Feet & a Half high: the upper Eleven Feet and a Half, and the Beames of the Upper Story to be Crowning Eighteen Inches & to have a Pitched Roofe: both Rooms to be Plaistered & whitewashed and well Glazed with Sash Glass, and to be Finished with Joynery Work according to the directions of the Committee that are & shall be appointed by the County & Town, and that the One Half of the Charges arrising in building & Finishing sd House shall be bourne by this Town."

Samuel Came and Jeremiah Moulton were appointed a committee acting on behalf of the town and their work was completed before December 26, 1735, as a parish meeting was held in the Town House on that date. This combined use continued until the beginning of the next century when dilapidations from age rendered it unsuitable for holding courts and the lack of accommodations for the bench and bar resulted in a transfer in 1800 and 1801 of the sessions of the Supreme Court to Kennebunk. This gave that town an opportunity to start a movement to make the change permanent. This attack on the old shire town was resented by Kittery and Berwick as well as our own people and by the financial aid of county and town appropriations, supplemented by individual contributions from residents of this town, Kittery and Berwick, the present Town House was built for the same joint purpose as before, and removal was thus forestalled for a while.

THE COURTS

As the Shire town of the Province, York was the scene of one of the persistent relics of authority which the pioneers could indulge while they were hewing out the forests to make their habitations and extend their planting fields. The courts were contemporary with their coming and developed in externals and importance as the population grew. The sessions of the courts were held, of necessity, in such places as the town could afford, usually in the private house of the local Magistrate or in the Meeting House as soon as one was available. The law knew only this necessity which converted a temple of divine worship into a secular hall where men would wrangle on week days after they had bowed in prayer on Sundays. The several Meeting Houses in turn furnished this accommodation until the first Town House was prepared for the purpose.

In accordance with the traditional attitude of the Englishman, the Judges of his courts were generally objects of reverence for their office and respect for their persons. The Usurpation, which brought in Judges from Massachusetts, was a signal for a decline in this attitude owing to the intense political objections to their presence and the controversies which it excited. After the purchase of the Gorges' Patent this feeling of hostility gradually wore off and the coming of the Justices to hold courts of Quarter Sessions and Common Pleas was always the occasion of as much pomp and ceremony as the primitive conditions of life at that period permitted. The members of the Provincial Court traveled from Boston and the local towns in Maine by horseback through woodland trails, fording rivers or crossing them by ferry when bridges did not serve.

The Shire Reeve or Sheriff was an important partner of the Justices in the administration of the law. His truncheon symbolized power and he was looked upon with almost as much awe as his superiors on the Bench, particularly by those in the clutches of the law. In the passage of time, when the changes in living conditions permitted development of more of the formalities of official life, the Sheriff was a picturesque figure in the business of the Court. In wig and cocked hat and surtout sparkling with brass buttons, knee breeches and buckled shoes he escorted the Honorable Justices from their lodgings at the Tavern to the Court House, and in impressive tones at the opening of the Court summoned the people to come and be heard. With a changed formula he announced the adjournments of the Court, as lunch or dinner closed this quarterly show for the townspeople. On special occasions the Sheriff would lead an escort of the Militia to meet the Justices at the Town line and convoy them to the Meeting House. The local occupants of this office were: Henry Norton (1653), Abraham Preble, Jr. (1713); followed by what might be called the Moulton dynasty, Jeremiah (1724), Jeremiah, Jr. (1752), Jotham (1771) and Johnson (1784-93). Nathaniel G. Marshall held the office from 1854 to 1857, but the glories of the office, in its spectacular phase, went out with wigs and buckled shoes, except that the silk hat, with its cockade, and the sword continued to be worn by the Sheriff on formal occasions until about 1860. The Sheriff of the County of Middlesex still opens Commencement exercises at Harvard College wearing this regalia.

Solemn as were these Judges on the Bench in full-bottomed wigs, they were ordinary human beings in their hours of relaxation. They dined informally at the taverns and were amply supplied from the tap-room to aid their enjoyment and enliven the conversation. Nor had they altogether forgotten that all work and no play makes Jack a dull boy. Judge Sewall relates a story of one of their dinners at the close of the term, showing something of the early manners of the Bench and Bar. It was anciently the custom when the business of the Court was finished for the Judges and members of the Bar to assemble at the tavern for a social meeting. On this particular occasion they would constitute a court among themselves, appointing one of their number "Chief Justice" for the trial of all breaches of good fellowship which had occurred during the term. At one of these meetings a member of the Bar from Kittery was accused of calling the High Sheriff a fool. The fact being proved or admitted, the moot court taking into consideration the time, manner and occasion of the offense ordered the accused to pay a fine of one pipe of tobacco to each member. They also ordered the High Sheriff, who is said to have been Samuel Wheelwright, to pay one mug of flip for deserving the appellation.

GAOL

If the early Puritan writers of Massachusetts on social conditions in the Province of Maine and their modern reverberators are to be accepted as authorities, there would not have been stones enough to construct prison walls to confine the alleged lawless element. Neither is it to be presumed that conditions were so ideal nothing of the kind was needed, and yet for twenty years after the settlement of York there was not a prison in the town or its next neighbor to the west. Apparently the remedy for this jail-less condition was required and

Court House, Gaol, and Punishments

at a General Court of the Province held December 30, 1651, it was ordered "that the towns of Gorgeana and Kittery are to build each of them a prison." As this was just shortly before the invasion of Massachusetts, and the consequent change of government, there is no evidence that this order became effective. The year 1653 has been locally accepted as the actual date of erection and publicly announced at the old gaol in this town, now used for exhibition purposes. It is not believed that this is the correct date. In answer to a petition from the inhabitants of Saco, Cape Porpus and Wells, the General Court of Massachusetts in November 1654, appointed residents of Kittery, York, Wells, Cape Porpus and Saco to make a "just and equall levy on each of the towns named and that they shall also take an account of the late Treasurer about the rate of the two late Courts and rectify the same, chargeing to each toune theire due proportion, according to the custome of the countrie rates." It appears that there had been disagreement among the various towns about the due proportion of costs chargeable to each, and in May 1655, four commissioners made their report, "not withstanding the person appointed for Kittery in this business refused to apply himself to the honnored Courts order, and hath not brought in the valuation of theire estates." In absence of the representative from Kittery the other members acted, as stated "fairely & favorably for them as for ourselves" with the following proportionate assessment:

Kittery	45: 15: 00
York	17: 17: 00
Wells	13: 10: 00
Cape Porpus	04: 08: 00
Saco	10: 05: 00
	91: 15: 00

From subsequent records it would seem that these amounts were for the estimated cost of a prison, not yet built, certainly not completed. It will appear from the following record of the Court proceedings in 1667, that the gaol was far from satisfactory at that date:

> In regard of the Couldness of the present season & the Inconveniency & unfitness of the pryson to Intertayne prysoners this winter tyme: It is therefore ordered that untill a more convenient pryson bee erected or the season bee more moderate, it shall be lawfull for John Parker, his Majestys Goaler at Yorke to remove his prysoners to his house, which untill the Court take further order shall bee allowed & computed as the lawfull pryson, provided the said prysoners do not exceed goeing out of the lymitts of tenn pooles from any part of the said Goalers house, which whosoever presumes to doe without lycence from the Goale keeper shall bee accompted as a breaker of pryson & lyable to suffer as such an offender.
> It is further ordered that prysoners shall have their lybarty to come to the meeting on the Lords days with the keeper of the Goale.

The new (second) Meeting House had just been completed, and as Parker the Gaoler lived close by, just across the Creek, the walk to meeting was not a long one. Acting upon this report the Provincial Court in October, 1666, made the following order:

> "Itt is ordered that this Western devision of the Province of Mayn shall build a sufficient pryson at Yorke before the last of September next, 1667."

In April 1669, John Bray of Kittery was committed to York Gaol by a Kittery Constable, from which it is possible to deduce that Kittery had no jail, and that the one here had been made "more convenient," for the new one had not yet been completed. At the same session the towns in the western part of the Province in arrears for their share of expenses in erecting the new jail were directed to fulfill their obligations so that the committee could "take speedie & effectual Course for the building of a new Jayle att Yorke, or maintaine that which is there." In 1671, another resident of Kittery was committed to the gaol at Falmouth, presumably because the one here was not completed or insecure, and in 1673, the Overseers of the Prison, Capt. John Wincoll, Richard Banks and Edward Rishworth were fined five Pounds apiece, "for not finishing it" as ordered by the Court. This fine was remitted the next year. It would thus appear that, twenty years after the original order, the gaol at York had not been completed. It was, however, in use, but owing to the "defectiveness" a prisoner in 1673, made his escape and the county was obliged to pay the creditor the amount of his bill against this escaped debtor. Either the responsible officials were continually amiss in this particular, or did not know how to build a structure that would hold its inmates, as in 1695, it was again reported as "much out of repair," and the Sheriff was authorized to designate any house convenient for a "common county Goale for the present." The next year Samuel Donnell, Abraham Preble and James Plaisted were directed to "forthwith view the Prison at York & see whats amiss in it, and cause it to be repaired." In April, 1707, the Court ordered the county to build a small prison in York as "the Gaol in Kittery is out of repair" and in October of that year Peter Nowell and Francis Raynes were employed to build it. The dimensions were specified as 24 x 16 and 7 feet between the floors, indicating a structure of two stories. As the dimensions of this "small prison" are not those of the foundations of the present one it is probable that this was the "House of Correction" referred to in the records of the next year when the prison-keeper was also designated as "Master of the House of Correction." It may be assumed that the "olde gaol" was completed at some time, but that it was never proof against the designs of ingenious prisoners is a matter of tradition as well as legal record. In 1750, a case of such gaol delivery was the basis of a long suit against the Sheriff for damages in allowing a debtor, through negligence, to escape. The verdict was in favor of the creditor and the case was finally taken to the General Court of Massachusetts on appeal. The prisoner was a shoemaker and allowed to work at his trade in the prison, having "his Tools and Billets of Wood for his fire by which he put away the wood and wrenched out the Grates in the window of the Room in which he was confined at which Window he made his Escape." In 1762, the condition of the old gaol was such that it was deemed necessary to build a new one which was completed the following year at a cost of 305-06-00 lawful money. Jonathan Sayward was one of the committee.

HOUSE OF CORRECTION

This introduces a secondary place of detention in the system of penology in the Massachusetts government. As stated in their plans adopted before emigration in 1629, these buildings were stated to be for

> "such as shalbe negligent and remiss in pformance of their dutyes or otherwise exorbitant our desire is that a house of correccon bee erected and set upp both for the punishment of such offendors and to deterr others by their example from such irregular courses."

In 1632 a "House of Correction" was built in Boston.

In this connection it is well to understand that prisons in the modern acceptation of the word were not built so much for felons as for the detention of debtors. In 1654, the General Court passed a law authorizing the imprisonment of debtors until their creditors were satisfied as to payment. It was not intended that they should be fashionable boarding houses for murderers and highwaymen where coddling them as heroes was permitted by the officers executing the law. As so many crimes were punishable by death under the Massachusetts laws and execution of the death penalty was prompt there was no occasion to afford means for interminable delays of justice such as modern legal contrivances to defeat justice permit. These prisons were almost exclusively used for the indefinite confinement of poor debtors as well as for the temporary detention of persons accused of crimes against life and property pending trial. In 1659, the County Court added to the existing complications by directing that another penal institution be erected in this town, without delay, in these terms:

> "Whereas the court hath considered the necessary use of an house of correction to be built in this county, as law hath provided to be in others, for the more constant & condigne punishment of obstinate offenders, as occasion from time to time shall require
>
> "It is therefore ordered that Maj. Nicholas Shapleigh, Edward Rishworth, Re: Cor: & and Mr. Abra: Preble shall take an affectual course for building of an house of correction for the town of York, according to such dimensions as they shall see meet for that use, & to order the finishing thereof before the next County Court, who are also impowered for defraying the charges thereof, to make a rate & levy it upon the whole county."

John Parker was appointed "to keep the house of correction when it is built."

The difference between a jail and a house of correction is not clearly apparent, especially in a sparsely settled country, but whatever it was the County Court wanted another one, and in July 1666, it was ordered that there should be "sett up a Pryson" at Falmouth immediately. This prison would, as a matter of space available, relieve the strain on the gaol here, if the pressure was too great, but the trouble seems to have been of a different character.

According to the newspapers of Boston there was a House of Correction here in 1765, and in April the *News Letter* prints a story of six women who were convicted of fornication and upon their confession were fined fifty shillings or ten stripes at the whipping post. Not being able to pay the fine they received the lash. They were called "veterans." Two of them were committed to the "House of Correction" and there they underwent

Court House, Gaol, and Punishments

the "Discipline of the House, which by way of Entrance was ten Stripes more each."

Escapes from either one of these places of confinement were common. Rewards for their apprehension were inserted in the *New Hampshire Gazette* as the nearest means of publicity. An example is here inserted:

> BROKE out of his Majestys Gaol in York on the Night of the 5th Instant, Samuel Richards and Benair Doore, imprisoned on Suspicion of making and passing Counterfeit Dollars; each of them of a midling stature and of about Thirty Years of Age. WHOEVER takes up said Prisoners and secures them, so that they may be brought to Justice, shall have TEN DOLLARS Reward and all the necessary Charges Paid by me.
>
> JEREMIAH MOULTON, Jr.
> Sheriff

York, March 6th, 1762.

At that time counterfeiting was punishable by death and the Sheriff was personally responsible for the safe-keeping of his prisoners.

In 1812, the use of the jail was granted to the County for one hundred years, or longer, if required.

The first keeper of the prison was John Parker who held the position until 1678, when he resigned. Richard Carter succeeded in 1679, and was followed by William Bray (1683), Thomas Harris (1685), William Bray again in 1690. In 1708, Thomas Moore held the office as well as that of Master of the House of Correction. In subsequent years the sheriff of the county became the responsible official with a resident assistant called a Turnkey. The salary of the Sheriff was 10 pounds annually, and the Turnkey had as his recompense 2 shillings and 6 pence for turning the key and was allowed 3 shillings and 9 pence per week for feeding the prisoners.

PUNISHMENTS

This formidable structure was not the only method of impressing evil doers or the evil-minded with the majesty of the law. There were other visible means of putting the fear of the law in their hearts. York had in its punitive equipment a pillory which consisted of two posts between which was a hinged board, or divisible in two parts with a hole in which the head was set fast, and two like openings for the hands. The prisoner stood locked in this on a raised platform looking down on passers-by. Usually a paper was affixed to this device stating the occasion for the punishment. It would be impracticable to enumerate the offenses for which the pillory was used. In 1671, Thomas Withers stood in our pillory for two hours for "putting in several votes for himself as an officer at a town meeting" and shortly afterwards for putting money into the contribution box and then "surriptisiously taking it out again." One of the first of these supplementary agencies was the whipping post. This was erected in the gaol grounds and probably had been in use even before the gaol was built. This method of punishment was reserved for the more serious offenses against morals, although violation of the Seventh Commandment was punishable by death. Small thievery received this form of punishment. In 1666, Mary Brawn of this town was sentenced to be whipped at the post "in publique meeting" with ten stripes for stealing sixteen pieces of pork from Sampson Angier. Young married persons, whose courtship had been carried on under the convenient and comfortable New England "bundling" device, and had anticipated events unwisely, found themselves in the hands of the law, when their first child appeared in advance of the physiological period of gestation. After labor was safely over both of them were haled into Court and ordered to the whipping post to receive a dozen stripes each at the hands of the public executioner. It is probable that many cases of premature delivery were unjustly punished. How long the whipping post was in operation is uncertain. In January, 1768, the Boston Chronicle stated that "a young man who had been in York gaol received 20 lashes at the whipping post for theft." The publication of this item as news would indicate that flogging had ceased to be a general practice by that time.

STOCKS AND BILBOES

Stocks were erected after 1665, at the York Gaol and were of the kind in which the unfortunate victim of the sentence sat with his feet and hands locked in the form for several hours where passing citizens could entertain themselves by jibes and possibly harmless missiles at the helpless man. This kind of punishment was meted out for small offenses like slander, cursing, etc.

In 1696, the Provincial Court ordered that the "Sheriff forthwith provide a payr of Iron Bilbows for the Prison." Bilboes were a kind of stocks generally used at sea. This was a simple, but effective restraint consisting of a heavy bolt or bar of iron having two sliding shackles something like handcuffs. The legs of offenders were thrust into these shackles and locked there. Lying with his back on the floor, the culprit's legs were attached to a post and in that position ample time was given him for considering the enormity of his offense. "Laying by the heels in the bilboes" was not a pleasant method of expiating misdemeanors.

There is no evidence that a cucking stool existed in connection with the gaol. York was fined in 1665 for having no "coucking stool." This was a device invented for the punishment of scolding or gossiping women by ducking them in the water when placed in a stool or chair fixed at the end of a long pole operated like a well-sweep. The origin of the word is involved in remote obscurity and it was later called the ducking stool. Whether the lack of it indicates that York had no such women is left for others to decide.

THE SCARLET LETTER

Hawthorne's immortal story of this title has no actual foundation as far as the color scheme is involved, but it is presumed that letters of a conspicuous color or in marked contrast to the clothing of the convicted persons were selected. It is a fact that persons convicted of various crimes were required to wear in public certain letters or words which described their offenses "cut in cloth and sewed on their uppermost garment on the arm and Back." The letter "A" for adultery; "B" for blasphemy; "D" for drunkard are examples. In other cases, the words were spelled out in full or a longer sentence written on paper in capital letters specified the crime more fully.

In 1651, the fourth wife of the famous Rev. Stephen Bachiler was convicted in a trial at York of adultery and the sentence of the Court was that she be branded on the cheek with the letter "A," and this sentence was carried out undoubtedly in York, by which she carried a permanent red scar for the rest of her days. This is the only known instance of the use of this permanent disfigurement in Maine. In fact, the records of the Province are singularly free from those awful cruelties inflicted by the Puritans of Massachusetts on those who happened to differ from them in matters of religion or politics. Cutting off the ears, pressing to death and endless floggings of Quakers at the cart's tail "from town to town" are some of the inhuman tortures which cannot be laid to the courts of justice in this town or Province.

BENEFIT OF CLERGY

One of the oldest customs in legal practice in England, sanctioned by law, is that of pleading the "benefit of clergy." It was in use as early as 1200, and was devised for the protection of the clergy when accused of crime, as it was claimed that they should be tried by Ecclesiastical Courts and not by the civil authorities. Thus arose the plea of "Benefit of Clergy" and the accused was turned over to the church authorities for trial and punishment if he could satisfy the judges that he could read the Holy Scripture. "The Book" as it was called was given to him to read in open court, and it came to be a custom to require the prisoner to read the first verse of the fifty-first chapter of the Psalms. From this circumstance that particular passage has been known for ages as "the Neck verse," as it has saved so many necks from the gallows. This verse reads: "Have mercy upon me, O God, according to thy loving kindness: according unto the multitude of thy tender mercies blot out my transgressions." Every clever criminal who could read invoked the "benefit of clergy," and if he could read this verse, or any other, the Ordinary or his Deputy said, "legit ut clericus" (he reads like a clerk), and he was then branded or flogged. It seems incredible, but it was a legal plea in England until 1824, when the statute was abolished. This plea was made by John Adams on behalf of the British soldiers tried in Boston for participation in the "Boston Massacre" and was allowed by the Court. It seems strange that this legal fiction was used here in York in 1736, at a trial for counterfeiting which, at that time, was punishable by death. William Patten of Wells was charged with "counseling, advising and assisting in forging and counterfeiting 25 shilling bills of New Hampshire and 5 pounds and 10 shilling bills of Connecticut Colony." John MacDonald of Wells had procured the engraving done in Dublin, Ireland, and some York people were involved in the transaction. Patten only was tried and, being found guilty, "prayed the Benefit of the Clergy which was granted him and Sentence was that he should be burnt in the Hand, suffer six Months Imprisonment and pay Costs." The Judges were Samuel Came, Jeremiah Moulton and Samuel Moody.

EXECUTION OF JOSEPH QUASSON FOR MURDER IN 1726

One of the Indians employed in the warfare against the Eastern tribes in 1725 killed another Indian, also a soldier named John Peters at Wells, and in due course he was tried here, found guilty and sentenced to death. The occasion was "improved," as contemporary phraseology would express it, by Mr. Moody to draw the usual moral lesson from the crime, and he printed his story of the affair detailing the conversion of the unfortunate man with a biography in the form of questions and answers between the "visitor" and "prisoner." He relates the visits of religious women to give him consolation and affords some interesting information regarding the execution itself which took place on June 29. He states that most of the ministers in the county and several others accompanied the prisoner from the gaol to the place of execution. He states that "the mile's Walk was improved in directing, encouraging & cautioning the Prisoner to Hope." When they came in sight of the gallows he was asked if he were not terrified, to which he replied: "Not at all." Again, this conversation ensued when they beheld "the first sight of the Sea, on the Shore of which was the Place of Execution" one of his escort asked him if he were not afraid to embark on the "Ocean of Eternity," to which he expressed entire readiness to take the journey. In this manner the time was occupied by these lugubrious suggestions of his approaching doom. "The Gallows was fixed in a Valley with Hills on the one Side and on the other so that the numerous Spectators (they were by Conjecture about Three Thousand—there having been no such Example in the country for more than Seventy Years), had an advantageous Prospect." When all was ready for the final act he ascended the ladder and made a short address, after which he offered a prayer of some length, and out of this scene Parson Moody has made an instructive picture of the way criminals were executed in his day. In June, 1704, Mr. Moody attended the execution of six pirates in Boston, in company of his cousin, Judge Samuel Sewall. He relates that there were in the river carrying spectators about one hundred and fifty boats and canoes. Evidently hangings had a fascination for the parson.

EXECUTION OF PATIENCE BOSTON, INDIAN, 1735

An unfortunate Indian woman, named Patience Boston, gave birth to an illegitimate child, of which she alleged one Trott to be the father, and she killed it at birth. She was tried and convicted in June of the above year and sentenced to death by hanging. As usual she underwent "conversion" which is related in a pamphlet by Parson Moody and his son Joseph, and went to her doom on Stage Neck, very cheerfully, according to these witnesses.

"EXECUTION" OF WILLIAM DEERING, 1749

Under date of February 16, 1749, Parson Smith of Falmouth wrote in his *Diary:* "Yesterday one Mrs. Deering of Bluepoint (Scarboro), was found barbarously murdered; it is supposed by her husband." She was Grace Pine before marriage. The suspicion proved correct and he was tried for the crime and convicted in June following the deed. He was to be executed here August 3, 1749, but when the fatal day arrived the prisoner's cell was empty. He was of a good family and had influential friends in and out of court. He was son of Joseph and Mary (Bray) Deering of Kittery. Among them was Sir William Pepperrell, who was related to him by marriage, his mother being a Bray, and it was generally supposed that the Baronet found means to save his relative from the gallows through connivance with the authorities here and in Boston. The prestige of Pepperrell prevented any public scandal arising and the affair was allowed to drop. It is supposed that he was taken to England in a mast ship belonging to Pepperrell.

EXECUTION OF TONY, A NEGRO, 1756

A Negro named Tony, living with his master in Kittery, murdered the young daughter of the family by throwing her down the well. He said that he did it to bring himself to the gallows, so that he would bring an end to his alleged hard usage.

Asked why he did not kill himself instead, he said that it would be wicked. Under the circumstances he was accommodated by a conviction for wilful murder in June 1756, and on July 29 following, the sentence was carried out at the usual place. "He behaved very penitently," as was reported.

CHAPTER

11.

The first military encounter between the British and Americans which took place in Maine in 1775 was at Machias. Local tradition claims that it was the first naval battle of the Revolution.

THE CAPTURE OF THE MARGARETTA*
The First Naval Battle of the Revolution
by
George F. Talbot.

The British attempt to apply military coercion to the American colonies aroused a feeling of resistance at Machias, just as it did at Lexington, Concord and Bunker Hill. The people of Machias of 1775, were Yankees of the Yankees. They belonged to Massachusetts politics and Massachusetts religion, just as they have till today. They entered enthusiastically and unanimously into the quarrel of their native state, and if Massachusetts was going to war with George III, they were going to war with him without one thought of the chances and without waiting to know whether another colony or another man was likely to back them.

When the American revolution broke out about eighty families made their home in the old town of Machias. With them the first consideration had been not that proximity so convenient for schools, for social visiting and the easy communication which roads and sidewalks afford, but a good site and plenty of land, which should give a homestead for themselves and their posterity. So with their two hundred and fifty acre first division lots they occupied both banks of the river, from the sea and its branches, East, West and Middle Rivers. The sixteen seven-acre lots of the first mill-owners made the nucleus of the village.

A lumbering community work energetically at stated seasons, but have many hours and days of idleness. We can fancy these first settlers, following a habit their children have never lost, gathered along the mill brow on the north bank of the river and sitting upon the great prostrate pines that here and there skirted it, talking over the affairs of the nation. Two coasters have lately got in from Boston. Captain Ichabod Jones, the prosperous merchant, who owns the vessels and a store, is too busy, perhaps too proud a man, to spend much time with the loafers who are whittling in their shirt sleeves. But the captain of the Polly, Jones' second trading sloop, is too full of intelligence to lose the opportunity of opening his budget before a crowd of excited listeners. It is difficult to exaggerate the importance of the captain of a coaster in those days. He was the newspaper, the mail and the telegraph, all combined. He brought to the people the news, the fashions and the opinions, as well as the hats and shoes they wore, and the bread, pork, fish, and beans they subsisted upon. His advent to the settlement, only a few times a year, must have been an event important enough to draw together from their scattered lots all the men of the colony. They came to trade for goods, for which they were always waiting, and to hear how the Boston people were getting along in their quarrel with the king. Getting along badly enough, they learned from the sloop's captain. From resisting the Stamp Act and throwing overboard the taxed tea it had come to actual war. A thousand men had been marched into the interior as far as Concord, when the farmers of the back towns gathered at the bridge and began to fire upon them. The regulars retreated, and militiamen, coming up from all the country round, chased

---

*George F. Talbot, *Collections and Proceedings of the Maine Historical Society,* II, Series II (Published by the Society, 1891), pp. 1-17.

them all day to Charlestown, killing and wounding hundreds of them. Perhaps the Polly's captain was at Charlestown, and saw the bleeding, haggard and dusty *redcoats* straggling in under shelter of the ships. Perhaps he was in Boston the next day and saw the wounded and stark corpses of the slain taken out of the boats. It was great news to hear and great news to tell; let us believe he told it well.

It has been too much taken for granted by the local historians that Captain Jones sided with the Tories in the struggle for independence. If he did, it is difficult to understand why Judge Jones, his nephew, who was admitted into all his counsels, was such a zealous patriot and republican. Captain Jones probably felt as merchants generally do when war, that interrupts all their commerce and threatens destruction to all their fortunes, impends. The difficulties with the home government he believed and hoped would be settled. Beside, he was in the enemy's power and had to make the best terms he could. He wanted to extricate his family and household effects, as well as his vessels, from Boston, then in possession of the king's forces under strict military law, and he could only do so by agreeing to take back in his vessels cargoes of lumber to be used in constructing barracks for the English troops, for which he was to be fully paid. That he stood well with the promoters of the revolution is evident from the fact that the selectmen of Boston furnished him with a petition to the people of Machias, desiring them not to hinder him in his enterprise. He seems to have proceeded with the prudence characteristic of his calling; for before opening his hatches and offering his goods for sale he exacted from the people a stipulation that they, on their part, would not molest him. He tried to get an obligation generally signed by the citizens by which they were to bind themselves to allow him to carry lumber to Boston and protect him and his property. But this many of the people refused to sign, and then, at his desire, a town meeting was called, which must have been somewhat stormy. At last a vote, not unanimous, was obtained to permit the vessels to load and sail, and Jones began to open his hatches and retail his goods to his old customers. But it is said he made a discrimination, refusing credit to those who had been prominent in obstructing his wishes, so that on the whole there was more exasperation of feeling than hearty accord produced by the vote of the town extorted under such circumstances. But it is probable that the permission granted in the vote would have been carried out in good faith had not the captain of the Margaretta unnecessarily provoked a quarrel with the inhabitants.

The Machias people had received notice in some way through the proclamation of the Provincial Congress that hostilities had commenced by an invasion into the very heart of Massachusetts and by the slaughter of its citizens, who had resisted the evident attempt of the British government to deprive them of the liberty and right of self-government they had enjoyed ever since their colonial charters. The Machias settlers responded to this proclamation with zeal and unanimity, and raised a liberty pole to stand as a symbol of their patriotism. Captain Moor, of the Margaretta, when he learned that the liberty pole had been erected and what it signified, ordered it to be taken down, under the threat of firing upon the town. A town meeting was held and voted with great spirit that the liberty pole should stand, but even then Jones induced Captain Moor to withhold hostilities until a fuller and larger town meeting, which he promised should be held on the fourteenth of June, and which should take final action in the matter. In the meantime the leading patriots, knowing that the town would never yield the point, looked round to see what means they had for defense and resistance.

There was then living at East River a sort of patriarch of the settlement, Benjamin Foster, the father of a numerous family, and a man, through his long life, of great consideration in both state and church affairs. The sixteen settlers of 1763 had brought his brother, Wooden Foster, with them to be their blacksmith—an artisan indispensable in an isolated lumbering community. He himself came in 1765, and, being a man of substance and enterprise, took up a lot at East River and built the first sawmill there. At the time of the event I am now reciting he was about fifty years of age, and having been present as a soldier at the first capture of Louisbourg in 1745, and having served under General Abercrombie in the French and Indian war ten years later, he was probably the man of the largest military experience in the whole settlement. As such he was made lieutenant of the first militia company in 1769, Judge Jones being its captain. Foster was the most prominent man in planning and organizing the expedition that led to the capture of the Margaretta. The sons of Morris O'Brien, six in number—one of them, Colonel Jeremiah, the leader—won the renown of the actual capture.

Their counsels were divided. Foster was in favor of taking possession of the now partly laden sloops of Captain Jones and making prisoners of the officers and men of the Margaretta, their convoy. More timid men must have urged that the town had voted to let the sloops be loaded and depart, and it was only on that condition that they had procured their supplies, and it was only by performing their promise that they could expect to be kept from starvation thereafter. But the coolness of Foster and the impetuosity of the O'Briens overwhelmed all calculations of prudence. Foster, weary of the debate, crossed a brook near which they were standing and called out to all who favored the capture of the Margaretta and the two sloops to follow him, and ultimately every man stood by his side. This was Sunday, the eleventh of June, 1775. Foster was a devout man, but no doubt he believed himself to be engaged in the Lord's business on that day.

A plan of attack was immediately agreed upon. The English officers would be at meeting that morning. A rude building, twenty-five by forty feet, had been built on the site of the present town hall and used for public worship. It had benches arranged on each side of a central aisle. It was decided to attempt to surround the church and seize the officers during service. Part of the company remained under Foster to do this at the proper conjuncture, and the rest dispersed, attending church as worshipers, though perhaps giving less heed than usual to the services. They had brought their guns and secreted them outside the building. John O'Brien says he hid his gun under a board and took his seat on a bench behind Captain Moor, ready to seize him at the first alarm. The day was warm and fine and the windows of the little tabernacle were wide open. A singular accident disclosed the danger of overlooking the Negro element. In our late great war we suffered everywhere delay, disaster, and defeat by not taking the Negro into our counsels. Just so it happened to the Machias patriots. I have no doubt Parson Lyon was fully possessed of the plot his flock was engaged in. The able, highly educated and eccentric Parson Lyon was called as the first settled minister at Machias, from Nova Scotia, and like many other people of that province who afterward fled to the States, was a zealous Whig. There were warlike sentiments in the old familiar psalms he might have selected that morning without exciting the suspicion of the English officers in their gay uniforms and decorous demeanor. But London Atus, the ancestor of all the Atuses, the colored servant of Mr. Lyon, had not been taken into the confidence of the military leaders. In some perch of a Negro pew, with a better outdoor view than the body of the congregation, he got sight of armed men—Foster's band—crossing a foot bridge that connected two islands on the falls, and giving an outcry, leaped out of the window. The English officers followed his example, and by the time Foster's force had reached the meeting-house they had reached their vessel and Jones, who was to have been made a prisoner, had fled and secreted himself in the woods. Captain Moor weighed anchor at once and proceeded down the river. The excited public followed on each bank of the river, keeping up a harassing musketry fire but at too long range to be dangerous, and shots were fired from the cutter. Foster and O'Brien then determined to seize Jones' sloops and pursue the cutter. One of these—the Polly—could not have been in a condition to be available. Perhaps she was already too heavily laden, but the O'Brien's took possession of the Unity, Jones' other sloop, and during the rest of Sunday mustered a crew of volunteers, numbering in all about forty men, and Foster went to the *East River* to get a schooner there and a volunteer crew to join in the enterprise.

Early the next morning they proceeded down the river from both villages. The East River vessel got a-ground and had no share in the battle. Of the party on board the Unity only half had muskets and for these there were only three rounds of ammunition. The rest had armed themselves with pitchforks and narrow axes. So sudden and impulsive had been the expedition that up to this time it had been an unorganized mob. But as, with a favoring wind, they sailed down the river they had leisure to complete their plans. Jeremiah O'Brien, the oldest of the brothers, was made captain, and Edmund Stevens, lieutenant, and knowing they had no powder to waste in long shots they determined to bear down on the enemy's ship, board her and decide the contest at once upon her deck.

Nothing can be more beautiful than the aspects in summer time of the trebly branching river and of the estuary inclosed between sheltering islands and steep and rocky cliffs that make its port. How much more beautiful it must have been before the ax had thinned the forest, and fires had bared the shores and islands, not only of the ancient forest, but of the soil that supported it, and left the blanched, bleak rock to be reflected upon the quiet surface of the sea, where the inverted woods once spread their margin of green! Little eye had those stalwart youths for all that beauty; the splendor of their heroism has fairly outshone it all, beautiful as it may have been.

Where was the East River schooner and its brave commander? These daring volunteers did not know; they did not wait for her. Forty undisciplined men are in chase of a vessel armed with sixteen swivels and four four-pounders, with a complement of men, without any thought of the peril of their adventure. The bravery at Lexington and Concord, where several hundred militiamen fired upon retreating regulars from behind trees, fences, and stone walls, or on Bunker Hill, where, mainly behind earthworks sheltered from shot, well-armed men resisted three successive assaults of a line of battle, was certainly not greater than that. I do not know of any feat in all the war, or of any war, that for daring and desperate courage can be compared with it.

As the sloop opened out into the broad river below Machiasport village the enemy they were in pursuit of came in sight and soon within hailing distance. Moor hailed the sloop and told her to keep off or he would fire. O'Brien shouted back a demand for surrender, and Stevens an emphatic defiance. Moor withheld his fire, and the breeze strengthening set all his sails and tried to escape. It is easy to see that Captain Moor owed the loss of his vessel and his life to his own hesitation—I cannot think to his cowardice.

When he stood out to sea again the sloop was close upon him and a collision had become unavoidable. So he opened fire and killed one man on board the sloop. The sloop answered with a volley of shot, and soon afterward the vessels came together and John O'Brien leaped on board the cutter. Then the vessels swung apart, leaving O'Brien alone on the quarter-deck of the enemy. He says seven muskets were fired at him without effect, and when the English marines charged upon him with bayonets he jumped over the rail and swam to the sloop. Captain O'Brien next ran the bowsprit of the sloop through the mainsail of the cutter, and twenty of his men armed with pitchforks rushed upon her deck. While in contact or at very close range musket shots had been exchanged, the assailants using all their ammunition. One man was killed, one mortally and one seriously wounded upon the sloop. Five were killed or mortally wounded on board the Margaretta—Captain Moor, who was shot through by two musket balls early in the action; the man at the helm; Captain Robert Avery, and two sailors or marines. When the man at the helm fell, the cutter broached to and was thus run into. Captain Robert Avery was the skipper of an American coaster lying in Holmes Bay and had been forcibly seized by Captain Moor and taken on board the cutter to act as pilot out of the river. The number wounded is not known. John O'Brien says the American vessel had four killed and eight or nine wounded, and the British ten killed and ten wounded. But he says himself that he does not remember the number, but gives it upon the authority of a letter of Captain Joseph Wheaton, written to O'Brien, in which he claims to have been present as one of the sloop's crew. Mr. Smith in his history, gives the name of John Wheaton as one of the heroes, mistaking the christian name which should have been Joseph. I have followed Mr. Smith's statement of the number of killed and wounded as more probably correct and more nearly agreeing with local tradition.

The error by which Captain Moor forfeited his vessel and his life was in not using his heavy guns while the sloop was at long range and had no effective means of returning the fire. When the vessels were in contact his superior armament had become unavailable. The firing of the Americans had been close and murderous, and when Moor fell, the midshipman Stillingfleet, next in command was panic-stricken and fled below and gave up the ship. The English officers did not know that the ammunition of their enemy had been exhausted, and the assault was too fierce and hot for the reloading of empty muskets. In a hand-to-hand contest a pitchfork—not the slender and elastic implement our factories now turn out, but such a stout and rude double spear as Wooden Foster would forge upon his anvil, set in a long ash pole—was a formidable weapon in the hands of a man who knew how to use it. The very novelty of the weapon, against which their tactics and drill had taught them no effective guard, may have dismayed the marines. At any rate the boarding of the cutter seems to have been the end of the strife, and there was nothing else to do but take care of the wounded, secure their prize, and return to the settlement to electrify their friends with the news of their success. They had purchased their victory by the death of two men—Coolbroth and McNeil. John Berry received a severe wound in his head, for which he afterward received a pension, and Isaac Taft and Joseph Cole were slightly wounded. John O'Brien relates that as soon as his brother Jeremiah was elected captain he gave leave to all who were afraid to join in the attack to leave and offered them a boat, and that three men availed themselves of his offer. He also says that the whole six of the O'Brien brothers—Jeremiah, Gideon, John, William, Dennis, and Joseph—participated in the action, and that Morris O'Brien his father was only prevented from accompanying them by the remonstrances of his sons.

Beside these, let us carefully recapitulate among the heroes every name that tradition has preserved. There was Edmund Stevens of Addison, who shouted back defiance when Moor threatened to fire; Samuel Watts, ancestor, I think, of the Englishman's River Wattses; Jonathan Knight, one of the first settlers of Calais, and who has descendants there; Steele and Merritt from Pleasant River (the name is still preserved in that region); Josiah Weston, forefather of the Jonesboro Westons; John Berry, Isaac Taft and James Cole, who were wounded; Nathaniel Crediforth, Josiah Libby, Joseph Wheaton, William Fenderson, Ezekiel Foster, son or grandson of Isaiah, brother of Benjamin called the *colonel;* Simeon Brown, Samuel Whiting, Elias Hoyt and Joseph Getchell, ancestor of those well-esteemed people who have chiefly made their home at Marshfield (he always claimed to have stepped on the Margaretta's deck foot to foot with John O'Brien), and, last of all, Richard Earle, colored servant of Colonel Jeremiah O'Brien, making good by his courage the indiscretion of his race that had defeated the bloodless enterprise of the day before.

Great must have been the exultation at Machias when the Unity and her prize came up with the returning tide to West Falls, sobered somewhat by grief for the slain and the general respect and regret, which was felt for the untimely death of the young English captain. As a part of the preparations of Sunday a messenger had been dispatched to Chandler's River to procure powder and ball, and as the men of that settlement were all absent at Machias—many of them, as we have seen in the expedition—two women, Hannah and Rebecca Weston, nineteen and seventeen years old, procured thrity or forty pounds of Rebecca Weston, nineteen and seventeen years old, procured thirty or forty pounds of blazed trees, and arriving at the settlement at two o'clock in the afternoon after the capture of the Margaretta.

A committee of safety was elected, who had the control of the military and civil affairs during the remainder of the war. The armament of the Margaretta was transferred to the sloop Unity, which was fitted up with bulwarks and named the Machias Liberty, and Jeremiah O'Brien, her commander, cruised for three weeks off the coast trying to capture the Diligence, a British coast survey vessel. The Diligence came into the lower harbor the middle of July, with an armed tender. The officers and part of the crew landed at Buck's Harbor as they said, to learn the fate of the Margaretta, and were surprised and captured by Captain Smith, grandfather of Bartlett Smith, the lamented historian of Machias, and the next day O'Brien in the Liberty and Foster in the Falmouth packet boarded and captured, without resistance, both the Diligence and her tender. On the twenty-sixth of June the Provincial Congress passed a vote of thanks to Captain Jeremiah O'Brien and Captain Benjamin Foster and the brave men under their command, for these heroic exploits, and placed at their disposal the two sloops and the Margaretta, which they had taken.

The enemy's wounded, as well as those of the expedition, seemed to have been as well cared for as was possible. A hospital was improvised out of a shop, and most of the wounded were placed in it and treated as well as they could be in a town, where was neither surgeon nor physician. Captain Moor, who was still alive when the prize was brought up river to the village, was received in the house of Judge Jones, nephew of Captain Ichabod Jones. A messenger was dispatched at once to Nova

Scotia for a surgeon, but Captain Moor could not profit by his long delayed arrival. His death occurred the day after the battle.

There is this pathetic relation of the unkindly fate of this young officer, who seems to have been a brave man, intent upon his duties, and who, as he must have believed, in a time of peace, did not consider that it would be actually necessary to turn his heavy guns upon a nearly unarmed party of fellow British subjects. It is asserted, that on his voyage to Machias, he brought as passengers from Boston two estimable young ladies, relatives of Captain Jones, to one of whom he was affianced, and that his service at Machias performed, and the two sloops at sea for Boston, he expected to sail to Halifax and there be married.

The expedition to Nova Scotia for a surgeon brought back Doctor William Chaloner, another Nova Scotia Whig, who continued to be a citizen of Machias, and was of eminent service and has left there a large and very respectable progeny.

This unique naval battle fought with such intrepid courage was the first naval contest of the revolutionary war. Its date is June 12, 1775. Only the Lexington and Concord fight had preceded it in that great struggle and the battle of Bunker Hill was not fought till several days later.

In briefly reviewing the event, our surprise and admiration pass alternately from the rash audacity of the project to the impetuous bravery of its accomplishment. There was a completely isolated lumbering community that did not raise its bread or vegetables, not even potatoes, and brought hay for the teams that were used in logging over sea from far away Nova Scotia, that was fed from hand to mouth, by supplies of provisions brought from Boston and exchanged for pine boards. Their only market and source of supplies was held by the whole British army in America. The cutter they seized was the convoy that had protected the sloops from whose cargoes they had just been fed, and that were to carry back the lumber with which they had paid for them, under a written permit obtained from the selectmen of Boston, who were of the patriot party. In flying at and seizing this vessel and her convoy they seemed to be arresting this trade and driving themselves and their families not only to invasion, burning, and pillage but to immediate starvation.

But we forget the grandeur of this sacrifice in our later admiration of the daring with which they accomplished their scheme. A trading craft without bulwarks or armed marines, or even sailors is pressed into service driven bows on to an armed cutter with forty trained men on board thoroughly armed and provided with heavy guns and ammunition, and commanded by a brave officer of the royal navy. Of the party of forty perhaps not a man was ever in battle, not more than twenty of them had muskets with only powder enough for them to be discharged thrice; and with this equipment they crowd all sail, rush at their prey, storm across her deck with no effective weapons but pitchforks and axes, for their ammunition had been spent. The captain of the assailed vessel is slain, the men borne down in the impetuous rush take shelter below, and the panic stricken officer who succeeds to the command surrenders his vessel to the assailants. Surely there is nothing like this in our early or recent history.

CHAPTER 12.

Shortly after the encounter at Machias, British power was leveled at the town of Falmouth. The British, of course, felt that they were justified in using force to quell an insurrection just as Americans today countenance the use of force to restrain unruly elements who challenge governmental policies.

THE BURNING OF FALMOUTH, 1775*
by
John C. Warren

"Often I think of the beautiful town
　That is seated by the sea;
Often in thought go up and down
The pleasant streets of that dear old town,
　And my youth comes back to me."

In these familiar lines one of Portland's most brilliant sons expressed the same affection for the scenes of his youth that animated the ancient settlers of Falmouth, causing them to long once more for a sight of the lofty promontory of Machigonne and island studded bay, while they were exiled from their homes by the desolating Indian wars of 1676 and 1690. For several years the peninsula had been uninhabited. The savage warrior had for a time banished the pioneer; and nature by slow degrees was repairing the same damage wrought by the axes of Tucker, Cleeves and those who came in their train.

But with peace established along the frontier, old settlers returned accompanied by others, who were not slow to recognize the natural advantages of the new settlement. Petitions soon flooded the executive office of the colony, setting forth convincing reasons why this or that "said humble petitioner" should be given grants of unoccupied land. The growth of Falmouth was rapid but healthy; along the water front several ship-yards were established and numerous wharves began to reach out across the muddy, grass-matted flats towards the deeper water, for the location of Falmouth made it essentially a commercial town. The harbor presented a constant scene of animation. Under the sheltering lee

"the eddies and dimples of the tide
Play round the bows of ships
That steadily at anchor ride."

Often in the harbor lay ships loading with masts for the Royal Navy, towering pines marked with the "broad arrow" obtained from the heavy forests of the surrounding towns.

Thus during the troubled period immediately preceding the outbreak of the American war of independence the village on the Neck consisted of something like a hundred and fifty families and supported three settled ministers. During the long period when the relations between the colonies and the mother country were strained, the spirit of resentment against English injustice ran high. Two prominent citizens, General Preble and Admiral Tyng, came to blows on the street over a difference in political opinions and several civil disturbances occurred. Of the manner in which the papers relating to the Stamp Act were received in Falmouth, Mr. Goold says:

> "In Falmouth the mob spirit was awakened and on the arrival of a brig from Halifax, in January, 1776, with the stamped papers for Cumberland County, they were demanded at the custom house. On receiving them, the people carried them through the town on a pole to a bonfire prepared for them, where they were burnt in the presence of a large concourse of approving people."

After Boston was placed under military law all knew that the crisis was rapidly approaching and that the time would soon come when the British regulars would measure their strength with the sturdy colonists. Parson Smith of the First Parish

---

*John C. Warren. *"The Burning of Falmouth, 1775." Pine Tree Magazine* VII, No. 2 (March, 1907), pp. 152-157.

of Falmouth writes under the date of April 19, 1775:

> "To-day our people in many hundreds are collected from all the near towns. The people are everywhere in the utmost consternation and distress."

The news of the fighting at Lexington and Concord did not reach Falmouth until the 21st of April. On the 23rd a patriotic town-meeting was held and it was voted to raise a company of sixty men under the command of Captain David Bradish to be despatched to the scene of hostilities. This was shortly afterwards enlisted and became a part of Colonel Phinney's regiment.

During such stirring times men will go to extremes. For the resolute nature there is no middle course. Today we can look back and respect the feelings of Admiral Tyng and Captain Coulson when they stood boldly facing the storm of popular sentiment, adhering in their loyalty to the crown. The former held a commission in the Royal Navy, well earned by services at Louisbourg and before the end of the Revolution sacrificed practically his whole wealth for this principle. Captain Coulson was an Englishman by birth but he had married the daughter of Doctor Coffin of Falmouth where he made his home. He was engaged in the mast trade between this port and Bristol, England. Outspoken in his views, he became very obnoxious to his fellow townsmen. Early in 1775, Coulson had launched a new vessel which was waiting to be rigged when it was the owner's intent to load her for England with a cargo of masts then lying ready. "The American Association," a patriotic society which had been established in Falmouth and had a large membership, forbade him to carry out these plans. Determined not to be defeated, Captain Coulson prevailed upon Admiral Graves to detail Captain Mowatt in the sloop of war Canceau to Falmouth that there might be no violent interference with his operations while fitting out the new ship.

This course awed the inhabitants of the Neck into sullen submission, for their dwellings lay under the guns of the British vessel. Upon the people of the outlying districts, whose homes were beyond the range of hostile shot, the effect was different, for these acts served only to inflame the country militia who were wild to emulate the deeds of their fellow colonists in Massachusetts and strike a blow at the hated flag of the oppressor.

May 19th, Colonel Samuel Thompson of Brunswick, a venturesome spirit, embarked down the Bay with fifty followers for Falmouth and landed without raising an alarm near a grove on the northern side of the Neck. The Brunswick company lay concealed in the dense growth until about one o'clock in the afternoon of the 11th, detaining in their camp several citizens who had accidentally discovered their presence, when Captain Mowatt, the surgeon of the Canceau, and Rev. Mr. Wiswell, the pastor of St. Paul's parish, chancing in that vicinity, were captured. Of this eventful day Parson Smith says:

> "Doctor _____ and Parson Wiswell (no mention of Mowatt) walking on the Neck, were taken by them (the Brunswick company) and made prisoners, which made a vast tumult. The Gorhamites, with some from Windham, and Captain Phinney, called Colonel, Hart, Williams and Steward joined them in the night."

The effect of this rash act may be imagined. General Preble says in a letter: "He (Lieutenant Hogg of the Canceau) clapped springs on his cables and swore that if the gentlemen were not released before six o'clock he would fire on the town. He fired two cannon, and although there was no shot in them, it frightened the women and children to such a degree that some crawled under the wharves, some down cellar and some out of town."

To all it was plain that unless some steps were taken the destruction of the village was assured, so General Preble, Colonel Freeman and other prominent citizens waited upon Thompson and urged him to release the prisoners, who had been conveyed to Marston's tavern. The doughty Brunswick officer would not listen to any proposition for a time, declaring himself the special instrument of Providence protecting American liberties. At length he agreed to set free the captives on condition that they return and deliver themselves up the next morning, and also that Preble and Freeman remain in his hands as hostages. Under this arrangement the English officers went aboard their vessel.

Morning came, but with it no prisoners from the Canceau. The militia threatened the sureties with violence and were only pacified with liberal allowances of rations and rum. Under the mellowing effects of these, a self-constituted court-martial composed of militia officers, prominent among whom were Thompson and Phinney of Gorham, summoned a number of inhabitants of known Tory sentiments for examination. Some pressure must have been upon those appearing, much like the conversions of Clovis, for Rev. Mr. Wiswell, a staunch royalist, declared himself a true friend of liberty and abhorred any passive obedience to a tyrannical monarch.

Captain Coulson's fine residence was used as barracks and much rum was found in the cellar so that patriotism ran high all night and one zealous defender of his country's rights, overflowing with good cheer, descended to the waterfront and discharged a couple of musket balls into the Canceau.

These were rude times and the actions of the raw militia should not be criticized from our modern standpoints, for despite their excesses, they were the sturdy country yeomanry who willingly laid aside the tools of husbandry for the musket; quitting the quiet and safety of the farm, made fertile by their toil, for the din and dangers of uncertain war and winning at last, and establishing a principle of human rights.

The country soldiers remained in town until Friday, when much to the relief of the villagers, they took their departure, the Brunswick company taking with them a small boat captured from the Canceau. Despite unpleasant experiences, the inhabitants of the town persisted in their loyalty to the American cause, as the following letter from Admiral Graves of the English North Atlantic fleet to the Admiralty Office will show:

> "The town of Falmouth having long been a principal magazine of all kinds of merchandise, from whence, besides supplying the scattered villages of the provinces of New Hampshire and Massachusetts Bay, large quantities of goods were usually transported in small vessels to Newbury port, and from thence to the rebel army around Boston."

H.M.S. Senegal of eight guns under Captain Diddington arrived in the harbor June eighth as an escort to Captain Coulson, who was after the cargo of masts, which he had prepared previous to his departure when Mowatt had sailed away. The masts were not obtained, owing to the hostility of the townsmen who had secreted them in a cove near Vaughan's bridge. The Senegal remained only a few days and when she left, the wives of Tyng and Coulson were passengers to Boston, in order to be under the protection of a royal governor.

Now comes the time when the people of Falmouth were destined to feel the heavy hand of a powerful nation upon rebellious subjects and fully realize the horrors of war. Acting under the orders of Admiral Graves, Captain Mowatt sailed into the harbor, October sixteenth, with a squadron made up of the Canceau of sixteen guns, the ship Cat of twenty guns, a schooner of twelve guns, a bomb sloop and a schooner loaded with supplies for the cruise. The armed vessels were ranged from the foot of King, now India Street, to a position off Union Wharf. Late in the afternoon while the people were wondering at the import of the visit, an officer was sent ashore with the following letter. Mr. Bradbury, an early Falmouth lawyer, read it before the court house to the people:

> "After so many premeditated attacks on the royal prerogative of the best of sovereigns, after the repeated instances you have experienced in Britain's long forbearance of the rod of correction, and the manifest and paternal entension of her hands to embrace again and again, have been regarded as vain and nugatory; and in place of a dutiful and grateful return to your king and parent state, you are guilty of most unpardonable rebellion, supported by the ambition of a set of designing men, whose insidious views have cruelly imposed on the credulity of their fellow creatures; and at last brought the whole into the same dilemma; which leads me to feel not a little of the woes of the innocent of them in particular, from my having it in orders to execute a just punishment on the town of Falmouth, in the name of which authority, I previously warn you to remove without delay, the human specie out of said town, for which purpose I give you the time of two hours, at the period of which a red pennant will be hoisted at the main top gallant mast head with a gun. But if your imprudence should lead you to show the least resistance, you will in that case free me of that humanity so strongly pointed in my orders, as well as my inclination. I do also observe, that all those who did on a former occasion fly to the King's ship under my command for protection, the same door is open to receive them."

At the risk of being for a time, if not constantly, tedious I have quoted practically the whole of this remarkable communication, of which Mr. Deane says, "a letter full of bad English and worse spelling."

Consternation reigned when the contents of the message became known. The town which had so bravely struggled ahead during seventy-five years of peace, was on the eve of destruction. A committee composed of General Preble, Doctor Coffin and Robert Pagan, all members of St. Paul's parish, Church of England, were appointed to wait upon Captain Mowatt. The following terms were made, the town would be spared upon delivering to the English the eight cannon in the village together with the small arms of the inhabitants. Safety could be obtained until eight o'clock the next morning by sending out to the fleet eight muskets. Upon the return of the committee it was decided to give up the eight small arms, that the impending destruction might be averted for a few hours, thereby giving time to remove the women, children and sick; also what personal property was capable of being easily transported to a place of safety.

The next morning, though the destruction of their homes would be assured, the townspeople voted to surrender no more arms, and at eight o'clock a committee was despatched to acquaint the English commander with the decision reached. No greater exhibition of cool heroism can be found in American history than that of the citizens of Falmouth freely sacrificing all their property and delivering to destruction comfortable homes, fruits, in many cases, of a lifetime's industry. The envoys had been instructed to linger as long as possible aboard the English vessel so that time might be gained.

By half past eight the representatives of the town, having exhausted their persuasive powers, were ordered to go ashore. At nine o'clock the dreaded signal was sent aloft on the flagship and fire was at once opened by all the armed vessels upon the defenseless town. A panic ensued in the streets, which were crowded with teams of all descriptions loaded high with furniture. Although the moving had been going on for twelve hours there was much that remained to be consumed. Inhabitants with bundles on their backs or with a few articles in their hands hastened through the storm of hot shot and bombs, seeking a shelter; oxen, mad with fright, ran plunging across the open lots, overturning loads and scattering valuable household possessions hopelessly about. It certainly seems remarkable that no one was killed by the bombardment.

Refuge was sought by many on the high ledges near what is now High Street, then open pastures; others fled to the surrounding towns. Among the latter was Thomas Smith, pastor of the First Parish, who had faithfully presided over his congregation through times of want and plenty for a period of fifty years. Though deserted by her neighbors and in danger of losing, not only her property but her life, plucky Widow Greele remained in her tavern, Falmouth's leading house of entertainment, located at the present junction of Congress and Hampshire Streets. Several times the building took fire, but as many times the flames were quickly extinguished by the undaunted mistress. On one occasion a bomb fell in her yard but Dame Greele hastily picked it up with a pair of tongs and removed it to a safe distance, remarking to a man who chanced to be passing: "They will have to stop firing soon for they have got out of bombs, and are making new balls and can't wait for them to cool."

For twelve hours the firing was almost constant, besides which several landing parties were sent ashore, putting the torch to buildings near the waterfront. One of these parties was attacked near the present site of the custom house, and tradition has it that several of the enemy were killed by the exasperated colonists. In all, about one hundred and thirty dwelling-houses were destroyed besides a public library, town house, St. Paul's church and two wharves. The night after the burning of the town a terrific storm arose, increasing the misery of the homeless inhabitants. Thus let us leave them in their greatest extremity. Ruined, but looking bravely into the future, for these were the men who erected from the ashes of ancient Falmouth a new town, the Portland of our Fathers' day.

CHAPTER

13.

The English plan to sever a portion of Maine from Massachusetts as a haven for loyalists never was consummated. It if had been implemented, most of Maine might today belong to Canada.

THE PROPOSED PROVINCE OF NEW IRELAND*

by
Joseph Williamson

The design of the British government during the Revolution, of severing a portion of Maine from Massachusetts, and of erecting it into a province to be colonized by Loyalists, under the name of New Ireland, has received little attention from historians. The earliest published account of it appeared in the seventh volume of our Proceedings, and it has since been briefly noticed by Bancroft, in the closing volume of his history of the United States. Through the Royal Commission on Historical Manuscripts, I have obtained copies of several documents which illustrate the origin and progress of the project. These were found in the private collections of the Marquis of Lansdowne, the present Secretary of State for War, and of Earl Dartmouth, whose ancestor was Secretary for American Affairs during the Revolution. The first, an order approved in Cabinet August 10, 1780, and by the King on the following day, is as follows:

> It being judged proper and necessary to separate the Country lying to the North East of the Piscataway River from the Province of Massachusetts Bay, it is proposed to erect so much of it as lies between Sawkno River and the St. Croix (which is the South West boundary of Nova Scotia) and to extend from the Sea between two North Lines drawn from the Heads of those Rivers to the Boundary of Canada, into a New Province, which from its situation between the New England Provinces and Nova Scotia, may with great propriety be called New Ireland, especially as the Era of its establishment is coeval with that of opening the trade of Ireland with the American Provinces. The remainder of the Country lying between the Sawkno River and the Piscatway it is proposed to throw into New Hampshire in order to give that Province a greater Front on the Sea than it now has, and for reasons of deeper policy.
>
> It is proposed that the Constitution of the New Province should be similar to that of East Florida at the outset, consisting of only a Governor and Council, a Chief Justice, and other Civil Officers, provided for by Estimate granted by Parliament, but that a declaration be made of the King's Intention to give it a complete local Legislative whenever the Circumstances of the Province will admit of it; and it may be proper to declare what that Legislative will be, as a Model of the Constitution wished to take place throughout America.
>
> It has been found by sad experience that the Democratic power is predominant in all parts of British America. It is in vain to expect the Governor to possess the Shadow even of the Influence of the Crown to balance it, and the Council in the Royal Governments holding their Seats at the pleasure of the Governor, Men of personal weight prefer being Members of the Assembly to seats at that Board, and therefore the Members of it being chiefly Officers of the Crown without property and but little of the Aristocratick Influence to the Regal Authority of the Governor, altho they form a sort of Middle Branch of the Legislature. To combat the prevailing disposition of the People to Republicanism, and to balance the Democratic Power of the Assembly, It is proposed to form a distinct Middle Branch of Legislature. The Members to be appointed by the Crown and to hold their Seats during Life unless removed by His Majesty in Council upon a charge exhibited by a Majority of the Assembly or by the Governor and a Majority of the Privy Council. To preserve the Influence of the Governor in this Upper House it is proposed that the Privy Council should all be Members of it, and to compose a Major part of the whole, and that in case of vacancies in the Privy Council they should be filled up out of the Members of the Upper House. It is also proposed that the Seats in the Privy Council should have Titles of Honor annexed to them or some Emoluments in the Place of them to make them desired, at the same time the Governor to have the same power over them, all the King's Governors now have of suspending them from their Seats and thereby from their Honors or Emoluments, and if any distinction in England could be given them it would have a most powerful effect.
>
> No Quit Rents have been reserfed to the Crown in any grants within the Charter of the Massachusetts Bay, but it is proposed that the Lands in New Ireland shall be granted subject to a Quit Rent, tho' it might be proper to declare that when the Legislature shall make a grant of a permanent Revenue for the Support of the Government the produce of the Quit Rents will be given to be disposed of by them. An exemption from the payment of Quit Rent for a certain Term would however be proper to be granted to distinguished Loyalists. To prevent the admission of the disaffected and to continue the Inhabitants in

---

*Collections of the Maine Historical Society, (Portland: Published by the Society, 1904), 3rd Series, I, pp. 147-157.

their Principles of Loyalty and Attachment to Great Britain, and perpetuate those Principles in their Descendants, it is proposed that a Declaration be required to be made by every Grantee before the Governor and Council in the following Words. I do promise and declare that I will maintain and defend the Authority of the King, in His Parliament as the Supreme Legislature of this Province, and that a Condition be inserted in the Grant obliging all persons who shall come to the possession of any part of the Lands contained in it, either by Inheritance or purchase, to make and subscribe the same Declaration before a Magistrate within Twelve Months after coming into possession, and to have it Registered in the Secretary's Office of the Province on pain of Forfeiture of the Lands to the Crown.

The Province to be divided into Counties or Circuits, and subdivided into Parishes, in each Parish a Glebe Land to be laid out and vested in Trustees for the Minister. The Church of England to be declared the Established Church, but the Governor to be the Ordinary and have the presentation to all Benefices. A salary to be granted to each Minister payable out of the general Fund, and issued by Warrant of the Governor and Council. The King to appoint one of the Clergy His Vicar General to Superintend the rest, to hold Visitations and report to the Governor their behaviour, who may suspend or dismiss any Minister the Vicar General and his Clergy in Convocation shall represent against. Application to be made to the Bishops to superadd to the Vicar General a Power to Ordain. This has been done of necessity, in certain cases and if it be done here the Church will have the Advantage of a Bishop and no Alarm excited by the Name, and when the Function is become familiar the Title may easily be assumed. The Ordination of the Unitas Fratrum Society is allowed as valid as ours, and yet their Ordainers are neither called Bishops nor Lords—The Vicar General however to have a handsome Allowance.

To reward or Indemnify the Loyal Sufferers from the other Province, and at the same time lay the ground of an Aristocratic Power, the Lands to be granted in large Tracts to the most Meritorious and to be by them leased to the lower People in manner as has been practiced in New York, which is the only Province in which there is a Tenantry, and was the least inclined to Rebellion. The poorest Loyal Sufferers should however have Grants from the Crown.

The Attorney and Solicitor General of England should be directed to report what of the Laws of England will of their own Authority take place in the New Province, and what Acts of Parliament The King may be His Proclamation introduce and give effect to therein, tho' they are not extended by express Words, to the Colonies—This has never been done, and much confusion has arisen in the New Colonies from the want of it.

These are the Things necessary to be done in the New Province at the outset, but if the present be judged a proper time to digest a System of Government for all America the occasion may be used for declaring the purpose of the Crown.

Estimate of the Civil Establishment of the Province of New Ireland.

Salary to the Governor in Chief Oliver		1200
Chief Justice	Leonard	400
Attorney General		100
Secretary and Register		100
Clerk of the Council	Dr. Califf	50
Receiver General of Quit Rents & Casual Revenue		100
Surveyor of Lands		100
Provost Marshal or Sheriff		100
Agent		Nothing
4 Ministers of the Church of England		400
A Vicar General in addition		200
Contingent Expenses		1000
		3750
Salaries to the 12 Counsellors		1200
		4950

The project had received attention from the Government during the preceding year, and was communicated to Governor Hutchinson, then in England. His diary, under date of September 3, 1778, recounts an interview with Mr. Knox, an official of the War department, who stated that the Penobscot district was "to be erected into a new province, and to be given to the refugees, ... as a recompense for their sufferings, and to ease Government of the expense it is now at for their support. It put me in mind of Mr. Locke's story of Lord Shaftesbury's friend, who, after he was privately married, sent for his Lordship and another friend, to ask their advice; and I observed the same rule so far as to find no fault with the most preposterous measure, because already carrying into execution." Probably the attachment which the Governor always retained for his native province of the Massachusetts Bay disinclined him to any plan of its dismemberment.

A latter entry says: "Called at Lord George's (Germain) office. Mr. Knox said I was the only man to go Governor of a new Colony at Penobscot, and that Dr. Caner should be the Bishop. I showed him a letter I had received from Mr. Weeks, which speaks in pompous terms of the benefits from the possession of this country. He was much pleased, as it is his own scheme, and few people here think well of it. I said to him I thought we had better stay until we heard more of D'Etaigne, before we thought any further on measures for restoring peace to America."

After slumbering for nearly two years after the royal approval, the plan was revived by memorials from Dr. John Calef, agent for the Loyalists on the Penobscot and others. The following is a copy of one of these documents and also of another, giving an account of the inhabitants whom he represented:

To the Kings most Excellent Majesty in Council.
The Memorial and Petition of John Calef Esquire
Agent for the Inhabitants of the territory of
Penobscot most Humbly Sheweth

That your Majesty's Memorialist did in the year 1773, petition your Majesty in Council for & on behalf of James Duncan Benja. Hawod and the several other Grantees named in Grants. A Copy of which petition is hereunto annexed. That before anything was done on the matter, the people of the Province of Massachusetts-bay committed such Enormitys, as that nothing has been done in this business to the present day.

Your Majestys Memorialist begs leave further to observe That, Although your Majestys subjects in the Province of

Massachusetts bay, have not returned to their allegiance to your Majesty, yet the people of the territory aforesaid, have, from the beginning of the Rebellion proved themselves firmly attached to your Majestys Government, and several of them took the Oath of Fidelity to your Majesty in April 1779, and when General McLean arrived at Penobscot with your Majestys forces in June following many hundreds of them took the same Oath, and it would seem, that by far the greater part of those Inhabitants are firmly attached to the Laws & Government of Great Britain, That there are upwards of Sixteen Thousand Souls within said territory, destitute of Law & Gospel, and having lived so long without either, and population increasing with amazing rapidity, many disputes have arisen and are still increasing, and their Children are growing up as Ignorant as the Heathen who dwell among them.

That the said Inhabitants have no desire of continuing a part & parcel of Massachusetts-Bay, and would think themselves happy should your Majesty be graciously pleased to sever this District from the Province of Massachusetts-Bay, and erect it into a Government under your Majestys own Authority. And should your Majesty be most graciously pleased to send over a number of faithfull ministers of the Established Church well affected to Government, it would have a tendency to lead the people to a more firm attachment to your Majestys Government, and bring the Indians also to a love of it, being fond of Ministers & forms of Divine Worship—A post Road to be opened from Halifax to Boston by way of Penobscot and travilled in summer in twelve days Also a Road from Quebec to Boston, and travilled in about the same time & way. If a small and well appointed sea force was sent to protect this Infant settlement, they would then be secure in their Cod & River fisherys & procure Masts for the Royal Navy, Lumber of all sorts, & in plenty, for other parts of your Majestys Dominion, and of great annoyance to your Majestys Enemies.

Therefore your Majestys petitioner humbly hopes your Majesty will see this District in such light, and so usefull to the Crown of England as to sever it from the Massachusetts Province and to erect it into a government under your Majestys own authority. And Confirm the Settlers in their possessions. Thereby they will take Courage, become usefull Subjects. Raise Oscen, Grain, Sheep &c to haul Masts for the Royal Navy, and provisions for your Majestys Inhabitants in other parts of the Dominion, and security to a most valuable part of your Majestys territory in America.

And your Majesty's petitioner as in duty bound will pray

John Calef Agent for the territory of Penobscot

Copy given to Lord George Germain
July 12 1780

The state of the Inhabitants of
the District of the Penobscot
March 1782

By the Charter granted by the late King William and Queen Mary to the Province of Massachusetts-Bay, among other things it is expressed. That all Lands lying to the Eastward of Sagadahock Granted by our said General Assembly, shall not be valid without the Royal Approbation. The said Assembly in 1763, did grant thirteen Townships of said District to thirteen sett of Proprietors, who laid out a plan of each, and returned the same to the Assembly, which was approved, and accepted, and have laid out the Townships into lotts, and settled more than sixty families on each township, and made great Improvements, at the expense of all they are worth. In 1764, & again in 1773, they sent Agents to Great Britain to pray for the Royall confirmation of the Grants, but hitherto without effect, except that of Mount Desert to Governor Bernard.

John Perkins, Joseph Perkins, & Mark Hatch purchased of the first settlers, the greatest part of the Peninsula of Majabigwaduce lying in one of the said 13 Townships—These three men were always esteemed friends to Government, a proof whereof they gave to General Gage when shut up in Boston, by carrying Picketts, Lumber, Wood &c, several times in vessels of their own, for which, and to prevent their doing the like in future, a large Mob headed by a Colonel Cargill, seized their vessels and carried them away, and robed them of their Cattle—They, were also first in sending to his Majestys Officers at Annapolis in Nova Scotia, to Invite them in the Kings name to take post at Penobscot as it is set forth in a Proclamation issued by General Mac Lean dated June 15th 1779, inserted in pamphalet entitled The Siege of Penobscot, page 26, 27, 34 & 35. They did everything in their power to assist the General in erecting the fort, by their own Labour, and that of Oxen, and supplying the Troops with Provisions to a considerable amount, for part of which they received prompt payment, a considerable sum remains due to them to this day, in the hands of the D, Qr. Mr., after the seige was raised, They, their wives and children, were grossly insulted by the more unthinking part of the Army, too grateing to every human feeling—They, thereupon went to Old York, the Town where they had been borne, hoping there to find an Asylum; no sooner was their arrival known, but they were ordered to joyn the American Army or they should be hanged up without favour, or delay, They resolved not to joyn them, but to return to Penobscot, which they did; When, they found that their absence had been construed a Desertion, their property all taken from them, and their persons confined in jail, untill they should under hand and Seal, give up all right, title and Interest, they have to the Lands at Penobscot, which they refused to do, and they are still held under confinement—By the Proclamation signed by Sir George Collier & General MacLean August 1779, Sixteen persons belonging to Penobscot were proscribed, the most of whom, were ever esteemed equally attached to Government as the aforementioned, all of them with their numerous familys are from a state of Affluence, driven to a state of Extreme poverty, & want, except one persons who sets quiet.

Last Summer, Shubal Williams a man of sober life and Manners, near 70 years of age, an Inhabitant of Long Island, having a wife and large number of Children, frequently carryed fresh Provisions to the Troops, was sentenced to, & did receive, five hundred lashes on the Oath of an intoxicated Soldier, (as it is said) the neighboring Inhabitants were ordered to be Spectators of the punishment, the Bostonians published this affair in their Newspapers with additions, many of the old Settlers have left their possessions fearing the like treatment however Innocent—Several persons now in England can attest to the truth hereof, when called.

These, and things of the like nature have done infinite prejudice to his Majesty's cause,—Should his Majesty be graciously pleased to Confirm the Grants aforesaid, to the Settlers, reinstate the three Men aforesaid, in their possessions, and order their property which has been taken from them, to be restored; it would remove the prejudices many have entertained of his Majestys intentions; give them satisfaction, and attach them more firmly to the Kings cause than ever before.

In Knox's Extra Official State Papers, it is stated that the proposed colony received its death-blow from an opinion rendered by the Attorney General of England, afterwards Lord Loughborough, who entertained scruples about violating the sacredness of the chartered rights of the Province of the Massachusetts Bay, arguing that these rights extended its limits to the river St. Croix, and that the eastern boundaries were not terminated at either the Saco, the Kennebec or the Penobscot. Up to this time Dr. Calef, who had remained in England two years, had been hopeful of success, but one morning, entering the office of Lord North, these hopes were ended by his Lordship's saying, "Doctor, we cannot make the Penobscot the boundary; the pressure is too strong." Yet long afterwards the British claimed that Massachusetts had no title west of that river, and in 1814 took possession of all the land between it and the St. Croix, not as conquered territory, but as rightfully belonging to the crown.

CHAPTER 14.

No finer piece of historical writing has ever been done on a Maine subject than Frederick Allis' monumental two volume work dealing with William Bingham's Maine lands. The following account of Maine's economic and political status between 1780 and 1820 is from that study.

THE MAINE FRONTIER*
by
Frederick Allis, Jr.

In the course of his extensive travels in the United States in the 1790's the French nobleman Francois Alexandre Frederic, Duc de la Rochefoucauld-Liancourt, paid two visits to the Maine frontier, the first in the summer of 1795, the second the following year. On each occasion the Duke was the guest of Major-General Henry Knox, who had just finished building an elaborate residence at Thomaston, and who, as the owner of extensive landed property in Maine, was most anxious to create a favorable impression of the country in the mind of his distinguished foreign visitor. Yet when Liancourt came to record his opinions of this part of the United States, he wrote the following appraisal:

> In short, of all America, the province of Maine is the place that afforded me the worst accommodation. And, considering how little reason I found to praise the accommodations of many other places, what I have now said of Maine must be regarded as an affirmation that the condition of human life in that place is exceedingly wretched....this country is still in its infancy, and in a languid and cheerless infancy.

The Duke's estimate of this New England frontier is probably a fair one. Throughout the eighteenth century, the eastern country had suffered from a combination of factors which had rendered its name unpopular among prospective settlers and which had hindered its progress toward a respectable position among its New England neighbors. The region had little enough to offer to the pioneer in actual fact; in addition, since accurate knowledge of the country was scanty, many misconceptions about the geography, soil, climate, and general productiveness had early been formed and had before long crystallized into a hard core of prejudice. The few settlers who had ventured east of Falmouth had found communication with the more settled parts of New England difficult and had in most instances disappeared into the wilderness. In short, for a variety of reasons, Maine had lagged behind other New England frontier areas until the close of the Revolution.

Among several factors contributing to eastern Maine's backwardness, its unattractiveness to farmers must occupy a prominent place. In comparison with other New England areas open to new settlement in the eighteenth century—for example, the Connecticut River valley and western New Hampshire—Maine's soil was less rich, its climate colder. The magnificent forests had early attracted lumbermen, but this only served further to discourage agricultural communities, for the lumberman and the farmer seldom settled happily in the same general area. One evidence of the lack of agricultural development down east can be seen from the fact that until close to 1790 it was necessary to import foodstuffs into many parts of the District. A characteristic attitude toward eastern Maine as a potential farming country was expressed by Rufus Putnam in 1790 when he wrote:

> ...And as to the eastern country it is a very fine place for lumber, and in that respect is of great service to Massachusetts: but any considerable number of people more in that district then

---

*Frederick Allis Jr., Ed., *William Bingham's Maine Lands* (Boston: Colonial Society of Massachusetts, 1954), I, pp. 3-34. Reprinted by permission of the author.

to carry on this business will be a diservice distroying the timber which ought to be preserved—that country in general is not fit for cultivation and when this idea is connected with the climate, a man ought to consider himself curst even in this world who is doomed to inhabit their as a cultivater of the lands only; however I cannot suppose the Ohio country will much affect the settlement of the eastern lands because those people who have not a double curse entailed to them will go to New York or Vermont, rather then to the eastward.

The natural handicaps for a farmer in Maine were real enough; yet the reputation of her lands was even poorer than actual conditions warranted. Lack of accurate knowledge of the territory had fostered the widely held opinion that the region was "an immense waste, unfit for the habitation of man." In particular, the area between the Penobscot and the Schoodic was termed "waste lands." As late as 1816 this opinion persisted, as the following passage indicates:

> ...the climate has been represented, and believed by many, to be most unfavourable to vegetation, and uncomfortable to man, and the soil barren and fruitless, in an uncommon degree. This was the chief complaint of the emigrants who lately flocked, like their birds of passage, in such numbers to the southern and western states; and...it had, indeed, become quite a prevailing sentiment, among the inhabitants of the District.

However much supporters of Maine might try to correct this impression, especially by urging that the climate was becoming steadily warmer as the ground was cleared, the popular concept of the eastern territory was anything but that of a "Vacationland," and with other more attractive frontiers beckoning, it is scarcely surprising that potential settlers should choose to seek their fortunes elsewhere.

Another important factor in explaining the backwardness of the Maine frontier was its position as a no-man's-land during the long struggle between France and England for control of North America. From the beginning of this struggle, in the latter part of the seventeenth century, until the final elimination of France on the Plains of Abraham, Maine had borne the brunt of frontier raids, Indian attacks, and Jesuit infiltration. As one writer put it:

> The depredations of the Savages, from the year 1675 to the year 1760, with but little intermissions of their wars, was the greatest injury to the settlement and growth of the country.... The contest between England and France, for territorial possessions, made the country of this District the theatre of savage wars, and for a long time together the principal place of those alarms and distresses, which arise from predatory parties.

Only the most venturesome of emigrants dared to risk his life and that of his family in such a country.

Another element which contributed to Maine's lack of progress was the confusion of titles which obtained throughout the seventeenth and eighteenth centuries. Until 1763 there was always the possibility that the territory east of the Kennebec might become French, with consequent loss to English adventurers. Even without the complications of French claims, the Council for New England, and later in a few instances the British government itself, had made a large number of conflicting and over-lapping grants which were not completely disentangled until well into the nineteenth century. Even after 1763, with the French menace removed, this problem continued, with Massachusetts and Nova Scotia presenting conflicting claims to the territory east of the Penobscot; and, throughout the whole colonial period, much acreage was claimed on the basis of vague and generally unsatisfactory Indian deeds. This state of affairs handicapped both the grantees in selling their lands at retail, and prospective buyers, who could never be certain of their titles.

As a result of these drawbacks, both real and imaginary, eastern Maine had been peopled by a pioneer stock which compared unfavorably with frontier folk in other sections of New England. The confusion of titles led to the growth of the squatter class, later to become an articulate and at times influential political and social force. These squatters did little to improve the reputation of the country, and by their presence discouraged potential buyers of Maine lands, who shied away from the dangerous task of either dispossessing the squatters or making them pay. The lack of well-established institutions of government had bred a disrespect for private property and for law and order generally that was to act as a deterrent to the more law-abiding settler who might develop Maine economically and socially. As will be noted below, the lumberman and the fisherman possessed few qualities that would make for the development of the region as a whole.

A final reason for eastern Maine's backwardness was its lack of capital and economic organization. A poor country, with few of its people living much above the level of mere subsistence, Maine as a province had never been able to find within its own borders the money necessary for its development. This condition made the eastern country, like other New England frontier areas, dependent on

Boston for the capital needed to bring about its economic growth. As a region, it was not an attractive area for investment, and monied men in the rest of New England were slow to provide the means of bringing Maine's latent resources into active development.

Immediately after the close of the French and Indian War, a moderate trend to the eastward was started by land-hungry veterans and other restless persons. This movement did not have time to reach significant proportions before the Revolution intervened. During this struggle Maine reverted to type, and became again a battleground of raids and reprisals which culminated in the Penobscot expedition and the British occupation of strategic points in eastern Maine. Again the tide of settlement ebbed, and while there was some immigration to Maine from Nova Scotia during the Revolution, it was not until 1783 that lands to the eastward could offer an attractive field for exploitation and settlement.

Though Maine's past development had been slow, there were many who had confidence in her future. The District had definite possibilities, once some of the unfortunate conditions which had retarded its growth had been removed. Maine's forests were already famous; the numerous good harbors together with the many navigable rivers and streams made transportation relatively easy; and, it could be argued, agriculture had not really been given a fair chance. Talleyrand, who must certainly be counted a shrewd observer, was sanguine about the eastern country's potentialities. On his return from a tour down east in 1794 he wrote:

> The general impression which the sight of the country left with us is...in favor of the province of Maine. One can only augur well of a great province, which combines healthfulness and fertility, whose whole coast is one vast harbor of the sea, which is watered by rivers, lakes, ponds, creeks, and streams in abundance according to the most fortunate distribution, and whose appearance continually recalls the alternating hills and valleys which form the attraction of Connecticut.

At the close of the Revolutionary period, the question was whether, at long last, the removal of the threat of foreign encroachment, coupled with expansionist forces in New England, would lead to a Maine boom, or whether the unfortunate reputation of the District, together with its physical disadvantages, would allow it to remain a sluggish backwater of American territory. Before the turn of the century, a sizable number of adventurers had become convinced that the Maine wilderness could be made to blossom like the rose, that enterprises on an extensive scale could be founded in Maine. It is with the most outstanding of these attempts that this volume is concerned.

THE EASTERN COUNTRY IN 1790

In the years following the American Revolution that part of the District of Maine lying east of Portland exhibited most of the characteristics of an American frontier region that had recently been opened to settlement. The decade of the 1780's was one of rapid population growth down east, According to an estimate based on the Massachusetts census of 1784, there were between fifty-five and sixty thousand people in the District of Maine as a whole in that year. By 1790, when the first United States census was taken, that number had increased to 96,540, which represented a gain of over fifty per cent. Of this latter number, it should be pointed out, about seven-eighths lived in the three western counties of York, Cumberland, and Lincoln, while over half resided west of Portland. In the newly created counties of Washington and Hancock, Penobscot was the only town with a population of over one thousand, the average population of each minor civil division in these two counties being 286. On the frontier, as in the District as a whole, the overwhelming majority of the people were of English, Scotch, or Irish descent; in all Maine there were only a little over a thousand souls coming from non-British stock. In 1780 there were forty incorporated towns in the District, not one of which was east of the Penobscot. During the following ten years, however, there occurred a rapid increase in the number of towns, paralleling that in population, with the result that by 1790 another thirty-one had been incorporated, nine of which were in Hancock and Washington counties.

In 1783 Maine was still under the political jurisdiction of Massachusetts, a position which she had occupied since the middle of the seventeenth century. As the 1780's wore on, however, several political developments testified to the fact that Maine was becoming a distinct political unit, conscious of a destiny separate from that of the Bay State. With these political developments the frontier areas had little to do: in most cases the settlers to the eastward were too busy struggling to maintain themselves in the wilderness to afford the luxury of political activity; and in those cases where attempts were made to participate in political affairs most of the eastern towns doubtless found themselves in the same position as that of the inhabitants of Blue Hill Bay, who had reported on an earlier occasion" . . .we are so as it ware out of the wourld that we dont hardley know wether we do rite or rong but we mean to do as well as we can." It would be some years before the people to the eastward would be sufficiently well organized to make their weight felt in local and state politics.

The abortive attempt at separation which began in 1785 was essentially Portland-conceived and Portland-led. As with most movements of this nature, the forces behind the campaign for separation are obscure, and it is doubtful if the announced platform of the separatists represented their real motives. At least some of the strength of the movement derived from the general unrest and economic dislocation that was characteristic of much of the back country of New England during the 1780's; and the drive for separation was in part Maine's answer to these distresses, as armed revolt was that of the farmers of western Massachusetts. There was present, also, in both the political and economic spheres, the same resentment of Boston and its ruling classes and of the dominant position which the capital occupied in the new Massachusetts government. The mere distance of Maine from Boston, coupled with the difficulties and expense of travel to the seat of government, led to a demand for political and legal institutions which would be near at hand and under local control. The time-honored attacks on bureaucrats, high taxes, government spending, and corruption were made with vigor down east, but there is reason to believe that they were voiced more for effect than because of deep-seated grievances. Maine's unique geographical position relative to Massachusetts made separation a possible remedy, where elsewhere in New England such a move could hardly have been attempted; and the Revolution was simply the most striking example of the use by Americans of that day of the technique of separation as a solution for their problems.

Whatever the forces behind the separatist movement, it received little support—or attention for that matter—east of the Kennebec. When Townships Nos. 4, 5, and 6 east of Union River held a meeting to consider the question, they came to the conclusion that the evils complained of were common to all governments and that even if redress were obtained, it would do little to change their situation. For the present they preferred to remain under Massachusetts jurisdiction, lest worse evils befall them. Even in the western counties of the District, support for the movement diminished rapidly after the convention which had been held at Portland in 1786, until at a final meeting there were only three Portland men present; and it soon became clear that Maine was not ready for so drastic a step. The failure of the movement was due in part to improved economic conditions throughout New England, to the by no means inconsiderable opposition to the proposal in Maine itself, and finally to the remedial measures taken by the Massachusetts government. The sentiment for separation remained latent, nonetheless, to be used for other political purposes in the early 1800's and eventually to be put into effect; and in these later movements eastern Maine would be ready to play a significant part.

Another example of Maine's independence, of a growing divergence between her and the mother state, is to be found in the struggle over the ratification of the Federal Constitution in Massachusetts. Here, as with the separation movement, it was the counties of York and Cumberland that played the most prominent part. To a large extent the Maine representatives to the Constitutional Convention were numbered among the opposition and while several of the more important of them were later "converted" and their opposition overcome, the line of cleavage promised more political fireworks in the future. In the debates themselves the down east opposition voiced a fear that was widespread among enemies of the Constitution, namely, that the new governmental system would deprive the people of hard-won liberties, that a strong central power, *per se,* was something to be dreaded. But there were complicating factors. Those favoring separation tended to oppose adoption, for it was believed that separation would be more difficult to achieve under the proposed Constitution. In addition, there is evidence of the first appearance of the Maine squatter class as a political power, the squatters on the Kennebec fearing lest the new Constitution would serve as an aid in dispossessing them of their lands. By and large Federalism was strong in the Maine coastal towns, while anti-Federalism flourished inland, but the pattern of voting varies enough to make any generalizations about social or economic cleavage, or any attempt to identify opposition to the Constitution with Shaysism, a dangerous business. Finally, and perhaps most significant as far as the frontier is concerned, no town east of Thomaston was represented at the Convention at all.

Economically, the Maine frontier, like the District as a whole, was a poor man's country. In 1782, according to Greenleaf's estimate, the relative per capita wealth in Maine was but a little more than half that of Massachusetts, while the total wealth of the region as a whole was little more than one-tenth that of the Bay State. While Maine's total wealth increased sharply in the succeeding decade, it did so less rapidly than did that of Massachusetts, and no striking change in her relative position occurred. Since the three most important occupations down east—lumbering, fishing, and farming—implied individualistic enterprises with a minimum of contact with the business world of the rest of the country, local economic institutions were slow in developing. What trade there was came under the domination of Boston markets and Boston finance. Money was scarce, and barter was the common method of doing business in the great majority of the communities. Maine was badly in need of capital if her economic future was to rise much above the level of subsistence enterprise.

The most widely practised occupation of those Maine settlers who lived east of Portland in 1790 was lumbering. If there was one thing which Maine had in abundance, it was timber, and in an era when wood was in high demand for fuel, houses, and ships, such resources provided a livelihood, if it can be called that, for many. White pine planks, boards, and shingles; spruce masts and spars; ash oars; oak staves, ton timber and scantling—all were produced in large quantities and formed an equally large proportion of the District's exports. Here again the price and much of the transportation were controlled by Boston, which in this, as in other matters, kept Maine in a satellite position. A possible by-product of the lumber trade was the manufacture of pot and pearl ashes, but the average down easter was yet to be convinced that it was to his advantage to develop facilities for this production.

The large number of rivers in Maine provided more than enough mill seats for the sawing of timber, the mills being usually owned in shares and operated as community projects. A good mill might cost as much as four or five hundred pounds but would produce 500,000 to 600,000 feet of boards annually if the water supply held and it was operated day and night. On the Kennebec River alone, there were seventy saw mills, half of them double ones. Attempts had been made to establish the cutting, sawing, transportation, and sale of timber on an equitable basis, but without much success. In some parts of the District a system had been developed whereby the woodcutter paid a definite percentage of the profits from the logs he cut to the owner of the land, the operator of the mill, and the owner of the vessel taking the wood to market. More often, however, the lumbermen had no respect for the ownership of the lands on which they worked; they preempted the best mill sites without possessing title to them, cut trees wherever they found them, and refused to recompense in any way the unfortunate, usually absentee, owner of the property. These depredations were to cause not only the landed proprietors, but the Commonwealth of Massachusetts itself, a great deal of trouble before they were finally checked.

The Maine lumberman of this period was a rough character at best. With little interest in the future of the country, with a commensurate disregard for property rights, he was content to fell enough trees to keep his family in provisions for a few months and then relapse into an apathetic state of sloth until the prospect of starvation again pricked him into activity. His only interest, according to Talleyrand, was the number of blows of an axe that he would need to use to cut down a tree. Restless, hard-drinking, always trying to change his present penury for some dubious future benefit, he and his ilk were one of the largest elements in the frontier population—an element that promised little for the future unless it could be controlled and organized. Timothy Dwight, writing at a later date and with a strong antipathy to the frontier as such, found the lumbermen a breed of men seduced by their life to "prodigality, thoughtlessness of future wants, profaneness, irreligion, immoderate drinking, and other ruinous habits," and was convinced that self-respecting New England farmers had been deterred from emigrating to Maine because the region was dominated by lumbermen. When the wood on one hundred acres of land could keep a family alive for many years, why worry about clearing and tilling, reasoned the lumberman. Such an element could only lower the reputation of the District and discourage the establishment of a more civilized way of life.

The fishing industry was second in importance to lumbering. Proximity to the Grand Banks was theoretically an advantage, but in most places large numbers of fish could be taken close to shore. In addition to the sacred cod and the herring, such fresh water fish as the salmon and shad were taken in great quantities, though the construction of mills on most of the rivers caused alarm among the fishermen and brought them into conflict with the lumbermen and farmers. Like most of Maine's economic activities, fishing was carried on on a share basis. Usually the captain or owner of the ship would provide the lines, bait, and food, and in return get half the catch. Once caught, the fish would be taken to some specified area for drying—for example, the Fox Islands—where the driers might get one sixteenth of the proceeds. The remaining seven sixteenths would go to the fishermen themselves. Maine fish, dried and salted, found its way to Europe and the West Indies and provided a source of revenue second only to that of the lumber trade. From October, 1790, to September, 1791, over two thousand tons of fishing vessels, most of them small craft of fifteen or twenty tons, are reported as entering Maine ports.

The fisherman was hardly a more estimable member of society than the lumberman. Needing only an arm to hang over the side of a boat, he followed the line of least resistance, satisfied, like the lumberman, to depend on nature for his needs. Attempts to organize the Maine fishing trade on a solid foundation, which had been made by Boston merchants, had met with failure, to a large extent because of the unwillingness of the fishermen to fulfill their contracts or to put forth the necessary effort to bring success to the venture. Like the lumberman, the fisherman was tied to no one spot for which he had any real affection; he was ever ready to pull up stakes and move on to a part of the country that promised better fishing. Thus he, too, was an unstable element in the population.

Most of those interested in the development of Maine were convinced that a stabilization of the region's economic and social life could be accomplished only by the establishment of traditional New England farming communities down east. Yet a survey of Maine's agricultural system in 1790 would reveal little to encourage such promoters. The Maine farmer of this period lived a grubbing existence. Except in the older and more settled parts of the District, the returns on what work he managed to get done were discouragingly small. His crop usually consisted of wheat, barley, rye, oats, or Indian corn, which provided his bread. This was supplemented by game and wild fowl, which were very plentiful. An occasional plot of ground for flax helped provide his clothing. While cattle, sheep, oxen, and a few horses were generally found, ignorance of stock-breeding, coupled with the difficulty of providing winter quarters and fodder for the animals, kept the herds at a low level. The majority of visitors to Maine during this period comment on the backwardness of the agricultural system, the hand-to-mouth existence of the farming folk. A few of the more enterprising produced surpluses, which were occasionally exported to Boston, the West Indies, or Europe, but for the most part a down east farmer was fortunate if he and his family could get through the year on what they produced.

Typical of the more successful agriculturist of this period was Farmer Nicholson of Belfast. An old-timer—he had lived in the same spot for thirty-four years—he had cleared eighty acres, had five under good cultivation, and cut one hundred and fifty cords of wood a year. His sons had caught a hundred barrels of salmon and cod, while his daughters spun wool from his sheep to make the family clothes, and made shoes from the hides of his cattle. Full of the prejudices of the old husbandman, he refused to grow wheat, depending on rye and corn for his bread, which Liancourt thought would have been given to dogs in other parts of the country. Twenty head of black cattle, as many sheep, and an acre of potatoes completed the picture. An occasional mug of grog made from rum or whisky, or the local spruce or birch beer introduced a little variation into the plain fare. Nicholson was content with his lot and had the reputation of being a good farmer, but Liancourt failed to see how his reputation had been acquired.

A more romanticized character sketch of the Maine farmer—one that would have warmed the heart of Rousseau himself—is given by the Italian traveller Luigi Castiglioni in his description of the Gregory family, who lived near Camden. The Gregorys lived in a log cabin thatched with hemlock bark. The dwelling consisted of one room, which served as both kitchen and bedroom, with a shallow attic, reached by a ladder, overhead. Outside, a straw fire was kept burning in the summer months to keep away the gnats, which, added to the July heat, gave the travellers a great deal of discomfort. The numerous Gregorys worked from morn to night, getting plenty of butter and cheese from their eight cows, making unleavened bread, slaughtering an occasional calf. On Sunday Father Gregory read the Bible to his children, and the family as a whole were virtuous and pious. Despite the many discomforts, Castiglioni could not see why these people should not be the happiest of mortals, practicing the useful and pleasant business of agriculture, unacquainted with the worry of poverty and in possession of the most enjoyable comforts of life.

Maine's foreign trade, in company with that of the rest of New England, had suffered in the years immediately following the peace, but by the late 1780's it was well on the road to recovery. Despite the British closure of the West Indies to American shipping, a thriving, if illicit, trade developed in that quarter, in which Maine products and Maine ships had their share. As early as 1784, Colonel Christian Febiger, making a tour of inspection to report on the supply and quality of masts and spars for a merchant in Copenhagen, described the whole Maine market from Portsmouth to the Penobscot as being glutted with mast timber. Since the English had adequate resources in Nova Scotia, and since the French fleets had stocked up during their recent tour of duty at Boston, almost unlimited supplies were available. The difficulty in carrying on this trade, thought Febiger, arose from the lack of an organized market to the eastward. Rum, sugar, molasses, and possibly metal goods were acceptable in exchange for lumber down east, but most of the trade passed through Boston, New York, or Philadelphia. Febiger commented on the practice followed by the Maine skippers of selling their goods in the West Indies, bringing West Indian produce back to New York, Philadelphia, or Boston, and finally heading east with cash in their pockets and their ships in ballast. Furthermore, Maine products were brought to market in Liverpool, Bristol, and Hull, as well as Belfast and Dublin. For the year ending in September, 1791, over 30,000 tons of shipping had entered the District from foreign ports, with an additional 10,000 tons in coasting trade. While Portland, Wiscasset, and Biddeford had the lion's share of this trade, entries were recorded at Penobscot, Frenchman's Bay, Machias, and Passamaquoddy as well.

Maine's returns from her foreign and coastal trade would always be limited so long as the vessels were owned and built outside the District. To meet this challenge, enterprising downeasters began a shipbuilding industry which was to crowd that of Massachusetts herself fifty years later. By 1790, the customs district of Portland had close to fifty vessels owned there which were engaged in foreign trade, while the district of Bath boasted five ships and four schooners totalling 1,364 tons. Charles Vaughan, one of the most enthusiastic boosters of the Kennebec region, saw shipbuilding as one of the coming Maine industries. A ship built down east at an average cost of thirty dollars a ton would sell in Boston for from forty to forty-five. Though the great days of Maine shipbuilding were still some years away, a promising start had already been made in this profitable form of enterprise.

An example of a successful mercantile venture in Maine at the close of the eighteenth century can be seen in the careers of two immigrant Irishmen, James Kavanagh and Matthew Cottrill. These two adventurers from the Emerald Isle arrived in Boston in the early 1780's, and after disappearing into the Maine woods for ten years, emerged as successful merchants at Newcastle on the Damariscotta. Starting business as proprietors of a general store or truck house, the two partners before long were prosperous enough to buy property along the river, open saw mills, found shipbuilding yards, and eventually watch vessels built at their yards, freighted with lumber cut on their lands and sawed at their mills, sail down the river for the West Indies. Another example is that of the two Alma brothers of Ducktrap (now Lincolnville). While one brother took the family ship to England, the West Indies, or along the coast to the westward with lumber or fish, the other remained at Ducktrap, buying up supplies, building ships, and dabbling in land jobbing. Yet despite a profitable business, the Almas lived in a miserable house and lacked many of what would be considered the barest essentials for comfort in Massachusetts. For every Alma, Kavanagh, or Cottrill, there were hundreds of would-be merchants who never emerged from the obscurity of the frontier.

Many of the travellers who visited the District of Maine during this period bore testimony to the fact that a large majority of the people living east of Portland were characteristic of the frontier type at a very primitive level. Talleyrand wrote of them: "Ignorant and grasping, poor but without needs, they resemble too much the natives of the country whom they have replaced." And the noted Frenchman went on to comment unfavorably on what he called the "moral disposition" of the population as a whole. The lack of specie, which made barter a necessity, bred a habit among almost all the people of making cunning, if not fraudulent bargains at the drop of a hat. Once a man could collect some rum, cloth, and a few tools and household utensils, he set up as a merchant, proceeded to encourage his neighbors to go into debt to him, and before long was able to dominate his immediate area economically, dictating to the unfortunates who had become enmeshed in the system. Nor did the debtors feel under any compunction to refrain from selling their wood or fish to the master of some vessel, newly arrived from the westward, who might offer more rum than their creditor. This system encouraged deceit and fraud among all classes and made everyone more interested in buying and selling than in producing. Once the bare essentials had been produced through a few days' labor on corn and potatoes, the settler would turn to the less onerous business of buying and selling, and would eschew further productive work. The result of this unwillingness to produce anything beyond their own most immediate needs was an almost complete absence of specialized craftsmen and a great superfluity of would-be merchants, contractors, and salesmen. And in the long run this meant debts, bad business, tedious law suits, and insolvency. Any traveller down east with a little hard money in his pocket could buy anything from anybody. "They wish to sell," said Talleyrand, "because they have done too little work around them to have placed their affections there."

The young Englishman, Alexander Baring, on the other hand, after having spent the summer of 1796 down east, could return with a very different impression. In contrast to Talleyrand, Baring was pleased with the "disposition and character" of the inhabitants and found less of the "wild and savage" than he had expected. He was gratified to discover a general respect for private property and a widespread interest in religion, though he was disturbed by "a pack of fanatical itinerant Methodist preachers" whom he thought "obnoxious." Even Baring, however, could find little good to say about lumbering and lumbermen. The lumbermen, he noticed, had no constant occupation, no tie to the country, no fixed homes; and he stressed the fact that they added no value to the land by their labor and thus could be of little benefit to a proprietor. Even so, Baring was convinced that the country and its inhabitants were developing rapidly and that a more balanced economy which would combine agriculture and shipping with lumbering would soon emerge.

Baring's testimony is perhaps less disinterested than that of Talleyrand and Liancourt. He had just finished investing a large sum of money in Maine lands for his principals in England, and his report to them would naturally want to justify what he had done; furthermore, his impressions of eastern Maine were gained while he was on a specially conducted tour, during which every effort was made to have him see the country at its best. While Baring's account must certainly be used to qualify those of Talleyrand and Liancourt, the chances are that the judgments of the two Frenchmen are the more accurate ones.

Exceptions there certainly were to these general characterizations. When the British naval officer, Lieutenant Bartholomew James, explored the Kennebec River in 1791, he found the people charming and the accommodations good. He had lodged at the home of Captain Parker in Phippsburg, where he was captivated by the "graceful, bewitching, angelic creatures," the Captain's nieces. At Rittle's tavern in Pownalborough he "sat down to as comfortable a meal as I ever remember to have fed on." Even when allowances are made for the bad food of the British Navy and the charms of the

Parker girls, there is no question of Lieutenant James's favorable impression of the country. Further up the Kennebec the Gardiner-Hallowell-Vaughan families had stately houses, landscaped grounds, and most of the amenities of the more established regions of New England. Down the coast at Thomaston Henry Knox was about to build Montpelier, probably the most handsome mansion in the District and an oasis of comfort, relatively speaking, among the establishments of Knox's less fortunate neighbors. It should be noted, however, that these exceptional families had all inherited their estates from ancestors who had been men of wealth and prominence in Massachusetts. East of Montpelier there were few families whose mode of existence had risen much above the bare subsistence level, nor would there be many until well into the nineteenth century.

Doubtless some of the comments made by visitors to eastern Maine during this period should be taken with the proverbial grain of salt. Many of the most detailed accounts were written by foreigners who may well have been deceived by appearances, if not actually hoodwinked by the natives. Present-day conditions in many parts of Maine give a superficial impression of being much worse than they actually are, and this same state of affairs probably obtained one hundred and fifty years ago. Furthermore, it is difficult to determine to what extent conditions down east during this period were typical of any frontier region in any part of the country, and to what extent they were characteristic of Maine alone. On the other hand descriptions of the District written by men who were bent on "puffing" Maine are so obviously prejudiced as to be almost useless in presenting a fair picture of the land and the people to the eastward. Even when one makes allowances for the inexperience of the foreign commentators, however, it is clear that the inhabitants of the eastern country represented a backwash of Yankee migration, with a standard of living and a sense of law and order below the average of that of other sections of New England.

Except for a few areas, then, eastern Maine was in the early stages of frontier development. The country was not a promising one; sparsely populated by a poorer than average pioneer stock, with a climate and natural resources appealing for the most part to lumbermen and fishermen, this region was, and is, a hard land. Its past history as a province had been one of bloodshed and confusion; its future prospects, when compared with those of other sections of America, were not auspicious.

On the other hand, there were favorable aspects, from the point of view of a land speculator, in the Maine scene. Lands down east were extremely cheap; thus a would-be adventurer could acquire large holdings for a relatively modest initial investment. Once such holdings had been acquired, additional capital would be needed to turn the tide of emigration—or at least part of it—from the westward to the eastward. But if, through man-made improvements and artificially forced "hothouse" settlements, a boom in Maine lands could be stimulated, the opportunity for profit to the speculator could be great indeed.

THE LAND POLICY OF MASSACHUSETTS

At the close of the Revolution, the Massachusetts Treasury was nearly empty. Although as a colony, Massachusetts had extinguished her debt in 1774, the expenses of war, with concomitant economic dislocations, now placed a heavy burden on her people. With a combined state and federal debt of close to three million pounds, with some twenty per cent of her taxes uncollected, with the poll tax bearing heavily on the poor and helping to produce the unrest that was later to flare up in Shays's rebellion, the state officials were naturally eager to explore and utilize if possible any additional sources of revenue which might ease the burden of the cost of government. It is scarcely surprising, therefore, that John Hancock, in his first message to the legislature in 1783 should have called attention to land sales as a substitute for taxation, or that early steps should have been taken to capitalize on the wild lands in Maine, a virtually untapped source of revenue.

Massachusetts was fortunate, in comparison with many of the other former colonies, in her land holdings. Though she agreed to surrender her claims to jurisdiction over land in western New York, she retained the soil, which she was able to dispose of to Phelps and Gorham, and later to Robert Morris and his associates for a considerable sum. As for the lands in Maine, there was no such trouble about title. True, the northeastern boundary of the District was still undefined and a confusion of grants to individuals was bound to retard development in some sections. Still, it was estimated that there were some seventeen million acres of land available for sale—sufficient to supply the demand for some time to come. Though at a later time Massachusetts was criticized by other states for not ceding these wild lands in Maine to the Federal government, there seems to have been no attempt to force her to do this in the 1780's. These Maine lands had not been included in the territory proscribed for settlement by the Proclamation of 1763, nor were they in any sense in the same category as the transmontane territory claimed by other states.

In 1781 the first step toward developing a policy for the lands in Maine was taken when a committee of five was appointed by the General Court to check the trespassing on unappropriated public lands and was empowered to prosecute interlopers. The committee was instructed to run lines so as to separate the unsold lands from those already sold, and to make maps of the tracts that could be put on the market. Though this committee struggled manfully with its difficult problems, by 1783 it was clear that the task was too big for it. Accordingly, in October of that year, a new committee was appointed to deal with land affairs in the County of Lincoln, which then included all land east of the Kennebec, leaving the counties of York and Cumberland to the old body. In the meantime, in an effort to preserve timber on these lands, it was made a penal offense to cut down white pine trees on public tracts, and the General Court acted to regulate the size and shape of boards and shingles exported from the District.

The Committee for the Sale of Eastern Lands in the County of Lincoln, composed of Samuel Phillips, Jr., Nathaniel Wells, and Nathan Dane, was to carry the major part of the responsibility for the sale of these lands in Maine for the next ten years. Early in 1784 it reported to the legislature a comprehensive scheme for disposing of the Maine territory: it recommended that townships be laid out between the Penobscot and St. Croix rivers; that alternate townships on the rivers be sold in five-hundred-acre lots at at least six shillings per acre; that the other half of the river townships be sold in one-hundred-and-fifty-acre lots at whatever the traffic would bear; and that three thousand acres in each of the non-river townships be given away in hundred-acre lots to actual settlers. After hearing this report, the legislature, in July, 1784, ordered the Committee to lay out as many townships as possible, to dispose of them either by private sale or public auction, and to receive in payment Massachusetts consolidated securities or Massachusetts notes to veterans. Apparently dissatisfied with the Committee's progress, the General Court, in November, 1784, urged the members to hurry with the surveys, ordered one of them to be in Boston at specified times each month to facilitate sales, and appointed Rufus Putnam surveyor. Later resolves ordering the state commissary to furnish the Committee's surveyors with pork, axes, soap, and other supplies show that a start had been made in that end of the business, and the Committee later reported that some hundred thousand acres had been sold in 1785 and 1786.

Since sales were still not rapid enough to please the revenue-hungry legislators, a new device was tried in 1786—namely, a land lottery. Lotteries had been frequently used in New England to raise money for charitable, educational, and similar purposes in the past; indeed Harvard College had conducted several. It was hoped that an appeal to the gambling instincts of the inhabitants of the Bay State might succeed, where a mere advertising of land had failed. Accordingly, in November, 1786, the General Court passed a land lottery act which, it was hoped, would bring into the state treasury the sum of 163,200 pounds.

The scheme devised by the legislators was a relatively simple one. Fifty townships of land, most of them the conventional six miles square, were set aside as prizes. These townships were located behind the coastal settlements in the area between the Penobscot and the Schoodic and were henceforth to be known as the "Lottery Lands." In keeping with the usual New England tradition, four lots were reserved in each township for the support of religion and education. Two thousand seven hundred and twenty tickets were to be printed and sold for sixty pounds each. Whenever a sale was made, the purchaser automatically acquired a tract of land, but the size of each tract was to be determined when the drawing of the lottery was held, presumably after all the tickets had been sold. The prizes varied in size from a whole township of land to a lot one half mile square.

Samuel Phillips, Nathaniel Wells, John Brooks, Leonard Jarvis, and Rufus Putnam were appointed managers of the lottery, were authorized to receive in payment for the tickets currency or securities of either Massachusetts or the United States—or specie, if anyone should be so foolish as to use coin for this purpose—and to give deeds after the drawing had been held. They were further instructed to advertize the scheme widely in the newspapers. Finally, the act included provisions against counterfeiting and other kinds of fraudulent activity and threatened lawbreakers with such punishments as being publicly whipped, not exceeding thirty-nine stripes, or being forced to sit on the gallows for one hour with a rope around the neck.

Despite the hopes of its proponents, the lottery failed to achieve its purpose. Only 437 out of the available 2720 tickets were sold, even after the date for the drawing of prizes had been advanced three months. The records of the managers of the lottery show that Harvard College led the list of purchasers, with nine tickets, followed by John Tudor, with seven, while the name of the Reverend Elisha Fuller of Ludlow on the roster shows that even the clergy were not averse to taking an occasional flyer. When the drawing was finally held in June, 1787, a certain William Dall won the largest prize—a tract of 5,440 acres—but most of the ticket holders received much smaller quantities, the total amount of land disposed of in this scheme amounting to a mere 165,000 acres. The managers of the lottery were now faced with a vexing problem; since the "fortunate adventurers" held land scattered throughout the lottery townships, sales of large tracts in the future would be the more difficult because of these encumbrances. Accordingly, the winners were urged to transfer their lots to four townships in the Passamaquoddy area, so as to free the other townships for unencumbered sale, but this the winners were slow to do. As a result the General Court was still extending the time limit for such transfers in 1790, and less than half of the acreage had been transferred when the Committee attempted to sell these same lottery lands in a single tract, a state of affairs which could cause troublesome complications in the future. Writing in 1835, a committee of the Massachusetts Senate appointed to review the land policy of the state, gave the following reason for the failure of the lottery:

> The partial success of this project was a striking instance of the high moral feeling of the community in regard to lotteries, as gambling institutions; and this rebuke of the plan of sale... successfully prevented the renewal of a project, at once fascinating and demoralizing.

However high the moral feeling of the Commonwealth in the 1780's, it is probable that the hard times of 1785-1786, and the poor reputation which the lottery lands had, played an important part in explaining this failure. In any event, the Committee for the Sale of Eastern Lands never again resorted to the lottery as a means of disposing of the wild lands in Maine.

With the failure of the land lottery, the committee turned again to the sale of lands by more orthodox methods. It busied itself with the nightmarish problem of untangling the confusing claims in the Kennebec region, defending its actions before the legislature, and surveying and preparing maps of the tracts at its disposal. The following Resolve, instructing the committee, may serve as a convenient summary of the legislature's policy at this time:

Resolve on the subject of unappropriated lands
   in the counties of Cumberland and Lincoln
   March 26, 1788

   Resolved, That a Committee be appointed to examine and adjust the accounts of the Committee on the subject of unappropriated lands in the counties of Cumberland and Lincoln to the time of the passing of this resolve.

   And whereas it is necessary that further powers should be given to the Committee on the subject of unappropriated lands in the counties of Cumberland and Lincoln:

   Resolved, that John Read, Esquire and Doctor Daniel Cony be joined to the said Committee, which Committee are also hereby appointed a committee on the subject of the unappropriated lands, belonging to this Commonwealth, in the county of York, for the same purposes, and with like powers, as have, by the several resolves of the General Court, been assigned to the said Committee for the counties of Cumberland and Lincoln, and their commission shall extend to each and every of the said counties: And that the said Committee be, and they are hereby directed to complete a plan or plans, as soon as may be, of all the located lands in the counties aforesaid, agreeable to a resolve of the General Court, of November the 5th, 1784, and as far as practicable to mark out the unlocated lands in the aforesaid counties, into townships or plats of six miles square, as near as may be, and where they shall think it to be for the interest of this Commonwealth, the said six miles square into lots.

   Resolved, That there be reserved in each township four lots of three hundred and twenty acres each, for public uses, *viz.*, one for the first settled minister; one for the use of the ministry; one for the use of schools; and one for the future appropriation of the General Court; the said lots to average in goodness and situation with the lands in such township, and to be designated in such way and manner as the said Committee shall judge proper.

Resolved, That there be, and hereby is appropriated to the building and supporting a public seminary of learning, upon such conditions as the legislature may hereafter direct, a tract of land six miles square, to be laid out to the northward of Waldo's Patent, and nearly central between the two rivers Kennebeck and Penobscot, as good a tract of land for that purpose, as may be found there; the same to be surveyed under the direction of the said Committee, and report thereof made to the General Court.

Resolved, That any of the lands belonging to this Commonwealth, in the counties aforesaid, may be sold to any foreigner or foreigners, who shall contract to settle thereon, within three years from the purchase, one or more families to each mile square of land; and any foreigner, having resided for the space of two years on such land, may, on application to the legislature, be entitled to an act of naturalization, he producing a certificate from any two justices of the peace, of the same county, or from the selectmen of the town nearest to such land, or from three respectable inhabitants of the same county, that such foreigner has, in their opinion, behaved himself during that time, as a good member of society, and is a proper candidate for naturalization.

Resolved, That each settler who settled on any lands belonging to this Commonwealth, before the first day of January, 1784, and who has not already been confirmed in his settlements, and who shall pay the said Committee for the use of this Commonwealth, before the first day of June, 1789, five Spanish milled dollars, shall be entitled to a deed of one hundred acres of land, the same to be surveyed, and laid out so as to include his improvements, and be least injurious to the adjoining lands; such survey to be under the direction of the said Committee and at the expense of such settler.

Resolved, That the Committee aforesaid, or the major part of them, be, and they are hereby authorized and directed to sell the aforesaid unappropriated lands, in any of the said counties, for the consolidated notes of this State, or otherwise in specie, and in such quantities, and on such terms as they shall judge most for the interest of the Commonwealth, any resolve to the contrary notwithstanding. And the said Committee, or the major part of them, are further authorized, to appoint such agents in the counties aforesaid, as they may judge necessary, to expedite the sale of the said lands; and the said Committee shall be allowed two per cent, in the same sort of pay as shall by them be received for lands they may sell as aforesaid, in full compensation for their services in the said business, and that of the agents which they may appoint; the expense of surveying to be borne by the State, and all the lands the said Committee shall sell as aforesaid, shall be exempt from taxes, for the space of ten years.

Resolved, That where a minute description of the quality and circumstances of any of the said lands cannot be ascertained without a greater expense, than would probably compensate the profits that may arise therefrom, in such case, the said Committee may dispose of the same, any resolve to the contrary notwithstanding.

After 1790, business picked up. As will be noted below, a speculative fever took possession of the country, and after the possibilities of the new government securities and the new bank stock had been exhausted, men with capital to invest turned to wild lands as an attractive field for speculation. Lands in the Georgia back country, Ohio, western New York, and Pennsylvania all boomed, and interest in Maine revived. As a result, the Committee, from 1791-1794 was able to sell some 2,300,000 acres for nearly 90,000 pounds and contract to sell about 1,300,000 more for close to 22,000 pounds. This burst of enthusiasm for Maine lands soon subsided, and in 1795 the General Court, dissatisfied with the Committee's conduct, especially their sale of land in very large tracts, took over the sale of wild lands themselves.

One other feature of the land policy of Massachusetts deserves mention—the practice of using wild land as a means of rewarding veterans, assisting educational and charitable institutions, and promoting industry and commerce. In line with this policy, for example, the General Court granted a township on the Passamaquoddy to John Allan and a group of his veteran associates, gave those inhabitants of Portland who had suffered from Mowatt's bombardment in 1775 two townships, and helped out Alexander Campbell of Narraguagus, who had fought hard in the Revolution, worked hard for the State since then, and was still in financial difficulties. In 1801, a blanket resolve gave all Revolutionary noncoms and soldiers who had enlisted and served three years, two hundred acres apiece on the upper Schoodic. Educational institutions profited even more: Williams and Bowdoin Colleges, Hallowell, Fryeburg, Leicester, and Marblehead Academies, to name but some, were given sizable grants, while one township was to be used to endow a chair in natural history at Cambridge, and the Boston hospital and the Massachusetts Medical Society were also beneficiaries. Industry and commerce came in for their share of help when land was granted to the Beverly Manufacturing Company, the proprietors of the Middlesex Canal, a group who proposed to improve the navigation of the Taunton River, and an agricultural society to establish a "botanic garden." One Lemuel Cox received a thousand acres for inventing a cardwire cutting machine, building the first powder mill, and suggesting that the criminals on Castle William make nails. Occasionally, special favors were meted out, as in the case of Joseph Inman, who had "suffered long confinement in close gaol on suspicion of having murdered one Oliver Holmes," and William Eaton, who collected ten thousand acres for his exploits in Tripoli. By 1821 over 1,200,000 acres had been thus granted away to foster objects believed to be of public concern. And this, it must be remembered, was in addition to the public lots regularly reserved in each township sold. There can be no doubt that these wild lands were a great boon to politicians;

without directly increasing the tax burden, the Massachusetts legislators were able to reward the faithful and promote institutions which were bound to be popular with the public. Still, this policy had an adverse effect on general land sales. The individuals and institutions that benefited from these public grants were nearly always anxious to turn them into cash as readily as possible. Speculators found it easier to acquire land from these sources than direct from the State. As a result, the market became gorged, values declined, and the State land sales suffered.

After being deprived of most of its powers in 1795, the Committee for the Sale of Eastern Lands languished. In 1801 it was replaced by two agents, who did little until about 1811, when speculative interest revived slightly. In 1816 these two agents were replaced by three commissioners and a surveyor-general, and these officials remained in office until the separation of Maine from Massachusetts. At this time, the remaining unsold wild lands were divided between the two states. Of the 17,000,000 acres of public land available for sale in 1783, some 4,700,000 had been sold for a little over $800,000 by 1821, not counting the 1,200,000 granted for public objects. The land sold had thus been disposed of at an average price per acre of a little less than twenty cents.

The policy of the Commonwealth of Massachusetts towards its Maine lands lacked the consistency which would have helped to encourage the growth of the District. Political pressures interfered time and again to prevent the adoption of a program designed to develop the eastern country. The insistence on the performance of settling duties—bringing a certain number of families on a given tract within a certain term of years—shows the Commonwealth desirous of encouraging emigration to the eastward. The reservations in each township for education and religion, as well as generous tax-exemption for ten years or more are further proof of an enlightened policy which envisaged the establishment of typical New England agricultural communities in Maine. On the other hand, the temptation to use the Maine property as a means of paying off the State debt, of distributing political favors, and of rewarding veterans seriously crippled attempts to adhere to the long-range policy which had the interests of Maine and its settlers at heart. The practice of selling land in huge tracts to speculators, initiated after 1790, further complicated the problem. The speculators were saddled with onerous settling duties, usually impossible of fulfillment, and no adequate provision was made for the squatters actually living on the land sold. With the assumption of State debts by the Federal government, some of the pressure on the Massachusetts financial structure was removed, but the Commonwealth made no serious attempt to revise its policy toward the Maine lands with an eye toward the needs of the inhabitants themselves. In short, the opportunistic course followed by the Bay State was to retard the progress of Maine and involve both settlers and speculators in endless difficulties.

CHAPTER

15.

Maine's first newspaper appeared in Falmouth in the year 1785. At one time in the 19th century Portland would publish as many as four newspapers.

MAINE'S FIRST NEWSPAPER*
by
Frederick G. Fassett, Jr.

The first newspaper published in the District of Maine, the *Falmouth Gazette,* set out under favorable auspices, as indicated in the address to the public appearing in Number I of Volume I, January 1, 1785, which declared:

> From the generous encouragement of a number of respectable gentlemen in Falmouth...we have undertaken to publish a weekly newspaper in this place. We hope it will meet with general approbation...and while we promise to use our best endeavors to make every future number useful and entertaining...we beg leave to express our wishes that every patron of the press will afford us that support which, in this infant country, will be peculiarly necessary to enable us to carry on the business with advantage to ourselves and those, to whom we shall devote our time and talents.
>
> Benjamin Titcomb
> Thomas B. Wait.

This address was followed by a statement from Samuel Freeman, who had circulated subscription papers for a journal to be published by Peter Edes and Thomas Baker Wait, and who informed the public that Edes had opened a shop in Boston and that "in his stead Mr. Benjamin Titcomb, a Person qualified for the business, has entered into partnership with Mr. Wait." Samuel Freeman was son of Enoch, previously mentioned as among the wearers of the cocked hat, bush wig, and red cloak, and was one of the most prominent members of the Falmouth community, serving as postmaster twenty-nine years, as member of the Committee of Correspondence during the Revolution, delegate and secretary to the Provincial Congress, clerk of courts, register and judge of probate, selectman for over twenty years, and president of the Overseers of Bowdoin College, and in various other responsible posts. That he should have been actively concerned in preparing the way for the establishment of the *Gazette* is direct evidence that the more stable part of the population desired such a paper. He was, however, a Federalist, for which reason we should hardly expect to find him working for a paper designed to aid the cause of separation, which the Federalists in the main opposed.

The theory that the *Gazette* was established to aid the separatist cause is based upon a direct statement to that effect by William D. Williamson, the historian of early Maine, who declares, "To aid the object (*i.e.*, separation), the first number of the 'Falmouth Gazette,' printed by Thomas B. Wait, appeared New Year's day, 1785..." North likewise, possibly basing the statement on William, says the *Gazette* "was first issued January 1, 1785, to aid the project of separation." Williamson was a carefully circumstantial historian, his work being rich in detail, for the most part well digested. That he would have dogmatically asserted the separatist origin of this newspaper without justification is decidedly improbable. Evidence in support of the contention is, however, lacking. The anti-separatist import of the Federalist Mr. Freeman's connection with the paper is offset readily enough by the fact that, once established, the *Gazette* displayed a strong separatist trend. Whether or not it was founded directly to aid the cause must remain a

---

*Frederick G. Fassett, Jr., *A History of Newspapers in the District of Maine* (Orono: University of Maine Press, 1932), pp. 29-43. Reprinted by permission of the publisher.

question. Mr. Freeman's statement about Edes, however, does indicate that the sponsors of the paper had planned to import men well qualified by previous experience to publish a newspaper, and that Benjamin Titcomb, Jr., the local partner, son of a member of the local aristocracy, was injected into the enterprise as a stop-gap. It is perhaps noteworthy also that both Edes and Wait had been connected with the dominant anti-Federalist newspapers of Boston at the time, Edes with the famous *Boston Gazette* published by his father, and Wait with the *Independent Chronicle* of Powars and Willis. Peter Edes, however, was a Federalist in politics.

Of four three-column pages about eleven by seventeen inches, the *Gazette* was rather above the average typographically, judged by the standards of excellence obtaining then. The words of the title, in an old English type, surrounded by the flourishes dear to the heart of the eighteenth century printer, occupied four and a half inches of the first page. The type and paper were firm and clean, the ink was evenly distributed, and the impression clear. Arrangement of contents was in the usual unsystematic manner, but was neatly done. Page 1 of the second issue was filled with a moral essay, entitled "On Entrance into Life, and the Conduct of Early Manhood." The second page carried various contributions, including a dialogue between a Briton and his son on the question of emigrating, a description of Antwerp, and miscellaneous short bits, with a quarter-column of advertising. "By the Western Post," a melange of foreign and domestic news, appeared on Page 3; what corresponded to the masthead of the present-day newspaper stood at the bottom of the second column on this page, leading a pseudo-editorial observation that "The present age seems to second every attempt to recover freedom, civil and ecclesiastic. . .Ireland has caught the fire of patriotism from America, and may heaven crown their efforts with the same glorious success." Announcement of the arrival in port of Capt. Christopher Dyer with £2,000 salvage money for bringing in a derelict was made on this page, which carried also three-quarters of a column of advertising. The last page, the literary section of the sheet, opened with a satirical poem, "The Matrimonial Creed," contributed by "Eliza." A "Comparative Sketch of the Dispositions of the Middle Classes in England, with Those of America," clipped from an Irish paper and sent in by a correspondent, was favorable to the Americans. A column of advertising filled out the page.

With a somewhat larger percentage of advertising, and wider variety of essay subjects, the contents of the *Falmouth Gazette* during its early days are fairly represented by the second issue. News, of course, varied with events, and the subjects which engrossed the contributors of essays likewise differed. The issue of January 15, 1785, for example, carried an essay written "For the Falmouth Gazette," dealing with the press. This contribution was to be reprinted some ten years later in the first number of Peter Edes' *Kennebeck Intelligencer*. Citing the worth of newspapers as aids to the government in circulating the laws, warning sessions of the legislature, and similar quasi-public functions, the correspondent declared that

> the value of them may, in some measure, be determined by the fondness of the people to read them—The moment the paper is published, the office is crowded with readers—the postriders flock from every quarter of the state and must go, let it rain or shine. For my part, I consider the money that is expended for two or three NEWS PAPERS in a week as paid out to the best advantage—as promoting my own interest and that of my country.

Medical letters, rebuses, and puzzles of various sorts were contributed. Daniel George, the schoolmaster who was later to become a publisher, offered a prize of one dollar to the first boy to solve a mathematical problem he set. For the first girl to solve it, the prize was four dollars. Three weeks time was allowed. James Hopkins, 13, of Falmouth, was the winner. "Preparation for Sunday" became a regular department on the last page, presenting brief moral essays on sincerity and similar topics, the *Gazette* being then issued on Saturdays.

The difficulties of news-collecting stand as sufficient reason for the publication of so large a proportion of non-news material as was usual in the early newspaper. In the *Gazette,* for example, a scant column or two contained matter justifiably to be defined as news, and the rest of the paper was filled with belletristic matter of various sorts. News was to be had from two sources, local and foreign. Local news in the present sense of the ordinary comings and goings of citizens was then not recognized; the ordinary daily doings of the town, scanty as they were, received still scantier space. Only local events of distinct significance were covered. Foreign news, by which is meant news coming from any point outside the local territory, from Boston or from London, was gathered in two principal ways: by clippings from outside newspapers, and by private letters made available through the generosity or public spirit of men of affairs; both of these depended on the mails, which were few and irregular. On April 29, 1785, Parson Smith noted: "The post at last got here, having been hindered near 5 weeks." Mail was sent once a week from Boston from June, 1775, to January, 1789, twice a week from January to May of that year, and thereafter three times a week. The postman sometimes travelled on foot, but generally on horseback, and the time of arrival was very irregular. In 1790, sixteen days elapsed in the passage of a letter from Philadelphia, thirteen days from New York, and three from Boston. Shipments of paper and ink also were dependent on an irregular transport, and for this reason the *Gazette* not infrequently appeared in smaller format than usual, at times on a half or three-quarter sheet.

The two men who undertook to produce a newspaper under conditions so unprepossessing were at the start of their enterprise still comparatively young, probably young enough to enjoy the difficulties they encountered. Wait was in his twenty-second year, Titcomb a year his senior, having been born in Falmouth July 26, 1761, the fourth son of Deacon Benjamin Titcomb and Ann Smith. His father had settled in Falmouth after having left his home in Newburyport, Massachusetts, to serve at the siege of Louisbourg in 1746. He was a blacksmith by trade, was for three years selectman of the town, and in 1780 was a representative to the General Court. The younger Benjamin was educated at Dummer Academy, Newbury, Massachusetts, and served his apprenticeship in a print shop at Newburyport. Returning to Falmouth probably in the 80's, he opened a business of his own, and was established there when Wait arrived from Boston and set up his stationery business. After his association with Wait and his subsequent career as publisher of the *Gazette of Maine,* Titcomb abandoned printing, about 1798, and began to act as preacher to the small society of Baptists recently established in Portland. Their first meetings were held at his house. In 1804 he went to Brunswick to become pastor of the Baptist church there. He served in this capacity for forty years, retiring at the age of eighty-three. In 1820 he was a delegate to the convention which drew up the Constitution of the State, and pronounced the opening prayer at request of Governor King. He was one of the original trustees of Waterville, now Colby, College. He died at Brunswick September 30, 1848.

His partner, Thomas B. Wait, was born in 1762, according to his daughter, in the part of Lynn, Massachusetts, known as Saugus. "He served an apprenticeship in the printing business in Boston," she says. According to Willis, Wait "had been connected in the publishing of the *Chronicle*" at Boston before coming to Maine in 1784. He carried on a business in books and stationery, as was common with early printers, and after the conclusion of his journalistic career was, according to his daughter,

> ...in the book-selling and publishing business at Portland, and was burnt out (probably in 1806), losing everything. He immediately issued proposals to reprint Blackstone's Commentaries, and received sufficient encouragement from his kind-hearted townsmen (who subscribed, many of them, for a book they did not need) to induce him to go to Philadelphia and engage a company of journeymen printers—Robert Lilly being the foreman. Soon afterward Mr. Wait moved to Boston, where he published the American State Papers. His three sons were with their father for a time; two afterward read law, and all three went to Illinois about 1817. His second son, William S. Wait, came back to Boston, and was in the book-business with Wells and Lilly. This brother afterward returned to the West. My father died in Boston in 1830.

Of Wait's edition of Blackstone, John Neal wrote, "It was wonderfully correct, and has ever been regarded by the profession as faultless. Tucker's Blackstone appeared long afterward." The edition was in four octavo volumes, with 1903 pages of text and 100 pages of appendix and index.

Wait, in Willis' estimation, "was a man of strong mind and great firmness and independence of character. He did much service to our community in procuring the establishment of post offices and mail routes, and in diffusing useful information. At the early period of his residence here he was very popular, and had great ascendancy over public opinion; he was alert and persevering in whatever he undertook and honest in his purposes."

Whether because Wait's popularity was too great, or because his editorial policies were distasteful, or for some other reason, Titcomb did not long continue as partner of the young Bostonian. Beginning with the issue of February 16, 1786, Wait was sole publisher of the *Gazette*, the title of which became the *Cumberland Gazette* with the issue of April 7, 1786. Part of Falmouth being incorporated as Portland on July 4, 1786, *Portland* replaced *Cumberland* in the imprint of the *Gazette* July 20, 1786. With the issue of January 2, 1792, it became the *Eastern Herald*. This title it retained during the rest of its independent career. That Titcomb had some animus against Wait, based perhaps on Wait's political attitude, is evidenced by later developments.

The contents of even a small weekly newspaper of four pages would so soon outrun the bounds of space imposed by a study of this sort that to give a few characteristic excerpts significant as indicating the editorial tendencies of the paper concerned, and to summarize briefly the general news policy observed is about all the commentator can do. The *Falmouth Gazette* during its earlier years was relatively dull in strictly news matter, since it depended for its coverage of national and foreign affairs upon clippings from outside papers which were several weeks, if not months, old when they reached the office. Even as late as 1804, the *Eastern Herald and Gazette of Maine,* lineal descendant of the *Falmouth Gazette,* declared, "It is now nearly 70 days since the date of the last accounts from London—owing, it is supposed, to the prevalence of strong westerly winds." For the reason here implied, a survey of local news and of the contributions of local correspondents who sent in verse, essays, letters, aphorisms, may be expected to provide a more accurate conspectus of the *Gazette* than could be had from a summary of its outside news.

First indication of the separatist sentiment in the District appeared in an acrostic on Falmouth, apostrophizing the town as mistress of a "rising state." This bit, contributed by "a benevolent Gentleman in a neighboring Town," called forth applause from "A Farmer," who urged the benevolent gentleman to use his talents to further discussion of the topic thus opened. "Impartialis," "A Farmer," "Ruricola," "Philanthropos" who wrote from Kennebec, "Philadelphos,""A Well-Wisher to the Eastern Country," "Civis," and "Orientalis," debated the question in succeeding issues. "Impartialis Secundus," "Senex," and "Benevolus" were also represented in the arguments. From Massachusetts papers were reprinted letters attacking the separatists, which were answered by members of the group. The editorial stand of the *Gazette* itself is to be gathered from a paragraph answering a Boston paper's sneer at separation:

> The above paragraph, while it proves the writer to be an ignoramus, with respect to the subject he scribles on, or a liar, or both—proves also, that, from interested motives, he fears the event;—and further, that notwithstanding he can offer no one, not even the most trivial argument against the measure, yet that he is *too thoroughly* NETTLED to hold his peace.—Happy, happy would it be for *certain characters* if the effects of these same nettles, were experienc'd at *Boston* only.

The ferment of discussion continued through the issue of September 17, 1785, which carried a notice to the citizens of York, Cumberland, and Lincoln counties, calling on them to assemble on October 5 to debate the question. The resulting conference named a committee to write to the towns asking that delegates be sent to a convention to be held in the following January. In the meantime the pros and cons of separation were argued by correspondents using a wide variety of pseudonyms.

The Stamp Act which Massachusetts passed in this year, laying a duty on newspapers, was denounced in material reprinted from Boston papers. The *Gazette's* own attitude was expressed thus: "This Act, so far as it relates to the suppression of public newspapers, is considered, by the Wise and Good, as *an ax laid at the root of our civil and religious liberties."* Falmouth in town meeting instructed Joseph Noyes, its representative to the General Court, to "labour the repeal of this act, or of that part thereof especially which imposeth a duty on newspapers," in which action may be detected perhaps the working of Wait's popularity with the townsfolk and Titcomb's prestige arising from the prominence of his father in the affairs of the place.

Daniel George, who was later to publish the successor of the *Gazette,* contributed verse to its literary section, as did Jonas Clark. "An Autumnal Elegy," by D. George, published in the issue of October 1, 1785, was in the correct melancholy vein. Still more lugubrious was "On the Accidental Death of Two Favourite Thrushes. . ."contributed to the issue of March 16, 1787. The anonymous mourner, with many "oh's" and "ah's," maintained that music had died with the thrushes, that no violin could console him now, and that it was bad enough to lose one, but to lose both was awful. The irreverent contributor who published in the issue of March 30 following, an ode "On the Accidental Death of Two Favourite Ram-Cats" was more robustious and wrote his satire with such evident enjoyment as to make it quotable. It parodied closely the ode on the thrushes:

> *What!—could grim death not spare me one?*
> *No—d—n it—both my Cats are gone.*
>   *Alas! my Ram-Cats! —O!*
>
> . . . .
>
> *And now to Pandimonium's land*
> *They're gone, to join th' infernal band*
>   *Of songsters grim and fell;*
> *Who meagre darkness, fire and pain,*
> *Tune the discordant banjo's strain,*
>   *And welcome them to H—ll.*

The closing stanza may be said at least to have deserved better proof-reading than Wait gave it.

Some idea of the sternness of justice in the early days is to be had from a report of the conviction of John Lowel for robbery and his being sentenced to pay three times the value of the goods taken and to suffer twenty stripes. The story of a holdup in the woods between Portland and Saccarappa, from which the victim escaped, carried the statement that another person also had been assaulted during the last week "in Saco woods."

The Congressional campaign of 1789, in which Josiah Thatcher of Gorham, Nathaniel Wells of Wells, William Lithgow of Georgetown, and George Thatcher of Biddeford were candidates for member of Congress from Maine, was virulent and personal. Wait strongly urged the election of George Thatcher, with whom he was friendly, and who was a frequent contributor to his paper. Thatcher was, however, opposed by the majority of the inhabitants of Falmouth. Says Willis, "There were at this time no party lines of division like those of the present day, but differences grew out of the local situation and individual character of candidates, which caused excitements as violent as those founded on differences of political sentiment." As a result of these "excitements," Wait was assaulted, Daniel George and Daniel Davis, correspondents of the *Gazette,* were threatened with personal violence, and Samuel C. Johonnot, another correspondent, was driven out of town. Their candidate, however, was elected.

During the troubles growing out of this election, which excited more personal abuse than Willis saw in any other campaign, Benjamin Titcomb, Jr., Wait's former partner, established the *Gazette of Maine,* second paper in the District, the first number of which was issued October 8, 1790. "Sustained by the opposition to Wait," against whom "some dissatisfaction existed at this time by a number of respectable people, who took offence at the freedom of his remarks," it was a dull sheet in comparison with the *Gazette,* which it resembled in general makeup. During the separatist agitation of 1792, Titcomb urged all people to consider the question, form an opinion, and abide by it, and published letters from various correspondents reviewing the arguments of 1785 and urging action in the plebiscite called by the General Court for the first Monday in May. That Titcomb, however, was not inclined to the partisan fervor shown earlier by Wait is evidenced by his comment on the election of 1796; listing the candidates, he said,

> The characters above mentioned are all good, as far as we know,—The good citizens will by their own judgment determine who among them shall be elected; and no doubt will, on the whole, make a wise and Judicious election.

An attitude toward governmental news somewhat less usual then than now appeared in a skit entitled "Shandyism," contributed by "Yorick," in which Tristan's father, Uncle Toby, and Corporal Trim discussed the publication in newspapers of reports of Congress, agreeing that too much was published, and that although events of major importance ought to be covered, much of the material included was not worth the space given it. A fortnight later, the paper reported the hanging on May 20 in the North Meeting House of a bell cast "by Col. Revere of Boston." We learn from Timothy Pickering's "Report. . .relative to the Fortifications and Harbours of the United States" that at Portland "the works consist of a fort, a citadel, a battery for ten pieces of cannon, an artillery store, a guardhouse, an air-furnace for heating that, and a covered way from the fort to the battery," and that £871 was needed to put the whole in good condition. The same issue contained, postponed from the week before, a report of the recommendations to colored people drawn up at Philadelphia by a convention of delegates from abolition societies. Negroes were urged to attend church, to learn to read and write, to teach their children trades' to be diligent, to shun liquor, to legalize their marriages, to save for their children, to be civil and respectful, and to "avoid frolicking, and amusements that lead to expense and idleness."

In connection with the earlier stories of crime already noted, there is interest in the *Gazette of Maine's* report that:

> One day last week as a Mr. *Trueman* from Boston was going from Wiscasset point up the Sheepscot river a few miles, (at the invitation of a Mr. Clark,) he was assaulted by five persons, one of which was armed—who stripped him of his clothes, beat and bruised him much, and robbed him of 200 Dollars in cash and sundry valuable papers.—Some of the persons were known to Mr. Trueman, although disfigured with paint. Some of the Banditti were for killing him—others for cutting and maiming him; and in this manner he escaped, having nothing on but a few of his clothes torn in strips.

Meanwhile the *Cumberland Gazette* had become the *Eastern Herald*, "Printed and Published by *Thomas Baker Wait* at His Office in the Main Street, opposite the Hay-Market, Portland." It changed relatively little, except as its advertising waned in comparison with that of better years. Wait and Daniel George, partners in a bookstore, advertised not only books, but shoes of all sorts. Frequency of advertisements dunning debtors of the paper increased in the issues nearing the time of Wait's sale of the paper. In June, 1796, he and J.K. Baker signed a proposal for publishing the *Herald* twice a week, the new system to start in July, new type to be used, and a price of fifteen shillings a year to be charged. The improved paper was to include

> the most interesting intelligence, of a political, philosophical, agricultural, and commercial nature, both foreign and domestic. Also the Federal and State laws...the Marine List shall be particularly attended to...whatever may contribute to advance the interest of the Farmer shall be carefully sought after...and the mechanic arts...shall not be forgotten...innocent wit, and humour, shall always find a welcome place; and a corner shall be consecrated to the Muses.

The rehabilitation, however, did not occur as scheduled. If Wait, as seems not improbable, had regarded this as a final effort to re-invigorate the paper, its failure may have made him more willing to dispose of the property, as he soon after did. Possibly the anti-Jacobin sentiment of a Federalist community in the early nineties cut into popular support of a paper the republican sympathies of which had built circulation a few years before.

Wait may have lost money in his brief excursion into publishing a paper at Hallowell—the *Tocsin*—with Baker; this sheet they sold in September, 1796, and it died soon after. Having on August 10, 1795, offered to accept "good English hay in payment any time before the 18th instant," by December 31, 1795, Wait was threatening to prosecute delinquents—quite a change from March 30, 1786, when "the Printer begs leave just to *hint*" that he wanted money.

Titcomb likewise was having difficulties. On December 31, 1795, he declared:

> It is now the third week since any papers from this Office have gone by the post from this to Warren, and below.—Not on account of any failure on the part of the Editor, but in consequence of a flat refusal of the post to carry them. It is hoped that some new arrangement will enable the Editor to supply his Customers at the Eastward, as usual, next week.

Collections probably were slow from subscribers whose papers arrived with such irregularity, if at all. Advertising in the *Gazette of Maine*, never so heavy as that in Wait's paper, fell off to two columns November 12, 1795. Opposition to Wait's paper was perhaps not a strong means of support after Wait had lost part of his prominence.

Whatever the cause, the *Gazette of Maine* for August 15, 1796, carried on Page 3 the following announcements, which are at once self-explanatory and characteristic of the men who wrote them:

To the CUSTOMERS

The Editor of the *Gazette of Maine* takes this opportunity of acquainting them that he has relinquished the publication of the same, of which intention they were apprized some time since.

Having by six years close application attended this business, he finds his health so far impaired, as to occasion the relinquishment of this employment.

Mr. John K. Baker having purchased the right of publishing the *Gazette of Maine*, together with the debts due therefor, it will in future be published in his name—to whom the Customers will in future apply to make payment of balances due, he being duly authorized to receive the same; and his receipt therefor will be their discharge.

The Editor presents his customers with his most sincere acknowledgements for their patronage and custom, and wishing them more satisfaction than they have ever yet experienced, bids them an affectionate Adieu!

To the PUBLIC

A proposal was issued some time since, to publish the *Eastern Herald* twice a week from the month of July. Circumstances which were unexpected at that time, have occurred to prevent hitherto the intended publication.

The public are now informed, that the *Eastern Herald* will continue to be printed once a week till the first of September, at which time the right of publishing said paper will be transferred to Mr. John Kelse Baker.

Persons indebted for Newspapers, advertisements, &c, are requested to make payment as soon as they can with convenience to their much obliged and very humble servant,

Thomas B. Wait
Portland, August 15, 1796

By the foregoing it will be observed, that the right of publishing the *Gazette of Maine* is already transferred to the subscriber, and that the right of publishing the *Eastern Herald* is to be transferred to him on the first day of September next. Till which time he has agreed with Mr. *Titcomb* to continue, as usual, the publication of the *Gazette of Maine.*

After the said first day of September the Customers for the *Eastern Herald* and *Gazette of Maine* are informed that the subscriber

PROPOSES

To supply them with two papers a week, to be entitled

The Eastern Herald and Gazette of Maine

It will be published on Mondays and Thursdays, and will be printed on good paper and a new type. The price to be but *Two Dollars and Fifty Cents* a year...

JOHN KELSE BAKER
Portland, August 1796

The specifications of the new paper, as they merely repeat those published in the *Eastern Herald* on June 10, which have been summarized previously in this study, are omitted here.

The merging of the two former opponents, comparable in its smaller way to the later union of the *Massachusetts Centinel* and the *Independent Chronicle,* was not, however, to clear the journalistic atmosphere in Portland. The issue following that which carried the manifestos recorded above offered the following, likewise characteristic of its author:

To the CITIZENS of MAINE

The subscriber, who has the pleasure to reflect that he was born in this rising District, and who has heretofore been concerned in the publication of the *Gazette of Maine,* a paper which he presumes to say has been conducted on the purest principles of republicanism, begs leave with due respect to inform his fellow citizens, that having been unfortunately disappointed of purchasing of Mr. Titcomb (the late Editor) the right of publishing said *Gazette,* which is now about to be incorporated with the *Eastern Herald,* he has, by the advice of many of his friends and former customers of the *Gazette* aforesaid, determined, if sufficient encouragement should be given, to publish, in its stead, a WEEKLY PAPER to be entitled The

ORIENTAL TRUMPET

He will particularly regard the Rights and Liberties of his Country, and stand in his place, a CENTINAL for their protection—When danger is apprehended, his TRUMPET shall sound the alarm; and when public proceeding or private information shall need be promulged, it shall be faithfully employed to spread them with the rapidity of a *Post-Boy,* throughout the now District, but speedily expected COMMONWEALTH OF MAINE!

JOHN RAND
Portland, August 13, 1796

Thus the scene closes on the independent careers of the two first newspapers of the District, leaving two new protagonists, whose activities are next to be considered.

CHAPTER 16.

The War of 1812 inflicted greater hardships on Maine people than any war in our national history. So traumatic was its effect when combined with Massachusetts' attitude toward Maine, that the war produced a feeling of alienation toward Massachusetts which would not end until Maine was erected into an independent state.

THE WAR OF 1812: A TURNING POINT IN THE MOVEMENT TO SEPARATE MAINE FROM MASSACHUSETTS*

by
Ronald F. Banks

The passage of the Embargo Act in December 1807, interrupted and in many cases reversed the growth and prosperity of the Maine seacoast towns from Eastport to Kittery which had grown relatively affluent from the profits derived from the neutral trade. It is true that many merchants circumvented the law by smuggling activities and the deliberate abuse of the privileges of coastal trading. There were even some whose ships, at sea when the law was passed, continued to trade with other countries. The majority of the merchant shippers, however, complied with the law and, as a result, suffered great losses. William King, one of the most successful shippers in the District, estimated that the Embargo cost him at the very least $5558 with each passing month. By the time the law was repealed in March 1809, sixty percent of the people of the seacoast towns were unemployed and in the largest town, Portland, where the Embargo was estimated to have produced losses in the excess of one million dollars, soup kitchens were set up for the needy.

Politically, the Embargo placed a severe strain on long standing alliances. Many Republicans in the seacoast towns, like King's former business associates, Moses Carlton Jr., Abiel Wood Jr., and Peleg Tallman, condemned their hand chosen representative to Congress, Orchard Cook, for his vote in favor of the Embargo. Nearly every coastal town sent anti-Embargo resolves to President Jefferson.

The Embargo, as is well known, revived the lingering corpse of Federalism in New England. In 1809, Christopher Gore won the governorship of Massachusetts over the hopeless efforts of Levi Lincoln. Gore's victory was due in no small part to the fact that he polled nearly 3000 votes more in the District than he had polled in a losing cause in the year before. It was difficult indeed to remain loyal to an administration that made life so arduous. Yet, by in large, the ranks of the Democratic-Republican party in Maine held together. With the repeal of the Embargo in March 1809, the worst was over, at least down to the outbreak of the war of 1812.

The news that Congress had declared war on England reached Massachusetts in late June, 1812. On June 26, Governor Caleb Strong issued a proclamation calling for a day of public fast and shortly thereafter affirmed his opposition to "Mr. Madison's War" by refusing to honor a request from Washington to allow the militia to leave the state. Strong justified his defiance of the national government on the grounds that the law of 1795, authorizing the President to employ the militia in times of national emergency did not apply in this instance since no such emergency existed. This was only the first in a series of acts, some of which contemplated secession, taken by the Federalists of Massachusetts during the course of the war.

In Maine there developed, also, a formidable opposition to the war particularly along the

---

*Ronald F. Banks, *"The Separation of Maine and Massachusetts: 1785-1820,"* (Unpublished Ph. D. dissertation, University of Maine, 1966), pp. 123-140.

seacoast. Though the leaders of the dominant Democratic-Republican Party, William King, John Chandler, William Widgery and others, were generally advocates of the national cause, there was little they were able to do to advance that cause.

Until the summer of 1814, the District was spared the ravages of war. Except for an occasional skirmish like the one that took place in Casco Bay between the *Enterprise* and the *Boxer* in 1813, hardly a shot was heard. The British, it appears, planned it this way, recognizing as one Ellsworth native reminded them: "New England may be conquered with kindness."

Many Republicans in Maine could not be so conquered. The *Eastern Argus* so angered anti-war Federalists in Portland: "that the war men in the Argus office, when they went home late at night, were obliged to arm themselves with the iron cross bars from their chaises, or other implements to protect themselves from attack."

William King, who in addition to his other activities was major general of the IIth Division of the Massachusetts militia, agreed to a request made by Washington to organize several units of volunteers to protect the coast of Maine and to discourage smuggling activities. In 1813, the War Department, in an attempt to embarrass Governor Strong for his contumacy, but which only alienated many of the supporters of the administration in Maine, ordered all the troops manning the United States garrisons in the District to the Great Lakes frontier. According to King, after the soldiers left, Maine was defended only by "a few invalids in various garrisons who were retained on account of their indispositions."

The defiance of Massachusetts' authorities encouraged many Maine citizens to cooperate with the British. General George Ulmer was appointed to command the United States garrison at Eastport. Ulmer was instructed to stop the thriving illegal trade with New Brunswick. Arrested on fabricated charges brought against him by irate citizens of the area who resented his effectiveness, he was placed in a Machias jail. He got his release only by appealing to Washington.

Peleg Tallman, who refused to vote for the war as a member of Congress, represented a large number of individuals in Maine who exploited the division of opinion in the District for their own advantage. In 1813, he was appointed Swedish Vice-Consul for the District of Maine in charge of the lucrative "neutral trade" which miraculously developed in the space of a few months.

For those who believed that the war was just, the illicit activities of their neighbors were traitorous. One can only conjecture the extent to which the jealousies and hatreds, generated by this abnormal situation, affected the lives of those involved and their relationships with one-another.

The year 1814 marked the crisis point of the war for the New Englanders. In June, the islands of Passamaquoddy Bay were occupied by the British. Further south, the expectation that the British attacks on Falmouth and Scituate would be followed by a bombardment of Boston caused even the Federalists to question the wisdom of further neglect of seacoast defences. The capture of Castine and the occupation of Eastern Maine during the first week of September must have come as a shock to the Boston bankers who had loaned money to the British while denying Washington access to their tills.

William King in his capacity as major general of the IIth Division of the state militia called out his men in June when news first reached him of British advances. Throughout the summer and into the fall his men remained on watch from Belfast to Bath waiting for what all conceded would be a British attempt to conquer all of Maine. West of Bath, other division chiefs did likewise. However, as events developed, the area west of the Penobscot, except for an occasional foray by the British, was spared.

Governor Strong commended King for his able generalship at the same time he worried over the expense. Washington revealed its unwillingness, to say nothing of its inability, to pay for the costs of the defense by the militia because of the failure of Massachusetts to cooperate with Washington, making it clear that no money would be forthcoming until such time as Governor Strong agreed to place the militia under federal direction. This, Governor Strong was determined to resist. Consequently, he was forced to convene a special session of the General Court in October 1814 for the purpose of raising needed revenues. The General Court, controlled by a large Federalist majority, dutifully authorized the Governor to borrow as needed from the banks of the Commonwealth.

Members of the General Court from the District were especially angered by the failure of Strong during this special session to recommend measures for the expulsion of the British from Eastern Maine. Most of the money to be borrowed by the Governor, it seemed, was to provide protection for Boston and surrounding towns. The District was to be given second priority. No event in all the previous history of the union of Massachusetts and Maine so blatantly and brutally revealed the extent to which the interests of Maine could be sacrificed to those of Massachusetts proper.

On October 19, Mark Langdon Hill of Phippsburg, senator from Lincoln County and friend of William King, joined by two new faces, John Holmes of Alfred and Albion K. Parris of Paris, asked the General Court to appoint a committee to investigate the possibility of a force being raised to drive the British out of Eastern Maine. After a number of days, Hill concluded that the General Court "meant to say or do nothing about it."

A month later, another attempt by Hill to obtain action on his request was again ignored. *Niles Weekly Register* reported that, in reality, however, it was not the General Court but Governor Strong who was refusing to "assist in rescuing a part of *his own state* from the hands of a foreign enemy."

At this point, the initiative was seized by Washington. President Madison had decided to exercise the authority invested in the executive branch by an act passed in 1795 to, in effect, nationalize a portion of the Massachusetts militia for the purpose of forming an expeditionary force to be sent against Castine. The troops of the militia were to be summoned, "without the intervention of the state authority," and the man selected to lead the expedition was none other than William King, Maine's leading Democratic-Republican politician.

There was only one problem: the national government was without funds to finance the expedition. The only part of the country having a surplus of money to lend was New England! Secretary of War Monroe, caught in a dilemma, instructed General Henry Dearborn to apply to the Boston banks for a loan but the banks which had liberally lent money to the British now found themselves without funds. Monroe was hardly able to contain his fury when he learned of their refusal. "A feeble invasion by a few thousand men only on any part of Massachusetts would have been expelled in a week, at any period of our revolutionary contest," the Secretary wrote to Henry Dearborn. "The cause is now the same and we look with equal astonishment and concern, at the change of conduct there."

At this juncture, Dearborn, commander in charge in the New England theatre of the war, ordered William King to Boston to confer with Strong. King was instructed to ascertain from the Governor what assistance he was prepared to offer to guarantee the success of the expedition. Specifically, the Governor was to be requested to advance a substantial sum of money from the state treasury to finance the expedition, the federal government promising to reimburse the state within two months if possible. The stage was thus set for a humiliating confrontation between an agent of the national government, King, and Governor Strong.

It was embarrassing enough for the national government to have to call on a governor of a state to bail it out of a difficult situation, but when the governor refused King's request, it became obvious to all the extent to which the Madison administration was paralyzed. Moreover, the failure of King's mission dramatized the extent to which the fate of the District rested in the hands of a stubborn administration in Boston. As if this humiliation suffered by the national government were not enough, the letter sent by Secretary of War Monroe to the Governor informing him of the planned expedition "in some treacherous manner" appeared in the Federalist [Boston] *Columbian Centinel* the following day after its reception "thus expressing to the enemy, the whole plan and with such celerity was the information thus promulgated, that the enemy, [at Castine] was apprised of it in forty eight hours."

Nor was the news of the expedition the only information "leaked" to the British. An anonymous gentleman whom General John Sherbrooke, British commander at Halifax, described as "a most respectable inhabitant of the country lying between the Penobscot and the boundary line of New Brunswick and who was a member of the House of Representatives of the State of Massachusetts," met with the General in his office on November 20, 1814. This man, who was known personally by

Sherbrooke and the commander of the British fleet in the northeast, Admiral Griffith, and who was greatly respected by them, announced that he had returned from the special session of the General Court held in October at which time he had met with Governor Strong. The Governor, he claimed, authorized him to make contact with Sherbrooke to determine if New England could expect assistance from the English should a secessionist course be taken by the New England states. Sherbrooke explained the proposition to his superior in London, Lord Bathurst, as follows:

> It seems that the New England states are very apprehensive that if Great Britain should conclude a Peace with the general Government their interests would be sacrificed—And as the President has refused to repay expenses already incurred by the Northern Commonwealth for the purposes of defence, the Executive of Massachusetts has resolved to withhold all pecuniary Aid from the General Government And to apply the Amount of Taxes raised for the defence of their own Frontier. . . .
> Notwithstanding the Custom which prevails of Calling these 'Federal States', It is right your Lordship should be informed that there is a very strong democratic Party in each of these Commonwealths [New England states] And as they will in the event of any attempt being made to separate New England from the Union most probably be assisted by the General Government in resisting the Measure. It appears that the Federal Party wishes to ascertain at this early period whether Great Britain would under these Circumstances afford them military assistance to effect their purpose should they stand in need of it.

Maine Republicans were not aware of this meeting between the Governor's emissary (if indeed he was the Governor's emissary for we have only his word that he was) and Sherbrooke. They suspected, however, that a number of prominent Federalists were in contact with the British. One of those whose activities came under suspicion was president Jesse Appleton of Bowdoin College. William King wrote Appleton the following note in the fall of 1814 which he signed not with his name but with the pseudonym "Enquirer":

> Sir, The object of your late visit to his Magistracy's [sic] Governor General at Castine [Sherbrooke] has become a subject of enquiry.
> The person who now addresses you has not the honor of a personal acquaintance [untrue—King was an Trustee of the College]. He therefore chooses to communicate with you in the way he deems most interesting to the country.
> Public men, sir, are the property of the Public; none more so than those literary men who have the charge of our youth; to you, Sir, as to a fountain whose streams are either pure or impure the public look with anxiety;—the least departure therefore from a correct course of conduct will not be submitted to.
> As our Country is now at war with Great Britain the following questions will not be considered uninteresting either to the public or yourself.
> Have you, sir, visited Castine since the British took possession of the place?
> Had you a passport or other document to authorize such a procedure?
> Was your object in making this visit Political?
> And if so, have you succeeded in your Negotiations?
> Will you state the conversation which took place between His Magistracy's [sic] Governor and yourself?
> And will you publish the results of your visit for the benefit of the people and the satisfaction of an Enquirer.

As a result of the foregoing actions and suspected actions, it is understandable that the news that a convention of New England Federalists was to take place in Hartford in December was received among these friendly to the war with deep concern. Maine sent two delegates, Samuel Wilde of Hallowell and Stephen Longfellow of Portland, father of the poet and the son of Stephen Longfellow Jr., who participated in the first phase of the separation movement, both of whom had a reputation of being the most staunch Federalists in the District. When taken together, all of these events produced in the District an atmosphere of extreme apprehension.

By December, many in the District were in desperate pursuit of some means by which the tide of events could be turned in a direction more to their liking. On December 8 and 9, 1814, there took place in the custom house at Portland a most significant meeting of several of these people. In attendance were many of the leading Republicans of the District and a few Federalists who were disgruntled with the actions of their more extremist brethren. Several of those present were William King, William Widgery, Joshua Wingate Jr., son-in-law of General Henry Dearborn; Asa Clap and Woodbury Storer, important shippers of the Portland area; and Samuel K. Whiting, Samuel Ayer, and William Pitt Preble, all of whom would become leading separationists within the year. Widgery was elected to preside.

The meeting produced a sober and frank appraisal of the defenceless position of the District. The conclusion was reached that only an appeal to the President of the United States could save the District from the "Treacherous" policies emanating from Boston. A committee was appointed, headed by Samuel Whiting, a Bangor lawyer, to draft such an appeal, the text of which read as follows:

> Three months have now transpired since the belligerent power with whom we are contending has had undisturbed possession of one third of our territory. Longer to remain silent upon the effects resulting from this state of things; and the conduct of our state authorities relative to the same, would be a tacit assent to all their measures—would be an abandonment of all our rights. We have seen the Executive of the Commonwealth tamely submitting to the invasion of his territory without making one effort to repel the foe. We have seen our state

legislature assembled for the express purpose of taking into consideration the peculiar state of affairs, and instead of calling out the energies of our country to drive out the invaders from our soil, instead of giving us that aid, rejected with indifference every motion urged for our relief; they passed over in almost total silence the occupation of our District by the enemy and adopted those measures only, which had tendency to embarrass the General Government—to organize faction—and encourage the enemy in their mad sickness of conquest.s,

And the more effectually to restrict our exertion, the governor, encircled by his Board of War, has it in contemplation of passing an order, that no Maj. General shall march his troops out of his own District, without an order from the Commander in Chief: thus bound we shall be destroyed in detail, we shall be presented a living sacrifice, without the power of resistence. Thus abandoned by the state authority, we view with serious alarm the situation in which we are placed—having the enemy in the bosom of our country—and an extensive seaboard unprotected; we shall soon become an easy prey to the savage attacks of our foe. Such is the situation of our District, and such the force of our laws, that the most unrestrained and unlimited intercourse with the enemy is carried on. We have become the general thorough-fare through which the unprincipled carry on the most illicit traffic—and thru which our domestic foes carry on their 'traiterous correspondence.' The collectors on our frontier in vain raise their arm of authority, our revenue laws are too insufficient to support them. The officers of the Militia call upon their Troops. Governor Strong controls their operations.

Significantly, several days later, after it became obvious that the national government was powerless to assist its friends in Maine, Samuel Whiting from his home in Bangor wrote King as follows:

> If Massachusetts won't cooperate and the Federal government is unable to, then the crisis has arrived when the District of Maine ought to Legislate for herself. Released from the thraldom of Boston influence, we would not suffer this Eastern section of the country to sink into the insignificance...if we can get no assistance let us make an effort ourselves.

On December 28, 1814, a convention of Republicans from several towns in Oxford county met at Paris and concluded that the authorities of Massachusetts had conducted themselves in a manner "unbecoming the representatives of a free people." It was further resolved, "that it is inexpedient that the District of Maine constitute a part of the state of Massachusetts—no longer than the state of Massachusetts gives support to the union."

This meeting, coming as it did during the winter session of the General Court, was designed, undoubtedly, to support the efforts of the Senator from Oxford County, Albion Parris. Parris, failing to obtain sufficient support for a proposal he had offered that would have resulted in the raising of a state force to drive the British from Eastern Maine, on February 6, 1815, (the war ended in December, 1814, but word would not reach Massachusetts until February 15), introduced in the Senate a resolution calling for legislative authorization of a district-wide convention to be held in Maine. This convention was to be given the power to "consult upon the expediency of the separation of the District...and the forming...of an independent state and it shall have further power, should such separation be, by them judged expedient, to frame and report a constitution of government, and to recommend all things:" necessary to effect the objective. While the resolve was being debated, news of the peace was received from Ghent and on February 25 by a 17 to 10 vote the Senate rejected Parris's resolve. The question now was whether the "separation fever" produced by the virus of war would subside, or continue to rise to a point where only major surgery would extirpate the cause of the illness.

CHAPTER 17.

Five men—William King, John Holmes, William Pitt Preble, Albion K. Parris, and John Chandler—all Democrats, launched a campaign to win the independence of Maine in the Fall of 1815. In May, 1816, their efforts produced a referendum on the question which saw those in favor of a separation obtain 10,000 of the 16,000 votes cast. However, the General Court behind Senator Harrison Gray Otis, contended that even though a clear majority had voted for a separation, too few of Maine's eligible voters participated. The Otis committee called for a second referendum to be held in September, 1816. This time the committee agreed to accept the verdict of the voters regardless of the size of the turnout. Opponents of separation managed to get the committee to require a five-ninths majority for a separation, a concession which at the time seemed inconsequential. The committee further authorized a convention to be called for October. If the five-ninths majority were obtained, then, and only then, were the delegates to draw up a constitution and petition Congress for admission to the Union. The debacle that became the Brunswick Convention marked a low point for the advocates of independence.

THE SEPTEMBER ELECTION AND THE BRUNSWICK CONVENTION OF 1816*
by
Ronald F. Banks

Never in the long history of the separation movement was interest among the citizenry of the District higher than in the summer months of 1816. Separationists appreciated the importance of the eight week interlude between the end of June and the September 2 election. There was, they realized, a limit to the number of opportunities they could reasonably expect, even from a sympathetic General Court, to effect their objective. A defeat in September would probably deliver the *coup de grace* to their cause. Similarly, the opponents of separation realized that failure to stop the separationists now would mean the end. There would be no appealing over the heads of the Maine citizens to a sympathetic Legislature. This was their last chance as well.

Cognizant of their "do or die" situation, opponents initiated a concerted effort to win the confidence of the people. Led by Moses Carlton Jr. and General David Payson of Wiscasset, a shipping town that suffered a severe economic setback during the War of 1812, the opponents at first stressed the time worn arguments that independence would result in higher taxes and a sharp decline in the profits of the coasting trade.

It soon became apparent to the opposition, however, that a criticism of the terms of the separation contained in the Otis Bill and accepted by the General Court had greater vote getting appeal in the District as a whole than did the traditional arguments. At a meeting held on June 22, at Castine, a seaport town that was evacuated by the British a year earlier, Carlton and Payson joined with gentlemen from Hancock, Washington and Penobscot counties to denounce the terms of the separation as "incompatible with the interest and highly derogatory to the honor of Maine." Meetings patterned after the one at Castine were held throughout the District during the summer. The most important one, however, was assembled at Brunswick on August 1.

Peleg Tallman who, with Carlton, was a former business associate of King was elected president of the Brunswick anti-separation meeting. In addition, a number of the leading Maine Federalists were in attendance including: Stephen Longfellow Jr., Benjamin Orr, a Brunswick lawyer who as Attorney for Bowdoin College was an avowed antagonist of William King; William Ladd of Minot, a former sea captain turned gentleman farmer who in 1828 was to found the American Peace Society; and David Payson of Wiscasset who had been associated with William King as a regimental leader of King's IIth Division of the Massachusetts militia during the War in 1812.

---

*Ronald F. Banks, "The Separation of Maine and Massachusetts: 1785-1820," (Unpublished Ph.D. dissertation, University of Maine, 1966), pp. 186-227.

The convention adopted a report that claimed separation would cost the people an additional $40,000 annually in taxes and would produce a debt of $180,000 just to construct the public buildings needed by a new state. These assertions were followed by an item analysis of the terms of the separation which were described as "ruinious to the people of Maine." The report pointed out that Maine would receive nothing from the value of public property and buildings located in Massachusetts proper, the cost of which had been borne in part by Maine people; that Maine would receive nothing from the money reimbursed to Massachusetts by the national government for expenses incurred by the state during the War of 1812 because the total amount that was due was encumbered by debts; and that the tax exempt status accorded the lands to be retained by Massachusetts in Maine was not only fiscally unwise but amounted to an abridgement of state sovereignty.

The greatest threat to the hopes of the *Argus* junto was not the machinations of the opposition, although these could not be taken lightly, but, rather, the overconfident attitude of some of the advocates of separation. The four thousand majority gained in the May election represented to many the irreducible minimum strength of the cause in Maine. William King, ordinarily an extremely shrewd observer, wrote to his brother Rufus in July that he

> "was inclined to think the majority in favor of the separation of Maine, will be much larger when the question is again taken, than it was last time. It is not considered a party question at all, and will, unless I am mistaken, have a tendency to do away with the asperity of party in the District: it is intended in the case of our being separated to organize the government without reference to the party and I feel confident it will be effected"

So sure of victory was King that he invited his brother to send him his thoughts on the kind of constitution that Maine should adopt.

John Holmes, a notoriously poor judge of such matters, reported to William Pitt Preble that separation was gaining many adherents in York County where a large pro-separation vote was needed.

The men in the *Argus* office were less sanguine. "Depend on it there is more reason to fear a failure than you seem to apprehend," Preble wrote Holmes. "There is an extensive organization of opposition and whatever zeal, desperation, juntoism and falsehood can do will be done." Samuel Whiting, a keen observer of shifting winds who had access to more intelligence than most in his capacity as one of the editorialists in the *Argus* office, informed King, "There is much of a current setting against the terms. The people are afraid and nothing will accomplish the object, but a constant, persevering and active exertion." So suspicious was the *Argus* junto of the presumed diabolical propensities of the opposition, that when the *Portland Gazette* offered to open its columns to pro-separation scribes if the *Argus* would reciprocate, the offer was rebuffed on the grounds that the *Gazette* people could not be trusted.

Throughout the summer, Whiting and Preble ground out articles in an attempt to combat the criticisms of the terms of the separation emanating from the reports made public by opponents of the several meetings held throughout the District. For Preble, the task appeared at times futile because, as he wrote King, "the truth is they are opposed to separation upon any terms. They would oppose it even if they could themselves make the conditions."

The "junto" made much of the fact that one of the most respected men in Maine, Cyrus King of Saco, the brother of William King, announced his support for separation at a York County meeting attended by over 300 people. King, a Federalist representative to Congress who had unseated Richard Cutts in 1812, condemned the arguments advanced by opponents as specious. King confessed that he had been always a separationist at heart who resented the fact that Maine had been originally taken over by Massachusetts by "forcible and violent measures." The speech by King was made all the more poignant by the fact that most people knew that he was dying from an incurable affliction that would take his life the following year while he was in the prime of his career. Consequently, what he said was considered the product of a disinterested man who only desired to leave the world in better condition than he found it. He concluded with this following impassioned appeal:

> Much as I venerate the institutions, much as I honor the statesmen of Massachusetts, I must be allowed to cherish a stronger attachment to Maine. I was born here. My family, my children were born and live here. The ashes of my father lie buried here. . . . It is but few weeks that I followed to her grave a much loved mother. And my feeble health and constitution

admonish me that the period cannot be distant when my dust must again mingle with theirs. I have no private plans or views to answer. As I said on a former occasion and in a different place, I can say with respect to any future government in Maine...I expect nothing—I ask nothing—I want nothing—God is my witness—I act from other and I trust higher motives. And may the God I envoke smile upon the doings of this meeting, that they may contribute toward effecting the INDEPENDENCE OF MAINE.

As welcome as Cyrus King's support was, it was no substitute for an offense vigorously pursued to convert large numbers of the people to the separation cause. To counteract the influence of the meetings held by the opponents required similar meetings. As a result, during the month of August pro-separation conclaves were held in such diverse locations as Belfast, Waterville, Whitefield, and Gray.

It was necessary as well to retain what support separationists had enjoyed, particularly from the squatter elements in the interior sections. This would necessitate reminding the settlers of the evil designs of their ancient adversaries, the proprietors. Many non-resident proprietors, including the Bingham heirs, were apprehensive over the possibility that independence would prove harmful to their interests. They especially feared that profits from speculation would decline because of higher taxes. Whether they actively supported the opposition to separation at the time is, at this date, uncertain. Whiting and Preble, however, believed they did or wanted settlers to believe so. The *Argus* readers were reminded of past "sins" committed by the men of "lordly dictation" who had made squatters pay as many as three times for their lands thereby contributing to their "over-grown fortunes." It was further charged by the *Argus* editors that a number of lawyers and sheriffs were the servants of the proprietors and deserved as much condemnation as their proprietor friends. Nevertheless, it was the men who lorded over the tenants who were the object of curses emanating from the *Argus* office:

> Gentlemen, your objects are apparent.... Startle not at my rudeness, for though your names are graced with high sounding titles, though you roll through the country with your guilded chariots and silver lackeys, you are not...elevated so far above the "ignoble throng" as to escape the weapons of truth.

Proprietors refused to be lured into battle by these provocative remarks; it was probably well that they didn't for there was little that they could have said that would have been received with any degree of understanding.

Hardly a voice was heard during the summer from Massachusetts. The Republican [Boston] *Yankee* persisted in lamenting the "narrowness, illiberality, and selfishness" of the authorities of Massachusetts which, the editor claimed, produced the separation fever in Maine. But even the *Yankee* found consolation in the belief that the Massachusetts Republicans would survive the loss of their Maine friends. It was certain, the newspaper asserted, that the corpse of Federalism would survive only a couple of years longer anyway. The Federalist press maintained an aloofness which betrayed their pleasure in contemplating the day when no longer would civilization be endangered by subversive elements from the District of Maine. For in truth, to paraphrase Adam Smith, the leading Federalists of Massachusetts, as well as of Maine, desired nothing more than the "preservation of their own importance." Verbal exchanges similar to those above continued down to the day upon which all were waiting, September 2, 1816 when Maine people would once again go to the polls to register their feelings on the question of a separation......

THE SEPTEMBER ELECTION

"It is greatly to be feared that we shall be under the necessity of continuing our vassalage to old Massachusetts," wrote the editor of the Portland *Gazette* sardonically as the returns from the September 2 election dribbled into his office. And it was true, for although the vote was close, 11,927 for to 10,539 against, it was clear that the requisite five-ninths majority was not obtained [Figure IX]. Instead of the 55.5% needed, the separationists had received only 53% of the vote.

An analysis of the returns of the September 2 election reveals that the separationists lost the election not because of the defections from their own ranks [Figures XII, XIII] but, rather, because of the spectacular increase in the vote of towns that had voted against separation in May. This was especially true in the counties of York and Cumberland where the pro-separation margin was cut from nearly a thousand in May to less than three hundred in September. Nearly five hundred votes of the May victory margin were erased in six towns located in the two counties alone [Figure XI].

FIGURE IX
VOTE BY COUNTIES—SEPARATION ELECTION SEPTEMBER 2, 1816, COMPARED WITH THE MAY 20, 1816 VOTE TOTALS

	September 2, 1816		May 20, 1816	
County	Yeas	Nays	Yeas	Nays
York	1,784	1,712	1,363	899
Cumberland	2,369	2,162	2,065	1,487
Lincoln	1,752	2,357	1,428	1,772
Hancock	407 ⎫ 911	1,257 ⎫ 1,461	906	684
Penobscot	504 ⎭	204 ⎭		
Washington	55	176	109	138
Kennebec	2,646	1,175	2,316	667
Oxford	1,563	828	1,448	566
Somerset	847	668	758	288
Totals	11,927	10,539	10,393	6,501

FIGURE X
SELECTED FEDERALIST-ANTI-SEPARATION TOWNS—VOTES FOR AND AGAINST SEPARATION MAY 20, 1816 AND SEPTEMBER 2, 1816

	September 2, 1816		May 20, 1816	
Towns	Yeas	Nays	Yeas	Nays
Wells	47	374	27	151
North Yarmouth	71	394	48	316
Waldoboro	11	306	8	262
Blue Hill	0	77	0	59
Castine	7	65	3	49
Totals	136	1,216	86	837

FIGURE XI
TOWNS IN YORK AND CUMBERLAND COUNTIES WHERE LARGE ANTI-SEPARATION VOTES WERE CAST—VOTES FOR AND AGAINST SEPARATION, MAY 20, 1816 AND SEPTEMBER 2, 1816

	September 2, 1816		May 20, 1816	
Towns	Yeas	Nays	Yeas	Nays
Wells	47	370	27	151
Freeport	74	160	59	107
Arundel	16	106	23	63
Lebanon	29	128	21	41
Minot	80	159	89	108
Brunswick	93	144	61	90
Totals	339	1,067	280	560

FIGURE XII
HEAVILY SEPARATIONIST TOWNS LOCATED INLAND— VOTE TOTALS FOR MAY 20, 1816, AND SEPTEMBER 2, 1816 ELECTIONS

Towns	September 2, 1816		May 20, 1816	
	Yeas	Nays	Yeas	Nays
Clinton	110	4	50	0
Dearborn	32	0	18	0
Unity	86	3	85	1
Mt. Vernon	135	1	127	0
Malta	56	0	50	0
Totals	419	8	330	1

FIGURE XIII
HEAVILY SEPARATIONIST TOWNS LOCATED INLAND AND WITHIN THE BOUNDARIES OF THE KENNEBEC PURCHASE TERRITORY—VOTES FOR AND AGAINST A SEPARATION—MAY 20, 1816 AND SEPTEMBER 2, 1816, ELECTIONS

Towns	September 2, 1816		May 20, 1816	
	Yeas	Nays	Yeas	Nays
Sidney	65	124	57	57
Vassalboro	76	64	84	52
Augusta	258	39	248	24
China	36	65	46	23
Albion	103	22	60	12
Winslow	57	3	59	1
Unity	86	3	85	2
Freedom	73	4	77	0
Palermo	78	20	70	8
Totals	832	344	786	179

In Hancock and Penobscot counties anti-separationists doubled their May total while the separationists gained only five votes [Figure IX]. As in the counties of Cumberland and York, the increase was due to the heavy turnout in anti-separation towns. For example, the towns of Deer Isle and Ellsworth, which had voted against independence in May, 154 to 0, recorded a September vote of 260 to 4, a net gain for the foes of separation of 102 votes.

Once again seaport towns contained the bulk of the opposition. Those that were nearly unanimously Federalist in politics produced one sided votes against separation [Figure X]. Even seaport towns which were generally Republican in politics continued to oppose separation, a fact that suggests that the coasting law objection was still an important factor in those towns. In seven southern Lincoln County towns [Figure XIV] which were generally Republican in politics and were seaport communities (except Alna, and even Alna depended upon commerce for its prosperity), separationists lost two votes while opponents gained over one hundred more votes than were cast for them in May.

In contrast to anti-separation towns where the votes increased sharply between May and September, the vote in Republican strongholds generally remained about the same or rose ever so slightly [Figure XII]. Separationist strength

FIGURE XIV

TOWNS IN SOUTHERN LINCOLN COUNTY WHICH WERE
GENERALLY REPUBLICAN BUT WHICH OPPOSED SEPARATION
VOTE TOTALS—MAY 20, 1816 AND SEPTEMBER 2, 1816

	September 2, 1816		May 20, 1816	
Towns	Yeas	Nays	Yeas	Nays
Wiscasset	68	123	78	95
Alna	22	65	24	48
Newcastle	22	67	21	52
Boothbay	12	64	10	52
Georgetown	13	33	17	35
Bristol	76	142	73	98
Edgecomb	24	32	16	28
Totals	237	526	239	408

continued to be greatest in inland communities. However, in a number of inland communities, the anti-separationists managed to cut into the margin of victory rolled up in May. This was especially true in the towns carved from the "Kennebec Purchase" where proprietor-squatter conflicts were historically most pronounced [Figure XIII].

In summary, the District remained divided along geographic lines in regard to separation, the coastal region being predominately opposed, the inland areas being predominately in favor. Politically, the lines were not so sharply drawn as in geography. Nevertheless, on the whole, with a few exceptions, the majority of the Republicans continued to support separation; the majority of the Federalists continued in opposition. Separationists lost the election of September 2, 1816 because anti-separation Federalists got their followers to the polls.

The increase in the anti-separationist Federalist vote was not matched by a corresponding increase in the vote of the Republican separationist towns. Federalists turned out nearly all of their voters; Republicans, as Samuel Whiting feared, could not claim as much.

Why this sudden reversal of fortune for the cause was not clear. One explanation is that the coastal towns feared the effect of the "coasting law" on their already greatly diminished prosperity. The difficulty with this explanation is that if people in the coastal towns were concerned why had they turned out in so few numbers the previous May? Another explanation that has some validity is that the opposition, for the first time, appears to have made a strenuous effort to defeat the measure. Certainly more anti-separation meetings were held during the summer of 1816 than at any time in the past.

The result of the election stunned the leaders of the separation movement. "I am as much disappointed...—and can hardly keep cool," declared Samuel Whiting, "but we must not desert the ship." Increduously, Albion K. Parris asked, "what shall we do if the majority should not be quite five-ninths? Will not a handsome majority decide the question as effectually, as if it amounted to that number?" Desperately the "junto" members searched for a way by which victory could be salvaged from what appeared to be certain defeat, and they soon deluded themselves that they had found it.

Believing that the official vote count would reveal that they had fallen short of the five-ninths majority required for a separation by a meager 200 votes, instead of nearly 1,000 as opponents claimed, several "junto" members were convinced that the General Court would take the position that the vote was close enough to justify granting a separation, especially if the delegates elected by the voters to attend the Brunswick Convention took a determined stand in favor of such a liberal view. The problem with this approach, as no doubt William King realized, was that it assumed that the people of Maine had elected a substantial majority of pro-separation delegates to attend the Brunswick Convention. If this were, in fact, the case, then there was a modicum of hope that victory might yet be realized. And, of course, there was always the possibility that such a majority could find enough illegal anti-separation ballots so that the five-ninths majority would be obtained. In any case, all hope rested on the complexion of the delegation and it was useless to make any plans until that complexion was determined.

Accordingly, William King furiously set about to make that determination. He decided that the Fall meeting of the District Court for Lincoln County scheduled to convene in Wiscasset on September 12, would provide a splendid opportunity to meet a large number of people. Lawyers and court officials from throughout the District, many of them separationists, would be assembled under one roof.

On the 12th, King, having traveled to Wiscasset, called a secret meeting of gentlemen who were at the Court, Thomas G. Thornton, United States Marshall for Maine was chosen presiding officer. King, undoubtedly, explained the purpose of the meeting to those in attendance. The session resulted in the appointment of one person from each county to serve as an agent "to ascertain the *names* and so far as possible the views of the delegates in his respective County," the information to be communicated to King and the other agents. The agents selected reveals to what extent the project was under the complete control of separationists:

YORK . . . . William Pitt Preble (Saco)
CUMBERLAND . . . . William Widgery (Portland)
OXFORD . . . . Albion K. Parris (Paris)
LINCOLN . . . . William King (Bath)
KENNEBEC AND SOMERSET . . . . John Chandler (Monmouth)
HANCOCK . . . . Benjamin Whitten (Belfast)
PENOBSCOT . . . . David Farnham (Brewer)

Before adjourning, the group also voted that it was "expedient that those friendly to separation although not members of the Brunswick Convention, should attend at Brunswick." A committee was chosen to invite such persons who fitted the description among whose members were Cyrus King of Saco, Thomas G. Thornton of Saco, Judah Dana of Paris and William Williamson of Bangor. Presumably those who accepted the invitation would engage in lobbying activity to persuade the unpersuaded of the justice of the cause.

Within two weeks King had received from the agents information that indicated a majority of the delegates elected to go to Brunswick were probably in favor of separation. John Chandler reported that in Kennebec County he believed that only one of the twenty elected delegates to be definitely opposed to separation. He added that he had seen "but few of them but believe that should there not be a 5/9 [majority] they would generally be in favor of pressing the legislature by memorial to give consent to a separation upon the [grounds of] the majority twice obtained. . . ." William Pitt Preble wrote King that in York County twenty-five delegates were in favor of separation while thirteen "will go to all lengths" to oppose, and three were "weake in the faith."

In spite of Preble's encouraging report to King, it is clear that he thought little of King's strategy. Either he was convinced that a majority of delegates to the Brunswick Convention, even though they were separationists, would refuse to ignore the fact that the five-ninths requisite majority had not been obtained, or he believed that the General Court would not ignore the fact. For Preble, the only certain way to victory was to make sure that the five-ninths majority was obtained, even though one had to resort to chicanery to produce such a result. The length to which the former tutor of mathematics at Harvard was prepared to go to obtain his goal is revealed in the following note he penned to King:

> Cannot the votes at Bath be helpful at home [forgotten] or lost? Though the majority is in our favor, by losing them we again gain twenty seven. Cannot the same be done in *Thomas Town* and Camden? You must not expect any aid from us this way for all our towns are sharply looked after—And stories about mis-conduct prove to be idle tales. I have made particular inquiries as to Wells [Wells defeated separation 374-4]. There is nothing which we can avail ourselves of. We must therefore depend on your quarter for aid and materials out of which to make a justification. The more I reflect the more I am convinced that if from a too rigid regard to punctilios the question is now lost—we have little to hope for from Massachusetts.

THE BRUNSWICK CONVENTION OF 1816

On September 30, 1816, 185 delegates representing 137 towns assembled at the Congregational Meeting House in Brunswick. Weeks of contentious squabbling in the press and rumors that separationists were prepared to resort to trickery, if necessary, to achieve their objectives, produced an atmosphere that was decidedly unchristian.

The convention was split into two major factions. There was the "junto" group at full strength represented by Parris, Preble, Holmes, King, Chandler, Widgery and Whiting, some of whom were resolved to achieve a separation even if the rules of the game had to be violated. Secondly, there were the opponents who were determined to veto any action designed to frustrate the will of the people, as they called it. Included in the ranks of the opposition were an undisclosed number of "mild" separationists who would have nothing to do with their militant brethren. Politically, as near as it is possible to determine, the opponents were mostly Federalists while the more determined of the proponents were Republicans.

On the morning of the 30th of September, the first day of the convention, confusion reigned. Neither faction seemed to know what move should be made first, mainly because neither side was certain of its relative strength. Finally, the convention recessed in order to allow time for the grouping of forces. Opponents met at Eastman Hall where they chose Colonel Lathrop Lewis of Gorham as their spokesman. Separation advocates chose William Widgery as their acting chairman. Presumably each group agreed on a strategy to be followed during the convention. At the adjournment of both caucuses the strength of the two groups was assessed and the separationists were found to have a majority of twelve, somewhat fewer than King had counted on.

The delegates returned to the meeting house where Widgery was declared temporary chairman of the convention "but he did not seem to know how to do it," so the convention was again recessed, this time until the afternoon.

At two o'clock, with Widgery again in the chair, the convention was finally declared in session. Peleg Tallman of Woolwich, an opponent of separation, introduced a motion to elect a secretary but was opposed by John Holmes and Albion Parris who suspected that the opposition had smuggled into its ranks a number of unauthorized people to increase its voting strength. Holmes demanded that a committee on credentials be appointed as the first order of business to seat only duly elected delegates. Tallman withdrew his motion, Widgery appointed the committee, and the convention was then adjourned until the following morning.

During the evening of the 30th, both sides caucused to choose their candidates for president of the convention. The anti-separationists, as a tactical move, indicated their willingness to support a "friend" of separation from their ranks "provided he were an honest and capable Man." Accordingly, they chose Ezekiel Whitman of Portland a Federalist member of the Governor's Executive Council of Massachusetts who would be elected to Congress the following November. The proponents, not surprisingly, chose William King as their candidate.

When the convention opened the next morning, King was elected President by a vote of 97 to 85. Balloting for secretary then followed, and Samuel Whiting, an observer at the convention and the man King backed, was elected. Jesse Appleton, president of Bowdoin and a devoutly "religious" man for whom King had little if any respect was permitted to invoke the blessings of the Diety on the delegates. It was his fervent wish, he said, that God would, "prevent animosity and strife from predominating, and that wisdom instead of cunning intrigue should be their guide."

With this formality disposed of, the separationists turned their attention to a more crucial concern—the official tabulation of the votes of the September election. If, as the unofficial returns indicated, the five-ninths majority had not been obtained, then, according to the "Act of Separation," the convention would have no choice but to adjourn. Obviously the "junto" had a stake in seeing that this did not happen. William King, who as President named the members of the committees, proceeded to appoint thirteen delegates to the "Committee to Examine the Returns." With Preble's admonition about a regard to "punctilios" doubtless fresh in his mind, he appointed nine separationists and four opponents. John Holmes was appointed chairman, and Chandler, Parris, Preble, and Widgery were also named members. Clearly, the committee was stacked. The minority complained that the committee was unfairly weighted against them but to no avail. Particularly galling to them was the appointment of the aged Dummer Sewall of Bath, a member of several conventions held in the 1790's and an old King nemesis, as one of the four minority members. Sewall, they complained, was worse than useless since he was deaf and could not as a result be expected "to do business or correct mistakes."

An attempt by the minority to add two of their own members to the committee failed of adoption, but a second motion was passed providing that the votes should be announced in open convention and recorded by the Secretary, before being delivered into the hands of the committee. The passage of the motion was certainly a defeat for the "junto" for it made the manipulation of the returns much more difficult, if, as Preble suggested, manipulation was contemplated.

For the next several days the convention was engaged in trivia. Behind the scenes, however, an interesting drama was unfolding as the "Committee to Examine the Returns" did its work. Preble was charged with collecting the returns from towns where known separation majorities had been polled; a member of the minority did the same for the towns that fell into the anti-separation column. William Allen of Skowhegan, a member of the convention, who later wrote an account of the preceedings of the convention, claimed that Preble was constantly on the look out for any evidence of wrong doing among the minority. When Allen received the returns from Avon and Phillips from a friend of his, both nearly unanimous for a separation, Preble accosted the friend and scolded him for his indiscretion. Allen, said Preble, was a known opponent and the "returns would be withheld or destroyed."

Allen claimed, further, that when the returns were all collected it was discovered that returns from five or six towns were missing, one of which was from Lyman in York County where separation had been rejected 179 to 6. "The return," continued Allen,

> was traced into two or three hands and lost in the fog. Preble was challenged and denied he had it. I thought he equivocated, and as he had suggested that I ought not to be trusted, I thought of the motto attached to the sign of the Order of the Garter. 'Evil to him who evil thinks.' When a committee was appointed the next day to make search for returns that were missing, I kept my eye on him until I saw him pass that from Lyman to a respectable clergyman, a member from the county of York, behind the corner of the meetinghouse as we were coming in at the afternoon session, and whisper a verbal message to him. I followed the bearer in and saw him lay the return on the Secretary's table without any ceremony. When the convention was called to order the secretary passed the document to the president and said he found it on his table, and did not know how it came there. The contents were announced and the return passed to the committee, but this was not the end of it. It was rejected by the committee.

Allen asserted that Preble was responsible for the burning or losing of several other returns. Whether Allen's account was accurate in its details is now impossible to establish. He wrote it fifty years later and if the reliability of other such reminiscences is any guide, it probably was not. However, considering Preble's willingness to disregard "punctilios," it is not, perhaps, unfair to presume that Allen was correct in the substance of his remarks. Indeed, one delegate who was appalled at what he observed at the convention supported Allen's charges when he wrote to the *Portland Gazette* that certain "desperadoes" may employ "fraud, violence, and usurpation" to achieve their end, but that there were enough men in the convention who favored separation "upon just and lawful grounds" only, so that those who would steal the prize would be frustrated. Further evidence that Preble was not above resorting to the very chicanery that he espoused in his letter to King, was provided in the report of the Committee to Examine the Returns which was presented to the convention on Monday October 6.

The report presented by Holmes was addressed to two major questions: the legality of votes cast and the determination of whether or not the five-ninths majority had been obtained. On the first question, the committee found "that a very large proportion of those votes are incorrectly or illegally returned." In nearly half the towns, the committee found, "the question which was to have been submitted to the people, was imperfectly or erroneously stated." In addition, evidence suggested that in a number of towns a large percentage of the votes cast were cast by non-qualified voters, i.e., voters who were ineligible to vote for state senators. In other towns eligible voters were denied their suffrage. The committee, thus discrediting the election returns, nevertheless, concluded that all the returns, except those from Lyman, should be certified. In the case of the town of Lyman, to which Allen referred, the committee felt obligated to make a judgment in as much as one John Low, Jr., of the town had sent a memorial to the committee demanding that the votes be rejected. According to the report, the situation in Lyman on September 2, was as follows:

> ...after the meeting [called for the purpose of balloting] was opened, a motion was regularly made, and put, and carried, that

the voters be polled to see who were for and against the separation; that though this course was objected to, it was carried into effect. Thus in a town where the majority was against the separation (179-6), were its advocates designated and pointed out, before they were allowed to carry their written votes. Thus were a portion of the citizens deprived the privilege of expressing their opinions *without inspection,* and subjected to the influence of powerful men, and the censure or disapprobation of a vindictive majority—your committee have therefore rejected the return from the town of Lyman."

The decision of the committee raised a storm in the convention led by John Low, Sr., the father of the memorialist, who charged that his son, in effect, did not know what he was talking about. The protest was ignored; the report was adopted.

On the second question—was a five-ninths majority obtained?—the committee dropped a bombshell. The majority on the committee decided, apparently, that the scrutinous eyes of the opposition made it unwise to attempt the manipulation of returns by various means to obtain a five-ninths majority. Consequently, it was necessary to adopt an alternative approach that would bring about the desired result while seemingly remaining within the bounds of legality. It was the ingenious mind of Preble, the former tutor of mathematics at Harvard, that produced the answer to the problem.

According to the Act of Separation, if it appeared to [the delegates at the Brunswick Convention] that a majority of five to four at least of the votes returned were in favor of a separation, then, and only then could the convention proceed to draw up a constitution. The report of the committee pointed out that it had been a "popular construction" that five-ninths meant five-ninths of the votes returned, but that this construction "has prevailed rather from the use of an expression not contained in the act, than from a necessary import of the words themselves." The report continued:

> The meaning of the word *majority is doubtful*—this word is sometimes understood to mean the excess of one number over another, and sometimes the excess of half the whole number. Exclude the words 'a majority of'—and no doubt remains but five yeas to four nays, or *five ninths* of the votes returned, would be required. But your committee [Preble] do not feel authorized to say that those words have no meaning.
> In the report of the Committee [the Otis Committee] prefixed to the act [of separation], it appears to have been the intention, that the expediency of separation should have been decided by 'an assembly of men'... meaning no doubt a *convention of delegates* chosen by towns. Here the delegates would have been in proportion to the aggregate majority of all the votes returned.
> It is understood that the bill as first reported to the Legislature authorized the delegates to decide on the *expediency*. It was however so far amended as that on the day of the choice of delegates, the inhabitants of the *towns,* districts and plantations, qualified to vote for senators, were to give in their written votes on the question proposed in the act, and a *majority* of five to four was required—as the delegates must be apportioned according to the respective majorities of their towns, so on the question of separation, the majority of *yeas* in the towns...in *favor* must be, to the majority of *nays* in those *opposed* as *five* is to four, of the votes returned. The corporate majorities of yeas must be placed in one column and those of nays in the other and each added. Then, as *five is to four* so is the aggregate majority of nays in those opposed.—In this way only can your committee give a meaning to the word *majority* as contained in the second...section of the act.

The whole number of votes returned...is:	22,316
The yeas are	11,969
The nays are	10,347
The whole aggregate majority of yeas in the towns in favor is...	6,031
The whole aggregate majority of nays in the towns opposed is....	4,409

> Then as five is to four so is 6,031 to 4,825, the nays required. But the majority of nays is 4,409 only. Hence it appears that upon this construction of the Act there is a majority of five to four at least....

The incredible audacity of Preble and of the committee that accepted his sophisticated reasoning was outdone, if this were possible, in the following portion of the report which contained the assertion that since Maine people had in May and September by majority votes elected to separate, it was inconceivable that their wishes should be denied by giving a construction to the wording of the Act of Separation that denied them what was rightfully theirs anyway. The committee, therefore, concluded that "where the act is doubtful, it should receive such interpretation, as shall best comport with the public will."

The report next recommended to the convention that before any action was taken the General Court should be consulted for its opinions and if the court accepted the construction offered, "as they undoubtedly will," or modified the law so that the construction would prevail then much disputation and contention would be avoided. However, if the General Court should refuse to honor the action of the convention, then the convention could reassemble to act "as may be thought proper."

Finally, the report recommended that president William King appoint committees to draw up a constitution; to apply to Congress for admission into the union; to appeal to Congress to amend the coasting law in a manner that would not leave Maine commerce inconvenienced as a result of separation; and to apply to the General Court for its consent to independence.

The opposition may have been dumbfounded as Holmes read the committee report but they soon regained their senses. After Albion Parris moved that the report be accepted, pandemonium broke loose. When the situation was brought under control, the opposition commenced an unmerciful attack on the report and on John Holmes whom the critics mistakenly thought to be its author. The substance of the attacks was represented by the remarks of the former sea captain, William Ladd of Minot, a Federalist in politics and an orthodox Calvinist in religion:

> I am more used to the tumults of the ocean, than of this assembly. I am a sailor, sir, and this is the first deliberative assembly I ever addressed. Sir, I cannot understand that report: I cannot catch the points of it. I might as well chase a mosquito in the Pacific Ocean. I wish the report may be made as plain as a pike staff, and straight as a hand spike, and capable of demonstration to every hand before the mast. Is it by a majority of 5/9ths, or 5/9ths of a majority, we are to be separated?...Now it is evident, that there are not 5/9ths of the votes in favor of separation. If I lay 9 dollars on your honor's table from which I take 4, are there more than 5 left? The case is self-evident. It reminds me of the philosophers of the dark ages, who decreed there was no motion, while their tongues incessantly moved to prove it. We now look on them and their arguments with pity and contempt. But a set of modern philosophers, by jumbling logic with mathematics come at a result still more contemptible. They are not to be argued against....Sir, the motives of the majority are to be found in the deception of the human heart. The heart is deceitful above all things, and I may add, desperately wicked. [Called to order by Holmes]. Our conduct shows a rotteness in the very bud, which like original sin, will stick to our posterity.

William Widgery in concert with John Holmes defended the report as a classic defense of majority rule and written with the best of motives. On Tuesday the motion of Parris to accept the report was carried by a vote of 103-84. On Wednesday, the day of adjournment, the opponents entered a minority opinion on the record. Signed by 71 of the 84 dissenters, the protest condemned the majority report as the work of ambitious and scheming men bent on obtaining their objective by any means. The minority report also condemned what they thought was the disrespectful attitude manifested by the majority toward the General Court and concluded by invoking the blessings of God on their virtuous stand against the forces of evil.

The last business before the adjournment of the now highly controversial Brunswick Convention was the naming of personnel to the committees recommended in the majority report. King complied with the expectations of his partisan friends by packing the committees with the friends of independence. To the committee to report a constitution, he named Holmes, Widgery, Chandler, and several others who outnumbered the opposition two to one; to the committee to make an application to the General Court, he appointed five proponents including Preble, Chandler, and John Davis of Augusta. Finally, he appointed himself, Holmes, and Chandler as a committee to make application to Congress. The convention then adjourned until after the winter session of the General Court when it would be known if a reconvention of the group would be necessary.

Before the "junto" left Brunswick to return to their homes, they held one last conclave at which it was agreed that Holmes, Preble, and John Davis should prepare an address to the people of Maine in answer to the protest of the minority and in anticipation of protests from the people at large which, they were sensible enough to realize, would be forth coming.

The abuse that greeted the result of the week long deliberations at Brunswick was unprecedented in its severity. The *New York Columbian* labeled the Holmes committee report a "very clever piece of sophistry." The [New York] *Courier* described it as "the greatest *Yankee,* trick ever practiced." From Boston, the *Yankee,* a Republican anti-separation organ called the entire proceedings "outrageous." Nathaniel Willis, former editor of the *Eastern Argus* turned mystic, wrote in his *Boston Weekly Messenger* that now history has the Brunswick Convention "the Rump Parliament will no longer be an object of derision, nor the National Assembly of France the subject of detestation." The [Boston] *Daily Advertiser* described the report "as one of the most contemptibly absurd documents that ever received the sanction of a public body of men." Predictably, only, the *Eastern Argus* stood out as a defender of the proceedings.

Many Federalists in Maine were elated at the storm created by Preble's arithmetic for he had given them a life that all their efforts could not have achieved. William Abbot of Castine, who signed the minority report, wrote to the Federalist supporter of separation in the Massachusetts General Court, Leverett Saltonstall of Salem. Saltonstall was a member of the Otis committee that drew up the "Act of Separation" and it is clear that Abbot knew he had an issue, perhaps for the first time in his life, that would cause his Federalist political friends in Massachusetts to bail Maine Federalism out of serious trouble:

> I hope you in Massachusetts proper will do your duty....I am surprised that you are willing to lose your consequence in the great national point of view. And to turn us over to be buffeted by Satan is not just. You see into what a state we should fall if left to ourselves—I hope you will take firm ground and all good men will consider the subject at rest. Let the union be perpetuated. You will want us hereafter. Maine is destined to save Massachusetts. If John Holmes & Co. will let the Governor issue his proclamation to disperse them [the convention], and if they refuse let them be accused of treason, tried and hung. As a legislator remember your oath to protect and defend the Commonwealth against traitorous conspiracies and all hostile attempts whatever.

From York, Isaac Lyman, also a Federalist member of the Otis committee, expressed similar sentiments. "We shall, at our next session, Lyman wrote Saltonstall, "give this subject its *quietus* and I hope an eternal one."

Most of the leaders of the separation movement in Maine were badly shaken by the criticism heaped on them. A number of them concluded that Preble's scheme was not only ill advised but would damage the cause irreparably. Others were more angry than regretful at what they thought was the amateurish management of the business. Still others were infuriated more by the fact that the leadership at Brunswick "did not now cut the cord, than because the report went too far."

Ironically, the man who was responsible for the awkward situation in which separationists now found themselves escaped the brunt of the abuse. It was John Holmes, as chairman of the Committee to Examine the Returns, who presented the report to the convention and was its most assiduous defender, who was considered by opponents the man responsible for the report. "Mr. Holmes," reported Sam Whiting, "feels himself placed in rather an unpleasant situation, but will not shrink. The federal lawyers (in Portland) all direct their malice against Holmes. Parris, Preble, and others escape." As for King, Whiting added, "his manner of presiding is approved, even by these Federalists, with the exception of appointing that committee on votes."

While Holmes stoically shouldered more than his share of the criticism, others were less willing to do so. William Widgery, who was criticized for his participation in the convention, and for his contention that the convention was, in reality, a confrontation of two classes, debtors and creditors, wrote a long letter that appeared in the *Argus* reaffirming that belief.

Nathan Weston of Augusta, later to become chief justice of the Supreme Judicial Court of Maine, thought it necessary to explain that while he had misgivings about endorsing the Holmes' committee report, he did so because he sincerely believed that old Massachusetts really intended that only a simple majority be required for a separation: that the five-ninths amendment was adopted to satisfy recalcitrant opponents of the independence of Maine. Weston was, undoubtedly, right in claiming that the General Court, as a whole, desired only a simple majority but if this were true it was irrelevant to the situation that arose at Brunswick. Separationists who held Weston's view had chosen the wrong battlefield. They should not have permitted the adoption of the five-ninths requirement in the first place, a requirement, ironically enough, that was proposed by John Holmes.

The Weston line of reasoning was adopted by Holmes, Chandler, Preble, and John Davis in the memorial that they drew up to accompany the majority report that was submitted to the Otis committee when the General Court convened on November 13, 1816. They also pointed out that opponents in Maine had shamelessly circulated lies in regard to the terms of separation which not only harmed the cause but reflected unfavorably on the intelligence of the members of the Otis committee. Significantly, the memorialists made no effort to defend the Preble construction of the five-ninths clause contained in the report itself. They did, however, appeal to the General Court to permit another test of separation sentiment in Maine on the principle of a simple majority, if separation were now refused.

The Otis committee found itself in an awkward position. Many of the members for political reasons, notably Otis, were not averse to letting Maine go. But to permit separation at this time and under present circumstances would have been to raise the lid on Pandora's Box. The committee would have exposed itself to the wrath of many in Massachusetts as well as Maine who would have charged that it accepted the specious reasoning contained in the Preble construction of the five-ninths clause. It came as a surprise to no one, therefore, when on

November 16, Otis for the committee, reported the following:

> ...the committee have no hesitation in expressing their full conviction, that the [majority of the Brunswick Convention] misconstrued the act by which their powers were defined: That the word 'majority' refers to the majority of votes returned, and not to the aggregate of local and municipal majorities: That this is a self evident position, resulting from a perusal of the act, and not susceptible of illustration or contravention by any argument. That of consequence, the contingency, provided by the act as prerequisite to the formation of a Constitution, and as a condition of the consent of this legislature, to the separation of Maine, has not occurred, and that the powers of said convention are at an end.

In respect to the request that another test of sentiment be arranged, the committee observed that such a request could not be honored for the reason that there was no evidence that opinion in Maine had changed since the September vote. As for revising the original bill to allow a separation on the principle of a simple majority, the committee noted:

> Should...the same Legislature which has once and so lately adjusted the principles, and with great deliberation fixed the terms and conditions which appertain to the dismemberment of the State, revise the fundamental provisions of its act without any new occasion, they might be considered as betraying an undue solicitude to accelerate the partition, and as regardless of the feelings and interests of a large and respectable class of their fellow citizens.

On December 4, 1816, the General Court passed two resolves, one dissolving the Brunswick Convention, the other declaring it inexpedient to adopt any further measures in regard to separation, and thus, the curtain fell on what proved to be the most bizarre episode in the long struggle to achieve the independence of Maine.

In retrospect, and even at the time, it is clear that the leaders of the separation movement very badly mismanaged the entire affair. It would have been wiser as well as more honorable to have accepted the defeat and to have returned to the General Court to try again unmarked by charges of corruption and fraud. The General Court, given the disposition of Otis and other Federalists toward separation might have conceivably permitted another test of separation sentiment in Maine or, perhaps, have recommended that a separation be permitted, notwithstanding the failure to achieve the five-ninths majority, on the ground that a majority bound to the jurisdiction of another state against its wishes makes for an unhealthy body politic. Moreover, even if such a strategy failed, the end result could not have been more injurious to the cause than the result of the course that was chosen. However desirable their objective, the means employed were inappropriate, morally and rationally, and once adopted, were employed with the dexterity of a first class bungler. In the first real test of their political leadership ability, the "junto" was found embarrassingly wanting.

CHAPTER 18.

After the fiasco of 1816, the separationists leaders allowed the atmosphere to cool down for the next two years. At the end of 1818 they once again moved to achieve independence. After very careful planning which involved such national figures as Senator Rufus King of New York and the Secretary of Treasury, William H. Crawford, the leaders succeeded in arranging another referendum on the question. This time, the people responded by voting 17,000 to 7,000 in favor of separating. In October, the Maine Constitutional Convention was held in Portland. What emerged was one of the most advanced democratic constitutions of that time.

THE MAINE CONSTITUTIONAL CONVENTION OF 1819*
by
Ronald F. Banks

On Monday morning, October 11, 1819, 274 delegates representing nearly all of the 236 incorporated towns in the District of Maine assembled at the Cumberland County courthouse in Portland to draw up a constitution for the new state. The delegates had been chosen by their respective towns on September 20 and reflected the overwhelmingly pro-separationist leanings of those who elected them. Conspicuously absent among the list of delegates were most of the inveterate foes of separation. Federalists such as Samuel Fessenden, Stephen Longfellow, Benjamin Orr, William Ladd, and others who had been present at Brunswick in 1816. Their absence was of considerable importance for without them, the views that they represented, views that were akin to those of Daniel Webster, Joseph Story and Chancellor James Kent, were not represented to any significant extent. Conspicuously present were John Holmes, Albion Parris, William Pitt Preble, William King, and John Chandler. Needless to say, these men had resolved to exercise a "decided controal [sic] and management" over the convention and the democratic document that emerged was the result of their handiwork.

The only effort to compile information on the delegates was made in the decade of 1890 by an Augusta school master, George Chamberlain. The result of Chamberlain's research was incorporated in a volume entitled *Debates and Journal of the Constitutional Convention of the State of Maine, 1819-1820*. Unfortunately, Chamberlain was unable to find information on nearly a hundred of the delegates. Nor was the information he did collect on the others always judiciously selected; the biographical sketches that he wrote, therefore, leave much to be desired from the point of view of the historian. Nevertheless, from Chamberlain's effort it is possible to identify roughly the occupations, trades, or professions of a significant number of the delegates. It appears that the largest number of delegates, forty-five at least, were involved in commercial pursuits oriented around the sea; shippers, shipbuilders, sea captains, and retail store owners who sold goods imported from abroad. Needless to say, several of the forty-five, like William King, were involved in more than one of these interests.

The second largest group, at least thirty-seven, were lawyers. Holmes, Preble, and Parris, for example, were from this group, many of whom were professional politicians. Thirteen physicians, seventeen civil servants—postmasters, sheriffs, and other comparable office-holders—, eight school teachers or principals, two editors, two surveyors, three lumber manufacturers (saw mill owners), and one shoe maker were also represented. Eight of the delegates were Baptist ministers; four were Methodist ministers; only one was a Congregational minister. The presence of so many dissenting clergymen reflected dramatically the extent to which the old orthodoxy had been superceded in the District between 1780 and 1820. Their presence also helps to explain why the convention

---

*Ronald F. Banks, "The Separation of Maine and Massachusetts: 1785-1820," (Unpublished Ph.D. dissertation, University of Maine, 1966), pp. 289-351.

adopted no religious tests of any kind in the constitution.

Finally, Chamberlain's sketches indicate that eight farmers were present. However, it is certain that there were many times this number of farmers selected as delegates. No doubt the nearly one-hundred delegates on whom Chamberlain could find no information of significance, were mostly farmers from the small inland towns, who, in spite of the convention, have remained obscure and unknown figures. Therefore, it is likely, that the largest group in attendance were farmers. Their influence in the proceedings, however, appears to have been negligible, no doubt because they felt themselves, as John Holmes observed, out of place in the presence of so many delegates with more legal experience.

The venerable Daniel Cony of Augusta who had participated in separation conventions in the 1790's was accorded the honor of opening the proceedings of the convention.

After John Holmes, Albion K. Parris, and three other delegates formed a committee to examine the credentials of the delegates and reported the presence of 274 members, the convention adjourned until 3:00 p.m. at which time balloting for president of the convention was to take place.

The office of president of the convention was more than a ceremonial office. The president not only named the committee members but recognized speakers from the floor. He was, in fact, the most powerful individual at the convention. In addition, the person elected president would serve as acting governor of the state between the time Maine was admitted into the union and the time of the first elections. And since all assumed that the acting governor would become governor by election, the delegates were to choose not only a president for the convention but a governor as well, a responsibility of some import.

It was, of course, no mystery that William King would be elected. When the votes were counted, the leader of the separation movement and the most powerful man in the District got 230 of the 241 cast.

After King offered the customary platitudes in an address to the delegates, his lieutenants, Parris, Holmes, and Preble, proceeded to organize the convention. Three resolutions providing for the creation of three committees were adopted. To the committee to prepare rules under which the proceedings would be disciplined, King appointed George Thacher Sr., associate justice of the Massachusetts Supreme Court; Benjamin Greene, chief justice of the Eastern Circuit Court which included Oxford, York, and Cumberland counties; and James Campbell of Harrington. Daniel Cony, Benjamin Greene, Benjamin Ames of Bath, Leonard Jarvis of Surry and Asa Clap of Portland were appointed to perform the perfunctory task of applying to Congress for admission. To the most important committee of all, the committee on the Constitution, King appointed thirty-three members including Holmes, Parris, Chandler, and Joshua Wingate of Bath. Holmes would become the chairman. In the meantime a number of minor committees were appointed and for the next two days the delegates were largely involved with their respective committee assignments.

On Thursday, October 14, the fourth day of the convention, the committee on style and title of the new state reported the recommendation that the state be named the "Commonwealth of Maine." The recommendation produced a spirited debate in which the name "Columbus" was offered instead. Finally, on Friday, it was agreed to name the new state "Maine." From October 18 to October 29, the convention considered the recommendations of Holmes' "Committee on the Constitution" which reported the various articles to the delegates for their consideration article by article.

The subject of a constitution for Maine had long been under consideration. In 1816, William King had gathered ideas from a number of sources anticipating that he would be called upon to help draw up a constitution at the Brunswick Convention. After that time he, and undoubtedly, others, continued to gather suggestions from some of the country's most distinguished minds including James Madison and Thomas Jefferson. Two months before the convention met in Portland, in 1819, King recommended that an attempt be made to write an entirely new constitution without reference to the Massachusetts constitution of 1780, largely the work of John Adams. Others, like Preble, thought King's suggestion was ill advised. The want of sufficient time, thought Preble, precluded such an ambitious undertaking; he recommended taking the Massachusetts constitution as a basis:

> I say taking the constitution of Massachusetts as a basis, because it is already rooted in the good feeling and affections of the public, and practical politicians ought always to keep an eye to public sentiment and not unnecessarily do violence to it.

Preble had evidently become more sensitive to public opinion than he had been in 1816. In any case, the sentiments espoused by Preble prevailed. The constitution reported by Holmes was, indeed, modeled after the Massachusetts constitution although the differences between the two were by no means insignificant.

What follows is an effort to deal with the provisions of the Maine Constitution as they were proposed by the Holmes' committee and as they were finally adopted. To avoid the pitfalls that usually result from the attempt to treat such subjects in a vacuum, the author has compared most of the provisions with their counterparts embodied in the Massachusetts Constitution of 1780, under which the District of Maine was governed for forty years. Thus compared, the Maine Constitution emerges, with the constitutions of several Western states, as one of the more democratic constitutions of the time, nine years before the inauguration of Andrew Jackson. The Constitution of Maine as adopted contained ten articles. Six chapters under two parts constituted the major divisions of the Massachusetts Constitution of 1780.

ARTICLE I

Article I of the Maine Constitution contained twenty-four sections devoted to a "Declaration of Rights." This article was patterned after Part I of the Massachusetts Constitution which contained thirty-three provisions. Both were devoted to the enumeration of "inalienable rights" that were to be enjoyed by all citizens but the Maine Constitution departed from its model in two important respects (1) The Maine Constitution [sec. 4] guaranteed freedom of *speech* and *press*. The Massachusetts Constitution, to the regret of John Adams, its chief architect, guaranteed only the freedom of the press. (2) The Massachusetts Constitution [part I, art. 2, 3] established a "quasi-religious" commonwealth, Article 2 stated:

> It is the right as well as the duty of all men in society, publicly, and at stated seasons, to worship the SUPREME BEING.... And no subject shall be hurt, molested, or restrained, in his person, liberty, or estate, for worshipping God in the manner and season most agreeable to the dictates of his own conscience....

Thus having stated the principle of the absolute freedom of religion, the framers in 1780 proceeded in article 3 to abridge that freedom. Article 3 required church attendance, and the taxation of all citizens for the support of public worship and "protestant teachers of piety." Article 3 further provided that a protestant could apply his tax to the support of a minister of his own denomination. In reality, however, the courts so narrowly construed this provision that until 1811, only incorporated Baptist, Methodist, and other non-Congregational religious societies were allowed to receive tax money. As has been noted, these court decisions produced a special hardship on dissenting groups in Maine.

The discrimination against Catholics and Jews reflected the anti-popish and Christian biases of the age. These peoples justifiably resented being singled out in such dramatic fashion as well as being under the necessity of paying "double taxation."

In the Maine convention, Holmes' committee reported a provision that guaranteed *absolute freedom of religion*. The provision followed closely the wording of article 2 of the Massachusetts Constitution but omitted the first clause of that article which described the worshipping of the Supreme Being as not only a right but a duty. No distinction, whatever, was made between Protestants and Catholics, Christians and non-Christians, reflecting the liberal attitude of most of those at the convention. This liberal attitude was demonstrated by the words of one delegate who addressed the convention as follows [paraphrased by Perley] during the debate on the provision:

> [He] ... trusted no distinction or pre-emmence would ever be given to any religious sect ... whether Catholics, Jews or Mahometans [sic]. The liberal principles of our government ought to make no difference between them, so far as we look to the investigation of truth by the force and effect of an oath, there is no ground for the exclusion of either of these great divisions. Does a court of justice rest satisfied when a Christian calls God to witness the truth of the testimony? and do not the descendants of Abraham call the God of Abraham, Isaac and Jacob to be present, while they depose, and is he not also the GOD and FATHER of our Lord Jesus Christ, by whom Christians swear? The Mahometans in their most solemn transactions, speak in the name of the MOST MERCIFUL GOD, who is the Jehovah of Jews and Christians. The Hindoos too, were there any in this country, would be entitled to give testimony in our courts of justice, tho' they were to call upon Juggarnant himself, as the God they feared."

In the debate over what became section 3 of Article I, no one contested the establishment of the principle of freedom of religion. The only disagreement came from those who thought that the omission of the phrase "duty to worship" was too permissive and would encourage some to seek freedom from religion. The convention, led by Holmes who declared that "To make it a *duty* to exercise a *right* is proposterous," defeated what Holmes described as an attempt to incorporate in the constitution "a whole body of ethics."

There was no discussion at all on the floor of the convention of the delicate question of the status of Catholics. The committee had received a memorial from James Kavanagh, Matthew Cottrill, and William Moony, leaders of one of the only two non-French and non-Indian Catholic communities in Maine centered around Damariscotta, begging the delegates to give Catholics equality with Protestants. Despite some backstage opposition to granting their prayer, especially from William King who harbored a deeply imbedded mistrust of "popish ambition," the convention would probably have given Catholics equality even if the memorial had not been presented.

ARTICLE II

Article II of the Maine Constitution established the qualifications for electors.

The Massachusetts Constitution of 1780, reflecting the notions of the classical republican theorists who abjured universal manhood suffrage in favor of a property qualifications for voting, established property requirements for electors. Electors for senators, house members, governor and lieutenant governor, and members of Congress were required to possess an estate of at least sixty pounds or have an annual income of three pounds or more derived from the possession of a freehold estate [Chap. I, Sec. 2, art. 2; Chap. I, Sec. 3, art. 4; and Chap. II, Sec. l, art. 3]. It may have been true that the qualifications "soon became a dead letter" but the provisions were there, nevertheless, and could be enforced by local officials who found it advantageous to do so.

In the summer of 1816, when it seemed likely that the Brunswick Convention would be called on to create a constitution, William Pitt Preble wrote to John Holmes his views on what a constitution should include. Among other comments, Preble observed that "pecuniary qualifications are a mere cloak for petty tyranny, as to the electors, what say you to make citizens of the U.S. of age, not paupers, resident in the town or plantation where they vote," eligible voters?

It is obvious that Holmes took Preble's suggestion seriously for Article II, as reported by Holmes' committee provided for universal manhood suffrage for those over twenty one excepting "paupers, persons under guardianship and Indians not taxed" having residence established in the state for three months preceding any election.

During the debate on Article II, no one objected to this departure from previous practice. Several delegates recommended the exclusion of felons and Negroes not taxed, both of which failed of adoption, but no one questioned the principle of universal manhood suffrage as John Adams, Daniel Webster, and Josiah Quincy did the following year at the Massachusetts Constitutional Convention. One reason for this was that the Adams, Websters and Quincys of Maine, men such as Samuel Longfellow, Samuel Fessenden, and other arch-Federalists were not delegates to the convention, either because they were not candidates or because they were defeated in the election held on September 20. Secondly, if it is true that the property qualifications written into the Massachusetts Constitution became a "dead letter," then the convention was simply recognizing *de jure a de facto* condition that had prevailed for years. And even if the qualifications were not a "dead letter," it is not certain that a significant number of people in the District were disfranchised. It is certainly significant that between 1780 and 1820 the question of property qualifications for voting was *never* discussed in the leading newspapers published in the District that the author has seen. For the people of Maine, it seems no problem existed. It is impossible to say for sure, but it is not unlikely that nearly every male owned enough property to qualify anyway.

ARTICLE III

Article III of the Maine Constitution established the principle of a separation of powers between the legislative, executive, and judicial branches of the state government. There is no evidence to suggest that any other arrangement was considered by the Holmes' committee. By this time, Maine people had come to believe that such a separation was "natural." Perley's account of the debates notes succinctly: "This article passed without debate."

ARTICLE IV, Part I

Article IV, Part I of the Maine Constitution describes the make up of the House of Representatives and prescribes the powers of that body. Of all the articles, submitted to the convention by the Holmes' committee, Article IV precipitated the greatest debate.

Sections II and III of Article IV, Part I, as drafted, provided for a House of Representatives of not less than one hundred nor more than two hundred members. The first legislature, however, would be apportioned between one hundred and one hundred and fifty members *only* based on the following formula:

Number of Inhabitants	Number of Representatives
1,500- 4,000	1
4,000- 7,500	2
7,500-12,000	3
12,000-17,500	4
17,500-24,000	5
24,000-31,500	6
31,500-	7

For towns with less than 1,500 inhabitants, the Holmes' committee recommended the adoption of the class system whereby two or more towns with less than 1,500 inhabitants would be joined and classified as one legislative district entitled to one representative who would rotate from year to year among the towns of the district. No town could have more than seven representatives no matter how large its population. Because the town of Portland with 8,000 people was the largest town in the District, this limitation did not pose a threat to any town at the time.

Objections to this plan were heard from two groups—spokesmen for the very small towns and spokesmen for the larger towns. The spokesmen for the small towns objected to the departure from the system under which they had lived for forty years. The Massachusetts Constitution of 1780 provided for corporate representation, i.e., for one representative at least from every incorporated town (a town could not become incorporated until it had 150 rateable polls). While the practice of making towns pay for their representatives' salaries kept the size of the House of Representatives usually within manageable limits, it was possible to have nearly 1,000 representatives according to the formula adopted in 1780. In 1812, after the Gerry administration had passed a bill providing for the payment of legislative salaries from the state treasury, the number exceeded 700, or roughly one for every 1,000 inhabitants. It was to avoid creating an unmanageable House of Representatives in Maine that prompted the Holmes' committee to so limit the size of the body.

Spokesmen for the larger towns argued that the formula, far from discriminating against small towns, discriminated against larger towns. Their criticism was valid enough for it was true that a town such as Portland, with 8,000 people, would have but three representatives though its population was more than five times as large as a town with 1,500 people. Holmes, whose vanity caused him to take criticism of the efforts of his committee personally, fired back at the critics that the committee had been faced with diametrically opposite demands—to limit the size of the House and to give every town equal representation regardless of population. He predicted that following the latter alternative, the House would someday "bear more the character of a mob, than a legislative assembly."

A motion to accept the committee's recommended draft was passed but a motion to reconsider the votes also passed. The debate was, therefore, revived and so protracted did it become that Holmes, at one point, threw up his arms and exclaimed that it was fortunate that the Massachusetts Constitution was to be provisionally operational in Maine "for I begin to doubt whether we shall be found capable of agreeing upon one for ourselves. Finally, patience was rewarded, and on October 22, the convention accepted Article IV, Part I, as drafted by the committee—or so it seemed.

A week later when Article X dealing with apportionment was reported to the convention the debate on the size of the House fixed by the adoption of Article IV, Part I, was again reopened, this time from delegates representing the larger towns who restated their objections to the weighting of the formula against them. Holmes admitted that their objection was a valid one but explained once again the dilemma with which the committee was faced. William Pitt Preble argued that the larger towns would receive their due as a result of the equal representation principle adopted in regard to the Senate. Finally, Holmes, in evident frustration, reminded the delegates from the larger towns, in true Jeffersonian manner, that there was nothing much to be said for larger towns anyway considering the tendency for them to become "great sores" on the body politic. However, in a gesture toward "conciliation," as Holmes put it, speaking for the committee, he agreed to accept the following revision of the apportionment schedule as a concession to the larger towns:

Number of Inhabitants	Number of Representatives
1,500- 3,750	1
3,750- 6,750	2
6,750-10,500	3
10,500-15,000	4
15,000-22,500	5
22,500-26,250	6
26,250-	7

ARTICLE IV, Part II

On Friday afternoon, October 22, the delegates turned their attention to a discussion of Article IV, Part II dealing with the description of the Senate and its functions. Holmes' committee recommended that the Senate consist of twenty-three members to be apportioned by counties according to *population*.

The Massachusetts Constitution, following the bias of many toward property distinctions among the population, had apportioned the Senate of the Commonwealth according to the wealth of the counties. As was intended by the framers, this provision gave Suffolk and Essex counties, both wealthy merchant dominated areas, almost a monopoly in the Senate to the consternation of the peoples in Western Massachusetts and the District of Maine. John Holmes was asked if his committee had taken into consideration the basis for the selection of senators and, if it had, why it had chosen population over property? Holmes tartly replied, "the answer to the first question is that we did. The answer to the other is equally concise—the reason why we established it upon population was, because we saw no good reason to do it otherwise." With that reply, history was deprived of what might have been a very interesting discussion in political theory. The committee report was adopted.

As with Article IV, Part I, a number of delegates were unhappy with Article IV, Part II. A week later, when a committee reported the allocation of senators for the first session of the legislature, the wisdom of limiting the number of senators to twenty-three was again questioned. The committee reported the following allotments based on the estimated population of each county according to the ratio of one senator for every 15,264 people:

Counties	Number of Inhabitants	Senators	Fractions Wanting	Excess
York	50,291	4	10,765	
Cumberland	56,043	4	5,013	
Lincoln	59,148	4	1,918	
Kennebec	54,992	3		9,200
Oxford	33,336	2		2,808
Somerset	30,790	2		262
Hancock	34,276	2		3,748
Penobscot	19,126	1		3,862
Washington	13,076	1	2,188	

The committee chairman proceeded to recommend the obvious to the convention, that for the sake of equity, one additional senator be authorized to be given to Kennebec County, making for a total of twenty-four senators. The reason that Kennebec had been penalized rather than York was not revealed. However, it probably was due to the fact that York County was the first county in Maine having been established in 1658, or, possibly, it was because Holmes was a resident of York County.

The recommendation of the committee produced another heated discussion with John Holmes again the object of most criticism. Eventually, the convention voted to accept the recommendation of the committee by a vote of 125-106. No sooner had the vote been taken, however, then the question was reopened by a motion offered by Alfred Johnson of Belfast to increase the allotment of senators for Hancock County from two to three. After a delegate from Castine made a similar request concerning the number of senators from

Penobscot County, an alarmed Holmes jumped to his feet to offer an amendment to fix the number of senators at twenty rather than twenty-three. The amendment passed unanimously, thus York, Cumberland, and Lincoln were deprived of one senator each placing them in equality with Kennebec. In order to admit some flexibility in the future consideration of the subject, it was further provided that subsequent legislatures could reapportion the Senate increasing the maximum number of senators to no more than thirty-one. With this, discussion concerning Article IV, Part II, ceased.

ARTICLE IV, Part III

Article IV, Part III, addressed itself to procedural questions and with certain rules defining the role of legislators.

ARTICLE V, Part I

Article V, Part I of the Maine Constitution, concerning the office of governor, was reported to the convention by the Holmes' committee on Saturday, October 23. The committee, once again, departed significantly from the Massachusetts Constitution of 1780. The Massachusetts Constitution [Chap. II, sec. 1, art. 2] stated that no person should be governor unless he had lived in the state seven years previous to his election and "unless he shall, at the same time, be seized in his own right, of a freehold within the Commonwealth, of the value of one thousand pounds; and unless he shall declare himself to be of the Christian religion." And the word "Christian" was not to be applied indiscriminately, for as the address to the people which accompanied the presentation of the Constitution of 1780 explained, it was intended to exclude from office those "who will not disclaim these Principals of Spiritual Jurisdiction which Roman Catholics *in some countries* have held."

Such restrictions did not, however, reduce the importance of the office. On the contrary, the absence of any restriction on the number of terms a governor might serve, combined with an extensive appointive power, and a veto power made the governor of Massachusetts "the most imposing and independent chief executive in the United States." The alleged negative reaction against the powerful office of Royal Governor was not so great as has been assumed, at least in Massachusetts.

The Maine convention accepted the recommendation of the Holmes' committee that no property or religious test be imposed on the governorship, only that the governor be not less than thirty years old, a natural born citizen of the United States, and a resident of the state for at least five years. As the "Address to the People" subjoined to the completed Constitution put it: "...merit, not wealth, is the proper qualification for office." As for a religious test, the same "Address" explained that "...vital religion cannot be regulated by human legislation." It was, however, "presupposed, that [office holders] believe in the existence and Providence of God."

The governor of Maine was given all of the powers possessed by the governor of Massachusetts, which, by the standards of the day, his Council willing, made him a potentially strong governor.

The Massachusetts Constitution of 1780 provided for the office of Lieutenant Governor [Chap. II, sec. 2]. The Lieutenant Governor was to meet all the qualifications for the position of governor and would succeed to the governorship if that office were vacated. In actuality, his duties were negligible, the most important being the assumption of the duties of the governor when the governor was absent from the state, an infrequent occurrence in the days of poor transportation. He was also a member of the Governor's Council. The Senate elected its own president. The Holmes' committee concluded quite logically, that Maine did not need a Lieutenant Governor. The office, it reported, "is given up [by] all hands." The President of the Senate was designated to succeed the Governor. No doubt, the committee was influenced in its decision by the advice of Rufus King written to his brother William. Rufus had been a member of the committee of the Constitutional Convention of 1787 which recommended the creation of the office of Vice President. Rufus wrote in reply to his brother's invitation to submit his ideas on a constitution for Maine, that in his opinion "a lieutenant Governor & vice President are equally useless. I don't think there w'd have been a vice President, had not Mr. Adams' friends devised the Place for him."

ARTICLE V, Part II

One of the more spirited debates at the Maine convention arose over the recommendation of the Holmes' committee that the executive council be retained in the Maine constitution.

The Governor's Council had its origin in the colonial period. Unlike councils in other colonies whose members were chosen by the King of England, the Massachusetts' Council was elected by the people. As the Revolution approached, the Council often opposed the wishes of the royal governor to his great frustration and from this conflict, no doubt, emerged the image of the Council as an institutional check upon the designs of an ambitious and tyrannical executive. It was likely that this image caused the framers in 1780, to retain the Council.

Under the Constitution of 1780, [Chap. II, sec. 3] the Council consisted of nine members and the Lieutenant Governor. The nine were chosen from the forty state senators by a joint ballot of the two houses of the legislature. If a senator refused to serve [eventually many did because their acceptance would weaken or erase the voting majority of their party in the senate], the legislature then elected councillors from among the people at large. The duties of the Council were loosely defined but included giving the governor advice on executive matters and giving advice and consent to many executive appointments.

The Holmes' committee recommended the creation of a council of seven members, one each from seven council districts to be chosen by joint ballot of the Senate and House. No member of the legislature, however, could be elected a councilor nor could a member of Congress, nor a federal or state employee.

The duties of the Council were the same as those prescribed in the Constitution of 1780 except that advice and consent to pardons was given to the Maine Council. The difficulty was, however, that the impreciseness of the statement of the powers of the Council in the Massachusetts Constitution of 1780 was carried over into the Maine Constitution. Article V, Part 2, Sec. 1 states, in part, that the governor "with the counsellors....may...hold and keep a council, *for ordering and directing the affairs of state according to law* [italics added]. This clause suggests that the Holmes' committee was placing the Council in a position of equality *vis a vis* the governor. Yet, Article V, Part 1, Section 1 states the "supreme executive power of this state..." rests with the governor. The Council is "to advise the Governor in the executive part of the government" and he is to assemble the Council "at his discretion." Although there has raged a controversy over which clause should be taken as giving the intent of the Holmes' committee, there can be little doubt but the committee meant the governor to be the "supreme executive power." In the context of the times, the delegates at the convention were unfamiliar with the theory, now so often advanced for partisan purposes, that the council is equal to the governor. This generally had not been true during the forty years during which the Massachusetts Constitution was the fundamental law of the Commonwealth nor did the supporters of the council imply as much during the debate at the convention.

Dr. Daniel Rose of Boothbay, later the first warden of the Maine State Prison at Thomaston and still later Maine's land agent, led the opposition that arrayed itself against the creation of a council. Perley paraphrased Rose's remarks as follows:

> Dr. Rose...thought a council unnecessary, and that dispensing with one would be a great saving of expense....The government of the United States had no established council. The President consults with the heads of departments, who are called his cabinet council; and the governor will have his aids; adjutant general and other officers to assist him in the discharge of his duties, with whom he may advise. The Executive of most other States, act without a council, and no complaint is made of want of one. New York has one, which they would be glad to be rid of.
>
> I believe, said Dr. R., we can get a Governor as capable of doing the business of the Executive alone, as other States. If we give him a council, we not only incur a useless expense, but divide the responsibility, and open a door for intrigue. The Senators will come from all parts of the State, and will give him all the information he could obtain from a Council. And besides, as has heretofore been the case, he may have a council in whom he has no confidence.

Rufus King, in a letter to his brother William, offered a similar criticism of the council describing it as "worse than useless, it is the scene of intrigue, and destroys executive Responsibility."

John Holmes asserted that he had urged the same arguments against the council in the committee "considering it a useless appendage to the government," but that he had been convinced by those who believed it a valuable and useful institution that it should be retained.

In the debate, two delegates [Ezekiel Whitman of Portland and James Bridge of Augusta] who had served on the Council of Massachusetts advanced now familiar arguments as to its great utility in regard to hearing pardons and as a watchdog over the treasury. A motion to have the council elected by the people was defeated for the reason that it would then be necessary to redistrict the state anew for that purpose. Finally, a vote to accept the committee report was passed.

[Article V, Parts 3 and 4, creating the positions of Secretary of State and Treasurer both to be elected by the legislature were lifted with minor amendments from the constitution of 1780 and passed without debate].

ARTICLE VI

Article VI, adopted without debate by the convention, established a Supreme Judicial Court only, leaving the establishment of other courts to legislative decision. The Constitution of 1780 [Chap. III, art. 1] provided that judges, with a few exceptions, should hold their offices during good behavior. However, "the Governor, with consent of the Council, may remove them upon the address of both Houses of the Legislature." The Maine constitution, for reasons not explained, provided that judges of the Supreme Judicial Court should hold their offices during good behavior but not beyond the age of 70. No provision was made at the time for creating a machinery for their dismissal.

ARTICLE VII

Article VII dealing with the militia of the new state was the subject of a protracted discussion over the wisdom of exempting Quakers and Shakers on religious grounds. The debate, of interest philosophically, was politically significant to the extent the convention voted to allow persons between eighteen and forty-five to buy their exemption from militia service. This was one of the few instances where the democratic inclinations of the delegates failed them.

ARTICLE VIII

It will come as a surprise to those who are accustomed to thinking that education, like theology, should be strictly divorced from politics, that the article in the Maine constitution which owed most to considerations of a partisan political nature was Article VIII prescribing the role the new state should play in the education of its citizens.

Bowdoin College in the year 1819 found itself under attack from those who believed it was the guardian of subversive elements and ideas. Like many institutions of higher learning in America in that period, the college had been established to transmit the traditions of ruling groups in society at large. These traditions were allegedly those that developed out of the Protestant Reformation, especially Calvinism with its emphasis on a rigorous moral life based on the teachings of St. Paul and after him St. Augustine. By the turn of the nineteenth century, the Calvinistic notion of predestination and its derivative, the elect, had largely gone out of style for a variety of reasons. However, the notion of an elect lived on in the belief that the clergy, in particular, constituted God's aristocracy on earth to whom the mass of mankind in general should look for guidance in the conduct of their lives.

Bowdoin was administered from 1805 to 1819 by Jesse Appleton. "The saintly Appleton," as he was affectionately called by his friends, was a man who believed as much as it was possible to believe in the mission of the Congregational clergy as agents of God on earth. To Appleton, Bowdoin College existed to provide these agents for Maine as Harvard had so nobly done for two centuries for Massachusetts and in so doing it would serve as a bulwark of orthodoxy.

As noted previously, there were many people in Maine who thought that Jesse Appleton performed his task too well. Baptists, who by 1812 were the largest denomination in Maine, charged that Bowdoin was a closed corporation. The sons of Baptist families were often denied admission or, they claimed, the few that were admitted were subjected to nothing but the most severe teachings of Congregational orthodoxy. It was, in part, due to this discrimination that the Baptists sought to establish their own institution at Waterville. Democratic-Republicans, behind William King, who had personal reasons for disliking the leaders of the college, complained that Bowdoin was not only a center of orthodoxy in the District but also the center of die-hard Federalist, elitist ideas. The leaders of the Democratic-Republicans admonished the leaders of the Brunswick college that unless they managed their affairs more "meritoriously," the consequences would be grave.

The example of Dartmouth College did not go unnoticed by Republicans. When in 1817, Dartmouth was "liberated" from "the thraldom of an oppressive hierarchy and aristocracy" and placed under legislative control, the Republicans on the *Argus* staff were elated. "Whoever tho't . . . a public institution, established for the public benefit," queried the editors, "by the force of a charter, and the appointment of certain persons as trustees to manage its concerns, thereby became the *private property* of the trustees?"

The answer was, of course, that only Federalists thought so, and their defeat at the hands of the Republicans of New Hampshire proved that they were not invincible. It was, doubtless, the Dartmouth experience that presented King and his cohorts with the idea to place Bowdoin under state control when and if the time presented itself. But as long as Maine was a mere "appendage" of Massachusetts, the Federalists of the state would protect the college from the corrupting influences of "illiterates."

As previously noted, the officers of the college during the winter session of the General Court in 1819, were determined to obtain increased assistance from the General Court because they "had no hope of patronage . . . from the government of Maine," should a separation take place. Nor did the defeat of the forces representing state control in New Hampshire as a result of the Dartmouth College decision bode well for Bowdoin, for it was John Holmes who was the victim of Daniel Webster's eloquence and John Marshall's disposition toward the sanctity of contracts, and, as everyone knew, Holmes did not take defeat gracefully. Jesse Appleton might assure his associates that "God has taken care of the college, and God will take care of the college," but others looked toward more reliable guardians, the Federalists of Massachusetts proper.

The more legalistically inclined Federalists such as lawyer Nathan Kinsman of Portland realized that the Dartmouth College decision, which held that a college charter was a contract and therefore unalterable by a state legislature, was of dubious value in the case of Bowdoin because Bowdoin's charter [sec. 16] gave to the legislature the authority to alter the charter. Consequently, Kinsman went to Boston in June 1819, during the time William King was guiding through the General Court the "Act of Separation.The Portland lawyer conferred with Senator Lyman of Hampshire County, a member of the Senate committee charged with framing the "Act," and Lyman, over the protest of King, got inserted in the bill what he considered a sufficient safeguard of the integrity of the college. King, reportedly, backed off from a showdown with the college at that time only because of appeals made to him from Republicans in Maine requesting that he take a moderate course.

The presumed safeguard was contained in article seven of the Act of Separation providing that the "President and Trustees and Overseers of the college, shall have, hold and enjoy their powers and privileges in all respects; to that the same shall not be subject to be altered, limited, annulled or restrained, except by judicial process, according to law." However Article nine of the "Act" provided that any of the terms of the "Act of Separation," including article seven might be modified or annulled by the agreement of the legislatures of both states. Article nine, as events proved, provided just the loophole that Maine Republicans needed to achieve their ultimate objective. The "Act" further provided that Bowdoin would receive from the State of Maine the sum of $3,000 until the year 1824.

Outmaneuvered for the time being by the friends of the college, King and his associates, between the adjournment of the General Court in June 1819 and the opening of the Constitutional Convention in October, considered different means by which the legal barrier erected around Bowdoin could be scaled or circumvented. One who played a significant role in these discussions was Judah Dana of Fryeburg. Dana, the grandson of General Israel Putnam of Revolutionary War fame, was a Dartmouth College graduate (1795). In 1798, he became the first lawyer to settle in Oxford County. The nearest lawyer to him was located in Portland, fifty miles from his home at Fryeburg. In 1801, Daniel Webster came to Fryeburg as preceptor of Fryeburg Academy and promptly became Dana's prize student in the law. Another was Samuel Fessenden whose son William Pitt Fessenden was the God-Son of "Godlike Daniel." In 1811, as a result of the Gerry revolution in Massachusetts, Dana was named associate justice of the Oxford County Court of Common Pleas. A man of unusual independence of mind, Dana left the Congregational church in a dispute over doctrine to become an active Methodist. It is obvious that Dana's hostility to Bowdoin College derived from his conviction that it was the home of religious privilege. A letter written by him in 1833, reveals that he was struggling even then with what he called "sectarian despotism:" "I become more and more convinced of the [necessity] of the government taking a still more decided stand against the *arrogance* and *dictation* of sectarian despotism." Above all, Dana understood the political dimension of the activities of a college.

It was Dana who wrote William King in July, 1819 that

> ...it becomes us as Citizens of Maine early to take a view of [college], and in our infancy, so to shape our literary establishments that the greatest possible benefit may be derived from them to individuals and the community, and that those placed over them should receive the patronage of the government and in turn, they should be attached to and support the same. In a country like ours, where its learning is mostly to be found in the desk [pulpit] and at the Bar, those orders of men have an extensive, steady and increasing influence over the public mind, hence the necessity of having them filled with Gentlemen friendly to the Government; this can only be done by that wisdom and foresight, which shall enable us to establish pure fountains of literature, so that the daily streams issuing forth, to replenish those professions, may not only be salubrious and healthful to the community, but also add strength and stability to the government .... the Instructors of our Colleges are daily instilling into the minds of the youth under their care, such principles as they themselves embrace—and as these youth are most generally destined to fill important stations in life, it becomes very necessary for the welfare of government as well as the community that these Instructors should possess sound principles and unbiased tastes and feelings; indeed, Sir, to a Gentleman of your experience and foresight, it will be needless to remark, that the literary Institutions of a Country, when arrayed against its government, are the most powerful engine to batter it down; but when favourably disposed, are its firmest and most desirable pillars.

King could not have agreed with Dana more but the problem yet remained—how could the barricade erected around the college be circumvented in order to implement any program designed to bring the college under state control? Dana had no answer to this question but he did have a proposal which he thought would constitute a beginning. He informed King that Chief Justice Marshall's decision that returned Dartmouth to the control of trustees would result in the unemployment of President William Allen who had been selected by the Republican forces of the State of New Hampshire to serve as Dartmouth's President. Now that President Appleton was nearing death why not persuade the governing boards to hire Allen?

> "I am aware that some of the Electors [the members of the boards] would secretly reject him on account of his politiks and the dread of his influence, in that way, among the Clergy—the Literati, and particularly among the youth, but when they reflect that the State will be highly republican, and that the College cannot flourish without state patronage, would they not overcome their prejudices and consent to appoint him? and would they not be brought to this measure from a conviction that the college as now organized, would not be a favorite with the new government.

King's immediate reaction to Dana's letter is not known but it is evident from subsequent events that the suggestion hinting at the possibility of withholding state patronage from the college, despite the clause in the Act of Separation which bound the state to pay Bowdoin $3,000 a year until 1824, was not unheeded. In addition, it is significant that Allen was hired in 1820 as Bowdoin's new president succeeding the deceased Appleton.

In the meantime, the rumblings within the ranks of the Republicans did not go unnoticed by the friends of the college. The more numerous Board of Overseers on August 31, 1819, voted to appoint a committee "to take into consideration that part of the law relative to the Separation of Maine, which applies to Bowdoin College, and to report at our meeting in May next what measures ought to be adopted in relation to the same." The Board of Trustees, of which King was a member, voted against the Overseers, producing an impasse which lasted for several months.

By the time the Constitutional Convention assembled in October 1819, a few of the more recalcitrant members of the governing boards of Bowdoin had reluctantly concluded that, legalistic safeguards notwithstanding, the future of Bowdoin College would be uncertain unless some effort were made to placate men like King and Dana who, after all, were going to be running the new state. One of these was William Vaughan of Hallowell, a friend of Priestly, Franklin, and other late eighteenth century luminaries. Vaughan, who was a member of the Board of Overseers, wrote King that he had concluded that it was wise, after all, to bend a little. As a result, he was now in favor of "throwing [Bowdoin] open to every sect ... [and] to all parties" but with this concession he expected the college to remain in the hands of "men of some property of a collegiate education."

What influence this apparent willingness of some of the college's more ardent defenders to relax their control over the institution had on the action taken at the Constitutional Convention is impossible to determine. King, there can be no doubt, remained determined to place the institution under state control. He appointed Dana and John Holmes to the committee to draw up a constitution. Holmes, the chairman of the committee, and the loser in his encounter with Daniel Webster before the Supreme Court in the Dartmouth College case, was in sympathy with both King and Dana on the subject of the future of the college, and was further angered by what he described as the "officious interference" of Massachusetts in the affairs of Maine by her erection of the legal barrier around the college.

On the evening of Monday, October 25, beginning the third week of the convention, the delegates received the long awaited Article VIII, entitled "Literature" from the Holmes' committee. The original draft of Article VIII read as follows:

> A general diffusion of the advantages of education being essential to the preservation of the rights and liberties of the people; to promote this important object, the Legislature are authorized, and it shall be their duty to require, the several towns to make suitable provision, at their own expense, for the support and maintenance of public schools; and it shall further be their duty to encourage and suitably endow, from time to time, as the circumstances of the people may authorise, all academies, colleges and seminaries of learning within the State: Provided, that no donation, grant or endowment shall at any time be made by the Legislature, to any Literary Institution now established, or which may hereafter be established, unless, at the time of making such endowments, *the Governor and Council shall have the power of revising and negativing the doings of the Trustees and Government of such Institution* [Italics added] in the selection of its officers and the management of its funds.

The first portion of Article VIII dealing with the establishment of public schools was modeled after a similar statement in the Constitution of 1780 [chap. V, sec. 2] which in turn was a lineal descendant of the "Old Deluder Satan" law of 1647, the first law ever passed providing for the compulsory support of public schools. It was, therefore, of historic origin.

The second portion contained the answer that William King provided for the question: how best can the barricade placed around Bowdoin be circumvented? The governor, which meant King, and his council would exercise a veto power over the actions of the governing boards of the college. If this were not permitted, then the state would be obligated to cease its contribution to the college, an action that, King knew, the college could not afford to allow.

The debate on Article VIII, as expected, centered on the delegation of this immense power to the governor and council. Those delegates who were friendly to the college and desired a continuation of past practices were represented by Calvin Stockbridge from North Yarmouth, a strongly anti-separationist and Federalist town. Stockbridge offered a motion that would have limited the latitude of executive power to cases where the governing boards mismanaged funds. The motion was defeated.

Ether Shepley of Saco represented a far larger number of delegates than had Stockbridge when he offered an amendment to strike out that part of Article VIII giving the governor and council a veto power over the actions of the governing boards of educational institutions, and substituting for it the following: that the state should not make grants or endow any Literary Institution

> [unless] the Legislature of the State shall have the right to grant any further powers to, alter, limit or restrain any of the powers vested in any such Literary Institution, as shall be judged necessary to promote the best interests thereof.

Shepley explained that he offered the amendment because he believed the legislature to be the proper regulator of such matters not the executive. Furthermore, he believed that such power should be employed only in regard to the management of funds, "having done that, let [such institutions] be managed by those to whom it properly belongs" [the governing boards].

No doubt recognizing that to insist on the original wording of Article VIII might jeopardize the ultimate objective of placing Bowdoin under state control, and that Shepley's amendment, regardless of his own views on how such powers should be employed, nevertheless gave to the legislature the power to act in any way it saw fit, Judah Dana rose to offer his support for the amendment. The important consideration, according to Dana was not that the executive must control such institutions but that they must be controlled by some public authority. On this principle he would never compromise.

The absolute and uncontrolled power given to Trustees to perpetuate themselves and successors in office, without any check upon them, in some future time will be considered as obnoxious to the community, and unfortunate to the institutions, themselves; as they can never expect the public munificence, without the public confidence. If the perpetuity of office is contained without a legislative control, favoritism, instead of merit, will decide the claims of candidates, and the successful recommendation to office will be political or religious sentiments, or family connections; and before the expiration of half a century, it will be found, that if our numerous Boards of Trustees are not converted into political junta or religious hierarchies, they will be twisted up into indissoluble knots of family connections, who will consult their own gratification and interest, rather than the public good.

At this juncture, the moderate voice of Albion K. Parris was raised in objection to Shepley's amendment and to Dana's reasoning. He was, he said, in favor of some control over Bowdoin College, "for it is Bowdoin College which is the object of this provision, and we may as well name it, as keep it out of sight," but he would not go so far as to allow the legislature to interfere with the charter rights of the governing bodies. More acceptable, asserted Parris, would be an arrangement by which officers of the state government would be appointed to the Board of Overseers. Instead of being punitive in intent, this proposal, continued Parris, would be preventative in that state officers would serve as watchdogs for the public interest preventing abuses of a private character from being perpertrated.

At this point, John Holmes, in his characteristically blunt manner, observed that he "felt mortified at the provision in the act of separation imposing on us shackles in relation to this subject. Sir, are we in leading strings? Are we too ignorant even to be made sensible of the importance of knowledge? And does Massachusetts *therefore* undertake to prescribe for us?" He supported the Shepley amendment and opposed Parris' alternative mode. Holmes, then, reminded the delegates that the amendment embodied a principle already well established. The charters of Harvard College and the charter of Bowdoin College did, in fact, contain provisions for legislative restriction on the power of the governing boards of both institutions. The problem presented to the delegates was not derived from the charters but from the provisions in the "Act of Separation" designed to insulate Bowdoin College from state control. Holmes continued:

What will be the consequence of this provision. To create a jealousy, and withdraw our patronage from Bowdoin College. I think the government of the College are aware of it, and will be willing to give up the odious provision. We cannot confide in those who are afraid to place confidence in us. Ought there to be a literary institution in a State not subject to the control of the laws, nor subservient to the government that protects it? Why should this institution, more than any other, be beyond our reach? It is dangerous to place too much confidence even in friends. Having acquired the power, they may defy the authority from which it was derived.

If the college at Brunswick prefers to proceed on its present basis, it has its choice. I am for letting it alone, until it shall come forward and ask for aid, and if it will couple its request with a relinquishment of this odious provision, I would grant it.

The Shepley amendment passed 151 to 18. With the amendment Article VIII of the Maine Constitution read, and continues to read for it is the only article that has never been amended, as follows:

A general diffusion of the advantages of education being essential to the preservation of the rights and liberties of the people; to promote this important object, the Legislature are authorized, and it shall be their duty to require, the several towns to make suitable provision, at their own expense, for the support and maintenance of public schools; and it shall further be their duty to encourage and suitably endow, from time to time, as the circumstances of the people may authorise, all academies, colleges and seminaries of learning within the State: *Provided,* that no donation, grant or endowment shall at any time be made by the Legislature, to any Literary Institution now established, or which may hereafter be established, unless, at the time of making such endowment, the Legislature of the State shall have the right to grant any further powers to, alter, limit or restrain any of the powers vested in, any such literary institution, as shall be judged necessary to promote the best interests thereof.

Article VIII, as adopted, provided the means that allowed the state to virtually place the institution under state control. It assumed correctly that the college could not survive without such support and that sooner or later, the governing boards would submit to superior power. What actually occurred was that the governing boards first accepted William Allen, Dartmouth's deposed president, as the successor to the deceased Jesse Appleton, and then, lured by the promise of King to establish a state medical school, Allen persuaded the governing boards that realism dictated that they submit to state control. In 1821, Governor William King, with legislative approval, increased the size of the Board of Trustees from a maximum of thirteen as provided in the college charter to a maximum of twenty-five. The Board of Overseers was increased in number by a third. To the Board of Trustees, King appointed only his closest friends, all Republicans, including John Holmes, John Chandler, James Bridge, Dr. Benjamin Jones Porter, and Ashur Ware. In addition, he appointed as trustees William P. Preble, Albion K. Parris,

Mark L. Hill, Judah Dana, Joshua Wingate, Jr., and Nathan Weston, all of whom had been members of the less influential Board of Overseers. To the Board of Overseers, the Governor, appointed, among others, Samuel Ayer, William Williamson, Daniel Rose, and three future governors of the state, Robert P. Dunlap of Brunswick, Samuel Smith of Wiscasset, and John Anderson of Belfast. Also to the Board of Overseers, King appointed his nephew William King Porter, a Somerset County lawyer.

The result of these appointments was to place Bowdoin not only under state control but the control of the Republicans as well, which, of course, was what had been really intended all along.

In 1876, Samuel Benson, who had attended a legislative hearing in 1834 concerned with the question of state support of literary institutions, recalled that William King had testified that Thomas Jefferson was responsible for the substance if not the exact wording of Article VIII. King, according to Benson, said that he had visited Jefferson before the Constitutional Convention and that "his old friend" had advised him to adopt Article VIII. Until now no corroborating evidence has been offered to support Benson's claim.

The following extract from a letter to Jefferson from King written after the convention adjourned supplies such evidence:

> The interest you are known to take in whatever relates to our institutions in every section of this country, is my inducement for forwarding the endorsed Constitution which we have presented to the people of Maine. [The] *Literary Article* we are indebted to you for, which received almost the unanimous support of the Convention, when at your hospitable mansion the last winter you may recollect naming the article of the kind to me as of the first importance, as calculated to perpetuate our Republican systems. I was convinced of the correctness of your opinions on that, as on every other occasion.

The unqualified manner in which King attributed the authorship of the Article VIII, should not detract, however, from the contributions made to the formulation of the article by others. In the first place, as already noted, while Jefferson was committed to public education, he was not the only one to be so committed. The injunction to the legislature to direct the towns to support public education had a long history in Massachusetts dating back to at least 1647, and was, in fact lifted from the Massachusetts Constitution of 1780. [Chap. V, sec. 2]. One contribution which Jefferson *may have made* was the insistence that the legislature "require the several towns to make suitable provision, at their own expense, for the support and maintenance of public schools." The Massachusetts Constitution described the provision of schools by the towns as a *duty* but did not specifically *require* such support, although the courts often interpreted the word duty to imply as much. Jefferson, as James B. Conant has noted, wrote in his autobiography of his utter disappointment at the fact that the Virginia legislature in 1796 had passed a bill to provide a free elementary education for all, but that it turned out to be a fraud because, by leaving the implementation of the bill to the courts of the counties, little in fact was done. Why Jefferson had more confidence in the good judgment of legislatures than local authorities, Conant does not attempt to explain.

It was with the second portion of the Article dealing with colleges which owed the most to the "sage of Monticello." Without doubt, Jefferson suggested to King the technique of withholding state support from Bowdoin as the most certain means of getting that institution to capitulate, although it was true that others, including Judah Dana, had come to the same determination independently.

Of course, it is probably true that Article VIII would not have been significantly different had King never traveled to Monticello.

After all, among men who shared Jefferson's political philosophy, the desire to bring private educational institutions, controlled by a few, under public control, was not uncommon. The belief that institutions, especially those that received public monies, should be free from sectarian influences was also widespread. One might say that the "ideas were in the air," and were the product of the enlightenment tendency to ridicule all pretentions to power based on a foundation of knowledge derived from sources other than "science." It is certainly clear that William King would have agreed with Jefferson's famous utterance, "I am of a sect by myself, as far as I know."

ARTICLE IX

Article IX, as reported, contained provisions for oaths and prescriptions, tenure of offices, and the impeachment of civil officers. In substance, these provisions were patterned after the Constitution of 1780. [Chap. VI]. There was an effort to deny public office to anyone who "denies the Christian religion," but Holmes, once again, rose to beat back the attempt on the grounds that such a requirement would be inconsistent with the Bill of Rights as well as violating the spirit of the constitution "which was not to require a religious test as a qualification for office."

Article IX likewise established what landed proprietors feared, a system of equal taxation as between improved and settled lands and wild lands held for purposes of speculation. However, if James Richards, one of the Bingham trustees' agents in Maine, was correct, the full impact of this measure was considerably blunted by King's agreement to keep the valuation on the lands low.

ARTICLE X

[Article X, among other subjects, dealt with the apportionment problem handled under the discussion of Article IV.]

With the settlement of the apportionment question, the last hurdle of the convention was surmounted. The remaining hours were taken up in routine matters such as the election of Ashur Ware as Secretary of State and the decision to convene the first session of the legislature in Portland. On Friday afternoon, October 29, 1819, the sixteenth and last day of the convention, 236 of the 274 delegates signed the completed constitution. Thirty-two members refused to sign and eight were absent. Preble and Parris, of the seven delegates from Portland signed; the others could not accept what they considered discrimination against their town in the apportionment of representatives. It is probable that four of Wells' five man delegation refused to sign for the same reason, although the fact that Wells had been historically one of the towns most opposed to a separation in District cannot be lightly dismissed. Among the delegates from the smaller towns who did not sign, the departure from the principle of corporate representation was said to be decisive. Of the twenty-five delegates, excluding those from Portland, who did not sign, it is interesting to note that fifteen came from Federalist towns that had voted heavily against a separation in July 1819. The greatest opposition was centered in York County which claimed thirteen of the dissidents. No explanation as to why this was true was advanced at the time. The county had always contained anti-separation strongholds, particularly those towns that bordered New Hampshire which argued that Boston was nearer to them than any location that had been proposed as a capitol for Maine. Possibly the same objection still pertained.

Most people, including Federalists, however, had nothing but praise for the efforts of the delegates. The *Portland Gazette* agreed with John Russel of the [Boston] *Columbian Centinel* who thought the Maine Constitution would not "suffer by a comparison with the best in the United States." Republicans were delighted with the warm reception of the Constitution. The more serious minded of them were more pleased that a significant step had been taken toward the creation of a thoroughly democratic community in which "artifical" distinctions based on religion, race, and property had no place. Martin Kinsley of Hampden who had been labeled a "jacobin" by Federalists because of his presumably ultra democratic leanings summed up the feelings of this latter group in a letter he wrote to King at the time the convention was still in progress:

> "We are all literally charmed with the mildness & wisdom with which you proceed in your Convention. Party spirit seems to have been lost in a spirit of Phylanthropy and Patriotism. We rejoice that you are not likely to shackle us with any *Religious Tests* or injunctions of *Religious Duties:* Those can never make us Christians; but will be pretty sure to produce Pharisees & Hypocrites. We need no *Pecuniary qualifications* for office. Was it ever heard of that a Senator or Representative refused to swear that he had such qualifications? Although some of his friends & creditors might have very serious doubts of the fact at the time. Go on my good friends! . . . Posterity shall "rise up & call you blessed."

Ironically, the man whose words were invoked most frequently throughout the convention, (especially by Holmes in justification of the decision to discriminate against the larger towns in representation), Thomas Jefferson, was not entirely pleased by the constitution, a copy of which William King sent him. Acknowledging the receipt of the Constitution Jefferson wrote King:

> Thomas Jefferson returns thanks to General King for his kind communication of the constitution of Maine which he finds marked with wisdom in every point, except that of representation. Equal representation is so fundamental a principle in a true republic that no prejudices can justify its violation because the prejudices themselves cannot be justified. The claims of the corporate towns in this case. [the small towns under 1,500 inhabitants, not the larger towns] like those of the barons in

England have formed the body of the nation to accept a gov. by capitulation there, the = rights of the people at large are forced to yield to the privileges of a few, however you will amend it bye & bye....

The Constitution, accompanied by an "Address to the People" explaining why the convention departed in many instances from the Massachusetts Constitution, especially in regard to religious and property qualifications for voting and office holding, was submitted to the people of Maine on December 6, 1819. The people responded by giving an overwhelming vote in favor of the Constitution. The aggregate vote was 9,040 in favor and only 796 against. Figure XVIII indicates that only in York County, where three towns, including Shapleigh which voted 132 to 25 against adoption, was there any appreciable opposition, and even there the vote was three to one in favor. In the entire District only nine of the 241 returns were recorded against adoption.

The Constitutional Convention reconvened on January 5, 1820 in Portland, at which time the votes given on the Constitution were officially recorded. A number of procedural matters were disposed of including the naming of John Chandler to succeed William King as acting governor in case of the latter's death. But what should have been a time of feasting and celebration was transformed into a time of great apprehension, for from Washington news was received that Maine's application for statehood had run afoul of the most inflammatory issue that the young republic had yet faced, the question of the extension of slavery into the areas beyond the Mississippi River. As a result, there was real doubt that Maine would be admitted before the March 4, 1820 deadline contained in the Act of Separation. If she failed to meet this deadline, unless Massachusetts agreed to extend it, Maine would revert back to the status she held between 1780 and 1819. For those who had worked for the independence of Maine for years, this prospect was a dreadful and depressing one.

FIGURE XVIII
AGGREGATE VOTE ON THE ADOPTION OF THE CONSTITUTION, 1819

Counties	Aggregate of Votes, Legally Returned			Aggregate of Votes, Not Legally Returned		
	Whole Number	Yeas	Nays	Whole Number	Yeas	Nays
York	1,411	1,094	317	135	118	17
Cumberland	1,814	1,675	139	70	57	13
Lincoln	1,553	1,496	56	110	110	0
Hancock	784	686	98	74	73	1
Washington	203	199	4	34	23	11
Kennebec	1,509	1,466	43	329	318	11
Oxford	1,350	1,262	88	88	88	0
Somerset	653	626	27	147	123	24
Penobscot	560	536	24	75	75	0
Totals	9,837	9,040	796	1,062	985	77

CHAPTER

19.

Maine did not come into the Union without difficulty. The Missouri controversy which Thomas Jefferson said alarmed him as a "fireball in the night" was an especially significant event in the history of Maine as the following account suggests.

THE MISSOURI COMPROMISE
"THE MOTHER HAS TWINS"*

by

Ronald F. Banks

With the resounding victory gained in the polls in July 1819, the separationists had every reason to believe, as they did, that they could now coast. To be sure, there had been concern manifested within the ranks of the leadership that the consititutional convention would present some challenges from the opposition but few doubted that the challenges would constitute any more than a nuisance. The application to Congress for the admission of Maine as a state was viewed as a mere formality, as indeed, it should have been. Consequently, it was with disbelief and shock that the news was received from Washington in December 1819, that the Maine statehood bill had encountered an unforeseen obstacle.

The latest difficulty was triggered by Republican Representative James Tallmadge of the Poughkeepsie District of New York. On February 13, 1819, less than a month before Congress cleared the way for the reopening of the separation question by the passage of the revised coasting law, Tallmadge "lit the fuse" to the most explosive controversy of the time by offering an amendment to the Missouri statehood bill to prohibit the further introduction of slaves into Missouri and to free all children born of slaves already in Missouri at the age of twenty-five.

The debate on the Tallmadge amendment in the House lasted through February and into March 1819, when it passed with the votes of northern representatives. Only six northern representatives, including John Holmes, voted against the amendment.

In the Senate where equality of representation favored the Southern states, the Tallmadge amendment was foredoomed to defeat. But Rufus King so ably led the exclusionist forces in that body that the Southerners for the first time bristled at the prospect that they might soon lose their power in the Senate to a new alliance of Northerners and Westerners united in opposition to slavery. When the Southerners succeeded in passing the Missouri statehood bill without any restriction placed on slavery, no one believed that this was the last airing of the question but simply the opening volley in what would prove to be a protracted stalemate that would, before it was broken, shake the very foundation of the Union.

The Sixteenth Congress that assembled on December 6, 1819, contained seven representatives from Maine: John Holmes of Alfred, Mark Langdon Hill of Phippsburg, Ezekiel Whitman of Portland, Martin Kinsley of Hampden, Enoch Lincoln of Paris, Joshua Cushman of Winslow, and James Parker of Gardiner. All but Whitman were Democratic-Republicans (although Cushman's allegiance to the Republicans was suspect) and all but Whitman and Cushman had been enthusiastic supporters of separation. Even Whitman, however, had grudgingly supported the cause. In addition, Prentice Mellon of Portland, a Federalist, joined

---

*Ronald F. Banks, *"The Separation of Maine and Massachusetts: 1785-1820,"* (Unpublished Ph.D. dissertation, University of Maine, 1966), pp. 352-387.

with Harrison Gray Otis to make up Massachusetts' senatorial delegation.

On December 8, 1819 John Holmes presented a petition to the House asking for the admission of Maine into the Union. Prentice Mellon did likewise in the Senate. By the end of December, it was apparent that all was not well. Mark Hill became so concerned that he sent for William King: "I wish you would come on this winter and if you can, come soon." Two days later, he informed King that "our difficulties appear to thicken....The speaker (Henry Clay) came out openly...in opposition to the admission of Maine without Missouri." Discouragement was increased by the news received from Prentice Mellon that in the Senate, General James Barbour of Virginia was determined to unite the Maine and Missouri bills. Mellon's plea that the admission of Maine should be considered on its own merit was to no avail. "The friends of Missouri have a majority and can defeat us if they unite," lamented Mellon. John Holmes, after a visit with President Monroe with several members of the Senate, reported to King that most senators, including Barbour, had expressed "a very friendly disposition towards our admission, but Governor Barbour and several others thought it would be best that the *Mother* should have *twins this time.*" Clearly, Maine had become ensnared in a net the escape from which bore absolutely no relation to the merit of her application. She was inextricably caught in the power play between contending forces. Her fate was now in the hands of the players.

The allusion to Clay's opposition by Hill was in reference to the debate that took place on the floor of the House on December 30. With Hill in the speaker's chair, Clay informed the membership that he could not accept any effort to restrict slavery in Missouri and that in order to assure that this would not happen he was supporting the uniting of the Maine and Missouri bills. John Holmes reminded Clay that if Maine were not admitted by March 4, she would revert to the control of Massachusetts. He hoped, he said, that Clay's strategy did not mean that Clay would sacrifice Maine in this contest. Clay succinctly replied: "yes it did." In spite of Clay's opposition, however, the House passed on January 3, 1820, the Maine statehood bill, and then turned its attention to the Missouri bill. Clay now turned his attention to the Senate where, he knew only too well, the axe would certainly fall.

The admission of Alabama on December 14, 1819, gave the Senate an evenly divided membership between the North and the South of eleven states each. However, because a number of northern senators, led by Jesse Thomas of Illinois, were opposed to restricting slavery in Missouri, the anti-restrictionist, pro-South element had a clear cut majority. When the House bill admitting Maine reached the Senate Judiciary Committee an enabling amendment was attached to it allowing Missouri to form a constitution and state government without restriction on slavery in either. Thus, Maine and Missouri now became formally joined. Both Harrison Gray Otis and Prentice Mellon objected to the action of the Judiciary Committee but their two votes were insufficient to block Senate passage of the committee's recommendation.

On February 17, the Senate paved the way for a compromise when it passed a second amendment, the Thomas amendment named after its sponsor the pro-southern senator from Illinois, providing that slavery be forever forbidden in the area known as the Louisiana Purchase north of the line 36° 30', excepting Missouri. The vote was 34 to 20 on the Thomas amendment with both Otis and Mellon among the minority. As one southerner explained, it would be difficult now for the Congressmen from Massachusetts and Maine to vote against the Senate compromise package. To do so would doom Maine as well. Joshua Cushman exclaimed upon hearing of the scheme: "Maine! Ill fated Maine! The story of her woes would make the angels weep."

Yet that was precisely what happened. When the Senate amended House bill was returned to the House, the House on February 23, after a debate that consumed over 600 pages in the *Annals,* rejected the Senate amendment uniting Maine and Missouri by a vote of 93 to 72. The Thomas amendment embodying the compromise proposal was similarly defeated by a resounding 159 to 18 margin. On each vote all seven of Maine's representatives voted with the majority.

To complicate matters the House now resumed consideration of its own Missouri statehood bill. An amendment proposed by John Taylor of New York, which would have barred slavery in Missouri, passed the House on March 1, by a vote of 91 to 82 with, significantly, John Holmes the only one of Maine's seven representatives voting against passage.

In the meantime the Senate informed the House of its unconditional commitment to the two amendments it had attached to the House Maine bill. Now, when the Senate received the House Missouri bill, it predictably rejected that bill as well and returned it to the House with the Thomas amendment appended to it. Both Houses were at loggerheads and Mark Hill wrote William King that, "it might take as long as two years for Congress to let us in."

However, at this juncture, the Senate requested a conference with the House and the House accepted. The Senate appointed three conferees: Jesse Thomas, James Barbour, and William Pinckney, all of whom were against the restriction of slavery in Missouri. The House designated five conferees including John Holmes and James Parker of Maine. All of the House members of the joint committee were moderates, chosen carefully by Clay who knew they "would be favorable to any reasonable settlement."

On March 2, John Holmes, whom Henry Clay later commended for his contribution in reaching a compromise, read to the House the report from the committee of conference. The report, which owed much to the efforts of Senator Jesse Thomas of Illinois, recommended: (1) that the Senate "recede" or withdraw the two amendments, one of them the Thomas amendment, from the Maine Bill thus returning it to its former unencumbered state; (2) that both houses be asked to strike out the clause restricting slavery in Missouri from the House Missouri Bill, (3) that both houses accept the Thomas amendment to be incorporated in the House Missouri Bill, which amendment would prohibit slavery north of the line 36° 30′ in the Louisiana Territory, excepting Missouri.

Actually, the House never voted on the compromise package as a whole. If it had believes Glover Moore, the historian of the compromise, the package would not have passed. Rather, the question was divided, each of the provisions taken up separately. On the second provision—the recommendation that the Senate strike the anti-slavery proviso from the House Missouri Bill—the House voted in favor, 90 to 87. Of the fourteen northern representatives who voted in favor, two of them, John Holmes and Mark Hill were from Maine. While the same could be said of any two of the remaining twelve, it is nevertheless true that had these two men not broken with their five collegues from Maine who voted against the second provision, the Missouri compromise would have failed of passage, a fact which both Holmes and Hill were not allowed to forget.

The third provision, Thomas' amendment to exclude slavery north of 36° 30′ excepting Missouri in the Louisiana Territory, was passed easily 134 to 42. Of the seven man Maine delegation, only Whitman, who was absent, did not vote for the third provision.

The House immediately sent to the Senate provision one which the Senate accepted on March 3, 1820, thus allowing Maine to be admitted into the Union on the same day.

Back in Maine, the news from Washington that the Maine's statehood bill was in trouble caught many unprepared. No one had foreseen any difficulty arising in Maine's application for admission; the prospect that those who had long sought independence would be further frustrated was almost too much to contemplate.

Throughout the month of January, before Jesse Thomas suggested what eventually became the Missouri Compromise, many Maine people saw the problem as one created by the slavocracy of the southern states—unless Missouri were admitted slave, Maine was to be denied admittance as a free state. The spectre of slavery being permitted in all the land beyond the Mississippi was even more frightening to many. As far as anyone in Maine knew, only John Holmes, among Maine's representatives, was at all amenable to such an arrangement.

Most men in Maine evinced feelings of shock that the Maine and Missouri questions had been joined. Dan Cony of Augusta could see no justice in the arrangement: "The spirits of pandamonium could not conjure up a plausible pretext" for rejecting Maine's application, he wrote William King, adding in a note to William's brother Rufus, the hero of the anti-slavery forces in Congress, that "We protest... against coupling the destiny of Maine, the civilized populous State of Maine... with the trackless regions, the dreary wastes, the sable tribes of the Missouri beyond the Mississippi." "How it is possible that men of high and honorable minds, men belonging to the most dignified body on earth can so far descend to adopt (such a course)," wrote Preble to John Holmes. "It is at least a *miserable, unworthy,* and *unwarrantable* course. The people of Maine deserve different treatment from the republicans of the South and West...." The venerable George Thacher of Biddeford reported to Holmes that the delegates to Maine's Constitutional Convention who met the first week in January agreed that Maine's admission ought to be postponed for a year rather than allow Maine to become "a mere *pack horse* to transport the odius, anti-republican principle of slavery" into Missouri. If necessary, advised Thacher, Maine's delegation should "suffer martrydom in the cause of liberty, rather than yield an inch in favor of slavery." Even William King, not usually a man to sacrifice all to principle, complained that John Holmes' willingness to compromise was disapproved of by the people of Maine as a dishonorable course of action. The *Portland Gazette,* a long time opponent of slavery, was disgusted at the entire proceedings in Washington and advised the Maine delegation to "hold fast to their political integrity, for as much as we wish success to the Maine Bill, we confess we had rather it would sink, than bear up so wicked a freight as the slavery of Missouri."

The men in the *Argus* office, namely William Pitt Preble and Ashur Ware, became alarmed by those who would sacrifice Maine's independence to a principle. They, with others, protested the manifest injustice of coupling the Maine and Missouri bills but to the question—"shall Maine yield to the admission of Missouri without restrictions?"—the answer was yes, "if she can become a state in no other manner." In response to a letter from John Holmes who by mid-January was one of the leading exponents of compromise, and who was seeking support for his efforts in Maine, Preble referred him to the *Argus,* which, said Preble, was taking a position agreed upon "after a pretty general consultation with our principal political friends and friends of separation." The position to which Preble referred was promulgated in the January 11, 1820 *Eastern Argus:* "...it is the duty of our delegates to see that Maine is admitted as a member of the union before the 4th of March. The people expect it, and will, we believe, take no excuse for the neglect."

Because of this "unprincipled" stand, the *Argus* came under fire from those who charged that the chief organ of the Maine Republicans was not only placing political expediency before considerations of morality but that it held a pro-slavery attitude. To this charge, Preble and Ware answered: "We admit in the fullest manner that (slavery) is both a moral and political evil. But having said this, it must be admitted on the other hand that it is an evil too deeply seated to admit of an immediate cure. No man in his senses, thinks of emancipation. All agree that it would be ruinous both to master and slave."

Independence must take, therefore, precedence over all other considerations. That others in Maine shared the *Argus* position is revealed in a letter written to Enoch Lincoln by a citizen of Oxford County, who reported that the leading figures of Paris supported the restriction of slavery in Missouri but that "there are some, who, either infatuated by the desire of public office, or instigated by the caprice of individual gain, would advocate the separation of Maine, let the sacrifice be what it may."

Not everyone was as certain as the editors of the *Argus* or *Gazette* as to the proper position to take in regard to the question. It appears that William King was one of these. As noted, King at first condemned John Holmes for his willingness to entertain the thought of a compromise. His brother Rufus, whom he greatly admired, was the leading figure in the restrictionist ranks, and William must have been deeply impressed by his brother's commitment to his cause. When the Maine delegation to the General Court (William was a senator from Lincoln County) met in Boston in January, 1820, it was King along with John Chandler who drafted instructions to the Maine delegation in Washington, instructions that manifested a sense of deep frustration as the following extract from them demonstrates:

> We ask you gentlemen to disentangle our question from the Missouri one. If this cannot be effected, the bill will no doubt be lost in which case we are instructed to request you to take up the bill which was postponed in the Senate, add to it a section prohibiting slavery in Maine and insist on the passage of the bill with that provision. You will in this way represent truely the opinions of an immense majority of the people of our District as well as the best interests of the country.

King, try as he might, could not, however, accept such a hollow victory. He might not compromise, but that did not mean that there was no alternative. To his brother Rufus, he wrote that he fully expected, if Congress refused to admit Maine, that a state government would be organized in Maine that would "obtain the assent of Congress when it is their pleasure to give it to us." This, William admitted, might be a regrettable course to take but the people of Maine would not consent to revert to the control of Massachusetts—"it is the only one they will be satisfied with if we are not admitted into the union." William Williamson of Bangor seconded King declaring that he was "about as willing to risk the untried consequences of sovereignty...as to have slavery indelibly graven on the frontlet of that bill, which shall make Maine a *member* of the great American Empire." The Republic of Maine!!

But not even King could long entertain such a radical notion as this. It is not surprising, therefore, that he led the effort to obtain a two year extension on the terms of separation from the General Court. He was successful and as a result the greatest fear of many—that Maine would revert to the control of Massachusetts if she were not admitted to the Union by March 4, 1820—was dispelled.

By February, however, King was beginning to question the wisdom of the doctrinaire anti-slavery position and it was not long before he rivaled even Holmes as an exponent of compromise. It is tempting to attribute his conversion to strains of personal ambition and well it may have been. Nevertheless, one cannot discount the cumulative effect of the many letters King received from both Mark Hill and John Holmes imploring him to throw his influence behind a compromise. The logic of their positions, given their premises, could not be refuted. After all, as Hill said, to be for a compromise was not to be for slavery but for the Union:

> I am for going as far as anybody to restrict slavery, if it can be done without setting the United States on fire, for I think the welfare of eight million of whites are of more importance than a question about the black population and that the preservation of the Union and the admission of Maine, of more importance, than the doubtful right by the constitution to meddle with state sovereignty in the present question.

It was certain, Hill informed King, that without a compromise Maine would "fall to the ground." And since he was convinced that southerners would never yield, an uncompromising position on the part of northerners would mean that Maine would, perhaps, never come into the Union.

The first hint King received that a compromise was a possibility was in a letter from John Holmes received the first week in February. Holmes wrote that there existed more hope for Maine's admission than at any time previously. "The ground of this hope I cannot communicate. If *we do*, you will know it, and after the storm is over, I will then tell you what I mean. Keep this to yourself...."

A week later, King heard again from Holmes:

> Inasmuch as the confidential hint which I gave you...came from a *very intimate friend* of yours it was communicated in perfect confidence. I am only at liberty to add that, if all other expedients fail, one may be resorted to, which will eventually succeed, altho the person making the intimation, who is of high influence where such influence would be necessary, would not be known to favor such a measure now. Perhaps I have already said too much.
>
> I *trust* we shall get Maine in, without compromising principle or interest.

What the expedient was to which Holmes referred is not known. It is possible that he meant the Thomas amendment which was introduced in the Senate on February 3, but it is not likely. In the first place, Holmes' second letter to King was dated February 7, three days after the Thomas amendment was introduced. It was, therefore, by February 7 public knowledge. The tenor of Holmes' letter suggests that the expedient about which he was concerned was not yet publicly known. Secondly, Holmes' confidence that neither "principle or interest" would be sacrificed would seem to rule out the Thomas amendment since the admission of Missouri without restriction, regardless of the other points of the Thomas compromise, could hardly be taken by restrictionists as a principled solution, at least at that stage of the controversy.

Whatever Holmes had in mind, it is apparent that King believed he was referring to the Thomas amendment. King wrote to a friend that nine-tenths of Maine people supported the Thomas solution as a means out of the impasse. To Holmes, King wrote that he now supported

Holmes' effort to achieve a compromise and would share with Holmes the responsibility in enacting one, based on the Thomas amendment. King had now come full circle.

Throughout February, Holmes and Mark Hill kept King informed of the progress of events. For Holmes, first William's brother Rufus was cast in the role of villain for his fanatical opposition to any compromise. Then the obstructionists became Maine's five other Congressmen, Whitman, Parker, Kinsley, Cushman, and Lincoln, all of whom refused to entertain any sympathy for an accommodation. "There is some chance for a compromise," Holmes, who now supported the Thomas amendment as Maine's only hope, wrote King. "If that fails, Maine must be admitted or rejected at last by her own members." After the House voted 94 to 86, on February 29, *not* to drop its insistence upon restriction of slavery in Missouri thus frustrating what seemed the only hope for a compromise, Holmes cursed the five representatives from Maine whose votes against the motion were decisive:

> It is strange...that our own members will compound for nothing. They can carry in Maine, if they will. Would it not be much better to restrict the territories where we *have* the *constitutional* power, and *propose* and *recommend* to Missouri to write a restriction in her Constitution, and get Maine admitted than to insist upon this point of doubtful policy and still more doubtful constitutionality and have our state?

The opposition to a compromise of the five Maine representatives, thought Holmes, was not due to moral considerations as alleged but, rather, to the fact that they had sold out to those who were "opposed to the admission of Maine." If something were not done to pressure them into line, it was Holmes' opinion that "we are gone." As events developed, the five votes represented by the Maine restrictionists were not needed even though they remained against the compromise to the end.

King, by now an ardent supporter of the compromise, attempted to persuade the five dissidents that the people of Maine would not tolerate their voting in opposition to the compromise. He reminded them that:

> The best informed people in Boston, as well as all the people of this section of the state of all parties with whom we have conversed are agreed in the opinion that a compromise on those principles would be highly proper, and more interesting to the north than anything which the most sanguine had ever contemplated. Considering the...interest which the people of our District have, we should consider ourselves wanting in attention to our Representatives should we withhold saying that such are the opinions entertained by the people of Maine at this time, that if they are kept out of the union in consequence of any of our Representatives opposing the compromise proposed by Thomas, the real interest of the District will be considered as abandoned to the pride of opinion on the part of such persons.

There can now be no doubt that the efforts of Holmes were instrumental in obtaining the Missouri Compromise. He was thoughout the debate in the House one of the more active exponents of compromise. His friend Henry Clay selected him to be a member of the conference committee that finally framed the compromise. In the debate on the House floor on the report of the conferees delivered by Holmes, it was he with Representative Lowndes who successfully convinced the members that the Senate had yielded as much as it would and that it was now up to the House to yield. Even Rufus King, the acknowledged leader of the restrictionists in the Senate, described Holmes as the "champion" of the compromise faction in the House. No less a person than Martin Van Buren remembered that Henry Clay, who is usually given the credit for arranging the final settlement, in a Senate debate with Daniel Webster in the early 1830's, said how "happy he was to find himself connected (again) with his friend from Maine with whom he had acted in the final adjustment of the Missouri Question." Holmes himself asked for and received no credit for his efforts. To him the entire proceedings had been a struggle with the result being in doubt until the last. He confided to William King that "an hour before or an hour after we should have lost the vote." Nor should the contribution of Mark Hill be overlooked. It was he who was instrumental in obtaining a conference of the two houses.

Four of the five dissenters from Maine, Cushman, Kinsley, Whitman, and Lincoln found it advisable to explain why they had not followed the lead of Holmes and Mark Hill. The address that they prepared, printed in the *Portland Gazette,* condemned the compromise as "insidious," a "scheme" to perpetuate the predominant power of the southern slavocracy well into the future. The people of Maine, they presumed, supported their decision to resist this effort.

The columns of the *Portland Gazette,* predictably, were filled with torrents of abuse aimed at both Holmes and Hill. They were charged with having "leagued themselves with southern slave drivers." Holmes was described by one correspondent as a "Demagogue and Parasite." The editor of the *Gazette* was less vitrolic; he was content to "let the result...be upon the heads of those, by whose means it has been procured."

For both Hill and Holmes, the severity and extent of the criticism heaped on them was alarming. Holmes, at least, seemed to believe that even his supporters might abandon him to the wolves. Perhaps he had heard that Samuel Ayer had recommended doing just that now that independence was finally secured. "I have no doubt that the republicans will defend us for getting Maine admitted," he wrote King in a tone that suggested he feared the worst.

Ashur Ware, who, more than anyone, had been responsible for putting the *Argus* behind a compromise, took note of the statements that Ayer and others were making and decided that a letter to King was in order: "We know how important their votes were to us. Ought we to suffer them to be sacrificed?"

The answer was soon forthcoming from William Pitt Preble. Preble, still a member of the inner council of the *Argus* staff, assured Holmes that the paper would commence "a regular *defense* of yourself and Mr. Hill...." King, likewise, informed Holmes that neither he nor Hill had anything to fear from the "howlings" of the opposition; their friends would protect them. As for the five representatives "who have done so much to embarrass and so little to aid us," Preble wrote King, "may they not be forgotten."

Holmes viewed the attacks directed at him as motivated not by the moral revulsion of men who could accept no compromise with an evil institution, but by the political ambitions of old line Federalists like Rufus King and the Clintonian wing of the Democratic-Republican Party of New York who, he contended, were attempting to use the slavery question to form an anti-slave state coalition from which a new political party would emerge along sectional lines. He was confident, however, that the passage of the compromise had foiled the plan on the national level for the time being, but on the state level he was not so sure. "I have strong reasons to believe," he wrote William King, "that the restrictionists of our delegation will either get up a newspaper or throw themselves into the arms of the federalists. Their object will be two fold—one to create a party against the *State administration* and the other to be looking towards a *northern combination* against the Presidential election after next (1824)."

There were others who agreed with Holmes' analysis of the situation. Lewis Williams from Washington, D.C. was one of these. He wrote William King in January that "The Missouri question I have no doubt will be conjured up into a kind of political hobby horse. I have been very much surprised that in some parts of the country it should be understood as a question of slavery. In fact the question of slavery has no imaginable connection with the Missouri Question."

William King, not one to be victimized by such schemes if he could help it, immediately upon learning of the alledged plan informed Holmes that the gentlemen who were making such plans would be disappointed in regard to their prospects for success in Maine for he was directing "all Republican Papers" to give all their efforts toward destroying their hopes in Maine.

Whether the slavery issue was the cause of the great debate or was simply instrumental to the larger goal of creating a Northern sectional party through which frustrated Federalists and disenchanted Democratic-Republicans could achieve their goals, depends on whom one believes. For some the first consideration was doubtless most important, for others, the second took precedence, and for still some others a combination of both influences worked to produce opposition to the compromise.

Despite the support given Holmes and Hill in the party press and by the leading party figures both men thought it advisable to issue public statements in their own defense in answer to the statement circulated by Cushman, Kinsley, Lincoln, and Whitman. This they did and both statements were circulated throughout the country.

In his remarks entitled "Fellow Citizens of the State of Maine" Hill explained that when he first considered the Missouri question, he was inclined to support restriction because of his contempt for chattel slavery, but that he was persuaded to change his mind. Claiming that he was "instrumental" in getting up the committee of conference that produced the compromise, he presented his reasons for doing so. The Louisiana Territory he asserted, was purchased out of a common fund;

Southerners, therefore, had a right to move to the area with their property. There were no constitutional means by which the rights of property could be abridged in a state. Missouri was created a first stage territory in 1805 and a second stage territory in 1812 without restrictions being placed by Congress on slavery; therefore, it was not wise, even if it were constitutionally possible, which it was not, to deprive Missourians of their property at the third stage. Critics of the compromise, said Hill, were not only unfair but unrealistic. Slavery now was forbidden north of 36° 30′ in the Louisiana Territory; if the stalemate had not been broken, Southerners would have taken slaves into this area in which event the institution would not have become even partially restricted. Furthermore, Maine would not have entered the Union. But Maine aside, "my vote would have been the same" for to deprive Missourians of slaves would have required force "which would have produced civil war; and probably disunion." For Hill, and there is no reason to question his sincerity here, the higher value was the preservation of the Union. Throughout the debates he had been haunted by the specter of a civil war; in the final analysis it was this fear that took precedence over his distaste for slavery. It is interesting to speculate on the position he would have taken had he been living in 1860. The choice then was inescapable: disunion or civil war—or capitulation to southern demands for no restrictions on slavery.

Hill sent a copy of his address to James Madison from who he hoped to receive commendation for his conduct. He was not disappointed. Madison who, with Holmes, suspected that the object of the restrictionists was in fact not the improvement of the condition of the slaves but "to form a new state of parties founded on local instead of political distinctions...." replied that in his opinion:

> The candid view you have given of the Missouri question is well calculated to assuage the party zeal which it generated. As long as the conciliatory spirit which produced the Constitution remains in the mass of people, and the several parts of the Union understand the deep interest, which every other part has in maintaining it, these stormy subjects will soon blow over; and the people, on the return of calm, be more disposed to consider wherein, their interests agree, than wherein their opinions differ.

In his remarks entitled "Mr. Holmes' letter to the people of Maine," Holmes took a more defensive and at the same time a more aggressive stance than Hill. "Apologies or justifications are extraordinary efforts and calculated to excite suspicion" he explained, while assuring the readers that it was not because he doubted the correctness of his actions that he prepared his defense. He denied, as he had previously denied, that the opposition to his stand was motivated by moral considerations. Rather, it was his conviction that the entire controversy was manufactured by calculating politicians to enhance their own selfish ends. It was not until an anti-slavery circular issued by a meeting of New York abolitionists in November, 1819, was circulated in Maine, claimed Holmes, that restriction became an issue in the District. In 1819, before the Maine bill was introduced, he voted against restriction in Missouri and "never received a letter in protest."

Holmes presented most of the same objections to restriction contained in Hill's letter, adding that by allowing slaves to be dispersed rather than confining them to existing areas avoided the evil of huge aggregates of slaves building up. Such aggregates, he contended, meant that control over slaves passed from benevolent owners who no longer could manage such large numbers to overseers who were notoriously cruel. The compromise, in short, would act as a kind of "anti-trust" solution to the evils of excessive concentration.

For Holmes as for Hill the legalistic arguments against restriction were unimportant compared to the threat to the union that the controversy presented. He assured his readers that he had incontestable evidence that the Senate would not have yielded, and that the practical politician was really faced with a choice between evils; the question was not was slavery an evil? "Slavery is a most dangerous evil," but to remove the evil without inflicting the greater evil of disunion was found to be impossible. Consequently, the compromise whose passage owed so much to Holmes' efforts, was, he believed, the most that could have been achieved given the existing political realities, and, added Holmes, was it not a prime example of how democracy resolves conflicts between contesting interests in a relatively peaceful manner: something for everyone, everything for no one? Holmes continued:

> Those who apprehended that slavery would be extended over the *immeasurable west*, will derive consolation that it is from thence excluded, and that settlements will be commenced and

continued, by a people who will never often consent to establish it. Those who claim the territory as a common property for a common retreat, will be satisfied with the reflection that though their portion is small, it is populous and valuable, and that they are excluded from a latitude where slaves could never be profitably employed. Those who saw, in this contest, an approaching storm with devastation and ruin in its wake, may rejoice 'with joy unspeakable' that its fury is assuaged, its clouds are scattering, and the sun of harmony is rising 'with healing in his wings and majesty in his beams.'

Holmes, like Hill, sought approbation for his stand. Accordingly, he forwarded copies of his statement to a number of leading men including Thomas Jefferson who replied with a now famous letter that contained the often quoted "fire bell in the night" phrase and revealed that even Jefferson preferred Union to all else. It also reveals Jefferson as an anguished prophet:

> I thank you, dear sir, for the copy you have been so kind as to send me of the letter to your constituents on the Missouri question. It is a perfect justification to them. I had for a long time ceased to read newspapers, or pay any attention to public affairs, confident they were in good hands, and content to be a passenger in our bark to the shore from which I am not far distant. But this momentous question, like a fire-bell in the night, awakened and filled me with terror. I considered it at once as the knell of the Union. It is hushed indeed for the moment, but this is a reprieve only, not a final sentence. A geographical line, coinciding with a marked principle, moral and political, once conceived and held up to the angry passions of men, will never be obliterated, and every new irritation will mark it deeper and deeper. I can say with conscientious truth, that there is not a man on earth, who would sacrifice more than I would, to relieve us from this heavy reproach in any *practicable* way. The cession of that kind of property, for so it is misnamed, is a bagatelle which would not cost me a second thought, if, in that way, a general emancipation and *expatriation* would be effected; and gradually and with due sacrifices, I think it might be. But, as it is, we have the wolf by the ear, and we can neither hold him, nor safely let him go. Justice is in one scale, and self-preservation in the other. Of one thing I am certain, that as the passage of slaves from one state to another would not make a slave of a single human being who would be so without it, so their diffusion over a greater surface would make them individually happier, and proportionally facilitate the accomplishment of their emancipation by dividing the burden on a greater number of coajutors. An abstinence too from this act of power would remove the jealousy excited by the undertaking of Congress, to regulate the condition of the different descriptions of men composing a state. This certainly is the exclusive right of every state, which nothing in the constitution has taken from them and given to the general government. Could Congress, for example, say that the non-freeman of Connecticut shall be freemen, or that they shall not emigrate into any other state? I regret that I am now to die in the belief that the useless sacrifice of themselves by the generation of '76, to acquire self-government and happiness to their country, is to be thrown away by the universal and unworthy passions of their sons, and that my only consolation is to be, that I live not to weep over it. If they would but dispassionately weigh the blessings they would throw away, against an abstract principle, more likely to be effected by union than by secession, they would pause before they would perpertrate this act of suicide on themselves, and of treason against the hopes of the worlds.
>
> To yourself, as the faithful advocate of union, I tender the offering of my high esteem and respect.
>
> Thomas Jefferson

But, for all the excitement created by the votes of Maine's seven Congressmen, the people of Maine appeared unmoved by it all. They sent Hill back to Washington for another term in 1820. Holmes was elected by the Maine legislature in 1820 as one of Maine's two senators (John Chandler was the other one). Yet, they also returned to Congress three of the four restrictionists, Cushman, Whitman, and Lincoln. No one, it seems, was punished for his participation in the great controversy.

The reason for this ambivalent attitude on the part of the people of Maine is not easy to identify. Perhaps, it was the result of a monumental indifference to public questions as Barnabas Palmer of Kennebunk contended in a letter to Holmes. Or, perhaps the explanation is more complex. It is entirely possible that many Maine people who professed to be morally offended at the thought of extending an evil institution further westward were, nevertheless, relieved that the passage of the compromise would not endanger the complementary economic relationship between Maine shippers and southern exporters of cotton and other commodities, a relationship that began about 1800, when William King became the first Maine shipper to enter the New Orleans-Liverpool cotton trade, and continued down to the Civil War. By rewarding both those who voted for and against the compromise, one could, so to speak, have his cake and eat it too.

On the fifteenth of March 1820, Maine became the twenty-third state in the Union. William King, by virtue of being president of the Constitutional Convention, was declared acting Governor until elections could be held in April. His election was certain, however, for not only was he unopposed but at a meeting held the previous January 6, in Portland attended by many delegates at the convention, Preble had called for his nomination. It was given him by a vote of 151 to 1.

PART
⌐ II ⌐

MAINE IN THE NINETEENTH CENTURY

In 1820 the Secretary of Treasury, William H. Crawford, wrote Maine's Governor, William King, that the federal government had spent $70,000 more in Maine than it collected during the previous fiscal year. This fact was due in part to a nationwide depression but also it was due to the fact that Maine was still thirty years away from her period of greatest prosperity. About the only asset of any significance which the state possessed in 1820 was land. Massachusetts retained control of 8 million acres; Maine held an equal number. The story of how she disposed of this domain and acquired the residue of the Massachusetts' lands is told in "Maine and Its Public Domain:—Land Disposal on the Northeastern Frontier,"(20).

Land also precipitated a minor international crisis involving Maine in the 1830's. Since 1783 the precise boundary line separating Maine from New Brunswick had been in dispute between England and the United States. In the 1830's, after arbitration had failed to settle the question, tension mounted in what is now Aroostook County as lumbermen from both Canada and Maine worked in the area which each claimed to belong to their country. The immediate cause of the Aroostook War was the arrest of an American surveyor by the New Brunswick authorities. Finally, the federal government became involved sending General Winfield Scott and Captain Anderson (of future fame as commander of Ft. Sumter) to quiet matters "Down East," (21).

The so-called middle period of American history (1830-1860) was noted for the ferment produced by many reform movements. Temperance, antislavery, women's rights, and peace were only a few of the causes to which many Americans became devoted. Maine had the distinction of giving to a number of these movements their leaders. For the first time in her history, Maine people made contributions to matters of national significance.

William Ladd of Minot, Maine, established an international reputation as an advocate of peace. It was he who founded the American Peace Society in 1828.

Dorothea Dix was born in Hampden, Maine. She moved to Massachusetts where she became the most important individual in the United States in the crusade to humanize the treatment of the insane and mentally handicapped.

The Temperance movement was launched in Maine in the year 1812 with the founding of the Cumberland Society for the Suppression of Vice and Immorality. By the late 1820's a number of such societies had been founded in towns in Maine. The Bath, Maine society was established in 1829 and for the next few years it experienced only partial success, (22).

One of the founders of the Cumberland Society for the Suppression of Vice and Immorality was the father of Neal Dow of Portland. A Quaker, Neal Dow became, as his biographer asserts, "the Napoleon of Temperance." Dow did not ride a white horse or a "pink elephant" but he did become the nation's leading prohibitionist. In 1851, he achieved his greatest triumph as Maine became the first state in the United States to become committed to prohibition. John Stuart Mill, the English liberal, thought the Maine Law an unwarranted infringement of individual liberty, but though many Americans were good Millians their liberalism did not extend to the use of alcohol. By 1920, when prohibition became a national policy, a majority of states, inspired by Dow's conquest in Maine, had prohibition statutes on their books, (23).

Maine had no nationally recognized leaders in the most important reform movement of all, but she did contain many anti-slavery advocates. One of the most important leaders was Samuel Fessenden, the father of William Pitt Fessenden. Actually, the movement in Maine paralleled that in the nation as a whole as the article "Anti-Slavery: Maine and the Nation" makes abundantly clear, (24).

Between 1830 and 1860 Maine experienced what was probably her period of greatest economic growth. If the Maine economy ever boomed, it did so at this time. For once the resources of Maine were economically relevant to national and international needs. The chief resource, as always, was lumber. Beginning in the 1830's, the demand for Maine lumber products seemed insatiable. A number of ports in Maine became lumbering centers but none compared to Bangor. If that city was not the lumber capitol of the world, then it was close to it. Stewart Holbrook captures the frontier spirit of this boom town in "The Flowing of a Lumber Town," (25).

Until the advent of refrigeration, Maine ice produced considerable wealth for those who lived along Maine rivers. A number of fortunes included that of the Morse family of Bath were made in the harvesting of "Frozen Gold," (26).

In addition to lumber and ice, there was also great wealth produced in the granite and lime industries as well as from fishing and shipbuilding. Nor should one overlook the contribution of textiles. The first textile mill was established in Brunswick in 1809 but it was not successful. In 1828, there was erected the first factory ever established in Maine. The York Manufacturing Company built at Saco the largest factory in the United States at that time, seven stories high and over 400 feet long. All of these industries produced goods which had to be transported. Thus, the period saw unprecedented ship building activity as every Maine coast town entered into the competition. The culmination of their frenetic building activity came in the 1850's with the appearance of the famous State of Maine clipper ships, some of which established speed records not surpassed until the 20th century, (27).

Today, one would hardly believe that during the boom period of the 1830's to 1850's Portland rivaled Boston for the distinction of becoming the economic capitol of New England. She did, nevertheless, and almost succeeded, (28).

The history of the construction and growth of Maine's railroads is as interesting and sordid as the history of railroads in other states. Even so, the story is a fascinating one from the time the very first road was chartered by the Maine Legislature in the year 1832, (29).

After the Civil War the national economy of the country, a product of great technical innovations, placed Maine's previous industrial and commercial gains in jeopardy. Steel ships put wooden vessels out of business. Refrigeration raised havoc with the ice industry. The introduction of concrete and the opening of stone quarries in other parts of the country put a damper on the Maine quarries. In addition, the introduction of structural steel, concrete, and other more modern building materials cut heavily into the market for Maine lumber. Even more disconcerting was the competition of the "New South" in textiles. Between 1880 and 1950, Maine's once great textile industry was gutted by the exodus of firms to the South. Finally, the post Civil War period witnessed the decline of Maine's once thriving fishing fleet and merchant marine.

Maine never has adjusted to the near collapse of her commercial and industrial economy after the Civil War. About the only new industry which developed to take up any of the slack was the pulp and paper industry. Again, capitalizing upon Maine's chief resource, the forest, the paper industry developed rapidly after 1880. By 1912, more capital was invested in the various paper mills in Maine than in all other manufacturing establishments, (30).

The history of Maine agriculture, as in New England generally, has been one of continuous frustration. Beginning as early as 1816 the West became a lure to New England farmers. The Maine Agricultural Society was begun in 1818 by leading Maine figures to reverse the out-migration of farmers but through the years the rocky Maine soil proved too much for even the most expert salesmen. Southern Maine has enjoyed some success in growing apples and blue berries. There has also been a thriving truck farming industry in the Portland area for many years. And there has been the poultry industry which has seen sporadic periods of prosperity. Above all, however, the potato has been historically Maine's chief agricultural cash crop though in recent years there has often been more crop than cash. The story of Maine's "Humble" potato makes for interesting reading, (31).

Few realize that the sugar beet industry which was brought to Maine in 1966 in an effort to diversify Maine's agricultural economy has a long history. As early as 1838 and again in the late 1870's and early 1880's efforts were made to develop a sugar beet industry in Maine. Whether success has finally accompanied virtue remains very much to be seen, (32, 33, 34).

Very little has been written on Maine labor. In fact, judged by the paucity of material in this area, one might conclude that labor has made no contribution to Maine's economy. Obviously, this is unfair and bespeaks more about those who have written on Maine subjects in the past than it does about labor. In the 1880's, Maine workers responded to problems created for them by industrialism by organizing into unions. The first important union in Maine was the Knights of Labor which by 1886 claimed 30,000 members in the state. After 1886 the Knights declined across the nation unable to cope with the challenge of the less radical A.F. of L., (35).

Beginning in the 1880's a number of Maine's seacoast towns became the summer preserves of wealthy families from the cities along the east coast, especially New York, Boston, and Philadelphia. Bar Harbor soon took its place alongside Newport and Saratoga Springs as a "cottage" town for the elite and near elite of the "Gilded Age," (36).

"History is made by people" a not so profound person once said. Never before or since have more Maine figures achieved positions of national significance than in the forty years between 1860 and 1900. The Civil War generation saw several such figures. Hannibal Hamlin was Vice-President from 1861 to 1865. William Pitt Fessenden was one of Lincoln's secretaries of the Treasury. Oliver Otis Howard was a distinguished Union general as was Joshua Chamberlain. And there were many more. One view of the contribution of Maine to the Civil War effort of the North is described in 37.

Finally, it is well known that Maine has long been a favorite of artists, especially painters. The cultural history of Maine has been an uneven one due mainly to the lack of financial support for the arts. Many poets have come from Maine, e.g., Henry Wadsworth Longfellow, Edward Arlington Robinson, and Edna St. Vincent Millay. And she has had her novelists such as Ben Ames Williams and Kenneth Roberts. But in reality, it is fallacious to speak of Maine writers or Maine artists for the truly creative mind belongs to his country and perhaps the world. Maine may contribute to the inspiration of a work of art but it is the merest kind of parochialism to claim any more, (38).

CHAPTER 20.

From 1820 to 1870 Maine relied on its public lands as an important source of income. The following article recounts the history of the disposal by the State of its vast holdings.

MAINE AND ITS PUBLIC DOMAIN—
LAND DISPOSAL ON THE NORTHEASTERN FRONTIER*
by
David C. Smith

Nearly all historians of land policy have directed their attention toward the federal public domain and its alienation. A complete story of the transfer of public lands into private hands would not be confined to this limitation, however. It would have to take into consideration the land holdings of the original thirteen states, as well as the lands under the control of Tennessee, Vermont, and Texas, all of which had lands not technically part of the federal domain.

Lands held by the original thirteen states passed, by and large, quite quickly into private ownership. Indeed, the disposition of the land is part of the colonial history of these states. Only one of the original thirteen states had land to dispose of during the greater part of the nineteenth century, and thus was in more or less direct competition with the federal government's land disposal plans. That state was Massachusetts. The disposal of the Massachusetts public domain, however, is really a story of the Maine public domain, since Maine split off from Massachusetts in 1819 and 1820.

The disposition of these lands offers an opportunity to study the movement of land into private hands at a time when lands were a drug on the market. Maine, faced with internal pressure and competition from outside, was forced to resort to many different methods to attract settlers to its lands.

Among the methods utilized by this northern state were the adoption of a type of homestead law, the granting of lands to academies and other institutions of learning, attraction of European immigrants by grants and gifts of land, and even the granting of a large tract of land to railroad promoters. All these efforts were undertaken in direct competition with the federal government, and although they served to transfer the land in question from public ownership to private, they did relatively little to fatten the treasury of the state, or to attract much population.

The failure was not entirely due to the competition. Location in northern latitudes, thinness of the soil, the lumbering economy, and the attraction of industrial developments elsewhere after 1860 all contributed to the failure of Maine's policy. It is the policy itself, and not so much the failure, which directly concerns us here.

Some of the area presently enclosed in the boundaries of the State of Maine was granted to prospective speculators and settlers before the Revolution. A line drawn due west from Portland would include to the south most of this land. After 1783 the ungranted land beckoned the citizens of Massachusetts as a solution to the monetary problems created by the war. A land office was set up, and sales of the northern lands commenced. They moved slowly, and in 1786 a lottery was started to raise money by disposing of some fifty townships between the Penobscot River and Passamaquoddy Bay area. The lottery was only partially successfull, as only 165,280 acres was disposed of by this method.

---

*David M. Ellis, et al, *The Frontier in American Development*, (Ithica: Cornell University Press, 1969), pp. 113-137. Reprinted by permission of the Publisher.

With the lottery promotion interest in the Maine woodlands did begin to rise, an interest which was increased first by the advertising efforts of General Henry Knox who owned land from one of the original grants, and later by the purchase of 2,000,000 acres—half on the Kennebec river and half on the Penobscot river—by William Bingham of Philadelphia. This interest caused many institutions, putative banks, canals, roads, and bridges, to apply for lands to be sold to defray the cost of construction, to provide them with working capital, or to set up an endowment fund for their continuance. By 1820 Massachusetts had disposed of 6,070,638 acres, which added to the land disposed of before 1783, 3,785,488 acres, for a total of 9,856,126 acres, meant that when Maine took control of its destiny about half the land area of the state had already gone into private hands.

When Maine became a state much of the land was not yet surveyed. Indeed, according to Greenleaf's map most of the area north of a line drawn from Magalloway to Vanceboro was unknown. Initially, Massachusetts offered the remaining land to Maine at a price which would have worked out to about .023¢ per acre, or $188,922 for the 8,000,000 or so acres. Maine refused the purchase, and so until 1853, when the then remaining lands were purchased by Maine, a dual land policy was pursued, one in which the land agents of both states had to participate. The 1820 independence agreement had provided for separation of the lands. Initially in the first five ranges (the so-called settling lands) the states took every other township. As the rest of the land was surveyed the agents divided the land in a similar fashion. Much of the correspondence between the agents of the two states was concerned with which lands to survey, the division of the lands, and the cost of maintenance, road building, prosecution of trespassers, and other such day to day work of the land office.

Trespass was the big problem. Over and over again the Maine land agent, who seemed at first to take the lead in the land business, wrote to his Massachusetts counterpart. Trips were taken to Moosehead Lake, to the St. John river, and up the Kennebec, both for surveying purposes, and for obtaining evidence of trespass. Oftentimes the exploration trips had both ends in view. In 1831, for instance, men were sent to Moosehead, across the portage to the Penobscot, and to Chesuncook Lake, thence to Umbazooksus Lake to the Allegash portage, and down the Allegash to the St. John. They were instructed to find out what settlements had been made, and by whose authority; what improvements were being contemplated, and on whose lands they were located. In addition the instructions went on:

> You will observe the lakes, ponds, rivers, and streams of water, the falls and millsites on them, and their capacity for navigation and floating logs and timber ...

The surveyors were instructed to observe the geology of the area, the soil, the production of the soil, and "especially the pine and other valuable timber."

Roads were built into the wilderness to ease the difficulty of access for prospective settlers. The land agent attempted to get private individuals to invest in improving the Penobscot for log driving. Border difficulties with the British were always part of the land agent's life. In addition to all these factors the agent was concerned with selling the land as he was directed, and obtaining the proper amounts of stumpage payments on the state owned lands. The bulk of his correspondence concerned these twin problems.

Prior to 1824 little activity took place. In 1823 a legislative resolve had called for sale of the land to actual settlers in 500 acre lots. The next year an act was passed which set up a policy to be followed with respect to the state lands. The land surveyed was to be designated in 100 acre lots, with the first forty contracts to go at 30¢ an acre, payable half in cash, and half in road labor. The settlers were to clear fifteen acres, plant ten in grass, and construct a house within the first four years. The rest of the land on each township was to go for 60¢ an acre, and additional purchases were allowed up to 500 acres, with the provision that for all purchases over 300 acres the buyer was responsible for settling two extra persons.

This first category was denominated as "settling lands." They were located in the first five ranges of townships west from the east line of the state north of the earlier purchases and grants. A second category was designated as timber lands, and were located generally on ungranted land, and mostly west of the settling lands. They were available only in 500 acre lots, with half payment due in cash, and the remainder in three equal installments. In addition the law provided that two hundred acres and a mill site would go to the person building the first saw and grist mill within three years time of the opening of a township for settlement. The law also provided for the setting aside of 1,000 acres in each township for public reserved lots to be used for educational purposes. It also provided for the protection of squatter's rights on the public lands. With this law a land policy was laid down, and land agents proceeded with their work under terms of the law.

This basic law was modified fairly often, but not in a wholesale fashion. In 1825 the prices were increased, and the land agent was instructed to dispose of meadow, hay, and waste land in mile square lots, at either public auction or private sale; he was also allowed to sell timber "where it was decaying." In 1826 payment was allowed in three annual equal amounts, with a third due down in cash. The state retained a lien on the land. In 1828 the law was overhauled, and the duties of the land agent were more closely defined. This law provided that no more than eight townships a year could be sold from the timber lands. The agent was to set an upset, or minimum price, hold a public auction, and sales were limited to one township per person per year. The settling lands could also go at public auction to stimulate sales, payment to be made in eight years, with the principal due in quarterly annual payments the last four years. In 1831 the minimum price was established at fifty cents an acre, with four years credit allowable. Stumpage permits could be granted for three years, but under strict regulation.

In 1835 the law was again modified. Townships were to be sold only after survey and lotting. The maps, plans, and field notes were to be open for all to inspect. Settling lands were to go to actual settlers only, at a minimum price of 50¢ an acre. These lands, however, could be commuted by road labor, so that they became a homestead grant, in fact. This introduction of the homestead principal, that is, that *bona fide* settlers should be virtually given lands in order to attract them to the state, marks a victory for those who felt agriculture would be the salvation of Maine. Little opposition was expressed to the new law probably because the large lumber operators and speculators were purchasing their lands west of the settling townships.

The other sale provisions of the 1824 law were restated. Other lands were to go at public auction, but if unsold the price could be lowered at the discretion of the land agent. Payments were to be made with one fourth in cash, and the rest in annual payments. No more than five townships a year were to be disposed of in this way. The settling lands were to be advertised in Boston, Concord, and all Maine newspapers. In 1838 the mill provision was reinstated.

In later years, as Maine lumbermen began to exert pressure to keep the state timber from the market in order to preserve higher prices, new laws usually applied only to sales of timber or stumpage.

In 1850 the duties of the land agent and regulations surrounding settling lands were rewritten. The most important provisions stated that the prospective entryman must be an American citizen, that 200 acres was the total to be granted, and that it was to be paid for in road labor, not cash, at the rate of fifty cents an acre, one third due each year. The older provisions for the construction of houses and the clearing of fields were continued. In 1853 Maine purchased the remaining lands from Massachusetts, and after this time little change took place in the basic policy. One change did come in 1853 when the state limited the sale of timberlands to ten townships annually, sealed bids to be proffered with a tender of 10% of the original purchase price. The terms were one third down and the remainder in three annual payments. Stumpage was due at the state's figures during the time the land was in the process of conveyance. Private sale was possible, however, at the discretion of the land agent.

How much land went into private hands from each category is difficult to say. Some of the records of the land office were lost in a fire in 1835, and before that time reports are sketchy. Also, before 1838 little distinction was made in reporting between settling lands and timber lands. The following tables give some idea of the sales and other business in the period 1824-1853.

Study of the tables reveals that Maine had fallen into the same trap as the federal government. Although it sought to sell its lands, or grant them, to actual settlers, and small holders, the bulk of the lands went into the hands of the great lumbermen

DISPOSITION OF SETTLING LANDS IN MAINE 1838-1855

Year	Acreage	Value Received
1838	12,825	$ 9,428.27
1839	6,642	4,903.88
1840	15,869	12,259.83
1841	24,183	16,251.12
1842	1,530	1,019.48
1843		4,157.51
1844		6,575.43
1845	Total Sales—	8,941.83
1846	1843-1852: in acres:	2,523.21
1847	58,152	1,734.22
1848		1,579.92
1849		767.65
1850		1,356.02
1851		2,141.81
1852		1,064.90
1853		
1854	5,050	1,431.00
1855	10,546	4,150.45
Totals	134,799	$79,691.89

LAND SALES IN MAINE 1825-1852

YEAR	AMOUNT	AVERAGE PRICE
1825	1,448	.84
1826	36,711	.50
1827	12,902	.40
1828	101,909	.22
1829	263,676	.31
1830	129,483	.21
1831	162,282	.28
1832	21,621	.68
1833	92,393	.66
1834	70,989	.42
1835	230,146	1.45
1836	2,630	.99
1837	3,274	1.66
1838	12,837	.74
1839	33,558	1.48
1840	18,050	.88
1841	17,868	.43
1842	1,661	.28
1843	147,657	.45
1844	48,459	.60
1845	47,310	.86
1846	105,625	.77
1847	101,220	.46
1848	145,708	.495
1849	342,913	.31
1850	39,823	.47
1851	310,802	.50
1852	297,413	--------

TOTAL SALES 1825-1852—2,800,029 acres

and speculators. Maine attempted to control this by limiting the acreage available in any year, but the incongruity of a land policy which promoted speculation and advanced the interests of the wealthy effectively limited the population growth to the areas specifically named as settling towns.

The state did go beyond its homestead policy however. Immigration on to its lands were aided by the expenditure of just under $170,000 for road building from 1825 to 1849. Many thought these roads would solve the problem of immigration. As one observer noted in 1837 when commenting on the completion of the proposed Canada road survey (a road still not built, incidentally.):

> The ease and novelty of the route, together with the romantic scenery of the lake [Moosehead], would make this a favorite tour for parties of pleasure and draw a large amount of travel through the state. This, however, is but of secondary consideration. Villages would spring up at each end of the lake, serving a *neuclii* [sic] around which in every direction, new settlements would cluster. Hamlets would soon be scattered along the Penobscot to the borders of Canada and the fertile shores of the Chesuncook would be covered with cultivated farms.

This comment was made just after the wild speculation of 1834 and 1835, a boom concerned primarily with privately owned land, and one which did not much affect public domain sales, but which, when it failed, did create a depression in both timber and land in the state. In fact, it was not until 1843 that the Land Agent could comment that settlement was prospering, although he was still complaining of squatting and trespass.

In his correspondence he was less sanguine. The land was good; he wanted to accommodate everyone; actual settlers would get preference; but, alas, his efforts met with "ill success." For those who would bring settlers, special help would be given. Even trespass was to be dealt with indulgently.

The officials of Maine and Massachusetts met several times to regularize their business, the most important occasion being in January of 1832. The land was all reclassified, but the agreement did not amount to much—settlement still lagged.

In 1842 it was estimated that 6,400,000 acres all together still remained unsold. Trespass remained a problem. From 1825 to 1843 each state expended about $12,500 to thwart these nuisances. Although some complained that land and stumpage were not available, and were, in fact, withheld for favored individuals, the evidence from the letter books is that both agents wanted to withhold the great amount of land from sale, and not sell stumpage either, as much timber was stolen, receipts were low, and logs were a drug on the market. Proprietors were given slightly better treatment, but the watchword was generally that, "I am very much afraid that so much land being sold, will cause a reaction, and bring another bursting up among the operators like 1846—which we should regret very much when too late to remedy...." Later the Massachusetts agent said, "Let us sell no more," at least until "the crooked times shall become straight." The Maine agent encouraged actual settlers and prospective small holders. For such individuals "... our State has adopted a very liberal policy ... which offers rare enducements to men of limited means...." In fact, he advertised that, "Good roads lead directly from here to there."

The pressures within Maine from Lumbermen and farmers grew throughout the first thirty years of the state's separate existence. It was felt that the Massachusetts control of some of Maine's land was detrimental to the state's future. Gradually these lobbies induced study of the possibility of purchase of the remaining equity from Massachusetts. In 1853 the purchase was completed. Few people knew the actual extent of the state holdings. In successive years official estimates differed by about 200,000 acres.

The following table gives some idea of the transactions in land from the time of the sale to the Civil War.

LAND CONVEYANCES—MAINE 1854-9

YEAR	HOMESTEAD LANDS*	TOTAL OF OTHER
1854	5,050 acres	
1855	10,456 acres	14,966
1856	10,394 acres	33,832
1857	23,337 acres	6,199
1858	34,279 acres	42,865
1859	46,350 acres	80,930
TOTALS	109,866 acres	178,792

*Extent of lands conveyed by payment with road labor.

During this time the land office continued its earlier policies. The agent answered questions from prospective settlers, dealt with the ever-present problem of trespass, sold his lands, and bargained with prospective purchasers over stumpage rates. Although Maine was apparently more strict in its dealing with prospective settlers than had been the case before, still the lands seemed to drift into the hands of the great land owners, that is, all except those which had been designated as settling lands.

The Civil War discouraged purchasers and land sales fell off except for a burst of activity in 1863. The following table indicates the amount of land transferred to private ownership from 1860 to the time of the great disposal to the European and North American Railway.

LAND CONVEYANCES—MAINE 1860-9

YEAR	AMOUNT	YEAR	AMOUNT
1860	39,712	1865	60,481
1861	9,967	1866	119,634
1862	21,857	1867	130,655
1863	145,336	1868	23,872
1864	55,930	1869	E. & N.A. Grant
TOTALS 607,438			

Much of the business now concerned stumpage sales on the public reserved lots (the 1,000 acres set aside for educational purposes), and on the unsold state lands. The state apparently did not care how the timber went as long as large amounts were cut, and the money promptly received. Trespass continued to be a problem, especially on lands not conveyed because of a lack of completion of the settling duties. The state lumber scalers were instructed to watch such timber thieves, as in the following letter:

> Attend to the lines enclosing the state lands in that vicinity, scale all ... timber, and be particular to see that no operations shall be made upon state lands except permitted as above. After getting the van(?) of all the teams and scaling up the lumber you will take a tour to Fort Kent and post up the office about operations thereabouts *in* the state.

Inquiries concerning the possibility of settlement on the vacant state lands continued to come in, but few people followed as western land opportunities also beckoned. Some pointed out the possibility of making good homes in the north country, as did the following letter writer just after the war.

> I am eighteen years old, have a good set of teeth and believe in Andy Johnson, the star-spangled banner and the Fourth of July. I have taken up a state lot, cleared up eighteen acres of it last fall, and seeded ten of it down. My buckwheat looks first rate and the oats and potatoes are bully. I have got nine sheep, a two-year-old heifer and two bulls, besides a house and barn. I want to get married. I want to buy bread and butter, hoop skirts and waterfalls for some person of the female persuasion during life. That is what is the matter with me. But I don't know how to do it.

Despite such plaintive appeals people continued to go west, and the newspapers were driven to editorialize urging people to "Stay at Home!" and "Stick by the State." As this last writer said,

> Farmers! Be of good courage. Study and Practice the economy of your Fathers. Maine's blighted interests and industries shall bloom again. Her happy and prosperous homes of the past shall yet be prosperous and happy in the future.

Editorials were also written to attack the west as an area in which confidence men, sharpers, and others waited to gull the innocent eastern farmer. Some writers claimed that in Maine, as well as in the west, crops of great extent and value could be raised. One needed only to practice thrift and hard work. Still the people went, as the advertisements of the glories of the west far overshadowed the promise of the "Garden of the North."

The state still owned lands; what to do with them became a question for many officials to ponder. Two methods were finally chosen, one designed to attract settlers from Europe to Maine's vacant acres, the second to let someone else do the attracting by making them responsible for the land.

As early as 1850 Governor John Hubbard had observed that perhaps free gifts of land to actual settlers might solve some of the settlement problems, and in 1858 it was proposed to the legislature that German immigrants might aid the state. It was suggested that a township be set aside for such immigrants, who would be granted the land upon completion of settling duties. Nothing came of this idea until William Widgery Thomas, a Maine native who had served Lincoln at the 1860 convention and who had been awarded a minor post in Sweden, returned to the United States to complete his eduation. He proposed that his native state grant a township to prospective Swedish settlers, whom he promised to attract. The state appointed him immigration commissioner, set aside Township 14, Range #3 (present New Sweden), built houses on the surveyed lots, provided cookstoves and utensils, and sat back to await its new Swedish citizens. After the first year a second town was set aside in the same way, but it was soon found that most of the state's settling lands had already been alienated. Although later many were to advocate this solution to the state's problems of shrinking population and vacant acres, it was not to be.

During this period the state continued its policy of grants to educational institutions, 35,721 acres in 1862-3, for instance. All together, the state granted, along with Massachusetts, some 945,214 acres in this way, although as late as 1869 close to 60,000 acres set aside for this purpose were as yet unsold. In the previous five years, however, close to 190,000 acres of the total had either been granted or sold.

The state and its officials did not know how much land was left. It was thought that perhaps close to a million acres remained. The slowness of disposal, and the failure to attract many immigrants caused older attempts at obtaining a land grant for a railroad to connect Maine with the Maritime Provinces was revived. "The short route to Europe," as it was called, might provide an answer to the question of land disposal. If the railroad were granted the land, it would then take on the task of obtaining the settlers, and the headaches of land ownership could be passed to others.

Attempts at providing a land grant, or some other state support of the railroad, had first come during the fifties, but it was not until 1864 that a grant of ten townships was made. This grant was apparently too small since the railroad was not built, and in 1868 the grant was cancelled. Then the remainder of the state's public lands, some 734,942 acres, was conveyed to the embryo railroad. The new road, named the European and North American Railway, was charged with selling its lands to actual settlers under the terms of the state's law in regard to the settling lands. It was to encourage immigration by appointing an immigration agent and by advertising the lands for sale. The railroad attempted to enlarge its holdings by claiming lands set aside for other purposes. Trespass claims against the road and their agents, however, were upheld, and the lands remained in the hands of the state. The road, running from Bangor to Vanceboro, via Winn and Mattawamkeag, was built within a year. It connected with a sister road in New Brunswick extending from the border to Saint John, via Fredericton. A steamship line was supposed to provide the European connections.

The road did make some attempt at selling its lands, but of its total holdings, less than one third went into private hands before the road went bankrupt, and the remaining lands were eventually sold at auction to pay part of the debt. Purchases were made by the road's successor, the Maine Central Railroad, and prominent lumbermen, in most cases. Before the auction sales occurred the legislature made one or two attempts to force the road to live up to the terms of the grant, but none of these attempts amounted to much. The road was too much of a gamble—the depression of 1873, the cost of shifting to standard gauge, the attraction of western lands, and, one suspects, the opportunity to alienate these lands to large holders were just too much.

Few lands now remained. They consisted of the timber rights on ten townships of the railroad land grant which had been reserved for school fund purposes, and a few settling lands. There were altogether 65,684 acres of timber lands, 126,844 acres of settling lands contracted for but not *proved* up, 246,843 acres of settling lands unsold and uncontracted for, and school fund lands of 86,685 acres. Lands with no incumbrances amounted to 399,270 acres.

The timber lands were soon sold, and the settling lands were then declared by the state legislature to be "unfit for settlement," and the land agent was instructed to dispose of them. An auction was held in Bangor and some 140,000 acres changed hands, at an average price of just over $1.00 per acre. As usual the large land owners were the biggest purchasers. Instructions were issued to close down the state land office as being wasteful, but when this occurred it was discovered that lands were still held by the state. Sales were begun again and in 1875 a further auction was held. All the lands did not sell, and the land agent held a private sale in his office a month later. One last auction was held in 1878, which disposed of another 10,000 acres or so of scattered holdings. By this time the land agent could report, "that all the public lands of the state having been disposed of, no further favors are now within the power of the state to grant for homesteads to settlers."

The business of the land office was now confined to rectifying mistakes, selling stumpage, protecting and caring for the public lots, quieting Revolutionary War claims, and winding up the business of transferring land for those who proved up their settling claims. In 1890 the office of land agent was submerged into the newly created post of Forest Commissioner, and since that time the business of land agent has been undertaken in that office. Before going on to recapitulate the Maine land policy, the following table will indicate the amount of sales and transactions which took place after the great European and North American Railway grant.

LAND DISPOSAL—MAINE 1870-1881
(Not Auction Lands)

YEAR	AMOUNT (ACRES)	YEAR	AMOUNT (ACRES)
1870		1876	
1871	11,773	1877	
1872	1,334	1878	1,029
1873	47,527	1879	3,517
1874	79,239	1880	410
1875		1881	431
TOTALS 145,261			

Altogether Maine disposed of close to 7,200,000 acres of land, of which about one million and three-quarters were sold in conjunction with Massachusetts. For the total the state received an average of about 35 cents an acre, as nearly as can be estimated. In addition it received money from stumpage before the lands were sold. The building of the European and North American railroad, and the movement of population into the eastern half of Aroostook County (nearly its entire population today is descended from homesteaders on Maine lands), are also benefits which cannot be included in ordinary ledgers.

It has frequently been fashionable to characterize the nineteenth century land policy as the "great land steal." This remark is fairly standard among many observers. Looking back, however, it is difficult to see what else the state could have done, other than keep the lands for its own use, and few, if any, advocated this policy until after the fact of disposal. The state was in competition with the federal government, with other states, and with private concerns. It was trying to move lands which lay in an inhospitable climate, and which generally had poor and thin soil. The only wealth was its timber cover, and lumbermen were not settlers. In attempting to move its lands the state adopted a homestead policy of a sort nearly forty years before the federal government, sold its lands on credit terms, designated them for different types of prospective purchasers, attempted to attract settlers to its lands from abroad, and finally used the lands to aid the growth of a railroad into the wilderness area. If these policies were not entirely successful, it was not the fault of the State of Maine, and concern over its lands was to be of some importance in establishing the forestry and conservation movements which have done much to preserve the Maine woods—movements which are closely associated with the Land Office and Forest Commission in the years since 1890.

CHAPTER 21.

The "Northeast Boundary" controversy which occupied British and American diplomats for nearly fifty years produced friction between Maine and New Brunswick loggers in the 1830's as both "invaded" the area under dispute. In 1838, friction produced fire in Aroostook which for a while threatened to get out of control. Locally, the abortive conflict was known as the "Aroostook War."

THE AROOSTOOK WAR*
by
Henry Burrage

While boundary matters thus remained unsettled, the earlier exhortations for the exercise of forbearance on the part of the representatives of the two countries in the disputed territory became less and less forceful. With the increase of population, alike in Maine and New Brunswick, both parties were increasingly in evidence, and, as their interests were divergent, clashings naturally followed.

Mr. S. S. Whipple, who had received an appointment as surveyor general of the State of Maine, proceeded in the summer of 1838 to the valley of the Aroostook River with a party of assistants, and was employed in the duties of his office in territory that had long been regarded as clearly within the limits of the State of Maine. June 27, 1838, Mr. James MacLauchlan, a New Brunswick official bearing the title "Warden of the Disputed Territory," addressed a note to Mr. Whipple, informing him that his work appeared to be "in violation of the existing arrangement subsisting between the British government and that of the United States," adding that his instructions made it his duty "to protest against any act implying sovereignty or jurisdiction on the part of any government or state, or of the subjects of any government or state, exercised within the territory in dispute betwixt the two governments of Great Britain and the United States and known by the name of the 'Disputed Territory.'" He accordingly warned Mr. Whipple to desist from further proceedings until the right to that territory had been decided by negotiation on the part of the two governments.

In reply, Mr. Whipple informed Mr. MacLauchlan that he was acting, under the authority and by the command of the government of the State of Maine, as a surveyor; but as to the location of settlers in the territory he had no further agency than to note the claims of different persons to certain tracts of land, making a return of the same to the land office in Bangor. There the matter seems to have rested. Complaints, however, with reference to encroachments upon timber lands within what was regarded as Maine territory continued to reach the authorities of Maine and Massachusetts, and on December 14, 1838, the land agents of both states sent George W. Buckmore to the Aroostook and Fish rivers with instructions to obtain information as to the extent of these depredations and such other facts as might come under his observation in boundary concerns.

On Mr. Buckmore's return, Governor Fairfield, in a confidential message, January 23, 1839, communicated to the Legislature the information which the messenger had secured. A large number of men, he said, many of them from the British province as reported, were trespassing extensively upon the lands belonging to the state, and they not only refused to desist, but defied the state authorities to prevent them from cutting timber to any extent they wished. From forty to fifty men were

---
*Henry Burrage, *Maine in the Northeastern Boundary Controversy*, (Portland: Printed for the State, 1919), pp. 257-275.

at work on the Grand River, from twenty to thirty on the Green River, and on the Fish River from fifty to seventy-five. The latter had with them sixteen yoke of oxen, ten pair of horses, and more were expected daily. On township H ten men were at work with six oxen and two horses. Seventy-five men, twenty yoke of oxen and ten horses were found on the Little Madawaska River, and at Aroostook Falls fifteen men with six yoke of oxen. The value of the timber which would be cut that winter by these trespassers was estimated at one hundred thousand dollars.

"These facts, it seems to me," added the governor, "present a case in which not merely the property, but the character of the State, is clearly involved. The supremacy of law, as well as the sanctity of right, cannot be thus contemned and set at nought with impunity without impairing the general authority of the government and inviting renewed aggressions on the part of daring and lawless men. Conduct so outrageous and high-handed, as that exhibited by these reckless depredators upon the public property, calls for the most prompt and vigorous action of the government." The governor accordingly recommended that the land agent be instructed to proceed at once to the place of operation on the Aroostook and Fish rivers, with men suitably equipped to seize the teams and provisions, break up the camps, and disperse those who were engaged in the work of devastation and pillage.

The Legislature took action on the same day, directing the land agent to employ forthwith a sufficient force to arrest, detain and imprison all persons found trespassing on the territory of Maine, bounded and established by the treaty of 1783; and the sum of ten thousand dollars was appropriated for the purposes mentioned.

Under this action of the Legislature the land agent, Rufus McIntire of Parsonsfield, with Major Hastings Strickland of Bangor, sheriff of Penobscot County, and about two hundred men, proceeded early in February to the Aroostook country. A few days later they captured about twenty men who had been lumbering farther up the river, also James MacLauchlan (already mentioned as "Warden of the Disputed Territory") and Captain Tibbets, of the Tobique settlement, sending the last mentioned to Bangor. In the night of February 12th, at a house where Mr. McIntire was spending the night, about fifty of the trespassers arrested the land agent, also two citizens of Bangor, and sent them to Fredericton, where they were lodged in jail. Colonel Ebenezer Webster, of Orono, was in Woodstock, New Brunswick, on the arrival of Mr. McIntire and the other prisoners, and endeavored to secure their release. Not only was he unsuccessful, but his efforts led to his own arrest and he was sent to Fredericton with the other prisoners and committed to jail.

Information concerning the arrest of the land agent and other citizens of Bangor was promptly carried to that important and busy community on the Penobscot, and soon reached all other parts of Maine, causing great excitement and awakening feelings of deep indignation. Governor Fairfield, February 15th, in a special message, conveyed to the Legislature the information he had received from the border. The company that arrested the land agent, he said, was at No. 10 on the Aroostook, fortified, and anticipating an attack in case any attempt should be made by the Maine civil *posse* to execute the recent legislative action with reference to timber encroachments. He accordingly advised sending a reinforcement of three hundred men to the Aroostook country, and asked authority to appoint temporarily a land agent in place of Mr. McIntire "to lead on the expedition." The authority was granted, and Mr. Charles Jarvis received the appointment.

Three days later the governor hastened a second message to the Legislature with reference to border concerns. A proclamation issued by the lieutenant governor of New Brunswick February 13th, had come into his hand, stating that a party of armed persons, to the number of two hundred or more, had "invaded a portion of this province, under the jurisdiction of her Majesty's government, from the neighboring State of Maine, for the professed object of exercising authority, and driving off persons stated to be cutting timber therein." The governor recalled the circumstances connected with this movement of the land agent's *posse,* designated by the lieutenant governor as an "invasion" and "outrage," and asked, "Could a greater indignity be offered to any people having a particle of sensibility to its rights and its honor, or to the sacredness of the personal liberty of its citizens? . . . . . How long are we thus to be trampled upon—our rights and claims derided—our power contemned—and the State degraded?" What the governor had done, under these circumstances, was mentioned. He had hastened the departure of the reinforcements then assembled at Bangor awaiting orders; and he had issued an order to Major General Hodsdon, commanding the third division of militia, to detach one thousand men by draft or otherwise to rendezvous at Bangor properly officered and equipped, ready to proceed at the earliest possible moment to the place occupied by the land agent's party, there to render such aid as would enable the land agent to carry into effect the resolve of January 24th. The Legislature gave the governor prompt support by the following action:

"Resolved, That the honor and interest of this state demand that a sufficient military force be forthwith stationed at the Aroostook River west of the boundary line of the state as established by the treaty of 1783; and on the river St. John, if found practicable, at such points as may be best adapted to the object, to prevent further depredations on the public lands, and to protect and preserve the timber and other lumber already cut there by trespassers, and to prevent its removal without the limits of the State.

"Resolved, That the sum of eight hundred thousand dollars be and hereby is appropriated for the purpose of enabling the executive to carry out the purposes of the foregoing resolve, and the resolve passed [approved] January 24, 1839. And that the governor be and hereby is authorized, with the advice of the council, to draw his warrant for the same from time to time as it may be needed for that purpose."

In a postscript Governor Fairfield informed the Legislature that since writing his message he had received another communication from Lieutenant Governor Harvey, in which the latter called attention to an alleged agreement by which the British government was to have exclusive jurisdiction and possession of the disputed territory, and urged the withdrawal of the land agent's party, stating that he had directed a strong force of troops to be in readiness to support her Majesty's authority in the disputed territory. "No such agreement as that alluded to by the lieutenant governor can be recognized by us," said Governor Fairfield; "it is an entire misapprehension, to say the least, that such an agreement has ever been made."

The governor's message and his report of this added communication from the lieutenant governor of New Brunswick, together with the report of the action of the Maine Legislature, found their way at once into every part of the state. No declaration of war could have stirred more deeply the hearts of the people of Maine. The spirit of '76 was again abroad. The state was being despoiled of its valuable timber by the subjects of Great Britain, and those in the service of the state who had resisted such intrusion had been seized and hurried to imprisonment in a British jail. The humorous side of the Aroostook war, as a bloodless war, appeared later. Now, in the lines of a lyric of that time, the cry was,

"Bring out the big gun made of brass,
    Which forges July thunder;
Bring out the flag of Bennington,
    And strike the foe with wonder."

Thus summoned, men hurried toward the border. It was midwinter, and only wood roads through the forest for lumbering purposes led thither. First came the hardy lumbermen, leaving their axes and their logging camps and hurrying to the support of the land agent's party on the Aroostook. Following them came other volunteers from towns, hamlets and farms, men and boys, armed with such weapons as could at once be secured, some of them with muskets used by men from Maine on the battlefields of the Revolution and were with Washington at Valley Forge, or with Pepperrell in the capture of Louisburg in 1745. Later, came the one thousand drafted men called out by the governor's order of February 16th. On February 19th, Adjutant General Thompson declared an added draft of ten thousand three hundred and forty-three officers and men, including field and staff officers, and directing them to hold themselves, fully armed and equipped, ready for an immediate call into the service of the state. This louder call was answered by an uprising not unlike that witnessed in all parts of Maine a little more than a score of years later at the opening of the Civil War.

On the 21st of February, Governor Fairfield was able to inform the Legislature that reinforcements had already reached the provisional land agent's party on the Aroostook River, and that the draft of one thousand militia had also arrived at the designated place of rendezvous. Other military movements were in progress. The governor also stated that, having learned from Sir John Harvey that Mr. McIntire and his fellow prisoners had been released on parole, pending a reference of the case to the British government, he also had released Mr. MacLauchlan and his assistants on the same terms. On the following day the governor wrote to President Van Buren concerning the threatening conditions that had influenced the state government in calling out such large reinforcements, inclosing correspondence and a copy of his message to the Legislature, and the president on February 26th, in a message to Congress, referred to conditions on the northeastern boundary occasioned by extensive timber depredations undertaken by New Brunswick trespassers on the assumption that an agreement existed between the two adjoining nations conceding to Great Britain, until the final settlement of the boundary question, exclusive jurisdiction over the territory in dispute. This, he said, was an error. The voluminous correspondence on this point had been carefully examined, but instead of sustaining the British assumption it entirely disproved it. "The State of Maine had a right to arrest the depredations complained of."

But while insisting on the right of the State of Maine to arrest "the depredations complained of," the president in his message informed the Senate that he might find it proper to propose to her Britannic Majesty's government a temporary arrangement for the "mutual exercise of jurisdiction" by means of which border troubles would be avoided. In fact, among the papers transmitted to Congress by the president was a copy of a memorandum, dated February 27, 1839, signed by the secretary of state of the United States and the British minister in Washington, stating terms on which it was believed that boundary collisions could be avoided consistently with the claims of both countries, the agreement having the force of a recommendation only. By the terms of this agreement New Brunswick officials were not to seek to expel by military force the armed party of Maine in the Aroostook country, while the government of Maine, voluntarily and without delay, was to withdraw, beyond the bounds of the disputed territory, any armed force at that time there.

A motion having been made in the Senate that these papers, communicated by the president, should be referred to the committee on foreign relations, Mr. Williams, of Maine, expressed doubts with reference to Maine's acceptance of such an agreement. Any temporizing expedient in the matter, he said, would avail little. If, however, the agreement should give opportunity for new negotiations, Maine would not complain. The time had come when the United States must bring the controversy to an end by negotiation or otherwise.

Maine has her rights and knows them. While she desires not to disturb or put in hazard the peace of the country, she cannot much longer suffer an important part of her territory to be in doubt or abeyance. While Mr. Ruggles of Maine, following Mr. Williams, was addressing the Senate, he was informed that there had been an actual collision on the border; that a battle had been fought and blood spilled. There was "great sensation and silence in the Senate for some moments." Then Mr. Webster rose. "I do not believe," he said, "there has yet been collision; I hope there will be none. But I do not wish to see Maine humiliated or disgraced. I believe that if something of her own spirit and feeling had pervaded us here, we should have now been through the controversy. There is yet, I have no doubt, time for pacific adjustment; but England must learn that she has nothing to gain by delay. Delay, while it can benefit neither party, every day endangers the 'peace of both.'" Before the debate closed, Mr. Ruggles informed the Senate that the report of a collision was unfounded.

The correspondence and documents relating to conditions on the northeastern border were then referred by the Senate to the committee on foreign relations. This committee, on the following day, reported a series of resolutions concerning these boundary disturbances. After stating in the first and second of these resolutions that the committee could discover in the documents and correspondence submitted no trace of any understanding, express, or implied, much less any "explicit agreement" such as was alleged, or that the State of Maine had violated the spirit of any existing understanding by sending, under the authority of the Legislature, her land agent, with a sufficient force, into the disputed territory for the sole purpose of expelling lawless trespassers, the third resolution added: "That should her Britannic Majesty's government, in violation of the clear understanding between the parties, persist in carrying its avowed determination into execution, and attempt by military force to assume exclusive jurisdiction over the disputed territory, all of which, they firmly believe, rightfully belongs to the State of Maine, the exigency, in the opinion of the Senate, will then have occurred, rendering it the imperative duty of the president, under the constitution and the laws, to call forth the militia and employ the military force of the United States, for the purpose of repelling such an invasion." A fourth resolution, on the other hand, declared, that should the British authorities refrain from attempting a military occupation of the territory in dispute and from enforcing their claim to exclusive jurisdiction over it by arms, then, in the opinion of the Senate, the State of Maine ought, on her part, to pursue a course of similar forbearance. Should she refuse to do so, and determine to settle the controversy by force, authority for which under the constitution belonged to the federal government, there would be no obligation on that government to sustain her by military aid.

On the same day, in the House of Representatives, the committee on foreign relations presented an extended report, denying, against the assertion of the lieutenant governor of New Brunswick, that the United States had ever consented to leave the exclusive jurisdiction of the disputed territory to the British authorities. The pretension was as unreasonable in itself as it was unsustained by any agreement between the two governments. As to the threatening conditions in that territory, the first appeal to military force was made by New Brunswick, and the subsequent proceedings of Maine were defensive merely. The committee also submitted a bill giving to the president additional powers, authorizing him to resist any attempt on the part of Great Britain to enforce by arms her claim to exclusive jurisdiction over that part of the State of Maine in dispute between the two countries, and to employ, for that purpose, the naval and military forces of the United States and such portions of the militia as he might deem it advisable to call into service; and the sum of ten million dollars was placed at the disposal of the president for the purpose of carrying the bill into effect. The president was also authorized, in case of actual invasion, to accept the services of any number of volunteers not exceeding fifty thousand.

On March 2nd, when the House bill came up in the Senate for action, Mr. Buchanan, in the course of the debate (there having been some opposition to the proposed appropriation), said: "Should Maine act in accordance with the spirit of these resolutions, then if war must come, it will find the country unanimous. On the part of Great Britain, it will be a war of pure aggression, waged during the pendency of peaceful negotiations for the purpose of assuming exclusive military jurisdiction against the clear understanding between the two governments, over a territory to which she has not even a color of title. In such an event, the only alternative is war or national dishonor, and between these two what American hesitates? . . . . . All we have to do is to stand on the defensive, and exercise forbearance until the shock of arms shall render forbearance no longer a virtue." In the Senate, the House bill was passed unanimously; in the House there were 201 yeas and six nays. The attitude and the action of the State of Maine had again been vindicated.

When the House bill was under discussion, March 1st, Mr. Evans, who had addressed the House at considerable length on the day the president's message was received, now again participated in the debate, replying to Mr. Biddle, of Pennsylvania, who had declared his opposition to the bill, deprecating "the getting up of this comparatively immaterial issue, more particularly as it is by no means certain that we have on it a clear and indisputable case," and asking, "What, then, is our course? To run into a new game of diplomacy about 'exclusive jurisdiction'? To shed American blood in an obscure and senseless contest in the Aroostook?" In his reply, Mr. Evans defended the course of the State of Maine in the boundary controversy, and asked, "What will you do in the present exigency? Will you make no demonstration in behalf of our rights? What can you then expect but that the most arrogant demands of Great Britain will be renewed and insisted on? Will you do nothing? Will you leave Maine to herself? Such is the course already predicted by one of the British presses in the country. The United States, they say, will abandon Maine to the consequences of her own folly. We are now to see how that is. I have already told you that Maine is in arms, determined to maintain her rights. She is solemnly pledged on this subject. She cannot retreat. She will most certainly maintain herself in the position she has taken. Will you stand by, and see her cut down? Will any man say that is a result which this nation can witness without disgrace and dishonor? . . . . . The question for you is, whether she shall be left alone battling for her rights—whether you think that is the way to preserve the peace of the country? You may see her trod in the dust by military power which she cannot resist, if you will; you may see her cut off from the Union, and incorporated with the colonial possessions of a foreign power; but you shall not see her quailing before the enemy, nor abandoning the high ground she occupies, while she can lift an arm to uphold her flag.''

The secretary of state in Washington, in a letter to Governor Fairfield bearing the same date as the memorandum already mentioned, and inclosing a copy of the same, earnestly urged an acceptance of the recommendation it contained, stating that the president desired it should be complied with by both the State of Maine and the Province of New Brunswick, satisfied that it was in harmony with the original understanding between the United States and Great Britain; and he asked the governor to transmit an inclosed copy of the memorandum to the lieutenant governor of New Brunswick as soon as it reached him. Both communications were intrusted to the care of Major General Winfield Scott, who was ordered to proceed to Maine. Taking leave of the president, having received his instructions, General Scott said: "Mr. President, if you want war, I need only look on in silence. The Maine people will make it for you fast and hot enough. I know them; but if peace be your wish, I can give no assurance of success. The difficulties in the way will be formidable." "Peace with honor," was the president's reply, and that being General Scott's own wish, as he has recorded, he went on his mission "with a hearty good will."

The general was accompanied by Captain Robert Anderson, later, as Major Anderson, the hero of Fort Sumter, and Lieutenant E. D. Keyes, later Major General E. D. Keyes, a distinguished officer in the Civil War. In Boston, he had an interview with Edward Everett, then governor of Massachusetts.

General Scott, March 5, 1839, reached Augusta, the capital of the state, and at once found himself in a highly excited community. The storm center was the Legislature, but he soon learned that the whole state, from Kittery Point to Quoddy Head, was in an excited state of mind occasioned by the proposed memorandum recently received from the state department in Washington, to which reference has already been made. The particular item in the memorandum arousing general hostility was the recommendation that the State of Maine should voluntarily, and without needless delay, withdraw from the disputed territory any armed force it then had there, thus leaving that territory wholly within the possession and jurisdiction of New Brunswick. What this meant, or easily could be made to mean apart from other items in the proposed memorandum, can easily be imagined. As General Scott viewed the situation at no loss of time after his arrival, the State of Maine and the Province of New Brunswick were very fast approaching a clash of arms. Besides its armed force in the disputed territory, Maine already had a considerable body of troops in the Aroostook country, while General Hodsdon had a detachment of a thousand men from the third division of Maine militia on the way thither; and ten thousand more from he several divisions of the state militia had been ordered to hold themselves in readiness for service on the border. In New Brunswick warlike preparations also were in progress.

In his conversations, General Scott at once found that rival political interests were very much in evidence. A remarkable degree of unanimity had thus far characterized the military preparations that were in progress throughout the state. The members of both political parties had laid aside their differences, and were loyally supporting the state authorities in their purpose to resist encroachments upon Maine territory. But the more he studied the situation at the capitol, General Scott found both Democrats and Whigs wary lest their opponents in some way should secure political advantage. In his endeavors as a peacemaker accordingly he carefully considered ways of approach, and first devoted his attention to the Democrats, then the dominant political party; and by degrees, as he tells us, he won them over, although they hesitated "lest the Whigs should shift about, agitate against any compromise, and thereby regain the state."

General Scott recorded an interesting story of the strategy he employed in one of his successful advances upon the leaders of the Legislature, alluding to the assistance he received from "Senator Evans, just from Washington," and from "the Honorable Albert Smith of Portland, afterwards a member of Congress, who, happening to be in Augusta, gave him the temper and bias of many particular Democrats, whom it was necessary to conciliate." General Scott wrote this story many years after the events to which he referred, and his memory was not wholly accurate. Mr. Evans was not then a member of the United States Senate, and the Honorable Albert Smith, of Portland, was the Honorable F. O. J. Smith, whose presence in Augusta at just that time, doubtless, was not altogether a matter of "happening"; but General Scott's account of the way in which he sought to carry out his instructions may be regarded as substantially correct.

In his work as a peacemaker the general soon found that the memorandum must be set aside as not affording a possible basis for a temporary agreement between the contending parties on the eastern frontier; and he at length suggested to the governor, and some prominent members of the Legislature, the basis for a compromise that had the promise of favorable action on the part of both the Senate and the House. The presentation of this suggestion to the Legislature was left to Governor Fairfield. Accordingly, in a special message, the governor laid the papers he had received from the president and the secretary of state, including the memorandum, before that body. As to the memorandum, he asked instructions, at the same time presenting his own views with reference to it. Replying to the question, "Shall we withdraw our forces agreeably to its recommendation?" he answered with an unhesitating negative. To the terms of the memorandum he saw obvious objections. It would make the state's action, he said, a retrograde movement. "What then shall be done?" he asked. "The people of this State surely are not desirous of hurrying the two nations into a war. Such an event is anxiously to be avoided, if it can be, without dishonor. We owe too much to the Union, to ourselves, and above all to the spirit and principles of Christianity, to bring about a conflict of arms with a nation having with us a common origin, speaking a common language, and bound to us by so many ties of common interest, without the most inexorable necessity. Under these circumstances I would recommend that, when we are fully satisfied, either by the declarations of the Lieutenant Governor of New Brunswick, or otherwise, that he has abandoned all idea of occupying the disputed territory with a military force, and of attempting an expulsion of our party, then, the Governor be authorized to withdraw our military force, leaving the land agent with a sufficient *posse*, armed or unarmed, as the case may require, sufficient to carry into effect your original design, that of driving out or arresting the trespassers, and preserving and protecting the timber from depredations. From such an act of jurisdiction—an attempt so right and proper in itself, and so imperatively called for by the circumstances of the case, we should not be driven by any power on earth. We ought not, however, wantonly to do *more than is necessary*. We want no military force in the territory if there be no military force against us."

By the governor's message, following General Scott's personal efforts as a peacemaker, the way was prepared for action by the Legislature; and a resolve was adopted March 23, 1839, authorizing the governor, when satisfied that the lieutenant governor of New Brunswick had abandoned all intentions of occupying the disputed territory with a military force, to withdraw the Maine militia, leaving the land agent with a sufficient *posse* armed or unarmed, carrying the resolve into effect.

Meanwhile General Scott had undertaken peace efforts with Lieutenant Governor Harvey, of New Brunswick. In the war of 1812, the general had made the acquaintance of the lieutenant governor, then a lieutenant colonel in the British army in Canada, and had been able to do him a kindness. The acquaintance formed in this way was continued after the war, and it was now of service to General Scott in securing Sir John Harvey's agreement to the proposed arrangement. General Scott's letter to the lieutenant governor was dated "Headquarters, Eastern Division, United States Army, Augusta, Maine, March 21, 1839, and contained the following proposition:

> "That it is not the intention of the Lieutenant Governor of her Britannic Majesty's Province of New Brunswick, under the expected renewal of negotiations between the Cabinets of London and Washington, on the subject of the said disputed territory, without renewed instructions to that effect from his government, to seek to take military possession of that territory, or to seek by military force to expel therefrom the armed civil *posse* or the troops of Maine."

This proposition received the assent of the lieutenant governor of New Brunswick. In a letter to General Scott, March 23, 1839, Sir John Harvey wrote: "I was gratified by the receipt of your very satisfactory communication of the 21st instant. My reliance upon you, my dear General, has led me to give my willing assent to the proposition which you have made yourself the very acceptable means of conveying to me; and I trust that as far as the Province and the State respectively are concerned, an end will be put by it to all border disputes, and a way opened to an amicable settlement of the national question involved."

On the 25th of March, because of General Harvey's agreement, Governor Fairfield signified in the following words his acceptance of the proposition conveyed to him by General Scott:

> "That in the hope of a speedy and satisfactory settlement, by negotiation, between the governments of the United States and Great Britain . . . . . it is not the intention of the Governor of Maine, without renewed instructions from the Legislature of the State, to attempt to disturb by arms the said Province in the possession of the Madawaska settlement, or to interrupt the usual communications between that Province and her Majesty's Upper Province; and he is willing, in the meantime, to leave the questions of possession and jurisdiction as they at present stand, that is, Great Britain holding, in part, possession of a part of the said territory, and the government of Maine denying her right to such possession; and the State of Maine holding, in part, possession of another portion of the same territory, to which her right is denied by Great Britain. With this understanding, the Governor of Maine, will without unnecessary delay, withdraw the military force of the State from the said disputed territory, leaving only, under a land agent, a small civil *posse,* armed or unarmed, to protect the timber recently cut and to prevent future depredations."

In this mutual understanding thus accomplished, the British claim of "exclusive jurisdiction" in the disputed territory received no recognition, one part of the territory, the Aroostook country, remaining in the possession of Maine, while another part, the Madawaska country, was left in the possession of New Brunswick.

On March 30th, Major General Hodsdon, in command of the state troops on the northeastern border, was ordered to leave one company of light infantry, one company of riflemen and two companies of infantry, under command of a field officer, at Fort Fairfield, for the purpose of protecting the public property until a sufficient civil force could be procured by the land agent; while General Hodsdon, with the remaining portion of the detachment was directed to report forthwith at Bangor, where the troops were discharged on April 26th. On April 4th the companies stationed at Calais were discharged, while the companies left in the Aroostook country, relieved by civilians, were discharged late in April or early in May, on their arrival at Bangor. The whole number of troops, whose services were required for the protection of the border, numbered three thousand three hundred and thirty-nine officers and men, who were in the service from twenty-one days to two months and twenty-five days. With their discharge the "Aroostook war" ended. There was no more encroachment on the timber lands of Maine, and there was no further seizure of Maine land agents or imprisonment of Maine citizens. What was intended had been accomplished.

CHAPTER 22.

Maine led the nation in the middle period in an effort to discourage excessive consumption of spiritous liquors. Before the Maine Temperance Society was formed in 1833, a number of local societies were established. The Bath Temperance Society was founded in 1829 and, as the following suggests, its leaders at first were not entirely successful.

ANNUAL REPORTS OF THE BATH TEMPERANCE SOCIETY*
by
(Anonymous)

TEMPERANCE

The Bath Temperance Society, held its annual meeting in the Baptist Meeting-house on the evening of Dec. 20, 1830. After appropriate religious exercises, the executive Committee presented its Report, which, on motion of the Rev. J. W. Ellingwood, accompanied by a highly interesting address, was accepted, and ordered to be presented to the Editor of the *Main Inquirer* for publication.

REPORT

A little more than a year has elapsed, since this society was organized. For some time previous to its formation, the friends of Temperance in this town, had looked, with deep anxiety upon the evils resulting from the immoderate use of ardent spirits; and rather wished, than expected, that a change for the better, might be produced. So many of our principal citizens were engaged in business, in some way or other connected with the manufacture, transportation, or vending of them; and so prevalent was the practice of purchasing, and using them, on almost all occasions, that but few were ready to act upon the principle of *total abstinence,* or to adopt any systematic operations to stay the progress of the wide-spreading evil.

Our attention was, however, in some degree aroused to the subject, by a powerful address from the Rev. Dr. Edwards, in which he portrayed the evils of intemperance, in its desolating effects, and threatening attitude, in relation to our Country. A new impulse was also given to our feelings and resolutions, by an address from the Rev. Mr. Mead, by which we were impressed with the importance of united and vigorous exertions, on the part of the friends of Temperance; and which finally resulted in the organization of this Society.

At first a Society was formed, consisting of about 60 members; but its Constitution not meeting the views of the public mind, this Society was formed, and its constitution subscribed by nearly all the members of the first; and *that Society* is now considered, as merged in *this.*

The number of members is now 286, viz: 137 *males,* and 149 *females.* This number we regret to say, is small, compared with the whole population of Bath, amounting, as it does, to 3773. Still, we have reason to believe, that a powerful and happy influence has been exerted by this Society.

Associated as its members are with the citizens of all classes, our object has not only been frequently discussed, in the social circle, and at the fire side, but has been also a subject of conversation and of solemn prayer to God, in our religious meetings. Believing as we sincerely do, that it must approve itself to every reflecting man's conscience, we doubt not, that many, who, a year ago, from various reasons, thought proper to decline becoming connected with us, will now be disposed to lend their names and influence, to advance a cause, so closely allied with the peace and order of the

---

*Maine Inquirer, January 11, 1831.

Community, the good of the rising generation, and the prosperity and glory of our Land.

The objections, usually urged against becoming members of Temperance Associations, were ably answered in Professor Newman's address, which, together with the excellent, and highly interesting ones, delivered by the Rev. Mr. Jenkins, and the pastors of the Churches in this place, has made an impression, deep and lasting, we hope, upon the minds of all, who heard them, of the magnitude of the evils of Intemperance; of the only remedies to be applied; of the futility of all objections to united and vigorous exertions to raise a barrier against the tide of desolation, coming in upon us; and of the duty of every friend of humanity to give his countenance, and personal aid to the common cause.

We believe that this cause has been steadily gaining ground, and that our members have no reason to be discouraged, or to relax their efforts. They are engaged in a high and noble work, designed to promote the good of themselves, their families, and their fellow men.

Even should they meet with opposition, let them not be disheartened. But on this ground they have no reason to complain,—They have not been much opposed or ridiculed; nor will they ever be, by sober, reflecting men. Already their influence is felt; their example is respected and many, who have not subscribed the Constitution of this Society, are exerting a powerful co-operation in the same cause, and will, we trust, soon not only adopt the *principle* of its members, but unite their *names* with theirs.

A great change has already been effected. The number of licensed retailers, in this town, has, within the last two years, diminished from *fifty-seven*, to *thirty-two;* and of this thirty-two, ten have taken only what are called *half licenses*. The taxes on the licenses have, in the same time, diminished from 342 dollars to 174, that is about one half.—*Eight or ten* traders in this town have from conscientious motives, during the *past year* wholly relinquished the sale of ardent spirits. Many families have discarded their use entirely, except as medicine. We no longer see them arranged on our sideboards, as a temptation to indulge. It is no longer considered, as an act of decorum to use them in the entertainment of visitants; or to celebrate the meeting or parting of friends over the social glass. And so completely odious and disgusting, has the practice of following strong drink become, that, we trust, ere long, there will be few, if any, found disposed to seek the gratification of a vitiated appetite in the inebriating draught.

Some of our merchants are nobly helping forward the work of reformation. Several vessels, during the last year, have been built in this place, and have sailed without any ardent spirits. And our physicians, knowing their pernicious effects on the constitutions and morals of their patients, dissuade from their use; and seldom prescribe them, when a substitute can be obtained.

We have not the means of stating accurately the quantity of distilled spirits consumed in this town during the past year; but we doubt not, that it has been much less than in any preceding year. A general conviction, *resulting from actual experiment,* now prevails, that men can transact the business, pertaining to any occupation, without the aid of these unnatural stimulants.

The public mind seems to be waking up to this subject, and, in proportion to the time, since effort, on the principle of *total abstinence,* began to be made, much, very much, has been accomplished.

It is less than five years, since the American Temperance Society was formed, consisting of a few individuals in Boston and its vicinity. It now embraces over *one thousand* auxiliaries, formed in every State in the union, and has enrolled on its lists, more than *one hundred thousand* members. Thus is this great cause rapidly gaining ground in our land. Medical, Ecclesiastical, and other bodies have passed resolutions, favorable to the object of this Society; many agents have been employed, and publications circulated and all are powerfully co-operating in the general reform.

Still, the reformation is just begun.—The evil, we wish to remove, is of immense magnitude, and portentous aspect. It is a pestilence, that walketh in darkness; a destruction that wasteth at noon day. Without help from on high, the great work will never be accomplished, but we trust that help will be afforded. It is estimated, that there are *three hundred thousand* intemperate persons in our country! What an army, led on by the demon of darkness! *Thirty thousand* fall in his service every year, not by the sword of others, but by a cruel suicide! According to this estimate, the number of deaths by intemperance in this town is nine annually! The loss to this town then, during the last 20 years, is *one hundred and eighty* persons who are gone down to the grave by this melancholy, degrading cause!

The annual expenditure in our nation, for ardent spirits, is computed at *fifty millions of dollars.* This expense would pay our national debt in one year. It is twice as much as the revenue of the United States. It would build a canal every year five times as long as the Grand Hudson and Erie Canal. It would pay the salaries of all the instructors of Schools and Colleges and support all the ministers of the gospel in our land. It would give a copy of the bible to every family on earth in less than two years.

But, who can calculate the vast amount of suffering endured; who can count the groans, and measure the tears of wives and children, of widows and orphans, caused by intemperance? Where almost is the family, that has not found sorrow from this cause? Who can brighten the clouded prospects, and revive the withered hopes, of disconsolate and broken hearted parents? Who can form an aggregate of all the pains of body and the stings of conscience, which the wretched victims bring upon themselves? Who can estimate the loss of property and reputation,—the lamentation, mourning, and woe, occasioned by this destroyer of human happiness?

Something has been already done to check its progress; but much more remains to be achieved. And we devoutly hope, that the time is not far distant, when all our professional men will advocate our principle; when all our merchants and inn-keepers shall find it consistent with their feelings and their interests to relinquish the sale of this *fiery ruin;* when the voice of the drunkard shall no longer be heard in our streets, nor our youth be exposed to his pestilential influence and when our nation shall wipe away its disgrace, and be no longer a hissing and reproach through the earth, for this vice.

In conclusion, let the members of this Society, relying on Divine aid, exert themselves in this cause. Let parents, who would have their children respectable and happy, be awake to this subject. Let them by example as well as precept, discountenance the use of these deadly poisons. Let the sober and temperate, of all classes, combine their efforts to banish the destroyer from this fair heritage, left us by our fathers; and to raise up a generation distinguished for sobriety and temperance. Let the *patriot* and the *philanthropist* throughout the land, as well as the professed christian, be aroused without delay, and put forth their noblest & united powers in this glorious cause; and, by the blessing of God, our country may yet be saved from *impending ruin.*

THE PROGRESS OF TEMPERANCE IN BATH, 1834

"But a few years since, although individual carpenters, and others, might here and there be found, who avoided spiritious liquors, one would no more have thought in this quarter of building or navigating a vessel without rum, than without the broadaxe or the compass. When, or by whom the first effort was made in this place, either to build or sail shipping, on the temperance principle, we have not been able to ascertain! Success however is shown in the following figures.

"Encouraging as these facts are to the friends of total abstinence, those which relate to the sailing of our ships are still more so. The merchants of this town owned last year, 24 ships, 28 brigs, and 36 schooners, registering 16,640 tons, of which all except something less than a quarter part of the schooners, were sailed as temperance vessels. What

	Without ardent spirits				With ardent spirits			
	No. Ships	Brigs	Schrs	Tons		No. Ships	Brigs	Schrs	Tons
1830	3	0	0	1020	1830	2	2	1	1277
1831	4	3	1	2156	1831	2	2	1	1340
1832	5	3	3	3372	1832	3	1	1	1502
1833	7	4	3	4137	1833	2	2	0	1305
1834	3	3	1	1620	1834	1	0	0	430

a difference between the output of spirits formerly provided and the one or two bottles that now occasionally go into the medecine chest."

SUMMARY OF THE FIFTH ANNUAL REPORT OF THE BATH TEMPERANCE SOCIETY, 1834

The fifth annual report of the Temperance Society of Bath appeared in the *Maine Inquirer*, December 19, 1834. The Executive Committee of the society revealed its regret that little progress had been made in 1834. Nevertheless, the Committee reported that the membership of the society was over six hundred, one hundred and eighty six of whom were new members.

The Committee reported that eleven licensed retailers of ardent spirits were operating in Bath. More disturbing to the Committee was the fact that thirteen unlicensed retailers were operating in violation of the law.

The Committee further noted that ten deaths in Bath in 1834 were attributed to intemperance. "One was a female who a short time previous to her death was seen lying drunk by the way side." At least fifty families were "rendered miserable by intemperance" and the number of individuals committed to the house of corrections for the same reason was eighteen. According to the Committee, the expense to the town for the support of paupers was $1,000, one half of which was due to excessive drinking.

Greater efforts were pledged by the Committee to convert the citizenry of Bath to temperance. "Give us every youth of fifteen years of age and under, and in ten years even gray headed drunkenness will be ashamed to show its face."

CHAPTER 23.

The most famous temperance leader in the United States in the 19th century was Neal Dow of Portland. The following extract from a recent biography describes Dow's successful campaign to obtain the passage of the first prohibition law in the United States history, the "Maine Law" of 1851.

THE NAPOLEON OF TEMPERANCE*
by
Frank L. Byrne

"Where is NEAL DOW? Can nothing be done? Is there no remedy?" According to a temperance writer, Portlanders of the late 1840's who believed that a wave of drunkenness was sweeping over their city, asked such questions. And, indeed, interest in suppressing intemperance was rising among many of Dow's fellow-citizens. On February 22, 1849, nearly 800 of them, including most Portland clergymen, petitioned the city authorities to enforce the Prohibitory Law of 1846 against 300 liquor-sellers. The city fathers agreed to try and also asked the legislature to enact a more stringent law. By temporarily stopping his own attempts at enforcement, Dow had encouraged other opponents of liquor-selling to take the field. As the century's first half expired, he was ready to resume his command of the aroused prohibitionists. Armed with a powerful new weapon, Colonel Dow would lead his army in his most successful offensive.

He first proposed to equip his followers with a device to overcome the liquor-sellers' last legal bastions. While he had deprived the dealers of their right to sell spirits as a drink, he had not yet been able to stop them from stocking and even displaying large quantities of liquor. And, from his futile attempts to enforce the Prohibitory Law of 1846, he had learned the difficulty of finding credible witnesses to specific sales of strong drink. In 1848, however, the Massachusetts legislature had considered and rejected a bill providing for the seizure of liquor to be used as evidence against its owner. At that time and again on June 12, 1849, at a meeting attended by Dow, his county's Washingtonian Convention had hailed the principle of the Bay State bill. Dow decided that seizure would solve his enforcement problems. On August 15, 1849, at Dow's request, the Democrat-controlled legislature passed a bill permitting justices of the peace to issue warrants to search buildings and seize liquor kept for illegal sale. Because the bill passed within three days of the lawmakers' adjournment, Governor John Dana was able under the Maine Constitution to withhold his decision on it until the next legislative session. Dow's weapon hung in helpless suspense.

While dependent upon Dana for the fate of his bill, Dow was in a strong position to counterattack against a possible veto. The disrupted condition of his state's political parties offered him the best opportunity of his long lifetime to throw the balance of power. In the 1848 presidential campaign, when the Whigs and Democrats had failed to endorse the Wilmot Proviso against the extension of slavery into the territory conquered in the Mexican War, elements of both major parties had bolted. Dow and other Whigs with antislavery leanings had joined Democrats and members of the abolitionist Liberty party in organizing the Free Soil party. While the Free Soilers met defeat in Maine and the nation, factions within the state's long-dominant Democracy continued to take sides

---
*Frank L. Byrne, *Prophet of Prohibition: Neal Dow and His Crusade*, (Madison: State Historical Society of Wisconsin, 1961), pp. 42-51. Reprinted by permission of the publisher.

on the question of slavery in the territories. In accordance with the policy of their party's national leadership, Governor Dana and other members of the office-holding clique called the "Wildcat" or "Hunker" Democrats opposed the Proviso. Another group within the party coalesced behind the controversial measure and called itself the "Antislavery Democrats." In 1848, overcoming the Wildcats, the Antislavery Democrats elected their leader, Hannibal Hamlin, to the United States Senate. In the following year, they controlled the nomination of Governor Dana's successor. Should Dana eventually veto Dow's bill, the prohibitionist leader could seek a bargain with the dissident members of the governor's own party.

Dow could easily work with the Antislavery or Hamlin Democrats. He had first met their leader in the 1830's when Hamlin, a swarthy, convivial youth, had studied law at the Portland office of abolitionist Samuel Fessenden. Like Dow, Hamlin had early learned to dislike slavery and had split with his party's Wildcat rulers on the issue. Having been elected to complete an unexpired term, the new senator faced an early reckoning with the vengeful Wildcats. In February and early March, 1850, while in Washington to attend a National Temperance Convention, Dow talked with Hamlin and found the Antislavery Democrat "particularly polite." Congress was then debating a solution to the problem of slavery in the territories. By the settlement, which became known as the Compromise of 1850, leading Democrats and Whigs hoped to quell both the Free Soil agitation and Southern threats of disunion. Dow and Hamlin agreed in opposing any extension of slavery to appease the Southern "chivalry." Despite his partisan differences with Hamlin, Dow had an ideological basis for an alliance.

The prohibitionist chief soon learned his practical need for the new tie. On May 7, 1850, outgoing Governor John Dana committed the Wildcat faction against prohibition by vetoing Dow's bill as an "ill digested outrage upon almost every right of our citizens." On May 16, the Democrats in the House of Representatives, of whom the majority were Hamlin men, declined to override the veto. Needing the help of the Antislavery Democrats, Dow helped them to get the legislative majority required to re-elect Hannibal Hamlin to the national Senate. In the crucial ballot on June 25, 1850, at the behest of Hamlin's lieutenant, Dow and other prominent Free Soilers persuaded several of their party's legislators to vote for the leader of the Antislavery Democrats. Two months later, in the same House of Representatives which had sustained the Dana veto, enough Hamlin Democrats voted with the Free Soilers and Temperance Whigs to pass an even stricter Dow prohibitory bill. By a tie vote, Wildcat senators blocked the measure. But Dow was close to revolutionizing Maine for his crusade.

To complete his control over the legislature, Dow conducted a final offensive. During the summer of 1850, by winning the presidency of the Maine Temperance Union, he had achieved formal recognition of his leadership of the state's anti-alcohol army. In the September election, the Temperance President and his followers attacked anti-prohibitionist lawmakers and often were able to throw the balance in favor of the anti-prohibitionists' opponents. As a means of organizing the necessary shifts across party lines, Dow found particularly useful a fraternal order called the Brotherhood of Temperance Watchmen. Members of the local Temperance Watchman Clubs, which for two years had been spreading through western Maine, pledged themselves to work for the enactment and enforcement of prohibition. After the votes of Watchmen and unorganized prohibitionists had purged some of the foes of his bill, Dow was confident that the next legislative session would grant him his longawaited victory.

Neal Dow was anxious to be in a position to enforce—and to advertise—his anticipated prohibitory law. He regarded the mayoralty of Portland as well-suited to his purposes. In the forty-six years of his life, his native city had quadrupled in size to reach a population of 21,000. From its central location on the peninsula, the little town of Dow's youth had spread out in both directions. Looking out his eastern windows, Dow could see, instead of open fields, some of the city's finest houses. Trade with the West Indies continued to help support the city's prosperity but distilling of rum was giving way to sugar refining. Railroads, in which Dow had an interest, controlled the trade of the backcountry. While no longer the state capital, Portland was in every other respect the metropolis of Maine. Once ensconced in its City Hall, Dow could choke off much of the state's liquor-trade and convert Portland into a model for the world's prohibitionists.

As the candidate of the locally-dominant Whig party, Dow ran for the Portland mayoralty. Though some of the Whig leaders were unwilling to give to a frequent bolter the post with its $1000 annual salary, the prohibitionist Whigs had controlled the nominating meetings. But on April 8, 1851, when Dow went to vote, he discovered that his party foes were distributing special Whig ballots headed by the name of another temperance man. The veteran bolter was tasting his own medicine. Because of the split among the Whigs, he received a plurality but not the required majority over Democratic candidate George F. Shepley. In preparation for a second trial at election, the Whig PORTLAND ADVERTISER urged all members of its party to vote for Dow as the regular nominee. On April 21, Dow received the support of most Whigs and of some prohibitionist Democrats. Only a few anti-Dow Whigs went over to the opposition. By 1332 votes to the Democracy's 986, he won his first major political office. While Dow admitted that having the endorsement of the city's major party had helped, he regarded his victory as an approval of his "zeal" and "methods" in fighting the Demon Rum.

Having obtained what he viewed as a mandate for enforced prohibition, Dow settled himself in the quiet study at the rear of his big brick house to write another bill to stop liquor-selling. By titling his new proposal, like his original bill of 1845, "An Act for the Suppression of Drinking Houses and Tippling Shops," he expressed its limited purpose. He forbade both wholesalers and retailers to manufacture liquor or to sell it as a beverage. To minimize opposition, however, he left several leaks in his dike. As under the Prohibitory Law of 1846, he permitted towns to appoint bonded agents to sell liquor for "medicinal and mechanical purposes." Moreover, in compliance with a decision of the United States Supreme Court, he exempted foreign liquor in the "original packages" from the law's operation. Anyone respectable enough to convince a bonded agent of his righteous intentions or wealthy enough to keep a cellar of imported liquor might continue to drink at home.

As Mayor Dow stated in his inaugural address, he favored a prohibitory law "sufficiently stringent in its provisions and summary in its processes to effect its objects." To adapt the bill to his first requirement, Dow increased the fines over those provided by the 1846 law and introduced a jail sentence of from three to six months for persistent liquor-sellers. By summary enforcement procedures, he attempted to satisfy his second requirement. He permitted any justice of the peace to try most violators of his proposed law. To discourage those convicted from appealing to the district courts, he required them to post appeal bonds with four sureties and to pay double fines if finally convicted. In general, Dow smoothed the path of the prosecution, multiplied difficulties for the defense and limited the discretion of often hostile judges. In so doing, he acted upon his early faith in the efficacy of stern, sure punishment.

As in his 1849 and 1850 bills, Dow's greatest innovation was the provision for search and seizure. He permitted any three voters, who suspected someone in their town of keeping liquor for illegal sale, to obtain a warrant to search any building used wholly or partly for business purposes. Eliminating the unlimited search permitted by his 1849 bill, he required evidence of an actual illegal sale from persons seeking a warrant to enter a dwelling. He threw upon the owner of seized liquor the burden of proving that it was legally imported or the property of a bonded agency. Dow punished those unable to give such proof with a small fine and destruction of their liquor. He thought that the search and seizure provision would make it easy for prohibitionist officials to transfer the Demon Rum from seller to sewer.

With his bill written, Dow pressed for its speedy enactment. On May 26, 1851, at Augusta, he appeared for the sixth time before a legislative committee to advocate prohibition. The reform leader, with his fashionably long brown curls, his blue jacket and his fancy vest, cut a dapper figure. As he had after the passage of the Prohibitory Law of 1846, he made a bold pledge of enforcement. He promised, while his deepset blue eyes sparkled with fervor, "If you will enact this bill, the sun shall not rise on Portland, January, 1852, and find there a single open grog-shop." Dow could count on the support of all eight Free Soil legislators and on some temperance men in the dominant Democracy and in the Whig minority. Besides, because of his aid to the Antislavery Democrats and his ability to control the balance in close districts, he could command the votes of other lawmakers. On May 29, eighty-one of his friends and allies in the lower house overrode forty opponents to order the engrossment of Dow's bill. The prohibitionist chief was on his way to overwhelming victory.

On the following day, under suspension of the rules, the Senate debated the engrossment of the prohibitory bill. Senator Shepard Cary, an Aroostook lumberman and a prominent Wildcat Democrat, spoke for the opposition. In bombastic style, he protested against a Democratic legislature's becoming "the registrar of the inquisitorial edicts of the temperance fanatics of Portland...." That city's "popinjay Mayor," Cary warned, intended "to overturn the democracy of the state and put himself at the top of the heap...." Nine Democratic senators backed the old Wildcat. But, disregarding Cary's prophecy, fourteen other Democrats joined three Whigs and a lone Free Soiler to order the bill's engrossment. On May 30, a smiling Dow watched both houses obediently vote the formal enactment of his measure. Letter for letter and word for word, he had attained his wish.

Dow personally carried his bill from the Senate Chamber to its last hurdle, Democratic Governor John Hubbard. A bushy-browed man with an upthrust shock of hair, Hubbard was a practicing physician. In 1849, with the backing of the Antislavery Democrats, he had won the governorship. Several Democratic legislators had already advised Hubbard, who was not a teetotaler, that he could safely veto the prohibitory bill. But the governor faced an uncertain political future. In 1852, after the Compromise of 1850 had finished calming the agitation against the extension of slavery, Hubbard's Wildcat opponents expected to retake control of the party and state. To gain the third term customarily awarded to Maine's Democratic governors, Hubbard might need the support of Neal Dow's well-organized prohibitionist army. On June 2, 1851, the tippling governor signed the prohibitionist's bill. While Dow knew that the reluctant support of some politicians had helped to give him his weapon, he was sure that the new law was "the will of the people."

Although the prohibitory law went into effect at once, Dow took the politic course of delaying the enforcement of the seizure provision in Portland. He wished, as he later recalled, to avoid friction with the holders of large stocks of liquor. On June 5, 1851, he proclaimed that he would allow dealers who sold no more strong drink a "reasonable time" to ship away their goods. Most of the wealthy wholesale merchants took advantage of Down's period of grace. The last of the city's once numerous distilleries also closed. On June 21, Dow's learned that one wholesaler, who had refused to ship away his stock, had sold some rum. The little mayor personally supervised the confiscation of the defiant dealer's spirits and later had them poured into the sewer. By this first seizure under the new law, he frightened the keepers of the hotels and "genteel saloons" into signing an agreement to sell no more liquor. Despite the muttering of some merchants about the effect of prohibition on the city's trade, Dow believed that he had successfully introduced his policy.

The prohibitionist mayor admitted, however, that he found some retailers to be remarkably persistent. Obtaining liquor from out-of-state wholesalers, they adopted new ways of doing business. Some began keeping their main supply of liquor off their premises. To conceal the small quantities of liquor needed for immediate sale, they learned to contrive increasingly clever hiding-places within their buildings. As Dow by publicity and legal action drove out of business some of the more "respectable" liquor-sellers, new types of drinking-places sprang up to fill the gap. A number of workingmen began selling liquor in their living quarters. Many of them were among the Irish attracted to the city by the railroad construction which Dow himself had enthusiastically supported. Young bloods also rented private rooms to house drinking clubs. Both groups were taking advantage of the provision of Dow's law requiring evidence of a specific illegal sale before the issuance of a warrant to search a dwelling. Dow had driven the Demon only a short distance underground.

To dig out the concealed violators, Mayor Dow relied, not on his novel search and seizure weapon, but on the traditional method of getting witnesses to actual sales. In the Brotherhood of Temperance Watchmen, which had helped him in past elections, he had a corps of volunteer agents. In addition, the prohibitionist mayor hired professional informers. By paying the costs of the "war" from the liquor-sellers fines, he avoided drawing on the city treasury and finally accumulated a balance of several hundred dollars. When some sellers pledged to stop, he ceased further prosecution for their past offenses. In September, 1851, however, he had a three-time offender sent to jail. By the end of the year, he had convicted seventy persons under his prohibitory law. Dow was putting to the test his belief in legal pains and penalties.

In three quarterly reports to the City Council on his enforcement of the prohibitory law, Dow claimed to have almost wiped out the Portland liquor-traffic. He admitted that a "few secret grog-shops" owned mainly by "foreigners" remained but argued that their small-scale operations were much less tempting than "open" sale. For the first time, he hinted that he might need "some additional provisions" for the "entire extinguishment of the traffic." The mayor alleged, however, that the reduction already made in liquor-selling had greatly decreased crime, drunkenness and pauperism. As proof, he cited reports from his police and almshouse master. "The watch house," he dramatically proclaimed in September 1851, "is now used to keep seized liquors instead of drunkards. . . ." All in all, the prohibitory law's author portrayed his creation as a thorough, almost automatic success.

Dow used varied means to bring his account of his law's triumph to the attention of the nation. He wrote personal letters. On August 4, 1851, he sent a copy of his law to a man outside Maine and exhorted him "to *reenact* it in your State—*you can do it if you try.*" In August, Dow also acquired a newspaper outlet for his propaganda. His supporters, the 5000 members of the prohibitionist Brotherhood of Temperance Watchmen, began to sponsor the MAINE TEMPERANCE WATCHMAN. Dow was friendly with the editor of the new Portland weekly, "Elder" Benjamin D. Peck. An ex-minister, the politically-ambitious Peck had been a power in the tiny Free Soil party and had become head of the Temperance Watchmen's Central Committee. He showed by his fat figure and by his taste for personal abuse that he limited his own practice of "temperance" strictly to abstinence from alcohol. Peck reprinted and sold bulk orders of Dow's reports on the new statute's remarkable results. Moreover, Dow's City Council distributed all three of his reports at public expense. Within a few weeks, Dow and his friends had scattered their documents across the northeastern United States.

By his publicity, Dow quickly won the backing of prominent American temperance agitators. One of the more influential of these was the Reverend John Marsh, the Corresponding Secretary of the American Temperance Union. In his fifteen years as editor of his organization's monthly JOURNAL, Marsh has endorsed successive panaceas for intemperance. He readily embraced Dow's new remedy. In the summer of 1851, when Marsh visited Portland, Augusta and Bangor, Dow convinced the elderly Congregationalist that prohibition was effective throughout Maine. Marsh and his Executive Committee called a National Temperance Convention to popularize Dow's law. In a letter to the delegates, who met on August 20 and 21, 1851, at Saratoga Springs, New York, Dow described the ease and completeness of his victory over the Demon Rum. Marsh pushed through resolutions urging the nation's temperance men to use both propaganda and the ballot box to gain for their own states the "Maine Liquor Law." Dow had acquired for his law the specific endorsement of the anti-alcohol movement's national leaders.

Through the efforts of Marsh and other publicists, Dow soon saw the "Maine Law" and himself become nationally famous. In addition to the American Temperance Union, the American Tract Society, the American Home Missionary Society and the rest of the complex of organizations closely associated with the Congregational and Presbyterian Churches threw their forces behind Dow's law. Before May, 1852, Marsh's society alone trumpeted the merits of the Maine Law in 235,000 copies of its adult and juvenile periodicals, in 10,000 pamphlets and in 80,000 pages of tracts. Marsh stressed the novel search and seizure provision of the Maine Law. In describing its results, he stripped every subtle qualification from Dow's glowing reports of Portland conditions and claimed for the Maine Law total success. Dubbing the law's author the "Napoleon of Temperance," Marsh cried that Dow had "brought into the battle-field every officer of State, . . . turned its whole artillery against the rum-fortifications, and in less than six months, . . . swept every distillery and brew-house, hotel-bar, splendid saloon and vile groggery clean from the State." Napoleon of Temperance! The little Portlander was gaining more than fame. He was receiving adulation.

Convinced by the widespread reports of the Maine Law's efficacy, most of the country's many temperance men joined Dow's crusade. As the fall of 1851 froze into winter in the New England and Middle Atlantic states, the evangelical clergy and temperance laymen met to vote their approval of the Maine Law. One ecstatic Massachusetts minister proclaimed "It is in harmony with the LAW OF GOD.... Its leading principles were taught by Jesus Christ." The clergyman argued, *"If God be for it, who can be against it?"* A Rhode Island Son of Temperance burst forth:

> Come all ye friends of temperance, and listen to my strain,
> I'll tell you how Old Alchy fares down in the state of Maine.
> There's one Neal Dow, a Portland man, with great and noble soul,
> He framed a law, without a flaw, to banish alcohol.

As the author of the much-praised Maine Law, Dow became within a few months one of his country's leading temperance men. On February 18, 1852, at New York, a short-lived National Temperance Society of the United States held a banquet in his honor. Among the notables present at the dinner was Horace Mann, promoter of public education, who regarded Dow as "the moral Columbus." Dow listened to the eminent educator tell the audience that the Maine Law ranked with "the discovery of the magnetic needle, the invention of printing, or any other of the great strides in the progress of civilization." General Sam Houston of Texas, who had become the temperance society's President partly to forward his ambition to become President of the United States, then presented to Dow a very large gold medal. Concealing his pride, Dow acknowledged the valuable gift as a tribute to his cause rather than to himself. He had received the first of many gold and silver laurels.

While the Napoleon of Temperance gained honor in distant places, he was adding to his detractors in his native city. John Neal became one of his more vocal critics. Dow had several times previously found his cousin, who had been an early temperance advocate, among those opposing his extreme measures. But Neal, after joining a Congregational church in 1851, had publicly supported his denomination's pro-Maine Law policy. Then, on January 12, 1852, the Portland Municipal Court convicted of liquor-selling Margaret Landrigan, "Alias 'Kitty Kentuck.'" Despite the Irish boardinghouse keeper's long record of similar offenses, Neal believed that she was innocent. Lawyer Neal and three of his friends signed the heavy bonds required under the Maine Law to permit an appeal. An anonymous writer in the MAINE TEMPERANCE WATCHMAN insinuated that the Landrigan bondsmen had a personal interest in "Kitty." Neal angrily attributed the article to his venom-penned cousin. In a later published defense, Dow did not disavow responsibility.

By writing another article entitled "History of a Neighborhood, A True Tale," Dow further infuriated John Neal and also other leading Portlanders. In this signed short story published in a New York temperance magazine, he told of the horrible results of intemperance in each of the households along a fine avenue in a city within sight of the White Mountains. John Neal recognized that Dow, again using real life illustrations, had clearly described the families of Neal and other residents of Portland's fashionable State Street. To expose Dow to his victims, Neal had the article reprinted in Portland. In a long controversy with his cousin, Dow later denied that his "True Tale" was a true account of any specific street. Moreover, he sneered that the able, influential man described in the story could not possibly be John Neal. His cousin shot back that Dow had torn up "the dead bodies of a whole generation, like a ghoul..." and had then said, "How could you ever suppose I meant you? Did *you* ever elope with your own mother?" Despite his bold denials, Dow had made his bitterest enemy.

The mayor also aroused less passionate but more powerful enmity among the Portland merchants. When he had suppressed wholesaling of liquor, he had received protests from wealthy Portlanders who feared that his action might injure their important trade with the backcountry. Then, on January 14, 1852, though his Maine Law contained no specific authorization for the policy, he had his police begin making regular searches and seizures on every boat and train entering Portland. As Dow later explained, he hoped to stop smuggling to illegal liquor-dealers in both his own city and its hinterland. On March 2, 1852, an "association of independent men" began publishing the Portland MAINE EXPOSITOR in opposition to Dow's enforcement policies. Both the EXPOSITOR and the Democratic EASTERN ARGUS alleged that the Whig mayor was hurting the business of the city-financed Atlantic and St. Lawrence Railroad. Though Dow denied it, his opponents also charged that he had permitted policemen searching for hidden liquor to bore repeatedly into boxes of valuable merchandise. Near the end of his term, Mayor Dow was under heavy fire.

The city's political parties prepared to fight out the 1852 municipal election on the issue of Dow and his methods. On March 20, the Democrats held a public mass-meeting, instead of their customary party caucus, at Portland's City Hall. Charles Q. Clapp, a leading Democrat and one of the city's richest men, harangued the rally against the mayor. The Democratic leaders secured the nomination by acclamation of the venerable Albion K. Parris, a former congressman, judge and five-term state governor. Seeking the support of moderate men of all parties, the EASTERN ARGUS claimed that Parris favored the Maine Law but would avoid Dow's "unwarrantable mode of executing it." Dow accepted his enemies' personal challenge. He and his Temperance Watchmen again took control of the Whig party machinery and secured his renomination. In two wards, however, the anti-Dow Whigs ran bolting tickets. Dow had begun to melt party lines. Indeed, as one of his Whig supporters admitted the prohibitionist chief had become the leader of a "Neal Dow party."

As in previous campaigns, Dow and his faction bid for the support of Portland's church members. Although Judge Parris had been an early temperance man and was a lifelong Congregationalist, Elder Peck of the TEMPERANCE WATCHMAN pontificated, "It cannot be denied that voting for Mr. Dow is voting for morality, virtue and religion, while voting against him is voting against all these interests." But Editor Asa Cummings of the Portland CHRISTIAN MIRROR undermined the Dowites' religious appeal. Since the days of Washingtonianism, Dow had publicly deplored Cummings' lack of enthusiasm for extreme temperance agitation. An early foe of intemperance, Cummings had expressed resentment at receiving such moral criticism from a man who was not a church member. He believed that Dow was arrogantly attempting "virtually to dictate to ministers and churches. . . ." In the last issue of his weekly before the 1852 election, Cummings commented, "A change in the administration of the law in a town or city, will not necessarily draw after it a neglect to execute the law." The knife-wielding reformer had received in his turn a subtle thrust into his vitals.

On April 6, 1852, despite a severe snowstorm, a record-breaking crowd of voters cast its ballots. While Dow got 1496 votes, a slight increase over the previous year, Albion K. Parris piled up a crushing 1900 ballots. The rueful Whig editor explained that the bulk of the city's Democratic minority had united with "church members and world's people, temperance men and rummies" to protect Portland's commerce and "to vote down Neal Dow." Elder Peck particularly blamed the aging "Father" Cummings' "Five Lines" for the defeat. To temperance men outside Maine, however, Dow explained that "the rum sellers of Boston" had spent $17,000 to defeat him. Although the Dowite Board of Aldermen had controlled admission to the voting lists, his followers spread through the country allegations that the Democrats had imported *"great numbers"* of Irish railroad laborers to create their majority. Dow and his local supporters thereby hid his unpopularity with many Portlanders from his increasing number of more distant converts.

On April 10, 1852, Dow invited his associates in the repudiated city administration to an oyster supper. As his baritone voice blended with theirs in the strains of "Auld Lang Syne," he had little cause for sorrow or vain regrets. Though defeated, he still had the ardent support of forty-four per cent of Portland's voters. In the 1852 mayoralty election, he had finally shattered the ranks of the old parties and had made enforced prohibition the decisive factor. Through his alliance with the Antislavery wing of the dominant Democracy, he had an opportunity to perform a similar feat in state politics. Elsewhere in the country his effective propaganda had made the Maine Law a rising issue. With Whiggery weak and Democracy divided, the Napoleon of Temperance strode forward to national conquest.

CHAPTER

24.

The antislavery movement was the most important of the various reform movements which occupied the country after 1830. The following article written by Professor Edward Schriver of the University of Maine discusses Maine's place in the activities of this movement.

ANTISLAVERY: MAINE AND THE NATION*
by
Edward O. Schriver

When the first Negroes landed in America in August, 1619, as bound servants, a problem was presented to colonial society—a problem the resolution of which came slowly until a place, albeit a lowly one, was found for the colored man. Because the Negro servant differed from the white indentured servant in color as well as in geographic and cultural orientation, he was treated differently. This difference was manifested in judicial enactments and legislative actions which were forthcoming. A Virginia act of 1661, for example, was based upon the assumption that some Africans were servants for life; but the decisive formulation, which applied particularly to the Negro, came with an act of 1670 which declared that all non-Christian servants who arrived by sea were slaves for life and that the children resulting from such unions acquired the status of the mother. So firmly did the Negro's subordinate position become a part of the customs and legal codes of colonial America that a later conversion to Christianity had no effect on his status as a slave. Dwight L. Dumond has claimed that colonial laws did three things to fix the position of the Negro: they held him in his place by force; they condemned his children to the status of the mother; and they denied him any real personal rights protected by law.

By the eighteenth century the Negro's color had become the evidence of his status and the badge of his degradation. American society had written chattel slavery, the caste system, and color prejudice into its customs and laws. The chattel principle was the capstone of this web of ideas, attitudes, and practices which made the servant a slave to be treated by the master as he saw fit, a thing whose fate hinged upon the caprice of his lord. At the close of the eighteenth century, a time when the slave system appeared to be in its death throes, the ingenuity of a Yankee inventor, Eli Whitney, may have helped to extend its life for over half a century. With the onset of the nineteenth century, it was clear that conscience had bowed to expediency and humanity to profit as the slave owners, and those involved in reaping the fruits of the system, became more sensitive to any threats to "their peculiar institution."

Still, some were not content to let the matter rest, nor to allow the chattel principle to stand unchallenged. As early as 1671, George Fox, founder of the Quakers, spoke out against American slavery after a visit to Rhode Island and, several decades later, another Englishman, Granville Sharp, was moved to argue that slavery was contrary to the Common Law. Some Americans felt uneasy as well. Anthony Benezet, a schoolmaster, and John Woolman, a tailor, both Quakers, believing in the equality of man and in the mental and moral capacity of the Negro for freedom, advocated that the slaveholders bear the cost of emancipation and that the slaves be given the benefit of retributive justice. Thomas Jefferson, basing his views on a theory of natural rights,

---

*Adapted from Edward O. Schriver, *"The Antislavery Impulse in Maine, 1835-1855,"* (Unpublished Ph.D. Thesis, University of Maine, 1967). Reprinted by permission of the author.

called slavery a "great political and moral evil," while Dr. Benjamin Rush, the Philadelphia physician, and the Rev. Samuel Hopkins of Rhode Island, a Congregational divine, declared human slavery to be inherently evil.

From these challenges to the chattel principle, two divergent approaches to slavery emerged. One addressed the issue of the free Negro, the other the means by which the whole slave system could be abolished. The first found embodiment in the American Colonization Society, the second in the antislavery societies.

The colonizationists were concerned about the Negro who had gained his freedom in a society which really had no proper place for the free colored man. He would never achieve equality in America, they reasoned, in spite of a limited capacity for self-improvement. The Negro would always be denied access to those things which were the everyday possession of the white man; therefore the only sensible course open was to encourage the free colored man to emigrate to Africa, to a place where he would fit into the social structure and where there was an opportunity for him to develop his talents among his peers. Included in the plan was a colony, and in 1821 a place was found for them at Monrovia, later to be the capital of Liberia. In its early years the American Colonization Society, which had been officially established in 1817, attracted the support of many well-meaning citizens, among whom were James Madison, James Monroe, and John Marshall.

Strenuously as the colonizationsts protested their good will in proposing their plan of emigration, they could not quiet, nor could they dispel, the charge made by their opponents that their motives were less than pure. One modern writer has gone so far as to assert that they sought to escape the responsibility for the whole slave system by shipping a few free Negroes to a colony on the coast of Africa. Other criticisms plagued their operation. How practical, the opponents of colonization asked, was the attempt to transport a small number of free Negroes to Liberia? Was it possible, they inquired, to ship enough to offset the natural increase in the slave population? Because of questions such as these, the officers of the Society were forced to spend much of their time, time which could have been used to implement their program, in merely proving the good intentions and the wisdom of their plan.

The other major approach to the issue of slavery in America was expressed first in organizations such as the American Convention for Promoting the Abolition of Slavery and Improving the Condition of the African Race established at Philadelphia in 1794 by delegates from several states, an organization which sought to emancipate the people held in bondage rather than ship them to a distant land. But out of deference to the property rights of the slaveholders, from a desire to protect infirm or old Negroes who would not be able to care for themselves if freed, and out of an unwillingness to assume the public guardianship of emancipated slaves, the framers fostered a platform which asked for gradual or slow emancipation. This step by step method for ending slavery did not produce any marked change in the condition of the Negro in the early years of the nineteenth century, nor did it give any promise of improvement in the future.

As a result of the slowness of the cause of emancipation, some of the more impatient enemies of slavery demanded a more direct course of action. In 1824 Elizabeth Heyrick, a resident of Leicester, England, provided an alternative to gradual emancipation in her *Immediate, Not Gradual Emancipation* which outlined clearly the principle that slavery was a sin and should therefore be exterminated without delay. Mrs. Heyrick pointed out the absurdity of efforts to end the slave trade so long as slavery was permitted in the colonies, so long as products produced by slave labor were consumed, and so long as the property rights of the slaveholder were given precedence over the human rights of the slave. Gradual emancipation, she argued, would result only in gradual indifference. There was no use to haggle with the slave owner because such a course would merely confirm him in his stubborn opinions. The only method to follow, she concluded finally, was to end the whole slave system—and to end it immediately! This message of immediate abolition soon reached America in the person of George Bourne, an English emigre pastor, who brought the urgency of immediatism to the attention of William Lloyd Garrison, a man who propounded it from any platform he could find.

The Colonization Society, which was organized sixteen years before the immediatists formed their first societies, presented their argument to the citizens of Maine first, even before separation from

Massachusetts was complete. In 1819 the Rev. William Meade, an agent of the Society, laid the foundations for further efforts in the state. Dr. Edward Payson, a Portland Congregational minister, also encouraged their work by endorsing the endeavors of Ralph R. Gurley, one of the leading officers of the Society. The efforts of Gurley were supplemented by those of Eliphalet Gillet, secretary of the Maine Missionary Society and the brother-in-law of Gurley, who labored as agent for Maine for the salary of eight dollars a week plus expenses. And to spread news of their organization to every corner of Maine, the colonizationists were able to depend upon *The Christian Mirror,* the Congregational weekly published in Portland and edited after 1826 by the Rev. Asa Cummings. The editor of *The Mirror* was certain that "no society in the land has juster or stronger claims upon the benevolence and the cooperation of our countrymen than this."

William Lloyd Garrison introduced the immediatist argument into Maine. Garrison, while working with Benjamin Lundy on *The Genius of Universal Emancipation* in Baltimore, became convinced that to abolish slavery gradually was to abolish it not at all. Finding no future in Baltimore, he returned to Boston and on January 1, 1831, began the publication of *The Liberator.* In the very first issue of the new paper, Garrison repudiated, and apologized for, gradual emancipation as a means to end slavery and by 1832 was ready to launch an all-out attack on the American Colonization Society, a stronghold of gradualism.

Garrison's offensive took him to Maine in the late summer and fall of 1832. He arrived in Portland on the first leg of his tour on September 24th and made the home of Nathan Winslow, a Quaker merchant, his headquarters while he was in town. The agitator made no secret why he had come to Portland; he was there to disassemble, brick by brick if necessary, the edifice which had been built by Colonization since it was introduced in the state. Among the men who listened eagerly to his lectures was one who learned the anti-colonization argument particularly well. Samuel Fessenden, a militia general and Portland lawyer of some ability, was so moved by the lecturer's attack on the Colonization Society that after one of the evening meetings, he waited for Garrison and accompanied him back to the Winslow house where the two men discussed the evils of colonization to a late hour.

From Portland the Boston editor moved north to Hallowell, where he was welcomed by his friends Ebenezer Dole and the Rev. George Shepard. The citizens of Hallowell, a few of them at least, listened to his attack on colonization; but most of the townspeople and the town press paid very little notice of his visit. The town press did, however, insert a note in one of its columns that Garrison had been there and that "He contended ably and eloquently, that the slaves had an undoubted right to immediate emancipation...."

Bangor came next on his itinerary; there he was the guest of the Rev. Swan L. Pomroy, minister of the Congregational Church. After the Bangor lectures against colonization were completed, Garrison moved south, stopping at Waterville and Augusta on the return journey. At Waterville College he was the guest of the president, the Rev. Jeremiah Chaplin. Apparently what he said to the students must have taken root later as an antislavery society was organized at the school in July, 1833. At Augusta Garrison came face to face with the Rev. Cyril Pearl, an agent of the Colonization Society, who had been sent to counteract the influence of antislavery in Maine. Pearl had worked hard to accomplish his mission; he had traveled six hundred and twenty-four miles and had given twenty-seven addresses in churches and camp meetings. And here he was in Augusta confronting the man whose influence he had set out to destroy. Garrison, who was present at one of Pearl's lectures, stood up to challenge the speaker and an exchange occurred which, if we can believe the testimony of his biographers, resulted in a clear victory for the Boston editor. But this first skirmish between a champion of the immediate abolition of slavery and a herald of emigration was not decisive; for the conclusive battle was yet to come. Leaving Augusta, Garrison returned home to Boston, ending his campaign against the Colonization Society in Maine.

From October, 1832, until June, 1833, the fires of controversy smouldered. In March Nathan Winslow, with some degree of satisfaction, was able to write Garrison from Portland: "The seeds of anti-slavery are sown in this place, and I trust that the cause of truth, righteousness and freedom will ultimately prevail over error, deception, and hypocrisy." But colonizationists were busy as well, moving from place to place, from pulpit to pulpit, promoting their cause. A confrontation between the two antagonists had to occur. It came in June and July, 1833.

The occasion for the Portland Colonization Debate was the appearance of the Rev. Joshua N. Danforth, the general agent of the American Colonization Society for New York and New England, who so impressed some Portlanders that they called for the organization of an auxiliary to the national society. On June 28th, after a Danforth lecture, enthusiasm was high. A motion from the floor recommended the organization of an auxiliary society on the spot; but no sooner had the speaker finished repeating his motion, when General Fessenden, Portland's most outspoken antislavery advocate, shot to his feet to protest what he considered to be an ill-conceived motion. Usually when the General spoke, Portlanders listened and this time was no exception. He pleaded for discussion, not organization; he called for reflection, not unreasoned action, before any positive steps were taken in so serious a matter. Most of the citizens present, even John Neal an arch-enemy of antislavery, agreed that he was right. July 8th was set as the date for a new meeting.

On that evening a large crowd assembled in the Third Congregational Church. Prepared before hand to get the jump on Fessenden, Neal read a draft of a constitution for the proposed society. After he had completed reading it to the audience, he suggested that it was time for the anti-colonizationists to voice their objections, while the pro-colonizationists remained silent speaking only when necessary to correct the errors of their opponents. The mantle fell to the General. Fessenden, who had read Garrison's *Thoughts on African Colonization* and who was in agreement with the argument presented therein, accused the colonizationists of impure motives and of acting upon unwarranted assumptions. His first thrust was mathematical. If the colonizationists wanted to end slavery as they claimed they did, how, the General asked, could they possibly do so by shipping a few free Negroes to Africa each year? How could a small number of emigrants, he queried, compensate for the new slaves who were born annually? It was not possible! More emphasis was given to Fessenden's cause when a free Negro, a Mr. Monroe, who had been preaching to the colored congregation in Portland and who, according to the colonizationists, was the type of man that they felt would be happier in Africa, incisively, and bitterly, impugned the motives of colonizationists. The whole thing, Monroe declared, was a plot to get rid of the free Negro, a conspiracy founded upon the basest sort of prejudice. The pro-colonization audience reacted so violently to these accusations that Fessenden was forced to take the floor to restore order. Once again on his feet, he eloquently presented his most deeply felt grievance against slavery; it was sin, he insisted, sin against God and man. Those who tried to portray it as anything else were moved by impure motives. Even Dr. Robert Finley of New Jersey, one of the founders of the Colonization Society, Fessenden observed, admitted that the society was moved by a desire to rid the country of the free Negro. At this point in the debate, when the fires of controversy were beginning to wax hotter, the chairman reminded the audience that the hour was late and that adjournment to another time was necessary.

The two sides returned to combat each other on July 10th and for several evenings after. On the occasions when General Fessenden was out of the city on business, the colonization standard-bearers, the Rev. Dr. Tyler, a Congregational misister of Portland, the Rev. Cyril Pearl, an agent for the Society, and John Neal, Portland writer and lawyer, held sway. These men presented the case for colonization by seeking to show that the antislavery argument was based upon unsound, even destructive, principles, while the plan fostered by their side was sound, reasonable, and, above all, humane. One evening, while Dr. Tyler spoke, he held a copy of Garrison's *Thoughts* in his hand and read from it, stopping from time to time to comment upon what he had read. "The object of this pamphlet is to prove the superstructure of the colonization society rests upon persecution, falsehood, cowardice, infidelity.... It did not take long using such an approach as this to classify Garrison as an extremist not to be heeded. Garrison was nothing more, they insisted, than a vile fomentor of confusion; all the man did was to collect bits and pieces of matter unflattering to colonization and then to fit them together to suit his foul purposes. Cyril Pearl, no doubt still smarting from his encounter with Garrison at Augusta, was unrestrained in his denunciation of the editor of *The Liberator*. The man, Pearl charged, was completely dishonest and his wild accusations were not worthy of the consideration of reasonable men. John Neal, one of the bitterest enemies of Garrison and antislavery in Maine, presented the climax to the colonization brief against Garrison and his friends when he joined the name of Samuel Fessenden with that of the Boston agitator:

> In the second place, the vice-president of the anti-slavery association of Portland has pledged himself to the views and opinions declared in these "Thoughts"; for in a letter to Mr. Garrison—the missionary—of December last, he says, "I assure you that I am with you *heart and soul,* and to the full extent of all your views."

Once Garrison and Fessenden were shown to be moved by the basest of motives and their works were unmasked for what they were, the champions of colonization offered justification for their plan of emigration. The Society deserved the support of the people of Maine, it was affirmed, for several reasons: first, the organization tended toward emancipation which was a moral influence; secondly, its aims did not "fly in the face of the law, nor did it interfere with rights established by the Constitution"; and, lastly, it tended to benefit the free colored population as well as Africa where they were sent. Slavery itself was a source of discord; the only way to end the disharmony was to ally with the colonizationists rather than with those who caused the chaos. Colonization men were entirely different from antislavery men; they were sane and reasonable, while the antislavery advocates were fanatical and irrational.

To the charge of their opponents that they ignored the great sin of slavery, the Portland colonizationists replied with an utter denial of the truth of the charge. The antislavery position, they argued, was based upon false premises. The primary consideration was not the alleged sinfulness of slavery as the abolitionists claimed, but the protection of the rights of property. The southern planter did not have anything to do with the souls of the slaves, nor did he claim property in their lives or limbs. The real threat to society, the colonizationists were certain, came when property rights were ignored, or, even worse, when they were violated. To conclude their argument, the colonizationists returned to an old theme. And was it not true, they confidently asked, that the free Negro was a misfit in white society? He was excluded from the very relationships which constituted the warp and woof of that society. What better blessing of fate could there be than to be shipped to a land where one did belong, where the people were one's own?

Only one man in Portland could present a rebuttal of the views expressed by the champions of colonization and expect to get a hearing. After his return to the city, another evening's debate was scheduled. The General did not muster any new arguments, but hammered at his opponents with the same ones that he had used before. Colonization was not worthy of support, he reiterated; its original aim had been to get rid of an unwanted class of citizens and, since its inception, this aim had not changed. To form a society for the purpose of removing free Negroes for their own benefit, besides being hateful, was not logical. Colonizationists formed themselves into a society for a purpose all right—to rid the slave states of a nuisance! Fessenden read excerpts from *The Liberator* to give more substance to his charges, then turned to a biblical example to conclude his case. Just as Moses could not be blamed for the reactions of pharaoh, so too the abolitionists could not be blamed for the excesses of those opposed to them. Slavery was a sin and God would have sinners leave off sinning immediately—this course of action, and no other, was the only just and proper answer to the problem so far as Samuel Fessenden and his friends were concerned.

The debate had continued well into July. It ended as it had begun; neither side had convinced the other of the truth of its case. Why such debates must end this way was clearly identified by an antislavery newspaper: "The truth is, they have not the same object in view. The one wishes to rid the country of the *free* colored people, the other the curse of slavery." For this reason the debate ended with General Fessenden and his small band of friends holding high the indictment of God against slavery and the Neal faction defending the reasonableness of shipping free Negroes out of the country.

But the Portland Colonization Debate was more than a drawn-battle; it was the turning point in the opposition to slavery in Maine. From the resolution of Samuel Fessenden and his followers the antislavery impulse was to spread throughout Maine and to become incorporated in the Maine Antislavery Society and its auxiliaries, in the Liberty Party which was organized in 1841, and in the Religious Antislavery Conventions which appeared at the state level in 1844.

Local antislavery societies had appeared in the state as early as March, 1833, but it was not until after the Colonization Debate that they began to blossom. The preamble to the constitution of the Hallowell Antislavery Society, the most important of the early societies, formed in that town on November 26, 1833, expressed the sentiments which were to permeate these societies for ten years:

> We, the undersigned, believing and adopting the following truths and principles, VIZ:
> That God hath made of one blood all nations of men to dwell on the face of the earth
> That all mankind are created equal, and that they are endowed by their Creator with certain inalienable rights, among which are life, liberty and the pursuit of happiness.
> That no man can rightfully hold property in his fellow man
> That the involuntary servitude and hard oppression of two millions of rational and immortal beings in our country (nearly one-sixth of the whole population) is a great political evil, and an atrocious personal sin
> That the only scheme of true rectitude and safety is to obey God and let the oppressed go free
> That the only justifiable and promising means of operating upon the evil, accomplishing redress for our injured and oppressed brethren, is the diffusion of the principles of truth and equity upon the heart and conscience, thus effecting, if anything can effect, a change in the public sentiment, which will sweep away the disgrace and inequity of slavery from our country.
> Adopting these principles, we do hereby agree with humble reliance upon Him who pleads the cause of the oppressed, to form ourselves into a society to be governed by the following...

When the American Antislavery Society was formed in December, 1833, at Philadelphia, several Maine men were present to sign the Declaration of Sentiments. Upon returning to Maine, these delegates worked to establish a state auxiliary society and finally reached their goal on October 15, 1834, at Augusta when a constitution was drafted for the Maine Antislavery Society. The constitution of the new society declared that

> The fundamental principles of this society are that slaveholding is a heinous sin against God, and therefore that immediate emancipation without the condition of expatriation is the duty of the master and the right of the slave.

The members of the new organization pledged themselves to carry out their stated purpose by moral and religious means, and no other, and to secure the immediate emancipation of "our enslaved brethren and sisters" for the sake of the master as well as the slave. They dedicated themselves to promote the intellectual, moral, and religious improvement of the colored people already free and to try to correct the wicked prejudice which stood in the way of the realization of this goal.

But the decade of the 1830's, besides being a time of heightened antislavery activity, was also a period of growing nationwide disapproval of antislavery agitation. Indicative of the extreme displeasure of the public was the treatment of Prudence Crandall of Canterbury, Connecticut and William Lloyd Garrison of Boston. Miss Crandall attempted to start a school for Negro girls at Canterbury, but she did not progress very far before the people of the town began to harass her unmercifully. They poisoned her well, broke her windows, and did all manner of hateful things to her and her girls. On June 27, 1833, she was taken into custody for violating the law and soon thereafter was tried, found guilty, and finally pressured to leave the town for good. William Lloyd Garrison also felt the wrath of the anti-abolitionists. In 1835 the Boston Female Antislavery Society had booked George Thompson, the English agitator, to address them at Julien Hall. Thompson was extremely unpopular in Boston and in the mob action which was generated by his rumored presence in the city, Garrison was pushed and tossed about, coming close to being trampled by the angry crowd. For security, he was taken to the city jail where he spent the night in borrowed clothes because his own had been torn from his body.

Open opposition to antislavery in Maine, while it did not display the intensity of feeling of the Crandall and Garrison episodes, was strong nonetheless. The most characteristic manifestation of disapproval was the antiabolition meeting, many of which were held in the summer of 1835 from Portland to Bangor. In Bangor the meeting was chaired by the mayor, Allen Gilman, who, like other men in the city, opposed the confusion created by antislavery agitation. The basic principles expressed in these gatherings were nearly uniform from one to the other: slavery had been forced on the South; the North had no constitutional right to interfere in the affairs of the states in the south; the South would eventually end slavery herself and the slaves had been elevated by the institution of slavery.

Despite this opposition the antislavery men continued their efforts in behalf of the slave. The Maine Antislavery Society maintained its cooperation with the American Antislavery Society and the agents of the national society were welcomed by their antislavery comrades whenever they came to the state. Chief among the lecturers who toured Maine was the Rev. Amos A. Phelps, who had been present at the founding of the state society and who reported his doings in the columns of *The Emancipator*. Among other things, Phelps observed that opposition to antislavery continued to be stubborn as evidenced by the refusal of churches in Wells, Freeport, Saco, and Kennebunk to allow him to use their facilities for an antislavery platform. But amid the signs of gloom, he saw also signs of hope in the formation of new societies and in the conviction and the dedication of those engaged in the cause.

Besides agents such as Phelps, the antislavery men employed other methods at the national and state levels to disseminate the principles of abolition. One of the most ambitious of these was the petition campaign, which, in Maine, was conducted by Ichabod Codding, later to be a political abolitionist in Illinois. The abolitionists believed, and wanted everyone else to recognize, that slavery undermined the Constitution and that terrible wrongs were committed because men allowed the Law of the Land to be violated. Typical of the character of the petitions drafted was the one submitted to the Maine House of Representatives for endorsement before being forwarded to the Congress which expressed confidence in the National Legislature to act against slavery in the District of Columbia:

> The Congress of the United States has the right under the Federal Constitution to abolish slavery in the District of Columbia; and it is considered that the exercise of this right would not be inconsistent with the good faith and lasting honor of the country.

Despite occasional approval by the Maine House of such petitions, they were never approved by the Senate, a smaller and more conservative body, which was controlled by those who believed the abolitionists to be rabble-rousers and who adhered to the principle that the Constitution did not give Congress the power to abolish slavery in the District of Columbia.

In Congress itself the petition battle reached white heat after 1836 when the number of petitions came to flood stage. Action was finally taken on the demands of the petitioners when Henry L. Pinckney of South Carolina, no friend of antislavery, successfully introduced a resolution to table all petitions pertaining to slavery. This Gag Rule, as it was called, awakened John Quincy Adams to the defense of the right of petition, a struggle which lasted until December 3, 1844, when the Rule was finally rescinded.

While much of the energy of the abolitionists was expended in supporting such causes as the petition campaign, much of it was dissipated in struggles within their own ranks. At the center of these controversies, and in great measure the cause of them, was William Lloyd Garrison who had embraced multi-reformism early in his career as an agitator and who worked for temperance, peace, and woman's rights with the same zeal that he pursued the goal of abolition. The division of opinion which developed over Garrison's views led to a bitter struggle in Boston where control of the Massachusetts Antislavery Society was the prize. The result of the clash between the Garrisonians and the anti-Garrisonians, besides a permanent bitterness of feeling, was the formation of the Massachusetts Abolition Society by the enemies of the editor of *The Liberator*.

But the battle did not remain confined to Boston; it was carried to New York in 1839 to the annual meeting of the American Antislavery Society at which Garrison introduced the following resolution: "Resolved that the roll of this meeting be made by placing thereon the names of all persons, male and female, who are delegates from any auxiliary society." The final stage of the struggle came in May, 1840, when the issue was raised by Garrison again. But this time he was prepared to outvote his opposition; he brought enough of his disciples with him from Massachusetts to give him victory when the time came to vote. Hours of debate occurred before the showdown, but when it came, it was William Lloyd Garrison who triumphed, while his opponents marched out of the hall in defeat.

The Maine abolitionists, despite the fact that it had been Garrison who had lighted the fires of abolition in their state, opposed his multi-reformism from the very first. Particularly opposed to the Garrisonian method was the Rev. David Thurston of Winthrop who completely disagreed with the Boston reformer. "I am utterly opposed," Thurston asserted, "to foisting in extraneous matter." Thurston, along with the majority of the Maine Antislavery men, felt that the single reform, antislavery, could best be served by concentrating on it, and it alone.

When Garrison brought up the question of the place of women in the American Antislavery Society, the delegates from Maine, except for Charles L. Remond of Salem, Massachusetts, who had been listed with the men from Maine, voted against his resolution. And when, after Garrison had captured control of the American Antislavery Society, the issue came up in the deliberations of the Maine Antislavery Society, the same anti-Garrison feelings persisted. At the Fourth Annual Meeting in February, 1841, Thurston again was the man to speak strongly against the views of the Boston editor. He introduced an amendment to the constitution of the society recommending a change of affiliation from the American Antislavery Society to the American and Foreign Antislavery Society, the new association created by Garrison's enemies. Most of the members present, not desiring to risk the chance of still another split in the antislavery forces, voted to remain independent of both national societies for the coming year. Their sentiments were revealed, however, in a resolution passed later in the meeting which promised unofficial cooperation with the American and Foreign Antislavery Society.

The year 1840, besides marking the split in the American Antislavery Society, also marked the rejection of another Garrisonian principle—the eschewing of political action. Experience had taught many of the abolitionists that more than moral persuasion, more than an appeal to conscience and reason, was required before any progress could be made toward emancipation. Believing that political action was the answer, a group of these men organized the Liberty Party at Albany, New York on April 1, 1840 and offered James G. Birney, a former slaveholder and colonizationist, and Thomas Earle of Pennsylvania as its first candidates for President and Vice-President respectively.

Those who were in sympathy with this new approach in Maine gathered a Human Rights Convention at Winthrop on July 1, 1841, and, as a consequence of the deliberations of the delegates there assembled, formed a Liberty Party for the State of Maine. The leaders of the newly established party believed, with the greater number of Liberty men around the country, that political action was a sacred cause, a cause which was blessed by God Himself. The Rev. David Thurston, a zealous advocate of religiously motivated political action, asserted that "We are at no time, in no place, on no occasion, to act otherwise than in love to God and to man. If these views are correct, then every qualified voter is under moral obligation to vote." Not only was voting itself a duty, it was a duty which required that votes be cast for men who were solid abolitionists. The Liberty Party offered such reliable men. In 1841 Jeremiah Curtis of Calais ran for the governorship of Maine on the Liberty ticket, but polled only 1,662 votes out of a total of 86,153 cast. From 1842 until 1848, when the Liberty Party died, Samuel Fessenden and James Appleton, both of Portland, alternated as the Liberty candidate for governor.

When the unsuccessful Liberty Party disappeared after 1848, Liberty men around the country, by and large, accepted the newly established Free Soil Party as the only viable alternative. The demise of the Liberty Party and the advent of the Free Soil Party commemorated the end of an era in antislavery politics based upon religious duty. An editorial in *The Emancipator* indicated the new emphasis: "The territories must be free. Nothing less than this will satisfy the free people of the North.... Freedom for the territories! That must be the rallying cry until the victory is won."

Indicative of the triumph of Free Soil over the minds of former Liberty men in Maine was the change in name of their state paper from *The Liberty Standard* to *The Free Soil Republican* on August 31, 1848. The Maine Free Soilers also reflected the abandonment of the biblically based call to political action for the more pragmatic cry of "free soil, free labor, and free men." This development was mirrored in the resolutions of the Free Soil State Convention held at Augusta on September 27, 1848, one of which declared that

Resolved, that it is the first duty of the freemen of this country, at every hazard and sacrifice, to arrest the further encroachments of the slave power, and restore their government to its proper sphere and action.

At the same meeting the past sins of Martin Van Buren, presumably committed when he was one of the leaders of the "pro-slavery" Democratic Party, were forgiven and his candidacy for President supported. The Maine Party also offered candidates for state office in 1849, 1850, 1852, and 1853. After 1853 the Party was lost as a separate entity in Maine in the welter of political confusion involving the Maine Law Party, the Know-Nothings, the Opposition Democrats, the Democrats, and the Whigs.

And in 1854, when the Republican Party was getting its start across the nation, the energies of the political abolitionists in Maine were absorbed in its antislavery orientated activities. Anson P. Morrill, who in 1854 ran for the governorship on the Maine Law and Know-Nothing ticket and who had gained the confidence and the support of the abolitionists, was almost returned to office as a Republican in 1855, the same year that political abolitionism disappeared as a separate and distinct force in the state.

A final, and underlying, part of the antislavery impulse, besides the moral element embodied in the antislavery societies and the political element incorporated in the abolition political parties, was the religious element which had been present since antislavery agitation began. Before 1830 there had been a religious consensus on the evil of slavery, a consensus clearly expressed by the General Assembly of the Presbyterian Church in 1818:

> We consider the voluntary enslaving of one part of the human race by another as a gross violation of the most precious and sacred rights of human nature: as utterly inconsistent with the law of God, which requires us to love our neighbor as ourselves, and as totally irreconcilable with the spirit and principle of the Gospel of Christ, which enjoins that "all things whatsoever ye would that men should do to you, do ye even so to them."

But after 1830 the situation changed radically; a vigorous antislavery movement began within as well as without the churches.

This agitation of the slavery question within the churches generated active opposition. Southern ministers were put in a particularly difficult situation and many of them searched for a scriptural sanction for slavery—and some of them found what they were looking for. Southerners pointed to specific texts in the Bible as their proof; a favorite was Genesis 9:25 "And he said, 'Cursed be Canaan; a servant of servants shall he be unto his brethren'." Three denominations were intimately involved in the dispute over slavery at the national level—the Baptists, the Methodists, and the Presbyterians—and eventually all three split into northern and southern branches over the issue of slavery.

In Maine the churches affected were the Baptists, the Congregationalists (who were closely connected with the Presbyterians), and the Methodists. Among the Baptists in the state the Hancock Baptist Association and its leader the Rev. James Gilpatrick of Blue Hill sounded the alarm in 1836, when at a meeting they labelled slavery a sin against God, advocated voting only for abolitionists, and called for the formation of a state Baptist antislavery organization. The Baptist press, *Zion's Advocate,* published in Portland, became mildly antislavery under the Rev. Adam Wilson. Perhaps the most spectacular, and least successful, display of antislavery sentiment among the Baptists in Maine was expressed in the gathering of the short-lived Second Church in Augusta which was formed by those who would have nothing to do at all with slaveholding churchmen.

The Congregationalists, while the most wealthy and influential religious body in the state, were far from vigorous in their denunciation of slavery. Their state organization, the General Conference of Maine, understood slavery to be a sin, but did not take any practical action on the matter. Its most positive efforts were a series of letter exchanges with churches and individuals in the South beginning in 1837 with the correspondence of Professor William Smyth of Bowdoin College with the Rev. Rufus W. Bailey of South Carolina. While the majority of the ministers taking part in the antislavery movement in Maine were Congregationalists, in their General Conference they followed the path marked out for them by moderates such as the Rev. Asa Cummings of Portland, editor of *The Christian Mirror* and a supporter of the cause of Colonization.

The Maine Methodists were plagued by the concern of many of their number to move slowly and to do nothing which might lead to a split. Even the discussion of slavery in a denominational meeting was going too far for some of them. But a small number of Methodist ministers felt otherwise. The Rev. Charles C. Cone and the Rev. Daniel B. Randall led a tiny band of men who were not afraid to call slavery what they thought it was—a sin of the worst sort against God and man! However, in spite of their gallant efforts, Maine Methodists spent most of their time trying to avoid controversy over slavery, rather than opposing the evil.

The most genuine expression of the religious objection to slavery came finally in 1844 with the advent of the first General Religious Antislavery Convention in Hallowell on January 9th, a meeting organized and promoted by antislavery leaders among the Baptists, Congregationalists, and Methodists who were making no progress within their separate denominations. These religious conventions, which had their heyday from 1844 to 1852, were taken up with spelling out exactly the duty of the clergy and the Christian layman with regard to the sin of slavery. The state annual meetings at which the issues evoked by slavery were discussed were usually lively and full of the fire of controversy; but, after 1852, when the political issue was coming to its climax, interest in the conventions faded. These meetings, while they lasted, did, however, provide an open forum for like-minded, religiously oriented men to air their views.

When Maine entered the Union in 1820, slavery was a major question and, not long after statehood, the problem of chattel slavery was debated in the state. The first antislavery sentiment expressed in Maine found embodiment in the American Colonization Society, which gave way in the 1830's, after the Portland Colonization Debate, to the organizations incorporating immediatism in their aims.

From 1834 to 1855 the antislavery impulse in Maine followed three avenues—the first, the humanitarian-religious, or moral avenue, which lasted from 1834 to 1846 and which was represented by the Maine Antislavery Society and its auxiliary units in the counties and towns the second, the political, which was incorporated in the Liberty and Free Soil parties; and the third, the religious, which was manifested most clearly in the General Religious Antislavery Conventions.

The year 1855 was decisive; it was the junction point for the three avenues, or antislavery impulses. The three were merged. They had been moving in the same direction; now they had completed their journey.

CHAPTER

25.

Bangor was known as the lumber capitol of the world in the 19th century. Stewart Holbrook, a well known historian, recounts in vivid detail the shape of life in the city of lumber in the days of old.

THE FLOWERING OF A LUMBER TOWN*

by

Stewart H. Holbrook

The rock-maple floors of Bangor's two hotels showed the impress of a thousand and more calked boots, and the proud plank sidewalks of the young city were deeply holed by rivermen's shoes, too, and splintered as well. For Bangor in Maine was to be the very first of the great lumber towns and in some respects the greatest of them all.

Conditions were perfect to turn the trick. Unwatered rum cost three cents a glass, a glass was a dipperful, and a thirsty logger helped himself with the tin dipper that was chained to the open barrel. And down Exchange Street, a piece, two rather pretty ladies had rented a house and put up a small sign announcing "Gentlemen's Washing Taken In"—a genteel and harmless euphemism. No chamber of commerce was needed to make Bangor; the lodestones were there already and talk in a hundred bunkhouses, back in the deep timber, would take care of the advertising.

Coordinating conditions also were magnificent. North from Bangor, and drained by the river that turned her sawmills, there stretched two and one-half million acres of black and wonderful timber. Once he saw it, the scene gripped the fancy of young Henry Thoreau, a-visiting here from Concord, down in Massachusetts.

There stands the city of Bangor (he wrote in 1846) like a star on the edge of night, still hewing at the forest of which it is built, already overflowing with the luxuries and refinements of Europe and sending its vessels to Spain, to England, and to the West Indies for its groceries—and yet only a few ax-men have gone up-river into the howling wilderness that feeds it.

A howling wilderness it was. The tall black spruce was dwarfed by the towering white pines that rose up, straight as masts and light as cork, close to two hundred feet above the ground. How far north of Bangor ran this forest, no man knew. Some said it reached to the Pole itself; everybody said it would last forever. It would take a small war and two pretty stirring orations by Dan'l Webster to learn where the Yankee pine left off and the Canuck pine began.

Through this vast forest ran the Penobscot, with all its lakes and tributaries, in season a swift-moving highway down which with no power other than brawn and a peavey the forest could be brought to mills and tidewater at Bangor. It was a temperamental highway, difficult to manage in spite of dams; but manage it they did and for a full century sharp-shod men walked fair down the middle of it on bobbing logs.

Fifty miles south of town, down the deep Penobscot, was the open sea. The tides in the river were remarkably high, and the deep-sea skippers liked the port of Bangor, for here they could, at low water slack, fill their casks easily from over ship's side and find the Penobscot water fresh and saltless, though in time it came to have the flavor of pine in it.

---

*Reprinted with permission of The Macmillan Company from *Holy Old Mackinaw* by Stewart H. Holbrook. Copyright 1938 by The Macmillan Company, renewed 1966 by Sybil Holbrook.

The Flowering of a Lumber Town

A numerous fleet, Bangor-built and Bangor-owned, carried lumber from here to the world and brought back rum, and molasses and sugar to be made into more rum to get more logs to make more lumber to trade for more rum. It was all a perfect cycle from the lumbermen's viewpoint, while from that of the practicing logger—the man who used the ax and saw—Bangor was nothing less than Paradise. Booze, bawds, and battle with roistering loggers—there was really nothing else in life, except timber, and that was handy by. Bangor set the classic pattern that would follow the timber line West to the Pacific shore, distant by three thousand miles, one hundred years, and two trillion feet of lumber.

God indeed smiled on the rising lumber capital of the world, and He caused one of His Apostles to name it. The citizens of the humming town on the Penobscot wanted a town charter, in 1791, so they drew up a highly official and legal application. The name of their new home in the forest, they decided, should be Sunbury, which handsome name was inscribed in the application and the document turned over to the Reverend Seth Noble to carry to Boston, where the Great Seal and the governor's signature might be put upon it.

The Reverend Seth Noble was a local divine whose voice was such that it could be, and often was, heard above the drone of four hundred and ten saws and the combined howls of wolves and loggers on carouse. But the Reverend Seth cared little for the chosen name, which smelled of paganism. He erased it and inserted in a neat round hand the name by which his favorite hymn was known in the old hymnals, "Bangor."

The name fitted Bangor, Maine, and so did the hymn itself, although the loggers probably did not realize how well:

> Hark from the tombs a doleful sound;
> Mine ears attend the cry—
> Ye living men, come view the ground
> Where ye must shortly die.

And die they did, up there in the gloom of the two million acres of tall black stuff—when a sudden waft blew a tall pine the wrong way; when there was the sickening slump in a mile-long landing of logs before they rolled Death over a man; or, the whiskered Old Fellow with the Scythe might hold off, jokingly, until the logs were fair in the stream, then strike you down into the white boiling water of the Ripogenus, on the west branch. Death always stood just behind the logger and very close to the riverman.

That's why loggers lived the way they did. Death might come out of the trees above, with the merest whisssh of warning, or it might wait in the form of a watered rock, just around the next bend in the river... Little wonder they pounded on the white pine bars of Bangor's groggeries and yelled for another drink all around.

The early years of Bangor saw only moderate progress. The first settler hewed out his home there in 1769, and within a year the first of a long line of sawmills was going. But Bangor didn't get its town charter for two decades, and the first ship with a Bangor house flag didn't go down the ways until 1811. Shortly thereafter, and suddenly, there came a brief era of speculation.

Indians, white hunters, and even a few landlookers had long told of the mighty trees in the vast forests of the Penobscot. These tales finally permeated to the populous cities of Portland and Portsmouth and even to metropolitan Boston and Philadelphia, where lived men of vision and substance. Good pines that were handy to streams, they knew, were already becoming scarce along the Connecticut, the Saco, and the lower Androscoggin and the Kennebec. Late in the eighteenth century men of means began buying Penobscot timber.

The District of Maine—there was no State of Maine until 1820—was happy to be shut of its timberland. It disposed of much of this by grants to colleges and academies and to soldiers of the Revolution; and it sold even more through lotteries. Money was hard to come by, for the provincial governments. Timberland not only was worthless, it was in the way. You had, as they said, to let daylight into the swamp before corn and potatoes would grow.

So the buying and granting went on. William Bingham, a wealthy Philadelphian, sent a timber cruiser on a voyage through the woods of central and eastern Maine, and then Mr. Bingham bought, for twelve and a half cents an acre, a goodly slice of Maine for himself. In one hunk Mr. Bingham purchased 2,107,396 acres of white pine and spruce in which no ax, save it be an Indian's stone tomahawk, had been heard.

It is beyond the minds of men today to conceive of two million acres of virgin timber in one solid block, owned by one man. For more than a century afterward a horde of loggers hacked away at the Bingham Purchase, driving part down the Kennebec, part down the Penobscot; and of a winter's work one logger would say to another that he had been working on the Kennebec Million, or the Penobscot Million.

There were many lesser but still large purchases, too, and Bangor soon became the scene of a land speculation that would be matched only in the Far West of later years. This was only proper, for the Penobscot country was really New England's last frontier, the only frontier in America where men moved from West to East to reach it.

In 1835 land brokers' offices crowded to the saloons and "gentlemen's washing" houses all along Exchange Street, and they ran like the water-front sawmills—all day and all night. Timberland that had brought six and twelve cents an acre a few years before was now changing hands at six dollars, eight dollars, and even ten dollars. Fast courier lines, a sort of Pony Express, were set up between Bangor and Boston. Smooth gents formed the somewhat diaphanous Bangor Lower Stillwater Mill Company, obviously more interested in lots than in mills, and staged a combination auction-banquet, the latter presided over by a caterer from New York. Champagne was poured from original bottles into washtubs, and all invited to belly-around and drink hearty. Fortunately, for the amazed loggers, this affair was held in June, when the drive was in and a man was handy—and thirsty.

The wildcatters turned over $127,000 in timberlands that day, and the loggers who would later cut the timber got ory-eyed on free champagne.

The speculation boom, of course, soon burst, but actual logging along the Penobscot was just getting a good start, for men of action had come along with the men of vision. Railroad construction had been pushed twelve miles upriver as early as 1836, to reach Oldtown and Orono. Its rails were wood, with scrap iron spiked along the top, and its locomotive had been made in England by Stephenson himself. The redoubtable General Sam Veazie bought this road and started out to make it go.

General Veazie, while perhaps the most aggressive of the early Bangor lumbermen, was quite typical. He soon built or bought control in nineteen mills at Oldtown, thirteen more at Basin Mills, and still twenty more in his own town of Veazie, which town he got a friendly legislature to set aside for him. The general thought it would be nice, and efficient, to elect men from his own company payroll to fill the rather important offices of tax assessors.

As early as 1825 the legislature had granted a charter to a company formed to collect the great mass of logs of mixed ownership that floated down from the woods and to segregate them for the various mills at and between Oldtown and Bangor. General Veazie bought this franchise and ran things in his own way, possibly to his own advantage, for there was hell a-popping and much fighting about logs until the other lumbermen got the State to appoint a three-man commission to handle affairs at the Penobscot log boom.

But Veazie was not alone in his aggressiveness. There was Jefferson Sinclair, a great figure to whom many gave the credit for starting the boom idea in the first place. There was Moses Giddings and old Arad Thompson, individualists from 'way back, and the Pearsons, the Lumberts, the Bruces, and a score of others, all of them up on their hind legs and r'aring to go. Among them, and aided by just such aggressive and prehensile logging operators in New Brunswick, they brought about what to this day in Maine is referred to as the Aroostook War.

The "war" took its name from the then vaguely bounded country known as The Aroostook. The international boundary was as yet undetermined, but not so were the intentions of the Bangor logging operators and timber owners. They wanted all that great straight pine, come hell and high water, and they charged that the New Brunswickers were jumping the claim and cutting in Maine woods.

The State of Maine sent its land agents up to investigate. They discovered many rafts of logs, allegedly cut in Maine timber, being floated down the Aroostook River and into New Brunswick. They seized some of the rafts, only to have the Blue Nosers cut them loose under cover of darkness. There was considerable hullabaloo, during which oxen were seized and stocks of wild hay burned. Among the actual loggers on both sides a heap of assault and battery took place, some of it naturally running to mayhem, through the loss of ears in combat.

Now the logging operators and timber owners set up a howl that was articulated through the Maine legislature loud enough to reach Washington, D.C. But Washington moved too slowly to suit long-memoried folk whose towns and cities—aye, and whose camps and sawmills had been burned by the British a few years before. In 1839 Maine loaded some old brass cannon onto oxcarts and scows and sent militia north to man Forts Kent and Fairfield.

Some excellent sniping was done back and forth with ball and cap rifles, but the artillery did not go into action. Sir John Harvey and Lord Ashburton had come forward as peacemakers for Great Britain, and General Winfield Scott and Dan'l Webster acted for the embattled Bangor lumbermen. The Webster-Ashburton Treaty (1839) setting the present boundary, was the outcome, and the Maine troops returned to their homes.

With the Aroostook Question officially settled, both Penobscot and New Brunswick lumbermen continued to poach upon each other's preserves, but the only actual fighting done was carried on by the loggers themselves, who enjoyed it hugely never allowing it again to become an International Incident but keeping it alive for local amusement and practice.

With comparative quiet restored along the border, Bangor went into the years of its glory. Williamsport, Pennsylvania, would later cut more lumber than Bangor. Saginaw and Muskegon in Michigan would cut more boards in a month than Bangor did in a year; and, in time, a single sawdust plant would rise on the Columbia River in the Pacific Northwest that could cut twice as much lumber as all of Bangor's four hundred and ten saws. Yet the fame of the Penobscot city became so great that no less than ten other Bangors were founded, hopefully, on the loggers' and lumbermen's trek South and West. A number of things contributed to this lustrous shining of Thoreau's star on the edge of night.

Bangor was the first city of size whose entire energies were given to the making and shipping of lumber and to the entertainment of the loggers who cut the trees. Then, too, it is from Bangor's canny and inventive men that stems so much that has been found sound and practicable throughout the years. And lastly, there were the sure-footed lads of Bangor who, spring after spring, walked two hundred and more miles on heaving logs straight down the middle of the Penobscot. These men made such a name for themselves, by their agility on a moving log and by their foolhardy courage anywhere, that west of Bangor a Penobscot man came to be known as a Bangor tiger—quick of foot and ready for battle.

Good as they were, the Bangor Tigers, like loggers elsewhere, lacked a forthright tool for driving the timber down rivers. For a century past, rivermen had got along the best they could with a tool as primitive as a stone ax. It was a swing dog, in its then most modern form, and a pretty poor rig it was. Around a short pole, some four feet long, hung an iron collar to which was attached a hook, or dog, for the rolling of logs. It was awkward, and dangerous, for the dog would move up and down and sidewise. Thus the dog was not always "there" when wanted, and a man giving a good quick heave on the staff might find himself flopping headlong over the log and into the stream. Rivermen cursed it, and it sent many of them into the water, not to rise until a million feet of logs had passed over them. Then they ceased to worry about swing dogs. But Bangor inventors didn't.

One afternoon in the spring of 1858, Joseph Peavey, a blacksmith of Stillwater Village, near Bangor, lay on his stomach in the old covered bridge that crossed the Stillwater branch of the Penobscot. Through a crack in the floor he was watching the efforts of a crew of rivermen below him to break a big jam of logs.

Old Peavey watched a while, and listened while the rivermen passed blistering remarks about the goddamn so-and-so swing dogs. Then, as he afterward told, the Big Idea came, like a shaft of sudden sunlight through a hole in a covered bridge. Peavey jumped up, shouting a blacksmith's equivalent of "Eureka!" and ran as fast as he could to the Peavey blacksmith shop. Here he directed his son Daniel how to make a rigid clasp to encircle a cant-dog staff, with lips on one side. These lips were drilled to take a bolt that would hold the hook, or dog, in place, allowing it to move up and down but not sidewise. Below the bulge in the cant-dog handle Daniel placed graduated collars of iron which added greatly to the strength of the handle. Then, as a piece of crowning genius, old Joe had his son drive a sharp iron spike into the end of the rig...Thus the tool was born that would in years to come roll untold billions of feet of logs into the many rivers that run between the Penobscot and the Pacific, and from Hudson's Bay to the Gulf of Mexico.

Old Joe Peavey's last name would soon be known wherever logs were rolled, though the greatest single invention in the technology of logging would bring him no fortune.

Peavey got William Hale, noted Penobscot river boss, to try out the new tool. Hale pronounced it the soundest rig ever put in the hands of a calk-booted man. So Joe Peavey made a drawing of it and set out on foot for Bangor and the post office, with the intention of getting it patented. On the way he stopped to see a blacksmith friend in Orono.

Joe Peavey liked a glass of Medford rum, sometimes two glasses. His Orono friend poured liberally and old Joe, his stomach warm, displayed the plans he was sending to the patent office. This called for another round of rum, and so on. When Joe awoke next morning and shook the fog out of his old gray head, drawings and application for a "Patent Cantdog," not a peavey, were on their way to Washington, submitted by the Orono blacksmith.

But regardless of first patents, the Peavey family went into the business of making the tool Joe had invented, and the fourth generation of them are at it today, in Brewer, just across the Penobscot from Bangor. The name had long been admitted to dictionaries and is a generic term applied by woodsmen to all cant dogs. Not one logger in a thousand today knows whence and how came its name.

Joseph Peavey didn't stop with the riverman's tool. He is credited with the Peavey hoist, for pulling stumps and raising the gates of dams, and with the hay press, by which loose hay could be baled into small tight wads for transportation into the logging camps.

The idea of a large sorting boom to handle logs for many mills has already been mentioned. It was devised at Bangor in 1825, and was copied later on the Hudson, the Saginaw, the Mississippi, and other streams in the West.

Bangor men invented the Bangor Snubber, a machine for regulating the speed of sledloads of logs on steep hills, and the log-branding ax, or hammer, was a product of Bangor, and it is the logger's one concession to Art.

A log with no owner's mark on it and floating down the public highway of a river is anybody's log, so the practice of branding logs came early in the industry. Before the Bangor invention of a branding ax, men who had to be marvels with an ax cut the owner's mark in the ends of the logs. These marks, by necessity of the tool used, had to be a grouping of straight lines. They ran to what were called, Dart, Double-dart, Diamond, Crowsfoot, Anchor, Short Forty, Long Forty, and such.

With the branding ax, its face a steel pattern of the brand's design, lumbermen could allow their imaginations free rein. Log brands have run to wondrous patterns since then, and include Derby Hats, Wine Glasses, Beerkeg-bungs, Aeolian Harps, and Hearts and Flowers. Thus did inventive Bangor devise an outlet for the long-suppressed artistic urges of logging operators.

During the period 1830-1860, sawmills grew and multiplied along the Penobscot. Bangor doubled, then redoubled its population to seventeen thousand. Ships for lumber came so thick that on many days small boys could walk across the harbor from Bangor to Brewer on their decks. The channel to the sea once got so full of heavy pine slabs that Army dredges had to come to clear it, making it even deeper; and monstrous great ships, like the graceful "Belle of Bath" and the staunch "Phineas Pendleton," could dock at Bangor with room to spare underneath the keel.

Below and above Bangor, the river was never empty. From the mills clustered at Oldtown and Orono came long rafts made of sawed lumber floating down to the docks, to be taken apart, board by board, and stowed in the holds. Log rafts, too, some of them half a mile long, came into Bangor for sawing in the city mills. As for men in calked boots—they simply swarmed over everything and everywhere.

On on a Bangor street one sniffed the air and found the perfume of pine in it. In the shops one smelled rum and molasses. It was pure affinity. Lumbermen sweetened the loggers' beans and tea with molasses; they made it into rum for the loggers' entertainment. And the logger, he put the pine dust in the air.

The big lumbermen built mansions all along State Street in Bangor, where some of the houses still survive. These first lumbermen were lusty fellows and they, too, set a pattern. It was a pattern that has been dimmed by the passage of time and dimmed again by the efforts of their scandalized descendants, but it is tolerably clear—and fascinating.

Most of these big lumbermen would drink Madeira, to be polite, when they entertained at home, but they liked Medford and West Indies rum, which they drank in vast quantities. They were kind to dumb animals, their favorite being the fast and tireless Morgan horse. These they imported from Vermont for themselves and their mistresses, whom they kept in semiregal style, if compared with the Spartan life enjoined on the young men and women of the Bangor Theological Seminary.

Nor was the calk-booted proletariat without its entertainment. Quite early in Bangor's life the Devil himself took possession of much of the property centering around Haymarket Square, on the west side of town, and held its own securely until the timber line had moved west to Michigan. It was here, on Harlow Street, that the noble Fan Jones built and operated her justly famous Skyblue House.

Fan Jones was a woman of wide vision, looking both landward and seaward. There was a huge chimney on the outside of her place and this she caused to be painted sky blue, the blue of the brightest sky ever seen. It was never allowed to fade, but was repainted twice a year, brighter and more lovely each time. And this chimney was so placed that its heavenly color served as landmark for women-hungry loggers coming downriver from the woods, and as a promise of snug harbor to the sailors coming upriver. If a man got lost in Bangor, whether by land or by sea, it was no fault of Fan's; and she did very well by this public-spirited service.

Haymarket Square came to harbor a score of hellholes where grog and other vice abounded. It was a fitting subject, close to hand, on which the young divines of the theologican seminary could practice calling down God's curse. Yet Satan had so well fortified it that in 1911, when Bangor suffered the worst fire in its history, the flames ate up five churches, a school, a bank and dozens of homes of the pious, but left the Haymarket with not so much as a blister of paint on its scarlet lights.

Bangor and the Penobscot did not reach the peak of lumber making and shipping until 1872, yet their importance in the lumber industry had faded a full decade before. By the time of the First Battle of Bull Run the bulk of Maine's white pine forests had gone through the saws, and Michigan, the next white pine stronghold, was the lumber colossus. A heap of spruce would go down the Penobscot just as some of it does in 1938—in tiny, four-foot sticks—but most of that spruce has gone into the chippers and digesters of pulpmills, to be regurgitated as long rolls of paper on which to print comic strips.

CHAPTER 26.

The Hudson and the Kennebec rivers produced more ice than any other American rivers in the 19th century. So profitable was the business at one time that ice was referred to as frozen gold.

FROZEN GOLD: THE ICE INDUSTRY ON THE KENNEBEC*
by
Ernest Marriner

On a New Haven railroad train in the 1880's a New York man fell into conversation with a man from Gardiner, Maine. "I've been down there on the Kennebec," said the New Yorker, "and I've often wondered how you Gardiner folks get a living. Hallowell has its big granite quarries, Augusta is the state capital, but how do you people in Gardiner pay your bills?"

"Well, I'll tell you," drawled the Maine man, "we get along all right. Our little factories don't hire many men, but they all help. Our shippin' ain't what it used to be, when Gardiner men owned and operated more ships than any other port on the river, except Bath. We pick up a lot of odd cents one way or another, but when it comes right down to it, I s'pose we pay our bills with frozen gold."

The first record of a shipment of frozen gold from the Kennebec concerns the city of Gardiner, for in 1824 the brig Orion of that town was loaded with floating ice in the early spring and sailed for Baltimore as soon as the river was fully open to navigation. In the Maryland city that cargo of ice sold for $700. When a product provided by nature itself could be so easily turned into cash, it took no great stretch of metaphor to call that product frozen gold.

The romantic side of the industry has been preserved for posterity in the poetic prose of Robert Coffin in his *Kennebec, Cradle of Americans*. Telling how the farmers, with their sons and their horses, gathered from all the lower Kennebec towns and from far into their hinterland, Dr. Coffin continues:

> Here you could reckon on a man's property in solid, tangible things, as in the days of Jacob and Laban. The richest man was one who had nine or ten strong men to follow the swing of his creasing trousers in ringing, ironed shoes. Or three or four spans of horses with the morning star in their foreheads and the music of steel under their feet. So the wealth of the Kennebec came down to the harvest of Maine's best winter crop in the eighties.

It was indeed a romantic industry. My first sight of it was in the winter of 1909-10, when I was a freshman at Colby College. I had seen ice harvested on Highland Lake in Bridgton and put into the little ice houses on its shore, but that was toy work compared with the Kennebec harvest. It was certainly a thrilling spectacle to see several hundred men out on the ice in section after section between Hallowell and Richmond; to watch the gougers marking the field, the saws worked by strong arms cutting the blocks, the picks guiding the big cakes through the open canals, the chains and hooks hauling the cakes up the run-ways into the huge ice houses. But romantic and spectacular as any stranger might find it, the practical economy was what appealed to the inhabitants of the Kennebec.

From time of the early settlements Maine had enjoyed one prominent winter crop—lumber. Trees cut down in the winter provided the long logs that came down the Kennebec on the spring waters and supplied hundreds of saw mills along the banks. That winter crop was profitable, but it was

---

*Ernest Marriner, *Kennebec Yesterday* (Waterville: Colby College Press, 1954), pp. 158-164. Reprinted by permission of the publisher.

harvested only by the hardest kind of labor over many weeks, and as time went on, the lumbermen had to go deeper and deeper into the big woods, far from the towns.

Kennebec ice, on the contrary, was to be had right at home. No artificial restoration was necessary, no waiting for twenty years for another crop to grow. The crop demanded neither seeds nor fertilizer; it just grew year after year. Its yield depended only on tricks of the weather. If the winter stayed warm or had too frequent thaws, the ice was thin and spongy; if there was a long spell of intense cold, it was thick and hard. But, in some condition and some quality, it came every winter. It was the Kennebec's cheapest and most available winter crop.

Somehow, whether deserved or just promoted by good advertising, Kennebec ice got the reputation of being the purest in the markets of the world. When we note the present-day appearance of the river, though we still contend it not so offensive as the Androscoggin, we wonder how its ice could ever have been considered pure. We can only conjecture that the chemical wastes now poured into the river from the big factories and the sewage from the growing cities had not then so badly polluted the stream.

Just how far the Kennebec ice travelled in those boom years of the industry from 1840 to 1900, no one can accurately say. Dr. Coffin may be right in his casual reference to cargoes of it going around Cape Horn. We have been unable to find any authentic reference to such a voyage. Perhaps loads of it went even to Calcutta, the destination (as Thoreau contended in *Walden*) of some of the ice from Walden Pond. We do know that ice from the Kennebec found its way into julep glasses at Savannah and the punch bowls at Port au Prince, that the feudal planters on Jamaica used a lot of it, and the Royal Bank of Canada on the island of Trinidad had a regular contract for summer supply. Doubtless occasional cargoes of ice from Hallowell or Gardiner or Richmond crossed the Atlantic to Mediterranean ports, and it is quite possible that it went to other parts of Europe and Africa.

By far the greater part of each winter's crop, however, went to our own Atlantic cities—to New York and Philadelphia, to Baltimore and Washington, to Norfolk and Richmond, to Charleston and Savannah. By 1880, the biggest operator was the Knickerbocker Ice Company, which had wholesale and retail outlets in a dozen major cities and which owned some of the biggest storage facilities on the Kennebec. It was in the ice business that the banker and financier, Charles Morse, accumulated the start of his considerable fortune.

After that experimental voyage of the Orion in 1824, the business developed fast. In 1826, Rufus Page of Gardiner put up in that town a building capable of storing 1500 tons of ice. Page filled the house with thick, solid ice. About the same time the Tudors of Boston, who had exclusive control of the ice trade with the British West Indies, built another ice house at Gardiner. Page arranged with the Tudors to transport his ice along with theirs. For some reason the market was not good, the venture failed, and Page had to turn his ice house over to the Tudors to pay his debts.

In 1832 the Tudors built a 3000 ton ice house at Gardiner, almost exactly where the bridge head now stands, and thereafter the industry grew fast. Ice houses sprang up at Pittston, South Gardiner and Farmingdale. It was not until 1867, however, that the first modern ice house was built on the Kennebec. This was at Pittston, where the Kennebec Land and Lumber Company erected a building with a capacity of 10,000 tons. Five years later a well established distributor known as the Independent Ice Company of Washington, D.C., built several houses at Pittston. One of the largest locally owned firms was the Haynes and DeWitt Ice Company, of which the head was J. Manchester Haynes of Augusta.

In 1896 The Gardiner Board of Trade, to promote industrial and business interests in the community, published an illustrated booklet with the title *Picturesque Gardiner*. This volume contains some excellent pictures of the harvesting, storage and shipping of Kennebec ice. There is a full-page scene of ice-cutting in front of the huge Knickerbocker plant at Gardiner; there are fascinating photographs of the trim, fast three-masted and four-masted vessels that carried the ice to distant ports. One view depicts the gigantic plant of the Cockran-Oler Company, with its almost unbelievable capacity of 175,000 tons. Altogether the booklet shows pictures of the ice houses and ships of six companies, whose combined annual output came to 6,000,000 tons. By way of boosting the town, the volume declared:

Today (1896) the largest and most convenient ice houses in the world line both banks of the river, with a total storage of 1,5000,000 tons. More than a third of this capacity is at Gardiner and Randolph. The average harvest, compared with the Orion's first cargo of $700 in 1824, is now $2,000,000.

Still preserved is a valuable record of the ice industry—a chart of all the ice houses on the Kennebec in 1882. It bears the heading: "Issued by T.B. Chase and Sons, Dealers and Brokers in Ice, 51 Commercial Street, Boston, and Gardiner, Maine, 1882." On the left side of the chart is a map of the Kennebec river from the Augusta dam to Bath, showing boat canals, position of buoys, depth of water, and the position, capacity and ownership of all ice houses. In the lower left hand corner is a list of tow boats on the river—the little steam craft that towed the big sailing vessels to the ice ports. Nine of those boats were owned by the Knickerbocker Ice Company and two by the Kennebec Company.

It was this chart which settled a dispute about the Knickerbocker Ice Company. When, on a radio program, I once referred to the Knickerbocker Ice Company of New York, several listeners took me to task. They admitted that, historically, the name Knickerbocker ought to be associated with New York, but they were very sure that the Knickerbocker Ice Company was a Philadelphia concern. One man told me he had, as a boy, often chased Knickerbocker teams through Philadelphia streets, to get small chips of ice, the way children used to do in every town.

The 1882 chart makes it clear that there were two Knickerbocker companies, or perhaps two branches of the same company. The Knickerbocker Ice Company of New York was by that time the smaller company, so far as its Kennebec houses were concerned, having only two with a combined capacity of 58,000 tons. The larger producer and distributor was called the Philadelphia Knickerbocker Company, and had six big houses with a total capacity of 188,000 tons. This Philadelphia company boasted one of the largest houses on the river, at Pittston, where 65,000 tons of ice could be stored under one roof. It took several different houses to store the 175,000 tons of Cochran-Oler, to which reference has previously been made. But the Philadelphia Knickerbocker house at Pittston, for all its 65,000 tons, was not the Kennebec's largest. That honor went to the ice house of Abram Rich of Farmingdale, where winter after winter Rich put up 80,000 tons. Haynes and DeWitt, the biggest of the local interests, had a house for 62,000 tons at Richmond, and the Baltimore firm of Ober and Son had a 50,000 ton house at the same place.

Altogether, between the Augusta dam and Bath, the chart shows 41 ice houses commercially operating in 1882. Those 41 were in addition to the numerous small houses used to store ice for local use. Although the Philadelphia Knickerbocker Company was by far the largest operator, not to be scoffed at were the four big houses of Russell Brothers on both sides of the river at Richmond and Dresden. At Pittston centered Washington interests, with the Great Falls and the Independence companies, both with headquarters in the national capital, accounting for 1,000,000 tons a year.

Among those giants, controlled from the big cities, local operators like Haynes and DeWitt strove valiantly for what was left of the holdings which, until after the Civil War, had been almost entirely in neighborhood hands. The Kennebec Ice Company, owned by Gardiner and Augusta interests, still had big houses at Richmond and Pittston as late as 1882. Even some of the small operators hung on tenaciously. G. E. Weeks, with a house just below the Augusta dam, stored a mere 2,000 tons. The White Brothers put up 5,000 tons at Farmingdale. George Brown, down near Merrymeeting Bay, rated a listing on the chart with 2,000 tons, while the smallest commercial ice house of all stored Thompson Brothers' 1,500 tons opposite Swan Island.

Thanks to this chart, we know that Kennebec ice held the record for all ice exported from Maine waters. On the right side of the chart are listed the names and capacity of commercial ice houses on the Penobscot and Cathance rivers, and at ports along the coast from Biddeford to Vinalhaven. On the Penobscot were fifteen companies, storing and shipping in 1882 a total of 146,000 tons. On the Cathance river were twelve companies with 39,000 tons. Along the coast were 34 companies turning out 349,800 tons. That made a total of little more than half a million tons of ice exported by all of Maine, except the Kennebec. From the Kennebec ports alone, in 1882, the ships carried 1,563,000 tons, three times as much as all other Maine ports housed and shipped. A million and a half tons is a lot of ice. It sold for a sizeable sum of money. No wonder they called it frozen gold.

The Kennebec's chief competitor was the Hudson, and the icemen of our Maine river watched the New York weather reports after Christmas almost as avidly as they watched the local forecasts. When, by one of those rare freaks of weather, thaws struck the Hudson valley while below zero cold held on the Kennebec, the faces of our Maine ice operators were spread with smiles. The news meant soft and spongy ice on the Hudson; sound, thick, solid, saleable ice on the Kennebec. The Knickerbocker Company, owning plants on both rivers, didn't care where its ice came from, so long as it got a good harvest. The right harvest conditions on the Kennebec simply meant several weeks of well paid employment for every able-bodied man or grown boy for many miles along the river. The big companies with their absentee ownership made plenty of money, but some of it stayed behind in the form of wages and purchase of local supplies. In those winters of seventy to eighty years ago, the Kennebec farmers and tradesmen watched the reports from the Hudson just as carefully as Aroostook people today follow the reports of Idaho potatoes.

Ingenious men sometimes went to a lot of trouble to keep up with the competition in ice. Such a man was Captain Eban D. Haley of Gardiner. Tropical ports needed ice the year round, in January as well as July. What the Kennebec needed and did not have were ice houses built where vessels could load at any time of the year. Captain Haley conceived the bold plan of cutting off an arm of the sea with a dam, then compel the water to leave the cove and return to the sea. He secured an act of legislature permitting him to build across Campbell's cove at Boothbay Harbor. The way Kingsbury tells it in his *History of Kennebec County,* Captain Haley constructed two complete dams of timber cribs filled with stone, forming two parallel walls eleven feet apart. Into this compartment gravel was dumped until the water was forced out, thus forming a solid road bed. Near the point of low tide Haley placed a spout 28 inches square through both dams and roadway. By a mere device of opening a gate in the spout at low tide, the water from the pond sought its level on the sea side of the dam, and it could enter the pipe only at its opening at the bottom of the deepest water. Kingsbury says that the result surprised the captain himself, for in fifty-four days the pipe was discharging only fresh water, with which land streams had entirely replaced the ocean flow. Captain Haley's scheme made it possible to cut ice in Campbell's Cove in 1881 and every subsequent winter as long as demand continued for the product. From it ice could be loaded on ships in any month of the year.

Winter after winter ice still forms on the Kennebec, but the sounds of gouger and saw, of shouting men and tugging teams, are no longer heard. The ice houses from Augusta to Bowdoinham have fallen into decay. Even the Maine Central's whistle stop called Iceboro has disappeared. Just as the iron horse put an end to the canals, just as the automobile abolished the trolley lines and spelled the doom of the narrow gauge railroads, so did electric refrigeration close the era of world-wide business in Kennebec ice. The crystals that now cool a Savannah julep come out of the freezing compartment in an electric box. But there are folks still living who can recall those days, sixty or seventy years ago, when all the way from New York to Key West, the crystals that cooled food and drink, that made ice packs for the sick, that preserved meat and vegetables and fruits, were chunks of frozen gold from the Kennebec.

CHAPTER

27.

The decade of the 1850's was Maine's golden age economically. Never before or since has the state reached the level of prosperity enjoyed at that time. Symbolic of the age was the Maine clipper known as one of the finest vessels ever to sail the seven seas.

THE STATE OF MAINE CLIPPERS*
by
William H. Rowe

A bully ship and a bully crew,
   Doo-da, Doo-da.
A bully mate and a captain too,
   Doo–da, Doo–da–day.
Then blow, ye winds, Hi–oh, for Californy O!
There's plenty of gold, so I've been told
   On the banks of the Sacramento.
   —Joanna Colcord, *Songs of American Sailormen*

"Clean, long, smooth as a smelt. Sharp arching head. Thin, hollow bow; convex sides; light round and graceful stern. A genuine East Indiaman or Californian. Aloft, large built, iron-banded lower masts; taut tapering smaller masts, long proportioned spars from lower to skysail yards. Above board, she towers up with strong fibrous arms spreading a cloud of canvas to the gale." This was what the mariner of the fifties had in mind when he spoke of clippers.—Carl C. Cutler—*Greyhounds of the Sea.*

Any attempt to sort out the clippers from among the sharp-built ships of the 1850's is likely to provoke controversy. Lloyd's had a rigid classification in which a given ship received in the register a rating of "C," "S," "M," or "F." The magic letter C, of course, stood for clipper. The S meant sharp ship, the M, medium ship, and finally the full-bodied ship received the rating F. Quite apart from these rigid ratings, if an ordinary merchantman had the good luck to make a more than average voyage, she and the magic talisman "clipper" came together and clung to each other like droplets of quicksilver. In this perhaps the advertising talent of her owners played its part. Then again even an old apple-bowed hooker that "beat her head three times against a billow and then fell off and sailed around it" is likely to turn up in the sympathetic chronicle of some member of her owner's or skipper's family as a "clipper ship."

And so casting close definition and technical classification aside, we choose to tell the tale of the fast, sharp ships of the fifties—some ninety of which were built and launched on the coast of Maine from 1850 to 1856. Commencing in the late forties, the clipper era lasted little more than a decade and came to an end in the financial debacle of 1857. The urge which impelled designers, builders, and owners—the entire shipping fraternity—was speed, more speed, and then still more speed. This desire received a powerful stimulus in the year 1849 with an episodic adventure which belongs to any account of the days of the clipper ships.

On a spring day in 1848 a powerfully built man bolted into the old Plaza in the little town of San Francisco. His shaggy hair was wind-blown and his flashy clothes were stained with the dust of travel. His black eyes flashed as he shook an old horse-radish bottle energetically up and down. In it were several good-sized yellow lumps. With a bull-throated bellow, he yelled:

"Gold! Gold! Gold! From the American River."

The bystanders recognized him at once as Sam Brennan of Saco, Maine, the manager of Captain John Sutter's store at his fort near Sacramento.

During the year ending April 1, 1848, but two ships, one bark, and a brig had come into San

---
*William H. Rowe, *Maritime History of Maine* (New York: W. W. Norton & Co., 1948), pp. 166-187. Reprinted by permission of the publisher.

Francisco from Atlantic ports. During 1849 there took place the gigantic migration which changed that city from a drowsy Mexican trading station into one of the busiest seaports of the world. There cleared for the Golden Gate from the eastern harbors some 775 vessels. Almost every port on the Atlantic seaboard was represented in this fleet. In the Maine newspapers the news had been published in late September, 1848. In this famous migration of the forty-niners, Bath led off with 19 vessels, Portland and Bangor each sent 13, Eastport 10, Belfast 3, Saco and Thomaston 2 each, and other smaller towns 1 each. This made a total of 67 sail. These argosies of the forty-niners were not the tall clippers so soon to be launched. All but one were brigs and barks, and the one ship, the *Andrew Scott,* was of only 318 tons burden.

The first band of gold seekers to sail direct from Maine to California set forth from Belfast. The owners of the bark *Suliot,* just off the ways in January, 1849, announced that she would sail for San Francisco so soon as a company of forty passengers was obtained. Fifty soon applied for passage. A mixed company it was and typical of those to come. There were fifteen mechanics, eleven lumbermen, five merchants, four farmers, three surveyors, two mariners, a chemist, a printer, a dentist, an apothecary, a hatter, a lawyer, and three who signed on as "gentlemen."

The freight brought in for shipment was equally quaint and varied. Some idea of the multitude of different articles may be gathered from the fact that the *Suliot's* manifest was fifteen feet in length. The merchants sorted over their stocks and sent out as ventures every imaginable kind of merchandise—dry goods, groceries, clothing, shoes, and medicine. Some of the passengers carried small frame houses knocked down and ready to be set up when they arrived. In order to fill the hold to a height suitable for the construction of cabins and staterooms, a large lot of hemlock boards was put aboard, they being the readiest thing at hand.

The sailing caused all manner of excitement along the Penobscot. On Saturday night a great banquet was held with Governor Anderson presiding. The speakers pictured the glorious future of California and its opportunities for development and unbounded wealth when it should be pervaded with the enterprise and thrift of New England. Sailing day, January 30, was bitter cold, but an enthusiastic crowd gathered to see the company off. After a voyage of 171 days they arrived in the following July at San Francisco. There the hemlock boards proved to be the most profitable venture of all. Bought in Belfast at $10 a thousand, they sold in San Francisco for $300.

Many forty-niners joined up with such men as William L. Hanscom, a member of the Piscataqua family of shipbuilders who built the schooner *Mary M. Wood* and sailed her round the Horn. Another favorite way to go to the gold fields was by the organization of a mining company. The Portland and California Mining Company was one of these co-operative enterprises. There were thirty-five shares, thirty-four held by men and one by two boys who were counted as one man. They chartered the little brig *Ruth*, of only 146 tons, under the command of Captain Jabez Stevens. The cargo, which had been bought by the company as a speculation, consisted of lumber and fitted house frames. Then there was a bountiful supply of provisions and tools to be used in mining. It was the custom of many of the mining companies to attend church in a body to listen to a sermon preached for their benefit on the Sunday before the voyage began. The favorite text, it is said, was Genesis 2:12–"and the gold of that land is good." The services in this instance were held on Long Wharf, whence the *Ruth* was to sail at midday on the eighth of September. There the Rev. William T. Dwight made an address appropriate to the occasion. Just at noon the *Ruth* slipped away from the wharf.

On the second of October the bark *I.A. Thompson* sailed from Bath with forty-nine passengers from Augusta, Hallowell, Sidney, Vassalborough, and Skowhegan. It was a gala day in Bath. Just before the *Thompson* cast off, the T.D. Robinson yards launched the ship *Old England,* and the Moses yard, the ship *New England.* As she slipped away down the Reach the *Thompson* fired a salute. It was answered by the brig *Anna C. Maine,* which was scheduled to follow her to California the next day. The price of passage was $150 to $200. A clergyman, the Rev. Amariah Kallock, was carried free and paid his way by preaching to the passengers. Daily prayers were also held after breakfast. The *Thompson* made her passage to San Francisco in 128 days from Bath to find over three hundred vessels crowding the harbor. This fleet was later augmented by the brig *Margaret,* which had sailed from Portland on October 12.

Not all these little brigs and barks of 300 tons burden and less had good luck in rounding Cape Horn. The *Condor,* commanded by Captain Long, sailing from Portland on the twentieth of August, was so buffeted by gales that she spent thirty-five days in getting around. Some tried to sail through the Strait of Magellan, with even less success. This route is especially treacherous, running from the Atlantic to the Pacific against the prevailing westerly gales. The more prudent captains who knew the hazards of this course carried abundant stores. But many underestimated their needs and suffered extremities of hardship and even failure. No tragedy was more terrible than that which befell the *Abby Barker,* a bark hailing from Yarmouth in Casco Bay.

Timothy Pratt was the eldest son of Master David Pratt, the first shipbuilder in old North Yarmouth. Like most of his family, he "had salt in his blood" and began early to follow the sea. In 1848 his home burned, and when rumors of the great discovery in California reached the East, he decided to go there with his whole family. He took one of his father's vessels, the *Abby Barker,* a bark of 259 tons, and loaded her with house frames. His eldest son, Timothy Augustus, a student in Bowdoin College and a poet of some promise, went as his first mate, and his next son Enos as second mate. With his wife and his twin boys, William and Henry, then about eleven, he sailed out of Royall's River full of hope.

To save time the *Abby Barker* attempted to pass the Strait of Magellan and spent the next eighty harrowing days in those terrible waters. Beset by fierce currents, she fought against the westerly gales and "willewaws" and could find no anchorages on the sheer rock coast of that inhospitable region. To add to the discomfort and anxiety, the *Abby Barker* ran short of provisions and water. But at last she passed out by Cape Pillar and entered the Pacific. Then there was further trouble. Soon after they had reached good water and were sailing up the west coast, the captain, worn out by the anxiety and the long struggle, suddenly fell dead on the deck.

Timothy Augustus, the eldest son, now took command. He succeeded in bringing the bark into Sacramento Bay. Here cholera broke out. The crew, taking all they could lay their hands on, deserted the ship. Augustus soon became sick and died. Enos and William, one of the twins, followed. The mother, either from the disease or broken-hearted by the loss of her family, next succumbed. This left only the surviving twin, Henry, of eleven years. All that the family at home had to tell them of these tragic days was an unfinished letter commenced by Augustus. In it he wrote, "Already the ravages of the dread disease are upon us."

Captain Talbot of Freeport happened to put into Sacramento. Recognizing the *Abby Barker,* he went on board, to find to his horror the dead bodies of William and Mrs. Pratt. Burying the dead, he took Henry with him. Two years later—for his voyage was a long one—Captain Talbot brought the lad back home to Yarmouth.

The experience of the only full-rigged ship to carry "forty-niners" around the Horn, the little *Andrew Scott,* was typical of the times. She had been financed by a group of Portland men who had heard that lumber was selling in San Francisco at $400 a thousand. Upon her arrival in May 1850, it was found that the bottom had dropped out of the lumber market. Her master, William Leavitt, was able to turn another item to account.

He had taken with him aboard the *Scott* a small two-masted sailboat, the *Naumkeag.* She had cost him $180. He sold her for $2,000. And the reason was this: Between San Francisco and Sacramento freight rates ran from $60 to $120 a ton. The demand for small, smart sailing craft was great. The purchasers of the *Naumkeag* cleared from $600 to $1,000 a week.

This small episode, coupled with the *Scott's* missing of the high lumber market, is the key to the clipper era. Indeed, with the term there goes as often as not its counterpart, the California clipper, and again the Australia and China tea clippers. The *Scott's* passage out had run in excess of 160 days. Had she been able to do it in 110 or better her cargo of lumber might have made its high market.

A desire for speed had been latent in the blood of every master builder worth his salt. With the rush for California gold and profits, swift passages became the profitable consideration and his opportunity to show what he could do had arrived. Owners ceased to be their own shippers. They found the greatest profit in rendering service to the merchant, whose success in turn lay in getting his goods to market in the shortest possible time. This was the reason for the sixty- and eighty-dollar freights. Capacity counted but little. Speed was the prime requisite, and to this end builders carved their models.

Although Maine had led the United States in the building of ships since the early forties, her builders were late in feeling this urge for speed. Their construction of sharp-built ships began in 1850, and the bulk of it was achieved in the four years from 1851 to 1854. By 1856 the demand for fast ships had evaporated as quickly as it had come. The greatest production was in four yards. There was Fernald and Pettigrew of Kittery, whose most famous ship out of eight, the 1,610-ton *Typhoon,* was long known as the "Portsmouth Flyer." At Bath there was Trufant and Drummond, who put over six, among them the *Flying Dragon,* which held the record on the Maine Coast for the run to San Francisco. She did it in 1857 in 97 days. Five came from the yards of Metcalf and Norris at Damariscotta, among them the first one, the *Alert,* launched in 1850. In Penobscot waters from Deacon George Thomas' yard at Rockland there came indubitably Maine's most famous ship, *Red Jacket*, together with three others. In this colorful period many other yards from the Piscataqua to the St. Croix launched one or more fast ships.

The output of the Maine yards in 1850 totaled 326 vessels. Only three of these could, in the light of their later performance, be called clippers. The first was the *Alert,* launched in November, and rushed to New York. From there, flying Crocker and Warren's blue and yellow house flag, she sailed under Captain Francis Bursley on December 29 for San Francisco.

She was followed out of New York two weeks later by the *Grey Feather,* built at Eastport by C.S. Husten. She sailed into the ranks of the record-breakers under two down-east captains: first, when Captain Daniel McLaughlin, a native of Grand Manan, in 1854 made the run from Melbourne to Calcutta in her in 36 days; and second, when Captain Bartlett Mayo of Hampden covered the 14,000 miles from New York to Australia in 84 days. This latter run, which was considered a record for ships of limited size, would be a credit to any. The *Grey Feather,* while listed in the registers as "full modeled" and of only 586 tons register, had lines approaching those of the out-and-out clippers.

The output in 1851 was but little larger. Of the 254 built, but 9 could be called clippers. At Rockland, George Thomas launched the little bark *Springbok,* a miniature forerunner of his famous *Red Jacket*. Trufant and Drummond began their notable fleet at Bath with the *Monsoon*. Alfred Butler at South Portland sent off Casco Bay's most notable contribution to the fleet, the beautifully named *Snow Squall*. Two others, authentic Maine-built clippers built on the east bank of the Piscataqua, were registered at Portsmouth, owing to a confounding of state and customs district lines. On Badger's Island at Kittery, Fernald and Pettigrew launched their *Typhoon,* and up river at Green Acre in the town of Eliot, Samuel Hanscom built the beautiful and romantic *Nightingale*. The last three deserve a careful scrutiny.

The *Snow Squall* was said to have cost $30,000. She was purchased when just off the stocks by Charles R. Green & Co. of New York. For thirteen years she held an enviable place among the smaller clippers. Even when she was twelve years old, she showed her heels to the Confederate cruiser *Tuscaloosa*. Her life was spent mainly in the China sea trade. Under the command of Captain Ira Bursley, a famous shipmaster of the packet and clipper era, she made the Australian voyage from New York to Melbourne in 79 days. In 1856, making a short detour in the coffee trade, she made a fine run from New York to Rio de Janeiro in 28 days. Returning in 34, she completed a round trip, including detention, equal to any made. Three years later she sailed a close race over the China course with the *Romance of the Seas,* one of Donald McKay's big clippers, a thousand tons larger than the *Snow Squall,* and reached Sandy Hook two days ahead of her.

Fully rigged with skysail yards aloft and all colors flying, the *Typhoon* slipped down the ways in February 1851. Owned by D. & A. Kingsland of New York and commanded by Captain Charles H. Salter, she made the passage from Portsmouth to Liverpool during the month of March in 13 days and 10 hours from wharf to dock, a feat unequaled up to that time. It was this voyage, her first, which gave her the sobriquet "Portsmouth Flyer." She was the maritime sensation of the year, being not only the first American clipper but also the largest merchant ship ever seen in Liverpool.

Back on this side of the Atlantic she sailed for California in August, taking part in one of the keenest and most interesting races ever sailed. Her competitors were the *Raven* and the *Sea Witch.* Sometimes one was ahead, sometimes another, and sometimes over the long course they fought it out tack by tack. The little *Raven* won. She slipped through the Golden Gate 105 days out from Boston, while the time of the *Typhoon* was 106. A later passage of the *Typhoon* from Calcutta to the Cape of Good Hope in 37 days was never beaten, and it was equaled only by the *Witch of the Wave,* which had been built the same year as the *Typhoon* in the George Raynes yard on the Portsmouth side of the Piscataqua.

One of the most beautiful of the extreme clippers was the *Nightingale.* Named for Jenny Lind, whose likeness she carried beneath her prow as her figurehead, she represented all that was lovely and exciting on the high seas in the glamorous fifties. From that fair day in June, 1851, when she slipped from the ways in Samuel Hanscom's yard under the hill at Greenacre, South Eliot, until she disappeared beneath the waves she had skimmed for nearly half a century, hers was a long life of adventure. She led off in a race to the Australian gold fields. She won the English tea races. Sold, she became a slaver and acquired "the taint of a musky ship." In the rebellion she saw service as a vessel of war. And again and again as a California clipper she rounded the Horn until she foundered in 1893.

The clipper builders never scrimped in their work. But Samuel Hanscom determined to surpass them all in prodigality. For his model he turned to his nephew Isaiah Hanscom, who was later to become chief of the Bureau of Construction in Washington. He designed her on the lines of a yacht. She was intended not for the Cape Horn trade but rather to carry passengers, who could well afford to pay for luxury, to the World's Fair in London. Also, Hanscom was ambitious to put his handiwork on exhibition in the Thames as the model American clipper. To this end she was fitted out between decks with luxurious saloons and staterooms which were finished with carved and gilded moldings and panels and furnished with upholstery and hangings of figured brocade.

Inboard and outboard all was richness and beauty. Besides the portrait bust on the bow, the stern was ornamented with the figure of Jenny Lind reclining with a nightingale perched on her finger. On stern, bow, and quarter the name *Nightingale* shone in a contrast of blue and gold.

All of this cost a deal of money, and she was launched heavily mortgaged and sent to Boston for sale. She was first bid in by ship brokers, to whom Sampson and Tappan were glad to pay $75,000 for her. She long sailed under the house flag of that firm—white over blue with a red ball in the center. So proud and confident were her owners that they offered to match the *Nightingale* against any British or American ship for a race to China and back for a stake of £10,000. The challenge was never accepted.

In the fall of 1851 came the word that gold had been discovered in Australia. The days of forty-nine were repeated. Although she had been advertised for the London run, the call was so insistent that the *Nightingale* joined the rush for the gold fields. The first to get away, she sailed from Boston on the eighteenth of October. This first voyage of 90 days to Melbourne, however, gave little promise of the fast passages whe was later to make. For examples there are her runs—in 1853 from Portsmouth, England, to Shanghai against the northeast monsoon in 106 days; in 1854 from New York to Melbourne in 75 days; and the next year from Shanghai to London in 91 days.

In 1860 she was sold and became a slaver. When under the command of Captain Francis Bowen, the notorious "Prince of the Slavers," and flying the American colors she was captured by the U.S. sloop-of-war *Saratoga.* After her cargo of 961 blacks had been liberated at Monrovia, she was sold to the government. She was armed and served during the Civil War with the Gulf Blockading Squadron as a supply and coal ship. At its close she was again sold and under various owners sailed in the California and China trades until 1876, when she went under Norwegian colors. Rigged as a bark but keeping her old name, she came to her end in the North Atlantic lumber trade. In 1893, when forty-two years old, she was abandoned at sea on a voyage from Liverpool to Halifax.

In 1852 the Maine yards launched some twenty fast ships. They were considerably larger than their predecessors. One, the *Defiance,* registered 1,690 tons, and six others exceeded 1,000 tons. Built by Deacon George Thomas in his Rockland yard from plans drawn by Boston's twenty-five-year-old genius of maritime design, Samuel Hartt Pook, the *Defiance* was the most extreme type of clipper. Her concave sides, with ends longer and sharper than those of the *Flying Cloud,* made her a supremely beautiful ship. Sensing the deficiencies of the earlier clippers as cargo carriers and taking a hint from the flat-floored Western Ocean packets, young Pook evolved a type which was almost universally adopted by later builders. On her voyage in ballast from Rockland to New York the *Defiance* logged twenty nautical miles an hour. Two Maine ships launched this year became record-makers. The *Rattler,* also from the Thomas yard, when twenty-six years old and known as the Costa Rican ship *Martha,* made an unsurpassed voyage in 28 days from Callao to San Francisco heads, and the *Red Rover,* built by Fernald and Pettigrew at Kittery in 1855, made the voyage to San Francisco in 110 days and equaled it again the next year.

In 1853 the high-water mark was reached in both the building and the sailing of clippers. Enthusiasm was at its height, freights were still good, and few eyes detected on the horizon the ominous signs of commercial depression. It is estimated that nearly half the number and more than half the tonnage of the clipper fleet was built this year. "Everybody who had capital to invest wanted one or at least shares in one," writes Captain Arthur Clark. The Maine yards which specialized in sharp ships built thirty-three, twenty-four of which were over a thousand tons. Some of the best-known vessels of the fleet were put afloat. Among them were the only five from Maine which made the voyage from Boston or New York to California in less than 110 days. These were the *Flying Dragon, Dashing Wave, Spitfire, Viking,* and *Oracle.*

Of the Maine-built California clippers the fastest was the *Flying Dragon,* built by Trufant and Drummond at Bath. Sailing from Boston under Captain Judah P. Baker of Brewster, on the twenty-first of July it took her 31 days to fight her way around the Horn into the Pacific. In the struggle she sprung her bowsprit and main yard and lost her jibboom. The grim battle off the Horn proved too much for the forty-six-year-old captain, who died before reaching San Francisco. This grueling voyage had taken 148 days. But better luck followed. Not counting that voyage, her average time for five successive years over this 15,000-mile course is 112 3/5 days. Moreover, the *Flying Dragon* is the only vessel from Maine during the days of the clipper ships to make a run of less than 100 days. In 1857 she did it in 97. In 1860 she sailed from Sydney, Australia, to Hampton Roads in 75 days. This is a record passage between these ports.

A close second to the *Flying Dragon* was the *Spitfire.* She was an extreme clipper launched in September 1853 by James Arey and Sons at Frankfort and commanded by John Arey. Sailing from Boston on the twenty-seventh of October, she put in to Rio de Janeiro the last week in November, where she remained twenty days. Here four men were discharged for incompetence. Elkanah Crowell, the mate, is credited with the saying that he "wished no man in his crew who could not jump over the foreyard before breakfast." These he must have had, for despite being baffled for fifteen days by gales off the Horn, the *Spitfire* arrived in San Francisco only 120 days out of Boston. This made her actual sailing time a few hours less than 100 days. The voyage around from Rio in 65 days is said never to have been beaten by any loaded vessel except the *Witchcraft,* and then only by three days. The *Spitfire's* best record was made in 1860, when she sailed a dead heat over the California course with the *Black Hawk.* They both arrived in 107 days.

This time was equaled by the voyage of Fernald and Pettigrew's *Dashing Wave* when sailing from Boston on New Year's Day, 1858. It is a tribute to this Kittery firm's fine workmanship and material that the *Wave* was the last of the clippers in active service. Like so many of the wooden ships, she spent the last of her days as a barge in the fishery business on the west coast. When sixty years old, in 1920, she was examined and her hull found to be in sound condition. She was lost the same year.

Metcalf and Norris of Damariscotta, the pioneer clipper builders of Maine, put afloat their most famous vessel this summer. The *Flying Scud* was of good size, 1,713 tons, and extremely sharp, calculated for speed. So quickly did she pass down the river after her launch that her officers could not believe it possible. They thought their chronometers must be out of order. Soon after her arrival in New York she was purchased by R.W. Cameron for his Australian Pioneer Line, for which he was using the advertising slogan, "Sixty days to Melbourne," and under Captain Warren H. Bearce she sailed on the ninth of September. In the Gulf Stream she was struck by lightning, which magnetized the cargo of iron in the after hold. This affected the compasses, and the needles whirled so rapidly as to make them useless. For a long time they could only be used by placing them on a board extending out from the port side. Despite this and despite the fact that she was so overloaded that her scuppers were nearly awash and she was trimmed by the head two feet, making her very crank, she made the passage in seventy-six days.

A notation in her log on November 6 stated that on that day she ran 449 nautical miles. If this fact could be substantiated, it would credit the *Scud* with the best day's run ever logged by a clipper. It is greatly to be regretted that the log book is not now available. The possibility of a mistake in the reckoning of Captain Bearce—although highly improbable in the opinion of those who knew the man—leaves Maine's claim to this record forever a matter of dispute. Her later performance is good evidence of her speed. To her credit is a passage of 19 days and 20 hours from New York to Marseilles and also one from the same port to Bombay in 81 days. The latter was a record at the time and was thereafter beaten by only a few days.

On the last day of November, 1853, Trufant and Drummond launched their second fast ship of the year, the *Viking,* built for George Hussey of New Bedford and bearing as her figurehead a northland warrior in full armor. Her best run to California was 108 days in 1858. The *Oracle,* the sole contribution to the clipper fleet by Chapman and Flint of Thomaston, made herself a place among the faster ships this year by a passage in 109 days.

At this juncture it seems appropriate to set forth the days run to San Francisco by fast Maine ships. With the yard from which they were launched and the year of their launching, they are as follows:

Flying Dragon	Trufant and Drummond, 1853	97 days
Typhoon	Fernald and Pettigrew, 1851	106 days
Spitfire	James Arey & Sons, 1853	107 days
Dashing Wave	Fernald and Pettigrew, 1853	107 days
Viking	Trufant and Drummond, 1853	108 days
Red Rover	Fernald and Pettigrew, 1852	110 days
Midnight	Fernald and Pettigrew, 1854	111 days
Euterpe	Horace Merriam, 1854	112 days
Talisman	Metcalf and Norris, 1854	112 days
Live Yankee	Horace Merriam, 1853	114 days
Golden Rule	William Hitchcock & Co.	114 days
Nonpareil	Trufant and Drummond, 1854	115 days
Mary Robinson	Trufant and Drummond, 1854	115 days
Golden Racer	Mortons, 1852	117 days
Anglo Saxon	Francis H. Rhoades, 1852	118 days
Flying Eagle	William Hitchcock & Co.	118 days

Another well-known run—from dock to dock, across the Atlantic to Liverpool, the *Typhoon* sailing from Portsmouth and the *Red Jacket* from New York—reflects the following:

Typhoon	Fernald and Pettigrew, 1851	13 days, 10 hours
Red Jacket	George Thomas, 1853	13 days, 1 hour, 25 minutes

The fast ships will always be best known by their records. For swiftness they were built, and their proper story is of how well they fulfilled their purpose. Some have an interest beyond the beauty of their lines, the list of their passages from port to port, and their best day's run. Two of those launched in 1853 have a prominence that does not rest on knots and miles, but on their stories, which are a part of the romance of the sea. Such are the *Wild Rover* and the *Wild Wave*.

The medium clipper *Wild Rover* was built by Austin and Hall at Damariscotta. She was long the property of Alpheus Hardy and Co. of Boston. In 1863, laden with lumber, she sailed out of Shanghai with a young Japanese hidden in her locked storeroom. He was the first of his nation to seek an education in the United States. In Boston he found a firm friend in the owner, Alpheus Hardy, by whom he was educated at Amherst College and Andover Theological Seminary. When he returned to Japan in 1874, he founded Doshisha College at Kioto and became its president. His own name combined with that of his benefactor is world-famous—Joseph Hardy Neesima.

The *Wild Wave* was a medium clipper. She was built this year by G.H. Ferrin of Richmond. In 1856 she made the run from Callao to Plymouth in 70 days, a record never beaten. The pluck and ingenuity of her captain when she was wrecked two years later made her story one of the classic epics of the sea. Josiah N. Knowles of Eastham, one of the most brilliant of the Cape Cod shipmasters, was in command. In March 1858 she was bound from San Francisco to Valparaiso with a crew of thirty, ten passengers, and two chests containing $18,000 in gold coin. Charts of the South Seas were then very inaccurate. At about one o'clock in the morning of March 5, the lookout saw breakers under the lee bow. Her people were unaware that there was land any nearer than twenty miles away. The *Wild Wave* attempted to come about but missed stays and, wearing, she struck an uncharted coral reef. Within five minutes she had lost her masts, bilged, and was among breakers so violent that they tore the copper from her sides and bottom and tossed it up on deck.

At daybreak it was found that she had struck a circular reef about two miles from a little coral atoll called Oeno. The island was nothing but a strip of sand half a mile wide. The crew and passengers were able to get ashore and land much of the provisions and livestock aboard the ship. Shelters were then built, using the sails of the ship. A dug well gave them water, and fish, sea birds, and their eggs were to be had in abundance. After about a week the captain with the mate, five men, and the two chests of treasure put to sea in an attempt to reach the settlement of the mutineers of the *Bounty* on Pitcairn Island.

This lay eighty miles to the south. After a hazardous three days' voyage they succeeded in reaching Pitcairn. On account of the surf they could not land in Bounty Bay and soon after getting ashore on another part of the island their boat was stove beyond repair. They salvaged the treasure, which was brought ashore and buried. Great was their disappointment to find that the island was uninhabited, the whole community having removed to Norfolk Island. There was plenty of food. Fruit grew abundantly, and there were chickens, sheep, and goats which had been left behind.

A boat had to be built. A diligent search turned up some discarded axes and other tools, and they set to work. They fashioned a schooner 30 feet long and of 8-foot beam. She was the result of immense labor and real Yankee ingenuity. Some of the small houses were burned and the nails which they contained were salvaged. This supply fell far short, and in many places wooden pegs had to do. Everything imaginable was used. An old anvil served as an anchor, a copper kettle as a stove, and their flag was made from the red hangings of the church pulpit, a cast-off white shirt, and a pair of blue overalls. Old rope was picked up, reduced to oakum, and spun again on an improvised wheel. The schooner was named the *John Adams* after one of the Bounty mutineers. She was finally put afloat and the treasure chests loaded in. Leaving three whose hearts had failed them on the island, they again set sail.

This time they had planned to go to Tahiti, but head winds increasing into a gale forced them to change course and head for the Marquesas. For eleven days they tossed about, suffering terribly from seasickness. At Resolution Bay they dared not land, the natives appearing hostile. They pushed on to Muka Hiva, where, to their joy, they found the U.S.S. *Vandalia*. The schooner they had built at Pitcairn was quickly sold to a missionary for $250, and the *Vandalia*, picking up the party on Oeno and the three men at Pitcairn, took them all to Tahiti. Those left on Oeno had constructed a large boat from the wreckage of the *Wild Wave*, but when finished it was so heavy they could not get it into the water. Their health had been remarkably good. Only one of the whole party had died.

On the second of November, 1853, in the presence of an immense crowd, some of whom had come from New York and Philadelphia to witness the event, there was launched at Rockland, the largest, and fastest, and one of the handsomest of the Maine fleet—the extreme clipper *Red Jacket*, of 2,306 tons. Designed by Samuel Hartt Pook, built by George Thomas, and commanded by Captain Asa Eldridge, she combined skills all but unsurpassable. Trim and sharp, the delicate beauty of her graceful lines, arched stem and exquisitely modeled stern were matched by her finely proportioned spars and standing rigging. Her figurehead was a life-sized likeness of the Seneca chief whose name she bore, while on her light, round stern, surrounded by heavy gilt scrollwork, was a bust of the same Indian warrior. To the end of her long life she was considered one of the more beautiful of the larger clippers.

No expense had been spared in furnishing her inboard and outboard with the best. The after cabin was finished in rosewood mahogany, satin, and zebra wood which was set off by black walnut and gilt work. Exclusive of the officers' quarters, with the forward cabin there were fourteen staterooms. And the forward house accommodated a crew of sixty-two men. A week after launching she was towed to New York, where she received her masts and spars, was rigged and her sails bent. Then on January 10 she sailed for Liverpool.

It was a memorable voyage with every sort of handicap. Uncoppered, with an indifferent crew, with hail, rain, or snow on almost every day of her run, the *Red Jacket* arrived on January twenty-third. Her elapsed time from dock to dock was 13 days, 1 hour and 25 minutes. This is a record that still stands for sailing ships. For six consecutive days her runs averaged over 343 miles, and on the ninth day out the crew "spliced the main brace." This was to celebrate a twenty-four-hour run of 413 nautical miles. Although Donald McKay's *Lightning* was to surpass this by 23 miles about two months later, it has been beaten on only two other voyages in the history of sailing ships, unless the claim of the *Flying Scud* to 449 can be established.

The *Red Jacket* created much excitement in Liverpool. Her arrival was dramatic. At least a day before she was expected by her greatest admirers, a steamer coming in announced that she was just behind. A crowd went down to Point Linus to greet her. Two tugs succeeded in getting lines aboard her but were unable to draw them taut. The great ship swept on up the Mersey with every stitch of canvas drawing in the brisk northwest wind, fairly flying toward her pier.

Then Captain Eldridge accomplished a feat not often attempted. The *Red Jacket* came about, threw her yards aback, and laid herself up to the pierhead with a precision that brought appreciative shouts from the spectators.

She never returned to America under the stars and stripes. The White Star Line immediately chartered her for the round trip to Melbourne. So pleased were they with her record—5 months and 4 days, with a spurt from the Cape to Melbourne in 19 days that was never equaled—that they were anxious to keep her in their fleet even at a cost of £30,000.

In 1854 the urge for speed began to lessen. Sobered by rising costs, falling freights, and long waits in port, owners and builders realized that the mad and merry days of these swift sharp ships were numbered. Trade conditions on the west coast had become stabilized, and it mattered little whether the voyage was made in 90 or 110 days. Conservative merchants began once more to think in terms of freight money, and many of the proudest of the tall ships were forced to find a cargo at the dusty Peruvian guano islands, at the southern cotton ports, or even in the wretched coolie and "black ivory" trades. Their days had been glamorous, but after all, afloat or ashore, it is a workaday world.

Maine builders were not slow in sensing this. During this year only fifteen ships were built that could be classed as clippers, and nearly all of these were of medium model and considerably less tonnage than their predecessors. George Thomas made no contribution to the fleet, for he had removed to Quincy, Massachusetts. Horace Merriam still built in Rockland. Although his *Live Yankee* of 1853 had shown up badly in comparison with the *Red Jacket* his *Euterpe* sailed into the fleet of the record-makers. Fernald and Pettigrew put afloat the *Midnight;* Trufant and Drummond, still optimistic, launched the *Mary Robinson* and the *Windward*, two beautifully modeled and sparred ships, and Metcalf and Norris sent off the *Talisman*. Of these the *Euterpe* made a record that stood for many years by running from Calcutta to the Cape in 39 days and thence to London, the whole voyage taking only 85 days. She was the first ship to enter the new Victoria Docks, none of the others being big enough to accomodate her 1,975 tons. The *Talisman*, the last clipper to be built by the pioneers, Metcalf and Norris, made her builders proud when in 1859 she led the *Great Republic* home from San Francisco by 4 days.

Of the new builders the most ambitious was Captain Nathaniel Blanchard. After having one vessel burned at great loss before she was launched, he built at the Thomas Knight yard at South Portland a beautiful and lofty vessel to which he appropriately gave the name *Phoenix*. She was very heavily sparred. Besides crossing skysail yards on all three masts, she carried the rather unusual moon-sails on her fore and mizzen. In 1859 she sailed what is considered by not a few authorities the best transatlantic voyage. Crossing from Savannah to Cork Harbor, she made the run in 14 days and 9 hours. When distance is considered, her admirers claim this equals a 13-day run from New York to Liverpool. Curiously enough, in 1860 she too came to her end in a fire.

By 1856 shipbuilding in the United States had reached its apogee with Maine leading all the states. Yet of the 215,904 tons built in the state in 1855, less than 5,000 was in sharp ships. They number five. There was the *Criterion,* by Hitchcock of Damariscotta, the *Midnight,* by Fernald and Pettigrew of Kittery, the *Dictator,* by Cox of Robbinston, the *Stephen Crowell,* by Burgess and Clark of Warren, and the *Young Mechanic*— built from a model whittled out by his son—by Rhoades of Rockland. Five only were registered in 1856. The full fury of economic depression in 1857 wrote finis to the construction of Maine-built clippers.

CHAPTER

28.

Portland has always been Maine's largest city. At one time she tried to become New England's largest. Boston, however, refused to relinquish her preeminent position to the upstart from "down east."

PORTLAND: RIVAL OR SATELLITE*
by
Edward Kirkland

"You know something of Maine. What are the first steps which a young and flourishing State should take who intends to embark upon a liberal and effective system of Internal Improvements?" George W. Pierce to James Baldwin, January 20, 1834. Baldwin Papers, Harvard Business School Library, XLVIII.

I

Boston enthusiasm for railroads in the early thirties was so boundless that projects of lines to the "Great American West" could not contain it. As some of its railroad leaders chartered the Western and imprudently explored the possibilities of a route to the Lakes, others were fascinated by the design of expediting and enlarging the trade between Boston and eastern New Hampshire and Maine. In engineering terms the proposals to cross the interior mountains to the Hudson or Lake Champlain were the more audacious; in commercial terms a railroad down East was the more daring project. The Western and the Vermont Central at worst confronted only indirect water competition by lake, canal, river, and sound; the roads to the State of Maine undertook the dangerous experiment of paralleling a coastal trade already well served by sailing packet and steamboat. As it turned out, however, not one but two railroads embarked upon the adventure.

The Boston and Maine had a three-year head start. Ostensibly it began as a local project for in 1833 the Massachusetts General Court chartered a seven-mile road, the Andover and Wilmington, to run from the latter place on the Boston and Lowell "so as to form a branch thereof, ... and to enter ... on the Boston and Lowell, ... paying, ... such a rate of toll as the legislature may from time to time prescribe"; and soon thereafter the directors induced Laommi Baldwin to lend his prestige to their little enterprise by viewing and selecting the most favorable route for it. Actually they had from the beginning a far larger objective than a mere local connection: their company was but "the beginning of a long line of travel." They proposed to extend their road to Haverhill on the Merrimack, bridge the river to a connection with the Boston and Maine, chartered in New Hampshire simply to build across that state to its eastern edge, and thus attain their object—"the accommodation of the general travel from eastern New Hampshire and the State of Maine." In this fashion also, a New Hampshire corporation introduced into New England railroad designations the famous "Boston and Maine."

On the whole all moved with celerity. James Hayward, fresh from his triumphs on the Boston and Providence, superintended the construction, and the Cranes of Haverhill, one of whom, Edward Crane, later became one of the most spectacular promoters and operators of dubious railroad enterprises in New England, secured the contract. When the panic of 1837 caught their enterprise

---

*Reprinted by permission of the publishers from Edward Chase Kirkland *Men, Cities, and Transportation,* Cambridge, Mass.: Harvard University Press, Copyright, 1948, by the President and Fellows of Harvard College. Vol. I, pp. 193-222.

unfinished and retarded the sale of securities and the collection of assessments, the corporation turned to the state for assistance. The General Court responded in 1837 and 1839 with the loan of state securities aggregating $150,000. To protect its advances, the state took a mortgage on the road and $100,000 of its stock. Thus aided, the tracks were driven forward until in 1843 they connected at South Berwick with those of the Portland, Saco and Portsmouth, a corporation chartered by Maine to provide the final link to Portland. By this time also legislation in Massachusetts, New Hampshire, and Maine had permitted the various little roads to blend and blend again into a single corporation, the Boston and Maine, the earliest and most conspicuous railroad consolidation in New England history. In later years when the Boston and Maine, incidental to its railroad tactics, attacked railroad mergers it did not favor, opposing counsel with fine irony adduced the early history of the protesting railroad.

So powerful an enterprise was not content to remain as a mere "branch" to the Boston and Lowell or forego the obvious convenience and advantage of a direct connection with Boston. Consequently, as soon as its route to Maine had been built and consolidated, the Boston and Maine petitioned the legislature to charter the Boston and Maine Extension Company and aroused thereby screams of protest from the Boston and Lowell. The latter corporation rehearsed the benefits which the Boston and Maine had drawn from their mutual relationship and stood immovable upon the provisions of a charter prohibiting a parallel railroad between Boston and Lowell. To the latter argument the legislature harkened to the extent of inserting in the charter of the Extension Company a clause forbidding the establishment of any station between Andover and Reading without previous assent from the Boston and Lowell. In 1845 the Boston and Maine reached Boston over its own rails. This achievement not only freed the Boston and Maine from the asserted extortions of the Boston and Lowell; it gave the former road a strategic position in its competition for down-East trade and travel.

This competition, at least on land, came primarily from the Eastern Railroad. Originally this line, too, was a local enterprise, designed to connect Boston and Salem, places already more closely and effectively united than any others in the Commonwealth by a modern turnpike, organized stage lines, freight wagons, and coastal packets. Under such circumstances it is probably just to regard the railroad as largely accessory to the ambitions of rival land speculators. Those, headed by General W.H. Sumner, who were profitably transforming Noddle's Island into East Boston, insisted the Eastern should make their holdings the site of its eastern terminus; those who had purchased lands in Chelsea thought the Eastern should locate its terminus in their area. For the road this rivalry was unfortunate. In 1833 a legislative committee dismissed petitions for its charter with the ironic comment, "Though the Committee highly appreciate the enterprise of those gentlemen who are desirous of bringing the lands of Chelsea and Noddle's Island into the market, and thereby enlarging the bounds of the city, they think that this enterprise ought not to be confused with the necessity of a railroad to Salem."

To convince doubting legislators of the public need for such a road the Eastern was now given a new tone and larger objectives. Any ostensible association with land speculation was buried beneath a tide of petitions signed by thousands and led by George Peabody, the rising merchant and banker of Salem and Baltimore. Not East Boston, but Salem craved the route. To refute the charge that the road was too short to be profitable, as well as to attach more localities to its chariot, the petitioners engaged to extend the route to Newburyport and then across New Hampshire to a railroad connection with Portland. Engineering talent of the highest caliber certified its success for John M. Fessenden, surveyor of the Boston and Worcester, laid out the line in Massachusetts with no grades of over thirty-five feet to the mile. Somewhat less successfully he attempted to settle the contentious issue of an eastern terminus by selecting East Boston. To his mind the ferry ride and the train ride were both somewhat shorter by that route. Furthermore the East Boston Company obligingly surrendered the management of its ferry connection to the Eastern and donated a right of way, extensive station grounds, and an area of flats. Though a new remonstrant, the "upper road"—as the vernacular of the day christened the Boston and Maine—challenged the proposed route as "unwise and inexpedient," the legislature, otherwise minded, granted a charter in 1836. One quarter of the shares could be subscribed by the Salem Turnpike and Chelsea Bridge Corporation, which the new road would put out of business.

Before the panic of 1837 the Eastern had barely a year of financial grace. When subscriptions, obtained largely in Boston and Salem, were inadequate to complete construction even to the latter place, the road appealed to the bounty of the state. The response was lavish. In 1837 the legislature appropriated $500,000 in state securities, and in the following year it granted a temporary loan of $90,000, seeking at the same time to throw additional safeguards of sinking funds and collateral around the advances earlier made. Thus succored, the Eastern was opened to Salem, reached Portsmouth in 1840, where it leased a like-named New Hampshire corporation laying track across the state toward Maine, and finally in November, 1842, joined with the Portland, Saco and Portsmouth to complete an uninterrupted communication between Boston and Portland. Thus at the very moment the Western was attaining Albany on the Hudson, Boston also reached down East by rail. Though no comparable celebration occurred, George Peabody had grasped the implications of the new era when the Eastern reached Salem. With a glance backward, he reviewed the historic methods of transporation between Salem and Boston and the necessity of their improvement. With a look forward he prophesied, "As we are accustomed to regard the discovery of America and the Protestant Reformation as two great events which have contributed largely to advance the interests of the human race; so [future generations], with perhaps a more clear conception and a more evident deduction of consequences, will point to the American Revolution and the Era of Steam Travel."

However stimulating such cosmic views were to "the contemplations of the patriot and speculations of the philosopher," the shareholders and officials of the road were soon aware of the unsatisfactory nature of their East Boston terminal. Passengers had to leave the cars and take a ferry ride to reach the business section and the transfer of merchandise was equally inconvenient. Upon these handicaps counsel for the Boston and Maine were wont to dilate with an amalgam of mockery and sympathy. They pictured the Eastern

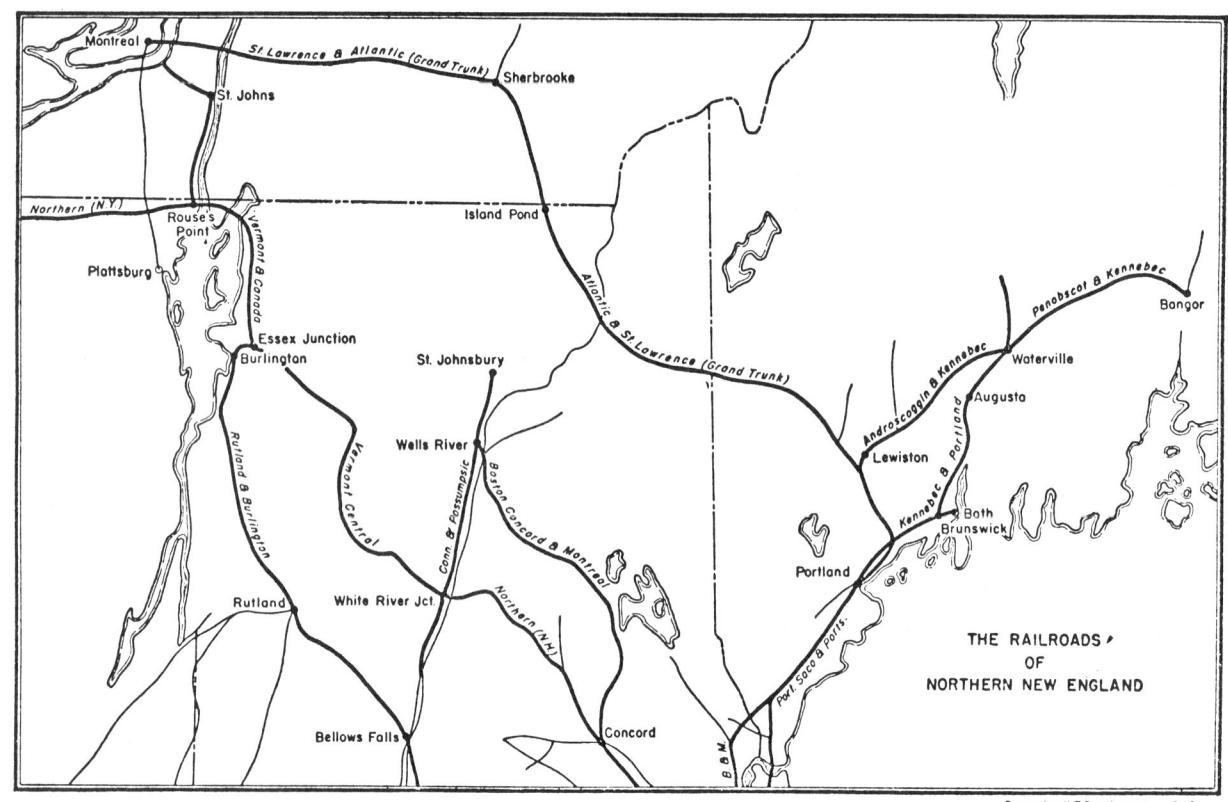

Drawn by W F Sharkey - Jan. 1948

as "creeping across a desert, plunging through a marsh, arriving at deep water at East Boston, where the ferry boat was exposed to all the detention of fog, ice and other impediments, and leaving at last the disconsolate passengers in an inconvenient terminus.... The necessity of steering by compass and the sound of the fog-bell is upon them, and they cannot avoid it or get rid of it." After a decade of trying to answer such arguments and erase such handicaps, the Eastern, over the opposition of the Boston and Maine, secured a succession of legislative enactments authorizing its extension into the city. In 1854 it finally secured an all-rail connection to a Boston terminal of its own. Whether Fessenden's engineering judgment had been at fault or the land speculators too powerful, the original termination at East Boston was unfortunate.

II

Competition between the Eastern and the Boston and Maine was inevitable. Fortunately for their welfare, the two forswore a cutthroat rivalry in Maine by negotiating in 1843, and again in 1847, common agreements with the Portland, Saco and Portsmouth for a joint connection, by guaranteeing the latter's dividends, and by joining in the ownership and operation of the steamboats which afforded connections at Portland to ports farther east. Thus there were no parallel rail lines in Maine. A far different condition prevailed in New Hampshire and northeastern Massachusetts. Here the Boston and Maine and the Eastern ran within twelve miles of each other and here each sought to encroach upon the territory of the other by branches and connections. It was riposte and counter-riposte; blow and counter-blow. The Eastern thrust lines westward to Lawrence, Haverhill, and other strategic points on the Boston and Maine; the latter pushed connections eastward to Lynn, Salem and Newburyport. Nor did the initiative for these enterprises always come from either company. Every ambitious town in the area wanted a railroad connection or railroad competition and, after convincing the legislature that public exigency demanded the granting of its request, secured a charter and blackmailed one rival or the other into assisting the construction of the road and into operating it. Rival directorates driven "by that first law of our nature, self-preservation and defence" were in no position to resist. Occasionally attempts were made to raise these squabbles to the level of high policy. David A. Neal, elected to the presidency of the Eastern as Peabody's successor, and his allies fought for months to convince the legislature of the folly, if not downright illegality, of parallels and universal competition. The attempt was a failure.

As the struggle continued, both the major contestants occasionally tired of exactions and soothed themselves with self-pity. The Boston and Maine was peculiarly vexed with the necessity of dealing with the legislatures of three states: "Composed as the legislatures usually are, of so much new and mixed material, it is not a little perplexing to your directors to guard properly the rights of the road from encroachment." On their part the officials of the Eastern bewailed the ingratitude of the Commonwealth and of the public. The "patriots" who built the road "became monopolists.... Men who refuse the first dollar to aid in the project while the slightest risk remains will spend hundreds to pull down the structure ... if ... they can save a sixpence in their fare, or put a shilling in their pockets.... The treasury of a Railroad seems to be considered like a city, carried by assault, the proper arena and admitted apology for plunder." Harassed and chastened by their own and others' excesses, the Boston and Maine and the Eastern at last formed an agreement in 1855. Neither was to carry the business of the stations on the other's main line or to cross it into the territory beyond; the area between the two roads was carefully apportioned, some to the Boston and Maine, some to the Eastern, and some on a half-and-half basis. If either road did business belonging to the other, it was to refund all receipts after deducting the expense of doing the business. But this provisional settlement—to last ten years—could not erase the millions in losses already incurred.

In its campaigns against the Eastern, the Boston and Maine had always the advantage of a superior location. Though it met water competition between Portland and Boston, it was on the whole an interior road, drawing traffic from both sides. With unusual sagacity it adopted a policy of low fares, particularly on season tickets, and thus built up a populous and dependent suburban territory. The Boston and Maine carried more passengers than any other railroad in New England and occasionally more than any in the nation. Furthermore it traversed a developing industrial area and with thoughtful timeliness relocated its main track through the new manufacturing center of Lawrence and secured there, over the Manchester and Lawrence, a connection with the route to the Lakes and a share in its traffic. On the other hand the Eastern throughout its length confronted water competition. Its industrial area, Lynn in particular, was so near Boston that wagons and carts continued to transport a large share of the freight traffic. It was a universal observation during the forties that, except in the carriage of ice, railroads could not displace teaming within fifteen miles of Boston; the latter was more flexible, teams picked up and delivered. The Eastern also earlier experienced the competition of interurban horse railroads. Figures talked. In the twelve months ending November 30, 1860, the Boston and Maine carried 1,893,185 passengers and 293,749 tons of freight; the Eastern's totals were respectively 1,460,653 and 128,566.

Inevitably finances reflected the disparity. The Boston and Maine was able to finance its construction by stock issues, even the construction of its intemperate extensions. This was the approved conservative practice of the day. Though the Eastern's financial expedients were discreetly concealed, its expenditures in the fifties and the general railroad prostration of that decade forced the sale of bonds at sacrificial discounts. Years later a thorough investigation revealed that the corporation from the date of its completion had recurrently increased its capital stock to pay dividends, interest, and even current expenses and had continually accumulated a floating debt which it recurrently funded. Nothing exhibited better the extent of its financial malaise than the comparative fate of the state loans to it and to the Boston and Maine. From its earnings the latter repaid the Commonwealth's advances of $150,000 somewhat before the due date. The Eastern cut corners on its sinking fund, requested and secured a postponement of repayments, and during the Civil War sought to discharge its obligations, in the hands of private investors as well as those held by Massachusetts, in legal-tender greenbacks rather than in gold.

Any other procedure was "not quite fair"; any other procedure was a sinister discrimination, since the state should not provide "gold for the rich, paper for the poor; gold for the capitalist, paper for the laborer."

III

At the Piscataqua or Salmon Falls rivers the probing railroads from Massachusetts touched the boundary of Maine and encountered the policy of a state determined upon railroad independence. Such an ambition was not entirely presumptuous. Maine had an area larger than that of the five other New England states, and her strategic location as a northeastern extrusion from the United States placed her squarely across the path of communication and commerce between Great Britain and the interior of Canada when the St. Lawrence was closed. Though in Maine an array of seacoast places aspired to capitalize these advantages, Portland was the pace setter. She was the state's largest city, her magnificent harbor was ice-free the year round, and, if Boston could dream of supplanting New York because she was nearer Liverpool, the same reasoning justified Portland's supplanting Boston. In truth there was soundness in these calculations. And for one brief, crowded, glorious interlude it seemed that, of all the cities of New England, Portland might be a rival, and not a satellite of either Boston or New York. As well as independence, the state's railroad policy for the moment promised system, for Maine, clearly imitating Massachusetts, established in 1834 a Board of Internal Improvements to conduct and finance surveys for canals, roads, and railroads. A policy of state aid was evidently envisaged, for the act specified that no funds were to be appropriated until the Board had determined the necessity and cost of the proposal. In the end this noble conception accomplished less in Maine than it had in Massachusetts. Although the engineers from the Board or the Army surveyed a number of routes from the seacoast toward Quebec in order to get "the immense trade of the two Canadas," each project incited the stubborn opposition of ports and communities left aside.

The appropriation of state funds, even the bonanza promised by the distribution of the national surplus, was prevented by a deep division of opinion within the state. Some felt that the Atlantic had already given Maine "a canal as broad as we can desire" and the state should remain a purely "commercial" and not a "producing" area. Others argued that Maine already was a "producing" state, that its agricultural products would increase in value if given a market, and internal improvements were necessary to halt both the damaging emigration to the West and the movement into the Maine wilderness. While the surveys and the controversy continued, the legislature incorporated the Portland, Saco and Portsmouth. The provisions of its charter, forecast by two general acts of the previous year, granted the corporation the conventional powers, including that of eminent domain, and permitted the legislature, if the tolls yielded a revenue greater than 12 per cent on the cost of the road, either to reduce the rates or appropriate the surplus for the public schools of the state.

Unhappily this first important railroad in the state was foreign in ownership and alien to the aims of Maine policy. Bostonians owned over 5,000 shares; Portland only 100 or more; the capitalists and places interested in the Eastern road were its real promoters. When the road was completed in 1842, though the editors of the Portland papers were given free passes for the opening-day excursion, they indulged in few superlatives. A month earlier a Boston correspondent had informed Maineites that the opening of the road would transfer the business of Portland to Boston. "It has been the fate of the small generally, from time immemorial, to be devoured by the large, and you must bear up as well as you can under the affliction." The disturbing purposes of this Massachusetts enterprise did something to cool the ardor of the state for railroads. A general hostility to all railroads, aroused as in New Hampshire by questions of land damages, tax favors, and other corporation privileges, did more. In addition, instructed by the unhappy experience of other states with internal improvements at government expense, Maine enacted in 1847 a constitutional amendment prohibiting the loan of its credit to private enterprise and limiting the size of the state debt.

IV

Though the setting was thus inhospitable, a group of Portland merchants and other civic leaders was gradually maturing the project of a railroad from their city to Canada. This new thoroughfare, probably terminating at Montreal, was to be the land link between interior Canada and Great Britain and western Europe. Portland was to blossom as an entrepôt and the merchant marines of the Atlantic were to throng her harbor. Though not yet a resident of Portland, John A. Poor of Bangor became the flaming evangel of her railroad greatness. Others connected with the Montreal railroad sank into obscurity and Poor acted and spoke as if a unique personal vision had moved him to originate the project. No doubt he was its colorful advocate and advertiser.

A lawyer, railway official, and journalist, Poor went on to become in the vernacular of the era the "philosopher" of the railroad and a self-appointed sovereign over the whole Maine system. In his native state he played the rôle that Quincy, Derby, and De Grand had in Massachusetts. With variations appropriate to his locale he saw in this new means of transportation an instrument for redeeming his native state from economic stagnation and for staying the emigration to Massachusetts and to the American West. For Maine agriculture it would give a market for bulky products. More important was the commercial prosperity with which it would bless her seaboard. "Maine will present at some future day, along our bays and harbors, a line of cities, surpassing those which are now found upon the shores of the English channel or the Baltic Sea." It would spur manufacturing enterprises. Maine had water power (and Poor was responsible for its first accurate appraisal); it had natural resources, stone and lumber, and would have more after a geological survey had unearthed them; and finally it had the climate. "The capacity of the human frame for labor is found to be greater in Maine, than in Massachusetts or any State, south or west of it.... The higher branches of industry, to be carried on with profit, must seek those regions of the earth where physical exertion is a pleasure, and continuous labor invigorates rather than exhausts the human frame." Incidentally Maine had a "low rate of wages." The attainment of this millennium depended upon the railroad, a Maine railroad system. Its construction was, like Maine's greatness, inexorable. As did most lawyers of the day, Poor inserted into his prophecies frequent references to laws, "natural" and "commercial."

Perhaps Bostonian energy might reverse nature. Already the citizens of that dreaded rival had turned their eyes northward to the fruitful Canadas, already they had projected not one but two routes to the St. Lawrence, already they had enchained Vermont and New Hampshire to their "interest," and already they had almost persuaded Montreal to an alliance. Defying this formidable phalanx, Poor and his fellow promoters launched a campaign to turn Montreal from Boston to Portland. They financed a survey which discerned a feasible route through Dixville Notch with grades of 80 to 90 feet a mile, heavy embankments and sidewalling, and a tunnel 1,500 feet long, to a triumphant union with a projected Canadian connection, and they sought a charter from the Maine legislature.. As affairs marched to climax, Poor in the winter of 1845 took off for Montreal by sleigh and, in spite of blizzard and sub-zero weather, reached it in five days, just in time to prevent the merchants there from committing themselves to the Boston route. A week later one of his associates, Judge William P. Preble, arrived with the charter which the Maine legislature had granted on February 10, 1845, to the Atlantic and St. Lawrence Railway.

Portland won the favor of Montreal. Whether the arguments of Preble and Poor mesmerized Canadian promoters, capitalists, and railroad statesmen or not, there were solid reasons for the decision. By ocean transport of that era Portland was two days nearer Europe than New York, a half day nearer than Boston, and the distance by railroad from Montreal to Portland was estimated to be at least a hundred miles less than to Boston. Since the Canadian portion of the line was also designed as a local route to serve the areas east of Montreal—the seigniories and the Eastern Townships—it traversed a wider Canadian territory if it connected with the Atlantic and St. Lawrence rather than with the Vermont and Canada or its alternates. Finally, in an alliance with Montreal, Portland was less apt to be master than was Boston. The latter was a rival to Montreal; it possessed routes to the West and to Canada, independent of her. Portland could achieve no higher destiny than serving as her winter port. So the Montrealers secured a charter for the St. Lawrence and Atlantic, the Canadian link in this Poor-christened "first international railroad of the world."

The whole project faced immense difficulties. For one thing it traversed a comparatively unproductive region. Years later a Maine man acquainted with the project recalled with a combination of lyricism and ruefulness the "sparsely-settled country and farther on a vast wilderness enclosing the hard-won farms which lay in the intervals along the streams, with pastures and tilled fields struggling up the sides of the hills, cleared from the adjoining forests, otherwise unbroken except by the inroads of the lumberman. Beyond these the forest primeval.... A line of stages ... led in the general direction of the desired railroad line, and was amply sufficient for the necessities of the public travel in that direction." In addition to its frontier aspect, the terrain was forbidding in the extreme since the Atlantic and St. Lawrence had to pierce, if not the heart, at least the rough outposts of the White Mountains. The charter wisely contented itself with the declaration that the road should run northwest from Portland "in the general direction of Sherbrooke and Montreal" and forthwith one surveying party after another tried to discover a feasible route. Eventually the road crossed from Portland to the valley of the Androscoggin, followed its valley into northern New Hampshire, crossed a divide to the Connecticut River, and finally joined with the Canadian connection at Island Pond in northeastern Vermont. Because of topographical difficulties and the decision of the Canadians to serve as large an area of their country as possible, the route was fifty miles longer than originally intended. "No grades above 45 feet to the mile were tolerated except for nearly three and a half miles of sixty feet."

More critical than the battle with geography was the ceaseless struggle against the wiles of Boston. The minions of Massachusetts had fought the charter of the St. Lawrence and Atlantic in Canada; with their allies they had almost persuaded New Hampshire and Vermont to forbid passage to the Portland road. The newspaper spokesman of the Vermont Central had declared of the enterprise, "The stock if subscribed for in America, would have to be taken by the Esquimaux, and the wolves and bears of these hyperboreal regions. The fox and beaver will cast their influence against the project; but the catamount and panther will come into the measure provided they can be made to believe that mutton and poultry will thereby become cheaper." But Poor and his cohorts had triumphed everywhere. To preserve the purity of their aim, an independent Maine system, they had carefully inserted in the charter a provision allowing connections with their railroad "but only on the easterly side thereof." Thus Boston was forestalled from tapping their river of commerce. In construction they took further precautions by giving their road a "medium gauge" of 5'6" rather than the standard one. The arguments of A.C. Morton, the engineer they imported from the Erie, itself a road with a peculiar gauge, gave the impression that their preference was dictated by considerations merely technological. Engines could have large drivers and still a low center of gravity, the multiplication of boiler tubes rather than their inefficient lengthening gave additional power, freight cars had a larger proportion of cargo space to their weight, and passenger cars would be more commodious. The real reason for the broad guage, however, was to inconvenience the interchange of goods and passengers with the Boston roads. This difficulty was enlarged when the Canadian roads west from Montreal, in spite of Boston's efforts, were built to conform to the Portland connection. Provincialism, Maine and Canadian, won the victory.

On July 4, 1846 at Portland, the governor of the state, President Preble, and a squad of distinguished spademen turned the first shovelfuls of earth. Soon thereafter the road was in financial straits. It proved impossible to collect enough subscriptions to meet even the modest estimates of $2,500,000 to $3,000,000 for a road only as far as the international boundary. Bostonians naturally did not invest; the bursting of a railroad bubble in Great Britain in 1846 blighted expectations of English assistance; and the first million, collected largely in Portland, apparently carried the road only eleven miles and partially built the Portland terminal. Recourse was now had to municipal credit. In 1848 Portland, permitted by the state to extend its credit to the road if two-thirds of the voters consented, granted $1,000,000; in later years the city loaned two additional sums of $500,000 each, and finally authorized $350,000 which, however, was not utilized. Though the protection given the city varied in different enactments, Portland eventually received a guarantee that the road would repay principal and interest of the municipal advance and, as collateral for its loans, $500,000 in the railroad's bonds and $1,500,000 in its stock; it could sell the latter only when annual contributions to the sinking funds fell behind schedule. More significant than these details, however, was the inauguration of municipal assistance to railroads. This policy was the means, then and later, by which the state secured "a liberal and effective system of internal improvements." Meanwhile, on the Atlantic and St. Lawrence, even municipal credit was not enough. When Poor in 1849 jammed through a construction contract with Black, Wood, and Company, a Portland firm which he admired, the contractors agreed to accept their payment of $26,200 a mile one-half in cash, one-quarter in bonds, and one-quarter in stock. The road was opened on July 18, 1853. It had cost nearly twice the estimates.

Three weeks later the Atlantic and St. Lawrence was leased for 999 years to the Grand Trunk Railway Company of Canada. Under the aegis of the latter, a monster corporation, Peto, Brassey, Jackson and Betts, the most famous English contracting firm of its day, had undertaken to construct and finance a Canadian rail network. They acquired the roads between Portland and Montreal as an outlet for their more extensive enterprises in the interior. For the Portland line their arrival was an unmixed blessing. They took over a partially unballasted road, with uncovered bridges and defective railroad furniture, and proceeded at great expense to put it into usable condition. Upon their association with the road the stock rose from $30 to $96 a share and the prudent Maineites gradually transferred their holdings to British purchasers. Consequently in the sixties when the Grand Trunk reduced the guaranteed rental from 6 to 4 per cent, momentarily omitted payments to the sinking funds for Portland loans, and funded rent arrears by an issue of scrip, the promoters, merchants, and capitalists of that city were not the chief sufferers.

Portland, alone among New England cities, had meanwhile gained a through route to the distant West. At Montreal, its line crossed the St. Lawrence by the Victoria Bridge. A tubular structure, over a mile long, with twenty-four piers, it was to Portlanders one of the wonders of the world, greater even than "the Pyramids of Egypt, the Parthenon of Athens, or the Roman Coliseum." West from Montreal the broad gauge carried its route to Sarnia on the St. Clair River and thence to Detroit, where it had "a complete and independent connection with the Western States." Boston had nothing like it. Nor was she likely to have the *Great Eastern* or *Leviathan,* building in Great Britain and promised on her maiden trip to Portland. Properly to receive this fabulous steamship, with its 18,914 gross tonnage and length of 692 feet, with its 112 furnaces raising steam for a double set of engines and driving both paddle wheels and screw propellers, and with its capacity for 4,000 passengers, Portland built a special wharf and began the erection of a marble hotel "of chaste architecture." Though the London *Times* sneered, "The steam monster, when it arrives, will dwarf hotel, landing place, and the town itself into utter insignificance," it was the moment of Portland's apotheosis.

> Portland is looking up, and all her spunk
> Is centered in those noble words—*"Grand Trunk."*
> That iron arm that links Atlantic *"Maine"*
> With Huron's waters, in a single chain;
> On whose smooth rail the swift, careering steed
> Shall cross Victoria Bridge, and onward speed,
> Defying time and space,—its journey o'er;
> Shall slake its thirst on the Pacific shore;
> While o'er our waters busy steamers ply
> With flags of every hue, in peaceful harmony:
> A neutral port with every flag unfurled
> That floats on merchant ships throughout the world.

Though some colorful anticipations, like the *Great Eastern,* did not materialize, the Grand Trunk benefited Portland in solid fashion. Clearances and entrances, imports and exports, population and property values, all increased remarkably. Portland became a Canadian city, at least part-time, for weekly steamship service to Liverpool, subsidized by the Canadian government, made Portland its terminus during the winter months. Through bills of lading from Liverpool to British Canada diverted the business in bond from Boston to Portland, and through Portland the products of the West even found their way to Boston. Its flour shipments Bostonward in 1860, 217,897 barrels, were greater than those from any other port and by any other railroad, except the Western with a total of 302,462. Confronted by this series of disquieting events, Boston had sulked and blustered. She pressed invitations upon the *Great Eastern*, chided Portland for cherishing "extravagant anticipations," and advised the Grand Trunk to extend by a third rail along existing roads to Boston, a metropolis and not a "ninth-rate town." Threats of this sort induced the Maine legislature in 1860 to pass an "act to promote safety of travel on railroads." Its only section forbade any road in the state to change its gauge or lay an extra rail without the consent of the legislature. This prohibition did not apply to the roads east of Portland.

V

For the area between the Grand Trunk on the west and the Penobscot Valley on the east, Maine promoters and planners had no railroad design of an imperial scale. In an almost offhand fashion the ruling railroad clique of Portland planned that a branch should diverge from the Atlantic and St. Lawrence at some point north of their city and move eastward to Lewiston and Bangor. If a road consecrated by Poor might be so regarded, this was the canon. To conform with it, the legislature in 1845 chartered two roads, the Androscoggin and Kennebec and the Penobscot and Kennebec; as their names imply they were to connect somewhere in the Kennebec Valley. When this project ran afoul of Augusta's unwillingness to be a way station and her preference for an exclusive and standard gauge connection with Portland, the Poor crowd located its roads farther inland along the "back route" and planned to connect them at Waterville.

Their rival, the Kennebec and Portland, appealed not only to Augusta, "a specimen of that profound selfishness for which *one portion* of the State is remarkable," but to a series of towns nearer the sea, of which Bath was the most important. Since it was to be a "narrow gauge" road—thus sneeringly christened by Poor and his associates—it connected easily with the Portland, Saco and Portsmouth and appealed to Boston investors.

Boston merchants subscribed $100,000 to its stock; the Portland, Saco and Portsmouth contributed another $100,000; private capitalists in Bath, Brunswick, and Augusta furnished additional funds; and in 1850 the towns along the route were authorized to advance $800,000 to the enterprise. In 1855 a second corporation extended the route northward along the Kennebec to a junction with the two official roads near Waterville. In 1855 these likewise had been completed. Bangor had contributed $800,000 in scrip to the Penobscot and Kennebec and, though it had cost 75 per cent over the estimates, the Bangor papers looked forward with delight to the time when "lecturers from abroad" could be brought over the rails, and celebrated with enthusiasm the first arrival of flour brought all the way by rail from Montreal.

Discord soon drowned such congratulations. A battle of gauges began. The Kennebec valley and coastal route, the standard gauge, insisted that the broad gauge must interchange through passengers at the junction near Waterville; the Androscoggin and Kennebec and Penobscot and Kennebec, the broad gauge, united to hamper such an arrangement. When the former summoned as allies the Massachusetts roads, which now refused to sell through tickets to Waterville and Bangor via the broad gauge route or to accept them from the same stations, the latter retaliated by connecting with the Boston boats rather than the Boston railroads. Of course the legislature was drawn into the quarrel. In 1856 it conditioned its assent to a merger of the Androscoggin and Kennebec and the Penobscot and Kennebec upon their giving "to all passengers their choice of routes at same rates of fare," and two years later, when the roads refused to accept this injunction, it established a Board of Railroad Commissioners to determine the terms of connection and the rates at which one railroad should carry the goods and passengers of another. This step the directors of the Androscoggin and Kennebec deplored: "The Railroad Corporations of this State are *private* corporations—*not public*—and whenever it is settled judicially that this act is the law of the land, you will have no future need of Directors to manage your affairs, except perhaps, to raise money to pay your debts."

This exception was no small one for the roads in question. Built at excessive costs, overlaid with bond issues, some kept from bankruptcy by the narrowest of margins, and the Kennebec and Portland did go into receivership. Although the investments by town and city were saved, private stockholders lost the whole or a large part of their holdings. All, however, was not dark. After the legislature in 1862 had withdrawn its conditions to consolidation, the broad gauge roads between the Grand Trunk and Bangor became the Maine Central Railroad Company. The rival Kennebec and Portland in the hands of trustees participated in the prosperity of the Civil War years. With the steamboat interests of Portland it steadfastly supported the state law prohibiting the laying of a third rail from Portland to Boston. Both were bent upon imprisoning the broad gauge within the state of Maine. The broad gauge sought to escape. Such was the ironic outcome of Maine's effort to create an independent railway system. In order to prosper it had to lose its independence.

VI

During the years of construction, squabbles, and merging in this middle region, Poor had suffered many humiliations. His advice had not been taken, his favorite contracting firm had been squeezed out of one of the corporations, and he himself was caught in contradictions of argument and attitude impossible to conceal. Meanwhile he had turned to happier pastures, eastern Maine, and larger prospects, the European and North American Railway. The latter was a railroad dream of inter-continental stature. In a petition of 1850 to the Maine legislature, Poor, other Portlanders, and Grand Trunkers revealed their plan for a railroad east from Bangor through New Brunswick and Nova Scotia to White Haven on Cape Canso and, if feasible, across the Gut of Canso to Louisburgh. Hence fast steamers were to cross the narrowed Atlantic to Galway. With the "Atlantic ferry" behind them, passengers would proceed by the Great Midland Railroad to Dublin, cross the Irish Sea to Holy Head, and speed thence by railroad to London. The journey between New York and London would shrink from ten days to seven or perhaps six. The European and North American would thus become the great avenue for passengers, mails, and freight between the United States and the continent. It also served local purposes. It would prevent the emigration of men and capital from Maine, increase the valuation of property and develop the eastern part of the state, and, taken in conjunction with the Grand Trunk, furnish the best connection between Montreal and Quebec and the Maritime Provinces. Though minor, this last objective was an urgent one, for already promoters and politicians were planning "the Intercolonial," a circuitous connection between the Canadas and the Maritimes entirely within British territory. Fortunately a lack of capital and local rivalries were for the moment retarding its construction.

As a prelude to the European and North American, Poor assembled in midsummer, 1850, the great Portland convention. It made a vivid impression upon its audience of legislators, judges, governors, businessmen, clergy, and delegates. The Star Spangled Banner, the Cross of St. George, and a huge map of the route decorated the hall. Solicited endorsements poured in from railroad and college presidents, professors, and statesmen. The speaking was a long oratorical marathon; a resolution declared "that the spirit of the Age and the progress of modern improvement" demanded the construction of the line; and the orgy of "repeated and prolonged cheers," "hearty cheers," "enthusiastic cheers," "rapturous cheers" and "ardent cheers" reached its climax on the last day, when three cheers were given for Queen Victoria, three cheers for the President of the United States, three cheers for the "Mother Country," three cheers for "her American Children," and finally "three notable and astounding cheers for the success of 'THE EUROPEAN AND NORTH AMERICAN RAILWAY.'"

Twenty days later the Maine legislature granted a charter for a line beginning at Bangor, crossing the river above it, and thence proceeding "over the most practicable route, in a line to the city of St. John, in New Brunswick, to the eastern boundary of the state." When the state also decided to finance the survey, A.C. Morton, engineer of the Grand Trunk, was detailed to make what he could of these specifications. His researches, published in 1851, were not entirely conclusive. Although he set the junction with the New Brunswick connections at Calais and St. Stephen, he rejected the approach by the coast as too precipitous and a direct overland route from Bangor as impossible because of mountains. Consequently the chosen route ran north along the Penobscot and then curved eastward through a lake region to tributaries of the St. Croix, which it followed to Calais. Although the country traversed was "unknown," the maximum grades and the cost were not—fifty-three feet to the mile and $2,266,577.

For nearly fifteen years the company in its own right never laid a rail. The difficulty was finance. Obviously it was a task for public rather than private capital, since no existing traffic could support a project of such magnitude, and the possibility of sluicing the trade between the United States and Europe along the coast of Maine and the Maritime Provinces, though it might dazzle talkers, did not convert investors. So Poor and his associates on "the Executive Committee of Maine for the European and North American Railway" tried to induce the state to give them a generous donation from its public domain or from the sale of its land in northern and eastern Maine. The people were not in the mood for such assistance. A similar appeal was directed upon Massachusetts, also the owner of lands in Maine. The European and North American, it was said, would enhance their value and also develop down East a manufacturing region and a market to compensate Massachusetts for the loss of western New England to New York. The Massachusetts General Court was deaf to the plea. Simultaneously the batteries were turned upon the national government, which had just granted lands to the Illinois Central and had paid $10,000,000 to Texas for an old land claim. Maine which had, under the Webster-Ashburton Treaty in 1842, surrendered her lands for a "merely nominal consideration," deserved federal funds as much as these western regions. When these claims produced no cash, Poor turned to those financial angels from overseas—Peto, Brassey, Jackson and Betts. They were willing to provide 80 per cent of the capital if they could have the whole line from Augusta to the border. Even if Maine interests could have been led to this surrender, the outbreak of the Crimean War definitely removed the further possibility of European assistance. The hopelessness of urban assistance was revealed when Bangor citizens refused to appropriate $500,000 in aid of one of the partial projects to which, during the fifties, Poor's grandiose conception had been whittled down.

The Civil War years, however, gave Poor an opportunity to revive the European and North

American Railway. Though he was unable to coax any assistance from the Federal government with the plea that the railway was a necessary military measure for the defense of Maine against British invasion, the hitherto hostile Bangorians summoned him to harmonize and promote their railroad interests. The following year, 1864, the Maine legislature authorized Bangor to loan $500,000 to the European and North American. Both the city government and the voters had to approve the grant. If it were made, the city would elect one director and receive a mortgage on the road as security. On behalf of the state the legislature granted to the railroad the proceeds from the sale of timber on ten townships, certain claims which she was still pressing upon the United States in connection with the losses of timber, and payments of money in the northeastern territory, once in dispute with Great Britain. Furthermore, if Massachusetts would assign to Maine certain joint claims against the national government and release Maine from further payments for the lands she had purchased from Massachusetts in 1853, the railroad could have all the public lands lying on the waters of the Penobscot and St. John Rivers with the exception of lands and timber set aside for public schools and "settlement." The railroad was to promote immigration by an agent and a campaign of education in Europe and America. Nearly all this was conditional. Incredibly, it nearly all came true.

CHAPTER

29.

As the previous chapter reveals, the laying of a railroad network in Maine between 1835 and 1890 produced some fascinating rivalries. Competition was keen and, one cannot help but conclude, shamefully wasteful. Yet, in spite of everything, the tracks were laid connecting Kittery with Eastport by the 1890's.

FROM KITTERY TO 'QUODDY*
by
Alvin F. Harlow

As early as 1828 a Maine legislative committee studied what information was available about the new form of transportation and reported their findings to an apathetic State Assembly. The public mind was not yet ready for any definite movement. The authorization of the first three short railroads out of Boston, however, reawoke the idea in Maine, and in 1832 its first two charters were granted. One went to the Calais Railway Company, which, after some years of toil in raising the needful cash, built and operated a two-mile horse railway between Calais and Milltown. The other was the Old Town Railroad, intended to connect Old Town with Bangor. The local enthusiasm over this project was so great that its shares are said to have sold at a premium before ever a spadeful of earth was turned. But so amateurish were both legislators and promoters at the time of these early charterings that the right of the corporation to seize land for its purpose was not assured, and a farmer could either chase the company's surveyors off his land with a pitchfork or have them arrested and jailed for trespass. The chartering had to be done all over again.

In 1833 the Bangor & Piscataquis Railroad and Canal Company, a rival enterprise financed in Boston, was chartered, with intent to run from Bangor through Old Town to some slate quarries thirty or forty miles up-country. The Old Town had done some grading and bridge pier building when, in 1835, it decided to sell out to the Bangor & Piscataquis. This company completed the road from Bangor to Old Town in November, 1836, and on it that year appeared the first locomotive in Maine, a Stephenson which stayed around for thirty years thereafter, and of which, fortunately, we have a crude photograph.

This road was not greatly successful and in 1848 was sold to a new company for a fraction of its cost. In 1854 it was extended to Milford and became the Bangor, Old Town & Milford, having attained a length of twelve and one-half miles. It was eventually taken over by the Maine Central. This was the first steam railroad in the state, and the only one until the Portland, Saco & Portsmouth was built in 1840-42. There was another small affair built in 1841-42, the Machiasport, a lumber railroad connecting Machiasport and Whitneyville, and this continued to operate until 1890; it was a friendly little affair, created solely for hauling timber, but it would carry passengers free whenever they desired. Its trains would even stop to pick up a woman or an elderly man. The Calais & Baring was another lumber road, chartered in 1837.

The building of the Portland, Saco & Portsmouth, to connect Portland and Maine coast towns with the Eastern Railroad coming up from Boston; the taking over of the Eastern by the Boston & Maine, and the leasing by the latter of the P.S. & P. have all been described in Chapter 7. Portland in particular was none too greatly interested in any line which would tend to draw off the commerce of the state toward Boston. Instead, knowing

---
*Reprinted with the permission of Farrar, Straus & Giroux, Inc. from *Steelways of New England* by Alvin F. Harlow. Copyright, 1945 by Alvin Fay Harlow. pp. 308-328.

Canada's lack of good Atlantic seaports, it hoped to accomplish the building of a railroad from its own harbor to Quebec or Montreal, and thus become Canada's seaport. The state lawmakers became interested in the idea and in 1835 passed a resolution requesting Maine's senators and representatives in Congress "to use their influence with the General Government to procure the aid of a corps of engineers for the purpose of surveying a railroad from Portland or some other point on the sea-board . . . to some point on the border of lower Canada."

Look at the map of Maine, and you will see that it is more than half surrounded by Canadian territory. It is no wonder that so much of its early railroad planning had to do with Canada. The national government saw the importance of Maine's request and sent a noted engineer, Colonel Stephen H. Long, to make the survey. After international consultations, Lord Almyer, the Governor-General, said that Canada would be happy to co-operate, and engineers were set to work on a survey southward from Quebec. In Maine there had been much argument over the question whether Portland, Wiscasset or Belfast would be the best terminus. Colonel Long, after several months of study and surveying, recommended Belfast, on the huge Penobscot Bay, and laid out a route from there to the border, near the headwaters of the Chaudiere River. The Belfast & Quebec Railroad Company was actually chartered in 1836, and Belfast sought state assistance for the building of the line, but Maine's constitution forbade the lending of its credit for such a purpose, and so few people in Maine liked railroads that enough private money could not be found. The Panic of 1837 finally stopped all efforts. An attempt was made a few years later to revive the project, but by that time Quebec's interest in the matter had evaporated.

The failure of this plan suited Portland to a T. In 1839 it begged $4000 from the Legislature for a survey from Portland across upper New Hampshire and Vermont to Lake Champlain, the ultimate target being Montreal, whom many now began to see as the coming great city of Canada. The survey was made and some boosting was done, but Maine, still primarily interested in such things as lumbering, fishing, shipbuilding and shipping, had not yet warmed up to railroads; hence no money could be raised there—and certainly Boston could not be expected to co-operate. And so matters drifted along for a few years more.

The building of the Portland, Saco & Portsmouth, however, was highly educational, and thereafter, a greater interest in railroads began to be noticed in Maine. Industry was developing rapidly, and businessmen had begun to realize how the railroad tentacles thrust out from Boston were siphoning the commerce of New Hampshire, Vermont, and even of Maine itself to the New England metropolis. And now arose a promoter, himself a vibrant enthusiast, who could stir the state to action—a young Bangor lawyer named John A. Poor. He had gone all the way down to Boston to see the Boston & Lowell launched. He was an evangelist, not only for railroads, but for Maine. In 1865, when he was advocating the broad-gauge railroad, he declared in an address: "The capacity of the human frame for labor is found to be greater in Maine than in Massachusetts or any other State south or west of it." He didn't say who had "found" it so, but there isn't the slightest doubt that he really believed it.

Poor was one of the early proponents of Maine as the natural sea-outlet for eastern Canada. He himself explored possible routes between the coast and the international boundary, following stream courses on foot through the mountains and through what was then a savage, tangled wilderness. He made little headway with his gospel until the early forties, when Portland and some interior towns began to thrill again to the idea. Poor's plan had now crystallized as a railroad from Portland to Montreal, and he urged upon the former city the desirability of aiding the enterprise with its cash. A preliminary survey by James Hall recommended that the White Mountains be passed via the Androscoggin River gulch and Dixville Notch. Hall figured the cost to the border at $2,250,000.

Simultaneously, Montreal capitalists were being stirred up by A.T. Galt—later Sir Alexander Galt—and were moving toward organization to build the Canadian end of the line. On February 10, 1845, the charter for the Atlantic & St. Lawrence Railroad was granted in Maine. But several days before this, word came to Poor that Boston emissaries had reached Galt and persuaded him that their city was the logical terminus. To tell the truth, Montreal didn't greatly care which was chosen: all it wanted was a good seaport that was open all winter, and it is easy to see that the big city of Boston would have some powerful reasoning on its side.

Poor did not lose a moment. He heard the news on the morning of Wednesday, February 5, and he decided instantly to start for Montreal, although a gale was blowing from the northeast, and snow, "almost a coarse hail," was falling heavily. The stableman who supplied the horse and sleigh "would not stir an inch with me," so a friend named Cheney volunteered to accompany him. In fur coats and caps and under fur lap-robes they started at noon, "& such a storm," wrote Poor, "I never before encountered.... To face the storm with our eyes open was impossible, & the only protection to them was the covering of ice which hung in masses from our eyebrows." The snow was drifted so deep and hard that they went right over stone walls and woodpiles and never knew when they were in the road. "Five times we called up the people on the way to get our road, which as many times we lost." Reaching a tavern seven and one-half miles out, after three hours of driving, they warmed themselves and pushed on.

Where they stopped for the night is not clear, but early next morning they started again with two horses tandem and a veteran stage driver to pilot, shovel and break drifts. As they proceeded through South Paris and Rumford, they sometimes had two, three and four horses pulling the sleigh. Skirting the south shore of Lake Umbagog and nearing Dixville Notch, "the cold was most cruel & intense." A Captain Bragg guided them through the Notch. "Two young men volunteered to go ahead and break the path, & as they approached the Notch, they started out other horses & riders, so that we had 4 horses & 5 men to put us through this wonderful chasm.... The wind howled fearfully" through the gorge, "and the drifting snow darkened the air." The intrepid young men helpers "penetrated the drifts with an apparent relish for the excitement, & would accept no compensation."

Beyond the Notch, conditions eased a bit. Through Colebrook and Canaan they hurried on, driving into Sherbrooke, Que., on Saturday. Leaving there at 5 A.M. Sunday, they pounded "through an untrodden road, with 18 inches of snow," reaching Granby, forty-six miles distant, at 5 P.M. But they did not stop there. With a change of horses they drove all night, arriving in Montreal at 5:30 on Monday morning, less than five days out from Portland. "The cold was intense, some 18 below zero, & in crossing the St. Lawrence [on the ice, of course] over 2 miles the mist of frost entirely prevented our seeing three rods ahead."

You have only to look at Poor's portrait to know that nothing would have stopped the indomitable man from accomplishing his purpose. After a three-hour nap at a hotel, he walked dramatically into a Board of Trade meeting, called to consider the Boston proposition. Talking himself hoarse, assuring the Board that Portland had a charter and would soon have the cash, he succeeded in getting postponement of action. About a week later, Judge William P. Preble, who was to be the first president of the A. & St. L., arrived, also by sleigh, with the charter; and with this evidence of good faith and determination, the Montrealers were won over. A gentlemen's agreement was made with Portland, and the Canadian company was promptly chartered with the name in reverse, St. Lawrence & Atlantic.

Back home, the war was being carried on merrily by the Portland and Boston editors. The former asserted that Boston harbor was silting up and would soon be unusable; also that it froze every winter. It was noted that with the mercury sixteen below zero, at Portland, the harbor was not frozen; but with impish glee they quoted a Boston paper as saying, "Our harbor is about as good, or rather, about as bad as closed up. It is filled with ice and snow, and it is with the greatest difficulty that a passage can be kept open for the East Boston ferry." Boston editors could only sneer back, "We would first inform the Maine editors that they and their readers have not sufficient enterprise and public spirit to accomplish such an object." Portland proceeded to disprove this during the following summer by raising a million dollars and effecting an organization. A resurvey was made and a route farther south than Dixville Notch was chosen, the one actually occupied by the road today.

Here for the first time we find a rebellion against Stephenson's accidentally-fixed gauge, which has come to be our standard. The track width decided upon by both companies was 5 feet, 6 inches. There are two conflicting stories as to the reason for this. One is that A.C. Morton, the engineer in charge of building the Atlantic & St. Lawrence, wanted a broad gauge and persuaded the Canadian authorities to revoke their original plan to use the Stephenson gauge, as had been done on the first few miles of railroad in the Dominion. The other is that the British Government—Canada then being still a mere colonial possession—not only favored Portland over Boston as the terminus but specified the broad gauge, different from all other roads in the United States, in order to make troop and munition movements into Maine difficult for our government in case of war—which has a slightly romantic and illogical sound to our ears. Whatever the origin, that decision caused a number of other railroads in Maine to be built on the broad gauge, and brought on a very annoying tangle in the years to come. Poor may not have originated the broad gauge, but he was as stubbornly in favor of it as if he had.

On July 4, 1846, construction was begun on the Maine project. Judge Preble, with a silver-plated shovel, filled a barrow with earth and the governor wheeled it away, while the populace madly cheered at this charming condescension. That same year the Portland Locomotive Works was organized, largely by stockholders of the railroad. Its first engine, however, was built for the Portland, Saco & Portsmouth, after which it turned out a number for the A. & St. L. and other roads.

But after two years, only twelve miles of track had been built by the A. & St. L., and money was increasingly hard to get. With Boston frankly hostile to the project, there was no chance of selling any stock there. Near the end of 1848, only fifty miles of track was ready, and a connection was made at Danville Junction with the Androscoggin & Kennebec, then building. Progress had been even slower in Canada, where only the thirty miles from Montreal to St. Hyacinthe had been accomplished. C.S. Gzowski, a Polish exile, later Sir Casimir Gzowski, was chief engineer of the St. L. & A., and its general manager after 1852. But both companies received an impetus in 1849, with England's reduction to a minimum of import duties on grain, which threw open the English market to American breadstuffs.

The Atlantic & St. Lawrence now made a contract with private builders for the construction of the road to the Canadian Boundary. The cost would be $26,000 per mile, to be paid one-half in cash, one-quarter in bonds and one-quarter in stock. The city of Portland lent its credit to the extent of $1,000,000 and a little later received permission to give additional assistance. But for two years more the thing dragged lamentably, and the railhead did not enter New Hampshire until July, 1851. Then it gained speed and reached the international border, north of Island Pone, Vermont, and 149 miles from Portland, in February, 1853. The Canadian company completed its track a little later, and the whole 292-mile line was theoretically open for use in July, 1853.

The promoters lost no time in bringing about the step which had long been contemplated. A new corporation, the Grand Trunk Railway of Canada, had been organized, and on August 5, it took a 999-year lease of the Atlantic & St. Lawrence (as well as its Canadian cousin), agreeing to pay all debts and 6 per cent dividends on the stock. Portland's loan was soon repaid, and that city profited handsomely by the investment. A year-round line of steamers to Liverpool was established, and large sums were spent in Portland for terminal facilities. Over a century has passed, but the Atlantic & St. Lawrence still has a corporate existence, most of its stock being held in Europe, though a small quantity of it still pays its comfortable 6 per cent to citizens of Maine.

The new Grand Trunk Company was rather supercilious about the plant it had taken over. In the annual report of 1854 the directors said that the line was supposedly open, but was unfit for use—

> Particularly the section between Sherbrooke and Island Pond, and the locomotive and carriage stock was equally deficient, but according to the terms of the amalgamation, one train had to be run every day. This was done during the winter of 1853-4 with the greatest difficulty, as there were no snow fences, the line was not ballasted in many sections, and the old company had used some sort of a metal crosstie that was unsatisfactory.

They said that the amalgamated companies had thirty-four engines, of which four were scarcely worth repairing, while most of the others required extensive repairs. The report added that new locomotives for the company were being built in England, which would indicate that the Portland works had completely lost its influence; but this did not prove to be true, for later, more locomotives were ordered from Portland, and it built, all told, one hundred and fifteen of them for the Grand Trunk.

The building of that broad-gauge line launched a quarter-century of trouble. In 1836, citizens of Gardiner, up the Kennebec, had procured a charter for the Kennebec & Portland, to create a line from Portland up the river through Freeport, Brunswick and Topsham to their town. But Augusta, still farther upstream, said, "Why not to me, too?" and as she held the seat of government and was in a position to exert considerable pressure, the terminus had to be changed to the capital, in one of several recharterings of the company.

This project was still lagging in 1845, when two other charters were issued, following in general Poor's dictum as to the necessity for a rail connection between Portland and Bangor. One of the two roads, the Androscoggin & Kennebec, was to run from a junction with the Atlantic & St. Lawrence through Lewiston to a point on the Kennebec somewhere between Waterville—north of Augusta—and Hallowell, south of it. The Penobscot & Kennebec was to build from that rail end to Bangor. Both lines were being promoted by the same group, and were essentially one. Both had at first thought of Gardiner, Augusta or Hallowell as their junction point, but jealousies and bickering arose among Lewiston, Augusta, Waterville and Portland, with the railroad companies involved. The Androscoggin-Kennebec-Penobscot twin companies depended upon the Atlantic & St. Lawrence for their western-southern outlet and therefore made theirs a 5-foot, 6-inch track, like the greater line. Augusta leaned toward the Kennebec & Portland, which contemplated a 4-foot, 8½-inch gauge, so that it might run cars through over the Portland, Saco & Portsmouth (also standard gauge) toward Boston. The P. S. & P., by the way, had bought, or rather, subscribed for (not always the same thing) one thousand shares of K. & P. stock. Portland, heavily interested financially in the A. & St. L., preferred the broad gauge, which seemed to promise it greater returns in traffic. There were other bones of contention, too many to list here, but it is enough to say that, in the end, the Androscoggin & Kennebec didn't touch Augusta, but passed to west and north of it, joining its Penobscot twin at Waterville.

Another group, among whom were some Augusta partisans, made the situation hotter in 1848 by chartering the Somerset & Kennebec, which was privileged to build north from Waterville to Skowhegan and beyond, and south to Augusta, *if* the Penobscot & Kennebec did not enter the capital. This was the best charter the company could get, says a local historian, "from the railroad power which then controlled the Legislature of the State" (meaning, no doubt, the broad-gauge roads) "and prevented Augusta from being connected with the upper Kennebec by rail during a long period of years." The Somerset & Kennebec did not get organized until 1852, and then wanted a charter amendment, assuring it of the right to enter Augusta with no stipulations. It was backed by 2700 petitioners and opposed by 1500 remonstrants from along the "upper route," as the Androscoggin-Kennebec-Penobscot was called. A major objection of the latter faction was the probability that the Somerset would be standard gauge, to make a continuous route with the Kennebec & Portland. There was a terrific battle on the legislative floors; eminent lawyers on both sides volleyed and thundered. One, W.B.S. Moor, for the upper route, threatened in the extremity of his excitement to plant cannon at a certain point (ever afterward known as "Moor's Battery") and "blow the Somerset road to hell."

But the Somerset road won through at last, a significant victory for the standard gauge. It was leased in 1853 and when completed was operated by the Kennebec & Portland. The latter in a reorganization in 1864 turned its name around and became the Portland & Kennebec. That this road was getting a foothold in state politics was proved in 1856, when the Androscoggin & Kennebec and the Penobscot & Kennebec begged to be permitted to unite, but had to be content with a lease of the latter by the former. For several years these two competitors between Portland and Waterville carried on a traffic war, with the Legislature, the Boston & Maine and the Eastern Railroads all putting in their oars. The A. & K. had trouble also with a feeder line, the Androscoggin, a vague little concern chartered in 1848, whose track left the A. & K. at Leeds Junction and crawled northward with much tribulation to Farmington, reaching that place in 1859. As a connection with the A. & K., its track was broad gauge, and it was fully expected that the A. & K. would take over and operate it, but it didn't. When the little road proved unprofitable, the directors planned an extension southward to the coast. They wangled a loan from the city of Bath, and in 1861 completed a line to Brunswick, near Bath. This extension was made standard gauge, the same as the Portland & Kennebec, with which it connected at Bath. Next the company planned to reduce its track between Leeds and Farmington to standard. The A. & K. procured an injunction against this action, but the Androscoggin officials dodged the process-servers (this was on a Saturday), and on the following day, when the Law was off the job, a force of men changed the gauge to standard. Three years of litigation over this episode ensued, the Androscoggin family finally being sustained. It eventually passed into the hands of the Maine Central.

And who was this Maine Central? Why, it was the consolidation in 1862—when the Legislature at last relented and gave permission—of the Androscoggin & Kennebec and the Penobscot & Kennebec; and what a relief it must have been to get at least two of those confusing "Kennebecs" off the record! The new corporation promptly announced that its life's aim was peace, that all bickering with the "narrow-gauge roads"—as the broad-gaugers always contemptuously called the four-eight-and-a-halfs—was at an end. It established friendly relations with the Portland & Kennebec and the Androscoggin, and evolved deep-laid plans for expansion. By 1869 it was ready. It leased the Dexter & Newport that year, and in 1870 it took the Portland & Kennebec and its dependency, the Somerset & Kennebec, under lease for 999 years. This was as much consolidation as lease, for Richard D. Rice, who had so ably headed the Portland & Kennebec for several years, now became president of the Maine Central.

Even before the union, it had been secretly planned that the gauge of the two original units of the new system should be reduced from broad to standard. Most stockholders were now taken unawares by the news, and John A. Poor, long the foremost champion of the broad gauge, brought suit in equity, seeking to prevent the change and even praying for a receiver for the company, but failed in his purpose. The broad gauge was on the way out. In 1871 the M. C. took over the Belfast & Moosehead Lake, running from its main line southeast to Belfast, and Maine's greatest railroad system was well under way. The management did not await the settlement of Poor's suit—which was not finally defeated until 1872, a year after the suitor's death—but completed its change to standard gauge in 1871. This left only two important broad-gauge lines in the state, the Grand Trunk (which became standard gauge in 1873) and the European & North American; and three smaller ones, the Somerset, the Bangor & Piscataquis and the Portland & Oxford Central. Let us notice the minor ones briefly.

The Somerset, chartered in 1860 to build from Waterville up the Kennebec Valley, was supposed to pass automatically into the hands of the Maine Central, but though that company bought $50,000 worth of Somerset stock in 1868, it did not actually take over the road until thirty-nine years later. Meanwhile, in the seventies the Somerset fell a victim to a common malady of the Maine woods in those days and saw itself as a link in an international railway from the sea at Wiscasset to Quebec, and a rival to the Grand Trunk. Three or four other companies, first and last, were chartered to become parts of this grand scheme; towns along the way pledged their credit; a Canadian company actually built track forty miles southward from Quebec—but the Panic of '73 halted all plans, and they never came to life again, the Somerset getting no farther north than Bingham.

The Bangor & Piscataquis was chartered in 1864 and organized three years later, with Hannibal Hamlin as its first president, to build from Bangor to Moosehead Lake, but it proceeded no farther than the Katahdin Iron Works. It later became a part of the Bangor & Aroostook.

The Portland & Oxford Central began in 1847 as the Buckfield Branch Railroad, to run from Mechanic Falls on the Atlantic & St. Lawrence to Buckfield. The stockholders lost their investment, and in 1857 the road passed into the hands of a Portland promoter, of whom Louis Clinton Hatch, in his *Maine, A History,* says, delicately but significantly, "The actions of the Hon. F.O.J. Smith in connection with this line would fill a volume." The Hon. Mr. Smith, known derisively the country over as "Fog" Smith, became what might be called notorious as a telegraph promoter, entitling us to some vivid guesses about his rail manipulations. Under Smith the road became the Portland & Oxford Central, was reorganized twice under new names, changed to standard gauge in 1878, and in 1890 emerged as the Portland & Rumford Falls, running far up the Androscoggin Valley. A subsidiary company built an extension to the Rangeley Lakes.

Now we turn back to the Maine Central. So important a system naturally wanted a good outlet from Portland toward Boston. It was not satisfied with its service via the Eastern, and began negotiating for control of the Portland, Saco & Portsmouth. That road had been under joint lease to the Eastern and the Boston & Maine since 1847, but it had the right to cancel the contract upon payment of $100,000 to each of the lessees. The Maine Central offered it a higher rental; its two lessees took alarm, and the bidding among the three ran up to 10 per cent per annum, where it stopped, everybody knowing that it would be ruinous to go farther. The P. S. & P., which leaned toward the Eastern, anyhow, thereupon paid off the Boston & Maine and leased itself to the Eastern. That road immediately began making overtures to the Maine Central, and a traffic agreement was presently effected. But it did not work satisfactorily, and as its next expedient, the Eastern began buying stock of the M. C., obtaining voting control by 1875.

And here it is time to notice a grandiose project which had become somewhat frayed and faded when the Maine Central got around to noticing it. But in 1850 something of a nationwide sensation was created when the plan for the European & North American Railway was made public, with a promise to shorten the traveling time between the United States and Europe! There was to be a railroad—broad gauge, of course, for John A. Poor was in the project up to his ears—over which you would speed through Maine, New Brunswick and Nova Scotia to the farthest point of land at Canso. From there, fast steamers, "larger than any yet seen," would run to Galway, Ireland, in five days! From there, trains would dash across Erin to Dublin; then a quick crossing of the Irish Sea to Holyhead and a rail jump to London, and there you were—and another couple of hours or so would put you in France.

The promoters thought of the Androscoggin & Kennebec and Penobscot & Kennebec as covering a part of the route: east of Bangor they would have to build their own line. Delegates from the New England states, New Brunswick and Nova Scotia met in Portland on July 31, 1850. The Canadians promised grants of land and money. Orators expatiated. General H.A.S. Dearborn of Roxbury made the hit of the day when he told how Cato had shown the Roman Senate a cluster of figs taken from a tree in Africa only four days before. "And I," he declaimed, "shall see the time when the Rose of England, blending the colors of York and Lancaster and plucked from the gardens of Windsor, shall be twined freshly in America with the beautiful prairie flower, 'the Queen of the West,' and bound together with the Lilies of Canada, shall compose a fragrant wreath wherewith to crown the Statue of Concord in the Temple of Peace."

The applause for that passage rocked the building, and when he sat down, three cheers were given for the General; but curiously enough, the ecstasy was not great enough to induce many people to invest money in the project. Maine and the two provinces soon chartered their companies, but investors were scarce. Another convention was held in 1852, at which Poor made golden predictions, but the fact was that slowness in building the Penobscot & Kennebec was a detriment to the promotion. Then came the Panic of '57 to make money tight, and next the Civil War. Relations with England became strained, and lo! there was a new argument for the building of the railroad—military necessity, the defense of the frontier! And this a project whose chief *raison d'être* only yesterday had been the cementing of international friendship! Upon this ground the company obtained a grant of 700,000 acres of land from Maine, while the city of Bangor in 1869 voted a $1,000,000 loan. With this aid and a bond issue of its own, the company finally succeeded in completing the 114½ miles from Bangor to Vanceboro, on the international border, and there was a great celebration on October 17, 1871, with President Grant, the Governor of Maine, Lord Lingard, Governor-General of Canada, provincial authorities of New Brunswick and other luminaries present. But John A. Poor, who would have been the happiest celebrant of all on that day, had died six weeks before.

The international road never approached the greatness predicted for it. The Canadian extension got no farther east than St. John, and it was soon bankrupt, a subject for reorganization. The Maine company scraped along until 1875 before going into the hands of trustees, of whom former Vice-President Hamlin was one. It had leased the Bangor & Piscataquis, whose track it used as a main line from Bangor to Old Town, and when insolvency came, the B. & P. took back its property. In 1877 the Maine Central agreed with the trustees to aid the company in altering its gauge to standard, and in 1882 leased the E. & N. A. for $125,000 a year and fixed charges. Simultaneously, the Maine Central declared the first dividend in its twenty-year history—2 per cent.

The E. & N. A. lease included the Bangor & Bucksport, a little road which had a curiously chameleon-like history. Originally built to broad gauge, it was drawn down to standard gauge in 1877, and in 1879 reduced to three feet width. Then when the Maine Central took full charge of it in 1883, it was widened again to standard. The M. C. next took over the incomplete Maine Shore Line, running from Bangor through Ellsworth to Mount Desert Ferry, across Frenchman's Bay from Bar Harbor. This road had the charter right to extend from Ellsworth to Calais, on the eastern boundary of the state, near the mouth of the St. Croix, but that line was at last independently built in the 1890's as the Washington County Railroad to Calais and Eastport, and the Maine Central acquired it in 1904.

Allusion has already been made to the Portland & Ogdensburg, which began construction in 1870 and was intended to connect Portland with the outlet of Lake Champlain, at the Canadian border, but which never quite got on its feet financially. The Central Vermont did what it could to make life difficult for the western end of it, and that portion eventually became a separate company, the St. Johnsbury & Lake Champlain, which passed through the hands of the Lowell into those of the Boston & Maine. The Portland & Ogdensburg thought it had scored a success when it arranged with the Eastern for through traffic over the latter's Great Falls & Conway—which touched the P. & O. at North Conway—while from a point farther north the P. & O. hoped to collaborate in the building of a line to Montreal. But nothing worked out as desired.

Next the P. & O. became interested in the Upper Coos Railroad, a little project in northern New Hampshire which the Boston & Maine had been aiding. The B. & M. would have liked to take over the P. & O., but the city of Portland, which had a stake in the road, preferred to see it go to the Maine Central; and so the latter leased it in 1888 for a miserable 1 per cent per annum on its capital stock for the first three years, and after that, 2 per cent for 996 years. (We wonder if any of these railroad officials ever paused to conjecture what the world may be like at the end of 999 years!) An extension of the P. & O., built in 1889, connected it with the Upper Coos, which was leased in 1890.

During all these years since 1874, the Eastern had held a majority of the stock of the Maine Central. But the Eastern was not of the stuff that endures, and in 1884 it passed under lease to the Boston & Maine, carrying with it the leased Portland, Saco & Portsmouth and stock control of the Maine Central. Talk that now began to be heard of a lease of the Maine Central to the Boston & Maine aroused such a furor in Maine that the B. & M. quickly dropped the idea. The Maine Central pursued its independent way, maintaining its own offices and officials, leasing and buying here and there, until in 1899 a significant development appeared: Lucius Tuttle, president of the Boston & Maine, was also elected president of the Maine Central. The camel's head had got a little farther into the tent.

A railroad designed to put Rockland on the map by connecting it with Bath was first chartered in 1849, and lived in a state of suspended animation for two decades thereafter, finally reviving in the latter sixties under the name of Knox & Lincoln. Cities and towns along its route agreed to lend it aid in sums ranging from $50,000 to $400,000; even the village of Nobleboro promised $25,000. On top of that, several bought from $25,000 to $125,000 worth of stock, the last-named figure being that of the city of Bath, which also promised a loan of its credit up to $600,000. Bath and Bangor were two cities of modest size which were extraordinarily generous in their aid to railroads. But the cost of this line along the rugged coast, bridging many rockbound estuaries and rivers, was far more than expected, and the communities all had to put up more money, so that by the time the road was completed in 1872, $2,395,000 worth of their bonds had been sold in its behalf, secured by first, second and third mortgages. An attempt to lease the road to the Maine Central found that company cold, and when the same expedient was proposed ten years later, it was defeated by popular vote in the bonded towns along the way. But unpleasant facts stared them in the face, and they decided to sell the property at a bargain price, if they could. A syndicate which included some Maine Central directors bought it for $1,300,000 in bonds and $200,000 in cash. Waldoboro at first shrieked, "No! We won't sell!" but, being small and alone, was forced to give in. In 1891 the property was leased to the Maine Central, which surprised nobody, and in 1901 was completely merged with it.

It was in 1907 that the Maine Central took over the Somerset and then the Portland & Rumford Falls when the latter began to talk big about building a through line between Portland and Quebec. The storm cloud from down Connecticut way which then threatened the M. C. will be discussed in another chapter.

The Portland & Rochester, originally chartered in 1846 as the York & Cumberland to build from Portland to South Berwick and there to connect with a road to Boston, had like some others "military importance" as an excuse for existence. Construction began in 1850. John A. Poor was briefly president and managed to push the track eighteen miles to the Saco River, where it bogged down. The bondholders took over in 1865, changed the name to Portland & Rochester and had visions of connecting with other roads at the newly proposed terminus, Rochester, N. H., to form a through line from Portland to New York. The city of Portland issued $700,000 in bonds to aid it, and it struggled on a few miles farther. In 1870 the city was persuaded to waive its first mortgage claim and permit $350,000 in bonds to be sold to the public. The next year a new issue was offered, but they couldn't be sold, until finally good old Portland heeded the cry of distress and bought them. The track crept on to Rochester, but the great western route did not develop, the Panic of '73 dealt it a fearful blow, and in the following year it couldn't even pay its interest. Portland now issued bonds to raise money to pay itself the interest on the mortgage held by itself, a device which would have delighted the author of *Pinafore*. The truth was that the P. & R. was a bottomless sink for money and had little excuse for being. At another reorganization in 1881, the stock held by the city passed into the strong box of the Boston & Maine, but an actual merger was not completed until 1900.

When in 1837 Canadian promoters talked of cutting through Maine with a railroad from St. Andrews to Quebec, the Down-Easters didn't like the idea of Britishers making a path across their dooryard. But by 1843, when the project took the form of a line from Halifax to Montreal, Maine folk had become more receptive, though they considered the 835-mile project beyond human power to accomplish. And sure enough, it didn't materialize for another forty years. A Canadian company calling itself the International Railway tried it in the seventies but stalled at the Maine boundary. In 1886 the Atlantic and Northwest Company bought out the International and immediately leased the latter's property in perpetuity to the Canadian Pacific Railway, which pushed the track across Maine to Mattawamkeag by 1888, used the Maine Central's rails from there to Vanceboro, and built its own line eastward through New Brunswick.

And this reminds us of another railroad, a remarkable piece of development which seems to represent the sturdy pioneer character of the Maine Yankee more than any other in the state—except perhaps one. The far northern county of Aroostook, a part of which Canada had once tried to ravish from us, was without rails save for two or three little branch lines from New Brunswick to Houlton, Caribou and Presque Isle, built between 1870 and 1880. Thus until 1892 the county, save for an extreme southern tip, was without rail connection with the outer world except through Canada. When the Canadian Pacific came streaking across the state in the eighties, Aroostookians thought they were about to fall into foreign hands again. Then a man arose who brought the gospel to them—Franklin W. Cram of Bangor, who had been general manager of the New Brunswick Railway from 1885 to 1890. He saw a future in Aroostook's lumber, pulp and agriculture, and he proceeded to create the Bangor & Aroostook Railroad, one of the soundest little rail developments in America. With the aid of Albert A. Burleigh, the company was financed, mostly with money from outside the state, chartered in 1891 and organized with Burleigh as president, for Cram at first modestly took the post of general manager.

The American Express Company, angry at being thrown off the Canadian Pacific, loaned $600,000 at a critical moment to this new railroad, which it believed would injure the C. P.'s business. The Bangor & Piscataquis was taken over as a starter, and from its line at Brownsville the system was shrewdly extended into Aroostook County, covering it in strategic areas and helping to develop there the wonderful potato and pulp industries and others as well. A branch was thrown out to Moosehead Lake, and from Bangor a line was built down the Penobscot to tidewater at Searsport, where a great ocean terminal was developed.

The other railroad which is typically Maine is the Belfast & Moosehead Lake. It was promoted largely by the little city of Belfast and never got any farther than Bingham Junction on the Maine Central, thirty-three miles distant. It was taken under short lease by the Maine Central in 1871, and until 1925 Belfast enjoyed a comfortable little income of $36,000 yearly from the rental. Then the M. C. gave notice that it was going to abandon service, as the road was losing $40,000 a year. Belfast was stricken with horror, and saw itself, its lumber, fish and potato industries ruined. Businessmen got together, borrowed $5000 for operating capital from a local manufacturer, rented three old locomotives and some cars from the Maine Central and started out on their own. For a few years the profit and loss curve zigzagged up and down bewilderingly; then it settled to a steady progress upward, and in 1944 the road on which the M. C. was losing $40,000 annually had a $50,000 surplus in its treasury—which proves something or other, if only we knew what. This, one of the two municipally owned railroads in the United States, is a beautiful example of co-operation. It has no vice-presidents; the president and directors serve without pay; the secretary receives twenty-five dollars a year and the treasurer one hundred dollars. Directors' meetings are now being held in the back room of a drugstore, the druggist being one of the directors. One train crew does all the freight and passenger work, and the conductor dons overalls and helps in the yard and roundhouse between times. Co-operation and the absence of lost motion make the small community a much more efficient organism than the big city or a giant government like the United States. And here may be a hint that there are too much overhead and brass headgear and formalities about the big railroads.

CHAPTER

30.

In 1912-1914 pulp and paper replaced textiles as the leading industry in Maine. It promises to remain the leader well into the future. The following article written by Professor David Smith of the University of Maine, deals with the early history of the paper industry in Maine.

WOOD PULP PAPER COMES TO THE NORTHEAST, 1865-1900*
by
David C. Smith

Although the period 1860 to 1900 was a time of tremendous development in the United States in manufacturing, it seems safe to say that few industries grew with quite the rapidity of the wood pulp and paper industry. Until 1866 most paper used in the United States was manufactured from rags. By this time, however, the increased use of paper and the growing scarcity of rags forced paper prices, and in particular the prices of newsprint, to nearly exhorbitant levels.

This great price rise triggered an almost frantic search for rag substitutes. Among the materials suggested were the bark and foliage of the mulberry tree, corn husks, manila hemp, agave of Cuba, cultivated hemp, cotton, acacia, Spanish broom, silk weed, hops, jute, down of the date tree, New Zealand flax, esparto grass, linden of basswood, yucca, white moss from Sweden and Norway, forest leaves, and many others.

The leading journal of the industry greeted most of these discoveries with skepticism,

> ...the vast majority of the so-called fibers fail... and people who are experimenting today with such materials will only have their labor for their pains. It may be truely said that this diligent search for new vegetable fibers is today unnecessary. Esparto, straw, and wood are the great substitute for rags in foreign mills. In this country wood and straw have the field to themselves.

The search was successful with the discovery of a workable wood pulp paper. This new source of paper triggered in its own turn an almost equally frantic rush as manufacturers hastened to shift their operations to wood pulp paper production. Two commercially viable processes appeared in the early years of the industry. The first of these was that of Henreich Voelter. This wood pulp, technically ground wood, was first used in Western Massachusetts. Voelter's research was done in Germany in the 1850's, and his American patent dated from August 10, 1858, antedated to August 29, 1856. Nothing was accomplished until the fall of 1866 when Voelter sold his patent for $6,000 a year for the length of the patent. The patent was extended for seven years on August 29, 1870. The royalties charged by the owners, which included by this time Senator Warner "Woodpulp" Miller of New York, were so high that when they applied for re-extension, controversy developed. A lengthy hearing resulted in no extension, but the hearing examiner was overruled, and the patent was extended until 1884. The first pulp ground under this process came from the machines on March 5, 1867, and the paper, manufactured by the Smith Paper Company, of South Hadley, was made on March 8, 1867.

The chief competition for the Voelter process came from the soda process which was developed at about the same time. The experiments dated from the mid-fifties, and again the inventors came to the United States in search for capital. After receiving an American patent in 1864, the inventors and others set up a firm called the American Wood Pulp Company to manufacture their product at Manayunk, Pennsylvania. The wood in both these processes came from the poplar tree exclusively, and the great success of the new

---

*David C. Smith, "Wood Pulp Paper Comes to the Northeast, 1865-1900, *Forest History*, (April 1966), pp. 12-25. Reprinted by permission of Forest History Society, Inc.

methods soon created a demand which far outran the local supply of poplar wood. By 1871 the wood used in the western Massachusetts mills was becoming expensive, and the process spread to other areas where the poplar was prevalent. Chester County, Pennsylvania experienced a boom, but soon the mills found themselves searching as far as Maine for their supply. The wood pulp paper was much cheaper and these processes could have revolutionized the paper business even more quickly, but the location of the first mills so far from the major supply of wood actually slowed the growth. The American Wood Pulp Company did locate a mill in Providence which was supplied with wood from Bangor and the Penobscot River, but this was unsatisfactory. It is curious, but apparently the firm believed that to locate further north was uneconomical. As their agent in Maine said when reviewing the early years:

> During two winters I traveled over the timberlands of Maine, New Brunswick, and Nova Scotia in the interests of this company, (nominally—in fact, in my own interest, and at the company's expense); to look up the best chances to get wood to ship to Manayunk, Pennsylvania, and Roger's Ford up the Schuykill, where their large mills were located. The idea of travelling all over Uncle Sam's and Queen Vic's territory to find wood had a ludicrous side to it and the next time I had a chance to talk with Buffum (the Treasurer) I said to him, "Why in the name of common sense don't you locate your mills in the State of Maine, either on the Kennebec or Penobscot rivers, where you can get your wood at a merely nominal price, instead of going all over the country collecting wood to be sent to Pennsylvania?" His reply was characteristic of the general opinion held concerning the State of Maine by New Yorkers and Providence men, "Oh, you are frozen up nine months in the year down in Maine," he replied. I could not help smiling. "Nevertheless," I replied, "if there is ever any money to be made in the business the mills must be located near where the wood grows."

This expressed the matter succinctly, and laid the basis for the history of the industry. The processes had been developed, now it simply remained to locate the industry in the most advantageous spots. Maine and New Hampshire were where "the wood grows," and they would be where the mill would grow. The proximity of the forest would determine the location, and the paper mills, already clustered in the northeast, would move farther north and east in their search for the new sources of supply.

I. THE FIRST COMPANIES

The first notice of a wood pulp mill in Maine was in 1864, but nothing came of the venture. The first mills in operation in Maine were at Norway, and at Topsham. The Norway mill will be treated briefly later. The Topsham mill began in the basement of a sawmill run by Charles D. Brown, and E.B. Denison. It utilized grinders from the machine shop of the Bath Iron Works. The mill produced one ton of pulp a day with Denison running the grinder and Brown the wet machine. Denison kept the books and Brown was the sales agent. The poplar which they used was sawed into one foot lengths, the bark was shaved off, the wood was then split, and knots and other blemishes cut out. The wood was then pressed against a revolving mill stone by a large iron weight. Water played constantly on the stone, carrying the pulp away. It proceeded through a series of sieves and rollers coming out at the end of the room in sheets of thick and rough drawing paper. The mill was quite successful, enough so that Brown and Denison branched out with other mills, and with paper mills in addition. Overexpansion and trouble with the Voelter patent holders, as well as a relatively poor location caused the firm finally to go out of business in the mid-seventies.

Many other small mills were started in the northeast during the early period. Few of them were successful as a lack of capital, over-ambitious promotion, poor location, the relatively small number of individuals who could handle the technical side of the business, and the ordinary business vicissitudes such as fire and the depression of the seventies militated against them. A number of Maine firms did begin to operate on the periphery of the industry, however, manufacturing paper machines, felts, and other necessaries.

A third process was developed at about this time, designed to utilize the resinous evergreens by application of sulphurous acid. The invention of this process, by Benjamin Tilghman, offered a great deal for the future, but not immediately. The first commercial success, after an attempt at Providence, came at a new mill built in Old Town, Maine, by the Penobscot Chemical Fibre Company. This was a very large mill, and when it began its operations, March 15, 1883, it employed 90 men. Garret Schenck was the treasurer of this firm, beginning the career which would take him to the Great Northern Paper Company. By the summer of 1884 the mill produced 19 tons of pulp a day. Even then the big mill used mostly poplar for its stock. Spruce would come later.

Paper had come to dominate the manufacture of many products now. Battery jars, house insulation, door and window frames, oil cans, chimneys, bathtubs, pots, skating rink floors, coffins, railroad wheels, and pipe all were utilizing paper. A store in Atlanta was constructed entirely of paper; a piano was exhibited in Paris made of paper; the ceiling of the Assembly chamber in Albany, New York was made of paper. Some thought the life of the future would be in a paper world. These paper goals have not all been reached, but the dominance of paper was unquestioned. For a discussion of this "paper world" it now is necessary to look more closely at some firms involved in the growth period.

The first of the Maine companies to grow beyond these small beginnings was the complex of firms controlled by Adna C. Denison of Norway, and Mechanic Falls. Denison actually experimented in substitutes for rags during the Civil War period in his paper mills. He ran and owned mills in Poland, Mechanic Falls, Canton, Norway, and Brunswick at various times, although he eventually went bankrupt because of over-expansion, and a poor investment in a rifle company. In his last years he was the New England representative of the National Sulphite Company, one of the early predecessors of the International Paper Company and the Great Northern Paper Company.

His Norway mill, which was opened in 1869, employed 20 men and 3 women, and produced about a ton of pulp, and a half ton of paper per day. This mill closed after the depression of 1873. The Mechanic Falls complex, consisting of five paper mills, which utilized pulp from elsewhere, was much grander. These Mills also had difficulty in stemming the tide of depression, and only did so with pay cuts. By 1878, though, the firms operations came to about 175 tons of book paper a month in the several mills.

Survival depended on government contracts, however, and when these were taken away, the whole edifice came down in June of 1879. The firm went into receivership for fifteen months time, coming out only when new contracts were received.

The underlying reasons for Denison's overall lack of success were his failure to understand the growth patterns of the industry. He was constantly over-expanded with his other mills, and further investments. After the Norway mills closed the firm was pressed for pulp sources. In 1880 it was decided to build a mill at Canton on the Androscoggin River to utilize mill waste from a nearly new steam saw mill. The town aided them with tax abatements and this mill produced 5 tons of pulp a day by the end of 1880. In 1882 its production averaged 200 tons a month. The wood was all poplar, and was driven down the Androscoggin on the rear of the regular drive. In 1883 about 4,500,000 board feet was chewed up for the paper machines. A railroad was built, more expansion took place, and by 1885 the capacity of the mill had doubled. In 1887 the mill failed. It could not stand prosperity. The men were not paid regularly, and were bound to the company owned stores. At the end of 1886 a payday was missed and the men complained. When another was passed by in January, the mills closed as the men refused to work. Bankruptcy ensued, and the entire operation went under the auctioneer's hammer in May. It was reorganized and still lives as the Poland Paper Company, but the Denison interests were all finished.

The Denison interests tell a good deal about the early days of the pulp and paper business after wood pulp had triumphed. There were many ups and downs in the industry, and those who were not reasonably conservative in their approach went under. Denison could obviously see the future in wood pulp paper, and he deserves much credit as a pioneer, but his vision was more elastic than his capital.

He was unable even to take his own advice. In 1882, 68 new mills were built in the United States, and 37 more were building. Howard Lockwood, founder and editor of *Paper Trade Journal*, thought the expansion was too rapid. He addressed some questions on this point to about forty manufacturers. All thought that there was too much expansion, and many predicted failure for the new mills. None was more pessimistic than Denison in his response.

He was right. A poem was circulating the trade during this period of expansion which told the story well.

> *Once of money I had plenty,*
> *and, friends, too, by the score.*
> *I went into the paper "biz"—*
> *Alas! It is no more.*

> *Men told me when my mill was built,*
> *and all my money spent:*
> *"Profits will be a mill a year—"*
> *But ten can't make a cent.*

Still with all this warning the trade grew, and Denison's mills were in the van of expansion. But because he failed to heed his own advice, he went down. Firms which were more cautious were more successful.

One such firm which held to a more cautious approach was that which is today known as the S.D. Warren Company. Just as in the Denison case the early story of the firm, and in this case the success of the firm was the impact of the founder, Samuel Dennis Warren. Warren progressed through the paper business in various steps and received invaluable experience in the early 1850's purchasing rags abroad to be used in New England paper mills. The success of the paper business caused the firm to branch out in Massachusetts and Maine in 1854, and in the next year Warren became sole owner of the Maine part of the business. Until his death in 1888 the founder remained active in determining the policies of his firm.

The firm grew steadily in size, employing 50 people in 1854, and 990 in 1888 at his death. Between times, S.D. Warren Co. purchased a mill at Gardiner, and a pulp mill at Yarmouth in Maine, as well as increased the size and capacity of the original mills at Congin Falls, Saccarappa, or Westbrook as the town was variously called. In 1873, it seemed to Warren that rag pulp was rapidly being surpassed by wood pulp, so the firm began to experiment with the manufacture of paper made from the new source. As a result of this investigation the Forest Fibre Company, in Yarmouth, was purchased. The mill produced 3 tons of pulp a day. By 1875 the importation of foreign rags on their own account was about over, and the firm had caught the new revolution at just the right time. Warren seemed to make his decisions with intelligence and foresight, and to move slowly enough so that the firm could meet any adversity.

The Warren mill was in an enviable position at Cumberland Mills, a place where the Presumscott River fell twenty feet. In 1870, it was estimated that the annual production was worth over a million dollars. From that time the mills grew in size, especially as the new wood pulp paper lowered prices and increased demand. By 1875 the water power owners on the river petitioned the legislature for the rights to increase the water storage in Lake Sebago. This was done by increasing the size and height of the dam which was owned by the Cumberland and Oxford Canal, a dam which had become defunct when the railroad made connections in 1872 at Sebago Station. The canal boats were used to haul stone from the canal quarry for the construction. The dam remodeling was completed in the fall of 1878 after a derrick and steamer on the lake had aided the work. The new dam, 300 feet long and 24 feet high, provided enough power for the present. In truth, though, the power problems of the company would not be solved entirely until the shift to electricity at a later time.

All during the depression the firm was prosperous. By 1877 the mill had seven machines running, and production was 15 tons a day. Even with this employees were forced to take two pay reductions, but apparently steady employment obviated any incipient labor problems.

Once the depression of the 1870 period was safely weathered, S.D. Warren Company began to grow even more extensively. The mill shifted over completely to steam power, and by 1880 was producing enough so that it was described as the largest paper mill in the world. Growth was arrested by a fire in 1882, but by 1885 the 700 employees produced 30 tons of book paper each day. The plant covered some 120 acres of land and was one of the largest firms in the state. Machinery was used wherever possible. A narrow-gauge railroad was constructed in the mill yards for the movement of materials, and it soon was connected with the railroads in town. The firm changed to the eight hour day, working three shifts in 1887. As the decade closed new buildings were going up.

Growth was evident in other ways. In the same year as the 8 hour day, electricity made its first appearance in part of the mills and S.D. Warren began to change over to hydroelectric power. The dam development which created this possibility was complete by 1890, but the firm did not change over entirely until after a serious flood in the spring of 1895. When it did come into use it marked a new era. The voltage generated was among the largest in the world at that time.

The Yarmouth mill was also rebuilt during this decade. In 1883 it employed 150 men. It produced nearly 10,000 tons of pulp annually shipping it all in railroad cars, 789 of them in that year. The mill consumed 10,000 cords of poplar wood, 6,000 tons of coal, and 6,000 cords of edgings and slabs from nearby sawmills in its work.

The 1890's was a decade of continuous increase in size, though the company did suffer heavily from the 1895 flood. The Forest Fibre Company (Yarmouth) expanded its production by 40% to nearly 40 tons a day in 1891, and in the next year the firm grew even larger by the purchase of the Richards Paper Company of Gardiner and Skowhegan. At the end of the century a modest land purchase program was underway for its wood supply, and the company had survived with ease the early and volative years of this industry. The secret of its success was slow, sustained growth, and growth in advance of the rest of the industry. Another factor in its success was an enlightened treatment of its employees. These two together provided a pattern substantially different from the Denison operations. Employee relations were an important key to success, and for that reason some discussion of this is relevant to the history of northeastern paper mills.

Warren was public spirited and he paid fair wages for his time, 75¢ a day in 1854, and $1 by the Civil War. In 1869, the firm gave a lot to a local church and contributed $5,000 to the building fund. This sort of semi-charitable activity was to be part of the company's relationships with the town, and by extension with its employees from that time on. During the time of building the extension to the dam at Sebago Lake wages ranged from $1.25 to $2.25 a day, plus board and room. Workers did find themselves under some restrictions. They were forced to live in company housing (boarding houses), unless they lived at home. Failure to abide by the regulations in the boarding houses was cause for dismissal.

In the early 1880's the employees decided to band together to form a Mutual Relief Society. Its object was "to aid and benefit such of its members as are, by sickness or accident, unable to work." All regular employees were members. An admission fee was charged of 50¢. On the death of a member an additional assessment was made of 50¢ on each member. The society paid death benefits of $200, and unemployment benefits amounting to $5 a week for males and half of that for females. The benefits did not start until the second week and were payable only for 26 weeks in any one year, or under any one illness. Benefits were payable upon presentation of a medical certificate. The society did, however, have the right to check with its own physician, and could expel members for malingering. Finally, no benefits could be paid for illnesses caused by intemperance or immorality. The society is still in operation, although the benefits are somewhat higher now.

Few problems in employee relationships occurred. Women employed as rag sorters went on a five day strike in 1880, but apparently no other work stoppages took place. Most of the employees lived in company housing, which by 1881 was furnished with running water. There was in addition a library and public reading room paid for by the company. In 1883, Warren testified before a Senate Labor Committee. He said the firm owned 150 houses, with rents from $75 to $200 a year. Electricity was provided in some at $35 per year; the water cost $10. A public hall was erected that year in Westbrook, with part of the money coming from the company. In 1889, the firm began work on a sewerage system for its property. In addition the firm loaned money to employees for purchase of houses, payment of bills, or even for the education of children.

Newspapers constantly held the company up as an example to others during the troubled times of strikes in the seventies and eighties. The following comment was typical of many:

> Here [Cumberland Mills] friction between capital and labor is unknown, affording the best practical example of the true solution to the labor question; and would that it might be more generally followed. Among the other evidences of the good will of the company is a fine popular library to which free access is had every week. Thus do they aim for the mental and moral improvement of the people.

The tradition of better living conditions and better pay continued. In the mid-80's women received 83¢ a day, and men $1 to start. Foreman went to as high as $3. In the early 90's men started at $1.25. Wages were increased by a profit participation plan for employees in this time as well. The plan started in 1891 and provided that those employees who worked a minimum of 75% of the working days would get a dividend credit determined by dividing a percentage of the net earnings in ratio to the total earnings of the employee. The company made it plain where they stood on the plan, urging the men to use economy in their work and not to fear the introduction of machinery. As a letter said,

> Under the plan now proposed, it will be for the interest of each man to work as he would on his own account; and a just regard for his own interest will make it right for him to point out to the management any failure in duty or inefficiency on the part of others.

The plan remained in operation throughout the nineties for the entire firm. Payments ranged from as high as 7½% to 2½%. Other paper companies in the northeast were forced to adopt similar plans. Wages themselves did not increase much in this period, but the dividend raised them above the average. The total story then shows a marked comparison to the policies of the Denison operations. On the one hand we have over-expansion, and poor treatment of employees; on the other careful and planned growth and solicitude for employees, at least in terms of the late nineteenth century.

Although S.D. Warren had begun a modest land purchase policy by the end of the period, most firms relied on other methods to procure their wood. Until the middle eighties the major source of wood was, of course, poplar. Farmers ordinarily cut the wood, peeled it, and hauled it by team to the nearest railroad station, or even to the mill itself. Occasionally a drive came down on the rear of the regular river drive of logs. It was not until mills began to take 2 or 3,000 cords a year (roughly 1 to 1,400,000 board feet) that more formal methods of procurement had to be found. S.D. Warren employed a man specifically charged with purchase of the wood supply. He eventually also acted for the Oxford Paper Company and the Penobscot Chemical Fibre Company. It was his practice to send out postcards to his farmer contacts stating the price for the year. They returned their estimates of their cut, and received their pay in quarterly installments, upon peeling, yarding, piling, and delivery.

Sometimes firms advertised for pulp wood, but ordinarily people cut it when they came to it in their regular operations and sent it to the nearby mills. As the local supply dwindled, more and more came in by railroad. A few lumbermen moved into this sort of supply work. The demand forced stumpage prices higher as the following squib indicates:

> C.B. and B.F. Smith of Denmark have another large contract this year, to furnish poplar for the Cumberland Mills, and pay $3.50 at the Brownfield Depot. They have had large lots peeled in Denmark, Bridgeton, Fryeburg, and Brownfield. Poplar four years ago could be had for 25¢ a cord stumpage, and now five times that price is paid.

Increased amounts came down in the drive. The Warren firm began to receive much of their wood this way. The drive came in on the Presumscott on July 18, 1884, May 1, 1885, and August 10, 1886. The river was last driven in 1906.

Other mills used a good deal of waste wood from nearby saw mills, especially on the Kennebec and Penobscot rivers. Some of the later pulp drives were immense. In 1890 a Lewiston firm took a contract to drive 36 million feet on the Androscoggin. By this time though consolidation had begun in the industry. The pioneer days were over. A quiet revolution had been consummated.

II. The Big Companies

The pulp and paper industry had come to the northeast by the mid-nineties. It only remained to be seen how large the industry would grow, and what form it would take. Observers were exultant over the soon-to-be-reached future. And, this was for good reason. In 1889, six mills manufacturing soda pulp rated at 92 tons daily capacity; six mills making 90 tons a day of sulphite pulp, and 13 mills rated at 157 tons capacity of ground wood pulp were either located in or were building in Maine. Five years later the growth had been even more phenomenal. In that year the state conducted a census of the mills in the state. It found that the industry now had a rated capacity of 1,036 tons of pulp and 508 tons of paper each day. When that part of the Androscoggin river in New Hampshire was added, the rated capacity climbed to 1,261 tons of pulp, and 608 tons of paper. Now came the major consolidation of some of these smaller plants into the International Paper Company. After this the only major change in the northeastern picture would be the construction of monster mills and monster companies in the wilderness such as the operation of the Great Northern Paper Company at Millinocket.

Consolidation had to come. There was over-production in the mills, and prices fell alarmingly.

Some mills closed; others went through bankruptcy, still others suffered from poor construction and poor management, and by 1897 or 1898 many mills were either loosing money, or were barely breaking even. As prices drifted lower, marginal mills were forced to the wall, or into the hands of their competitors. (Ground wood pulp prices went from 4¢ a pound at the end of the seventies to as low as 6¢ near the time of consolidation). The savage competition which ensued began to weed out the weak and incompetent, and owners fearful of the possible consequences began to participate in attempts at controlling the markets. These efforts led directly to the formation of the International Paper Company.

Several combinations and trade associations had been attempted earlier, in 1870 and in 1878. Little could be done until the rights ran out on the Voelter patents in 1884. Various attempts in 1884, 1888, 1889 were tried. The winter of 1893 and 1894 mark the first serious discussion, however. Little came of even this though until February, 1895 when a series of meetings were held to discuss the possibility of a firm to either control production or to form a selling agency to control prices. In July and August of that year meetings were held nearly every week at New York, Boston, and Saratoga Springs. Apparently the plans failed as a result of disputes over the valuation of certain mills. Prices rose slowly under the impact of the consolidation rumors, and by January, 1896, the "giant news combine," as it was usually called, was quiescent, at least for the time being.

When trade slackened again, as it did in late summer, the consolidation talks revived. It was not, however, until after the passage of the Dingley tariff that the combination became active again, and this time it was more than just talk. By early September, 1897, a committee was created to set a formal valuation on the mills. With this some became disturbed at the prospect of higher paper prices. Anxious editorials, like the following, were written.

> It is claimed, however, that there is no intention of forcing up prices unduly or even materially. A large part of the benefit claimed for the proposed consolidation, it is said will result from greater economy, particularly in selling the product. Some advance in prices is generally predicted, and in fact there is a firmer market at present, but exceptionally high prices, it is asserted, are not aimed at.

At the end of November a meeting was held in New York City to discuss the valuations. At this meeting, apparently, it was agreed to set up a new firm, to be capitalized at $25,000,000. When the actual capitalization was completed, it amounted to $45,000,000. A successful marriage had been consummated, between the Fourdrinier paper machine and the counting house. The future of the industry seemed to lay in this direction.

The growth of the new firm was steady, and the profits created in part by the impact of the Spanish-American War were excellent. The first president said in his initial report to the stockholders that the firm controlled 90% of the newsprint production in the east. "Our competition is not of a serious nature," was his comment. The Treasurer of the firm later remarked on the opening of a new mill that, "It has been the policy of the directors to purchase woodlands and to place all our surplus earnings in betterments, so that we will begin to obtain larger profits in a few years." The era of the huge firm had arrived.

The mills of consequence to this account of the new firm were located in Maine and New Hampshire. These, in addition to some small and minor plants, included basically the large operations at Livermore Falls and Berlin Falls, both of which dated back to the earliest days of pulp manufacture, and the new plant which had been recently created in the wilderness of Rumford Falls.

The big investors in all these mills, and the men who were instrumental in causing the International Paper Company consolidation were Hugh J. Chisholm of Portland, its first president, and early investor, and promoter of the Rumford development. Most of the others on the Maine scene were co-investors with Chisholm, but with perhaps less money than he had in the new firm.

Although the formation of the International Paper Company had a great effect on the Maine economy, and the member mills are still of importance to the area, the impact of these mills is not great compared to the effect of the other great giant of this time, the Great Northern Paper Company. To a very great extent much of the study of Maine lumbering in the twentieth century is the study of this firm. With this firm, even though the founding took place less than seventy years ago, much of its history is shrouded in obscurity. To a certain extent this is apparently due to the fact that some of the reasons for founding may have been purely speculative in nature. It was not until the firm became successful that long-range planning became its hallmark. Much of this obscurity also evolves from the fact that the firm really goes back much further in history than the usual 1899 founding date. Its beginning dates actually to the fall of 1889.

In that year Isaac M. Weston, a one-time Maine man who had gone west to Detroit, where he became, among other things, state chairman of the Democratic party, came back to his home state to make an extended visit to look over the timber supply preparatory to setting up a pulp mill which would use a new and supposedly revolutionary process. Weston was the advance agent for a larger group which toured Maine in late November, 1889, to inspect the areas which he had pinpointed. The touring group were a wealthy lot, and closely associated with Grover Cleveland and the national Democratic party. It included Henry C. Payne, H.C. Twombly, former secretary of the Navy, H.C. Whitney, Daniel Lamont, Pierpont Morgan, George N. Fletcher, and Don M. Dickinson among others. These men, with Cleveland, were the founders of a firm, capitalized at a million dollars, and known as the Manufacturer's Investment Company of New Jersey. While in Maine they visited Rumford, Livermore, Berlin, all on the Androscoggin, Madison on the Kennebec, Howland, Enfield, and Bangor on the Penobscot, and Calais, Milltown, and Baring on the St. Croix. They decided to erect their new mill at Madison.

Although Maine newspapers welcomed the new addition, and reported construction details as rapidly as they became known, other trade journals felt the company began on shaky ground. When the Madison mill began operations *Paper Trade Journal* saluted it, but commented, in addition, that:

> It is a matter of remark in the trade that the capitalization of this company is excessive and that any ordinary individual or firm could have put up either plant for about one-third of the money which they cost....

The trade magazine also went on to say that the office of the new firm was on Broad Street in New York and this was suggestive of the speculative atmosphere surrounding the new firm.

The mills were uneasy, and press notices reflected the situation. Cleveland and others came to inspect once when unstable rumors were very high. The firm had difficulty with Madison over tax abatements. Experiments in cheaper Canadian wood were attempted, but in June of 1893 the plant manager was relieved of his post, and the plant shut down for repairs. The Appleton plant also closed, and the firm went through a reorganization in the front office. It was found that the Madison mill was badly constructed and it was not until June of 1894 before manufacture again began. When it opened, the manager of the Appleton mill had been brought east, and that mill closed permanently. The owners began to purchase timber lands and apparently the mill was successful through most of 1896 and 1897.

The mill ran until the spring of 1899 when it went into a receivership. Death resulted from that event, but reincarnation occurred in the Great Northern. That story, as is true of most of the early Northern story, is the story of Garrett Schenck. He was a man of forceful personality and great breadth of imagination, and a man who left two memorials, the Great Northern, and the town of Millinocket.

Schenck was born in Trenton, New Jersey, in 1854. He, like S.D. Warren, worked with an uncle in the rag business in Massachusetts. By 1886 he was the resident manager of the Penobscot Chemical Fibre Company in Old Town. He also served as agent for a mill in Lincoln. He was patentee, and part-owner of a process used to reclaim liquids from the digester. J. Fred Webster, a name in early Maine lumbering, J. A. Kimberley, of Appleton, Wisconsin, and Edward Ames of Bellows Falls, Vermont were associated with Schenck in a firm engaged in making digesters to use this firm. At one time or another he apparently owned part of a pulp mill in Orono, and was an early investor in the development which became the Eastern Corporation in Brewer. When the Rumford development came about he moved to Rumford as manager and part-owner of the Rumford Falls Paper Company, and was a member of the first board of directors of the International Paper Company, until he resigned in August, 1898, to set up the Great Northern Paper Company.

At this point it is necessary to introduce a very obscure firm, the Northern Development Company. This was apparently an organization founded to purchase and locate lands in Millinocket after the success of the Chisholm development of

Rumford. The firm was made up mostly of Bangor men, and included representatives of the Bass, Appleton, Prentiss, Rice and Mullen families, all famous in Bangor logging history. The firm never amounted to much primarily it seems for financial limitations, but they did apparently own the important land in the Millinocket area.

Dissatisfaction with the International Paper Company and their virtual monopoly of newsprint production had led several to suppose that some attempt to control them might take place. In 1898 Schenck, D.F. Emery, and Joseph Pulitzer were rumored to be negotiating such a competitor to build a mill at Millinocket. In 1898 Schenck replaced Prentiss on the Board of the Northern Development Company. In the early spring of 1899 a further reorganization took place and such men as Oliver Payne, A.G. Payne, E.H. Haskell, R.H. Hayes, A.H. Paget (the son-in-law of ex-Navy Secretary Whitney), and representatives of the Wall Street firm of Grant and Schley were also added, and most of the Bangor figures dropped out. What apparently happened was that the cost of the development of Millinocket was so great that the firm had to appeal to Wall Street, an appeal which caused the removal of most of the Maine men.

The new firm moved rapidly, purchasing land and beginning its operations. In the first year it bought acreage amounting to 252,060.87 acres, for a price of $1,042,575, or $4.136 an acre. While this was happening the Manufacturer's Investment Company was ending its days. From its death bed announcement was made that the firm's liabilities amounted to $2 million over the assets, and Oliver Payne was chief creditor. Payne had been one of the biggest investors in the first Millinocket organization, but now more money was needed, and apparently this time he told Schenck and his associates to take his Madison mill as payment. They apparently forced the receivership as a result, paid off the other creditors, and took over the mill as a collateral branch of the Great Northern Paper Company. In retrospect it seems that O.H. Payne performed a clever piece of surgery at a time when such operations were common-place.

Maine welcomed the new firm, whatever its antecedents. Some thought newsprint would drop in price. Others thought this was Bangor's big chance. New wealth would come to its citizens; the retail and wholesale trade would both benefit.

"Isn't that a pleasant outlook for citizens of eastern Maine?", asked one observer.

Once the financial arrangements and the land purchases were underway the company began its building preparatory to the manufacture of paper, which was scheduled to start approximately September 1, 1900. The promoters of the new firm met with representatives of the Maine railroads to determine competitive rates to and from Millinocket. To accommodate the builders the Bangor and Aroostook relocated its depot. Some men went in to start clearing the land in February and large crews were on hand by the end of April. Once the contract for the construction was let, John N. Merrill, of Bangor, who supervised the construction, went to Boston to secure Italian contract labor for the building. In addition immigrant Poles, Finns, and Hungarians were employed. Men from downeast railroad construction also were hired, and by June 1, 500 men were at work in the Millinocket area.

A large steam shovel was brought in to do the bulk of the excavation. Lodging was primitive at best. Forty-five men slept in a room, and paid $3.50 a week for the privilege. Elsewhere it was $7 weekly for more private accommodations. Many slept in jury-rig tents out doors. As yet there was little home building. A newspaper commented, "there is a Bohemian air about everything here which cannot be described. There is really no town but there is an army of people working and camping."

At the end of August the Bangor and Aroostook railroad planned a train excursion for the curious to see what was being done. Three hundred from the Bangor area went on the trip. By this time 1,000 men, 2 locomotives, a rock crusher, and 2 steam shovels were hard at work. (In addition the firm employed 250 men on the Madison mill adding new machinery, and strengthening the old masonry).

The traffic to Millinockett was so heavy that the county commissioners were forced to construct a road from Medway. It was open for foot travel in June, and for horses and wagons by October.

One of the more interesting features was the impact of all the building on the port of Bangor. By the time the river was closed with ice in 1899 more than a hundred vessels had veen involved in the new trade. Eighty cargoes of bricks and twenty of cement arrived that fall. Bangor's "mudlarks," as the stevedores were called, had a difficult time with the huge machinery for the new mill. The city fathers rebuilt and strengthened their piers and wharves because of the business involved.

By June of 1900 Millinocket had really grown. One hundred houses, and many business establishments were open. According to the land agent, no house could be erected for less than $750, and no liquor was to be used in the city. A thousand men were working, 400 of them Italians, who lived mostly in shacks in what was known as "Little Italy," across the stream. These, the visitor was assured, were to be torn down when the construction was complete. The Italians were paid $1.50 a day and board, which consisted of bread, potatoes, macaroni, beans, and rice. The company also announced its payroll—$1.50 a day for laborers, $2.00–$2.50 for skilled workers, and $3.00–$5.00 for machine men.

In the summer more strides were made. Forty new houses were built. Streets were constructed; a combination school and interdenominational church was in operation. The company had promised a good school by spring. A good hotel was being built, and a town sewer and water supply were underway. On the eve of the mill opening, 2,000 people lived in "The magic city of the North." The streets were nearly finished, and the water system was nearly complete. The Great Northern Paper Company had truly wrested a town from the wilderness. Maine's pulp and paper industry was practically complete.

The plants themselves were huge as well. The Madison plant produced 55 tons of newsprint, 50 tons of sulphite fiber, and 40 tons of ground wood pulp a day, while the Millinocket mill produced 240 tons of newsprint, 120 tons of sulphite fiber, and 240 tons of ground wood pulp each day. To create this paper, in addition to the winter's cut, the Northern purchased 275 cords of pulp wood a day which arrived by railroad. More expansion was planned.

Other large firms were talked about, and a few firms were built, such as the St. Regis plant at Bucksport, or the large St. Croix Paper Company mill in Washington county, but by and large the story was complete. In a little less than thirty-five years this industry had taken giant strides. It was a long way from the one ton daily of pulp production in Topsham to the monster mill in Millinocket, but a paper revolution had taken place in the country meanwhile. Pioneers may have caught a glimpse of the future in their discussions in the 1870's, and some, such as the Warrens, and the Chisholms, had seen most of it come in their lifetime. What no one really foresaw was the impact on the Maine economy, and the whole scale revolution on Maine's rivers and in her woodlands. That, however, is the twentieth century, and it is a story of a different nature than the one told here. This story is the story of enterprise, hard work, and luck. Of course, as H.A. Morrell had remarked, "... if there was ever any money to be made in the business the mills must be located near where the wood grows." That was exactly what had happened in these halcyon years before the turn of the century.

CHAPTER

31.

The orange is synonymous with Florida, oil with Texas, and tobacco with North Carolina. To "outsiders" Maine and the Irish potato have always been considered together. The role played by the "humble potato" in the Maine economy is the subject of the following article.

THE HUMBLE POTATO*
by
Clarence A. Day

Potatoes have been Maine's principal cash crop for a century or more and Maine has always been one of the leading states in their production. Soil, climate, and location have all contributed to this result. The potato, called by botanists Solanum tuberosum, was first found in the Andes Mountains of South America. The Spanish conquistadors carried it to Spain, and from that country the crop spread slowly over Europe. In Ireland it became the staple food for man and beast.

Historians believe that potatoes were first grown in New England by Scotch-Irish immigrants who settled at Londonderry, New Hampshire, in 1719. However, potatoes came to Maine nearly, if not actually, as soon as they came to New Hampshire. A few members of the same group of immigrants settled in or near Falmouth, now Portland, and the next year another company came to Wells and brought potatoes with them. Other Scotch-Irish who a few years later located along the Maine coast from Brunswick to Belfast also raised potatoes.

However, many years elapsed before the crop became popular. Wrote the Reverend Samuel Deane in his *New England Farmer*: "No longer ago than about the year 1740, we had but one sort, a small reddish colored potato, of such rank a taste that it was scarcely eatable." Varieties of better flavor were introduced later, so that, again quoting Deane: "Within twenty-five years (previous to 1790) they have been much cultivated." Still it would seem that even then most farmers raised only a few bushels for their own use. But by 1820, potatoes were being shipped from Belfast, Portland, Saco, and other ports both "Down East" and to Boston and beyond.

The First United States Census to record data on crops was that taken in 1840. The previous year, six Maine counties, Kennebec, Lincoln, Cumberland, York, Somerset, and Waldo, each produced more than a million bushels of potatoes. The whole crop for the state was 10,392,280 bushels, or about 250 bushels per farm. New York was the only state that raised more potatoes than Maine that year.

Almost every farmer grew potatoes. There were many varieties; but, said Dr. Holmes, "The Long Reds and the Chenangoes were the lords of the potato field." The prolific Long Reds were grown principally for livestock. and the Chenangoes for home use and for market. Farmers liked potatoes. They were easy to raise, they were not much troubled by insects or disease, and they usually sold for a fair price. They also did well in the more northern counties where corn was an uncertain crop. Dr. Holmes estimated that by early November 1838 more than half a million bushels of potatoes had been shipped from the Kennebec Valley at an average price of 38 cents a bushel to farmers, which was considered a good price in those days.

Then came disaster. The cause was late blight. This disease of potatoes seems to have reached the United States from South America early in the 1840's and spread with lightning-like rapidity. The

---
*Clarence A. Day, *Farming in Maine, 1860-1940* (Orono: University of Maine Press, 1963), pp. 117-139. Reprinted by permission of the publisher.

outbreak was serious in Maine for the first time in 1844, when in some places nine-tenths of the crop rotted in the gound or in the cellar after it was stored. The next year the disaster was repeated. One keen observer stated that "probably not one-fourth part of the crop was secured." One result was that a promising starch factory was nipped in the bud and did not again become important until long afterward in Aroostook County. Another was that hundreds of farmers ceased to grow potatoes. The crop grown in 1849 was only about one-third of that of ten years earlier, and not until 1909 did Maine produce as many potatoes in a census year as in 1839.

However, by 1860 farmers had regained their courage and were planting a fair acreage. No one had discovered an effective way to control late blight; but growers had learned that some varieties were less susceptible than others, that early varieties planted early often matured before blight became prevalent, and that there was usually less rot on high, well-drained fields than on low, wet, clay loams. Dr. Holmes was saying once more: "Maine is the home of the potato, and our potato crop rules the market in half the states in the Union." A year or two later a member of the Maine Board of Agriculture reported that farmers were receiving a larger income from potatoes than from any other crop.

The census of 1860 credited Maine farmers with having raised 6,374,617 bushels of potatoes the previous year. The crop was being grown in all parts of the state, although the leading counties were Penobscot, Oxford, and Somerset. Bethel, with 72,675 bushels, raised more potatoes than any other town. The next in rank, Poland, Corinth, and Paris, all exceeded the 50,000 bushel mark. The area where most of the potatoes were grown extended lengthwise in a broad belt from Dover, Bradford, and Bangor on the northeast to Paris, Poland, and New Glouster on the southwest, with a few small sections elsewhere. Areas of greatest production included one in the counties of Penobscot and Piscataquis centering about Garland, another in Oxford County that included Bethel, Rumford, and Paris, and a third in the Kennebec Valley from Solon to Augusta. The smallest acreage was to be found east of the Penobscot, along the north woods, and in the coastal counties.

The principal shipments of potatoes from Maine to other states in 1860 were made over what is now the main line of the Maine Central Railroad and from the ports of Bangor and Belfast. An article in the Maine Farmer says that one fall a few years earlier, 500,00 bushels of potatoes were shipped from Bangor before ice closed the Penobscot to navigation. In 1869 a Mr. Ingalls, of Bangor, told the Maine State Board of Agriculture that shipments from that port had averaged 300,000 bushels annually for the previous fifteen years. "Maine," said he, "has a wonderful reputation for the quality of her potatoes. That was earned by the Jackson, and the Orono has come to take its place, because people abroad are hardly able to distinguish between the two, and the Orono yields more. All the orders that come to purchasers contain this phrase underscored, 'a cargo of Jackson Whites.' It is not only the white skin that is wanted, but the white flesh."

Shortly afterward, John W. Lang, of Brooks, wrote in his Survey of Waldo County: "The favorites most cultivated in our county are the Orono, Early Rose, Davis Seedling (a red potato), and Harrison. The Orono is our great market potato, yields well, is a superior table potato, keeps well and is not especially affected by rot... It is medium for earliness, white, had a medium top and is prolific in blossoms and seed balls, eyes sunk, flattened, oblong, and handsome."

Indeed the style in varieties had changed. Both the Chenango and Long Red, once popular, had fallen victims to the onslaughts of late blight. The Orono and Jackson White had replaced the Chenango for the table, and the California had taken over as feed for livestock. Many thought that Orono and Jackson White were two names for the same potato, but both Dr. Holmes and Secretary Goodale believed them to be distinct varieties. Although the tubers looked very much alike, "one could easily tell the difference in the growth of the vines," said Goodale. "The Orono," he added, "is the potato most largely grown in the state, especially for export." He also found that it was grown under various other names, such as Reed, Carter, Foote, and Holmes. The variety was said to have been originated by a Mr. Reed, of Orono, who named it for the town in which he lived.

Other varieties which were more or less popular in the 1860's were older ones like Early Bluenose,

Early Sebec, Garnet Chili, Davis Seedling, and Peachblow; and newcomers such as Harrison, Early Goodrich, General Grant, and Early Rose. Indeed the number of varieties was legion. Students at the State College at Orono made, in 1870, field tests of 61 varieties, and about the same time a grower exhibited 140 varieties at a farmers' meeting. All but a few of them soon ceased to be grown, doubtless to the benefit of the industry.

Not much information seems to be available as to the fashion in varieties for the remainder of the nineteenth century. However, as early as 1870, Secretary Goodale thought that the popular Oronos were running out. In 1887 and again in 1888, the Maine Agricultural Experiment Station made field tests with fifty or more named varieties. The Orono was not among them. Neither was the Green Mountain, which was soon to become Maine's leading potato and was to hold that position for two score years.

Growers in western and central Maine were raising more potatoes in 1870 than in 1860. Then began a long decline that by 1900 had cut production in half. Reasons for this decline are not readily apparent, but a few seem indicated. Among them are the increased interest in dairying, orchards, and sweet corn; the slow but continuous decline in potato prices; and the gradual trend from diversified to specialized agriculture. "Potato bugs" must also have had some effect.

This scourge of Maine potato fields did not come like a thief in the night. His approach was well heralded. He came from the Rocky Mountains and his advance was slow but determined. He was the Colorado potato beetle. As his name suggests, he was a native of Colorado, where he had fed for ages on a wild plant of the same genus as the potato. When settlers took potatoes to Colorado, the beetle sampled the new food, found it very much to his liking, and began the long journey east.

The Colorado potato beetle was first described in its native haunts by an entomologist, Thomas Say, and was sometimes called the ten-lined spearman. Apparently it started on its eastern journey about 1850. At first its advance was slow, but after it reached the railroads its progress was more rapid. Colorado beetles were reported west of Omaha in 1859, in Iowa in 1861, Illinois in 1865, and Ohio in 1870.

In 1866 the then editor of the *Maine Farmer* thought he had found specimens of the invader. But a Maine man versed in entomology, George E. Brackett, showed that they were specimens of a native beetle with similar feeding habits. The Colorado beetle, he wrote in the *Farmer,* would not reach Maine for about ten years. He proved to be a true prophet. They were first reported here in 1876, and by the end of the next year they had spread quite generally over the state.

During the beetle's long progress eastward, Paris green sprinkled, sprayed, or dusted on the potato plants had proved an effective means of control. But certain farmers preferred other methods, perhaps because of the cost of the material, perhaps because they were conservative minded. For a long time the barefoot boy with cheeks of tan, and with a pan containing a little water or kerosene in one hand and a wooden paddle in the other, was a familiar sight in potato fields. Sometimes the boy paddled the bugs from plant to pan, sometimes he had no pan and knocked them onto the ground in vain hope that they would stay there and starve. Although potato bugs were easily destroyed if taken in time, they did untold damage until it became the custom to include poison with the sprays that were being applied to control late blight.

During the first decade of the present century there was a brisk revival of the potato enterprise in nearly every part of the state. Every county except York increased its acreage of potatoes. Totals for the state, except Aroostook, were 29,812 acres in 1899 and 60,001 in 1909. The increase was greatest in Penobscot, Piscataquis, Somerset, and Waldo. This time the reasons were more obvious. Said Augustus W. Gilman, Commissioner of Agriculture, in his annual report in 1913: "The potato crop in the state was the largest in years. Not only has the crop in Aroostook been such as to awaken new interest, but some of our practical, wide awake farmers in central and southern Maine have demonstrated that the soil in these sections, with the aid of proper fertilization and cultivation, can be made to produce potatoes equal in quality and quantity to those produced in the more favored northern sections. Their success has stimulated others to an enlarged production." Other reasons probably included higher prices for potatoes in the markets, greater use of commercial fertilizer and horse-drawn machinery, and a more satisfactory control of the late blight through spraying.

However, time proved that Commissioner Gilman was mistaken in thinking that climatic and soil conditions were as favorable in southern and central Maine as in Aroostook. Fields as a rule were smaller, the surface more broken, the quality of the soil more variable. Often underdrainage was defective, and droughts, not so common in Aroostook, were sometimes prolonged and severe. On the whole production costs were higher and yields per acre were lower than in the potato empire. Dairying also offered real competition by giving a continuous income and year round employment.

Whatever the causes, the results are well known. The mild boom did not last. The acreage devoted to potatoes dropped drastically between 1909 and 1919, and then more slowly for the next twenty years. In 1939 the crop "down state" was 3.8 million bushels, or only half of the crop in 1859, eighty years earlier. Potatoes were no longer an important crop in central, western, and southern Maine, except in a few small isolated areas.

Aroostook is a land by itself. Situated in the extreme northeastern section of the state on the Canadian border, and separated from the rest of Maine by a broad barrier of woodland, it differs from other areas in soil and climate. The winters are both longer and colder than farther south, but they do not "linger in the lap of spring" as they do along the coast. Farmers can often work the land before the last traces of snowdrifts have melted and gone. There is less rainfall than elsewhere in Maine but during the growing season it is generally adequate. Severe droughts are rare. The short, cool growing season limits the production of tomatoes and corn but favors that of oats, grasses, clover, and potatoes.

Caribou loam is the prevailing type of soil. It is well drained, friable, free from boulders, and seldom bakes. It is excellent for any crop grown in this latitude, and especially for potatoes. Nearly all other types of soil found there will produce good potato crops. Long, broad ridges with gentle slopes abound where machinery can be operated to advantage. Soil and climate have combined to make Aroostook the ideal home for the potato.

Dr. Ezekiel Holmes first visited "the Aroostook" in 1838. He was much impressed with the fertility of the soil and the abundance of the crops that were being grown on the newland farms. Wheat was the staple crop in the southern part of the county and buckwheat in the St. John Valley. Potatoes were equal to those grown anywhere. "The climate and soil both seem congenial to this root. Nothing is wanting but geater facilities for getting them to market to make their culture one of the most profitable branches of agriculture that can be pursued there. The variety most approved is called the Christie potato from their having been introduced by a Mr. Christie who lives there. Many assert that they have obtained 300 bushels per acre by common management." Dr. Holmes recommended that the state establish a farm where livestock, crops, and methods of culture could be tested for the guidance of the new settlers who would soon flock into the county. Thus he foreshadowed the Aroostook experimental farm over seventy years before it became a reality.

"Should I take up a farm in Aroostook?" he was often asked. His answer to men comfortably situated at home was an emphatic No. To the lazy, shiftless, and criminally inclined it was also No. "Better stay where almshouses and prisons are more abundant." But: "Are you a young man just starting in life, with no capital save a strong arm, good courage, and a narrow axe? Go to the Aroostook. . . and with the blessings of Providence you will in a very few years find yourself an independent freeholder, with a farm of your own subduing, and with capital of your own creating."

Before we consider the agricultural development of Aroostook after the visit of Dr. Holmes, it will be helpful to glance at the early history of the county with map in hand.

The first permanent settlement there was made at Madawaska by the French in 1785. They were children and grand children of the Acadians whom the English had driven out of Nova Scotia in the days of Evangeline and the son of Basil the Blacksmith. Soon they were joined by other French from the Province of Quebec. Here they lived for several decades in almost complete isolation, while their settlements spread out in either direction along both banks of the St. John. They had very little intercourse with the English in New Brunswick, not much more with their companions in Quebec, and none at all with the Americans in the rest of Aroostook.

Their agriculture was primitive and self sufficient, as one would expect from pioneers in a new land and without contact with the outside world. Buckwheat was their principal grain crop. They probably raised potatoes for family use, although early writers seem not to have mentioned the fact.

Like some of the older settlements in Maine, Madawaska more than once faced famine. The most serious occurred during the winter of 1796-7. Heavy frosts the previous autumn had severely injured the food grains. They were followed by an early snowstorm that buried deeply that portion of the harvest that still remained in the fields, and ushered in an unusually severe winter. Some of the people sought refuge among friends along the St. Lawrence and the lower St. John. Others remained at home and suffered almost intolerable hardships. Only a successful hunting expedition saved the settlement from starvation.

It was during those days of distress that a remarkable Acadian woman, Marguerite Blanche Cyr, won by her heroism and unselfish devotion the proud title of "la Tante du Madawaska"—the Aunt of Madawaska. Already aunt to numerous nieces and nephews, after that terrible winter she was aunt to everyone in the valley. Madame Cyr was of great vigor and greater charity. Depriving herself, she became a veritable angel of mercy, feeding the hungry, clothing the freezing, preparing the dead, and cheering the living with her own contagious courage. When she died years later, all Madawaska was plunged into mourning.

Farther south, the first settlement in Aroostook by people who spoke English was made at Houlton in 1805. The little band of pioneers from New Salem, Massachusetts, was led by Joseph Houlton, for whom the town was named. It was then the custom of Massachusetts to encourage the establishment of colleges and academies by granting them townships or half townships of land in the wilderness, several of them along Maine's eastern border. In Aroostook these grants included the present town of Weston to Hampden Academy, Hodgdon, to Westford and Groton, Houlton to New Salem Academy and Williams College, Littleton to Williams College and Framingham Academy, New Limerick to the academy at Limerick, Ludlow to the one at Belfast, Bridgewater to the academies at Bridgewater and Portland, and Westfield to those at Deerfield and Westfield.

The grant to New Salem Academy was the only one to be settled promptly. Not only was Houlton the first English settlement in Aroostook, but for many years there were no others nearer than those about Calais and Bangor, and no road connecting Houlton with the rest of the state. The only way to the outside world was through New Brunswick. Agriculture was of the most primitive type and crops were sometimes a near failure. The worst season was that of the cold year, 1816, which was just as disastrous in Aroostook as elsewhere. Snow fell deeply in June and young birds were frozen in their nests at both Houlton and Madawaska. No grain ripened. The government of New Brunswick found it necessary to send food supplies to its own subjects along the St. John, and with fine international courtesy came to the relief of the people at Houlton.

The earliest pioneers in the valley of the Aroostook River came across the border from New Brunswick shortly before 1820. They came singly rather than in batallions and built their little log cabins far apart along the banks of the river. By the time of Dr. Holmes' visit a few Yankees had entered the valley, among whom was Dennis Fairbanks, the first settler in Letter F, now Presque Isle. His luxuriant crops, especially of wheat, made a firm impression on his few visitors from southern Maine.

The fifty-mile barrier of dense forest that barred Aroostook from the "outside" was first broken shortly after the United States Army established a post at Houlton in 1828, when the Military Road was built from there to Lincoln. This road was, and still is, the main thoroughfare from Aroostook to the rest of Maine. A few years later another road was "grubbed out" from Houlton to Calais, and along both roads settlers began clearing farms. As yet there were no roads between Houlton and the Aroostook Valley, or between there and the Madawaska settlements. They came shortly after the Aroostook War when the Military Road was extended from Houlton to Presque Isle and Fort Fairfield, and another road was built from the Military Road at Molunkus through Masardis to Fort Kent.

Aroostook was now ready for rapid settlement. Dr. Holmes' report had awakened interest in the new northland, and the Aroostook War fanned it into flame. This is not the place to tell the story of that brief and bloodless struggle, but it influenced the settlement of Aroostook, so here are the facts in capsule form. Both the United States and Great Britain claimed an immense tract of land north of a line running westerly from Mars Hill to the western boundary of Maine. Several attempts to settle the controversy failed, and all the while lumbermen from New Brunswick were cutting valuable timber and floating it down river to St. John. During the winter of 1838-9, Maine sent a posse to the Aroostook River to stop these depredations. New Brunswick's Governor Harvey then declared that his province had been invaded by a foreign foe and posted troops all along the eastern border. Maine reacted by sending its own militia into the disputed area, and for a time it seemed that an armed conflict was imminent.

However, a truce was declared, most of the armed men were withdrawn, and the dispute was finally settled by the Webster-Ashburton treaty of 1842, which established the present boundary line and opened the Aroostook Valley to settlement by the people from Maine.

Thousands of Maine militia men had caught glimpses of the rolling hardwood ridges, with their towering maples and birches, and had listened to the reports of the lush crops that sprang from the fertile soil. Many of them returned to carve farms out of the forest especially in the central part of the county. Settlement was encouraged by the liberal land policy of the state of Maine, which sold land to actual settlers for fifty cents an acre and permitted them to earn most of the purchase price by working on the new roads in their neighborhoods.

By 1860 there were 22,000 people in Aroostook and traffic over the Military Road to Bangor was heavy—both then and for many years afterward. Traffic was less in summer, when the low places were sloughs of despond where the laden wagons sank to their axles in mud; more in winter, when the well-packed snow made the best of roads, except when piled in huge drifts after a storm. The four-and-six-horse teams often went in caravans that they might help each other, if need be, through the mud or drifts or up the steep hills. Twenty miles was a good day's journey for the freighted teams. The faster four-horse stages made the trip with passengers and the mail from Bangor to Presque Isle in three days.

Into the county went hardware, groceries, dry goods, and other commodities needed by the growing population. Out came the more valuable and less bulky of the products of forest and farm-shaved cedar shingles, buckwheat, grass, and clover seed, butter, and wool, and at one time honey. 'Tis said that Leonard A. Blaisdell, of Westfield, once known as the "bee king" of Aroostook, once shipped five tons of honey in a single year. Great droves of cattle and flocks of sheep plodded over the military road to the outside markets. But there was no place on the road for potatoes. They were too bulky.

Aroostook continued to grow rapidly. By 1870 it had 3,209 farms and 133,024 acres of improved land, 5,072 horses, 28,744 cattle, 39,615 sheep, and 6,638 swine. The previous year the farms had produced 48,052 tons of hay, 380,701 bushels of potatoes, 532,151 bushels of oats, 46,946 bushels of wheat, and 360,450 bushels of buckwheat. Already the county ranked first among its sister counties in the production of wheat, oats, buckwheat, and grass seed. In fact it produced twice as much grass seed and three times as much buckwheat as all the rest of the state.

During the preceding thirty years the economy of the region was based on the lumber industry and it was to be so for some time to come. The Webster-Ashburton treaty contained a clause that permitted lumber to be driven down river to the city of St. John and then shipped, duty free, back into the United States. Lumbermen were active and needed all the grain, hay, and potatoes that farmers had for sale.

In addition to the local market, farmers raised a few things for export. As we have seen, these included buckwheat, clover, and timothy seed, and honey, which could profitably be "toted outside" and also cattle and sheep which could make the long journey on their own four feet.

Grass seed, because of its high value in proportion to its bulk, was a staple commodity. As early as 1850 the county produced twenty tons of clover seed and twenty-four tons of timothy. A few years later, John Allen, of Maysville, raised over a ton of clover seed that he sold for fifteen cents a pound. And one year Freeman Hayden, of Presque Isle, raised 5,800 pounds of clover seed and 230 bushels of timothy.

Aroostook even then had livestock equal in quantity to that in any other part of the state. There were a few purebred Durham cattle and numerous grades, also some Herefords and Devons. As for sheep, farmers preferred mutton breeds to the little, wrinkled Merinos. There were a few Cotswolds and Southdowns, but the large, long-wooled Leicesters were most in evidence.

One of the leading breeders in this period was J. Wingate Haines who moved, about 1846, from Hallowell to Fort Fairfield and brought part of his excellent herd of Durham cattle with him. Another was Charles Perley of Woodstock, who had one of the finest flocks of Leicester sheep in New Brunswick. Many specimens from his flock were brought across the border for breeding purposes, and were known far and wide as the Perley sheep. Quite a few farmers raised colts, and there were in the county stallions of both the Messenger and the Morgan strains. Said the editor of the *Maine Farmer* in 1864: "Aroostook is ahead of the rest of the state in the quantity and quality of its colts." Active in the advancement of agriculture were two fair associations: The Aroostook and Penobscot Agricultural Society and the Aroostook Agricultural Society (now the Northern Maine Fair).

Stories of big crops of potatoes were even then in circulation. In 1852, for example, J. Wingate Haines harvested 417 bushels from one acre; and John Knight, of Presque Isle, had grown a 350-bushel crop. Both crops were grown without fertilizer among the stumps in the newly cleared land then planted for the first time. Such yields seem to have been fairly common. A correspondent for the Maine Farmer was only expressing the general opinion when he wrote: "Of all the places in Maine where potatoes will pay best, Aroostook will excel as soon as it shall have railroads."

"What we want is a railroad to Bangor. Then Aroostook will become the garden of the State of Maine," wrote George F. Whidden of Presque Isle, to Secretary Goodale in 1858. All Aroostook agreed with him, and the cry, "We want a railroad," was continued from the day that the first iron horse chugged into Bangor until the railroads became reality.

The call was first answered from Canada. The New Brunswick and Canada Railroad (now part of the Canadian Pacific) reached Richmond, near Woodstock, in 1862 and slowly worked its way up the St. John Valley not far from Maine's eastern border. Next a branch was built from Debec Junction to Houlton Village in 1870, and Aroostook had a railroad—three whole miles. By 1878 the Canadian road had reached Edmundston, across the St. John River from Madawaska, and a branch had been opened through Fort Fairfield to Caribou that was later extended to Presque Isle. Meanwhile the European and North American Railroad (now a part of the Maine Central) had been completed from Bangor to Vanceboro where it connected with the road from St. John. Thus Aroostook had a rail connection of sorts with the outside world, although in a roundabout way and through a foreign country.

The effect was immediate. Houlton began shipping potatoes at once, and Fort Fairfield, Caribou, and Presque Isle as soon as the rails reached them. It is said that Kimball & Co., of Boston, shipped the first carload from Houlton and James M. Oak the first one from Presque Isle. On the heels of the railroad came the starch factories, and by 1880 twenty were in operation, scattered all the way from Frenchville to Sherman.

Although new in Aroostook, the manufacture of potato starch was by no means new in Maine. The first starch factory in the state was probably the one built in Mercer in 1842 or 1843. Then followed a regular epidemic of factories. During the next two or three years, fifteen or more were erected, all in a narrow belt of towns extending from Bethel and Weld to Solon and Skowhegan. Hardly had they become established when Dame Nature inflicted upon them a major disaster. Late blight struck Maine's potato crops with venomous vigor, and nearly all of the infant factories were forced out of business for lack of raw material.

However, the industry survived, although on a much smaller scale. In 1860 six factories were making potato starch, one in Oxford, two in Franklin, and three in Somerset Counties. In 1873 there were eight in the same general area, one each at Rumford, Peru, Strong, Mercer, and Madison, and three at Andover. All were very small. The largest then at Madison, used only about twelve thousand bushels of potatoes a year. All these factories eventually closed.

Alba Holmes, who had been connected with the starch business in New Hampshire for some years, came to Caribou in 1871 and opened a factory there the following year. Most authorities consider that this was the first starch factory in Aroostook, although one states that two brothers, Elmer and George Hibbard, also from New Hampshire, built and opened a factory in New Limerick in 1871. The next factory seems to have been the one opened in Presque Isle in 1874.

The Holmes factory could grind about a thousand bushels of potatoes a day and ran for about a month the first year. Farmers received about twenty-five cents a bushel for potatoes, field run, delivered at the factory. There was no railway station in the county nearer than Houlton, and the heavy casks of starch had to be trucked by team about twenty miles to Tobique in New Brunswick. Most of the product was sold in Lewiston where it was used in the cotton mills for sizing cloth.

Starch factories increased rapidly in number. Those in operation in 1880 were located in Ashland, Bridgewater, Caribou, Easton, Fort Fairfield, Fort Kent, Frenchville, Grand Isle, Houlton (two), Limestone, Mapleton, Monticello, New Limerick, Presque Isle, Van Buren, and Washburn. All were private concerns and nearly all were owned by men who lived in Aroostook. The principal manufacturers were Johnson & Phair, of Presque Isle, and Alba Holmes, of Caribou. A few years later Thomas H. Phair bought the interests of his partner, C.F.A. Johnson, and for many years was known as the "starch king" of Aroostook.

As to production in those early days, seven factories in 1876 made 1,480 tons of starch and the output in 1878 was estimated at 2,000 tons. In 1881, 3,400 tons of starch were shipped from the railroad stations in Fort Fairfield and Caribou alone. Counting nine pounds of starch to a bushel of potatoes, that would mean that farmers in the area sold 760,000 bushels of potatoes to the factories.

For a number of years the manufacturers contracted with the farmers to grow potatoes for their factories. The price was usually twenty-five cents a bushel for the potatoes "field run," that is just as they grew in the field. Later when potatoes were being shipped in quantity to the city markets, only the culls were made into starch, except in years of a surplus and low prices. Thus the amount of starch produced varied greatly from season to season.

Census figures show that the potato crop increased more than seven fold between 1869 and 1889, or from 380,701 to 2,746,765 bushels in the twenty years. Other enterprises shared in the increase. The number of horses rose from 5,072 to 13,348, of cattle from 17,202 to 31,484, and of sheep from 24,369 to 39,006, the number of farms more than doubled and the acreage devoted to both hay and oats made still larger gains.

Two new crops were tried in central Aroostook, sugar beets and hops. Farmers proved that they could grow sugar beets successfully; but the sugar refinery, at Portland, was too far away, and the enterprise did not get beyond the trial stage. Hops were grown for several years, but apparently the market was too uncertain and the crop was abandoned. On the other hand, the butter factories established at Houlton, Presque Isle, and elsewhere remained in business for a number of years.

The need still existed for a direct line that would serve the whole county, and agitation began anew. The Northern Maine Railroad Company was chartered in 1887 but could not command sufficient capital and failed. One reason was that financiers and the public knew very little about the northland and its possibilities. As a Boston newspaper man remarked while viewing an exhibition staged in that city to show the resources of the county: "Why all this fuss about Aroostook? There's nothing but bears and Indians up there anyway."

The struggle continued. Under the able leadership of Albert A. Burleigh, a prominent Houlton business man, and Frank W. Cram, an experienced railroad man, the Bangor and Aroostook Railroad was chartered in 1891 and opened to Houlton January 1, 1894. The road was continued to Caribou and Fort Fairfield the same year, and subsequently branches served other settled parts of the county. After fifty years of agitation, Aroostook had a direct line of railroad, and its future as "the Potato Empire of the East" was assured.

Again the effect was immediate. Nearly a thousand new farms were occupied between 1890 and 1900, and the value of land and buildings jumped from 7.5 million dollars to 11. Potato acreage leaped from 16,641 to 41,953 acres, and production increased two and one half times. Aroostook was growing more than half the potatoes in the state. The grain and hay crops shared in the increase, but dairying made only small increases, and the number of sheep declined. During the next ten years the area planted to potatoes increased to 75,738 acres and the yield to 17,514,491 bushels.

Several factors besides Aroostook's favorable soil and climate and new direct access to market contributed to this extraordinary growth. Prominent among them were the favorable economic conditions in the country as a whole which resulted in better prices, the development and increased use of potato machinery, the greater use of commercial fertilizers, and the growth of a thriving seed trade with the Atlantic and southern states.

Previous to 1890, the only special horse-drawn potato implement was the winged horseshoe used to cover the seed and to hill up the rows at hoeing time. Then came the Hoover digger that enabled farmers to handle more acres with less manpower at harvest time, and the planter which gave the same result at planting time. Bordeaux mixture for the control of blight was first applied with knapsack sprayers that the operator carried on his back, or with barrel sprayers drawn by one horse and equipped with a hand pump. However, it was not long before traction-powered sprayers came into use.

Moreover, when farmers began to use commercial fertilizers, they made very small applications compared with those of the present day, perhaps two or three hundred pounds per acre. But as they found it paid to use larger amounts, they did so, until by the time of World War One many were using a ton per acre. Not only that, but the plant food contained in the popular brands for potatoes had practically doubled. Naturally yields per acre increased. In fact the average yield per acre was 170 bushels in 1889 and 230 bushels in 1909. All these advances, however, added to the cost of conducting the enterprise, which in years of low prices gave promise of possible disaster.

These average yields were far below the maximum. For example: in 1889 the Bowker Fertilizer Company and the American Agriculturist offered prizes for the best acre of potatoes grown in the United States. Farmers in Presque Isle won three of the first five prizes. Charles B. Coy won the first prize with a yield of 738 bushels; Fred S. Wiggin, third, 537 bushels; and Delano Moore, fourth, with 523 bushels per acre. While these examples were extreme, Aroostook was soon far ahead of the rest of the state in yields per acre, just as Maine was leading all other states in that respect.

Again, the seed industry is based on the fact that northern grown seed is more vigorous and gives better yields in warmer climates than that grown locally. This fact was well known even before Aroostook came into the picture. According to the Maine Farmer: Moses Hussey, of North Berwick, "well known as the largest dealer in seed potatoes in the state," exhibited twenty varieties of potatoes at the State Fair in Augusta in 1870.

The seed business began in Aroostook soon after the first railroads were built. Among the leading growers and dealers during the pioneer period were Edward L. Cleveland, of Houlton; Elisha E. Parkhurst, of Presque Isle; and George W.P. Jerrard, of Caribou. As early as 1885 Jerrard was issuing catalogues describing the numerous varieties that he had for sale. Parkhurst sometimes grew as many as forty varieties for the southern trade and shipped in quantity as far away as Texas. The seed business gradually grew until thousands of carloads were sold annually to the southern states, especially Virginia, Florida, and Texas, as well as growers nearer home.

By the turn of the century the industry had three important market outlets—for table stock, for seed, and for starch. Low prices were paid for potatoes to be ground into starch, and in most years after the coming of the Bangor and Aroostook Railroad the factories received culls only. But in years when the markets were glutted, they took merchantable stock as well, and thus put a floor of sorts under the potato price structure.

In 1904 there were 64 starch factories in Maine, 62 in Aroostook County and two in Penobscot. Thomas H. Phair was operating 14 and John Watson, of Houlton, six. The others belonged to smaller concerns. The banner year before 1904 for the manufacture of potato starch was 1895, when the potato crop was very large and the price for seed and table stock was very low. About 10,000 tons of starch were produced that year.

The boom in the potato industry had a marked effect on the economy of Aroostook County. Men who had planted three or four acres of potatoes annually increased their acreage to 15 or 20; men who had been planting 15 or 20 increased to fifty or more. Most farmers adopted a definite system of crop rotation of potatoes followed by grain and hay, with a large proportion of clover in the hay. Thus the acreage of grain and hay also increased and more land was brought under cultivation, all subordinated to the potato industry. In 1910 more oats were grown in Aroostook than in all the rest of the state. It was during this period that farmers began buying the heavy work horses from the West for which the county became famous.

As potato production prospered, farmers lost interest in other farm enterprises, including dairying. Even in the 1890's many a farmer was saying: "As long as I can raise a hundred barrels of potatoes on an acre and sell them for one or two dollars a barrel, I'm not going to tie myself down to milking cows." This widespread attitude foretold the doom of the butter factories that had once seemed such a desirable source of income. It also adversely affected other farm enterprises. Aroostook was approaching an economy based on a single money crop.

Eugene H. Grubb, a prominent potato grower in Colorado, sensed that when he visited the county in 1910 in search of material for a book on the potato industry, later called facetiously "Grubb on the Potatoe." He found the people prosperous and progressive and noted that: "The potato dominates every sentiment and idea. It is the sole topic of conversation where two or three men are gathered together... They talk about them in the streets, in the offices, in the banks, and, I have no doubt, in the schools and churches, and even in their sleep...Houlton...is the only place where I have been talked to a standstill on the subject of potatoes. I never met people so eager for knowledge in connection with potatoes." Grubb must have discovered, as did many other discerning visitors, that Aroostook's success in growing potatoes was due not only to climate and soil but also to the "Western spirit of enterprise" of its citizens.

During the decade marked by World War One, the production of potatoes increased and continued to absorb most of the energy and attention of farmers. The production of hay and nearly all grains also increased, while wheat made startling gains, from 76,126 bushels in 1909 to 167,323 bushels in 1919, the largest yield ever recorded in the county at a census period. This was the result of strenuous efforts to produce more wheat as a war measure. When the stimulus was removed, wheat again resumed its retreat from Aroostook fields.

The number of dairy cows also reached nearly an all time high in 1919, (17,570) for much the same reason. Products not used by the farmers themselves found ready sale in the nearby villages, but they offered little competition to potatoes as a source of cash income. Orcharding, which had once seemed promising in a few small areas, was by this time practically forgotten. The sheep population continued on its way downward, but during the war and for some years afterward farmers kept more hogs.

It was during this period that people were forcibly impressed with the fact that the national potato crop, and not that of Aroostook, governed prices. Aroostook's crop in 1912 was about normal while that of the United States as a whole was the largest crop ever recorded up to that time. The monthly price of that crop to Maine farmers averaged $1.37 a barrel. In 1916, the Aroostook crop was somewhat larger than normal while the crop nation-wide was the smallest in ten years. The average monthly price was $5.23 a barrel, and along toward spring potatoes sold as high as $10 a barrel. One dealer in Presque Isle paid over a million dollars for potatoes that season. He paid $10 a barrel to one man for 50,000 barrels. The next "ten-dollar year" came with the crop of 1919. This time Maine had a crop above average, but that of the nation was much below normal. Prices started high in the fall, went higher before spring, and averaged $6.18 a barrel for the season. Said a veteran dealer: "Everyone connected with the potato business was rolling in wealth." This was a pardonable exaggeration, but it had a solid core of truth, nevertheless. Another point might be noted that continued to hold true: When the crop in the country was small, it paid to hold potatoes in storage for the spring market; when the crop was large, it did not.

During the 1920's Aroostook reached the point where it could truly claim to be not only the Garden of Maine but also the Potato Empire of the East. Acreage, yield per acre, and total yield all made marked gains over those of the previous decade. The crop of 42 million bushels in 1929 was double that of 1919 and the largest grown in the county to that time. First Maine established the record of raising more potatoes than any other state; then Aroostook broke the record by growing more potatoes than any state except Maine. These records were maintained nearly every year until World War Two and long afterward. They came because of a special combination of favorable climate, well-adapted soil, and skillful farmers. A contributory cause was the increasing use of trucks and tractors that enabled growers to enlarge their acreage. By 1930 the county was already the leading producer of certified seed potatoes and made the lion's share of potato starch in the United States and Canada.

Another result was the development in the county of three fairly distinct sections as far as agriculture was concerned, northern, central, and southern Aroostook. Previous to the 1890's agriculture was of a fairly uniform type and just emerging from the self-sufficient stage. The principle sources of cash income were supplies sold to the lumber camps, some shipments of potatoes over the Canadian Pacific Railroad, and cattle and sheep driven to the "outside" markets. Later the potato industry grew most rapidly in central Aroostook, until by the time of the First World War the area including Caribou, Fort Fairfield, Presque Isle, and the neighboring towns had become a commercial farming section with a single money crop-potatoes. Both northern and southern Aroostook grew potatoes, of course, but as a whole their farmers were still more inclined toward the self-reliant type. There was a small sheep industry in the St. John Valley and a small dairy industry in southern Aroostook. Conditions were somewhat similar in 1940, although all areas were raising more potatoes.

Everything, however, was not always rosy. Aroostook's commitment to a single money crop brought upon it all the problems that perplex a one-crop area: the danger of overproduction and the lack of supplemental income in the "poor" years, fluctuations in yield and fluctuations in prices, fat years and lean years, and financial problems ranging from bank credit to finance the crop to a desperate struggle to save the old homestead from foreclosure. On the other hand there were "ten-dollar" years when money flowed in a golden flood; when farmers paid off old debts, bought big horses, cars, and tractors, repaired their buildings and bought more land; and when the persuasive voice of the salesman was heard in the street. The situation was well-described by a couplet in Aroostook's own song: "When the price is high enough, we have a little cash; and when the market's on the bum we eat a lot of hash."

The depression that followed World War One was a time of trial for potato growers. The second "ten-dollar" year was followed by three years of ruinously low prices, one of fair returns, and then the worst year of all. Some farmers lost their farms, others were burdened with mountains of debt. But Aroostook potato growers had a saying: "The place to find your money is where you lost it," and so it proved in this instance. Wrote Frank P. Washburn, Commissioner of Agriculture: "With characteristic tenacity and courage our growers planted in 1925 an acreage only six thousand below that of the previous year, and the result makes one of the happiest chapters in the story of Maine agriculture... The crop of 1925 returned sixty-eight million dollars, based on the December first report, and was the largest in both volume and value produced in any state that year.... Many potato farmers were able to discharge obligations incurred during the preceding years and in some instances to make substantial improvements in plants and equipment."

The next few years were fairly prosperous. The average crop planted was about 125,000 acres, the yield per acre about 270 bushels, and annual production about 34 million bushels. Farmers were climbing out of the depths of debt and making needed improvements. Then they ran head on into the Great Depression, and plunged deeper into debt than ever before.

During the four crop years, 1930 to 1933 inclusive, the average annual "cash to grower" income was less than 13 million dollars as compared with an average of 23 million dollars for the whole period from 1920 to 1929 with its years both good and bad. Then came the 45 million bushel crop of 1934, of which farmers sold 37 million bushels for 5.5 million dollars, or a farm price of 42 cents a barrel (15 cents a bushel). Farmers received less than six million dollars for growing the crop; the railroads collected ten millions for carrying it to market. Farmers owed 28 million dollars, which was more than half the value of their real estate.

Late in 1935 the Aroostook County Council, which included in its membership the railroads, fertilizer industry, bankers, growers, shippers, Granges, and other interests, and the Aroostook County Farm Bureau (now the Aroostook Extension Association), appointed a joint committee to take account of stock and recommend action. The committee sought and received the assistance of the economists of the Maine Extension Service, Donald W. Reed and Smith C. McIntire. All recognized the fact that the country would recover from the depression. They also saw that some of Aroostook's problems would sit on her doorstop for a long time to come.

The basic problem was over production; and while farmers were producing more, consumers were eating less. In fact consumption per person had decreased sharply since 1925. Research also revealed that during the ten-year period, 1921-1930, farmers received about twice as much for their potatoes when national production was less than 3.5 bushels per capita than when it was more. Competition for the consumer's dollar was growing keener both with other food products and with other potato areas.

What could be done? There was no panacea. However, the committee recommended a long-time program in which it urged all interests to take part. This program, in brief, included the study and adoption of methods of producing, handling, and marketing potatoes of better quality at lower cost, soil conservation, grower representation in the terminal markets, more adequate methods of farm financing, more intensive advertising, the use of supplementary crops such as peas for canning, poultry, and dairying wherever practical, and the development of new uses for potatoes not sold for human consumption.

The need for more careful handling was shown by a study made by the Maine Agricultural Experiment Station in city stores. Station workers found some type of injury on nearly half of the potatoes they examined. Major injuries threw seven per cent out of grade and caused a reduction in price. Accordingly the Extension Service urged the padding of diggers and barrels in the field and precautions against bruising while the potatoes were being stored and shipped.

Since larger yields per acre would result in lower production costs per bushel, Extension demonstrated the value of green crops to increase the humus in the soil, and also the accurate placement of fertilizer for the best use by potato plants. Enormous amounts of clover were plowed under instead of being cut for hay, and for several years quite an amount of crimson clover was seeded for that purpose.

The Federal Land Bank provided more adequate credit both to growers and for cooperative marketing. The U. S. Soil Conservation Service and the Agricultural Adjustment Administration assisted farmers in preventing soil erosion and in maintaining the fertility of their fields. A cooperative, Maine Potato Growers, Inc., was already doing a business that grew until, during the coming war years, it handled a large slice of the crop and helped to stablize the market.

Two laws enacted by the Maine Legislature proved helpful. The first, known as the Potato Branding Law, was passed in 1935. It required that potatoes must be packed for shipment in accordance with the United States standard grades, and that the package must carry a statement as to contents and grade and the name of the person or firm responsible for the packaging. The purpose of the law was to assure the customer that she was getting what she purchased and to keep inferior grades off the market.

The other law was enacted in 1937 and was known as the Potato Tax Act. This law imposed a tax of one cent (later two cents) a barrel on all potatoes marketed. The receipts were used for two purposes—for advertising the commodity and for research in handling and merchandising potatoes and potato products. The advertising was done by the Maine Development Commission and the research by the Maine Agricultural Experiment Station. Both brought good results.

The potato industry has been developed most intensively in central Aroostook. In 1939 six adjoining towns each raised more than a million bushels of potatoes. Fort Fairfield, with 3.9 million bushels to her credit, was the champion potato town in Maine. Caribou came next with 3.3 million bushels, and Presque Isle third with 2.5 million bushels. The other three towns were Easton, Limestone, and Mars Hill. The extent to which the farmers in these towns were engaged in the potato enterprise is shown by the fact that their potato acreage was nearly equal to that of all other crops combined.

The last five years of the 1930's saw a gradual recovery in the nation's economy and were less difficult for potato growers. Production remained high (about thirty-five million bushels a year), debts were being paid, and the farmer was looking with confidence toward the future.

As a prominent grower and shipper from Aroostook County told leaders of the potato industry at a conference in Chicago during the depths of the depression: "The Aroostook farmer has the dogged inertia of the English squares which Napoleon's charging grenadiers could not break. He knows the potato game more completely than any other spud specialist on earth, as witnessed by his yield per acre.... We stand humbly before his never-die spirit. 'Under the bludgeonings of chance, his head is bloody but unbowed.' He will stick it out and, like England, win the last encounter."

CHAPTER 32.

Like other one-crop agricultural states, Maine has always sought a second cash crop to supplement the potato's contribution to the economy. As the next three chapters reveal, the sugar beet has played a prominent role in the search beginning as early as 1838. The 1870's saw an abortive effort to grow beets. Finally in 1965, the 125 year old search ended with the assistance of the United States government.

MANUFACTURE OF BEET SUGAR—1838*
by
Anonymous

The culture of the sugar beet is a subject which demands our candid consideration. It is a business which holds out to the farmers of Maine, the most flattering inducements to embark in it. Our soil,—our climate,—our internal and external resources are all peculiarly suited to the production and manufacture of beet sugar. A man of no ordinary experience, who has looked deeply into this subject, says, with regard to the soil: The beet root penetrates low into the ground, and therefore a deep loose mould should be provided for it, in which it will vegetate without obstacle its radicles easily collect the nourishment necessary for its support, and it thrives luxuriantly. Decomposed animal matter mixed with lime is the best manure for the beet crop. But well rotted manure from the stable and barn yard is also favorable to its growth. The land should be ploughed deep, and the manure well incorporated with it.

In all the countries in Europe where the sugar beet is cultivated, it is now admitted that the north, all things being equal, is far more favorable to its production than the south. It is observed in a notice on the sugar beet, "that the north of France has been found more congenial to the beet than the south. Germany, Prussia and Silicia, where this manufacture had its origin, produce a root more productive in sugar, than France; and there is every reason to believe that Russia is among the highly favored countries for the culture of the sugar beet." Although the experiments made with us are very limited, yet they are sufficient to remove all reasonable doubt that New England, and particularly the State of Maine, will not prove inferior to the best districts in Russia for this important object.

The beet has been found favorable as a crop to follow wheat, oats, potatoes, Indian corn and ruta baga, and some cultivators in France have raised good crops upon the same ground for eight years in succession.

Much inquiry has been made about the process of making sugar from the beet. We do not profess to fully understand the whole proceedings, but according to the latest discoveries with which we are acquainted, it appears that slicing and drying the beet, and then grinding it to a powder, and steeping this powder in boiling water, to which it readily yields its saccharine matter, constitutes all that is peculiar to its manufacture. The remainder of the process is precisely the same as that of making sugar from the sap of the maple tree.

Nearly every article of machinery necessary for performing this operation on a large scale, is already made and in use among us. All that is wanting is to bring them together and apply them to this use. In the first place, a machine is wanted to slice up the beets—and you have it in the Straw Cutter invented, *but not patented,* by our worthy fellow citizen, Dr. E. Holmes. By making very trifling alterations in this machine, a man will be able to slice 100 bushels a day without excessive labor. The cost of the machine will not probably exceed ten or twelve dollars.

---

*Maine Farmer and Journal of Useful Arts, October 9, 1838.

The hop houses that are already built in many parts of our State, will answer admirably well for drying the beets after they are sliced. Spread them upon the cloths much in the manner that you would hops. Build in one corner of the lower part a furnace, and set a boiler for extracting the saccharine matter, and boiling down the syrup,—and let the smoke and steam be conducted through funnels along under the flooring on which the beets are spread to dry,—and in this way the same fire that makes the sugar will dry the beets. In the other corner set a mill, similar to those used by tanners for grinding bark; or one of the horse power grist mills may be found preferable. To either of which the common horse power can be attached, and the grinding performed with ease and facility. Thus you have the whole appendage for a sugar manufactory.

At present, one manufactory of this kind will answer for a School District, or even a whole Town; but the time is not far distant when we shall find one, on a plan something like this, on every third or fourth farm of any magnitude in our State.

The pulp, after having been steeped, may be again dried, and kept for feeding cattle and store hogs through the winter,—for which purpose it is said to be as valuable, pound for pound, as oatmeal, either used alone, or mixed with boiled or steamed potatoes.—This business is yet in its infancy, and, as it advances, improvements will continue to be made in the process of manufacturing the sugar and new and valuable uses will be found for the pulp.

What hinders our farmers from embarking in this busines? It cannot be the want of soil or climate suited to its culture. The former we have, that is second to none in the world, and the beet grows in so short a time that even our coldest seasons will produce good crops. It is not certainly a want of enterprise, energy or industry, all these the farmers of Maine possess in an eminent degree. It must be mainly attributed to a want of information which however, we believe has already been given through our agricultural newspapers sufficient to enable any one to commence on a small scale. Let three or four of our best farmers in each town commence with a quarter of an acre for the use of their land, and it will not be many years before the importation of sugar into this State will cease.

CHAPTER

33.

THE BEET SUGAR INDUSTRY IN MAINE, 1875-1880*
by
Ernest Thomas Gennert

Months have passed by since I had the pleasure of addressing you on the question of planting sugar beets, and pointing out to you the probable result the trial might have, and the sure result which would follow success. The leading and most enterprising farmers of Aroostook county have shown by their readiness to try the experiment, as it is termed, that they are well aware something has to be done if they will not follow in the wake of nearly every other farming community in the State of Maine, in fact, in every New England State, and every State in the Union, exhaust their land and make it comparatively speaking, nonproductive. Even in Aroostook county we find plenty of land which was cleared not more than twenty years ago, and which today does not pay to farm because it has been cropped too much, it is worn out, and farmers investing their hard work on such land find but very poor compensation in the scanty harvests they can take off.

But in speaking of the production of sugar beets, we have to take in a wider scope; we have to examine the question of raising root crops, and their relation to general farming, and in pointing out to you the influence which the cultivation of sugar beets will exert on Aroostook county if successfully introduced, a few words on farming in general are necessary. The idea which has done so much mischief to our farmers who have been the pioneers, has been, that newly subdued land which they called virgin soil, was inexhaustable, and could be cropped for an indefinite time, yielding always bountiful crops, requiring nothing of the farmer but stirring the soil, sowing and harvesting. This idea has been exploded long ago, yet but few farmers have taken the necessary stops to return to the land sufficient of what they carry from it, in order to be reasonably sure of good paying crops in general.

Accepting the fact which every farmer has to admit as true, and which is the foundation of all successful and remunerative farming, that without manuring there can be no paying farming, the question of successful farming has been reduced to the production of plenty and cheap manure. With plenty of good manure, judiciously applied year after year, it does not require an extra smart man to raise well paying crops; on over-cropped, worn out land, with manure applied in homoeopathic doses, or none at all, the most intelligent and industrious farmer will find it up-hill work; he will find, notwithstanding the greatest exertion, he grows poorer every year. But without raising and feeding roots to your cattle, it is useless to expect large quantities of good and cheap manure. Anything which will lead the farmer in the right direction to root-raising, will bestow a lasting benefit on him and his farm, and this the cultivation of sugar beets most undoubtedly has done. Whatever the financial result of the first year's cultivation of sugar beets has been to the farmer, it has shown to him the right direction to successful

---
*Written by Ernest Thomas Gennert, Supt. Maine Beet Sugar Company, Portland. From *Agriculture of Maine: Twenty-third Annual Report of the Secretary of Maine Board of Agriculture for the Year 1878.* Augusta: Sprague, Owen & Nash, 1878.

farming, in making roots one of the general farm crops.

The farmer in nearly every State of the Union, has labored under the disadvantage of starting in the wrong direction, and once entered into the wrong system it has been kept up, and we have tried to make up in acreage what we lacked in yield from a given extent of ground; this applies as to Aroostook county as to any other locality. But this starting in the wrong direction has not been without a natural cause. The pioneer who enters the wilderness to clear and subdue wild land, with very rare exceptions does so with very slender means; he has to provide shelter for himself and family, and also provide food. He cannot, therefore, be expected to start with the inauguration of a system of permanent improvement which calls for the outlay of large sums of money, and the waiting of years for returns from the same. What wonder, than to find on most farms in Aroostook county, barns or cattle sheds in which roots would freeze as hard as a rock in less than an hour after they were put in, in winter? What wonder to find these barns entirely too small to contain sufficient cattle for the proportion of acres under tillage? What wonder to find the manure piles not only of the poorest quality, but also of the smallest dimensions? And what wonder, finally, to find plenty of land in Aroostook county which will hardly produce a crop of buckwheat, or a crop of potatoes, which is worth gathering? It is all very well to say build warm barns, keep plenty of cattle, raise roots to feed to your cattle, with other feed which is generally wasted on the farm, in order to produce plenty and cheap manure to enrich your land with, to bring it to a high state of fertility.

All this is very easily said, but not so easily inaugurated; and here it is where the production of sugar beets for the manufacture of sugar comes in to help the start in the right direction, by first of all giving the farmer a cash crop on which he can rely as an income as soon as he takes it from the field to the factory, and secondly, by introducing on our farms a crop which leads to better and deeper cultivation; while being a feed crop, will furnish to the cattle the kind of feed so much needed on our farms in order to utilize much which goes to waste now. Of all the straw grown in the State of Maine, not 10 percent is utilized, while combined with the beet pomace it would fatten many thousands of cattle, doubling and trebling the manure at present produced on our farms. But the farmers in Aroostook county have found out by this time that the cultivation of sugar beets means high farming, means rational farming, it means the reverse from surface farming, which we have so long pursued. Root farming means subsoil farming, bringing into play a strata which has so far never been exposed to either sunlight, warmth or air; which, though it has received for years the leachings of the upper strata of soil, yet has so far contributed very little, if any, towards the growth of crops which were grown on the surface. The result of some of our farmers has shown most conclusively that both the soil and climate of Maine is most excellently adapted for the cultivation of root crops, especially for the sugar beet.

But we have to pass from the considerations of general principles regarding root and beet raising, to the special features which we observed during the summer in the vicinity of Presque Isle, where the cultivation of sugar beets has received the most attention in the state of Maine. Every farmer has been aware the enterprise was from some unavoidable cause started too late in the season, which left no choice in the land as to its adaptability for producing a root crop or even a crop of anything, the farmer generally takes his best land for the crop on which he counts most, using his manure there, and attending to this crop first and foremost; the cultivation of beets coming rather late in the season to the notice of the farmer, had to be done on land left for no special purpose, though as a general rule the farmers have done the best they could under such circumstances. The late opening of spring was soon followed by several weeks of severe drought and intense heat, which put the whole beet culture to a severe test. Taking a general view of the state of affairs as they developed from day to day, it could be easily observed that on land in a good state of fertility, or land which had been manured the previous fall, the young beet plants showed their usual vigor, whole acres having hardly a wilted leaf during the hottest mid-day sun, while on land which had no fertility or cultivation, the beet plants, after sprouting well, perished for want of available nourishment. The same was the case with land which had been manured in the spring with coarse unrotted barnyard manure. Some fields had started so well that the rows were full up and had been once hoed, yet when the tender plant with its tiny rootlets could find no nourishment, it had to perish, and whole acres disappeared within a few days. That this was due to no other cause was, in some cases, most clearly demonstrated.

A three acre field had been manured and ploughed well last fall, with the exception of about one-half acre, which, tongue-like, run into the square field. This half acre had no manure in the fall because the stock was completely exhausted. In the spring some fresh manure had accumulated and was placed on the half acre, in the same proportion as on all the rest, and the beets planted. The whole field came up well but in about one week every plant from the tongue-like piece had disappeared, leaving the land completely bare, while on the other two and a half acres almost surrounding it, the crop looked well, and when harvested, gave a good yield. A second field came under my observation bringing the same features out very prominently. Two acres of poor land were well prepared and planted and came up well, but in less than a week every plant disappeared, because it had perished; thinking something might be the matter with the seed, the field was worked over with a cultivator and freshly planted, when to the great delight of the young men, in eight days the beet rows were all up again. They informed their parent of the fact, expressing their confidence that they would yet reap the reward of a good crop for their labor, but alas for worn-out soil, in a few days they had all perished again.

In judging from these fields, the conclusion forces itself upon the close observer, that every field which was in a good condition and would have given fair returns of any other crop, gave a good yield of sugar beets, while overcropped and ill-prepared land, even if manured in spring, did yield but little if any crop; between land in a good state of fertility and land even too poor to produce a crop of buckwheat, there were fields in every stage of fertility and poverty, most or at least many were abandoned, some ploughed up, others not. To the surprise of many farmers, a struggle ensued between the crop and the weeds and in many cases the former predominated.

The more favorable summer season which followed the bad spring, brought out many a neglected and backward field, and many farmers who had given up only too readily, came to the conclusion from observation on their own fields, that a good crop of sugar beets can be raised with proper care on any land which will produce any other good field crop. A great many farmers who thought that early planting would be injurious to sugar beets, have been convinced of their mistake, and in planting the crop another year, it should be the great aim of every farmer to have the sugar beets planted early enough that the leaves cover the ground by the fourth of July, that no more work has to be done on them, which will ensure a good and early crop and give the farmer ample time to attend to his hay crop.

When farmers entered into the enterprise this year, they did so with a great deal of good will but with no experience, and no very great result could be expected; the general opinion expressed by farmers is to benefit by their experience for another year. Though the result has fallen short of the expectation the fact that good beet crops have been raised after fields had been given up and partly ploughed up, shows that with proper care, and under ordinary favorable circumstances, Aroostook county will prove one of the finest beet growing districts in the world. As everything was a trial, and new, hardly any machinery has been used; while it is but reasonable to expect as the cultivation of sugar beets is carried on on a larger scale, machinery will be almost exclusively used. Most parties appear to agree now that early planting is essential to success, and that the European principle considering the danger from too early planting, by far less than from too late planting, is the correct one there as well as here.

On the following page is the account from Geo. A. Parsons of Presque Isle.

If, then, the actual self cost after every part of the work performed has been well paid is $2.58, the result has been satisfactory.

Mr. Alex. Johnston, in Wiscasset, has raised sugar beets for seven or eight years in succession; the crop has never failed, and this year, though not as good as generally, he harvested by actual weight 24 tons, 700 lbs. per acre, while his neighbor, who had the field of beets almost adjoining his, whose soil is fully as good as his, but who appears to labor under the impression because a kind Providence provides rain and sunshine, perhaps Providence will also attend to the weeding and cultivating; he

Three acres of sugar beets.	Dr.
Plowing twice	$ 9.00
Harrowing and smoothing	2.25
Marking	.60
Planting, 1½ days	1.50
Thinning, 12 days	9.00
Weeding by hand	4.50
Horse hoeing	4.00
Harvesting and delivering to dry-house	30.00
Thirty-six pounds of seed	7.20
Thirty-six loads of manure, half of said value	36.00
Quarter value of last year's manure	8.00
Interest and taxes	15.00
	$127.05
	Cr.
By tops fed to milch cows	$ 15.00
43 2-5 tons of beets sold, cost $2.58	112.05
	$127.05

harvested not quite 11 tons by actual weight and measurement per acre.

Mr. Libby, President of First National Bank, Portland, harvested from his farm 17 3/4 tons per acre. Mr. Westworth, Superintendent of the Reform School, Cape Elizabeth, had a still better yield, though he thought in the earlier part of the season, which was very unfavorable, he would have no beets at all. I might continue the list of parties who have done well in beet raising, but this is enough to show that beets, when properly taken care of, on land well prepared, will yield as large a crop in the State of Maine as anywhere in the world. But while grass or hay farming is in reality the lowest stage of farming, requiring the least brain, the least care and attention, the least work, and gives the least returns, barely keeping the farmer from starvation, root crop farming, especially sugar beets, means high farming, requires the most brain, a good deal of care and attention, and a good deal of work; it will give, if all these are properly applied, the largest cash returns, and will bring the farm into the highest state of productiveness for every crop the farmer may afterwards wish to raise.

We have proved by our experiment this year, that large crops of beets can be raised in every part of the State of Maine, because what many can do, all can do, if they will only profit by the experience of their neighbors; we have proved that the beets produced in any part of the State of Maine yield as much sugar as the beets raised in any part of the world; and we have proved that the sugar from beets raised in Maine can be as easily extracted, and is of as good quality as the best in any country.

Without root crops no production of manure, to any great extent, is possible. Sugar beets will bring cash and plenty of feed, consequently plenty of manure, without which farmers will always have hard work, while plenty of manure will restore lost fertility to our worn out lands, and eventually make farming easy, and above all, remuncrative.

CHAPTER

34.

AROOSTOOK'S "SWEET" POTATO*
by
Editors of *New England Business Review*

The name Aroostook has long been synonymous with potatoes. But a sweeter image is in the wind. The people of the County are trying to put New England into the sugar beet business.

The Background

In all the world, there's no place exactly like Maine's Aroostook County. Oh, it has a few similarities to other places, of course . . . some that are obvious, some less so.

Aroostook is, in a way, the "Alaska" of the East. The area it covers gives some balance to maps by tending to compensate for Alaska's thrust toward the upper left hand corner. But Alaska has 1,000,000 acres of land for every day of the year, and by this yardstick, Aroostook, big as it is, has only a four-and-a-half day supply.

Aroostook's area, both in total size and in available crop land, is almost the same as that of the Hawaiian Islands. But for anyone familiar with the Islands or the County, the similarity ends there.

Perhaps the one thing Aroostook has in common with most other farming regions is that here, too, it is hard to make a living. But even this likeness doesn't go much deeper than the skin on a potato.

Aroostook's combination of especially fertile soil, relatively short growing season, large area of crop land, and distance from consuming markets has reinforced the county's increasing dependence on potatoes. Indeed, few farming areas are so dependent on the production of a single perishable crop.

There's no denying Aroostook knows how to grow potatoes. While potato yields, nationally, have doubled since 1944 to reach about 17,000 pounds per acre, Maine harvested some 26,500 pounds per acre in 1963. With people eating fewer potatoes, this kind of productivity has sent potato prices bounding like a ball rolled down the cellar stairs.

In recent years, farm prices per hundred pounds of potatoes in Aroostook have varied from $3.03 to $.74 . . . and farm receipts from potato sales have fallen from $110 million in 1948 to about $40 million.

Paying for the Privilege

More of the potato growers have been producing more potatoes for less money over the past few years. In fact, a recent University of Maine publication indicates that some growers may have "paid" up to $68 an acre for the "privilege" of growing potatoes last year. A current survey estimating the agricultural debt of the County at some $44 million tends to confirm the fact that Aroostook's potato economy has fallen on hard times.

The relative isolation of the area has truly tied the people to their real estate. There are few opportunities for alternative land use which would allow growers to recover their investments. There just aren't the pressures of population or industrial development here to encourage growers to "sell out and move to town" as is the case in some other areas.

---

*From *New England Business Review*. Boston: Federal Reserve Bank of Boston, March, 1964. pp. 6-10. Permission to reprint granted.

A logical solution might be for growers to transfer to some other types of production. Livestock, for example, could presumably use the tremendous acreage if it were in forage crops ... the county was a major source of hay for many metropolitan areas back when transportation depended on four legs rather than four wheels. But dairying opportunities seem largely limited by the restricted potential of local markets for milk. Beef and sheep production have shown limited returns, too.

From this it appears that Aroostook, far from being different, is very much like the rest of America's agricultural countryside ... falling prices, soaring production, farmers pinned to the land by the weight of their own productivity, with little opportunity for making a helpful change.

Lifting the Lid

And yet Aroostook is trying to be different!

After more than five years of depressed prices and chaotic markets, growers in the County have moved to diversify. They plan to live with the potatoes they grow so well—but to supplement farm income with another crop. Instead of shifting into products already in oversupply ... they've decided to put New England into, of all things, the sugar beet business.

It Comes in Bowls

Of all the kinds of "Sugar," the principal one is "sucrose" ... derived primarily from sugar cane and sugar beets. Sucrose is also found in the sap of sugar maple trees, in sorghum, in carrots, and, of course, in sugar bowls throughout the world. No matter where it comes from, one sucrose crystal is indistinguishable from another.

Because sugar cane requires a semitropical climate in which to grow, sugar beets are of increasing importance as the countries of the temperate zones find their needs for sugar expanding.

Like most crops, sugar beets are usually planted in the spring, and then harvested at the end of the growing season. At that time, the foot-long wedge-shaped, silverish-white root weighs about two pounds, and has the equivalent of about 14 teaspoonsful of sugar in it.

Efforts to grow and process sugar beets were made earlier in New England's history. Abolitionists, protesting the importation of slave-produced cane sugar, built sugar beet processing plants in Massachusetts in the 1830's. These plants were apparently unable to compete successfully with the West Indian product, and were relatively shortlived.

Since then, times and techniques have changed. Now more than 60 sugar beet processing plants are in operation in the United States ... extracting and refining sugar from beets grown on over 1,000,000 acres of land in 22 states from Ohio to California. In 1963, the Nation's growers produced over 23 million tons of beets, while the industry marketed over 5½ billion pounds of refined sugar ... a little over one quarter of our total sugar requirements.

Sugar—Who Needs It?

The people of the world now use some 60 million tons of sugar a year. In the United States and many western countries, per capita consumption runs about 100 pounds, while in poorer countries it tends to be considerably less—ranging from under 1 pound per person in Nepal, through 61 in Russia, and 83 in Brazil. Production throughout the world during the past two years has been slightly less than consumption. Adverse weather ... drought in the USSR and hurricanes in Cuba ... reduced the Sino-Soviet Bloc's output, while free world production increased almost 4 million tons. As the world's population continues to grow, and living standards rise, the need for sugar moves apace.

Shifting Crystals

Like the potato, sugar is pretty much taken for granted. Yet sugar has probably been more closely controlled over a longer period of time than any other crop. As in most "sugar deficit" countries, the United States exercises control over both domestic production and imports. The effect of this is to maintain sugar prices at a sufficiently high level to make domestic sugar growing a profitable business. Early control of imports was largely through tariffs, but since the mid-1930's we have relied on a quota system. In fact, quota arrangements are so extensively used by the importing countries that only about 10 percent of the world's sugar ever reaches the world market as sugar-without-a-home.

Under our quota system, the Secretary of Agriculture estimates what the Nation's requirements for sugar will be during the following year, and then apportions this total between domestic suppliers—including Puerto Rico and the Virgin Islands—and some 25 foreign countries. The allocation of foreign quotas is determined according to historical export patterns and foreign policy considerations. In the past, about 40 percent of our total requirements came from foreign sources with Cuba supplying almost three-quarters of those imports. After trade with Cuba was suspended in the middle of 1960, our pattern of imports had to be modified. About half of Cuba's former quota was reallocated to other suppliers, while the remaining 1.5 million tons were set aside in an unassigned global quota. This has the effect of reserving this tonnage as an instrument of foreign policy in the event of Cuban disillusionment with Communism.

When the United States sought to replace the tonnage formerly supplied by Cuba by entering the world sugar market, the current tightness of the world supply was dramatically demonstrated: the wholesale price rose 50 percent over the level of the previous ten years.

Booming Beets

This situation resulted in a push by the domestic sugar industry for more "at home" production—and in 1962, Congress amended the Sugar Act of 1948 increasing the domestic producers' share of the market.

Now the Secretary of Agriculture estimates requirements by applying the earlier 60:40 allocation of shares between domestic and foreign suppliers to the basic 1963 U. S. consumption. The tonnage required in excess of that base is to be divided so that 65 percent will be furnished by domestic producers. Three-fourths of this increased allocation is to come from sugar beet sources, and one-fourth from cane.

As a further inducement to the expansion of the sugar beet industry, Congress decided that acreage for new sugar beet production should be established each year through 1966 sufficient to yield 65,000 tons of raw sugar annually. This increase in the beet industry's allotment is to be awarded by the Secretary of Agriculture with preference given to growers in new areas who will be supplying new

SOURCES OF U. S. SUGAR FOR 1964

Mainland Beet	2,698,600
Mainland Cane	911,400
Hawaii	1,110,000
Puerto Rico	965,000
Virgin Islands	15,800
Total Domestic	5,700,800
Republic of the Phillippines	1,137,900
Dominican Republic	343,900
Mexico	313,500
Peru	220,300
Australia	215,400
Brazil	182,400
South Africa	122,200
British West Indies	117,100
India	116,500
Other 15 Countries	452,500
Unallocated	877,500
Grand Total	9,800,000

refining plants. This acreage from the reserve, once allocated, is to become a permanent part of our domestic capacity, and will be included in all future determinations of domestic production quotas. To give them a good start, new allotments are guaranteed against serious cutbacks for a three-year period.

So far, the government has been highly successful in matching needs and supplies. The effectiveness of the import control system, which in effect regulates prices, is indicated by the stability of sugar beet prices from 1949 to 1961. In that period the price per ton of sugar beets varied only from $10.80 to $12.00.

The future yield is, of course, another matter. It is currently estimated that improved seed as well as better growing techniques and cultural practices are capable of increasing production by some 50,000 tons of sugar annually on acreage now under cultivation. Since the country's sugar requirements are increasing by about 150,000 tons each year—with around 76,000 tons of this scheduled to come from sugar beet producers—the capacity built into the industry by the reserve program seems to provide an excess of about 44,000 tons, if this rate of "technological expansion" continues. Ordinarily, this excess supply would result in the imposition of proportionate shares—that is, acreage controls—on the industry.

Until the world supply-demand situation gets back on a more even keel however, such action seems unlikely.

Cane and Codfish

New England consumers are currently served by two cane refineries. Although some cane sugar from other areas does move into the area, the amount is negligible. Until very recently, no beet sugar has been sold here. As a result of the region's distance from suppliers combined with the limited number of refineries, the price of sugar has tended to be somewhat higher in New England than in other parts of the country.

New Englanders use about 850 million pounds of sugar each year with a little over half of that going into commercial channels. A preliminary survey made to support Aroostook's application for a sugar beet allotment indicates that commercial usage in the Boston area alone amounts to almost twice as much of the types and grades of sugar as the Maine refinery would produce.

Sugar beets are probably the surest crop a grower can produce for a cash return. Not only are the returns relatively high per acre... but the contract between the grower and the refinery is practically "money in the bank," barring outright crop failure. Estimates from growing trials completed in Aroostook indicate that, given a quota, producers should net around $70 per acre from beet operations. Top yields in both beet tonnage and sugar content could increase this figure to the $100 per acre range.

Added to this high level of profitability is the bonus of income stability sugar beets provide, as contrasted with the expectations from potatoes.

In all, the sugar industry should supplement the $40 million potato crop by adding about $5.5 million to Maine's $190 million farm marketings. By-product sales—largely beet pulp and molasses—could contribute another $1 million to the economy.

It's obvious that sugar beet operations should be attractive to other agricultural areas—and Arizona, Minnesota, North Dakota, and Texas growers are competing with Aroostook for acreage allotments. The Department of Agriculture must choose among them and is expected to announce the allocation of the two remaining acreage quotas in April.

The Aroostook Gambit

With so much to gain, the county has made an all-out effort in its application for an acreage allotment. "All-out," not only in the sense that it has tried hard to come up with the very best answers to all of the questions on the application forms, but, more significantly perhaps, in the sense that growers, potato people, banks, local and state government people, railroad people, equipment people... all have worked and contributed to put Aroostook in the sugar beet business.

Test conducted in cooperation with the University of Maine show that sugar beet yields well above the national average are possible in the area.

Special legislation was enacted to extend the loan capacity of the Maine Industrial Building Authority to allow an $8 million first mortgage loan guarantee for plan construction. Promise of second mortgage financing up to $6.9 million has been obtained from the Area Redevelopment Administration. To complete the construction financing, growers and industry sources have oversubscribed a $2.6 million issue of third mortgage bonds.

The favorable production results, the firm commitments for financing, the enthusiastic cooperation of the area—led to an agreement on the part of one of the country's major beet processors to provide the required working capital and to operate the refining plant.

If all goes well, the sugar beet may, indeed, be Aroostook's "Sweet" potato!*

[Editor's Note]: In 1965, the U.S. Department of Agriculture alloted to Maine 33,000 acres for sugar beets. A $17,000,000 refinery has been constructed by Fred Vahlsing. In 1966, only 3200 acres were harvested. In 1967 and 1968, this was substantially increased. Yet, whether Maine keeps its allotment and finally becomes a successful sugar beet raising State depends on the willingness of Maine farmers to avail themselves of this significant new development. The outcome is by no means certain.

CHAPTER

35.

As industrialism in a small measure came to Maine, so too did the union movement. A much neglected subject in Maine history, labor has finally found an historian, Professor Charles Scontras of the University of Maine. The following is an account of the political activities of the Knights of Labor, a forerunner of the A.F. of L.

ORGANIZED LABOR AND POLITICS IN THE 1880's*
by
Charles A. Scontras

The Knights of Labor are going to be a powerful factor in the next State election and both parties are coquetting for their support.

Into the present campaign in Maine a new element has entered. For the first time a labor organization of unknown strength but powerful in point of numbers is in the field and has announced its intention of taking part in the election.

It was inevitable that the Knights of Labor would enter politics, for the reforms proposed by the Order presupposed political and legislative action for their realization. The basic question was whether the Knights in Maine would enter the political arena as a pressure group, or whether they would form a labor party as a means of attaining their objectives. They tried the former with some degree of success. Those who were not satisfied with "moderate" gains drifted into independent political action, specifically in the form of the Union Labor Party and then the Populist Party.

The Knights of Labor, representing as they did individuals from various segments of society, were theoretically well structured to foster political education and political action in the interests of labor. The mixed assembly gave numerical strength and cut across narrow class lines. These same characteristics made the mixed assembly suited to the activities of striking, boycotting, and forming cooperatives. In the constitution of 1879, the basic regulations concerning the behavior of the Knights in political activity were set forth:

A district assembly or a local assembly under the general assembly may take such political action as will tend to advance the interests of the Order or the cause of labor. But when political action is contemplated, the regular business of the district assembly or the local assembly shall be concluded, and the district assembly or the local assembly regularly closed. Local assemblies may properly use their political power in all legislative elections, and it is left to the discretion of each local assembly to act with that party through which it can gain most. An assembly shall not take political action unless three-fourths of the attending members are united in supporting such action. No members, however, shall be compelled to vote with the majority.

The Order in Maine did not formally endorse any particular party, nor was it bound by the political views of any of its individual members. A legislative committee to exert influence upon the Legislature in behalf of labor reform was created.

That the Knights in Maine would take an interest in politics was not surprising; not only because legislative action was necessary for labor reform, but also because many Knights had been Greenbackers.

When the Greenback Party declined in Maine, many of the Greenbackers and labor reformers responded to a call for the formation of a People's Party in Maine organized on October 7, 1884. Ossian C. Phillips, later District Master Workman, joined, as did others who would become members of the Knights. The People's Party was designed to bring together the two factions of the Greenback Party, i.e. the "Straights" and "Fusionists" and the various labor reformers. The bitterness between the two factions had eroded the power of the Greenback movement and forced some labor supporters to stand aloof from both sides. The factionalism encouraged laborers to remain with the major

---

*From: Charles A. Scontras, *Organized Labor and Labor Politics in Maine*, 1880-1890, Orono: University of Maine Press, 1966. pp. 16-47. Reprinted by permission of the publisher.

parties. It was hoped that the new party would attract laborers by "voicing every demand of organized labor."

The call for the convention of the People's Party was addressed to "all voters who believe that labor, the creator of values, is entitled to and should receive a just share of the wealth which it creates..." and who felt that they had been deprived of a fair share of production by the corrupt major parties. It sought the support of those voters who adhered to the doctrine that the government had the exclusive right to establish and issue legal tender money to the people; and finally, the appeal advocated economy in government, equal and exact administration of justice, and an end to special privilege. The People's Party failed to swing many voters to Benjamin Butler and the West in the general election. He received only 3,952 votes. By the time of the next election in 1886 it had disappeared. Also, the Greenbackers of the State failed to present a ticket. It was against such a background that the Knights of Labor assumed the leadership of political reform on behalf of labor.

Many who joined the Order during its period of rapid growth recognized its political significance. One Knight wrote to Powderly:

> We are sorry to say that we are unfortunate enough to have a number of politicians in our assembly from whom we apprehend some trouble. We have been growing so fast that we (have) not had the opportunity to educate the members as they should be, and you can understand how easy it is for a few scheming men to lead them astray.

When asked for advice as to how to proceed, Powderly succinctly replied, "Watch them."

The State Convention of the Knights in January, 1886, took formal action to prevent political infiltration. District Master Workman Ossian C. Phillips warned the delegates to be on guard against those who joined the Order, not for principle, but because "they think they see a chance to obtain our assistance in some political or business enterprise for their own selfish ends." Probably with the intent of preventing those with political motivations from manipulating the Order, the Maine Knights passed a resolution in January, 1886, instructing the Executive Board to ascertain on the first of each month whether any Local Assembly attached to the District Assembly had on its rolls a large number of persons who were not wage workers as required by the constitution of the Knights of Labor, and to report at each meeting of the District Assembly the names of any locals that were guilty of violation.

On the state and national levels, attempts to organize labor reforms parties largely gave way to "fusionist" politics; on the local level labor frequently presented its own slate of candidates. But even in the latter case, fusion was not unknown.

The municipal elections in the spring of 1886 gave an indication of the potential strength of the Order in the State and Congressional elections. In Bath the Knights were relatively unsuccessful in their attempt to elect Charles A. Pattern, a Democrat, as mayor. In Gardiner, where the Knights were reported to be in "controlling force," they nominated and elected the Prohibitionist Joseph E. Ladd as mayor. Ladd was successful in gaining a second term. In Rockland, Alexander A. Beaton, later District Master Workman, lost the mayorality campaign to a Democrat in a close election, but was elected Clerk of the city. Oliver Otis, another prominent Knight, was elected auditor for the city. In Lewiston, the Knights were also unsuccessful in the mayorality race, but undoubtedly many of them voted for the victorious Democrat and labor reformer D.J. McGillicuddy. In Auburn, Knights Rodney Foss, Secretary of the District Assembly, was chosen clerk; Charles S. Yeaton was chosen president of the Common Council; and Isaac W. Harris was elected alderman.

In Camden the Knights elected Daniel Andrews third selectman and Orris B. Wooster, prominent labor politician, as auditor and member of the school committee. All other candidates lost. In Oxford the Knights elected their entire slate, while reports from Richmond and Minot indicated some success. The extent of the Knights' success was dramatized when a newspaper reported that the "...potency of the Knights of Labor in local (Waterville) politics has incited other secret societies to try their hands (at it)..." The foregoing examples are illustrative of the political activities of the Knights in early 1886.

The major parties began working for the support of the Knights before their conventions were held later in 1886. A dispatch to the *Daily Eastern Argus* noted the irony of the actions of the Republicans, who on the one hand appealed for labor's support, while on the other, through its leadership and press, attempted to break up the Order.

Both parties included labor planks in their platforms. Of the two groups, the Democrats made the stronger commitment. Its platform provided:

> *Resolve,* that the Democratic party as in the past, so in the present, is the friend of labor and the laboring man, and sympathizes with labor in the impending struggle for its rights against aggressive capital and associated wealth; that it is in favor of all legislation which will tend to an equitable distribution of property, to the prevention of monopoly and to strict enforcement of individual rights against corporate abuses; and especially favors enactment of laws by which labor associations may be organized for arbitration of all differences between employed and employer; for the establishment of co-operative institutions; for introduction of a co-operative industrial system; for the establishment of a national bureau of labor for reserving what is left of the public domain for actual settlers, that the lands of the people may be held by the many and not the few; for abolition of that relic of barbarism, imprisonment for debt; for repeal of the odious trustee process by which a heartless creditor may snatch the wages of a laborer from the hand of his employer before it can be converted into bread for his wife and children.
>
> *Resolve,* that we oppose the system of long hours of labor in many of the factories and workshops in this state, and favor the enactment of a uniform ten-hour law. . . .

The Republicans stressed their general sympathies for labor, and then passed the following resolves:

> *Resolve,* that labor and capital must be in harmony to insure the prosperity of either. Every conflict between the two tends to the injury of both, and wherever differences arise, we believe that they should be submitted to impartial arbitration, to the end that friendly adjustment may be properly reached and suffering to all classes prevented.
>
> *Resolve*, that in the judgment of the convention, no manufacturing establishment in Maine should extend the length of a day's labor beyond ten hours.
>
> Recommends a revision of the prison labor system, so as not to compete with the honest calling of any citizen.

The Democratic Party clearly presented a more inclusive and militant program patterned on a class appeal.

Individual Republicans, in running for office, sometimes went beyond the Party's commitment. Joseph Bodwell of Hallowell, granite quarry owner, and candidate for Governor, advocated a ten-hour law, abolition of imprisonment for debt, and repeal of the trustee process. Whether he was sincere is debatable.

Because organized labor was a new dimension in Maine politics, it was uncertain what its political strength, strategy, and success would be. *The Portland Advertiser* estimated the strength of the Order to be 35,000 in August of 1886, and sought to compute mathematically its voting strength.

> The whole vote cast at the last gubernatorial election was 142,107. With one-quarter of the voters of Maine already in the labor organization, and with the prospect that before another year the fraction will be increased to nearly one-half, it is easily seen what a power in politics the organization might be made should the reins be allowed to pass into the hands of politicians.

The Industrial Journal took issue with the *Advertiser's* assessment of the political importance of the Order in Maine and prophetically asserted that the influence of the Knights was " . . . largely imaginary . . . destined to be slight, and short-lived." Even assuming the membership figures cited by the *Portland Advertiser* to be correct, the *Industrial Journal* recognized that the large number of women and unnaturalized citizens within the Order would subtract from its voting strength. Of the remaining twenty-five percent or more who were eligible to vote, the *Journal* argued that they had " . . . no sympathy whatever with the leaders of the movement or their aims." Thus loyalty and allegiance to the traditional parties were assured. In any event, the *Journal* continued, should 35,000 Knights vote as their leaders dictated, the Maine voters would vote "almost to a man" against the Knights of Labor. The candidate who endorsed the Knights of Labor was inviting failure, for the Knights were engaged in warfare against the most important and sacred rights of workingmen—"the right of any man to earn his livelihood by honest labor, under such conditions as he may choose."

Although the *Industrial Journal* relentlessly opposed the Knights of Labor, it recognized the political consequences of the labor protest and thus counseled candidates seeking election " . . . to lay special stress upon their sympathy with the workingmen and their intention to see to it, that, so far as their action may count, his right will be promoted and maintained."

The forces of labor, however, produced their own aspirants for political honors. Delegates from the local assemblies of the third district initiated the movement for active political participation. They met in Waterville on June 26th to consider the advisability of taking political action, deciding, finally, upon a policy of fusion by nominating the Democratic candidate, Joseph E. Ladd for Congress.

In the second district, labor reformers had issued a call for a mass labor congressional convention to meet at Auburn on July 22nd, for the purpose of nominating a candidate for Congress. Notable Knights in attendance were: acting chairman, and one of "the principle movers" of the call, Alexander A. Beaton of Rockland, Isaac W. Harris of Auburn, William H. Simmons of Rockland, a perennial candidate of the labor ticket throughout the eighties, and Rodney Foss of Auburn, District Secretary, who served as secretary at the labor convention. There were, no doubt, many other Maine Knights among the fifty delegates present.

Since the mass convention was poorly attended, it voted to issue a new call for a delegate convention to meet August 5, 1886. The Knights felt that the "mass convention" had not been adequately advertised and that people of the rural districts knew nothing of it. Perhaps a more important reason for dissolving the convention was the dissension caused by the efforts of some to manipulate the nominating process. The *Maine State Press* was of the opinion that the real Knights of Labor in Auburn were strongly opposed to congressional political action and that it had " . . . been engendered by (Democratic) politicians of Lewiston . . . who care nothing whatever for the 'poor laboring man,' but are taking this method, as a last resort, to defeat (the Republican candidate) Mr. Dingley." The Knights as a body did not endorse the meeting.

The labor convention met as rescheduled amidst new political charges that the Knights of Labor movement was being manipulated " . . . by a few disappointed Democrats, so-called, and a number of Republican and Greenback wire-pullers, who were unabled to join the Knights of Labor when it was in its infancy." Such charges were common and verified in large measure by the fact that many of the Knights had been Greenbackers. When the convention adopted resolutions favoring the traditional position of the Greenback party on monetary policy, the political complexion of the convention became more obvious. The convention also denounced the importation of foreign labor. Although resolutions concerning child labor and the ten-hour law had been introduced, the Chairman of the Resolutions Committee ruled that such issues were matters for the State Legislature. The mass convention was convened specifically for the purpose of nominating a Congressman from the second district.

The convention then turned to the task of naming its congressional candidate. William T. Eustis, prohibitionist from Dixfield was nominated by Charles S. Emerson, a Knight from Auburn. Alexander A. Beaton was placed in nomination by William Simmons of Rockland. Many Knights of Labor who were present preferred Beaton, but since the Order had not formally endorsed the meeting, the other delegates favored Eustis. In the official tally, Eustis received eighty votes, Beaton thirty-two, with one each for Alonzo Garcelon and Nelson Dingley, the nominees of the Democratic and Republican parties.

The *Portland Advertiser* charged that "the so-called labor convention," by adopting Greenback monetary resolutions and nominating a Prohibition candidate, did not endorse the Knights of Labor movement. "These are subjects," argued the *Advertiser,* "with which the Knights of Labor do not meddle." This was true, in part. Not only did the Knights refuse to formally support the Auburn convention, but they also refused to endorse the principles of prohibition. The Knights of Labor did have an interest in currency reform, however, and the currency plank adopted at the Auburn convention was almost identical to that contained in the declaration of principles of the Order.

About 300 labor reformers from the first district met in convention in Portland on August 24th to nominate their candidate for Congress. Charles E. Halliday of Saccarappa, a prominent Knight, was chosen to preside. W.F. Eaton, of Cape Elizabeth, Treasurer of the Knights of Labor District Assembly, was the most notable Knight serving on the Committee on Resolutions. The Convention nominated labor leader Daniel O. Moulton of Falmouth.

The preamble and resolutions adopted by the convention included all those principles and demands upon which the Knights of Labor in the nation, and in the state, had been founded. A resolution endorsing the candidates of the two major parties who showed greatest interest in the principles declared at the convention was indefinitely postponed by a vote of 70 to 20.

As the election approached, efforts were made to assess the labor vote and the political entanglement occasioned by the labor movement. *The Industrial Journal* remarked:

> This so-called labor element—composed of doctors, ministers, tradesmen, political bummers and loafers as well as laborers, with a large sprinkling of women and children—has caused the two political parties so much uneasiness that in order to secure the vote real and imaginary which it controls, their leaders have practically announced their willingness to support all the measures it demands. In fact, each party seems to be endeavoring to outbid its rival in the price it is willing to pay for the support of this element.

The *Journal* became more concerned as election day approached. It identified the Knights of Labor with industrial depressions, social anarchy, riots and bloodshed, and tried to warn the citizens of the state "that a very serious danger menaces the State the the Republic." The time had arrived to choose men from the ranks of both traditional parties which would "consider the interests of the whole people as more important than the imaginary wants of a small faction." Advising against bolting the two party system, the *Journal* argued that "the duty of the hour" called for united action against the new social forces.

The *Daily Kennebec Journal* was not as alarmed as the *Industrial Journal*: "... the labor vote does not look more promising than the Greenback vote in 1884." Yet it reminded its readers that it was "an unknown quantity." It was precisely this element of uncertainty that frequently caused anxiety among the sensitive political observers.

Ralph Beaumont of New York, Chairman of the Congressional Legislative Committee of the Knights of Labor, traveled through Maine during the election year and gave the Maine Knights the benefit of his oratorical abilities. Beaumont had been in Maine on previous occasions, supporting Benjamin Butler and organizing local assemblies for the Order. Addressing "at least 3,000 Knights of Labor," on Peaks Island, he criticized James G. Blaine for referring to the eighteen planks of the Knights of Labor platform as "side issues;" and argued against protectionist principles. Of Thomas B. Reed, Beaumont said: "... he is corporation every time ... there isn't a man in the United States who is now running for Congress whose election would be so dangerous to the labor cause ..." Beaumont was apprehensive about the possibility of Reed's election, for if the Republicans carried the House of Representatives, Beaumont was certain that Reed would become its Speaker, with the consequence that every committee would reflect the interests of corporations. Beaumont continued this general line of attack against Reed in Cumberland Mills, Brunswick, and undoubtedly elsewhere in the first district. Beaumont, as chairman of the Congressional Legislative Committee of the Order, had had frequent contact with Reed and feared the consequences of his election.

The results of the election of 1886 were not particularly encouraging for the labor candidates as Table I indicates:

On the State level, the Knights sent a number of labor reformers to the Legislature. Most notable among them were Republican Representatives Thomas J. Lyons of Vinalhaven and John H. Eells of Camden. In the Senate, the Knights of Labor were represented by Democrats Stephen J. Gushee of Appleton and Harry A. Weymouth of Saco.

Clearly, the labor forces of Maine were not united in political action. Some played the game of fusion when they thought it was to their best interest. But fusion was not acceptable to other labor leaders as events were to show.

The Union Labor Party was the solution for those labor leaders who disliked fusion. The first

TABLE I

NAME	PARTY	DISTRICT	VOTE
Thomas B. Reed	Republican	First	15,486
W.H. Clifford	Democratic	First	14,298
T.B. Hussey	Prohibition	First	756
D.O. Moulton	Labor	First	328
Nelson Dingley, Jr.	Republican	Second	18,137
Alonzo Garcelon	Democratic	Second	11,930
William T. Eustis	Prohibition and Labor	Second	3,939
Seth L. Milliken	Republican	Third	17,992
Joseph E. Ladd	Democratic	Third	12,781
H.H. Harvey	Prohibition	Third	761
....	Labor	Third	......
C.A. Boutelle	Republican	Fourth	17,372
John F. Lynch	Democratic	Fourth	13,657
C.S. Pitcher	Prohibition	Fourth	685
....	Labor	Fourth	......

information concerning the birth of the Union Labor Party was given by the Lewiston Labor *Advocate* in December of 1886 when it announced

> ... that a new party is about to arise in this State, which will include all the Butler men of 1884, and those Straight Greenbackers who voted for Solon Chase in 1882. The platform is to be the platform of the Knights of Labor with a few additions.

The new movement was launched in the same month at Prospect, in Waldo County, under the leadership of Thomas Clark and one hundred and seven "fishermen, sailors, farmers, mechanics and laboring men of all trades." A committee was appointed to coordinate activities in the counties. Although the elections were two years away, the organizers were determined to establish a solid basis. The Union Labor Party as a national organization originated in the summer of 1886. At that time the Chicago Express issued a call to the Knights of Labor, the Farmers' Alliance, Grangers, Greenbackers, and Anti-Monopolists, which brought about a convention and the Union Labor Party in February, 1887. The program of the new party contained only two provisions that were new to the Knights of Labor—woman suffrage and the direct election of U.S. Senators.

In the interim before elections in 1888, further agitation came through the formation of the Land and Labor Clubs based upon Henry George's theories of taxation. The first such Club was organized in Portland in January, 1887. The Club distributed literature on the single tax rather widely, and also sought to have Henry George visit Maine in the interest of his cause. Plans for forming a second club at Lewiston were made, and rumors prevailed that other Maine cities had sent in applications for charters.

Meanwhile, the Knights of Labor as a national organization had focused on Reed and Blaine again. Newspapers were reporting that Powderly would not continue in his office in the October meeting of the General Assembly. It was Powderly's intention, the reports show, to take an extended tour through the State of New York "... where he will take the stump for the purpose of beating James G. Blaine and the Republican Party in 1888." Powderly was preparing to attack Blaine on the tariff question should Blaine receive the nomination for the presidency in 1888.

Organization of the Union Labor Party in Maine was completed in 1888. A preliminary meeting of labor leaders in Augusta issued a call for a mass convention to be held at Waterville on June 12, 1888. The call was addressed "... to all voters, who are opposed to the hypocrisy of old party rule, monopoly, trusts, caste, corruption at the polls and class legislation ..." The purpose of the mass convention was to nominate candidates for governor and Congress and adopt a platform of principles. The preliminary conference had chosen H.S. Hobbs, a prominent Knight from Rockland, as a delegate to the National Union Labor Party Convention held on May 15, 1888, in Cincinnati. On his return from the Union Labor National Convention, Hobbs reported that there were few delegates from the east—most of the delegates representing western and southwestern states. Hobbs undertook to organize the Union Labor Party in Maine and met with apparent success.

The mass convention scheduled for Waterville on June 12 was transformed into the Union Labor Party. Though some Knights opposed the organization of an independent party, other members of the Order were active in the convention. All officers and candidates were Knights of Labor. Frank A. Howard was elected chairman, and Alden H. Wooster was chosen secretary. William H. Simmons of Rockland was nominated by acclamation as the candidate for governor, while Dexter W. Smith, editor of the Lewiston *Labor Advocate*, along with H.S. Hobbs, both Knights, were nominated electors at large. Charles E. Halliday of Saccarappa was chosen elector from the first district, while J.L. Cummings of South Paris and George W. Gillette of Gardiner were selected as electors from the second and third districts. Candidates for Congress from the second and third districts were E.A. Howard of Bath and F.A. Howard of Belfast.

The convention adopted a platform favoring a national monetary system, an income tax and service pensions, favored greenback postal banks, government telegraph and railroad service, secret ballot, homestead laws, denounced the importation of foreign labor, declared in favor of a per capita distribution of the surplus revenue, and declared against fusion with either of the two dominant parties.

The following day Volney B. Cushing of Bangor, member of the Prohibition State Committee and Prohibition candidate for governor, appeared before the convention and sought fusion of the two parties, claiming that they were similar in their ideas!! But with advocates of independent labor politics were not in sympathy with the fusion.

The Union Labor Party perfected its organization in thirteen counties. William H. Simmons, the candidate for governor, reported Maine to be the only New England state to have a ticket in the field. He expected to poll about 5,000 to 7,000 votes, and he said, "Thus in time we shall be one of the predominating parties in this state. After the state election we propose to perfect our organization in every town and hamlet in the state."

Another element in the campaign of 1888 was the attempt of the major parties to attract labor support. Alexander Beaton reported to Powdery in June that "the Democrats are very friendly to me while I never voted the ticket in my life." As District Master Workman, Beaton felt that he could not attempt a nomination on any ticket, for a nomination would "... be construed by the people as an affiliation with the party nominating me and D.A. 86 would also be construed as an annex—which I cannot—aye will not permit." Of the Republican Party, Beaton informed Powdery that "leading Republicans" sought his withdrawal from the Knights of Labor and offered him high positions within the Republican ranks. Beaton gave his appraisal of the Republican Party when he wrote:

> ...In fighting the battles of organized labor I have endeavored to show the people of Maine the shallowness of the pretense that the Republican Party was friendly to labor and have thus incurred the eternal enmity of the Republican Party and as far as is concerned the Democratic Party as well.

Beaton had issued a scathing address to the Republican Party because of its legislative performance on labor reform in 1887. This was the theme of his address to the Knights of Labor delegates assembled in convention in January 1888. It contributed to resentment on the part of the Republican Knights who formed a "large majority" of the delegates present, and doubtless contributed to the movement for the Union Labor Party.

Labor leaders had good reason to be disappointed about the election returns. The Union Labor Party's ineffectiveness at the polls was obvious: [Table II].

Some Democratic sources were of the opinion that the Union Labor Party was put into the field

TABLE II

NAME	PARTY	DISTRICT	VOTE
For Governor:			
Edwin C. Burleigh	Republican		79,401
William L. Putnam	Democratic		61,348
V.B. Cushing	Prohibition		3,109
William H. Simmons	Labor		1,526
For Congress:			
Thomas B. Reed	Republican	First	18,288
William Emery	Democratic	First	15,849
T.B. Hussey	Prohibition	First	829
....	Labor	First	......
Nelson Dingley, Jr.	Republican	Second	21,075
Charles E. Allen	Democratic	Second	15,614
E.A. Howard	Labor	Second	782
William T. Eustis	Prohibition	Second	731
Seth L. Milliken	Republican	Third	30,562
S.S. Brown	Democratic	Third	14,026
B.S. Kelly	Prohibition	Third	537
F.A. Howard	Labor	Third	352
C.A. Boutelle	Republican	Fourth	19,823
T.J. Stewart	Democratic	Fourth	15,481
John Barker	Prohibition	Fourth	973
....	Labor	Fourth	......

as part of the Republican Party strategy, particularly after the Union Labor Party failed to score any significant success in the State elections. The Rockland *Opinion* wrote that the Union Labor Party " ... ticket was run solely in the interest of the Republicans ... " and that the character of the new party was revealed " ... by the fact that the whole strength of it was directed to this county (Knox), the only county in the state that it could give to the Republicans." The paper charged that the leaders of the Union Labor Party did not vote the ticket, and those that had generally led in the movement had never done any creditable work in the cause of labor. The true workers for labor reform, argued the *Opinion,* were to be found within the ranks of the two party system, and that independent labor politics had set back the cause of labor reform. The position of the *Opinion,* a Democratic newspaper and strong supporter of the Knights of Labor objectives, illustrates how the forces of labor were split on political action. Such dissenters merely diluted the political power of labor.

Another Democratic source also analyzed the Union Labor Party movement as a political conspiracy. It charged that the Union Labor Party was placed in the field by the Republicans in 1888 " ... by trading with several of the more prominent agitators at Augusta, and contributing a fund for the traders' and dickers' sole benefit," and that "when the Republican politicians decide that this faction is no longer necessary for their salvation, it will go as the Greenback party did."

Ralph Beaumont, once more in the State of Maine, wrote very discouragingly of the desire for reform among the people of Maine. In his judgment, they were suffering from mental slavery. Beaumont did not see politics in Maine as centering around issues and principles. The firm base of the Republican Party discouraged adequate discussion of vital questions. It was probably because Beaumont was witnessing the decline of a great order that he spoke critically of Maine and the lack of interest of its citizens in political reform. His dismay with Maine was further revealed when he was discussing the rates charged between various points by the Boston and Maine Railroads—"A great big railroad monopoly":

> Now four-fifths of the people of Maine are farmers, and I am told that over one-half of the legislature of that State is composed of farmers, and they allow this corporation to charge them 4 cents per mile for riding on that road. Thomas Carlisle (Carlyle) once said that there were 17,000,000 people in England, principally fools. I should say that four-fifths of the people of Maine were farmers, principally fools.

Charles E. Allen gave a brief and succinct explanation of labor's lack of success in politics when he wrote there was " ... too much voting the Democratic ticket because it is Democratic, and the Republican ticket because it has been the Grand Old Party." The voting patterns of Maine laborers had been too well established, and lack of sufficient discontent, or the lack of greater aspirations, prevented a greater response along the lines of a single purpose party.

The Knights of Labor who favored independent political action were not discouraged. The Union Labor Party held a State Convention on May 20, 1890, in the City of Waterville. Eight counties were represented. F.A. Howard was elected chairman, while the editor of the Lewiston *Labor Advocate,* Dexter W. Smith, was chosen Secretary. Isaac C. Clark of Bangor was chosen as labor's candidate for governor, and Luther C. Bateman of East Searsmont was labor's choice for Congress from the third district. He was also the Prohibitionist's candidate for the third district, indicating a return to political fusion. Because of the lack of attendance from certain areas of the state, no other nominations were made in other districts at that time.

The platform adopted by the labor convention declared in favor of the establishment of a national monetary system; of distributing the surplus millions in the treasury among the people on a per capita basis; in favor of a savings bank institution for the use of people in connection with the post-office service; and government ownership and control of telegraph and transportation facilities. The platform declared itself against the granting of lands to corporations and the sale of lands to aliens. It favored a graduated income tax; opposed dealing in futures in agricultural products; declared in favor of strict enforcement of all statutes without discrimination for political purposes; favored pensions for soldiers and sailors who served in the Civil War; and the Australian ballot. It opposed contract labor and fusion with other parties.

While the Union Labor Party held its county conventions throughout the state, efforts again were made to bring the Union Labor Party within the ranks of the two party system. The Democratic Rockland *Opinion* admitted that the Union Labor Party held the balance of power in some localities. It pleaded for merger between the Union Labor Party and the Democratic Party, noting that "... the division between the Democracy and the U.L. party is not so deep and radical as that between the latter and the Republicans..." In fact, argued the *Opinion*, the "... parties are in purpose and principles to a great extent one: it is more a division of two Democratic parties than the formation of a new party..."

The Union Labor Party may have held the balance of power in some instances at the local and county level, but its efforts to secure votes at the state and national level were to no avail, as they could only secure a handful. Reform politics in the name of the Union Labor Party was a complete failure. [Table III]

With the growth and success of the Farmer Alliances of the West, and the rise of the Populist Party in the nation, a new dimension to reform politics emerged in the State of Maine. The possibility of union between the Knights of Labor and the Grangers in Maine was given some consideration by the Order in 1885. A writer from East Union felt the idea of union an "admirable one," but did not think the consolidation of the two organizations a wise one because:

> ...the methods of organization of the farmer are better suited to the needs of farmers and those of the latter (Knights) better adapted to the condition of mechanics and laborers in cities and villages. But it would be quite practicable for the orders to cooperate and practically unite in this work without merging the organizations.

To this end, the Knights of Labor passed a resolution in January, 1886, authorizing the legislative committee to cooperate with the Patrons of Husbandry. The Patrons of Husbandry of Maine expressed sympathy for the Knights of Labor but declined to merge with the Order. While they recognized the existence of certain common goals, the Grangers insisted that the two organizations were not identical, and that "...we must not lose sight of the fact that an unfair, uncompromising and unnecessary warfare against capital is injurious to every interest." Farmers in Maine joined the Knights of Labor movement, however, and in some areas formed local assemblies.

TABLE III

NAME	PARTY	DISTRICT	VOTE
For Governor:			
Edwin C. Burleigh	Republican		64,259
W.P. Thompson	Democratic		45,360
Aaron Clark	Prohibition		2,981
I.C. Clark	Labor		1,296
For Congress:			
Thomas B. Reed	Republican	First	16,797
M.P. Frank	Democratic	First	11,971
T.B. Hussey	Prohibition	First	557
D.G. Weeks	Labor	First	51
Nelson Dingley, Jr.	Republican	Second	16,499
Charles E. Allen	Democratic	Second	11,187
William H. Foster	Prohibition	Second	745
....	Labor	Second	......
Seth L. Milliken	Republican	Third	14,477
Charles Baker	Democratic	Third	11,011
Luther Bateman	Prohibition Labor (fusion)	Third	995
C.A. Boutelle	Republican	Fourth	15,716
Josiah Crosby	Democratic	Fourth	11,144
V.B. Cushing	Prohibition	Fourth	962
....	Labor	Fourth	......

Ralph Beaumont, now a very familiar person in the state, was sent into New England by the Secretary of the National Farmers' Alliance to create local branches of that organization. Beaumont and "sockless" Jerry Simpson of Kansas visited Maine in March of 1891. In Portland, Simpson informed his audience of some of the purposes and goals of the National Farmers' Alliance; an economical government, free silver coinage, prohibition of alien ownership of lands, government control of transportation and communications, an income tax, return of land from railroads, the reduction of all national and state taxes to a minimum, and the direct election of U. S. Senators.

On September 8, 1891, seventy-five delegates representing twelve counties met in Lewiston to launch the People's Party in Maine. A committee appointed by the National Convention in Cincinnati, consisting of H.S. Hobbs, Frank A. Howard, and D.W. Smith, directed the formation of the new party. Alexander A. Beaton, District Master Workman of the Knights of Labor in Maine, was made Chairman, and D.G. Richards and N.W. Lermond were chosen Secretaries. A State Committee consisting of three members from each county was formed. The names of several Knights were included. The platform adopted by the assembly of reformers was that of the National Convention of the People's Party which had met at Cincinnati. The *Maine State Press* summarized the political complexion of the new organization:

> It was a strange and suggestive assembly. The grey heads and grizzly beards of the remnants of the old Greenback party made up the larger part of the assembly, while the younger and more aggressive element seemed to be furnished by those who belong to what little labor agitation there is in Maine.
> ...In short, it was a regular reunion of the old guard Greenbackers, who have kept the fires of their faith in cheap money burning for a dozen years, and now come out in response to the slogan cry of the Alliance in the West. It must be admitted that the old fellows seemed as full of ginger as in the days when the tramp of the cowhide boots was heard in the land.
> While the enthusiasm seemed to be furnished by the grizzled old Greenbackers, the direction of the meeting seemed to be in the hands of the younger Union Labor men ...

The paper reported that the old Greenbackers, with the memories of past victories in the State, expected to carry the State easily. But it noted that the younger Union Labor men were more conservative. "W.H. Simmons of Rockland, in the course of his speech, admitted that the laboring people of Maine were 'not hungry enough' to make the People's Party successful at once."

When the People's Party of Maine met in Gardiner on May 3, 1892, Alexander A. Beaton was again elected Chairman. D.G. Richards and N.W. Lermond were chosen Secretary and Assistant Secretary, respectively. Nearly 100 delegates were present at the convention, "including many prominent labor men."

The Populists in Maine drew up and adopted a platform endorsing that of the Industrial Conference held in St. Louis on February 22, 1892, but also added equal suffrage and prohibition planks. They nominated the Prohibitionist Luther C. Bateman for governor; I.C. Clark and W.H. Harris were chosen electors-at-large; while J.B. Swan of Camden, G.W. Soule of Livermore, William Hobbs of Milo, G.L. Walker of Biddeford, J.E. Canpion of Portland, William Harris of Auburn, and Henry Betts of Ellsworth were elected delegates-at-large to the National Convention at Omaha.

The Populist's chose D.O. Moulton of Gardiner, and O.D. Chapman of Plymouth as congressional candidates for the first, second, third, and fourth districts respectively.

The platform commitments of the Populist Party of Maine produced further dissension among labor reformers. A.F. Wooster, Secretary of the State Committee, issued a call for a state convention of the Union Labor Party to be held at Rockland on June 23, 1892, for the purpose of nominating a candidate for governor, choosing the state committee, presidential electors, and delegates to the Populist Convention in Omaha.

The call for the Union Labor Party was aimed primarily at the members of that organization, and at all voters who supported the National People's Party, but particularly those who were opposed to the action of the People's Party in their convention at Gardiner. The Union Labor Party opposed the Populist planks on woman suffrage and prohibition. It further opposed the nomination of a prohibitionist for Governor who did not identify himself with the Populists until just prior to the convention. The suffrage and prohibition questions had caused much friction at earlier national conventions and labor meetings, so it appears that the Union Labor Party wanted to avoid renewal of such conflicts. For these reasons the labor party bolted.

The Union Labor Party convention chose William H. Simmons as temporary chairman and nominated Edgar F. Knowlton of Auburn for governor, and the Rev. G.R. Sanford of Camden for congressman from the second district. For electors, the convention chose the following: William H. Simmons, Edgar F. Knowlton of Auburn, Marshall A. Ripley of Matinicus, Joseph Bradley of Union, A.R. Allen of Thomaston, and William M. Merrill of Berwick. The new State Committee consisted of Edgar F. Knowlton, William H. Simmons, S.D. Sanford, and E.E. Chaples of Rockland. The delegates to the Omaha National Convention were W.H. Simmons, William P. Thurston, and W.A. Ripley of Rockland, George E. Church of Cherryfield, John M. Todd of Portland, M.M. Merrill of Berwick, J.S. Simmons of Gorham, S.D. and G.R. Sanford, Roland Allen of Thomaston, and Marshall A. Ripley.

The platform of the St. Louis Industrial Conference was adopted, and resolutions were passed expressing the sentiment of the Union Labor Party on the issues of woman suffrage and prohibition.

The Union Labor Party further resolved that if their candidates for electors were elected, they were to cast their votes for the Presidential and Vice-Presidential candidates nominated by the Omaha Convention which was to meet on July 4, 1892. Thus, both state conventions had adopted the St. Louis platform, but the Populist Party had gone beyond the St. Louis commitments. As both state conventions chose delegates to the Omaha convention, a contest seemed inevitable, giving one or the other of the organizations the stamp of regularity. The Union Labor Party was, in essence, primarily a faction of the People's Party in the State. Its recognized standard bearer was William H. Simmons. At the Knox County convention of the Union Labor Party, H.S. Hobbs accused Simmons of causing the split at the instigation of one of the old parties—this was now a traditional charge where third parties were concerned. The convention endorsed the Omaha platform.

TABLE IV

NAME	PARTY	DISTRICT	VOTE
For Governor:			
H.B. Cleaves	Republican		67,900
C.F. Johnson	Democratic		55,397
T.B. Hussey	Prohibition		3,864
Luther Bateman	Populist		201
Edgar Knowlton	Labor		
For Congress:			
Thomas B. Reed	Republican	First	16,312
D.H. Ingraham	Democratic	First	14,635
W.A. Tucker	Prohibition	First	691
. . . .	Labor	First	. . . . . .
Nelson Dingley, Jr.	Republican	Second	17,194
D.J. McGillicuddy	Democratic	Second	13,546
N.W. Lermond	Populist	Second	1,193
Ammi S. Ladd	Prohibition	Second	803
G.R. Sanford	Labor	Second	99
Seth L. Milliken	Republican	Third	15,582
W.P. Thompson	Democratic	Third	13,700
G.W. Gillette	Populist	Third	883
A.D. Knight	Prohibition	Third	790
. . . .	Labor	Third	. . . . . .
C.A. Boutelle	Republican	Fourth	16,549
D.A.H. Powers	Democratic	Fourth	12,261
Ira G. Hersey	Prohibition	Fourth	1,277
O.D. Chapman	Populist	Fourth	550
. . . .	Labor	Fourth	. . . . . .

In August of 1892, E. Gerry Brown, a member of the People's Party national committee, visited Maine in behalf of the Populist movement. While in Knox County, he was informed by telegram that the National Committee would send its best speakers in the State, among whom were Edward Bellamy, Mrs. O.V. Treat, and H. Baldwin. But the Maine Populists needed more than oratorical assistance from some notable reformers. The election returns for 1892 again demonstrated the weakness of the third party movement in the State. [Table IV]

When the People's Party of Maine met in convention in March of 1894, Alexander Beaton again served as chairman. Also, the District Worthy Foreman of the Knights of Labor in Maine, A.W. Boynton of Augusta, served as chairman of the State Committee. Prohibitionist Luther C. Bateman was again nominated for governor, and the convention reaffirmed its position on Populist principles.

On June 5, 1894, M.J. Bishop, General Worthy Foreman of the Knights of Labor, was in Maine lecturing on the "money question" while the District Worthy Foreman of the Order, E.W. Boynton spoke of

> ...the folly of being any longer led astray by the delusive promises of the old political parties, and called upon all present to become active participants in the movement for a new industrial system.

Indeed, the vision of "a new industrial system" was what the decade of the eighties was all about, but Maine's rank and file were not seeking it through third party methods.

The Greenback Party was the last successful effort at reform politics. Remnants of the Greenbackers and labor reformers failed in their efforts to revive the spirit of political reform that characterized the late seventies.

CHAPTER

36.

Coastal Maine has long been a favorite of summer visitors. There is hardly a town along Maine's 1700 mile coast line which does not see its population rise significantly in June. The most famous of the Maine resort towns is Bar Harbor.

BAR HARBOR: THE SUMMER COLONY*
by
Richard W. Hale, Jr.

The summer colony of cottagers had become deeply rooted in Bar Harbor by 1890, though "cottage" may seem a misleading description of some of the houses that had been built. One such was Mrs. Bowler's "Chatwold," that had been passed on to Joseph Pulitzer, and to which had been added his famous but not too successful "tower of silence," where the almost blind old wizard of the newspaper world could be at peace from the noises that disturbed his sensitive ears. Another such, more modest by far but still hardly a cottage, was "Stanwood," from which James G. Blaine had opened his campaign for the Presidency in 1884, and which his biographer calls a "mansion." Yet others, built or building, were "Kennarden Lodge," first owned by John P. Kennedy and now by Mrs. John Dorrance; the Edgar Scott house, torn down after Major Scott's death in the Philippine Sea, in the tragic sinking of a Japanese prison ship by an American submarine; the Vanderbilt house at Point d'Acadie, still a center of hospitality, but in other hands; "Bogue Chitto," whose building by John A. Morris of Louisiana evoked a burst of applause in the *Mount Desert Herald;* and many another house to which the word "cottage" might not seem to apply.

Yet though it might seem, "mock humility," of which De Quincey wrote, to speak of a "cottage with a double coach house," in one sense of the word "cottage" still fitted the homes of the Bar Harbor summer colony. The old free-and-easy spirit of the first summer visitors still hung over its life—and, for that matter, it still does. On social matters no one, not even a historian looking back, can be authoritative. Every social group has its own estimate of its own importance, and will, automatically, disagree with any rating or estimate; just that sort of special reason probably brings that social group together. But it is possible to say that such and such a resort has such and such general reputation and shows such and such general tendencies. And with that point in mind, it is possible to say that Bar Harbor stood in the top rank in America in fashion—if that is the right word—and linked in popular estimation with Newport. Of all the summer resorts that were then fashionable, it had perhaps the easiest and most tolerant social life.

The reasons for this go back into the early history of the summer colony. As has been told, originally it had been a colony of artists and their friends, and of scientists and hunters. The pleasures of early days had been "rocking," sketching, and canoeing. The more permanent summer residents, as contrasted with those who came for short week-end trips, had first lived in hotels or near hotels, before moving into cottages that were true cottages. They had built up their social life on the assumption that anyone who took the trouble to make the then long trip to Mount Desert Island shared common interests and could be trusted to live up to common standards. Consequently, when whole families took to coming to Bar Harbor, the chaperonage rules of the Victorian era were

---

*Richard W. Hale, Jr., *The Story of Bar Harbor* (New York: Ives Washburn, Inc., 1949), pp. 167-189. Reprinted by permission of the publisher.

relaxed, though still formally in force. Girls were allowed to walk, drive, and canoe with young men far more readily than at home. For, as Robert Grant pointed out, in his "Plea for Bar Harbor" a tippy canoe was in itself a chaperone, which automatically prevented a young man from being too forward. Naturally enough, marriageable young women passed the word around, so that to Bar Harbor came the sort of person who wanted the combination of freedom and decorum to be found there. As the summer colony made itself permanent, it set up institutions that furthered this combination of decorum and ease. In their turn, those institutions preserved the old atmosphere for later times.

Prominent among those institutions were the old Oasis Club, which grew into the Reading Room, the Canoe Club, the Kebo Valley Club, the Pot and Kettle Club, and, later, the Swimming Club. Institutions—in another sense—were certain private houses, such as that of "Aunt Sue" Dimmock (Mrs. Henry F. Dimmock of Washington), where parties were traditional. Such houses, and the last three of the five clubs mentioned above, exist today, and the life of the summer colony can perhaps best be told in terms of the clubs, whose history is a matter of public record. But it should be realized that these were outward manifestations of an inward social life that cannot yet be recorded. Perhaps, when in the future some diarist publishes his or her Bar Harbor memories, or some novelist sets down the life of the present, we shall have such written record to go on. But until then, the story of the summer colony can be most fittingly told in terms of the institutions that have already directly or indirectly published accounts of themselves.

The Reading Room, historically the oldest of the meeting places, since it stems from the Oasis Club, was in its heyday much what the Reading Room at York Harbor is today. Originally, as the Oasis Club, it was a place where the men of the summer colony could be free from women's control and find newspapers and, in circumstances winked at by the county enforcement officials, liquid refreshment. In 1881 it moved from its original brown cottage to a new and more splendid building, designed by the Boston architect, William R. Emerson. This building has had an interesting subsequent history, having been taken over by the Maine Central Railroad and used first as a yacht club, then as the "Shore Club," and, finally, after a period as United States naval quarters in World War II, it now forms the base of the new hotel. In front of it stood a steel latticework pier, at which yachts could land their passengers, and on the upper level of which tea could be served. In front also stood a flag pole, that once, to the horror of all but one concerned, flew a Boer flag. The horror came from the presence, during the Boer War, of a visiting British squadron, mingling cordially with an American squadron. The flying of that flag, the angry representations of the American admiral, the indignation of the members of the "Gentleman's Club," and the expulsion of the offender, naturally became a front-page story in the press. And for many years, from 1881 to its collapse for financial reasons in 1921, the Reading Room served a useful purpose.

The economics of the Reading Room—all social institutions have an economic side—were simple. In days of low costs and plenty of visitors to Bar Harbor, the average summer resident of social standing was glad to pay ten dollars a year or so for a masculine hide-out, to which he could give his house guests a card, and which could contain a locker into which the sheriff might not inquire. And as long as these conditions existed, the Reading Room flourished. But when Maine's prohibition law was differently enforced, and when costs went up, the Reading Room was not worth the dues, and slowly sank away.

In the matter of prohibition and temperance Bar Harbor has seen fluctuations of opinion. In 1825 Elder Hunting founded the Mutual Temperance Society of Eden, with only fourteen members, against "much opposition ... even by Deacons and members of the church." By 1835, after the Elder had left town, it had 202 members. In the 1880's the Templars were strong, so strong that once, outraged by a drunken driving carriage accident they stormed through town forcing all liquor dealers to spill their stocks on the ground. Yet Sproul's Restaurant became nationally famous for the way it served wine in defiance of the "Maine Law," and by 1916 the *Bar Harbor Times* could editorially attack the appointment of sheriff's deputies as a waste of money since it was clear that they had no intention of earning their pay by enforcing the law.

Perhaps Bar Harbor's most typical club was the Canoe Club. For some reason unknown to present-day yachtsmen, men and girls who feared with reason the cold waters of Frenchman's Bay, and who refused to sail, confidently embarked in canoes, which cannot have been too safe, and paddled around among the Porcupines. Of course, it soon became a minor local industry to rove among the Porcupines in rowboats, rescuing those who had fallen overboard or who had forgotten that the tide rises and had left their canoes to float away while they explored an island. Just the same, it is amazing to look back at the years in which ladies now less young and never of the reckless type had their swains paddle them about Frenchman's Bay, and never thought it out of the ordinary. Such is the effect of fashion. It was the thing to paddle a canoe, and one did so. Almost the only legend left is not a canoeing but a boating one, of how X landed on what is now called Bald Rock—but was then known by three other names. Smullidges', from time immemorial, "Isola Bella" to the lady who had bought it to preserve it from the desecration of that name, and _____'s Rock to those who could not quite see "Isola Bella" as the name for a piece of granite off the Maine coast. Many a dinner party has been regaled by the story of how X's boat and his clothes floated away on the tide, and how he struggled after it, fearing telescopic observation and shivering every time a gust of a light norther blew the gunwale out of his grasp. The informal boating of those days soon became formalized. The ever-useful Rodick family had a site on Bar Island on which was established a canoe house, safely away from the waterfront of West Street and to be reached at low tide by a walk or carriage ride, at high tide by a fee and a ride in a hired boat. At the Club House were established the ever-present Indians of the Penobscot and Passamaquoddy tribes, who would give instructions in the fine art of paddling or themselves furnish propulsive power. And at least thrice a year, the ladies of the Canoe Club would entertain at tea, sending out engraved cards to announce the event.

This club, too, flourished as long as it served a need. When there was still a large visiting population, some of which came by yacht, the full harbor offered a great inducement to canoeing. When the New York Yacht Club fleet was in, one could in one afternoon easily see a large number of one's friends from New York and the rest of the Atlantic seaboard, by lazily paddling around Bar Harbor from Bar Island to Sheep Porcupine. Then, as the hotel life lessened, and as the Passamaquoddy and Penobscot Indians found other things to do, the Canoe Club died away, being replaced in the scheme of things by the Swimming Club. For the Canoe Club depended on young men who wanted to paddle canoes, and in these days young men either drive cars or go to the north woods. And so Bar Island saw less and less social life. As late as the 1920's, there was still one cottage on the island, but the daughter of the house found, after one sad experience, that her swains did not like to drive her home through the rising tide on the bar, even in a car with a high clearance.

Perhaps the most colorful Bar Harbor institution is the Pot and Kettle Club. It was founded in 1888 by members of the so-called Fishhouse Club of Philadelphia, and their friends. In the winters they had been accustomed, of a Sunday, to retire to the freedom of an island in the Schuylkill River. There, in their "State in the Schuylkill," free from the outside world, they would cook their own meals, to their own taste, and then, stimulating their appetite with "Fishhouse Punch," in which brandy, rum, tea, and certain secret ingredients are so mixed as to be comparatively harmless, they would enjoy the food they had cooked and each other's company. In such company, with men of affairs who knew one another well, talk is frank and free. In the summers, on another day in the week, the members of the Pot and Kettle enjoyed the same pleasures, in similar ways.

The customs of the Pot and Kettle resemble those that the Fishhouse has allowed the *Saturday Evening Post* to describe. The presiding officer for the day is the "Caterer," who is responsible for both physical and mental entertainment. He settles questions of menus and sees to it that there is a member or a guest who has something to say that is worth hearing. What is there and then said is "off the record." What has been said can be inferred, after the passage of time, from the guest book, where are to be found, among others, names of William Howard Taft, Theodore Roosevelt, Warren G. Harding, Franklin D. Roosevelt, and Harry S. Truman. (There was some to-do about adding Mr. Truman's name. He visited the club as Senator

Truman of the war investigating committee, when on a semi-secret trip with his colleague Senator Brewster, and happened not to sign as a guest. It later occurred to the club secretary that this omission was a huge mistake, when such a tradition of Presidential visits had been built up, and the book was, for once in the club's history, taken from the clubhouse; then, in the White House, the President added his signature.)

There are many ways to reach the Pot and Kettle—when invited. In the old days many a yacht managed somehow to drop anchor off its pier, and the Bar Harbor Yacht has been known to call off a race at Googin's Ledge when a majority of the race committee belonged to the Pot and Kettle. Or so the legend goes—and who would stop a good legend for want of facts? And on days of the meeting, many a member managed to sail up, no matter how rough the seas. Buckboards drove others up, as today automobiles. During all this time the Pot and Kettle has preserved its combination of privacy and hospitality, and should be left in that privacy. In the strictness of its membership rules and the cordiality of its welcome to visitors, it typifies the aspects of the social life of Bar Harbor which are part of the history of the town.

Another club that survives is the Kebo Valley Club. Today this is a golf club, though in 1889 it began, at Arcadia Park, as a racing club. Then, as golf grew in favor—this was in the days of America's only seven-hole course, which Herbert Jacques laid out at Schooner Head, where three holes were dangerously close to the tees of the opposite pairs of holes—the Kebo Valley Club left to Edward Morrell the patronage of racing. It built a nine-hole course on the slopes under Cadillac Mountain, survived a fire in 1898, and flourished steadily. The racing that was otherwise organized evolved into the well remembered Bar Harbor horse shows. Year after year, until 1922, the horse show was one of the great events of the season. Many a house shows with pride the cups won in competition; many a fine handler of the "ribbons" showed his or her skill at that August event. It drew together many who would not otherwise enter into the social whirl, and made a focus for local life. It was only to the horse show that the children in Helen Train's *Mile of Freedom* went, in that happy summer she described, of idyllic peace away from the gay life of the resort. And, in a sense, it was the horse show that caused the great automobile war, whose story is a part of the history of the summer colony.

Bar Harbor, like Detroit, the other place that Cadillac founded, early saw automobile building. In the days when daring people put engines in buggies, took off the shafts, and smoked their way about, Paul Hunt, who is still among the living, varied his interests in architecture by building an automobile; this was in 1896. In due course of time, automobiles increased in number, and consequently in disturbance to the horse-loving public. Men and women who came to Mount Desert Island for peace and quiet were vexed by this. They arose, being people of influence, and secured legislation to keep automobiles off the island. Just how this was done is not known, as the participants in the effort are now dead, and did not write down what happened. Presumably, all sorts of influence was used. By that time Bar Harbor had established good connections at Augusta, and the legislation that was drafted had about it the marks of deft political handling. But this was not a purely Bar Harbor venture; the island summer colony was almost unanimous for it, under the leadership of such men as President Eliot of Harvard. And so it was that while much of the rest of Maine had cars, the horse lovers of Bar Harbor could drive on their roads in peace, confident that no "gasoline bug gies" would frighten their favorite steeds.

This state of affairs did not meet with complete approval. The people of Bar Harbor were divided in mind. Some wanted to do as their customers wished. If summer folks wanted a haven for equines, and would pay for it, why not let them have the haven, and pocket their money? Others felt that the automobiles had rights, and that they, too, had money. Those it was who sniped at the law.

The first draft of the law had been softened, to ease its passage, by having a limit on the roads which could be used, those roads being the only ones by which the island could be reached. Obviously, the thing to do was to bring cars in by boat—and, of course, all that meant was a legal change. No automobiles on wharves. At that challenge, Leslie Brewer, in the spring of 1907, built a car locally, with a motorboat engine for power, but without a differential. This moved legally about the unrestricted streets, with some difficulty in steering, until the law was changed again. Mr. Brewer prizes the photograph he made of his automobile; the engine has long since returned to the sea whence it came. In 1909 a New York honeymooner took his turn and had his Oldsmobile towed by horses over the hills, keeping the motor running as he did so. The testimony, as given before Judge Clark in the municipal court was amusing, the result inevitable.

However, change had to come. It was perfectly easy to take a selected poll of summer residents and find them ninety-five per cent against cars. It was fun for Arthur Train to take time off from more serious fiction to write a futuristic skit about the death and destruction that would ensue when cars raged about the streets of Bar Harbor. It was feasible, when Mr. Sherman presented a petition for cars, to employ the late Luere B. Deasy as counsel in the hearing, and have him tie Mr. Sherman up with quotations from his own guidebook. But the fact was that a growing number of the people of Bar Harbor wanted two things—the automobile tourist trade and the chance for local doctors to get to their patients in time. Pressure grew. It was, for a time, held back by influence. This time it is known how—for the late George B. Dorr wrote down the story—by money used in the legislature; it was, to use President Arthur's indiscreet phrase, "spent where it would do the most good." Here it was, Mr. Dorr relates, that he stepped in. In his many schemes for the island, he had secured a route for an electric railway, never built; this he offered now as a potential automobile road, to allow access to the town. He persuaded the anti-auto group in the summer colony to drop their more drastic methods and adopt the plan for a special road. By the quick action that was Dorr's characteristic in any lobbying he did, he secured partial consent from the group, and had the bill submitted before a recalcitrant element could talk their fellows into renewed stubborness. In effect, this plan for a special road kept automobiles out for another year, for the road was never built. Though the Town of Eden voted its share of the cost, the expected contributions did not materialize. And the next year, permissive legislation allowed the towns of Mount Desert Island to vote for or against automobiles, and Eden voted for them. Soon the rest of the island followed, after a death had occurred because a doctor had had to drive by buggy from the town line. And, not unnaturally, the horse show withered and died.

To return to the change in the summer colony in general: As the 1900's came on, both the cottage colony and American life altered. As canoes went out, and as hotel after hotel closed, the summer life acquired a more permanent basis. A substitute was needed for "the Fish Pond" as a natural meeting place, and a substitute was needed for the old and not too good swimming baths. The natural answer was the Swimming Club, metamorphosed in 1929 into the present Bar Harbor Club. Its original purpose was to provide good salt-water swimming, at bearable temperatures, and tennis courts. Using the site to which the Oasis Club house had moved, when the Reading Room was founded, it put up a brown clubhouse, dug a pool, and became the equivalent of a local country club.

Having built such institutions as these, the summer colony by 1910 had established itself as a permanent element in the Town of Eden-so permanent an element that Eden soon changed its name to Bar Harbor. And, as a result, there are many who look back to the 1900's as the "golden age" of Bar Harbor's social life. Such a retrospect is natural. That was the time when there were still enough hotels to afford prosperity and extra sales for local market gardeners and shopkeepers, so that the cottagers could have their cake and eat it too, could have the advantages of an exclusive colony and of a populous resort. In retrospect, too, it is surprising to note how long the old service industries held on. The Rodick House lasted on past 1900, to come down only because the successor to Daniel Rodick did not have either his personal touch or his clientele. Sproul's restaurant, still defying the Maine law—hung on, too, until it also went the way of all service enterprises that rely on the touch of one aging person. And so, one by one, went the landmarks of the old pre-cottage era.

Meanwhile, the cottage era bloomed. Tales are still told of how an ambassador of a country now seeking a loan from the United States (this should be inclusive enough for concealment) put lights all over Bar Island for a party to honor the young lady he was courting but did not succeed in marrying. The fire of 1947 destroyed a dining table made in that golden era, whose center used to sink through the floor to the kitchen, and, usually, rise again with another course; legend happily dwells on an occasion when it allegedly sank not to rise again, leaving guests eating while looking into a void. It was in Bar Harbor that Mrs. John Jacob Astor, widowed by the sinking of the *Titanic,* chose for the scene of her remarriage. Rightly, she felt that she thus could escape the publicity, and succeeded in doing so, thanks to excellent co-operation by the authorities of St. Saviour's Church. The waiting cameramen, hoping for one of the first motion-pictures of news events, were foiled, deftly, by the use of an alternative door. Such are randomly chosen stories of that era that may help illustrate the background of the summer colony.

There are other ways for taking a somewhat objective look at the summer colony. One is through real-estate transactions. Now that deeds no longer tell the price of land but run "for one dollar and other valuable considerations," the Hancock County registry of deeds no longer tells at which price who moved in and who moved out. But an eager follower of the real-estate transactions on the *Bar Harbor Times* can learn the steady flow of new personalities into the Bar Harbor summer colony. Former owners died, and the next generation had, perhaps, other ideas. Yet in their places came new buyers, bringing new life to the community. As long as fluctuations in value are not too extreme, either a rise or a fall in property can be helpful. When good houses are cheap, new owners move in, induced by bargains to settle permanently. When houses are hard to get, building takes place, and higher standards are set as modern improvements come in. But though there has been a flow of new blood into the summer colony, there has been a surprising loyalty to it. Families come year after year, generation after generation. They will cling to their property, renting instead of settling, and pay flying visits off season. Then, suddenly, they will reappear. Naturally, many things attract them; one is the special character of the life. This serves to bring in new blood as well as to keep loyal the old supporters of the colony.

Here again, there is another means for observing the summer colony with some objectivity, this time through the fiction of the past that has dealt with cottagers. It shows that Bar Harbor, for all the high standards it sets, accepts newcomers readily. The ways in which new blood comes in vary. Usually it is a matter of introduction by visiting friends, or residence at a hotel, then gaining a liking for Bar Harbor and buying. Bar Harbor's social ease has done its work again. (This does not mean that John Doe can walk into Bar Harbor, ring anyone's doorbell, and be invited in to make himself at home; it does mean that John Doe, when he has made proper contact, will feel at home quickly.) Francis Marion Crawford, the novelist, in the 1890's wrote not one but two books about this cordiality. One was Number Three, of Harper's summer resort series. It tells the usual stories about boardwalks and buckboards and canoes and flirtations. The other was a pot-boiler novel, *Maidens Call it Love in Idleness,* which winds up with the lady accepting the gentleman in a canoe. In both, one can see how Bar Harbor of the 1890's led the social world in ease—or, as an editor of the Harvard *Lampoon* put it, in effect Bar Harbor was a place where nice Philadelphia girls taught slowgoing Bostonians how to flirt. It is noteworthy that Crawford, as did Robert Grant, made it perfectly clear that the standards of behavior were high. Similar evidence, though of an earlier time, is to be found in Henrietta Rowe's *A Maid of Bar Harbor,* with its thumbnail sketch of the cordial little dandy who explains life to the returning Civil War veteran, after a chance introduction. A different slant, but the same basic idea, is to be found in a letter which Professor Barrett Wendell, of Harvard, wrote to the Boston *Transcript* in 1896; in it he asserted that Bar Harbor was the place in America where the best conversation was to be found. A similar—though not, in that case, unprejudiced statement—is to be found in the writings of Secretary of the Interior Franklin K. Lane, after a visit to George B. Dorr made in 1918.

All this adds up to the fact that several keen observers saw that in the early cottage days Bar Harbor had a catalytic effect on people, and made it easy for them to get together. This is just as true for the period after World War I. Much of the summer population changed. The names of Astor and Vanderbilt drop out of the cottage directory, to be replaced by others as prominent. But the cottage directory that records the names has the same general effect. An American social historian could consult it and say: "Here is a paradox; here are the owners of very varied industries, some highly competitive, the managers of certain great fortunes, who come from cities a thousand miles apart, living cheek by jowl." He could then expatiate, if he wanted to get away from the point, on the curious combinations that were neighbors. But in doing so he would go wide of the mark. What the cottage directory shows is a social and not an economic process at work. And to understand the meaning of neighbors living beside neighbors, emphasis should not be put on wealth of some, but on the mingling by all. The names in the directory that do not have economic importance have equal social importance.

Here it might not be amiss to put in a paragraph or two of philosophical reflection, which may be skipped by those who care not for such things, and read by those who want a few words on "social significance," in the other sense of "social," in the Bar Harbor summer colony. For Bar Harbor is a national phenomenon, even an international one, and the name is sometimes used as a by-word for wealth at ease, such is the reputation it has acquired. What does such a reputation mean to a community, what effect does it have on the community?

An answer is, recreation can be considered just as much an industry as any other. To the extent to which Bar Harbor is a one-industry town, which it is not, or a town with one major industry, which it is, the circumstances of that industry control the town. Since many citizens of Bar Harbor sell their services during a short period of the year, they tend to provide in the summer for the winter's income. Or, conversely, they follow their clients from summer resort to winter resort. Because there is much purchasing power in town, it has become a shopping center. These tendencies are what might be expected.

There is, however, another tendency. The cottage trade, compared with the hotel trade, is a long-term one, and long-term businesses demand a reputation for integrity. There are constant arguments as to costs, but, generally speaking, the free-market economy of the United States in general and Maine in particular sees to it that the customers stay satisfied and the suppliers of recreation stay in business. For so long as there is no monopoly or monopsomy—all one seller or all one buyer—the workings of competition will go on.

Now, in a competitive market, quality goods must be distinctive. What, then, does Bar Harbor have to offer as high-quality recreation? There the argument turns full circle, for what is offered is ease and relaxation, caused by and combined with natural beauty. So Bar Harbor sells a double brand of goods. On the one hand it sells fashion. It has its houses with butlers and footmen, where the young guests are awed by splendor—or amused, as the case may be. On the other hand, it has simplicity, so that a society magazine could jest that the custom of Bar Harbor was to have a big house and then a camp to get away from the house, and that soon the leaders of society would have camps in which to get away from their camps. Bar Harbor's essential qualities are still those which attracted to it the artists of the 1850's. And the "cottage economy" of Bar Harbor, distant as it is from sources of wealth such as New York and Chicago, can attract the owners of wealth only as long as the type of freedom and ease marked by, say, the Pot and Kettle Club, sets the tone of the resort. Such a tone of freedom and high standards will remain as long as the purveyors of recreation keep their high Maine standards of integrity, and as long as the summer residents continue, through public opinion and the management of their special institutions, to uphold lofty standards of social behavior.

These thoughts, as applied to the present, are of course, the author's own interpretation. They are based on personal observation over a period of years, and the close parallel of what goes on today with what writers have seen in the past. They also fit in with the facts of the summer colony's institutions, as recently made public.

Within two years, Major George McMurtry, who has since become the president of the Bar Harbor Club, compiled an interesting history of its first fifteen years. Since he has used names, the owners of those names may not mind their being used again. That history tells how certain men—be it noted, many of them newcomers to Bar Harbor—decided to put the bankrupt Swimming Club on its financial feet. One of them, the late E.T. Stotesbury, purchased the majority of the stock of the Swimming Club. As a partner in a Morgan affiliate, it was doubtless not the first time he had bought a working control to put his ideas across. This was done in the summer of 1929. Subscriptions were obtained from various members of the summer colony who could afford to make them, an opportunity being given to the former members to "get in on the ground floor." With Mr. Stotesbury were associated, among others, a newcomer to Bar Harbor. A. Atwater Kent, of radio manufacturing fame, and the late Potter Palmer, of Chicago, a member of a family that was returning to Bar Harbor after an intermission; the family had founded the famous firm of Palmer and Leiter, and the Palmer House hotel, and had long been legendary figures in Chicago society. This group floated a loan and proceeded to build a club-house as quickly as might be, wisely not waiting for bids, in the knowledge that they had better spend their construction money fast while it was still available, before the stock market misbehaved further. It might be suggested, in passing, that this action may explain the good showing made by Bar Harbor in the study of relief made in 1939 (see Thorndike and Thorndike, *Survey of the Town Relief Situation,* 1939). It seems a good description to say that the kind of clubhouse that was built was the kind that Messrs. Stotesbury and Kent and Palmer wanted and could afford. That club became what they intended it to be, the social center of Bar Harbor. For dances, swimming meets, and tennis tournaments, they extended its facilities on a broad basis, throughout the summer colony. The control they kept in the hands of those who were paying the bills, being perfectly willing to let who would do so join them. (Anyone who wishes to confirm these statements need only go to Major McMurtry's well written brochure and a copy of the published club rules.)

The Bar Harbor Club, as the brochure shows, has been managed as a club of rich, shrewd business men would be managed, when its directors aim at a balanced budget and their money's worth of comfort. It has slowly but steadily retired its bonded debt, and has served to make Bar Harbor a more enjoyable place, even for those who grumbled at the scale on which it was run. The published facts about the club suggest that the same social spirit as that of the 1890's is still at work. And a little genealogical research into the connections and interconnections of the old families of the summer colony will show that both new blood and old blood share in the management.

Again, take the Kebo Valley Club and its adventures. Captain John J. O'Brien, of the Hudson Motor Company, recently published its history, to celebrate its fiftieth anniversary and its second rebuilding after fire. That history tells much the same story as in the case of the Swimming Club. Again and again those who loved the club made good its deficit. It was discovered, that, speaking in terms of economics, Bar Harbor could not support a public golf links. In 1916 there was a genuine attempt to start a public course, in which the management of the Kebo Valley Club heartily joined. George B. Dorr provided much of the needed land, from his purchase of the Harden farm. T. DeWitt Cuyler put up the funds, amply, and persuaded the Town of Eden—as it still was—to share in the investment, in order to keep the course public. But the venture did not succeed, and the Kebo Valley Club bought the land to make its second nine holes.

In all the account that Captain O'Brien has given, what stands out is that after every "down" of the club there has been an "up" because its members were so fond of it. It is an unusual sign of vitality to have funds raised by dedicating holes to former members and have all the holes endowed, including one hole dedicated to the manager, who has been made an honorary member.

The Yacht Club, or clubs, show another side of Bar Harbor's life. Here a meteorological phenonenon comes into the picture. Ever since the days when Benjamin Church came to one side of Mount Desert Island with his whaleboats, while Le Moyne D'Iberville and his frigates and Father Thury and his canoes came to the other, sailors have known that the two sides of the island favored different types of vessels. At what used to be called Mount Desert South Harbor, between the Cranberries and the main island, there was always enough wind and not too much, thus affording the type of conditions needed for open-boat sailing, whether whaleboats in 1690 or the A and B boats of the North East Harbor Fleet. To the north, in the roadstead of Mount Desert, as Cadillac truly pointed out, a whole fleet could lie as if in a box, and canoes could safely ply their way, whether with Father Thury and his Indians or with Robert Grant's young lady safely chaperoned by the tippiness of the craft into which her swain had put her. Off Bar Harbor winds have tended to be lighter, but the swell has come from the mouth of the bay. Sailing there has demanded the qualities that length gives a vessel, of higher speed and ability to keep moving when waves roll.

Consequently, for two reasons, one meteorological, one financial, Bar Harbor has favored large-size yachts. There was one period, of the Mount Desert Racing Association, when the Bar Harbor Thirties, a very sound type, as their subsequent owners realized, raced regularly. These were big enough to move through the water as did D'Ilberville's frigates. Legend has it that when the fleet broke up in a law suit, when an irate competitor discovered that the rules of the road for racing and the rules of the road under United States law were different, and that, in one set of circumstances, you could ram a man who was winning a race from you, and collect damages. Unfortunately, the source of this legend is no longer alive, and it can be set down only as an example of what good legends exist. Anyway, after 1913 the association died a lingering death, the Thirties were dispersed to serve as cruisers, and, finally, no one could be found to pay the annual corporation fees; the association was listed in the secretary of state's files as a "dead corporation."

In the late 1920's a new club arose. It hoped to have two boat classes, one for learners, one for the older and more expert sailors. The late Edsel Ford subsidized the design and construction of the very safe Mount Desert Island class for the smaller size. These, too, were good boats. In a light wind and no sail at all, they had surprising speed, and would then overhaul vessels of reputedly swifter and larger classes. But this happened about once every two years. Usually, since they had no overhang to speak of they just bobbed up and down safely, while other boats knifed ahead and left them far behind. And enough of the young sailors had enough money behind them so that when they were not interested in a docile learning period they either started out with the S class or moved into it quickly. Thus, when the depression came, the Yacht Club gave up its lease of the old Reading Room and the hopes of building up younger sailors by small boats was given up. The Yacht Club had a surprisingly successful life when it consisted of a few enthusiasts, some buoys for courses, and a rented mark boat.

This Yacht Club was an accidental casualty of World War II. Its officials went off to fight and forgot where they put the club's records. So it automatically expired. Then, aided by a town subsidy a new organization, humorously insisting that it was the Bar Harbor Yacht Club, Inc., was created; it took no responsibility for the loss of the records, and incurred no legal penalties for not making an annual report. This new club hopes it has found the answer to the meteorological-financial problem of yacht racing, with its new Luders class that is both safe in sea and has a long overhang to make it move, with ability to carry sufficient sail, and yet small enough for amateurs to sail—in short, a combination of the virtues of canoe and frigate.

Here again, present events show something typical of Bar Harbor throughout the years. Here a combination of wealth and weather has hampered small-boat sailing and the sporting pleasures of yachtsmen. Wealth and weather have brought the use of a type of boat that is too expensive to allow a big sailing group, and lack of that group has weakened racing. But twice the demand for yachting has come to the fore, in spite of these handicaps; Bar Harbor, not thought of as a sportsman's resort, still has a yacht club in full activity.

Each of these accounts seems to have the same moral: The Bar Harbor summer colony, as seen through its active institutions, has had true vitality, and keeps to this day the special characteristics that were created in the 1880's and 1890's.

This whole account is a generalization of the story of the summer colony. It has avoided personalities, except where names are already in print. There is another story of the summer colony—indeed, several other stories—containing personalities whose rich flavor has made the summer colony what it is. That story can be obtained, or part of it can, from any summer resident who, not bound by the laws of libel, will talk "off the record." Indeed, if it be assumed that there are about 19,500 living summer residents, of the present or the past, it may be assumed also that a researcher or team of researchers could in the course of time get about 19,500 different stories. All would have a flavor that can only be hinted at here. Perhaps some day, fifty years or so from now, one or two of them will be set down. And then future readers will know why it is that people have continued to buy land at Bar Harbor.

CHAPTER

37.

Maine people have always taken pride in the contributions made by their ancestors to the Union cause. The following, written by John Pullen, describes the various components which went into the building of Maine's most famous regiment, the Twentieth Maine.

HOW D'YE DO, COLONEL*
by
John J. Pullen

When, in August of 1862, Colonel Adelbert Ames went to Portland, Maine, to take command of a new volunteer infantry regiment, he was a little more than fourteen months out of West Point and a year out of the first battle of Bull Run, where he had received a painful wound. Thus it had been impressed upon him in two ways—one theoretical and the other practical—that discipline is a mighty good thing to have among your soldiers when the shooting starts. And therefore Colonel Ames was disgusted and horrified when he arrived at Camp Mason, near Portland, and got his first look at the troops gathering there for the 20th Regiment Infantry, Maine Volunteers.

Instead of saluting, a man would say, "How d'ye do, Colonel!" often as not leaning against a wall or tree with legs crossed, for a Maine man will not ordinarily waste energy holding himself erect if there is an inanimate object handy to do that for him. The military posture of one man, standing in ranks, was so abdominally atrocious that Colonel Ames roared at him, "For God's sake, draw up your bowels!"

The men wanted to act like soldiers but obviously none of them had the slightest notion of military affairs. They had no uniforms or arms and little equipment. Yet they had organized a guard and were trying to hold formations. At one guard mount, the Officer of the Day was clad in brown cutaway, striped trousers and silk hat. He carried a ramrod for a sword.

Both the officers and the men seemed to think that a regiment should be run something like a town meeting. Orders consisted of long explanations, then there would be conferences and discussions and, finally, agreements between the officers and enlisted men. True, the agreements seemed to be carried out; the men themselves took a great deal of responsibility for this, and in cases of disobedience the offender was likely to be knocked down and perhaps kicked if the offense was of a particularly flagrant nature.

Colonel Ames, not a mild-tempered man to begin with—and with so much to be done, the Union to be saved, a brigadier generalship to be won, and all that—found himself losing what patience he had. He barked, "This is a hell of a regiment!" Then he straightaway set about putting the 20th Maine into some semblance of a military organization.

After a little preliminary drilling, the Colonel attempted to hold a parade, so that he could get the 20th Maine lined up and see what he had for soldiers. This was interrupted, noisily. In their martial ardor the men had organized a fife and drum corps in which the fifers and drummers all seemed to fife and drum independently but with great power. Just as the Colonel took his place in front of the drawn-up troops, the fife and drum corps suddenly and prematurely moved from its position and came tweetling and thundering down the line, making an appalling racket. To the

---

*"How D'Ye Do, Colonel" from *The Twentieth Maine* by John J. Pulien. Copyright ©1957 by John J. Pullen. Published by J. B. Lippincott Company. pp. 1-17.

324

company commander nearest him Colonel Ames shouted, "Captain Bangs, stop that damned drumming!" Captain Isaac S. Bangs couldn't hear him for the noise, nor could anyone else. In a rage, Colonel Ames charged the drum corps with his sword and scattered it sufficiently to make himself audible.

If Ames had been asked to pick a regiment that was earmarked for great deeds, he certainly wouldn't have picked the 20th Maine in that August of 1862 as having any date with Destiny. Yet in numbers, at least, Ames could see that he had a regiment that conformed to the table of organization prescribed by law. The Civil War volunteer regiment consisted of ten companies, each having from sixty-four to eighty-two privates, thirteen non-commissioned officers, a wagoner, two musicians, a captain and two lieutenants. The regiment was commanded by a colonel, aided by a lieutenant colonel, a major, and a small regimental staff of commissioned and non-commissioned officers.

All these positions had been filled by individuals with varying degrees of competence. Starting at the top there was Ames himself—a West Pointer and a Maine man, thus both able and eligible to command the regiment. Ames had already made a distinguished record for bravery and what Maine people would call "stick-to-it-iveness." Serving with a battery at the first battle of Bull Run, he had taken a Minié ball through the thigh, but had refused to leave the field, being lifted on and off a caisson as the battery changed position, and continuing to give fire commands until his boot ran full of blood and he keeled over from exhaustion. Able, intelligent, intensely ambitious, Ames had been mentioned in official reports and marked as a young officer who was on the way up. For his performance at Bull Run he would later be awarded the Congressional Medal of Honor.

The lieutenant colonel of the regiment was a man worth looking at twice. This was Joshua L. Chamberlain, age thirty-three, a graceful, erect gentleman of medium but strong build, with a finely shaped head, a classic forehead and nose, a moustache that swept back with a distinguished flair, a resonant and pleasing voice. To Chamberlain the war would be a great adventure. He was destined to become one of the most remarkable officers in the history of the United States—a veritable knight with plumes and shining armor. He came of English and Norman stock; his people had been among the earliest settlers; and he combined a great deal of solid strength and common sense with a dash and gallantry that may well have come to him from the French roots of the family tree. Chamberlain also had a talent for doing the impossible which seems to have been encouraged by his childhood training. One of the tenets of this training was that if something was said to be impossible, a man was supposed immediately to go at it, and do it. Clearing stones from the family farm in Brewer, when Joshua and his brothers reported to their father that they'd left a rock in the field because it was too heavy to move, the elder Chamberlain would say simply, "Move it," and the boys would go back and move it. (One of these brothers, Thomas, was also in the 20th Maine as a sergeant.) As another instance of this unwonted perseverance, when young Joshua wanted to learn to play the bass viol but couldn't afford to buy the instrument, he made a crude viol and bow, and sawed away until he could play tunes. And when he desired to learn Greek, he shut himself up in the attic and studied from morning until night, until he had learned the complete grammar textbook by heart.

After graduating from Bowdoin, Joshua had taken a three-year course at the Bangor Theological Seminary, meanwhile teaching German language and literature to classes of young ladies, serving as supervisor of schools in Brewer, running a Sunday school, and leading a church choir. Later he had joined the faculty of Bowdoin College, where he had taught rhetoric, oratory and modern languages. The college had not wanted Professor Chamberlain to go to war, so he had taken a two years' leave of absence for the purpose of visiting Europe and had instead visited the state capital in Augusta, where he secured a commission as lieutenant colonel of volunteers. The Governor had wished to make him a colonel and give him a regiment, but he'd said no, he'd start a little lower and learn the business first.

Although trained to be a minister of the Gospel, Chamberlain seemed to show a most un-Christian aptitude for military affairs, and Ames thought he might do well.

The major, Charles D. Gilmore, had seen service as a captain in the 7th Maine, a regiment that went into the field in 1861. Gilmore was evidently a man of some managerial ability. He had contrived to get himself a transfer back to Maine, a leave of absence and a promotion to major in the 20th Maine all at one stroke. For some time he had been the only uniformed person in camp and had looked extremely lonesome.

Among the company commanders one of the most notable, as it would turn out, was Ellis Spear of Wiscasset. A frail-appearing, bearded young schoolmaster, Spear didn't look as though he could withstand the rigors of army life a month, but he was actually tough as leather and what he lacked in physical stamina he would make up in determination. In many ways, Spear was much more typical of the good volunteer officer than was Chamberlain. To him, war was far from being romantic; it was instead a dull, ugly job that had to be done in spite of all its horrors and official stupidities. Possessed of a dry sense of humor and a Yankee gift for understatement, Spear was the type of Maine man who, if you ask him how he is doing and he happens to be doing very well indeed, will reply, "All right." Ellis Spear always took the conservative view of both men and events.

As for the enlisted men, as Colonel Ames walked up and down the ranks of his first parade he could begin to see certain possibilities. There were many—obviously passed by patriotically blind examining physicians—who had no business in the army. But there were others who looked very rugged indeed. These were flat-bellied, hard-muscled fellows from the farms, forests and coast towns. There were among them many who eked out a living on the farms in summer and in the woods in winter, and it was a muscular life in both places. On the farm power was provided by the man, the ox and the horse, and the work—lifting rocks, pitching hay, manhandling the crude farm tools—was a personal struggle against the laws of inertia and gravity. In the woods it was all axe work. Even that doubtful laborsaver, the two-man crosscut saw, was not in general use. Men who worked in the lumber camps of that day got up before dawn, walked through deep snow four or five miles to their work, started chopping as soon as there was light enough to see, ate a frozen lunch, and worked until the light faded. To many of Ames' soldiers hardship was not strange; it was the ordinary and accustomed way of life.

So there were tough men in the ranks of the newly formed 20th Maine. Not many six-footers among them; a good guess would place the average at about five feet eight inches, but that was all to the good; experience had shown that tall men did not stand up as well on the march as the small- or medium-sized soldiers.

In addition, many of the Maine soldiers were already familiar with firearms. And they *were* volunteers, even if strong persuasion had been involved in their enlistment. The year before, in 1861, Maine had had no trouble in raising regiments; young men had rushed to the colors in the first flush of war excitement, when it seemed that the rebellion would be put down within a few weeks. But in July of 1862, when Father Abraham called for "three hundred thousand more," it was a little harder to round up the requisite number.

Usually, ordinary citizens, with authorization from the Governor, did the recruiting and paid their own expenses. The recruiters were men of all classes: ambitious young lawyers, budding politicians, schoolteachers who thought they knew something about discipline, farmers, clerks, youngsters just out of college. There was a sort of understanding with the Governor that if they succeeded they would get commissions. In the Civil War volunteer regiment, all the officers were appointed by the Governor—often on the basis of political rather than military merit. Regular Army commanders contemplated the system with positive horror. Referring to the commissioning of untrained officers by governors, Major General Emory Upton wrote, "In no monarchy or despotism of the Old World do the laws give to the ruler such power to do evil." Once the regiment was in Federal service, higher commanders had ways of getting rid of incompetent state officers, but then the Governor might appoint another one just as incompetent as a replacement. Within the regiment itself there was much political activity—manipulation of influences and supposed influences in order to obtain commissions or promotions from the Governor. And not only was politics active in the regiment, but the regiment was active in politics. The 20th Maine, for example, in 1863 would hold a meeting and send a resolution back to Maine approving one candidate for governor, and roundly condemning another.

Ellis Spear, who helped raise Company G of the 20th Maine in Lincoln and Sagadahoc counties, could foresee some of the complications. He described the work as a process of "log-rolling" among the neighbors. There had to be persuasion, promises, and deals of various kinds which would not leave him an enviable position when it came to future discipline. Thus, the test of a line officer was whether or not he was an effective salesman and diplomat. In military matters, he was as green as the men he was trying to enlist. Thinking about it later, Spear could only credit the recruiting officers with great enterprise and audacity, "for such certainly were required in a young man given to serious reflection, who should propose to organize a military company, and to command it in the field, when he scarcely knew a line of battle from a line of rail fence."

There were other and more immediate perils, such as wrathy mothers. One woman charged with a pitchfork and drove the recruiting officer from the premises. And there were additional difficulties that could be overcome only through methods that would not bear strict investigation, in the absence of adequate methods for raising troops.

Like most of the states, Maine had entered the war in a woeful state of unpreparedness. Only twenty years before there had been a thriving militia—699 organized companies in the state. And this had been militia in the old "minute man" sense of the word, as originally envisioned by the framers of the Constitution and by Congress. The men had armed and equipped themselves at their own expense, had elected their own officers and held musters in the spring and fall for training and inspection. The older men in the 20th Maine remembered the muster, an occasion which was a sort of combined Fourth of July and country fair. Around the drill field there had been refreshment booths, dancing floors, shows, games, sleight-of-hand performances, auction sales and wrestling matches. And there had been martial splendor of a safe and satisfying kind—soldiers parading up and down to the music of fife and drum, officers resplendent in their fancy uniforms, a few old soldiers of the Revolution watching critically from the sidelines. It had all been a great event—one of the few holidays of the year, looked forward to for weeks, talked about for weeks afterward. But by the time of the Civil War, musters and other training had long since been discontinued and the militia was little more than a memory of plumes and epaulettes, sideshows, cider and gingerbread. As John Hodsdon, Maine's Adjutant General, put it, "Long years of uninterrupted peace had led us to believe that it was our privilege to enjoy all the advantages of a free government, the best since the world began, without adopting any measures for its protection and perpetuity, just as we enjoy the light and the heat of the sun."

Actually, the situation was even worse than it looked on the surface. Until the passage of the Enrollment Act, calling for national conscription in 1863, the basic legal authority for the raising of a large army was the Federal government's ability, under the Constitution and existing laws, to call out the militia, or state troops. (Expansion of the government's own force, the U. S. Regulars, was also possible but was never seriously considered; the specter of a large standing army still haunted the nation.) In order to provide for a uniform militia establishment throughout the states, Congress in 1792 had enacted legislation which ordered, among other things, that all qualified men in the nation between the ages of eighteen and forty-five, with certain exemptions, were to be enrolled by the captains or commanding officers of their local militia companies.

At the outbreak of the war there was a nominal enrolled militia in Maine of around sixty thousand. But most of these men were subject to no peacetime duty or training whatever. Aside from a few volunteer companies, the militia existed on paper only. And there was even some doubt about the legal validity of the paper. As the Federal law then stood, the men were supposed to be enrolled by military officers—the captains or commanding officers of the local companies. But most of Maine's militiamen had been enrolled simply by the assessors of the towns and cities, in conformity with a section of the state law which did not agree with its Federal counterpart.

Fortunately the insubstantial nature of the militia was not an immediate danger in the early days of the war. In 1861, men were trying to get into military service, not out of it, and the government was hard put to find places for all the patriots who came forward. This gave rise to the authorization of a third type of military organization for the Civil War—the volunteer force. But

Congress was still unwilling or afraid to invade states' rights too far. Although in the service of the United States, the volunteers were still considered by many to be another form of militia. The volunteer regiments were raised and officered by the states. They took their names from the states, and while making up almost all of the armed force, still remained essentially state troops.

In the meantime, while the first volunteer regiments were being raised, a somewhat tighter legal net was being cast for the militia. By midsummer of 1862, when the 20th Maine was being assembled, there were provisions for properly enrolling men in the militia and for drafting them from the militia into Federal service. This served primarily as a threat. If enough troops could not be raised through volunteering, they could be drafted as militiamen. Thus, the Federal government could put pressure on the state, and the state could put pressure on its towns and cities in the form of quotas for required numbers of men. Every possible effort was made to avoid the draft. A quota, being a number, could be filled by a number; and getting the equivalent in live bodies became the chief consideration of everyone from the Governor down to the town officials. Examining physicians could be persuaded that patriotism was sufficient evidence of physical fitness. If a man was warm, moving under his own power, and patriotic enough to sign his name on the enlistment papers, certain defects could be overlooked. One man, for example, was too short; but he got into the 20th Maine by virtue of a pair of high-heeled shoes. As the heels wore out, he shortened down considerably, but it is recorded that he made a good soldier after all. Another passed muster in a beard dyed glistening black; shortly afterward a widening band of gray appeared and he grew old prematurely.

The first problem, however, was to ignite the necessary feeling of patriotism. It was soon discovered that there was nothing like money for doing this. Bounties were offered by the cities and towns in addition to those from the Federal and state governments. A dollar was hard to come by in Maine, and if a man could be patriotic and lay a little away at the same time, he might as well. In an attempt to fill their quotas, many of the towns were in effect bidding against each other, so it paid to shop around and there was much switching of names and numbers on papers.

This led to some real headaches for the man who was supposed to keep the records straight, Adjutant General John L. Hodsdon, and when he wrote his report at the end of 1862, he was burning up about it. Although he fought the war with pen and paper in Augusta, Maine, General Hodsdon appears to have been one of its unsung heroes. He complained that statistical records of all kinds were sadly deficient and incomplete in America. He could remember old soldiers of the Revolution and the War of 1812 who had died in want because their rights to pensions and other claims could not be established for lack of adequate records. He had, in addition, a deep sense of historic justice in thinking of the men who were going to bleed and die and disappear in this big new war, and he wanted, as he put it, "to present a continuous and perfect record of the share of our State in the present glorious struggle for the honor and integrity of the union, and afford, so far as practicable, the due meed of praise to every person participating in it, however humble his position."

As he struggled to compile and publish his "continuous and perfect record," Hodsdon was beset by many difficulties, such as illegible, lost and neglected returns from careless and forgetful correspondents. But some of his worst troubles were caused by the bounties. The papers turned in to his office were supposed to show the recruit's place of residence as well as other needed facts. Each volunteer for three years' service was enlisted upon a separate contract, and these papers were usually sent along with a group of recruits to their regimental rendezvous in charge of a recruiting officer or some other authorized person. It was usually upon delivery and mustering-in of the men in camp that the bounties were paid, although in some instances the recruits were paid in advance.

Hodsdon described what often happened: "Upon their arrival at the camp, the officer in charge finds the agent of some city or town 'where wealth accumulates but men decay,' prepared to pay a much larger bounty than that offered by the place from which his squad was sent; by supplying him with the men under his charge, he secures a larger bounty for them than that which they had contracted for, with a bonus to himself usually, of from twenty-five to one hundred dollars per man. To effect this arrangement, either the place of residence given on the enlistment papers was changed, or new enlistments were substituted from the assertion of the recruits, upon due instruction, that the quotas of their towns were full, or that they had no legal residence in the State. Not infrequently during the negotiations, the agent of some other town offered a larger bounty, occasioning the substitution in the enlistment papers of still another place of residence, so that some papers when they were deposited in this office exhibited three or four different towns as the residence of the recruit, all but one of which shows an attempt at obliteration."

Endless confusion resulted. Often, when the authorities of a town from which recruits had been sent came into camp to pay them the bounty agreed upon, they found them credited upon the quotas of other towns. Or worse yet, where quotas were filled and bounties paid in advance, towns were often surprised to get notices that they were short a number of men. Controversies arose between towns which, as Hodsdon said, "embodied all the zeal, bitterness and contradictory evidence usually attending pauper lawsuits."

In his report for that year, 1862, Hodsdon estimated that in addition to bounties paid by the Federal and state governments, Maine cities, towns and plantations had paid more than $1,500,000. This money even corrupted some of the earlier volunteers, who presumably had enlisted for pure patriotism in 1861. Many procured discharges by any available means and came back to Maine. Here they re-enlisted to get some of the gravy.

A great deal of the bounty money went into the pockets of brokers and agents who negotiated between the towns and the available recruits. Often broker and volunteer divvied up the money half and half. The municipal authorities themselves were not above reproach. Many of them were interested in filling their quotas in any way they could, without regard to the interests of the nation. The system of voluntary enlistment was proving itself to be unrealistic, and the bounty payments were in Hodsdon's opinion a deep and lasting disgrace.

And yet most of the volunteers were far from being crooks or mercenaries, and not all the towns lagged in their responsibilities. The Adjutant General cited seventy-nine towns, cities and plantations that not only sent their quotas but sent from one to twenty-five more soldiers than they were asked for. The town of Enfield, with 329 inhabitants, had fifty-four in the service. One Enfield man sent six sons, then went himself. The town of Portage Lake had only one able-bodied man left in it. And again it must be remembered that people were persuading, but no one was forcing these men to go; they were volunteers.

It is difficult, at this distance in time, to analyze their deeper motives. Many undoubtedly enlisted from boredom—to get away from bleak farms, lonely forest clearings or ugly wives. Many volunteered simply because there was a war on and men were going to it. But many enlisted in a sort of patriotic frenzy. It can well be imagined what emotions would be aroused today if there were an attempt to break up the United States by force. That feeling, comparable to the instinct of the hive or the herd to save itself, was perhaps intensified by the fact that the nation was smaller, younger, and at that time not too far removed from foreign domination.

The regimental staff did not include an Information and Education officer to tell the men what they were fighting for. None was needed. Many of the men of the 20th Maine seem to have been well informed, surprisingly well educated, and fully cognizant of the main issue. If the South won, there would be no reason to expect a continuance of the United States of America. And they might soon have no country.

This was an intolerable thought. Just how intolerable it was we can probably never understand, unless some day we unhappily find ourselves in the same position. But judging by the letters these men wrote, the efforts they put forth, and the hardships that failed to deter them, we can understand that they were very much in earnest in their devotion to the Union.

As the war progressed and they saw that Southern men were fighting for ideas that seemed to *them* equally important, the Maine soldiers thought more deeply, and some of them realized that it was not a simple question they were fighting to settle. But through it all they clung to their determination that the Union must be preserved, and in this resolve—as they would prove in the election of 1864—they identified themselves very closely with the President.

In the character of its men, the regiment approached a fairly good cross section of the entire state, although its volunteers came mostly from the smaller villages and rural sections. The 20th Maine was the last of the three-year regiments raised in Maine in response to the President's call for three hundred thousand volunteers in July of 1862. Apparently it was formed from detachments originally enlisted for the 16th, 17th, 18th and 19th regiments, and afterward found to be unnecessary to complete those organizations. The "leftovers" came from scattered localities. Companies E, G, I and K came from many little towns lying in the arms of the ocean along the deeply indented coast. Companies A, C, D and F were harvested from the farmlands of south-central and western Maine. Company B came from a big-woods county, Piscataquis—as also did Company H, journeying down from Aroostook County, forest-sequestered region from which it was a one-hundred-mile trip by stagecoach before they came to the railroad at Bangor.

Geographically, this was the background of the 20th Maine, and when the regiment had left home far behind, it could dream of many things: of gulls crying and green waves crashing on a stony shore; of forest silences so deep they seemed to have an audible presence; of oxen and bow-necked horses pulling plows and turning the green sod of spring, with birds foraging behind in the furrows; of axes ringing in a winter dawn and tall trees falling with lingering smashes; of deer running in high bounds and partridge rocketing up over hardwood ridges; of endless crops of stones, and stone walls lined with hazel bushes; of one-room schools with a water pail in the corner, a stove in the center, and scholars studying with a drowsy hum; of white farmhouses with lilacs in the yard; of gristmills and blacksmith shops; and fishing boats bobbing on a wind-swept ocean.

Racially, with few exceptions, the men were what the people of Aroostook, borrowing an expression from the terminology of the potato, would call "the old seed-ends." After the war the Adjutant General tabulated the nativity of all Maine troops, and it figured out that about eighty-five per cent had been born in New England. The rest were overwhelmingly English, Scotch and Irish in their origins. The same report classified occupations as around thirty-two per cent agricultural, twenty-nine per cent mechanical, twenty-four per cent laborers, eleven per cent miscellaneous (which included seamen), two per cent commercial and two per cent professional. With so few men from the cities and larger towns, the 20th Maine probably was composed of an even larger percentage of native stock, with farming, fishing and lumbering predominating among the occupations. The names in the muster rolls also reflect an old-time character of population, culture and way of life. Along with the Georges and Williams, there were the Aarons, Abials and Arads, the Ebenezers, Elijahs, Elishas, Ephraims and Ezekiels, the Isaacs, Isaiahs and Israels, the Jobs, Joshuas and Josiahs, and so on down to the Zachariahs.

In age, the men of the 20th Maine (just under one thousand in all) ranged all the way from eighteen, the lower legal limit, to forty-five, the upper. Sixty-seven of them were forty and over. The oldest rifleman listed on the records was Glazier Estabrook of Amity, forty-five. Glazier was a small man but full of fight and terribly strong. The older people in Amity remember stories. One: Long after the war, when Glazier was getting on in years, he got into a fight with a man at a lumber camp on Jimmy Brook, got him down, and began beating him with his fists. When bystanders dragged him off he cried, "Oh! Let me give him just another touch of the live oak!" Glazier fought all through the war and, after Gettysburg, made corporal and the color guard.

All this was the raw material waiting for Colonel Ames. The men, he soon realized, would never be regulation, government-issue soldiers. They were too independent, for one thing, and although acknowledging the necessity for obeying orders, they could not help resenting invasions of their "rights." For example, a private, when admonished by his company commander for a lack of personal cleanliness at inspection, would retort that he thought it was "cussed mean business to go around and peek in other folks' ears." But they were enthusiastic and willing. Many of the officers showed promise, even though they had not been selected on the basis of military merit. (Ellis Spear believed the Governor commissioned them after thinking it out in this fashion: "These fellows who have recruited so many men and have actually landed them in camp must have military qualifications.")

In the few days Colonel Ames had before the regiment was to move to the theater of war, everything seemed to happen all at once. Commissions for the officers arrived from Augusta. A Regular Army officer appeared and mustered the regiment into the Federal service. The uniforms came and were issued. The usual uniform in the Civil War was dark blue coat and light blue trousers. But initially the 20th Maine wore *all* dark blue—coat and trousers alike. This effect must have given the regiment, as seen in the distance, something of the appearance of a group of railway conductors on an outing. Ellis Spear recalled that "the diverse effect of all these new clothes was remarkable. Of course there was no such blaze of glory as that which now appears upon the Avenue on occasions of official display; but compared with the sober drabs of civil life, the blue cloth with the gold buttons and the new shoulder-straps were comparatively gorgeous. Some whose youth was more easily affected by the unusual display assumed airs of importance; others wore their honors with meekness, and some went about with a settled determination expressed upon their faces to attend to business and to ignore as far as possible these honors and glories thus suddenly thrust upon them. The camp put on a military appearance, and regiment, if not a lion, was at least clothed in the skin of that formidable beast."

The skin was too tight in places, and at others it hung loosely. One soldier wrote later that he was sixteen years old (his age appears on the rolls as eighteen) and stood over six feet and weighed 150 pounds. To get a uniform that was long enough to cover his beanpole frame he had to take one that billowed out around the waist, leaving room enough for another soldier inside.

The regiment would be equipped partly by the state, partly by the United States government. In addition to his uniform, each man would get from the state a woolen blanket and a rubber blanket ... a haversack, knapsack and canteen ... a tin plate, tin dipper, knife, fork and spool ... and if he were lucky he would get a towel. From the Portland peddlers the men were also buying patented drinking tubes, pencils, stencil plates and ink, stationery, combs and brushes, revolvers, murderous-looking knives, money-belts, patent medicines and everything else that could possibly be imagined as helpful in crushing the rebellion. Colonel Ames knew that most of this stuff and much of the government-issue material, too, would probably be scattered along some Virginia roadway on the first hard march.

As for arms, the 20th Maine was scheduled to draw muskets and ammunition in Washington. Colonel Ames went through the list of other regimental property, and it didn't take him long. He noted such items as camp kettles ... wall tents ... spades ... axes ... hatchets ... mess pans. With no time for training, with 965 officers and men who were completely raw militarily, and with scanty equipment that included ten drums, five bugles, ten pounds of nails and a handsaw, Colonel Ames was supposed to represent himself as the commander of an infantry regiment and report, forthwith, to the Commanding General, Army of the Potomac.

The 20th departed quietly from the State of Maine. Probably because of the scattered nature of its origin, it was not, as Joshua Chamberlain noted, one of the state's favorites; no county claimed it; no city gave it a flag; and there was no send-off at the station.

As the troop train rattled southward and Colonel Ames brooded upon the military shortcomings of its passengers, the young West Pointer might have been reassured by the prophetic words of Alexis de Tocqueville, a perceptive Frenchman who had visited America some years before. De Tocqueville had observed that discipline for many European soldiers was only a continuation of social servitude, but the American fighting man would be another breed of cat. He wrote, "A democratic people must despair of ever obtaining from soldiers that blind, minute, submissive, and invariable obedience which an aristocratic people may impose on them without difficulty. The state of society does not prepare them for it, and the nation might be in danger of losing its natural advantages if it sought artificially to acquire advantages of this particular kind. Among democratic communities, military discipline ought not to attempt to annihilate the free spring of the faculties; all that can be done by discipline is to direct it; the obedience thus inculcated is less exact, but it is more eager and more intelligent. It has its root in the will of him who obeys; it rests not only on his instinct, but on his reason; and consequently it will often spontaneously become more strict as danger requires it. The discipline of an aristocratic army is apt to be relaxed in war, because that discipline is founded upon habits, and war disturbs those habits. The discipline of a democratic army, on the contrary, is strengthened in sight of the enemy, because every soldier then clearly perceives that he must be silent and obedient in order to conquer."

But all this could be clearer to a foreign observer than it was to natives facing the nation's first big war. There was still a picture of battle wherein brilliantly uniformed men moved to the music of bands and executed Napoleonic maneuvers—with a smaller picture of the soldier saying "Sir" to officers, clicking his heels, and turning to carry out orders without question or hesitation even into the jaws of death. If he had reflected upon it, the Maine man would have agreed with de Tocqueville. He had about as much chance of being the classic soldier as he had of becoming a ballet dancer in the Paris Opera. For he certainly wasn't going to say "Sir" to the officer who was just old Tom or Joe from down the road. Clicking the heels was just plain silly. As for carrying out orders without question, sometimes old Tom or Joe didn't show very good sense. So the glamorous picture would begin to disintegrate even as he first thought about it.

As many men have been, the volunteer was somewhat enamored of war. He had read of war. He had heard of war. But he knew absolutely nothing about it, except that there was a war on; that it was a serious thing for the country; and that it had better, some way or other, be won.

CHAPTER

38.

Maine's cultural history has been uneven in its development. In the summer of 1964, Colby College focused on the achievements of "Maine" artists through the years. The following article describes some of those achievements as they were publicized at Colby.

MAINE AND AMERICAN ARTISTS, 1710-1963*
by
Jacqueline Davidson

What can an individual state offer to the cultural heritage of the nation? Colby College, in the central Maine town of Waterville, commemorated the one hundred fiftieth anniversary of its founding with a three-part program that establishes the importance of that state in the history of American art. More than 125 paintings and sculptures by Maine artists of Maine subjects, as well as several examples of indigenous folk art, were exhibited this past summer in the college's Bixler Art and Music Center. The exhibition will also be shown at the Museum of Fine Arts in Boston from December 18 until January 26, 1964, and at the Whitney Museum of American Art in New York, from February 10 until March 22, 1964.

Maine and Its Role in American Art, published by The Viking Press, is an expanded survey of the state's art from 1740 to 1963. Seven authorities introduce chapters on the historical periods, each of which is profusely illustrated with black and white and color plates, including works in addition to those in the exhibit. As a result of the research for the exhibition and the book, an Archive of Maine Art has been established by Colby to become a center for the collection and preservation of documents relating to art produced in this state. Files of biographical information, photographs and colored slides of paintings and sculptures, and personal papers will be housed permanently in the art center.

The earliest painting in the exhibit, a portrait of Jane Pepperrell, was painted about 1710 by an unknown artist who also portrayed six, and possibly nine, other members of the same family. Maine was not yet a state but remained a province of Massachusetts until 1820. In those early decades of Maine's history, the leading portraitists of Boston were commissioned by the wealthy landholders and military leaders of the region. The names of many of the sitters still flourish in the names of the towns which they helped settle: Gardiner, Hallowell, Waldoboro. Robert Feke portrayed Brigadier General Samuel Waldo whose daughter-in-law, the former Sarah Erving, sat to John Singleton Copley. Gilbert Stuart pictured William King, who later became Maine's first governor, and James Bowdoin III and his wife Sarah, benefactors of Bowdoin College which still owns their portraits. John Smibert, Joseph Badger, Joseph Blackburn, and the miniaturist Edward G. Malbone, also captured likenesses of the province's leading citizens.

The less well-to-do also enriched their homes with portraits and decorative objects. Artists traveled by foot, horseback, wagon, and boat, often exchanging a completed painting for lodgings or services. Prices for portraits varied: William Matthew Prior painted traditional formal portraits—as well as flat unshadowed likenesses for one quarter the price. Townscapes were painted by itinerant artists as well as by local residents, many of them amateurs. In the prosperous mid-nineteenth century, traveling artists stenciled walls, decorated signboards, depicted shipping scenes, and carved figureheads.

---

*Jacqueline Davidson, "Maine and American Artists, 1710-1963," *American Artist* (December, 1963), pp. 32-39; 63-67. Reprinted by permission of the publisher.

With Gilbert Stuart's death, artistic attention focused on the Hudson River School. Thomas Cole, a founder of the movement, traveled to Maine as did his first pupil, Frederick E. Church, the first artist to extensively study the state.

The end of the Civil War and the beginning of the Industrial Revolution altered the artistic atmosphere of Maine. Mass production and specialization nudged out the local artist. At the same time Maine became a vacationland, a reputation so lasting that every state license plate still carries that legend.

In 1884, at the age of 48, Winslow Homer moved to Prout's Neck on Saco Bay, twelve miles below Portland. Brother Arthur had "discovered" the area and suggested that the family buy up the waterfront and start a summer resort. As the area developed, Homer withdrew more into his studio on the shore. Here he painted the *oils* for which he is famous. He remained here for the rest of his life, leaving only in the bleakest winter months for trips to the south—Florida, Cuba, the Bahamas. The surf on the rugged coast, the fishermen against the sea, the struggle of animals in a frozen wasteland; the scenes he pictured are still, for many people, the very image of Maine.

A very different view of Maine life is that portrayed by Eastman Johnson, a native whose father was Maine's Secretary of State for thirty years. Born in Lovell, Johnson lived in Fryeburg and Augusta, the state capitol, with his family before moving to Washington, D.C., and subsequently to Germany to study painting. Most important of the genre subjects for which he is noted is the maple-sugaring series he painted in 1865 and for several years thereafter. He returned each spring to Fryeburg, forty miles inland from Portland, and made studies of the activities, probably completing many of the paintings in his New York studio. In the 1870's he often visited his sister in Kennebunkport where he painted *In the Hayloft*.

The coast attracted many artists. The American impressionist Childe Hassam spent many summers on the Appledore, portraying the light effects on rocks and calm sea. Frederick J. Waugh and other younger artists were concerned with the naturalism of waves and rocks. Waugh went to Bailey Island, where his sister owned property, and built his house on a cliff above the breakers. He also painted on Monhegan Island.

By that time, Monhegan had attracted a number of outstanding artists. Robert Henri, leader of the "Ashcan School" and one of *The Eight* as well as a popular teacher, summered on Monhegan in 1903 where he painted the two canvases in the Colby exhibit. He recommended the island to several of his students, including George Bellows and Rockwell Kent who painted his famous *Winter* there in 1907. Kent spent a part of several years on the island, living in a house which he built himself. Carpentering, lobstering, and tending the lighthouse were his means of income.

George Bellows spent the summer of 1911 on Monhegan with the Henris and returned for two more summers. Subsequently, he painted at Ogunquit, Camden, Matinicus, and Criehaven, the latter two small islands off the coast. *In the Country* by Leon Kroll, another frequent Maine visitor in those years, portrays the Bellows family in Camden in 1916. John Singer Sargent, so noted for his society portraits, painted informal oils and watercolors of the family of artist Dwight Blaney at Ironbound Island near Mt. Desert.

Claiming that he was the only artist painting Maine who was a native-born son, Marsden Hartley was also determined to be the finest painter on the subject. Born in Lewiston in 1877, he returned there in 1900 and spent almost ten summers in Maine while wintering in New York City. In 1917 he was attracted back to Maine by the folk art of painting on glass and worked in that technique himself. After twenty years of self-exile to Paris, Germany, the south of France, the Southwest and Mexico, Hartley returned to Maine for the last six years of his life. He painted in Georgetown, notably Robin Hood Cove, and at Vinalhaven, a sizeable island east of Rockland. But he also penetrated to the northern part of the state to portray Mt. Katahdin, the highest point in Maine. Here he continued to develop the pyramid form that had intrigued him earlier in France and in Mexico. His rather blunt technique complemented the unfinished character of Maine's landscape and was the first break with the realism of the preceeding generations of artists who worked there.

Another modern artist closely linked to Maine, and one no less awed by it, was John Marin. Though his permanent home was in New Jersey, he spent many summers on the coast—at West Point,

Small Point south of Bath, and at Stonington. For twenty years, until his death in 1953, his summers were spent at Cape Split, Addison, only forty miles from the eastern boundary between Maine and Canada. Here he painted the oils that only recently have been appreciated. Marin marveled at the fierceness and beauty of the state, and lamented the passing of the schooners he painted off-shore and the creeping modernization that he felt was spoiling the villages. His painting, in contrast to Hartley's, is filled with energy and motion, and movement is a prime consideration in much of his work.

Not the dramatic forces of nature but the loneliness and desolation of isolated lighthouses, back country roads, and frugally ornate Victorian houses were depicted by Edward Hopper. His interest was painting the effects of sunlight on houses. His *Lighthouse Hill* and *Libby House, Portland* date from the late 1920's when he summered at Rockland and at Cape Elizabeth, a few miles below Portland.

A few years earlier, Ogunquit, a small town on Maine's less rugged western coastline not far from New Hampshire, began to attract young modernists. Hamilton Easter Field, founder and editor of *The Arts* magazine, ran a summer art school there to which he invited many of the artists whom he encouraged. A number of paintings in the Colby exhibition originate from this period. Peter Blume's *Maine Coast* is concerned with the relationship of the figures, as is *Maine Family* by Yasuo Kuniyoshi. Yet, as was true for most of Maine's history, it was the ocean and the land that drew the attention of most artists. *Wave Night* by Georgia O'Keeffe shows a new vision of Maine—a highly simplified stylized semiabstraction of a wave slowly and silently approaching a sandy beach. Niles Spencer's *The Cove* is of Perkins Cove in Ogunquit, but the artist's emphasis is on the boxy buildings and the structure of the landscape. Maurice Sterne did a series of rock studies in a cubist vein. Not all these artists continued to paint Maine, but the works they produced there show the influence of its unique geography.

Maine's unlimited supply of varying land and seascapes has provided material for unknown numbers of painters; sculptors, on the other hand, came to the state only in recent decades. Some were attracted by the colonies. Others, like William Zorach, discovered the state before becoming sculptors. He and his wife Marguerite, both painters, experimented, like many artists in the early decades of this century, with fauvism and cubism. In 1923 the Zorachs bought a farm on the edge of the sea at Robinhood, near Bath, where they still spend part of each year. During summers there, while his wife painted Maine landscapes such as *Rockport Bridge,* William Zorach experimented with direct carving in stone which subsequently replaced his painting. His affection for Maine goes deeper than just the carving materials he finds on its surface: he has written poetry about the state—and each summer does a group of water colors of the Maine landscape.

More than one third of the artists represented in the Colby exhibit have worked in Maine in the past twenty-five years: this statistic emphasizes the increasing attraction of the state and its growing importance to American Art. Though the styles of these artists are widely divergent, each has been affected by the atmosphere of Maine.

The abstract, expressionistic and non-objective movements have not been ignored but have been subordinated to the powerful Maine landscape. In John Heliker's *White Landscape* and in William Kienbusch's *Seagrass* not the details of the landscape are pictured—but the effects of nature on them. Maine was still the inspiration. In *Eclipse of the Moon* Reuben Tam, a younger painter of Monhegan Island, shows not the surf on the rocks or the massive cliffs but the eerie half-light peculiar to the phenomenon. Jason Schoener's feeling for Maine is so strong that he comes to his summer home on Georgetown Island from San Francisco every year. Again, while the exact setting for his *Lunar Tide* may be difficult to identify, it is unmistakably Maine. William Thon of Port Clyde portrays impressions of the woods of the Pine Tree State as in his *Early Frost.*

Another resident of Port Clyde and nearby Cushing, during the summer, is Andrew Wyeth. Son of the noted illustrator N.C. Wyeth who painted local fishermen and lobstermen during many summers in these same towns, he pictures the weathered barns, barren rocks, and scraggly meadows with a stunning realism unattained by other artists. In *Wind From the Sea,* with its tattered lace curtains billowing into a deserted room, he fills the desolate scene with a sense of loneliness that a camera could not capture. Wyeth discovers the details overlooked by other artists who are awed by the grander aspects of Maine.

By far the greater amount of work being produced in Maine is in the representational mode. And the same places have remained most popular: Ogunquit, Monhegan, the coast. The interior is not neglected, however. Carl Sprinchron, for instance, lived with woodsmen for three years, painted Katahdin region. Monhegan, like Ogunquit, has become a famous summer art center and appeals to those who relish the "arty" atmosphere as well as to more serious artists. Ernest Fiene's Lobster Shacks, Monhegan Island pictures the shingled cube-like shacks on stilts that are part of the island's appeal. In Ogunquit Henry Strater continues to paint landscapes and still lifes while directing the Museum of Art of Ogunquit. Exhibits there are devoted to twentieth century American art and include many pieces produced in Maine. John Laurent, painter son of sculptor Robert Laurent, works nearby.

Family ties have brought some artists to the state. Waldo Pierce was born in Bangor, the son of a wealthy lumberman. After years of travel and painting in Europe, he returned to Maine in the 1930's where he developed his present style, still spends summers in Searsport. Henry Varnum Poor was named after a great-uncle in Maine though he was raised in the Midwest. When he was in school he visited relatives in Andover, Maine; after the war he moved to Skowhegan, fifty miles to the east, to join the faculty of the new Skowhegan School of Painting and Sculpture. The school has attracted many artists, either as faculty or as students, and a body of work has been produced around the inland town. *Farm Composition, Number v, Skowhegan* was painted by Abraham Rattner during a teaching summer. Edwin Dickinson painted his small *The Chair* at the school. Alex Katz, a former student, spends his summers painting near Lincolnville.

More sculptors have come to Maine, and their work has become more influenced by the environment. Charles Gordon Cutler's *Maine Lobsterman* was carved from granite obtained near the artist's South Brooksville home. William Muir works instead in wood; he lives on Stonington near the Haystack Mountain School of Crafts with which he is associated. While his themes are not so dependent on the forms of nature, Abbott Pattison has nonetheless found an agreeable atmosphere in Maine. He has spent summers in Lincolnville for many years.

The art of Maine will continue to parallel the development of American art, but the unique qualities of the state will be evident. James M. Carpenter, chairman of the Art Department at Colby College, concludes the final chapter of *Maine and Its Role in American Arts*.

"We close this section of our book with some feeling of inadequacy in attempting to give a just account of the art leading up to the present. There are facts which do not make themselves known and there is the difficulty of judging the art of today while keeping an outlook broad enough to include the diversity of styles and objectives. But one thesis, we feel sure, will stand the test of time as it has when applied to previous periods: that artists who have worked in Maine have felt the impress of a place and that their works, when gathered together, bear witness to this."

PART III

MAINE IN THE TWENTIETH CENTURY

In comparison to the preceding sections, this third and last section is an abbreviated one. This is explained by the dearth of historical studies dealing with Maine in this century. What is included, therefore, is not for the most part history but commentary.

It is significant that much which has been written in recent years falls within the category of what one might describe as the "problems approach." Preoccupation with social and economic problems accompanying the industrialization of America has been especially obvious in the last decade or so. This has been true in Maine as well even though industrialism has largely by-passed the State. Yet, that is precisely the point. While Maine has escaped many of the problems resulting from industrialism, she has also failed to share as fully as some parts of the country in the material prosperity which has been one of the blessings of industrialism.

Thus, a debate rages. Is Maine fortunate that the natural beauty of the State has been left largely intact or is she cursed by the fact that national economic development seems to have passed her by? There are many who seem to hold both positions simultaneously in schizoid fashion.

There are several approaches to the enigmatic situation in which Maine finds herself economically. One approach is that of the clever journalist who finds the paradoxes and confusions of Maine life reinforced by a conservative outlook, as essentially pathetic, (39). A second approach calls for a concerted effort at industrial development building upon the experience of states in southern New England, (40). A third approach attempts to resolve the paradoxes and to eliminate the schizophrenia by plotting a strategy of economic development through conservation. This third approach is well presented by a special message on conservation and economic development presented by Governor Kenneth M. Curtis to the 104th Legislature in 1969, (41).

There can be no doubt that Maine has an economic problem. The incidence of poverty is the highest in Maine of the New England States, (42). From another angle an examination of Maine's "income gap" reveals the same picture, (43).

There are those who feel that education holds the key to economic prosperity. They feel that the creation of the new University of Maine system by the Legislature in 1968 is as significant a move in the direction of high quality education as was the enactment of the Sinclair Act in 1957, which encouraged secondary school consolidation, (47).

Finally, there are those who believe that only through the creative assistance of the federal government can meaningful economic progress take place. These persons pushed for the Quoddy Project in the 1930's, and the Machiasport Project more recently. Thus far, such ambitious federally supported programs have run into great opposition in the country as a whole and have failed to materialize. The Dickey-Lincoln hydro-electric project on the upper St. John River serves well as an illustration of the problems surrounding such efforts, (44).

Undoubtedly, each of the approaches has much to commend it. In the final analysis any breakthrough is likely to occur when the proper mix has been prepared and the time is right. Above all, what is so encouraging is the apparent eagerness on the part of so many Maine people to find solutions to their problems in recent years. In the final analysis, it is this eagerness which holds so much hope for the future.

CHAPTER

39.

Written in 1963, the following is an example of critical writing about Maine which has appeared frequently in the twentieth century. The underlying assumption of most such criticism is that Maine people are bound by tradition and convention—that what is needed is for the people to get shaken out of their time-worn ways. Such a view further assumes that too many Maine people refuse to look reality squarely in the face, preferring to escape into a blur of rhetoric about past and present virtues.

THE TROUBLE WITH MAINE*
by
William S. Ellis

In these enlightened times, when all good Shahs parcel out their royal hunting preserves to the peasants, we have, in our own country, a state so oligarchical in character as to suggest that the Chief Executive may one day be forced to flee to Miami.

Dismiss those that come first to mind: Montana, and the Anaconda Copper Company omnipotent atop its Butte Hill throne; Virginia, and the dedication of moldy First Family aristocracy to the Byrd barons. Turn instead to the far Northeast, to that spread of magnificent wilderness offering what is perhaps the last refuge from the oppressive busyness of the East Coast. Turn to Maine.

It has become good sport for outsiders to take potshots at Maine: to rewrite the old political saw, as Jim Farley once did, and have it read, "As Maine goes, so goes Vermont"; to keep the *Reader's Digest* posted on the quips of the natives; to suspect that the old sea dog who poses for pictures on a pier at Boothbay Harbor doesn't really know a lobster pot from a double boiler. Maine accepts these gentle knocks in good humor because, with Yankee individuality having disappeared with the last clipper ship, the state has to settle for being merely "quaint."

To look beyond this facade of simplicity, however, is to see a state gasping for breath, bogged down in the muck of supreme depression—a state dedicated seemingly, to the humiliation of its own people. Substandard living conditions are widespread; wages (when work is available) are appallingly low; mills are shuttered and farm machinery stands abandoned in fields no longer worth working. In the tidy villages with their white churches banked in clusters of Cape Cods, people gather on the streets not only to talk about yesterday's Grange meeting or tomorrow's Rebekah Lodge social, but also to wait for allotments of government surplus food.

And yet, not many people in Maine are exercised about the situation; they give all indications of being content with their unenviable lot. Since this is so, it is understandable that the controls of government in the state are entrusted to persons who are more or less sworn to oppose major changes. Thus, Republican Governor John H. Reed, a man who makes a virtue of indecision, was able to say, after touring the state on a campaign junket, "I like what I saw."

Surely the Governor must have been referring to the scenery, or else he "likes" the sight of cancerous poverty. Governor Reed saw what he wanted to see, for, if nothing else, Maine is a kaleidoscope of heady illusions. To feast on the enchantment of mountains pressing against the sea is to forget that those caught in the middle are having to exist on a per capita income of $1,843 a year. This hardship is compounded by the fact that living expenses in Maine are fairly high. It is true that a man can buy a ten-room farmhouse, a massive barn and 250 acres of land for less than he would pay for a new Thunderbird. It is also true that he can get his hair cut for as little as seventy-five cents in many of the towns and

---

*William S. Ellis, "The Trouble with Maine," *The Nation* (June 22, 1963), pp. 527-529. Reprinted by permission of the publisher.

villages. What strangles him is the cost of such basic essentials as fuel, electricity and food.

In a way, the high utility rates in Maine represent everything that is wrong with the state. They tell of old-line reactionary legislators who, in their empirical wisdom, regard the development of cheap, public power as too sweet a taste of honey for their constituents. Just as Ezra Pound expressed fear at what would happen if the classics had a wide circulation among the masses, so do these government figures fear the possible effects on the state's political structure in the event that the people are given what should be theirs.

Lobbyists representing the private utilities command considerable influence in Augusta, although not as much as in previous years. For example, in 1958, the Central Maine Power Company asked the state's Public Utilities Commission to authorize a rate increase amounting to more than $3 million. The PUC said that an increase of $860,000 was sufficient. Central Maine Power, not one to have its request weighed as simply a request, turned to the state Supreme Court with an appeal and came away with authorization for an increase more than double that which the commission would have allowed.

More recently, the National Rural Electric Commission Association charged in Washington that Central Maine Power had overcharged its customers by more than $2.5 million during the period 1958-1960. Less than two weeks later, Frederick N. Allen, chairman of the Public Utilities Commission, made this statement: "After completing further studies into the matter, the Commission will issue a final report which will indicate beyond any doubt that Central Maine Power Company's rate of return for the period questioned was well within the limits prescribed by the Commission under Maine law."

And with that, Allen let it be known what the final findings would be, even though the investigation was not yet completed. He was also clear on the point of law: it is perfectly legal for the Central Maine Power Company to charge anywhere from 5 to 30 per cent more than the average private-utility rates outside of New England.

Typical of the power-company executives who kept the reins of government in their hands for so many years was the late Robert Braun. In addition to being a director of Central Maine Power, Braun, who died in 1953, had interests in banks, the state's largest department store, and paper and textile companies. Because his influence seemed to spread to all corners of the largest of the New England states, he was sometimes referred to as "The Spiderman." Naturally, Braun's economic power overlapped into the political field, and he was responsible in great measure for putting various individuals in high state offices. However, the decline of Maine had its beginning long before Robert Braun's time. He simply did what others are doing today, and that is to prolong the survival of a few at the expense of many.

The strategy can be seen at work at almost every legislative session: a bill to raise the minimum hourly wage in the state to $1.15 is tabled for "further study" after an opponent warns that such a measure would be of "major economic importance" (i.e., harmful to employers); it is proposed that a person eighteen years of age be allowed to vote provided he is not a "pauper"; legislation to raise the current 3 per cent sales tax to 4 is put into motion, while suggestions that what Maine needs at this point is a more equitable personal state income tax are knocked down with arguments that such a tax would pose "a threat to our economy."*

Another tragic example of this strategy can be seen in what were once rivers and streams of classic purity. For some time now, Maine, along with New Hampshire, has been feuding with the federal government over the pollution in the Androscoggin River. The government wants the states to clean up the river, and last September, representatives of the Department of Health, Education and Welfare came to New England for a conference on the matter. The representatives of Maine and New Hampshire walked out on the meeting. Another meeting was held early this year, but nothing of any real value was accomplished.

Maine's defiance of the federal government in this matter stems from the fact that the state's most powerful industries, the paper and pulp companies, are responsible for most of the pollution in the river. To cooperate with the federal government in this effort would mean pressuring the economic giants. Maine is not about to do that, or at least not until every fish in the Androscoggin dies and the river stench makes even the birches wilt.

---

*An income tax was adopted by the 104th Legislature in July 1969.

And yet, the pulp and paper companies are the so-called "responsible" industries in Maine. The accolade is well placed when most other manufacturing operations in the state are taken into account. There are, for example, the manufacturers who deal in leather products, mostly shoes. In many cases, the method of operation in this field is riddled with here-today-gone-tomorrow movement. An operator can move into a small Maine town, take over the vacant textile mill (there's certain to be one) for practically nothing, rent the equipment he needs and hire a handful of women willing to work for salaries on a par with, say, garbage collectors in Addis Ababa.

Women play a vital role in the economy of Maine. During the period from 1950 to 1960, there was a gain in manufacturing employment in the state of 2,600 persons. Of that number, only 600 were men. Said an engineer employed by the Fairchild Semiconductor Division plant in South Portland: "Our company came to Maine, quite frankly, because we knew there was a large force of women with nimble fingers and soft brains here. Such a person is perfect for assembly-line work in a semi-conductor plant."

A great many of the 960,000 residents of Maine refuse to accept the fact that blue-ribbon industries—those not engaged in nimble-finger-soft-brain work—are not going to locate in a state served by just one passenger train a day that comes from Boston and terminates in Portland; a state with inadequate—nay, non-existent—facilities for research in such fields as electronics; a state that places more store in the illiterate pretentiousness of Rotary fellowship than in development of a creditable system of state-supported higher education.

What Maine needs, of course, is a thundering voice of dissent—someone in authority to stand up and announce that a man is a damn fool to work sixty hours a week and take home a $55 paycheck. More important, Maine needs someone who can, without concerning himself with "Yankee heritage" and other such cobwebs in this nation's northeast corner, bring to light the true value of the state. For example, it may well be that Maine has an important role to play in the world's ever-increasing need for intelligent use of the sea. At the present time the legislature is less interested in the possible development of a major oceanographic research center than it is in resolving a quarrel between lobstermen and skin-divers, the latter having been accused of catching the crustaceans by hand.

There are those who say that Maine should concentrate on building up its "Vacationland" image. Surely, the several million vacationers who come to the state every summer do provide a substantial, though seasonal, prop for the economy. But it may be too late for development even in the area of recreation. Maine catered too long to the turn-of-the-century financiers who could afford to build seashore mansions and call them "cottages." The Rockefellers, for instance, named their Seal Harbor cottage "The Eyrie," and if one cared to count the rooms, they would add up to eighty. "The Eyrie" is now in the process of being demolished, and when that work is completed, an era will have ended—an era that saw some villages in Maine collect as much as $10,000 each year in taxes levied on a single "cottage."

During that era, Maine allowed too many of its beaches to be closed to the public, too many of its wilderness acres to go into private ownership. Today, the federal government would like to make a National Recreation Area of the splendid expanse of rivers, lakes, and dense timber growths known as the Allagash. Most of the 300,000 acres comprising the Allagash, however, are owned by paper-manufacturing interests, and they, of course, would rather have the area remain a private preserve with a primary function revolving around pulp rather than play.

From where, then, is the voice of dissent to come? Democrat Edmund S. Muskie might have been the answer had he not moved on from the governorship to the U.S. Senate. Now and again, the editorial writers on the sanguine Portland *Press Herald*, the state's most influential newspaper, flirt with reform, but they are somewhat like bilious turtledoves. Besides, the editorial page of the *Press Herald* features its own lovable May Craig and her regular accounts of how naughty the Negroes in Washington are becoming. "After reading May Craig," said a high school English teacher in the village of Gorham, "I can't take anything else seriously on the editorial page."

Maine has much help in projecting a pleasant, homely image of itself. *The Christian Science Monitor* regularly prints lengthy communiques from old-timers who recall how much fun it was to hike through the snow to grandmother's farm at twilight; John Gould's dispatch from Lisbon Falls, also appearing in the *Monitor,* cautions against putting too much white flour in corn bread; again in the *Monitor* (it's a wonder they have room for all those Dutch and Portuguese translations), a Mr. Ronald D. Billings writes: "When I think of Maine, I think of the inland country of the North and Northwest; that land of endless green forests, studded with boulders, laved with rivers and streams, and spotted with lakes and ponds; that land where there is a mountain on every horizon."

Maine is indeed all those things. It is a state where hunters can kill 40,142 deer in a single season. It is a state where citizens can gather at their town meetings and, if they so choose, vote down the $54 appropriation for keeping the town clock wound for the rest of the year. It is a state where, if you want to travel by Greyhound bus from Portland to Concord, N.H., a distance of eighty-five miles, you have to go 200 miles south to Boston and then back up.

Most of all, though, Maine is a state in trouble. And, as the perplexed friends of the wealthy kleptomaniac are invariably told in the television dramas, nothing can be done until she recognizes her own problem.

CHAPTER

40.

Mr. George Ellis, formerly president of the Federal Reserve Bank of Boston and a Maine native analyzes Maine's economic future in the following article. Central to his analysis is the contention that faced with a national economy, Maine must make a concentrated effort to reorient itself economically to the needs of such a national economy.

ISSUES AND DECISIONS: MAINE'S FUTURE*
by
George H. Ellis

Maine is not, as some of our rugged individualists seem to think, an independent nation—separate, distinct, self-contained and self-sufficient. It is just the reverse—almost entirely dependent on the rest of New England and the nation.

For example, the standards of living which prevail in lower New England—wage and salary levels, social services, cultural opportunities—have direct bearings on Maine's economic and social progress. Maine cannot safely ignore the changing trends of other parts of New England and the Northeast. It must not only adjust to them but, I believe, swim with them. To those who say "we like ourselves the way we are," I can only answer, you must force progressive change or you very soon will *not* like the way you are.

If Maine is less fortunate in some respects than other New England states, what is there in the experience of those states, or of New England as a whole, which can assist Maine in achieving its full potential?

For the eighty years for which there are accurate figures, New England's per capita income has consistently led that of the country as a whole. To the basic question—how has New Englnad sustained this leadership?—there is a quick and easy answer: the intelligence, education, foresight, skill and adaptability of the New England people. This *is* the answer. But it's an answer so amorphous as to have little value for this discussion.

The region's per capita income, the foundation of social and cultural progress, is solidly based on manufacturing. To be sure, we raise broilers and potatoes, milk cows and vacationists, teach the young from all over the nation, insure any and everything, and help finance new enterprise and the nation's underdeveloped states. But it is primarily what we make and sell to the rest of the world that keeps us an eminently going concern.

Until the 1930's there was a more-or-less common pattern of manufacturing activity prevailing throughout the New England states. Let us call it the classical pattern, concentrating heavily on nondurable goods—textiles, apparel, shoes and leather, food processing, paper making. Subordinate to these, New England produced assorted durable goods, such as machinery, fabricated metals, lumber and wood products, building stone and the like. While each New England state ran variations on this pattern, this is generally how things were for the region as a whole at the end of World War I. It is how things still are here in Maine.

With the outbreak of World War II, there developed a new and increasingly important second line of manufacturing activity which we may designate as the research-based pattern. As an economic scientist, I thoroughly disapprove of over-generalization, but for purposes of discussion let's say that Maine and Rhode Island continued to adhere to the older, classical pattern while Massachusetts, Connecticut, and to a lesser extent New Hampshire, switched over to the new one. Vermont stands by itself, as it always has. For the breakaway states, the research-based pattern

---

*George H. Ellis, "Issues and Decisions," *Down East Magazine* (March, 1963), pp. 46-47; 57-60. Reprinted by permission of the publisher.

brought a significant reorientation and revitalization of manufacturing, with healthy increases in new jobs, wage levels, purchasing power and tax revenue. Herein lies a lesson for Maine.

In this new pattern, the leadership formerly held by nondurables, especially textiles, has passed to durables. These include machinery and electrical machinery, which embraces electronics, transportation equipment in the form of nuclear ships and aircraft and components, instruments, and a dozen subdivisions in atomics, nucleonics, metallurgy and optics.

Let us compare the results during the 1950's of these two opposing manufacturing patterns—the research-based as exemplified by New England as a whole, and the classical as exemplified by the State of Maine.

In the decade of the 50's New England manufacturing employment slid off by 2.2 per cent. The loss came entirely through the still declining textile industry. Had textiles merely held the line instead of dropping 148,000 jobs, the region's small sag would have been converted to a gain of over 100,000 in manufacturing employment.

Now contrast this with the decade's developments in the new research-based durables. Total New England employment in durables was up by 17.2 per cent, a figure which exceeded that for the nation. There were gains of 6,000 jobs in machinery, 10,000 in instruments, 13,000 in ordnance, 45,000 in electrical machinery and electronics, and 52,000 in transportation equipment.

There is a factor in here of even greater significance than simply "new jobs for old." All through the 50's there was a steady upgrading of New England workers, both in skills and from lower to higher paying jobs. In the region, as in the nation, workers in durable goods industries are paid a higher average hourly wage than are workers in nondurables. The movement during the decade of more than 100,000 New England workers from nondurables to durables resulted in a substantial increase in their purchasing and taxpaying powers.

What I hope emerges from this hasty review of the new pattern in New England manufacturing is the picture of a region substantially stronger than at any time in our generation. In my view, all this was made possible by the New Englander's capacity for adaptation to change. Even more, by his capacity to foresee and prepare for change. The critical elements here are breadth of understanding and flexibility of mind and talent. Both are products of education.

I have devoted so much space to manufacturing, and the nature and results of the *new* New England pattern, because I believe that therein lies Maine's only road to progress. The state's present manufacturing structure is still that which prevailed in New England before World War II. Considered in terms of the structural shifts I have just described, Maine's manufacturing structure is old-fashioned and vulnerable, top-heavy with nondurables—particularly shoes and leather and textiles.

Between 1950 and 1960, Maine's manufacturing employment dropped as did New England's, but Maine dropped more—4.5 per cent as against 2.2. Here again the principal loss was in textiles—12,000 jobs. This was partially offset by a 5,000 job pickup in shoes and leather, 1,000 in paper, 600 in food processing. And, in sharp contrast to all New England, what happened in durables? Absolutely nothing. More than half of Maine's durable employment is in lumber and wood, in which employment has hung stationary since the war. Nearly half of all the remaining jobs in durables are in transportation equipment, largely shipbuilding. Here again no significant change. Collectively, Maine's machinery, electrical machinery, and primary and fabricated metals industries have never been important in terms of total employment—but even so, instead of growing they showed a collective job loss of more than one-third.

Recently the Boston Federal Reserve Bank studied New England's changing industrial skill requirements. The study showed that those industries requiring the highest skills are also the industries growing fastest in the region. Skilled craftsmen's jobs grew at the same rate as total employment, while semi-skilled and unskilled jobs declined steadily. Similar shifts in labor requirements took place in other expanding industries.

In Maine, during the decade of the 50's, employment of professional, technical and kindred workers increased by 30 per cent. Skilled workers increased by 16 per cent and clerical and similar employment by 24 per cent. In sharp contrast, operatives—that is, semi-skilled—grew in number by only two per cent, and unskilled, including farm help, actually declined by 31 per cent.

By 1970, only eight years from now, the Reserve Bank estimated that New England's need for professional and skilled workers will increase by 233,000, with the need for skilled workers alone rising by 165,000. In this situation Maine is in competition with the other New England states. It cannot hope to attract desirable new industries without greatly increasing its own skilled labor force. Unless the new industries are acquired or developed, Maine's skilled labor will continue to be lured to adjacent states by more job opportunities and higher pay. The end result, under such circumstances, might well be an increasing handicap to existing industry, a solid roadblock to industrial expansion, and eventually a contribution to unemployment.

To meet Maine's future needs, then, young people must be given more and better formal education. They must also be given the opportunity to acquire skills *before* entering the labor force. Finally, those now at work must be enabled to improve existing skills and acquire new ones.

Part of the answer to this problem is to be found in the publicly-supported vocational training school. Since such schools are expensive, they are best established on an area basis. Maine has only one area public vocational school, that in Portland, in contrast to fourteen in Connecticut. Massachusetts, which already has fifty-five vocational high schools, is now turning to the area or regional concept. Two such schools opened this fall and more are in the planning stage. I understand Maine is also considering additional area vocational schools. Obviously the need is great—and the time is now.

I urge expansion of state support of education at all levels, with particular attention to vocational training and post high school education. I propose this partly for the direct values to the young people themselves, but also as a technique of economic development with broad and indirect effects.

To make such a recommendation is tantamount to asking for increased public expenditures in total, since significant opportunities for reduction of other outlays do not seem apparent. Obviously, then, more spending on education can occur only if public revenues are expanded—by additional taxes, but only with a sense of fairness and equity in the taxation process. In considering the means of securing new tax revenue, we must make sure that the measures taken do not in themselves impede the economic development which will further broaden and strengthen the tax base. We must also observe fairness and equity in the taxation process.

We all agree that holding the tax line or even reducing taxes is desirable, yet we must of necessity also agree that state needs can be met only by an increase in tax revenues. We could achieve this by reducing exemptions allowed under the sales tax, raising the sales tax rate, or by miscellaneous other devices. In my opinion, however, the soundest long-run approach is to adopt—now—a personal income tax.*

I believe that adoption of a state personal income tax will not act as a significant deterrent to the state's continued economic development. It seems improbable to me that Maine residents would move out of the state to escape such taxation. For one thing, they would find that thirty-five other states already have personal income taxes of some sort, including the immediate neighbors of Massachusetts, New Hampshire, and Vermont. Twenty-one states already have both a personal income tax and a retail sales tax. Nor does it appear reasonable that Maine businessmen will change their minds about expanding their operations as a result of the new income tax. The federal income tax long ago acclimated businessmen to sharing their increased income with the government. Finally, I point out that most of Maine's new manufacturing employment is likely to come from the establishment of branch plants by out-of-state firms. The decision of a national company to locate a branch in Maine will not be materially inhibited by the fact that Maine, like thirty-five other states, will expect the local manager and employees of the Maine branch to pay income taxes for the support of state needs.

As to plant location decisions, one must also remember that the burden which concerns business most is the property tax. It must be paid year in and year out irrespective of the relative profitability of the operation. If a new source of tax revenue is not established, industry inevitably will be loaded with paying for higher local government outlays through increasing property tax rates. In the long run, the income tax alternative, insofar as it would relieve cities and towns of increasing tax

---

*An income tax was adopted by the 104th Legislature in 1969.

rates or assessment or both, would be a distinct advantage to business.

My second reason for favoring the adoption of a state personal income tax is that such a tax would be more equitable than the alternatives. Removing food as an exemption from the sales tax, for example, would hit hardest at those low income families that spend relatively high proportions of their income for food. In final analysis, all taxes are paid out of income. What is needed now is a tax that rests primarily on income not devoted to paying for necessities. This could be achieved through an income tax with reasonable deductions by size of family.

Furthermore, by associating the liabilities of such a tax with federal income tax calculations, marked efficiencies of definition, administration and enforcement become possible.

To summarize the foregoing:

1. Maine's future economic strength will be governed largely by Maine's ability to transform its manufacturing operations into the newer research-based industries, as demonstrated by the experience of southern New England.
2. An adaptable labor force, moving steadily into higher skills, is essential if manufacturing is successfully to negotiate such a transition.
3. An enlarged public effort (more taxes) in support of more and better education, particularly vocational education, will be necessary if Maine is to achieve its highest potential.

CHAPTER 41.

It is asked frequently if Maine can experience economic and especially industrial development while preserving its natural environment. The experience in other states would suggest that in practice the two objectives are incompatible. Maine has an opportunity to demonstrate that the two goals are compatible through planning as the following written by Governor Kenneth Curtis demonstrates.

CONSERVATION AND ECONOMIC DEVELOPMENT*
by
Governor Kenneth M. Curtis

Introduction

The subjects of Conservation and Economic Development are inseparable, a fact that was not always understood in the past. Recognizing this relationship, we have adopted the guide of "Development through Conservation." We know that further industrial development is coming to Maine. The only question is the terms under which that development will take place. What kind of industry do we want to attract? What kind of land use pattern do we accept as orderly? What controls on the defacing and pollution of the environment do we care to impose?

With this policy of development through conservation we recognize that a certain level of economic growth is a prerequisite to the exercise of effective development controls. And we recognize the parallel principle that the proper exercise of controls, the proper use of land, and the proper protection of our air and water resources, are prerequisites to sound economic development.

Certain resources that we have long taken for granted in America are coming into short supply. Clean air, clean water, open space, recreation opportunities—these elements, in which Maine abounds, are becoming more valuable every day. Nevertheless, demands are beginning to mount on these precious resources of ours, and Maine must, therefore, plan and pass intelligent legislation in order to avoid the despoiling effects of chaotic, helter-skelter growth that has left such gaping wounds in other states and in a few locations here in Maine. We have the opportunity now to act. To fail to grasp this opportunity would be a failure to live up to our responsibilities. The Maine that we bequeath to our children depends upon our decisions.

Mining and Drilling Controls

Several bills will be presented to the Legislature to establish standards of conservation and regulation for industries that are just beginning to come to Maine. I am speaking of the mining industry, which is expected to increase its investment in Maine in the very near future, and of the oil and gas industry, now on the threshold of searching for resources off our shores and creating refineries and other facilities upon our coasts.

A *Mined Land Rehabilitation Act* before you would require the rehabilitation of all land surface areas that are disturbed by mining operations. Before beginning to mine in Maine, a company would submit a rehabilitation plan to the Maine Mining Bureau and have it approved. The company would also provide a bond of up to $1,500 per acre to assure completion of the work as outlined in the rehabilitation plan. A conservation engineer would be hired by the Mining Bureau to help supervise the provisions of the bill. Violations of this bill, as well as violations of other conservation measures, would be prosecuted by the Attorney General's Office.

An *Oil and Gas Control Act* would authorize the Mining Bureau to supervise the oil and gas industry

---

*Message of Governor Kenneth M. Curtis presented to the 104th Legislature, February 19, 1969.

in Maine and establish pollution control standards for all facets of operation—including exploration, development, drilling, production, transportation and refining. Regulations would be specifically aimed at preventing waste, spillage and pollution.

One of the biggest, but probably least recognized, problems in the State in terms of land damage is the current form of sand, gravel and other earth material extraction. Such operations are a form of open pit mining, and they have never been the subject of state law. Here, too, there is a need for establishing standards and assuring methods of rehabilitation. A *Surficial Materials Conservation Act* would cover the extraction of sand, gravel, clay, loam, etc., and, much like the Mined Land Rehabilitation Act, would require the extracting company to post a bond to insure site rehabilitation. However, because of the limited staffing of the Mining Bureau, supervision of this law would be left to municipal officials, with the Mining Bureau and technicians from the Soil and Water Conservation Districts acting in an advisory capacity.

A fourth bill to be considered in this area calls for a revision of the Maine Mining Law. The changes proposed will streamline the law, and establish conformity with the laws of other states and Canadian provinces.

Water and Air Pollution Controls

In September of 1968, I appointed a Pollution Abatement Committee to begin an intensive investigation of the status of the fight against pollution in Maine, and especially water pollution. This committee was made up of private citizens, legislators, and state officials.

The report of this committee, recently issued, presented a series of recommendations that must be translated into legislation if we are to tackle our water pollution problems effectively.

Our pace in dealing with water pollution has been too slow. One unhappy illustration of this fact can be seen in the following statistics. Five years ago, it was estimated that the total need in Maine for municipal construction of sewage treatment facilities amounted to $130 million. During the past five years, we have spent $10 million but our needs have increased by $50 million. Consequently, we now need $170 million, and we are losing ground. Moreover, these figures represent the estimate only for municipal costs. The total clean-up bill for Maine's water is now estimated to be in the range of $250 to $320 million.

Possibly the most basic problem in our slow fight against water pollution is the continuing unavailability of Federal funds to meet the Federal share (up to 55% in some cases) of the total cost of any project. Despite our total needs of $250 to $320 million, the Federal money available is $1.8 million for this current year.

The time is now approaching when we cannot wait for authorized Federal funds to be appropriated. There are many situations where State and local governments are ready to move, industries have made their commitment, and the only input lacking is the Federal one. Inaction costs money. The costs of not dealing with a problem become greater than the costs of dealing with it. We in Maine should act now to authorize the advancing of State funds to cover the authorized Federal share. The cost to Maine in interest payments while we wait for eventual Federal reimbursement will, in all likelihood, be offset by the lower costs of construction now as compared to construction 3, 4, or 5 years from now.

The Pollution Abatement Committee has recommended a $50 million bond issue to finance pollution abatement projects. In my Budget Message, I proposed this course of action for a referendum vote at the 1970 election. I reiterate my support for this all-important measure.

It is also incumbent upon us to release the balance of the 1963 pollution abatement bond issue for immediate obligation. Some $12 million of the original $25 million bond issue has already been spent or earmarked. Under the pre-financing authorization passed by the 103rd Legislature, only $3,500,000 of this was released for projects already authorized but not funded by the Federal Government. Proposed legislation would authorize use of the remaining $13 million for prefunding as well as the State share of projects.

I further support the Pollution Abatement Committee's recommendations for reorganization of the Water and Air Environmental Improvement Commission. The proposed plan would reduce the eleven man commission to a more workable five man commission, double the staff of the agency by adding twenty members, provide for an Executive

Director, provide for improved hearing and licensing procedures, and plug loopholes in current legislation. This measure would dramatically step up the fight against pollution.

A bill to establish civil liability for unlawful pollution, making the pollutor responsible for expenses incurred by the State in tracing pollution sources and restoring quality, will also be proposed, as will legislation to have the WAEIC license treatment plant operators.

Air pollution is another serious problem in Maine—more serious than we had suspected. A preliminary study by the University of Maine has detailed the extent of the problem and set forth recommendations, most of which are incorporated in legislation submitted to you.

The most important need is for establishing air quality standards similar to those that we have established for water, insuring, at the same time, that these standards will be reached and maintained. Ambient air quality standards would be established for regions and sub-regions in the State, and because of the complex technical nature of air pollution, the Water and Air Environmental Improvement Commission, rather than the Legislature, would handle this task. Power to set standards for enforcement, licensing, prohibition and hearings will also be vested in the WAEIC, requiring an expanded staff in the air pollution division.

Land Use Controls

Slightly more than one half of the total land mass of the State currently lies in the unorganized territories and plantations, where there is no effective mechanism of local governmental control. A bill presented to the 103rd Legislature called for wildlands zoning to correct the injurious effects of inadequate planning, and for development standards in our wilderness areas, now subject to increasing pressures from a recreation-minded public.

The Legislative Research Committee has now completed an extensive study of this problem, and refinements have been added to the old bill. In its present form the bill would establish a Wildlands. Use Regulation Commission with power to set zoning and other standards for all land in this area within 500 feet of access roads and shorelines of accessible rivers, streams, lakes and other bodies of water.

Changes in taxation policies are also incorporated in this bill, directing the State Tax Assessor to consider the effect upon value of any enforceable restrictions to which the use of the land may be subjected. Such a provision should help prevent the taxing of wildlands at residential property rates, a practice which forces the use of this property for hasty, unwise development.

The Wildlands Bill is far-reaching legislation, aimed at launching an early attack upon a disease before it advances to an incurable stage. This is a step that we must take now, while the problem is manageable.

We must also improve the control of development in coastal marshes (wetlands), with their great scientific value as breeding grounds for marine species. The 103rd Legislature provided a mechanism for control, but difficulties have arisen in carrying out the bill's provisions because of a failure to supply funds for enforcement personnel. A bill will be introduced to facilitate administration, and limited personnel increases are recommended in the Executive Budget.

The Legislature should also give serious consideration to a bill that would extend the area of responsibility for wetlands control to inland waters.

In the area of subdivision control, I support legislation to establish minimum lot sizes in unsewered and unwatered areas and mandatory zoning and subdivision in areas bordering lakes, streams and coastal waters. More specifically, the legislation would require that in all areas of the State where there is no public sewer and public water supply, lots used for single family residential use would not be less than 20,000 square feet. In cases where there is one but not the other of the public sewer and water facilities, the minimum lot size is reduced to 15,000 square feet. In the case of multiple dwellings, there are other provisions on a proportionate basis.

Another part of this legislation would require the zoning of all land areas within 500 feet of normal high water of any navigable pond, lake, river, stream or body of salt water. Municipal governments would be given until June 30, 1971 to adopt zoning and subdivision control ordinances for these areas. If such ordinances were not completed by that date, authority would be given to the Water and Air Environmental Improvement

Commission to adopt suitable protective measures. At the same time, the State Planning Office will be working on a coastal use study, to establish a model plan for the best utilization of these resources.

Control of outdoor advertising has become an important component of efforts to preserve the best features of our natural environment. A bill will be presented to you which offers a reasonable approach to providing information needed by a travelling public without detracting from the State's roadside beauty. It is, in part, a revision of the current law, but also incorporates changes in our law required by the Federal Highway Beautification Act of 1965. It amends the present law by providing for the *removal* of signs already erected that do not conform to the Highway Beautification Act requirements. Such removal also qualifies the State for increased bonus payments from the Federal Government.

A complementary bill establishes a Scenic Highway Board with responsibilities for declaring a system of scenic highways in Maine and preserving the scenic values along this system.

Solid waste disposal has become an increasing problem for Maine communities. The location of dumps and the disposal of trash constitute pollution hazards throughout Maine. Open dump burning is one of the chief causes of air pollution in the State. Dumps located within the view of motorists are a blight upon our landscape. To meet these problems, I propose legislation that permits the Department of Health and Welfare to coordinate State efforts to regulate solid waste disposal activities, which now affect the interests of 8 departments of State government. The legislation also requires the filing and approval of a written plan before any new disposal area can be initiated.

Our increasing consciousness of the importance of proper sewage treatment and sewage systems requires an overall State approach to this program. I therefore recommend a bill that permits the Public Utilities Commission to regulate and assist the numerous sewer districts and utilities now existing in Maine.

Another important measure related to development and the conserving of our environment regulates the cutting of timber within 100 yards of any body of water, or any highway. The bill specifies certain methods of cutting and requires that no unsightly conditions remain as a result of such cutting.

State Park Development

As part of the State's effort to preserve the natural beauties of our forests and seacoast, the 103rd Legislature and the people at referendum approved a 4 million dollar bond issue for the purchase of lands and waters. To complement this effort, I have recommended a capital improvement program of $1,667,000 for the development of park lands and historic sites now owned by the State. The program includes the development of Poland Spring State Park near Lewiston, the expansion of Popham Beach, completion of initial development at Peaks-Kenney, and the development of park facilities at Damariscotta Lake, Ferry Beach, and on the Saco River. These projects will generate $1,288,400 in federal funds.

Development of these parks will give great pleasure to our citizens. It will also encourage valuable tourist trade.

Economic Growth

The housing situation in Maine is now an object of study and attention. The State Planning Office, in cooperation with the Citizens Advisory Committee on Housing, issued a report that documents the critical need for a massive campaign to build new housing in Maine. An alarming percentage of our dwellings are substandard, dilapidated and obsolete. The availability of decent, reasonably priced housing is severely limited.

Many steps must be taken to correct this situation, most notably the creation of a State Housing Authority with the powers to sponsor housing projects for low income families and for the elderly, to purchase or partially guarantee home mortgages, and to coordinate research on a variety of housing projects and to provide technical services to these housing projects.

Increasing the State's efforts in housing, which are now practically nonexistent, will help meet an urgent need and will stimulate our economy through the increase in construction activity. Construction could also be encouraged if, as being studied by the Credit Research Committee, we use State guarantees to builders for tract development. This would require a Constitutional amendment, which will be presented to you.

Legislation will be introduced to modify the organizational structure of the Department of Economic Development, the agency with primary responsibility for increasing economic activity in the State. I support these changes. The bill, among other things, would change the name of the Department to the Department of Development, emphasizing the interrelated nature of all development in the State.

The laws administered by the M.I.B.A. and M.R.A. are two of our major tools for stimulating economic growth. The functions of these two agencies are similar, and the agencies often work together. In order to effect further economies, we should consider combining the housekeeping functions of the above agencies and providing a single secretariat and office operation. We should also consider broadening the potential usefulness of M.I.B.A. by extending its guarantee powers to so-called "service industries," in addition to manufacturers. This change, which would require an amendment to the Constitution, would place the State in a position to assist this important form of development.

Power rates and fuel costs in New England are the highest in the nation and they are particularly high in Maine. In our efforts to find relief, either through the medium of the Dickey-Lincoln electric project or the Machiasport Oil Refinery Project, we have been frustrated by certain lawmakers and lobbyists in Washington. Without public power in New England, we will continue to suffer high rates and short supply, with the continual possibility of losing industrial prospects. For this reason, the State must consider a Maine Public Power Authority that would be authorized to study and ultimately build appropriate projects to help Maine and all of New England in our quest for better service and lower rates.

Our tax structure in all areas needs reform. One of the most difficult problems we have is that our present property tax system discourages home improvement. The more a homeowner improves his residence, the more property tax he pays. Increase in value to the home, and individual homeowner pride, have kept improvements from dwindling to nothing, but we know that the tax system has prevented much modernization. The result is a loss of economic activity. The dollar and cents loss to the State is incalculable. Recognizing that the problem is a difficult one, not easy of solution, I would like to have a study authorized to seek ways to encourage home improvement without diminishing the property tax revenue of the municipalities.

Studies have been undertaken of our liquor laws, which directly affect the revenue of the State as well as our extensive tourist industry, and it seems clear that reforms must be made. It is estimated that one reform package consisting of a bill to allow the sale of wine in grocery stores, eliminate the licensee discount, increase license fees and eliminate the Government beer tax refund would return to the State approximately $1.2 million. Clearly, we must have as much additional revenue as possible. A measure will also be introduced to establish "agency stores" or, in other words, to allow the sale of liquor in stores not 100% operated by the State, yet under State supervision and control, in communities too small to support a "State Store." Many communities have voted to have State stores, but the Liquor Commission cannot afford to build and stock these stores, with a resultant loss of potential revenue.

It is time also that we consider raising the amount of working capital available to the Liquor Commission. No business can operate efficiently without enough capital. Finally, we should consider a modest and reasonable Sunday Sales Law that will be a boon to our tourist industry and a further source of increased revenue.

Transportation

Transportation improvements are directly linked to improvements in economic development. Measures to provide for a Department of Transportation have been advanced. A study of this complex, potentially beneficial consolidation of different agencies is now underway, and I recommend the continuation of this study to allow full exploration of the implications of this step.

In air transportation Maine has lagged behind, but it is now catching up with the establishment of new routes, such as the Maine to the Middle West run by Northeast Airlines, and the entry of new third level airlines on the scene.

We should authorize the establishment and regulation in Maine of an expanded third carrier system to encourage this flight service to communities not now reached by regular service. Four third level carriers operate in Maine now:

Aroostook Airways, Downeast Airlines, Executive Airlines and Trans East Airlines. Under the proposed third carrier legislation, the Maine Aeronautics Commission would have the power to license third level carriers, issue route accreditation certificates, provide assistance to these airlines, and lay the groundwork for expansion of the system.

In line with Maine's plan to increase its role in aviation transportation, we should act now to make the former Dow Field at Bangor more attractive as a possible International Airport for jet travel. A major function of Dow as an International Airport will be its position as a refueling stop for transatlantic flights. We should therefore consider an exemption of taxes on jet fuel to make Bangor more competitive as a site for refueling jets.

We must also improve the quality of our airports throughout the State and develop new ones. In my capital improvements program I recommended $2,124,000 for airport development, which, along with $371,000 already available, will generate $3,851,000 of federal money. The program includes a new terminal building and other facilities at Bangor; general improvements at Portland and Auburn; new airports at Livermore Falls and in the Madawaska area; and other important aviation projects. These developments and improvements, increasing accessibility to all areas of the State, will contribute greatly to our economic development.

With respect to boating, a uniform system of fees for registration should be enacted in place of the personal property tax. A portion of the money collected would be turned back to the municipalities.

Finally, our highway program, which I discussed in detail in my Budget Message, remains the basic element in our transportation system. I simply wish to reaffirm the need for the program outlined in my budget.

Conclusion

I have discussed legislation affecting many areas—mining, oil and gas development, water and air pollution, land use, housing, transportation, and others. The problems in each of these areas are enormously complex, susceptible, in their complexity, to much debate and many solutions. I realize that the measures I have proposed today do not provide all the answers, and I encourage discussion and legislation that will evaluate and supplement these proposals. But, whatever the final solutions, we must act now, lest we expose ourselves to chaotic development that despoils our natural resources and destroys our potential for healthy economic growth.

As I have indicated, conservation and economic development cannot be regarded as independent or antagonistic goals. They are, in reality, the same goal. Our people will be less hostile to some forms of industrial development if we have laws, vigorously enforced, that demand protection of the environment. We will, with strong conservation laws, attract industries that value our environment and that want to share the benefits and costs of its protection. We will, through our commitment to conservation, protect natural resources of incalculable economic value. In short, development without conservation is unthinkable and illusory. We would destroy resources as rapidly as we gained them.

We can avoid such a futile course, and we must. Our people demand better jobs and services. They seek a share of the prosperous life of the nation. Only economic development, through conservation, will meet these demands.

CHAPTER

42.

America can be said to have "discovered" the poor among them about 1960. Since then, considerable research has been done both describing the problem and prescribing solutions. The following is an analysis of the situation as it appears in Maine.

POVERTY IN AFFLUENCE
by
the staff of the
Maine Business Indicators

The extent and characteristics of poverty in Maine were explored at a series of discussions held at six different campuses throughout the state between October 8 and December 10, 1968. This series of nine sessions, led by economists, sociologists, and political scientists, was sponsored by the University of Maine and assisted by the federal government under Title I of the Higher Education Act. Each discussion was preceded by a relevant program on the Educational Television Network. The following paragraphs contain highlights from two of the sessions conducted at Bates College by Carl E. Veazie, Staff Economist of the Public Affairs Research Center at Bowdoin College.

What is Poverty? Poverty generally is defined as the relative absence of money or material possessions. Standards for measuring poverty have changed over the centuries, due to the vastly increased affluence of the industrialized countries of the world. Nevertheless, various amounts and quality of food, clothing, health, housing, and education may be established as minimum standards acceptable in our present-day society. Due to the great difficulty in obtaining statistics on the above criteria, however, poverty usually is measured in respect to personal income alone. The most precise measure is the one devised by the Social Security Administration which indicates the amount of income needed to support families of varying size in cities or on farms at a minimum nutritional level. These poverty levels are adjusted annually to reflect changing prices of food and other necessities.

Based on this definition, 226,000 persons or about 24 percent of the population of Maine were classed as poor in 1960. Over half of all single adults and 40 percent of those in families of seven or more persons were listed as poor, while only 13 percent of those in three-person families were below the poverty line. Although no data on income by family size for Maine have been published since the 1960 census, it seems likely (because of the substantial subsequent rise in per capita income) that the poor have declined to about 20 percent of the present population. Recent figures indicate that residents of Maine filing federal tax returns on less than $3,000 adjusted gross income comprise 34 percent of the

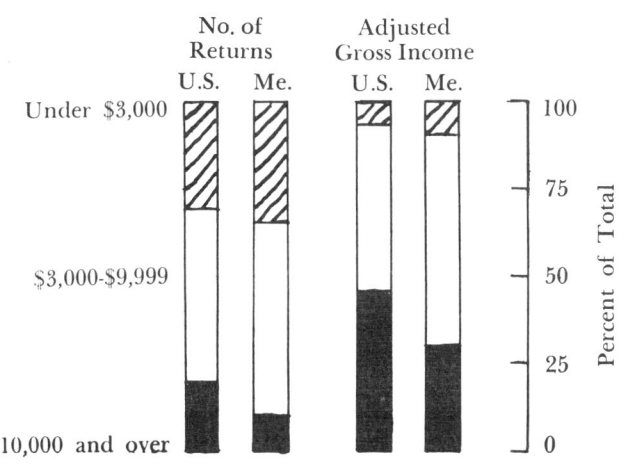

DISTRIBUTION OF PERSONAL INCOME
IN U.S. AND MAINE 1966

Maine Business Indicators, March 1969. Reprinted by permission of the Public Affairs Research Center at Bowdoin College, the publishers.

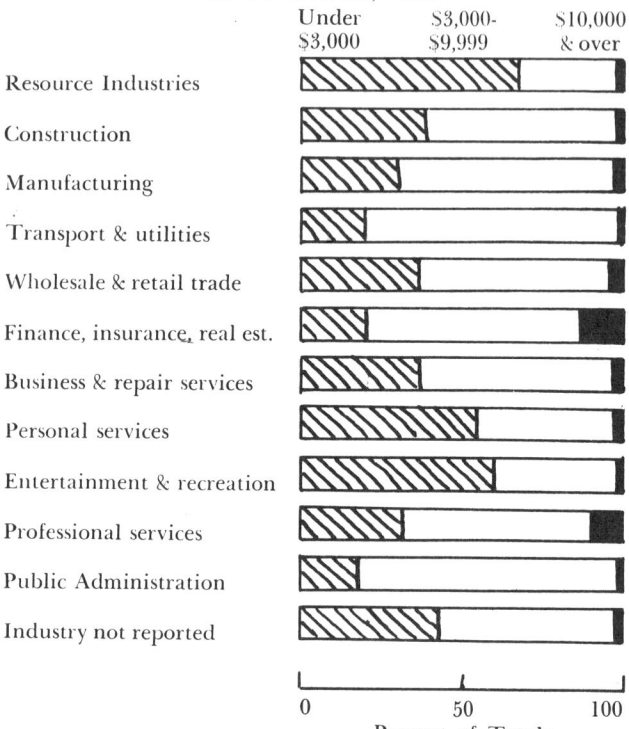

INCOME DISTRIBUTION IN MAINE BY INDUSTRY, 1960

total number paying income taxes, although they earn only 9 percent of total adjusted gross income. Both of these figures are considerably worse than comparable U. S. averages.

Who Are the Poor? The incidence of poverty varies according to family size, age, sex, educational attainment, race, occupation and industry of employment.

Age. Over three-fourths of Maine's young adults (14-24 years of age) and older citizens (65 years and over) earned less than $3,000 in 1960, while only one-fourth of those aged 25 to 64 were in that low income category.

Sex. Eighty-five percent of the state's females aged 14 years and over with income received less than $3,000 in 1960, although only 45 percent of all males were in that class.

Education. Of all the state's males aged 25 years and older, those earning less than $3,000 in 1960 attended school a median of only 8.8 years, in contrast with the 13.6 years attained by those earning over $10,000. There was a similar, though less marked, relationship among females in this respect.

Race. The proportion of Maine's 6,000 non-whites (mostly Negroes and Indians) earning less than $3,000 in 1960 was twice as high (46 percent) as that of whites (23 percent).

Occupation. About two-thirds of the state's males employed as farmers, farm laborers, and unskilled industrial laborers earned less than $3,000 in 1960, while approximately one-third of the professional and managerial workers, craftsmen, and operatives were in that low income class. Almost 80 percent of all females employed as clerks or operatives (in factories) received less than $3,000 that year.

Industry. Over half of all males employed in Maine's resource industries (agriculture, forestry, fisheries, mining), personal services (including motels) and entertainment and recreation earned less than $3,000 in 1960. On the other hand, less than one-fourth of those working in government, transportation and utilities, and finance, insurance and real estate were in the lowest income category.

Where Are the Poor? Generally speaking, the rural areas of Maine have a greater degree of

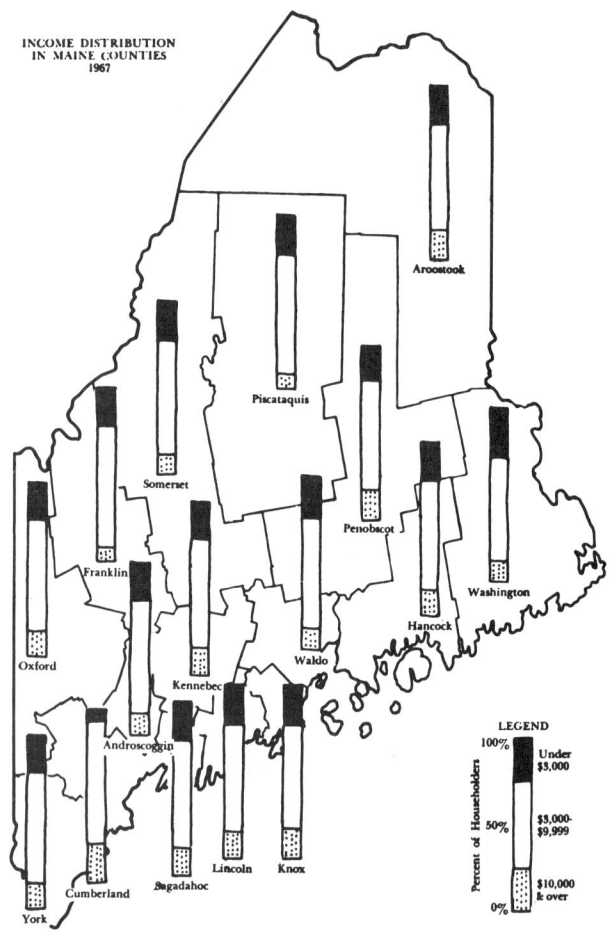

INCOME DISTRIBUTION IN MAINE COUNTIES 1967

poverty than do the cities. 40 percent of the state's rural farm families earned less than $3,000 in 1960, while 27 percent of the rural nonfarm families and only 18 percent of urban families (living in places of over 2,500 population) were in that low income class. More recent (1967) estimates reveal that the share of households receiving less than $3,000 varied from a high of 29 percent in poverty-stricken Washington County to a low of only 6 percent in more affluent Cumberland, with all others ranging from 20 to 24 percent.

The *unemployment* pattern in Maine's counties is somewhat similar to that described above, although many rural areas have small urban centers that are relatively affluent. In 1967, unemployment varied from highs of 12 percent in Washington and 7 percent in Knox, to lows of less than 4 percent in Franklin, Penobscot, York, Oxford, and Kennebec Counties. The remaining counties had unemployment rates ranging from 4 to 5 percent of their respective work forces.

Due to high unemployment in some cases and to high birth rates in others, there has been a substantial and continuing *net out-migration* of people from most of Maine's counties. This is a particularly serious problem because of the great exodus of a large share of the state's younger, more ambitious workers. The highest rates of net out-migration have occurred in Aroostook, Washington, and Penobscot Counties, each of which lost over 10 percent of its population between 1960 and 1966. On the other hand, Lincoln and Knox enjoyed a small net in-migration and York had no net change. Although the others experienced a small degree of net out-migration, it was offset in several counties by even higher rates of natural increase (births minus deaths).

The condition of *housing* in Maine's counties is a significant reflection of poverty. Over half of the housing units in Washington, Piscataquis, Waldo, and Franklin Counties were classed as sub-standard in 1960. Those with less than one-third in that class were Cumberland, Androscoggin, and York Counties, while the others varied from 35 to 49 percent. Housing units with median values of only $5,000 in 1960 were recorded in Washington and Piscataquis Counties. Androscoggin, Cumberland, and Kennebec had medians of more than $10,000, while all other counties had less. There was a similar pattern in respect to median gross rentals,

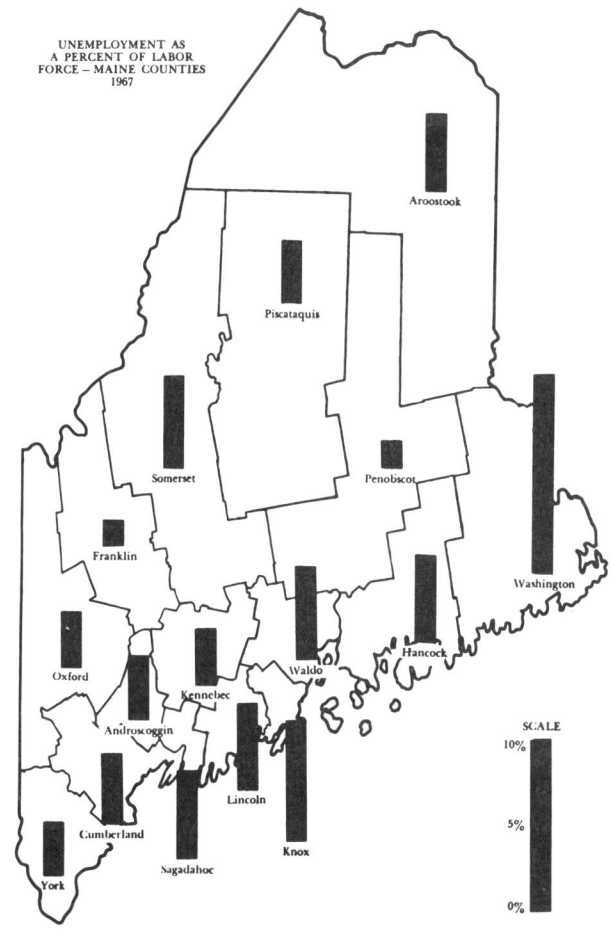

which were only $55 in Washington and Piscataquis Counties and less than $70 in all others except Aroostook and Penobscot (which were higher because of the effect of military bases at that time).

What Causes Poverty? In general, poverty is caused by the scarcity or poor utilization of economic resources, as well as personal handicaps.

Although Maine is relatively rich in land, water, timber, fish, shellfish, potatoes, and scenery, it lacks most foods, fuels and minerals to support a diversified economy. In addition, the state's access to raw materials and markets is inhibited by its somewhat isolated location in one corner of the nation. This is reflected in the fact that Maine's average per capita income has been consistently lower than the comparable U. S. figure. (Maine's per capita income is now 84 percent of the national and 76 percent of the New England average.) Nevertheless, this state's underutilized manpower resources and ample land for future use by additional industries, homes, and tourist attractions offer the possibility of further growth in income. A Maine location for business firms, service industries, and homes will be increasingly attractive as "Megalopolis" becomes more crowded, but only if stringent land use controls are adopted to prevent incompatible uses of land.

Other factors which induce economic development at different rates in different areas are the relative availability of capital and managerial skill, the cost and availability of private and public services, and living conditions such as housing, education and recreation. By optimal use of the various factors of production, Maine's economy can become more adaptable to long-term and short-run fluctuations and can produce rising real per capita income.

Personal handicaps also induce poverty by preventing many persons from employing their potential talents. There has been exploitation or discrimination against relatively disorganized groups such as women, children, immigrants, migrant farmers, Negroes, and Indians. Many poor families also are handicapped by lack of a father, large numbers of children, chronic illness, malnutrition, mental retardation, lack of education, poor work habits, and a feeling of hopelessness. The "hard-core" unemployed generally have multiple handicaps which prevent them from obtaining or keeping a job. Only a massive continuing effort by government and industry is likely to break this vicious circle and permit underprivileged people to become productive members of our affluent society.

CHAPTER

43.

A way of analyzing the economic well-being of Maine families is to look at the "Income Gap."

MAINE'S "INCOME GAP"
WHAT IT IS AND
HOW IT CAN BE CLOSED*
by
Edgar Miller

What Is the Income Gap Problem in the State of Maine?

The per capita income is the best overall measure of how well the economic system of any state compares with itself and other states over time. A good source of statistical information on the per capita income is the *Sales Management* Magazine's annual Survey of Buying Power. All per capita statistics developed in the Survey are labeled Effective Buying Income (EBI), which is Personal Income less state and federal taxes. The EBI then approximates the take home income that is available for the purchase of goods and services.

The per capita income of Maine is increasing relatively faster than New England, which is a good sign, but the dollar income gap per capita is still increasing. Table 1 shows that in 1967 the per capita income in Maine was $2303, which was $636 below the New England average and increasing slightly compared to 1966. One of the specific goals of the Department of Economic Development is to change the direction of this income gap ($636) and do everything possible to close the income gap. If the population of Maine in 1967 was 985,000 and the per capita income equaled that of New England an additional EBI of $626 million would have been added to the State's 1967 total of $2268 million.

Table 2 shows that Massachusetts and Connecticut are consistently above the New England average EBI, while the remaining states are below the average. In 1967 the lower New England states were above the U. S. average per capita income of 2697, while the upper states of Maine, New Hampshire and Vermont were below the U. S. average.

TABLE 1
Per Capita Income of
Maine and New England
1965-1967

Area	1965	1966	1967
New England	$2639	$2778	$2939
Maine	$2029	$2154	$2303
Income Gap — Maine & N.E.	$ 608	$ 624	$ 636
Rate of Change 1965 = 100			
New England	100.0	105.3	111.4
Maine	100.0	106.2	113.5

Source: Sales Management Survey of Buying Power.

TABLE 2
Per Capita Effective Buying Income
New England States
1965-1967

State	1965	1966	1967
MAINE	$2029	$2154	$2303
Vermont	2114	2293	2507
New Hampshire	2240	2483	2655
Rhode Island	2380	2616	2786
Massachusetts	2711	2794	2955
Connecticut	2953	3146	3292
New England Average	$2637	$2778	$2939

Source: Sales Management Survey of Buying Power.

The low per capita income is not the only income problem of Maine. The distribution of

---

*Edgar A. Miller, *Maine's "Income Gap,"* Augusta: D.E.D., 1968.

income is very high toward the lower incomes as shown in Table 3.

TABLE 3
Percent Cash Income by Household, by State, New England 1967

State	Hslds. (000)	0-$2999	$3-4999	$5-7999	$8-9999	$10-15000	$15-25000	$25000
Vermont	115.9	19.6%	15.4%	27.2%	15.0%	15.5%	5.4%	1.9%
Maine	288.8	18.7	18.4	32.4	14.4	11.0	3.9	1.2
N.H.	201.5	17.9	13.7	29.8	16.2	14.9	5.6	1.9
R.I.	277.6	17.3	13.8	29.0	15.9	15.8	6.1	2.1
Mass.	1643.2	11.2	13.1	32.8	16.8	16.3	7.2	2.6
Conn	879.3	10.6	10.0	28.9	17.6	19.4	9.5	4.0
N.E.	3406.3	12.8	12.9	31.1	16.7	16.5	7.3	2.7

Source: Sales Management Survey of Buying Power.

The northern New England states and Rhode Island have a higher percentage of households than the New England average of 12.8%, with less than $3,000 cash income. Vermont has the highest of 19.6% and Maine is second with 18.7% of the households under $3,000 cash income. Although other years are not shown the percentage breakdown shows very little change. This means that Maine has approximately 54,000 households that fall within the poor classification of the Federal government. If you accept that any household with two or more children with a cash income of less than $5,000 cannot enjoy the benefits of our productive economy, then approximately 107,000 households can be classified as being poor. The basic problem of Maine is to close the income gap but also reduce the proportion of households that have very low incomes.

Employment and Sources of Income in Maine

Table 4 shows the major source of employment and the changes in employment from 1960 to 1967. The greatest gain is in the non-manufacturing group, especially in personal services and state government which includes teaching. The second greatest growth over the period is in manufacturing, especially non-durable manufacturing.

TABLE 4
Employment in Maine by Major Source, 1960-1967
(thousands of employees)

Source Employment	1960	1961	1962	1963	1964	1964	1966	1967
Durable	29.3	28.7	29.0	27.5	28.1	28.8	31.7	32.8
Non-Durable	75.2	74.5	75.3	75.3	75.9	79.2	83.3	83.8
Total Mfg.	104.5	103.2	104.3	102.8	104.0	108.0	115.0	116.6
Total Non-Mfg.	173.0	173.9	175.2	176.8	181.1	187.4	194.2	200.2
Agriculture	21.9	20.2	20.5	20.1	19.0	16.8	16.4	16.2
Non-Farm All Other	44.7	45.7	44.2	42.6	42.0	42.0	40.9	39.7
Unemployment	27.5	30.3	25.4	25.2	23.0	18.3	16.1	15.3
TOTAL	371.6	373.3	369.6	367.5	369.1	372.5	382.6	388.8

Source: Maine Employment Security Commission.

Table 5 shows the sources of employment in Maine from 1960 to 1967. Within the major subgroups manufacturing and non-manufacturing jobs are listed in order of magnitude of 1967 employment. Leather is the largest source of employment with 28,680, Paper and Allied Products second with 17,990. After these two largest groups employment levels seem to stratify into three sizes—11000 to 13000, 2400 to 4500 and less than 1300 employees. Electrical Machinery, Machinery and Ordnance, Rubber and Plastics are the fastest growing industry groups with a more than 3 times growth in the eight year period.

When looking at the entire picture of employment several important relationships appear. About 1.6 people are employed in non-manufacturing for every person employed in manufacturing. The national average is 2.4 non-manufacturing jobs for every manufacturing job. The ranking of absolute growth in jobs was

State and Local Government	11,800
Service	8,000
Wholesale and Retail Trade	6,100
Leather	4,970

from 1960 to 1967. This indicates that the fastest growth in actual jobs in the last eight years has been mostly from segments of the non-manufacturing group. In relation to national averages it would seem that this non-manufacturing growth in jobs will continue in the future.

The low per capita income in Maine partly arises from specific kinds of manufacturing employment. Let's examine the types of employment, plant size and industry size and determine the relationship of each on income.

In Table 6 we see the number of employed and gross average wage by durable goods industries and non-durable industries. In each grouping the individual industries are arranged by magnitude of employment in 1967. In the durable goods industries Transportation is the largest employer and Lumber and Wood second. The gross average wage of the Transportation industry is $7015. The weighted average gross wage of $5460 in 1967 is computed with industry employment as weights. A

TABLE 5
Sources of Employment, Maine, 1960-1967
(Number of Jobs)

Source of Employment	1960	1961	1962	1963	1964	1965	1966	1967
Leather	23950	23980	23980	24880	26060	27890	29090	28680
Paper & Allied Prods.	17110	17450	16970	16370	16520	16790	17510	17990
Transportation	14650	15430	15190	13170	12320	11520	11960	13140
Lumber and Wood	12820	11660	11680	12630	12990	12550	13100	12920
Food	11910	12010	12200	11910	11520	11990	12020	12730
Textiles	13430	12440	12690	12380	11950	12020	12290	11930
Electrical Mach.	1280	2050	2500	2300	1900	2450	3590	4510
Machinery Ordnance	1200	1210	1600	2360	2560	3050	3600	3810
Apparel	2660	2370	2760	2890	2840	3110	3240	3190
Rubber and Plastics	630	990	1080	1380	1680	1820	2300	2640
Printing	2310	2250	2300	2330	2320	2300	2320	2460
Fabricated Metals	1530	1640	1700	1950	2190	2060	2020	2400
Stone-Clay-Glass	1110	1180	1240	1220	1260	1300	1300	1280
Chemicals	780	840	790	690	800	920	980	910
Furniture	1130	780	780	760	810	790	770	770
Misc. Mfg.	650	580	650	680	680	840	790	770
Primary Metals	430	400	430	400	400	420	460	520
Instruments	120	90	110	150	170	180	200	220
Petroleum	15	60	60	150	150	180	220	210
TOTAL MFG.	107715	107410	108710	108600	109120	112180	117760	121080
Whsle. & Retl. Trade	53900	53500	53000	53500	54300	55600	58000	60000
Government	48200	49500	50300	51500	52900	54300	57400	59600
Federal	18500	18900	18500	17800	16900	16100	17000	18100
State & Local	29700	30600	31800	33700	36000	38200	40400	41500
Service & Other Non-Manufacturing	30200	30600	31900	32500	34000	35700	36700	38200
Transp. & Pub. Utils.	18100	17700	17300	17100	17000	16500	16900	17000
Contract Const.	13600	13300	13100	12500	13100	15400	14800	14500
Finance—Real Estate—Insurance	9000	9300	9600	9700	9800	9900	10400	10900
TOTAL NON-MFG.	173000	173900	175200	176800	181100	187400	194200	200200
Non-Farm—All Other	44700	45700	44200	42600	42000	42000	40900	39700
Agriculture	21900	20200	20500	20100	19000	16800	16400	16200
TOTAL EMPLOYED	347315	347210	348610	348100	351220	358380	369260	377180
UNEMPLOYED	27500	30300	25400	25200	23000	18300	16100	15300
TOT. LABOR FORCE	374815	377510	374010	373300	374220	376680	385360	392480

Source: Total Manufacturing—Census of Maine Manufacturers, (rounded to tens), 1960-1966 revised data, 1967 current data—the remainder from: Maine State Employment Security Commission.

TABLE 6
Number Employed and Gross Average Wage, Maine, 1964-1967

TYPE OF EMPLOYMENT	NUMBER EMPLOYED				GROSS AVERAGE WAGE			
	1964	1965	1966	1967	1964	1965	1966	1967
Transportation	12300	11390	11940	13150	$6730	$6590	$6910	$7015
Lumber & Wood	12600	11970	12700	12920	3755	3890	4200	4450
Electrical Mach.	1900	2440	3570	4510	3430	3420	3460	3670
Machinery & Ordnance	2550	3040	3600	3810	5185	5390	5760	5700
Fabricated Metals	2180	2060	1990	2400	5150	5310	5665	5950
Stone-Clay-Glass	1260	1300	1300	1280	4380	4460	4850	5020
Furniture	800	790	770	770	3650	3820	3930	4360
Primary Metals	400	410	460	520	4780	5060	5170	5640
Instruments	170	180	200	220	4360	4590	5010	4700
Durable Total and Weighted Average Gross Wage	34160	33580	36530	39580	$5040	$5030	$5280	$5460
Leather	25640	27340	28750	28680	3610	3750	3840	4070
Paper & Allied Prods.	16520	16780	17510	17990	6290	6560	6690	6880
Food	11480	11890	12010	12730	3680	3870	3960	4260
Textiles	11940	12010	12140	11930	3945	4130	4410	4560
Apparel	2840	3100	3030	3190	2920	2950	3020	3220
Rubber	1670	1820	2310	2640	3790	4090	3880	4160
Printing	2300	2180	2310	2460	4450	4690	4730	4880
Chemicals	790	910	980	910	4400	4290	4590	4500
Misc. Manufacturing	660	820	770	770	3590	3570	3710	3840
Petroleum	150	260	280	210	5710	6680	6570	6800
Non-Durable Total and Weighted Average Gross Wage	73990	77110	80090	81510	$4290	$4455	$4580	$4795

Source: Census of Maine Manufacturers.

similar analysis exists for the non-durable industries. The important relationship in this table is the difference in the gross average wage in the durable industries and the non-durable industries. Over the four years the weighted gross average wage period is between $575-750 higher in the durable industries. Specific industries in either group are above or below the gross average wage but still durable goods industries on the average offer higher wages than the non-durable industries.

One of the problems of low income in Maine is the generally very large number of firms employing 10 or less employees. In a separate study by the Department of Labor and Industry of 1965 data indicated that 45.5% of all Maine firms employed 10 or less employees. All the industry groups had 20% or more firms within the industry group with 10 or less employees with the exception of Textiles, Paper, Rubber and Leather. Small firms then in Maine cross the most of the industry groups and are not isolated within a narrow segment of the economy.

It is interesting to note that the average wage paid in the firms with 10 or less employees during 1965 was $3400 compared to the average wage paid to all employees which was $4693. These many small firms then tend to contribute to the low income problem in Maine. Fortunately, perhaps, these firms account for 3,580 employees or only 3.1% of the total manufacturing employment.

There is another interesting relationship, however, in comparison of the plant size and the average gross wage. There is a continuous relationship between the small plant size and lower income and the larger plant size and larger income. The tabulation shows this relationship for 1966 and 1967 data.

The plant size and earnings relationship fits well into the general body of economic theory. Larger firms generally employ more capital equipment in the production process. This usually enables an individual employee to be more productive and turn out a greater value of product within a given unit of time. In addition there is a much greater tendency toward full year employment which will increase the annual wage of an employee. A firm can definitely be too small an economic unit for the benefit of the employees, and the total state economy.

From the previous discussion one might hypothesize that there is also an association between industry group employment and average gross wage. That is, the Leather industry being the largest employer in Maine would also have the highest wage, and the Paper Industry being the second largest industry would have the second largest wage, etc. The Spearman rank correlation is a convenient method of testing if a relationship does exist between these ranks.

Ho = There is no relation to employment in an industry group and income.

H1 = Large industry groups pay higher wages.

	1966 Employment	Rank	1966 Avg. Wages Paid	Rank	d^2
Leather	28,750	1	$3,839	9	64
Paper	17,510	2	6,687	2	0
Lumber & Wood	12,697	3	4,203	6	9
Textiles	12,142	4	4,410	5	1
Food	12,013	5	3,959	7	4
Transportation	11,945	6	6,906	1	25
Machinery & Ordnance	3,595	7	5,756	3	16
Electrical Machinery	3,571	8	3,461	10	4
Apparel	3,030	9	3,024	11	4
Printing	2,307	10	4,729	4	36
Rubber	2,304	11	3,877	8	9

$$Rs = 1 - \frac{6 \sum d^2}{m(m^2-1)}$$

$$= 1 - \frac{6(172)}{11(121-1)}$$

$$= 1 - \frac{1032}{1320}$$

$$= 1 - .7818$$

$$= .2182$$

CONCLUSION

ACCEPT H_0

The conclusion of this test of hypothesis is to accept Ho. That is, there is no relationship between size of industry and average gross wage. The magnitude of the wage paid by an industry is dependent upon something other than the number of people employed. However, do not confuse this relationship with that of gross wage and plant size. In this relationship there is good evidence that the larger plant sizes yield larger average gross wages. Also, the average gross wage of durable goods industries is higher than non-durable goods industries.

1966	
Plant Size (Employees)	Gross Average Wage
0 - 50	$3909
51 - 100	3955
101 - 200	4076
201 - 300	4272
301 - 400	4341
401 - 500	4002
501 - 700	4874
701 - 1000	5806
1001 & over	6293

1967	
Plant Size (Employees)	Gross Average Wage
0 - 50	$4149
51 - 100	4260
101 - 200	4192
201 - 300	4406
301 - 400	4554
401 - 500	4706
501 - 700	4971
701 - 1000	5638
1001 & over	6565

What are the likely causes of the low income problem?

1. Low hourly pay rates that can be caused by some factors like:
   a. unskilled employment;
   b. industry characteristics in substituting capital for labor;
   c. type of product handled does not lend itself to skilled labor or capital equipment;
   d. seasonal employment especially unskilled;
   e. for any reason the value of a unit of product of a unit of labor is low;
   f. inadequate competition within an area bidding for the supply of labor, therefore, no market force in a local labor market to bid up labor cost.
2. Employment in older industries, small firms, firms cost inefficient, etc.
3. For any business (mfg., recreation, retail, or government) the relationship of the cost of output and size of operation. That is, where does a specific cost center fit on an average cost curve. Any firm can be too small to be a good contribution to an economy. Any business enterprise should be large enough to employ some degree of capital equipment which makes labor more productive and therefore worth more. This is true for white collar employment as well as blue collar. In the factory the value of capital equipment is easy to understand in relation to wages. In the office, government and teaching capital equipment is perhaps less easy to see. As the cost of labor increases and the demand for output increases the efficient use of mechanical equipment is essential. Examples: electric vs. manual typewriters; mechanical record keeping vs. manual; computer computation vs. manual, etc.

The basic problem is how to increase the total real income of the current members of the work force. In any sector of the state's economy wage and salary income in the long run will be dependent upon the value in product of a unit of labor. This value of product can be increased by making a unit of labor more valuable, which generally means either greater skill level or greater use of capital equipment or both. Small, short run gains can be made by a greater distribution of a yearly revenue to wages and salaries, but this could be disastrous in the long run if it prevents adequate recapitalization, investment in research and development, and new product introduction. It will do little good to encourage the current industry within the state to expand operations *with the same distribution of employment skills as currently in use,* since in many firms it will only tend to increase the number of households with minimal income.

Methods of Increasing Household Income

Three general methods of increasing household income exist: increase the skills of those employed so that they are worth more, employ more members within a household, and shift the members of a household from seasonal to full time employment. Let's examine these in somewhat more detail.

Increase the skills of those employed is oftentimes limited in our thinking to upgrading the factory employees. It is indeed true that a more skilled factory employee, in marketable skills, can earn more than a less skilled employee. The problem is, however, that something less than 30% of total Maine employment is in factories. What then ought to be done in the non-factory employment to increase skills and household income. Consider top management of any business firm, government position, or any employment that allocates resources. The attitudes, skill level, knowledge, motives and incentives of this group can very largely affect the structure of employment within the entire State's economy. If top management is not oriented to expansion, new product development, production efficiency, training programs, and generally the efficient allocation of resources, structural employment changes are likely to be slow if they come about at all. By structural employment we mean skills involved and use of capital equipment. Some results can be low wage rates, little economic development, out-migration of younger people in search of better opportunities, and general underdevelopment. The problem of growth in skill level rests with every individual, not a specific group only.

Increasing household income by more members of a household working will certainly raise the income but it can also create other social problems that must be given consideration.

Seasonal employment for the head of the household is generally at low income levels. This source on low income can be largely reduced by expanding many small firms to full season operation and expanding the skills of those seasonally employed to alternate full time employment.

We need a consolidation, of some kind, of the many small firms into larger, more economically healthy enterprises. The size of the firms for economic health is related to products produced, cost of capital equipment, and size or potential markets for product.

Who is involved?

The causes of low income are basically those involved in the entire economic system of the State. Specifically involved are Government at all levels, banking-finance institutions, educational system, top management attitudes of individual firms industrial organizations and anyone concerned with resource allocation.

Government
  a. Department of Economic Development
  b. All other departments whose spending or resource allocations are made without consideration of effect upon other segments of the total State economic system.
  c. zoning laws, building codes, pollution controls, city planning, attitudes, etc., that affect individual decisions of investment among those in the private sector.
  d. investment and expansion environment created by the tax structure.
  e. the total transportation system expressed by highways and railroads, etc.
  f. the total educational system and its ability to prepare people for productive employment. This includes public schools and colleges, as well as all adult continuing education programs and vocational education.
  g. expectations of private individuals concerning investment to the progress of the State government.

Banking-finance
  a. bank services and working hours.
  b. lending policies and acceptance of risk—security oriented vs. expansion oriented.
  c. home loan policies, and policies toward home building and repair industry.

Top management of the private sector—both Manufacturing and Non-Manufacturing.
  a. management orientation toward expansion-research, new product development recapitalization, and mergers.
  b. in-plant training programs to promote cost efficiency.
  c. attitudes of firms toward industry advertising, research development, and sales organizations.

What alternatives are available to close the problem of the "income gap"?

Relatively short run solutions

1. Continue to work in the promotion and industry contact of recreation and industrial groups that might be attracted to a location in Maine. This is essentially the current program.

2. Sponsor a continuing education program sponsored by industry and government to expand the skills of management levels of industry and government. This program should include topics on the skills of managing people, the total economic system and the functions of each segment, company organization requirements for growth, etc.

3. Rebuild State banking and finance laws with new legislation ability to provide more capital resources for expansion and development of the State's economic system. This alternative would require a research project of capital needs within the State, sources of capital, and some formula for legislation and allocation of the relatively scarce capital resources. A team approach to the research ought to be considered. An economist-banker or finance-industrial specialist should combine skills toward the final analysis.

4. Establish, as a sub-operation with DED, a unit to offer professional services to the management development and growth of individual firms within the non-manufacturing group within the State. This group could function similar to the current industrial group, and provide similar services. If this were done, there would be complete coverage of some kind of assistance to the entire State economy—the agricultural extension service for agriculture, the DED manufacturing group for manufacturing employment,

and a new DED group for the non-manufacturing employment.

Relatively long run solutions to the "income gap" problem. Long run measured in terms of development time and time required before any results can be anticipated.

1. Develop an extensive research structure inventorying the resources of the State in terms of population, education, work skills, etc. Much of this information is already available from past research projects. Develop an input-output table to study the total economic system and explain its operation. From this information one should be able to plan with a fairly high degree of accuracy the types of firms that could prosper and grow within the State. In addition information should be available to determine what State programs in re-education, highways, etc., should be developed to promote the development of the economic system in some sort of optimum fashion.

2. Develop economic areas oriented toward substate economic systems. Define skills, resources, need for growth, potential for growth, etc. Select one or two areas of greatest need or potential and develop a State task force toward solution of the area's problems. The solution should be oriented to measurable objectives and the budgets established toward these objectives. The task force by each division of State government should be charged with specific objectives and a system of measuring results.

3. Careful analysis of the tax laws and other incentives possible to encourage industrial and non-industrial expansion within the State. Approximately two people are employed in non-manufacturing jobs for every person employed in a manufacturing job within the State. Expansion incentives should be oriented toward both sources of employment, with perhaps special provisions for each.

4. The State should buy land for industrial parks that fit into a planned system that can be most economically fit into the communities in consideration of the entire package of Federal, State, and local government services, such as roads, water, sewage, education, etc. The planning should include manufacturing and non-manufacturing activities which tend to link together and grow in some compatible sequence. In this allocation of resources careful delineation should be defined concerning what resources will be supplied by government and what resource allocations can be best left to the open market and price system for optimum allocation. This alternative will involve a very careful team approach and involve a very high degree of cooperation of different levels and agencies of government. Success could very well be dependent upon the degree to which this cooperation and coordination takes place.

CHAPTER

44.

A forward step in educational policy was taken in 1957 with the passage of the Sinclair Act. In the decade that followed its passage many school administrative districts were formed to consolidate the many small unions into larger units.

MAINE'S SINCLAIR ACT*
by
Bailey, Frost, Marsh and Wood

The Nature of Legislative Power

Representation in both houses of the Maine legislature is determined to a considerable extent by population. Constitutionally, the membership of the House of Representatives is fixed at 151, pro-rated to the counties on the basis of their respective shares of Maine's total population. For instance, Cumberland County, with about 175 residents, has twenty-seven representatives in the House while Lincoln County, at about 18,000 has only three. No municipality within a county may have more than seven representatives, regardless of the percentage of the county population within the city limits. Only Portland is in this class. Below this arbitrary maximum, the apportionment procedure is consistent: the county's total population is divided by the sum of representatives to which the county is entitled, giving a ratio of one representative to every so many constituents. Representation is then granted to municipalities within the county in the same proportion that their populations bear to the county population. Only thirteen municipalities have more than one representative of their own. At the other end of the scale, a number of small municipalities may be lumped together into one legislative district. In such cases, these towns, by gentleman's agreement, pass around among themselves biennially the honor of producing their district's one legislator.

The Maine Senate also responds to population, but more precisely. Each county has at least one senator. If the county population is between 30,001 and 60,000, it has two; between 60,001 and 120,000, three; between 120,001 and 240,000, four; and over 240,001, five. No county yet has five. In recent sessions, the Senate has had thirty-three members; during the next decade it will have thirty-four. Senators chair all legislative committees, all of which are joint; the vice-chairman is always the senior committee member from the house.**

The actual working of this system tends to concentrate its power. Half or two-thirds of Maine's representatives at any session are freshmen. The bulk of this turnover occurs among the representatives from the consolidated county-towns conscientiously living up to their gentlemen's agreements. This means that, while rural legislatures have an absolute majority in the House, they have no seniority, and being new to state politics, no disciplined organization through which to express common rural interests. Furthermore, this constant disorder makes committee recommendations doubly important—and senators and "big city" representatives run the committees.

This is not to say that the Maine legislature is run by a clique, but it certainly is clubby. Given the state's political complexion, the legislative

---

*Bailey, Frost, Marsh, Wood, *Schoolmen and Politics: A Study of State Aid to Education in the Northeast* (Syracuse: Syracuse University Press, 1962), pp. 73-82. Reprinted by permission of the publisher.

**Since 1962 both of the Senate and House have been reapportioned. Thus, much of the material contained in the first two chapters is no longer factual.

experience of leaders may well count for more than partisanship in determining the outcome of policy proposals. Collaborating or locking horns, legislative sessions give rise to a comradeship among veterans that is intensified through being surrounded every two years by greenhorns and countrymen. Experience counts, and in 1957, as now, experience lay with Maine's senatorial committee chairmen and their "big city" vice-chairmen from the House. Knowing their way through the legislative maze, these veterans could not help but lead the newcomers.

Party discipline is a standard vehicle for organizing a relatively disorganized legislature. It is often hard, however, to crack the party whip when there are no clear partisan sanctions. In a one-party state, this discipline is, by definition, personal. It can be responsibly partisan only when there is a clear threat from a strong and coherent opposition. For most of the twentieth century, Maine has been a one-party state: Republican. After World War II, the legislature was blessed with at least a handful of strong leaders, mostly Republican, directed by Senate President Robert Haskell. In the mid-fifties, however, Democrat Edmund Muskie won the governorship and led into the State House more legislators—almost sixty—of his party than had been there in decades. The Democrats did not capture the House, but the strongest minority in history gave the House a coherence it had never before experienced. Like his Republican colleagues, Muskie was experienced, bright, quick—and strict. Roger Putnam, assistant Attorney-General at the time, recently recollected with glee and grim approval having watched a Democratic caucus file whitefaced out of Muskie's presence. Putnam was told, in hushed tones, that "somebody zigged when he should have zagged." During Muskie's governorship, with Haskell ruling the Senate, the Maine House of Representatives was more tightly disciplined than it had been in years.

By the mid-fifties, school subsidy revision had another factor in its favor. The groundwork had already been laid by a state tax revolution devised and carried out by Mr. Haskell in 1951. In 1950 Maine had a state tax on real property which brought in $5,187,000, 8.5 per cent of the state's revenue. Not only was this tax limited, it competed directly with hard pressed local jurisdiction in an obvious and painful way. In 1951, Mr. Haskell got a Republican governor and legislature to swap the state property tax for a 2 per cent sales tax. By 1955, the sales tax was producing about a quarter of Maine's tax revenue, some $17,000,000. The President of the Senate had secured the state some badly needed fiscal elbow-room. He had done more than that; municipalities had been handed a valuable financial competence. By 1959, 98 per cent of all local taxes, almost half of all tax dollars collected in the state, were based on real property. Both state and local tax structures were more solid than they had been in years. Each could withstand increased fiscal commitments.

The Legislative Background

Seth Low of Rockland, Maine, Chairman of the Joint Committee on Education in 1957, has remarked that he did not know just how the Sinclair Bill got through the legislature even though he had led the floor campaign for it. All that he could say was that it took a combination of men, timing, and resources.

In 1957, Maine had all three, but 1957 took a long time coming. Nobody had ticketed it years in advance as education's session, and, in fact, other major legislation was on the docket. Senate President Robert Haskell, however, knew that sooner or later school subsidies and school districts would have to be thoroughly revised. The creation of a General Purpose Aid Bill in 1951 had been a step in the right direction but more—much more—needed to be done. Haskell had a single basic objection to the 1951 formula and it was devastating: it gave Maine's school districts a blank check. The formula put no upper limit on the amount of state aid to which a district was legally entitled. By that statute, the state was obligated to subsidize a calculated percentage of every district's annual operating costs, however luxurious they might become. In some respects a decade ahead of its time, the 1951 act looked to conservative legislators in the mid-fifties, as an open-handedness which would encourage frivolity in many schools. Worse yet, it would encourage—indeed, underwrite—existence for small ones, particularly tiny high schools. These institutions were demonstrably bad, not because they gave a bad education (Mr. Haskell saw this as a fruitless and futile argument), but because they produced drop-outs and did not prepare Maine's boys adequately for college. This formula and the small high schools it perpetuated would both have to go.

On the other hand, inflation aside, Mr. Haskell believed strongly that Maine and its school districts needed to spend more money than they did on education. In 1955, the voters of Maine gave the Republican President of the Senate an invaluable ally, a Democratic Governor. The two men were much alike. When they agreed to disagree, they had a hard, clean fight; when they agreed to agree, they were invincible. They agreed on increased school subsidies and on district consolidation. This meeting of minds took place personally; neither the State Board of Education nor the Commissioner was consulted on these decisions of fundamental policy.

During the legislative session of 1955, Haskell and Muskie presided over a revision in the general purpose aid formula. The classes of aid were refined from nine to twenty-four and the percentage of subsidy for each class was raised. These changes, however, did nothing to the formula nor did they add much to the state's appropriation for state aid. What they did do was acknowledge with greater precision than was previously possible the state-wide equalized valuations of the Board of Equalization. Since these valuations were upwards, subsidies had to increase by a like amount to keep school districts from losing money. The real opening came late in the session when a senator from southern Maine complained that some schools in his county really did not find themselves helped very much by their new state aid. He wanted the legislature to do something about it.

The Marriage of Politicians and Experts

The legislature did something. It passed a resolution that the Joint Legislative Research Committee study the financing of public schools in Maine and report its findings and recommendations to the next legislature. The legislature appropriated $25,000 for the Research Committee budget.

This Committee's six-man Subcommittee on Education was a powerhouse. Its chairman was Senator Roy U. Sinclair, an experienced legislator and highly respected specialist in finance. Seth Low, proprietor of a small printing firm in Rockland and a senator who had been Haskell's right hand in getting the sales tax, was also on the committee. So was Robert N. Haskell, *ex officio* as President of the Senate. The Research Committee hired two consultants, Mr. William O. Bailey, retired Deputy Commissioner of Education, not yet at work as Professor at Maine's College of Education, and J. L. Jacobs & Co. of Chicago, consultants in public administration and finance.

These consultants worked hard during 1956. Mr. Bailey got in touch with an old friend of his, Mr. Fred Beach, Director of Research in the U. S. Office of Education, and got copies of the proof sheets for a government publication on public school foundation formulae in the forty-eight states. He wrote to fourteen states whose programs seemed most appropriate for Maine, asking for copies of their laws. With these laws in hand, he moved to his summer place on the beach, admired the ocean, and began to hammer out the provisions of the Sinclair Bill.

Mr. Thomas Jacobs of J. L. Jacobs & Co. virtually commuted between Chicago and Bangor. He had, in a way, more work to do than Mr. Bailey, since his firm had to write the report to justify the Bill. This assignment required the compilation and analysis of a host of statistics on schools and finance. Through Mr. Sinclair and Mr. Haskell these figures were forthcoming from the state. The harder job was to determine what statistics to use and what precise line of argument to pursue. Ironing out these matters took hours of discussion in the subcommittee, with Mr. Bailey on hand. While the report and the bill did not agree in all particulars, Mr. Jacobs had no trouble in recommending a minimum foundation program and the consolidation of school districts. Indeed, he insisted that the bill include construction grants as the best practical way to encourage district reorganization.

By the fall of 1956 both the report and the bill had begun to take definite shape and structure. Neither was finished, but each was far enough along to need exposure to a wider audience. The Subcommittee on Education, therefore, called in an advisory committee of friends of education— other members of the Legislative Research Committee, Mr. Russell of the Maine Teachers' Association, Mr. Bowen of the PTA, and the University Women. This group took its responsibility seriously and its advice on particulars was discussed, weighed, and acted on. For the most part, the advisors concentrated on the report, rather than the bill, since the former had the earlier deadline. By the middle of December, the Jacobs Company formally handed over its finished document to the Legislative Research Committee. Within a week, the report was transmitted to the incoming Legislature. Shortly after the first of the year the "Jacobs Report" was public property, so members of the State Board of Education finally got copies.

Structural Strategy

In the meantime, Mr. Haskell was deploying his forces for the legislative campaign. He had long since consulted by mail with the administrators of all Maine's school districts to give them ample time to get involved in the impending legislation. Through a new Commissioner, the Department of Education worked up tables for every school district in the state, showing the aid it was getting under the General Purpose Act and what it would expect to get under the Sinclair Bill. With a "safe-harmless" formula added, no district lost money under the new proposal. Aside from these slight bows, Mr. Haskell refused to go to the grass roots. He wanted to fight this fight in the State House, where he held the advantages, not in the towns, where the opposition was strongest. Even in Augusta, however, he could not afford weakness. He put Senator Sinclair into the chair of the Joint Appropriations Committee and he gave the Education Committee to Seth Low. The latter assignment outraged senatorial seniority, but the man due for that post was not up to the job—and Haskell told him so. (Toward the end of the 1957 session, the bypassed senator thanked Mr. Haskell for having protected him from what Mr. Low was having to take.) Representative Lucia Cormier, Democrat from Rumford, led her party's—and the bill's—forces in the House.

The Governor and Legislative Strategy

This arrangement was really not so anomalous as it appears, for Governor Muskie wanted the Sinclair Act. He had already determined to raise the sales tax. By taking it up a whole percentage point and committing a very healthy share of the added revenue to schools, he strengthened his own hand and his party's program substantially. The Sinclair Bill was sound legislation, quite appropriate in his estimation to Democratic ideals, and Republican leadership was committed to it. The governor saw no need to look this gift horse in the mouth. But his interest went beyond partisanship. Education may not have been Mr. Muskie's specialty, but Maine's schools clearly needed help and the Sinclair Bill, unpalatable as some of its provisions might be to Yankee localists, was about the best help the state had in its power to give.

The big problem in 1957 was to get the legislature to take it. As the 98th session opened, the bill still needed final polishing. There was time for this work, however, for the bill's timetable had already been set. It was to be introduced after the revenue bills but before they came to votes. Appearing at that time, the bill could be tied to the sales tax so as to make the tax a school matter and school support an act of prudent statesmanship. The Sinclair Bill, of course, would not come out for a vote until after the revenue was assured. This timing was not necessarily routine politics, but it was sound.

The governor, however, was more than planner and policy-maker or party leader. Every Monday he entertained the legislative leaders of both parties at dinner and an evening of shop-talk. Mr. Haskell and Miss Cormier were regular guests; *ex officio,* Mr. Low and Mr. Sinclair almost as much so. Mr. Bailey, Mr. Haskell's liaison with professional education during the legislative campaign, was a frequent diner-out at Blain House, the governor's residence. During these free and friendly winter evenings, the legislative tactics of the 98th legislative session were ironed out.

The Debate

The Sinclair Bill did not get through without a fight. It came in on schedule and was referred to the Joint Committee on Education. Mr. Low promptly and properly called a public hearing at which attendance was good and reaction overwhelmingly favorable. At this hearing, the State Board of Education had a chance to put its views on record. Mr. Frank S. Hoy, the Chairman, approved of the principles of the bill but offered suggestions on its procedures, especially those for getting out of a Sinclair School Administrative District. Towns could join or create districts easily by simple majority vote at town meeting. Then the District became a political entity and could contract debts for buildings, teachers, and the like. The bill stipulated that towns at this point could not get out because such a move would free them of financial obligations they had voted for. Mr. Hoy saw trouble ahead on this issue. His remarks were unheeded at the time, but the next two sessions of the Legislature and three years of litigation by the town of Liberty have been required to establish an orderly process for district dissolution.

In one way, Mr. Hoy's comments were typical; debate in Augusta centered on mechanics and marginal adjustments rather than policy. In another sense, his concern was his own, almost alone. What the 1957 legislature really struggled with was the scope and equity of the recommended formula. The bill set 700 as the minimum student population for which the state would subsidize a high school, clearly intending to lead towns with small high schools to band together. Miss Lucia Cormier, leading the big city representatives, opposed these standards on the grounds that in the whole state there were only two high schools that large and that both were in single districts already. In a word, the bill failed to reward those schools which had already achieved its goals. She carried the day; single districts were given construction subsidies on a par with consolidated districts. Since then the minimum student population requirement was cut to 500. But the fight was important. More than forty "big city" votes were involved. Since they were almost all in the lowest subsidy group, the cost to the state would be slight. Miss Cormier had upheld the right of large, relatively wealthy municipalities to enjoy state support.

The Final Vote

After the Committee had resolved this issue—at 1:00 A.M. one morning late in the session—the bill went to the floor with Committee endorsement. There were complaints from the floor but they were isolated and unorganized. Debate ignored the principles of the act; nobody opposed getting more school subsidy, especially since they had already voted an additional 1 per cent to the sales tax, the revenues from which would more than cover subsidy costs.

What the rural representatives objected to was what they had to do to get the money. They did not like the mandatory salary scale for teachers. Their localism concentrated, however, on the very nice legalities by which a school administrative district was to be organized. Several hasty and ill-conceived amendments were made on these procedures, but the leadership accepted them to get the bill through. (They turned out to be unconstitutional in the judgment of the Attorney-General. His office rewrote the Act, which was passed without a murmur at a special session of the legislature in 1958.)

In the end, the long, hard, careful work paid off. The power of grass-roots localism had been weakened, if not blocked, by organized and coherent friends of Maine's public schools. The educational "brain trust" had produced a responsible and feasible program for the state. Powerful party leaders capitalized on the discipline of their respective political assets to make sure that the legislature did right by the state.

The Sinclair Bill passed in the House by roll call: 109 to 23. In the Senate the bill passed by voice without objection. Not one Democrat voted against the Act.

Postscript

In the five years since the passage of the Sinclair Act, problems associated with its implementation have emerged. For three years the Town of Liberty fought the Act in court in order to stall the creation of School Administrative District 3, into which the town had voted itself and out of which it wanted to get. This litigation held up bond issues by all the other districts until the courts declared the Act constitutional. Now there are sixteen districts at work* on nineteen construction projects, only one of which is finished and in use. Meanwhile, other towns have been busy backing and filling, grouping and regrouping. At last count, eight new districts were in the process of formation. But the process has been slow, and the Sinclair Act cannot remain long in its present form. Some of the districts now being created voluntarily are poorly laid out. There is an expressed sentiment favoring state determination of district membership.

The more basic problems, however, lie in the workings of the minimum foundation program.

---

*By 1969, this number had increased to seventy-five.

Experience since 1957 reveals that standards are too high for some conscientious poor towns and too low for some niggardly rich ones. The Maine School District Commission is beginning to push for an equalized tax effort rather than for an equalized foundation expenditure as the basis for state aid. The Department is beginning to wonder if the number of teachers in a district rather than its number of pupils is not a more sensitive measure of the schools' financial needs.

Sooner or later, but in due course, Maine will resolve these questions. The Sinclair Act solved more fundamental ones five years ago. Within its essential framework, the educational statesmen in Maine should be able to bring about the refinements they need.

CHAPTER

45.

The issue of private or public power is the subject of the last two chapters. In a real sense, the arguments of both representatives reflect a fundamental difference in political philosophy. Since these articles appeared in 1967, events have cast doubt on the possibility that Dickey-Lincoln will ever be constructed. This article should be read in conjunction with the following article (46).

"THE BIG QUESTION?"*
DICKEY-LINCOLN IS JUSTIFIED!

by
Senator Edmund S. Muskie

New Englanders are traditionally hardnosed about innovation. Before we give approval to a new plan or project, we want to know whether it will work, whether in fact it is an improvement, whether we can afford it, and whether it is economically justifiable.

This common sense approach served us well in the development of our region and in the pioneering of a nation. I am confident that if New England exercises this same judgment today, our region will continue to support the development of the Dickey-Lincoln School hydroelectric project on Maine's St. John River.

By every standard, Dickey is justified.

It will produce the cheapest peaking power in New England, and the cheapest base energy for Maine. At the same time, Dickey will pay for itself more than twice during its lifetime in direct benefits to consumers.

Dickey will be a flexible power source, compatible with present and all future power facilities.

Dickey will give New England a "yardstick" for efficient power production and an opportunity to catch up with other regions of the nation where Federal multi-purpose hydroelectric power plants have stimulated economic growth.

Dickey will be a large power source which can buttress our region and assure a strong electrical interconnection between the United States and Canada.

Dickey will develop and tap one of New England's great water resources, the St. John River.

DIRECT SAVINGS

Dickey will produce peaking power more cheaply than any alternative or combination of alternatives planned by our region's privately-owned utilities. Based on figures from the privately-owned utilities, the Federal Power Commission provides us with the following comparisons:

In Maine, Dickey will supply 100,000 kilowatts of base power at $15 per kilowatt as compared with $24.50 charged by the privately-owned utilities. (In each case the energy cost per kilowatt-hour is the same.) That represents a saving of $950,000 a year, or $33,250,000 over the 35-year life span of a steam plant.

The remaining Dickey power—618,000 kilowatts of peaking power—can be sold for $15 per kilowatt as compared with $22.50 from a combination of privately-owned pumped storage and steam plants. That represents a saving of $4,635,000 a year, or $162,225,000 over the 35-year life span of such facilities.

Thus, the total direct savings to New England customers would be $195,475,000 over 35 years.

However, Dickey's lifetime will exceed 100 years which means that total savings from the project will be more than $500 million.

During the first half century, Dickey will return $1.83 in benefits to consumers for every $1 invested. After the investment has been repaid *with*

The New Englander (February, 1967), pp. 15-17. Reprinted by permission of the publisher.

interest in 50 years, Dickey's power will be sold even more cheaply.

READY MARKET

There already exists a ready market for Dickey's power. The municipal and rural electric cooperatives in Massachusetts have expressed interest in buying all of the Dickey power to be marketed outside of Maine. And I am confident that the privately-owned utilities also will want this efficient, low-cost power. Experience throughout the nation has shown that there are more customers—public and private—for power from projects like Dickey than there is power to sell.

OTHER BENEFITS

Dickey will fully develop the water resources of the St. John River—a waterway shared with Canada. It will provide the opportunity for mutually beneficial power integration with the Canadian Maritime Provinces.

It will mean jobs for New Englanders while it is being constructed—and equipment orders for New England manufacturers and suppliers.

Dickey will help meet the soaring power demands of the future, demands which the FPC says will more than double by 1980.

Especially significant, Dickey will supply badly needed inexpensive peaking power for the rush hours at nightfall, and it will be a flexible power source which can be drawn on for base power and for protection against emergency demands like the one which darkened the Northeast in November, 1965. Hydroelectric plants have the advantage of being able to respond instantly to crises. They react as quickly as the turn of a water faucet.

Dickey will complement the nuclear and pumped storage plants proposed by the private utilities.

Dickey will bring to our region the much needed "Federal yardstick", or competition by comparison, the same yardstick which has brought the lowest power costs and highest power use to the Northwest, the Tennessee Valley and other areas served by public power from Federal dams. This comparison is the same stimulus which motivates innovation and efficiency in other industries.

The benefits of the Dickey yardstick already are evident. Recent rate reductions and plans to develop a $1.5 billion program utilizing nuclear and pumped storage plants were announced by New England's privately-owned utilities after Congressional authorization of Dickey.

The yardstick comparison will work to lower power costs throughout the Northeast, not merely in those areas served directly by Dickey power. This has been the impact in every region where a Federal power project is located.

And we should remember that in regions served in part by Federal power, the privately-owned utilities and their stockholders have prospered since the initiation of public power. Because of the lower power rates, homeowners use more electricity—meaning higher sales for private companies and for manufacturers of home appliances.

THE PROBLEM

At the heart of New England's power problem is the fragmented group of privately-owned utilities. They frequently serve small areas and are unable or unwilling to fully implement new cost-cutting techniques. As a result, we find duplication, inefficiency, highest consumer costs and lowest power use. The companies are beginning to recognize this—principally because of Dickey which will accelerate conversion to modern methods of electric production.

Surely, in our region where we pay the highest electricity bills in the nation, we will not turn our backs on Dickey, the first Federal power project in the Northeast.

On a cost-per-customer basis, our electrical costs are 26 per cent above the national average. Compared with the Tennessee Valley, Colorado and the Northwest, our power costs are greater still.

For instance, New England homeowners pay $4.56 for a 100-kilowatt-hour bill. Tennessee Valley homeowners pay $2.85.

If our power rates were reduced to just the national average, our manufacturers alone would save an estimated $71 million a year, or 31 per cent.

FAULTY ARGUMENT

In discussions of public power developments, we frequently hear the argument that a project like Dickey is an unnecessary or unfair infringement on the private sector. This argument fails on two counts.

First, public power is not a new concept in our region or elsewhere. Scores of municipal and cooperative power agencies already serve New England.

Second, privately-owned utilities have been granted protected monopolies by states for the explicit purpose of serving the public as efficiently and effectively as possible. In reality, privately-owned utilities are public utilities, created with the blessings of State governments and carrying the prime obligation of serving the public

We should not make the mistake of placing privately-owned utilities in the same category as automobile manufacturers, for instance, whose primary responsibility has traditionally been to the stockholders. Legally and historically, privately-owned utilities are and have been subject to government regulation to protect the public interest. Public power has developed where this interest has not been efficiently or economically served.

When we build an economically sound Federal power project like Dickey, we are strengthening our economy, meeting a longstanding commitment to the public welfare, and encouraging and enabling the privately-owned utilities to better fulfill their responsibilities.

We are not talking about an abstract concept of infringement on private enterprise. Rather, we are developing a natural resource to meet a public need in line with long-established national policies. Because we are economically weakened by the highest electrical costs in the nation, we must develop our total power potential and lower costs to consumers.

Dickey will do both and will do so economically. Dickey completely satisfies every national standard for public power development. Dickey has been given detailed engineering, design and economic study by the Army Corps of Engineers, the International Joint Commission, the Interior Department, the Federal Power Commission, and the Bureau of the Budget. All endorse Dickey. President Johnson endorses it. The Congress—House and Senate both—voted to construct the project.

COOPERATION NEEDED

New England's economic vitality in the decades ahead depends in large measure on the supply of low cost electrical power. The combination of Dickey, as the least expensive source of both firm power and instant peaking power and as a stimulus for lower power costs, plus private power development of the scope envisioned in the Big Eleven Loop program offers the greatest promise for meeting New England's energy needs of the future.

CHAPTER

46.

DICKEY—LINCOLN
IT'S OBSOLETE BEFORE IT'S BUILT!*
by
Albert A. Cree

To some New Englanders the words "Dickey-Lincoln School" still sound like a remote railroad station or another of the many, fine New England prep schools. But as the facts become better known each day about this wasteful Federal power project in Maine the name is becoming better known, also.

A brief history and review of this project is in order at the outset, but perhaps even more important is a statement why the investor-owned electric industry in our region opposes this project. Let me make it clear at the outset that this opposition is not based on the traditional philosophical battle of private vs. public power. The industry has consistently taken the position before the Congress that its opposition is based on economic grounds—the simple fact of the matter is that the project does not make economic sense whether it were to be built by the United States government or private industry!

EARLY BEGINNINGS

The history of the project really goes back to the early part of this century when some engineers originally conceived the idea of harnessing the tides of Passamaquoddy Bay near the mouth of the Bay of Fundy. From 1919, through the days of the Roosevelt administration, innumerable studies were undertaken concerning the production of electric power from the tides. Time and time again the studies indicated that it could be done but only at an exorbitant price.

In the 1950's and the early 1960's the project was unearthed again—linked with a power development on the St. John River at Rankin Rapids, *below* the confluence with the Allagash—and studied some more with the same end results. By 1963 the economic nonsense of the scheme had become so evident that the Interior Department shifted gears and began to talk of a much larger Quoddy tidal power development, for peaking power production, tied to a more conventional hydroelectric development at the Dickey site on the St. John River *above* the confluence with the Allagash River.

The hue and cry which had been raised by conservationists concerning the desecration of the Allagash wilderness, and the further deterioration of economic logic to the Quoddy project brought forth still another scheme for hydro power to be produced by the Federal government—the proposal to build a $227 million project at the so-called Dickey-Lincoln School sites on the St. John River with the Quoddy tidal power project once again placed in moth balls entirely. It almost seems that the Interior Department and their public power allies were determined to build a hydroelectric station somewhere in New England—anywhere and at any cost.

ECONOMICALLY UNSOUND

Unfortunately for the taxpayers of the United States the latest proposal is little better than any of its predecessors. But the proposal was there and in

---

*The New Englander (February, 1967), pp. 15-17. Reprinted by permission of the publisher.

1965 became a part of the Federal budget, battle lines were drawn and the debate started in the Congress. One of the little known facts concerning this project is the opposition of 20 out of the 25 New England Congressmen. New England can well be proud that these members of the House had the courage to oppose this wasteful project in the face of strong counter-pressures from many areas.

In brief, the Dickey-Lincoln School project is a mammoth Federal hydro-electric generating station to be built on the St. John River in Maine, in combination with a smaller re-regulating station at Lincoln School, at an estimated total station cost of $227 million. There will be an additional $80,000,000 expenditure for the 400-mile transmission line to be built to carry the power output from the remote, sparsely-populated region on the Canadian border to the load centers of southern New England.

HIGH COST—LOW OUTPUT

For the government's $300,000,000 investment it will get an output of about 700,000 kilowatts for approximately two hours a day. As a comparison the small, 180,000 kilowatt Yankee Atomic plant built for $40,000,000 in Rowe, Massachusetts is today turning out more kilowatts of electricity in a year than the Dickey project will do in the mid-1970's.

Despite its many obvious shortcomings and a substantial lack of sound engineering and economic information the project was authorized by the Senate in 1965 without even a recorded vote. But when it reached the House side there was a considerable inquiry in depth and on September 22, 1965 the House voted 207 to 185 against authorization and for a further study of the project.

Through a subsequent involved legislative procedure, and one that was to be seriously questioned by many members of the House later, the project was finally authorized by a close vote in the House and an initial appropriation of $800,000 was passed for preliminary engineering.

In the recently completed 1966 session of the Congress the battle was rejoined, an additional $1,100,000, again only for preliminary engineering, was voted, but this time the House established its own study, independent of any Senate action.

This study, by the House Appropriations Committee, is now underway and will go a long way toward providing the answers to the many questions that the proponents of this project have been avoiding.

THE INDUSTRY'S POSITION

The basic position of the electric industry in New England has been clearly stated a number of times:

(1) The Department of the Interior, which has proposed the project has no marketing plans for the power to be produced. This was so despite the fact that more than 90 per cent of the output would have to be marketed outside of Maine.

(2) The Department of the Interior did not consult with the electric companies in the New England area in the planning (such little as there was) despite the fact that they would be the only logical customers for the power, and in the face of the certain knowledge that the cost of the power to be produced will be so high that no one will want to buy it.

(3) The power to be produced by the Dickey project will be more expensive in the 1970's than that now being produced in some New England steam-electric generating stations.

(4) The private power companies of the New England region have offered not just opposition but a tangible and more economical alternative to the production of power for the region, *without the expenditure of any public funds.*

Nuclear power is now completely competitive with fossil fuel (coal and oil) plants in most areas of the United States.

In the field of nuclear power generation New England has much more to gain than any other region. In the past, generating costs have been higher here than in the rest of the country because fuel, which has to be transported farther, has cost more. Fossil fuel costs in New England average about 34 cents per million BTU compared with a U.S. average of 26.1 cents per million BTU.

Nuclear fuel being essentially weightless wipes out the disadvantage arising from transport costs and puts New England on a par with any other region—a gain greater than any other region has the opportunity to secure in this field.

To achieve lowest cost power, the power supply for New England and for its separate political and geographical parts must and will now be provided *on a regional one-system basis* with only large-size and the most economic and reliable of generating plants placed in diverse locations close to the major loads to be served.

As a dramatic initial step towards this goal the electric companies of New England have announced the "Big 11 Powerloop" as the pattern for the provision of the region's low-cost, coordinated power supply through 1972.

THE BIG 11

The "Big 11 Powerloop" comprises 11 large-capacity generating plants to be tied to each other and to New England load centers as well as to other parts of the country, by 700 miles of a heavy 345,000 volt transmission grid reaching into every state in New England and into the heavy interconnections with the rest of the country through New York State.

All of this new construction is scheduled for completion during the 1966-1972 period and will represent an investment by the companies involved of about $1.5 billion, a new investment in seven years equal to more than half of the total capital employed by all of these companies in 1965.

The 11 new power plants to be added in the "Big 11 Powerloop" will consist of five new nuclear plants, including the new Vermont Yankee Nuclear Power Plant, with an aggregate capacity of 2,900,000 kilowatts; five new fossil fuel-fired plants with an aggregate capacity of 2,350,000 kilowatts, and the new low cost pumped-storage plant of Northeast Utilities, Inc., planned for service in 1971, at Northfield Mountain, on the Connecticut River just south of the Vermont border, with an aggregate capacity of 1,000,000 kilowatts,—a total of 6,250,000 kilowatts of new generating capacity to be put into service between now and the end of 1972.

These eleven new power plants will constitute about 43% of New England's power capacity by 1973 and will be generating more than 65% of the area's kilowatt hours in that year.

FOR THE FUTURE

For the long pull, presently all signs point to a combination of large nuclear and hydro pumped-storage plants as offering the most economical and reliable source of New England's growing energy requirements.

Continuing to follow in the years beyond 1972, this developing pattern of generation and transmission growth for the future power supply for New England, will result by 1980, if not before, in a reduction of the cost of electricity to consumers of not less than 40%.

New Englanders have a long and hardy tradition of independence, ingenuity and insight. The independence has already been well demonstrated by the 20 New England Congressmen who rejected a Federal largesse for the area and particularly when it would harm and not help our problems. The ingenuity is being demonstrated every month with the announcement of new nuclear power plants that will balance the resource disadvantages of our region with the rest of the nation. The insight will, I feel, be finally demonstrated by the Congress of the United States when they have all the facts.

Neither State nor Federal public power has yet come to New England and I do not believe it will. The dreams of the ambitious politicians are not supported by the desires or will of the people.

10